Excavations at Newport Street, Worcester, 2005

Roman Roadside Activity and Medieval to Post-Medieval
Urban Development on the Severn Floodplain

Excavations at Newport Street, Worcester, 2005

Roman Roadside Activity and Medieval to Post-Medieval Urban Development on the Severn Floodplain

by

Peter Davenport

with contributions by

Martin Allen, Steven J. Allen, Angus Crawford, Hal Dalwood, James Dinn, M. Felter,
Laura Griffin, Christopher Guy, Katie Head, Pat Hughes, Alan J. Jacobs, Robin Jackson,
Ian Panter, Allan Peacey, Elizabeth Pearson, Nicola Rogers, Huw Sherlock,
Penelope Walton Rogers, Sylvia Warman and Keith Wilkinson

Cotswold Archaeology/Worcestershire Archive and Archaeology Service

Cirencester 2015

Cotswold Archaeology Monograph No. 4

Published by Cotswold Archaeology
Building 11, Kemble Enterprise Park, Cirencester, Gloucestershire GL7 6BQ

Copyright © Authors, Cotswold Archaeology and Worcestershire Archive and Archaeology Service 2015

All rights reserved. No part of this publication may be reproduced, stored in a retrieval system, or transmitted in any form or by any means, electronic, photocopying, recording or otherwise, without the prior permission of the copyright owner.

ISBN 978-0-9553534-9-9

The following images are supplied to Cotswold Archaeology for use in this publication:

Figs 2.4, 2.7–2.12, 4.7, 4.10, 4.24, 4.30, 4.32 © Worcestershire Record Office
Fig. 2.5 © National Archives
Fig. 2.6 © Society of Antiquaries
Fig. 2.13 © Worcester City Museum Collection

Front cover: Extract from 'Newport Street, 1905' by Evacustes Phipson © Worcester City Museum Collection
Back cover: Photomontage of excavations at Newport Street, 2005 © Michael Hallett

Cover design by Rosanna Price, Cotswold Archaeology
Produced by Past Historic, Kings Stanley, Gloucestershire
Printed by Henry Ling, Dorchester

CONTENTS

List of Illustrations — viii
List of Tables — xi
Acknowledgements — xiii
Summary — xiv

Chapter 1: Introduction, by Robin Jackson
1.1 Introduction — 1
1.2 Site location — 2

Chapter 2: Archaeological and Historical Background
2.1 Previous major archaeological investigations in the city, by Robin Jackson — 3
2.2 Archaeological and historical frameworks, by Hal Dalwood and Robin Jackson — 3
2.3 The documentary history of Newport Street, by Pat Hughes — 8

Chapter 3: Project Objectives and Methodology
3.1 Project objectives and research priorities, by Robin Jackson — 19
3.2 Methodologies — 20
   3.2.1 Excavation — 20
   3.2.2 Assessment and updated project design — 20
   3.2.3 Structural evidence — 21
   3.2.4 Documentary evidence, by Pat Hughes — 24
   3.2.5 Artefactual evidence, by Robin Jackson — 24
   3.2.6 Leather conservation, by Ian Panter — 25
   3.2.7 Bone and ivory conservation, by M. Felter — 25
   3.2.8 Geoarchaeological survey, by Keith Wilkinson — 25
   3.2.9 Pollen remains, by Katie Head — 26
   3.2.10 Sampling and plant macrofossils, by Elizabeth Pearson — 26
   3.2.11 Animal bone, by Sylvia Warman — 27
3.3 Retrospective view, by Huw Sherlock and James Dinn — 27
   3.3.1 The consultant's perspective, by Huw Sherlock — 27
   3.3.2 The curatorial retrospective, by James Dinn — 28
3.4 Archive content and location — 29

Chapter 4: Site Narrative
4.1 Introduction, by Peter Davenport — 30
4.2 Geoarchaeology, by Keith Wilkinson — 31
   4.2.1 Stratigraphy — 31
   4.2.2 Discussion — 38
   4.2.3 Conclusions — 40
4.3 The archaeological sequence, by Peter Davenport — 40
   4.3.1 Plot 1: the northern part of no. 32/34 Newport Street — 40
   4.3.2 Plot 2: the northern part of nos 26 and 28 Newport Street (including nos 35 and 37 Dolday) — 43
   4.3.3 Plot 3: the southern part of nos 26, 28 and 30 Newport Street — 48
   4.3.4 Plots 4 and 5: no. 24 Newport Street — 61
   4.3.5 Plots 6 and 7: no. 22 Newport Street — 67
   4.3.6 Plots 8 and 9: no. 20 Newport Street — 73
   4.3.7 Plots 10 and 11: nos 18 and 16 Newport Street — 76
   4.3.8 Plots 12 and 13: no. 14 Newport Street — 78
   4.3.9 Plot 14: no. 12 and a small part of no. 10 Newport Street — 85

Chapter 5: Specialist Reports
5.1 Documentary evidence for individual properties, by Pat Hughes — 93
   5.1.1 Introduction
   5.1.2 Properties west of the excavated area (nos 54–36) — 93
   5.1.3 No. 32/34 Newport Street (Plot 1; Figs 5.3 and 5.4) — 97
   5.1.4 Nos 26, 28 and 30 Newport Street (Plots 2 and 3; Figs 5.3 and 5.4) — 99
   5.1.5 No. 24 Newport Street (Plots 4 and 5; Fig. 5.4) — 102
   5.1.6 No. 20 Newport Street (Plots 8 and 9) and no 22 Newport Street (Plots 6 and 7; Fig. 5.3) — 104
   5.1.7 Nos 14, 16 and 18 Newport Street (Plots 12 and 13; Fig. 5.3) — 105
   5.1.8 Nos 10 and 12 Newport Street (Plot 14) — 108

5.1.9 Nos 2, 4, 6 and 8 Newport Street (to the east of excavated area)	109	5.16 Glass, by Angus Crawford and Alan J. Jacobs	189
5.2 The Roman pottery, by Alan J. Jacobs	110	5.16.1 Medieval and post-medieval glass, by Alan J. Jacobs	189
5.2.1 Analysis	110	5.16.2 The later bottle glass, by Angus Crawford	190
5.2.2 Discussion	111	5.17 Ironworking residues, by Robin Jackson	191
5.3 Medieval and medieval/early post-medieval pottery, by Laura Griffin	111	5.17.1 Analysis	101
5.3.1 Analysis	111	5.17.2 Discussion	192
5.3.2 Discussion (by period)	119	5.18 Leather, by Ian Panter	192
5.4 Post-medieval pottery, by Alan J. Jacobs	121	5.19 Cloth hose fragment, by Penelope Walton Rogers	193
5.4.1 Analysis	121	5.20 Wooden small finds, by Steven J. Allen	195
5.4.2 General discussion	126	5.21 Bone and ivory objects, by Nicola Rogers	197
5.5 The modern pottery, by Alan J. Jacobs	129	5.22 Pollen, by Katie Head	198
5.5.1 Analysis	130	5.22.1 Results	198
5.5.2 Discussion	130	5.22.2 Discussion	199
5.6 Ceramic building material: medieval floor tiles, by Laura Griffin	130	5.23 Plant remains, by Elizabeth Pearson	201
5.6.1 Analysis	131	5.23.1 Results	201
5.6.2 Discussion	132	5.23.2 Discussion	214
5.7 Ceramic building material: Roman roof tile, by Laura Griffin	134	5.24 Animal Bone, by Sylvia Warman	216
5.7.1 Analysis	134	5.24.1 Results	216
5.7.2 Discussion	135	5.24.2 Analysis	219
5.8 Ceramic building material: medieval, post-medieval and modern roof tile, by Laura Griffin	135	5.24.3 Discussion	223
5.8.1 Analysis by fabric type	136	5.24.4 Conclusions	224
5.8.2 Discussion by period	139	5.25 Synthesis of environmental evidence, by Elizabeth Pearson and Sylvia Warman	225
5.9 Ceramic building material: bricks, by Angus Crawford	140	5.25.1 Early deposits, build-up of alluvium and phases of flooding, and the site over time.	225
5.9.1 Analysis	142	5.25.2 Environment of the site during the medieval period	225
5.9.2 Discussion	144	5.25.3 Medieval industry on the riverside	225
5.10 Fired clay artefacts, by Angus Crawford	146	5.25.4 Introduction of new crops, crop varieties and animal breeds	225
5.11 Architectural stonework, by Christopher Guy	146	5.25.5 Trade and imported exotics	226
5.11.1 Introduction	146	5.25.6 Information on specific documented households	226
5.11.2 Discussion	151	5.25.7 Comparison with similar sites, locally, regionally and nationally	226
5.12 Other stone, by Angus Crawford and Alan J. Jacobs	157		
5.12.1 Spindle whorls, by Alan J. Jacobs	157	**Chapter 6: Thematic Discussion**	
5.12.2 Rotary querns and millstones, by Angus Crawford	157	6.1 Chronological overview, by Peter Davenport	228
5.12.3 Other stone objects, by Angus Crawford	158	6.2 The river, the floodplain and its transformation, by Hal Dalwood	229
5.13 Metal artefacts, by Alan J. Jacobs	163	6.3 The development of the street system and medieval town planning, by Hal Dalwood	231
5.13.1 Period 2: medieval metal artefacts	163		
5.13.2 Period 3: post-medieval metal artefacts	164	6.4 Colonisation and property division, by Peter Davenport	234
5.13.3 Period 4: 18th-century metal artefacts	166	6.5 Buildings and houses, by Peter Davenport	236
5.13.4 Period 5 and unassigned metal artefacts	166	6.5.1 Period 1: Roman	236
5.14 Coins, tokens and jettons, by Alan J. Jacobs (identification by Martin Allen)	166	6.5.2 Period 2: medieval	237
5.14.1 Analysis	166	6.5.3 Period 3: post-medieval (c. 1550–1700)	239
5.15 Clay tobacco pipes, by Allan Peacey	169		
5.15.1 Analysis and discussion	172	6.5.4 Period 4: 18th century	241
5.15.2 Conclusions	188		

6.5.5 Period 5: 19th to mid 20th century	241
6.6 Industry and craft, by Peter Davenport	242
6.6.1 Period 2: medieval	242
6.6.2 Period 3: post-medieval (*c.* 1550–1700)	245
6.6.3 Period 4: 18th century	246
6.6.4 Period 5: 19th and 20th centuries	247
6.7 Consumption and urban households, by Hal Dalwood	247
6.7.1 Period 2: medieval urban households and trade	247
6.7.2 Period 3: post-medieval households and trade	248
6.8 Patterns of wealth and social change, by Peter Davenport	249
6.8.1 Period 1: Roman	249
6.8.2 Period 2: medieval	249
6.8.3 Periods 3 and 4: post-medieval and 18th century	250
Chapter 7: Conclusions, by Hal Dalwood	252
Appendix: The Brick Catalogue	255
References	277
Index	287

List of Illustrations

Fig. 1.1 Site location. Scale 1:2500 xvi
Fig. 1.2 Aerial view of excavation and City (from the north). The site lies in the foreground with the 'new' bridge to its south-west. © Mike Glyde 1
Fig. 1.3 Partnership in action 2
Fig. 2.1 The site in relation to other major excavations in Worcester. Scale 1:7500 4
Fig. 2.2 The site in relation to Roman Worcester. Scale 1:6666 6
Fig. 2.3 The site in relation to Medieval Worcester. Scale 1:6666 7
Fig. 2.4 Version of the 1660 map of Worcester as it stood fortified 3rd September 1651 (from an original plate re-engraved in 1723). © Worcestershire Record Office 9
Fig. 2.5 Extract from Broad's map of Worcester (1768). Note the boats at the bottom of Dolday and the channel and water-house for the waterworks below the bridge. © National Archives 10
Fig. 2.6 St Clement's Church and the 'new key(e)' at the west end of Dolday (by H.B. Leigher; *c.* 1825). © Society of Antiquaries 11
Fig. 2.7 Map of the city redrawn from Young's map of Worcester (1779). Note the insertion of Bridge Street and the site of the newly built bridge. © Worcestershire Record Office 12
Fig. 2.8 Medieval bridge and houses built at the west end of Newport Street. The house at the end of the bridge was once the King's Head. The new bridge is visible through the arches (from the E.F. and T.F. Burney watercolour collection). © Worcestershire Record Office 13
Fig. 2.9 Demolition of the medieval bridge (*c.* 1780). Buildings visible at the end of Newport Street include the building now known as the Severn View and, to its left, the King's Head and St Clement's Church (from the E.F. and T.F. Burney watercolour collection). © Worcestershire Record Office 13
Fig. 2.10 The upper end of Newport Street (1930s; looking east). © Worcestershire Record Office 14
Fig. 2.11 View from the top of Newport Street (*c.* 1967; looking west). © Worcestershire Record Office 15
Fig. 2.12 The central part of Newport Street (1930s; looking east). © Worcestershire Record Office 16
Fig. 2.13 The upper part of Newport Street in 1905 by Evacustes Phipson, showing from the left nos 32/34, 30 (with the creeper), 26/28, 24 (The Boar's Head), 22 and 20 (the tallest building). © Worcester City Museum Collection 16
Fig. 2.14 Extract from the 1:500 1886 Ordnance Survey map of Worcester, showing the site location. Scale 1:1000 17
Fig. 3.1 Excavation areas and location of deeper excavations (West and East Sondages). Scale 1:500 21
Fig. 3.2 Location of boreholes across the site. Scale 1:500 22
Fig. 4.1 Plan of structural features and courts superimposed on the OS 1886 map. Scale 1:500 31
Fig. 4.2 General view of Plots 1, 2, 4 and 6 under excavation, looking south-west 36
Fig. 4.3 Composite site section through Bore-holes BH1–6 37
Fig. 4.4 Modelled thickness of made ground and archaeological beds (for borehole locations see Fig. 3.2) 39
Fig. 4.5 Plot 1, Period 3.1, piles under Building 1a, looking south 41
Fig. 4.6 Plot 1, Period 3.3, Building 1b, looking south 42
Fig. 4.7 Dolday, 1936 photograph. © Worcestershire Record Office 43
Fig. 4.8 Plot 2, Period 3.1, hearth S107, looking north 44

Fig.	Description	Page
Fig. 4.9	Plot 2, Period 3.1, cobbling and kerb G366, looking south	45
Fig. 4.10	Plot 2, cottages (Building 3) leading to Court 8, 1930s photograph. © Worcestershire Record Office	46
Fig. 4.11	Plot 2, Period 3.3, cess pit S113, looking north-west	47
Fig. 4.12	Periods 1 and 2.1/2.2, west end. Scale 1:250	48
Fig. 4.13	Sections 1 and 2. Scale 1:50	49
Fig. 4.14	Period 2.3, west end. Scale 1:250	50
Fig. 4.15	Periods 2.4 and 2.5, west end. Scale 1:250	51
Fig. 4.16	Plot 3, Period 2.4/2.5, hearth 2706 and cellar G55, looking south-west	52
Fig. 4.17	Plot 3, Period 2.4/2.5, cellar G55 west wall, looking west	53
Fig. 4.18	Period 3.1, west end. Scale 1:250	54
Fig. 4.19	Plot 3, Period 2.5, cess pit S263, looking north-west	55
Fig. 4.20	Plot 3, Period 2.5, oven S256 in Building 5, looking south-east	56
Fig. 4.21	Period 3.2, west end. Scale 1:250	57
Fig. 4.22	Period 3.3, west end. Scale 1:250	58
Fig. 4.23	Period 4, west end. Scale 1:250	60
Fig. 4.24	Plot 3, Court 4, 1936 photograph. © Worcestershire Record Office	62
Fig. 4.25	Plot 5, Period 2.3, small beehive oven G44, looking north	63
Fig. 4.26	Ovens G368, G203 and G267. Scale 1:50	64
Fig. 4.27	Plot 4/5, Period 2.5, oven G368, looking north-east	65
Fig. 4.28	The Malthouse, Plots 6/7. Scale 1:150	70
Fig. 4.29	Period 5. Scale 1:250	71
Fig. 4.30	Plot 6/7, Court 3, Building 16, 1936 photograph. © Worcestershire Record Office	72
Fig. 4.31	Plot 6, Period 3, millstone capping well G84 in Building 15, looking north-east	73
Fig. 4.32	Dolday 1930s photograph. © Worcestershire Record Office	74
Fig. 4.33	Periods 1 and 2.1/2.2, east end. Scale 1:250	78
Fig. 4.34	Sections 3 and 4. Scale 1:50	79
Fig. 4.35	Plot 13, Period 1, road G349 and pit G350, looking south	80
Fig. 4.36	Period 2.3, east end. Scale 1:250	81
Fig. 4.37	Periods 2.4 and 2.5, east end. Scale 1:250	83
Fig. 4.38	Plot 13, Period 2.4, oven base G139, looking south-west	84
Fig. 4.39	Plot 13, Period 2.5, oven G146, looking south-east	85
Fig. 4.40	Period 3.1, east end. Scale 1:250	86
Fig. 4.41	Plot 14, Period 2.4, hearth G234 under excavation, looking south	87
Fig. 4.42	Period 3.2, east end. Scale 1:250	88
Fig. 4.43	Period 3.3, east end. Scale 1:250	89
Fig. 4.44	Period 4, east end. Scale 1:250	90
Fig. 4.45	Plot 14, Period 3.3, oven G267, looking west	91
Fig. 5.1	Reconstructed street frontage and property ownership, c 1550 to 1925	94
Fig. 5.2	'West View of the City of Worcester', engraving by J. Ross (from Green 1796)	96
Fig. 5.3	Annotated extract from 1:500 1st Edition Ordnance Survey map (1886) showing nos 14–38 Newport Street	97
Fig. 5.4	Nos 24–37 Newport Street, as shown on plans accompanying sale documents of 1936	98
Fig. 5.5	Plan and Elevation survey of nos 16 and 18 Newport Street prior to demolition, as recorded by N.A.D. Molyneux, 1978. Scale 1:100	107
Fig. 5.6	Medieval pottery (Nos 1–18). Scale 1:4	118
Fig. 5.7	Medieval pottery (Nos 19–26). Scale 1:4	119
Fig. 5.8	Post-medieval pottery (Nos 1–17). Scale 1:4	127
Fig. 5.9	Post-medieval pottery (Nos 18–29). Scale 1:4	128
Fig. 5.10	Post-medieval pottery (Nos 30–42). Scale 1:4	129
Fig. 5.11	Decorated floor tile (Nos 1–9). Scale 1:2	133
Fig. 5.12	Roman roof tile. Scale 1:4	134
Fig. 5.13	Medieval and post-medieval roof tile (Nos 1–10). Scale 1:4	141
Fig. 5.14	Bricks (Nos 1–4). Scale 1:5	145
Fig. 5.15	Fired clay counter. Scale 1:1	146
Fig. 5.16	Worked building stone (Nos 1–2). Scale 1:4	147
Fig. 5.17	Worked building stone (No. 3). Scale 1:4	148
Fig. 5.18	Worked building stone (Nos 4–6). Scale 1:8	149
Fig. 5.19	Worked building stone (Nos 7–8). Scales 1:4 and 1:8	150
Fig. 5.20	Worked building stone (Nos 9–14). Scale 1:8	151
Fig. 5.21	Worked building stone (Nos 15–17). Scales 1:4 and 1:8	152
Fig. 5.22	Worked building stone (Nos 18–20). Scale 1:8	153
Fig. 5.23	Worked building stone (No. 21). Scale 1:4	153
Fig. 5.24	Worked building stone (Nos 22–23). Scale 1:4	154
Fig. 5.25	Worked building stone (Nos 24–25). Scales 1:4 and 1:8	155

Fig. 5.26	Worked building stone (No. 26). Scale 1:4	156	
Fig. 5.27	Worked stone objects: spindle whorls (Nos 1–4). Scale 1:2	159	
Fig. 5.28	Worked stone objects: querns (Nos 5, 6, 8 and 9). Scale 1:5	160	
Fig. 5.29	Millstones (Nos 10–13). Scale 1:15	161	
Fig. 5.30	Worked stone objects: mortar (No. 14). Scale 1:4	162	
Fig. 5.31	Worked stone objects: candleholders (Nos 15–16). Scale 1:4	162	
Fig. 5.32	Stone troughs (Nos 17–18). Scale 1:15	162	
Fig. 5.33	Period 2: Metalwork (Nos 1–8). Scale 1:2	164	
Fig. 5.34	Period 3: Metalwork (Nos 9–21). Scale 1:2	165	
Fig. 5.35	Period 4: Metalwork (Nos 22–24). Scale 1:2	166	
Fig. 5.36	Clay pipes (Nos 1–13). Scale 1:1	173	
Fig. 5.37	Clay pipes (Nos 14–26). Scale 1:1	174	
Fig. 5.38	Clay pipes (Nos 27–40). Scale 1:1	175	
Fig. 5.39	Clay pipes (Nos 41–52). Scale 1:1	176	
Fig. 5.40	Clay pipes (Nos 53–64). Scale 1:1	177	
Fig. 5.41	Clay pipes (Nos 65–76). Scale 1:1	178	
Fig. 5.42	Clay pipes (Nos 77–87). Scale 1:1	179	
Fig. 5.43	Clay pipes (Nos 88–100). Scale 1:1	180	
Fig. 5.44	Clay pipes (Nos 101–114). Scale 1:1	181	
Fig. 5.45	Clay pipe stamps (Nos 115–168). Scale 2:1	183	
Fig. 5.46	Clay pipe stamps (Nos 169–202). Scale 2:1	184	
Fig. 5.47	Glass (Nos 1–5). Scale 1:4	190	
Fig. 5.48	Fragments of cloth hose from cess pit S263. Scale 1:4	194	
Fig. 5.49	The slits for the foot inserts and a reinforcement strip (Photo: The Anglo-Saxon Laboratory)	194	
Fig. 5.50	The hose from Quintfall Hill, near Wick, and its pattern, after Orr 1922 (Illustration: The Anglo-Saxon Laboratory)	195	
Fig. 5.51	Wooden objects: comb and bowl (Nos 1–2). Scales 1:2 and 1:4	196	
Fig. 5.52	Ivory combs (Nos 1–3). Scale 1:2	197	
Fig. 5.53	Bone pin and buzz bone (Nos 5–6). Scale 1:2	198	
Fig. 5.54	Pollen percentage diagram for Monolith 1 spanning above and below the Romano-British metalled layer in the East Sondage	199	

List of Tables

Table 3.1	Summary of data recorded from boreholes	23
Table 4.1	Concordance of buildings and land-use by plot	34
Table 5.1	Purprestures 1662 to *c.* 1780 with some additional information from deeds (D) and wills (W)	101
Table 5.2	Summary of stratified Roman pottery assemblage	110
Table 5.3	Quantification of the medieval and early post-medieval pottery by fabric type (after Hurst and Rees 1992)	112
Table 5.4	Quantification of the analysed later post-medieval pottery assemblage by fabric type	121
Table 5.5	Analysed modern pottery by fabric	130
Table 5.6	Quantification of medieval plain floor tiles by glaze colour	131
Table 5.7	Quantification of the ceramic roof tile by fabric and type	135
Table 5.8	Metalwork assemblage (count and weight) by metal type and period	163
Table 5.9	Medieval coins, tokens and jettons	167
Table 5.10	Post-medieval coins and tokens	167
Table 5.11	Late post-medieval and modern coins and tokens	168
Table 5.12	Illustrated clay pipe bowls	169
Table 5.13	Illustrated clay pipe stamps	185
Table 5.14	Glass	189
Table 5.15	Summary of iron slag assemblage	191
Table 5.16	List of environmental samples from bulk samples	201
Table 5.17	Summary of environmental remains from bulk samples	203
Table 5.18	Plant remains from Period 1 (Roman)	204
Table 5.19	Plant remains from Period 2 (medieval): quantified data	204
Table 5.20	Plant remains from Period 2 (medieval): scanned results	207
Table 5.21	Plant remains from Period 2/3 (medieval to post-medieval)	210
Table 5.22	Plant remains from Period 3 (post-medieval): quantified results	211
Table 5.23	Animal bone from Period 1 (Roman): hand-collected material	217
Table 5.24	Animal bone from Period 1 (Roman): sieved assemblage	217
Table 5.25	Animal bone from Period 2 (medieval): hand-collected material	218
Table 5.26	Animal bone from Period 2 (medieval): sieved assemblage	219
Table 5.27	Animal bone from Period 3 (post-medieval): hand-collected material	220
Table 5.28	Animal bone from Period 3 (post-medieval): sieved assemblage	221

Acknowledgements

The excavations at Newport Street and this publication were generously funded by Cabot Homes Ltd. We are grateful to Matt McCabe and Mike Race of Cabot Homes, Huw Sherlock of Archenfield Archaeology and to James Dinn of Worcester City Council for their help and support. The fieldwork project was managed by Simon Cox of Cotswold Archaeology (CA) and Robin Jackson of Worcestershire Historic Environment and Archaeology Service (WHEAS). The excavation was directed by Richard Young and area supervision was undertaken by Kate Cullen, Derek Evans, Mike Rowe, Simon Sworn and Jon Webster. The watching brief was undertaken by Simon Sworn. Lisa Moffett, the English Heritage Regional Scientific Adviser, advised on sampling policies on site. The post-excavation was managed at CA by Mary Alexander and Martin Watts, and at WHEAS by Robin Jackson and Derek Hurst. Figures 4.1 and 4.2 were prepared by Keith Wilkinson (ARCA), the rest of the figures for Chapter 4 and Figure 3.1 were prepared by Peter Moore, Lorna Gray and Jemma Elliot (CA). Figures 2.1, 2.2, 2.3, 3.2, and those in Chapter 5 were prepared by Carolyn Hunt, Steve Rigby and Laura Templeton (WHEAS) with the exception of Figures 5.36–5.46 (the clay-pipe figures) prepared by Allan Peacey (freelance clay-pipe specialist), and Figures 5.11–5.13 (floor tiles and roof tiles), 5.28 (querns), 5.30 (mortar), 5.31 (candleholders), 5.52, 5.53 (combs and bone objects), which were prepared by Jerneja Kobe (freelance illustrator).

Keith Wilkinson (ARCA) would like to thank Robin Jackson and Dr Katie Head (University of Plymouth) for their help during the borehole survey.

Our thanks go to Lisa Moffett (the English Heritage Regional Scientific Adviser) and Nigel Baker (Project Officer, Hereford Archaeology) for refereeing an earlier version of this text and to James Dinn (Archaeological Officer, Worcester City Council) for invaluable and detailed comments on the same. The text was edited by Martin Watts and copy-edited by Rachel Tyson. The contribution of field and finds staff and the specialists is gratefully acknowledged.

Permission to use historic photos and maps was kindly arranged by Pat Hughes.

Permission to use the Evacustes Phipson image from Worcester City Museum Collection was kindly arranged by Philippa Tinsley, and the photomontage of the site under excavation was kindly provided by Michael Hallett.

Summary

Between August and December 2005, Cotswold Archaeology (CA) in partnership with Worcestershire Historic Environment and Archaeology Service (WHEAS) excavated an area of approximately a third of a hectare at Newport Street, in the north-west part of the historic core of Worcester, in advance of the redevelopment of the site for residential and commercial use. The site lies on the northern side of Newport Street within the parish of All Saints, bounded to the north-east by All Saints' Road and to the north by Dolday, near to the eastern bank of the River Severn on the edge of the former floodplain. The work was funded by Cabot Homes Ltd, the developers.

The excavations revealed evidence for activity dating from the Roman to the post-medieval and early modern period. The deepest deposits were recorded in geotechnical and archaeological borehole surveys and were investigated in two deep sondages. The rest of the site was excavated to the depth of formation level for the new development, which is supported on pile foundations. Excavations revealed evidence for a Roman road running on the approximate alignment of the present-day Newport Street. Deposits relating to road construction and ground consolidation mainly comprised metal-working waste in the form of slag. Finds from these deposits suggest occupation in this period spanned the later 2nd and 3rd centuries, and possibly continued into the 4th century AD, although no *in situ* evidence of occupation was excavated. The Roman levels were sealed by a depth of alluvial deposits interspersed with evidence of episodic activity dating from the 11th to the 13th century. The ground was consolidated again in the early 13th century, and shortly afterwards the area was divided by boundaries, which were consolidated during the subsequent medieval and post-medieval periods into a series of building plots with frontages onto both Newport Street and Dolday. The layout of medieval buildings indicates that the alignments of both Newport Street and Dolday were established in the medieval period.

The excavation took place across a number of historic plots which conformed to the later street numbering of nos 10 to 34 Newport Street, although some plots fell only partially within the excavation area. Other than within the deep sondages, the full sequence of archaeological deposits was not excavated. The Newport Street frontage was developed from the 13th or 14th century with substantial stone buildings as well as early timber construction, over stone-built cellars. A series of ovens, hearths, structures and surfaces suggest a mixture of craft and domestic activities took place in the back plots of these properties. Although smithing was the only clearly identified medieval activity, documentary sources suggest that the parish accommodated a high proportion of the medieval city's leatherworking, tanning and textile-working trades. The style, construction and layout of some of the medieval buildings, coupled with artefactual and environmental evidence, suggest the occupants were relatively prosperous. Fragments of architectural stonework, mostly of medieval date and probably derived from an ecclesiastical source, were re-used in the foundations of the earlier and later buildings.

The excavations showed that major plot boundaries changed little throughout the post-medieval and early modern period, although documentary research indicates a complex history of ownership and holdings featuring sub-division, amalgamation and multiple occupancy. The street frontages of both Newport Street and Dolday continued to be occupied throughout the post-medieval and early modern periods. Open spaces and structural remains, including wells, hearths, ovens and cess pits, in the back plots reflect a variety of activities associated with trades and domestic activity. Analysis of finds and environmental evidence has helped to link some of these structures to trades associated with the owners and occupants of properties known from historical records. The remains of bread-ovens, a bakehouse, a malthouse and a warehouse for hemp have been identified, and there is more tentative archaeological evidence for cordwaining, cloth-making, brewing and distilling, the latter trades replacing cloth-making in the 17th and 18th centuries as this trade declined. The sub-division of properties and the crowding of small cottages into the back plots during the 18th and 19th centuries reflect the increase in residential occupancy that resulted in over-crowding and a decline in status for this area of the city.

The excavations at Newport Street represent the first

large-scale archaeological investigation of this part of Worcester, within a chronological framework that spans the construction of the Roman road through to post-medieval urban development and decline. The results complement those of previous major investigations of the Roman and medieval town, in particular the excavations at Deansway (Dalwood and Edwards 2004), and provide valuable insights into the economic and social status of the medieval town's expansion onto the former floodplain. An integrated approach, analysing all aspects of the archaeological evidence in combination with detailed study of the available documentary and historical sources, has been particularly valuable in achieving an understanding of the site in later periods, providing the first major archaeological study of the post-medieval development of the city.

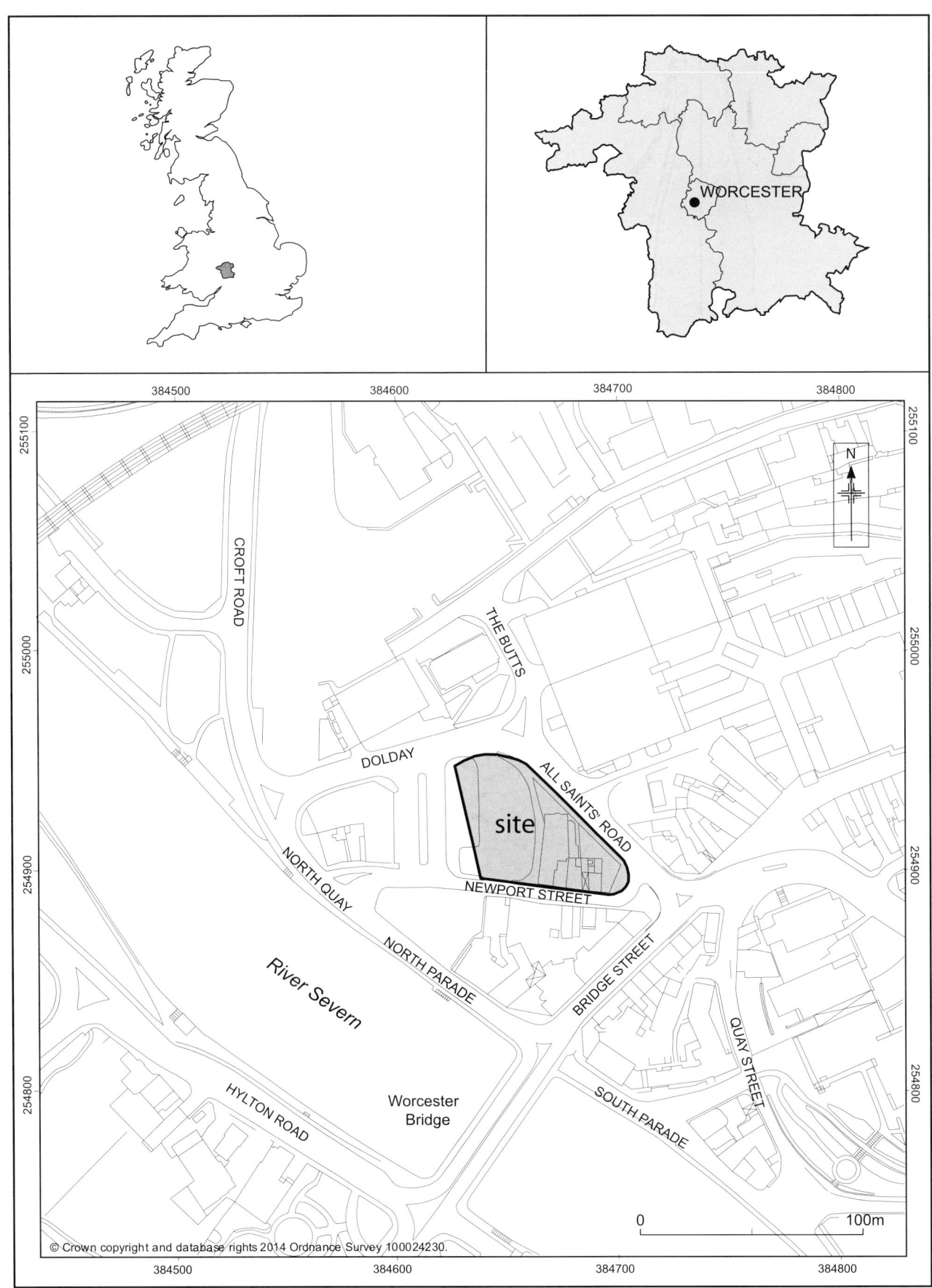

Fig. 1.1   Site location. Scale 1:2500

Chapter 1
Introduction

Robin Jackson

1.1 Introduction

The Newport Street excavations were undertaken between August and December 2005 by Cotswold Archaeology (CA) in partnership with Worcestershire Historic Environment and Archaeology Service (WHEAS; now Worcestershire Archive and Archaeology Service or WAAS) in the north-west part of the historic core of Worcester (Figs 1.1–1.3). The work was undertaken at the request of Archenfield Archaeology (AA) acting as archaeological consultants for Cabot Homes Limited, and was designed to fulfil a condition attached to planning consent for the comprehensive residential redevelopment of the site.

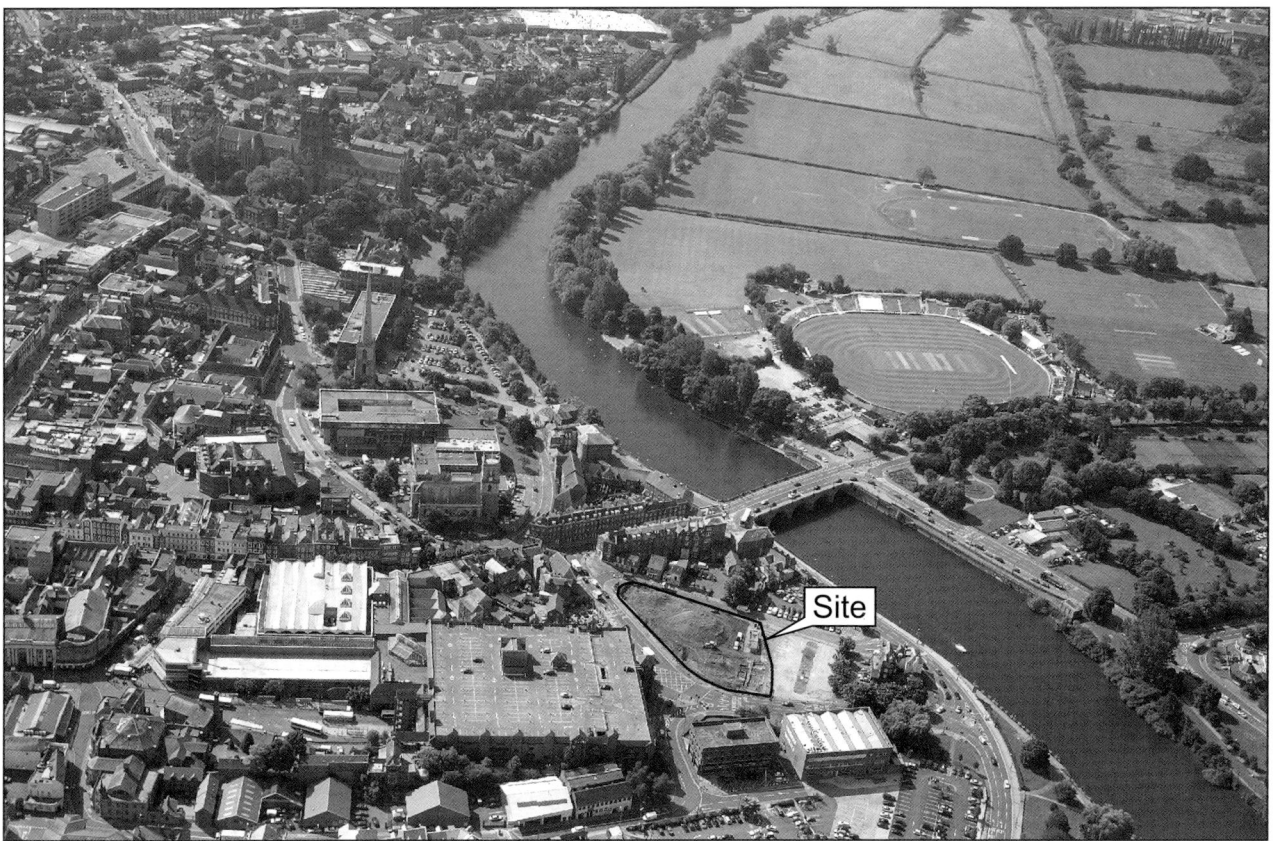

Fig. 1.2   Aerial view of excavation and City (from the north). The site lies in the foreground with the 'new' bridge to its south-west. © Mike Glyde

Prior to the excavation, a number of archaeological investigations relating to the redevelopment had been undertaken. These included a desk-based assessment (AA 2004a), a field evaluation (WHEAS 2004), an assessment of the standing buildings (AA 2004b), an archaeologically monitored geotechnical borehole survey (Soiltechnics 2003; AA 2003) and an assessment of the potential impact of construction on archaeological deposits (John Parkhouse Partnership 2004).

Of particular importance were the results of the geotechnical borehole survey, which indicated a depth of between 2.70m and 4.70m of archaeological deposits present from 0.70m below ground level. The high potential of these deposits was demonstrated during the subsequent evaluation, which recorded well-preserved structures and deposits representing a sequence of building and rebuilding from the 14th century onwards. In contrast, the buildings assessment concluded that none of the above-ground remains merited any more archaeological attention than a basic photographic record.

The strategy for the subsequent excavation was detailed within a Written Scheme of Investigation (WSI: WHEAS/CA 2005), designed in the light of these investigations and according to a brief prepared by James Dinn, Archaeological Officer, Worcester City Council (Worcester City Museum Archaeology Section 2005). Details of the methods adopted are presented later in this report.

1.2 Site location

Newport Street is located on the north-west side of the historic centre of Worcester near to the eastern bank of the River Severn (centred on NGR: SO 8468 5849; Figs 1.1 and 1.2). The site, which covers an area of approximately 0.3ha, lies on the northern side of Newport Street, and is bounded to the north-east by All Saints' Road to the north by Dolday. This area encompassed the greater part of eleven historic properties, but immediately prior to excavation the western half of the site was a car park and the eastern half was occupied by modern buildings and areas of hardstanding.

Prior to excavation the site sloped down towards the river, from a height of *c.* 17m AOD at its south-east corner to *c.* 15m AOD on its western side. To the east of the site, a sand and gravel terrace forms a ridge of higher ground, running from north to south, on which the core of the historic city of Worcester lies. The underlying geology of the site consists of deep beds of alluvial drift over the Eldersfield mudstone formation (BGS 1993).

Fig. 1.3 Partnership in action

Chapter 2
Archaeological and historical background

2.1 Previous major archaeological investigations in the city
Robin Jackson

The origins of Worcester in the Roman period were first suggested by 18th-century antiquaries, and the basis in archaeological evidence for the Roman settlement was established in the mid 19th century by Jabez Allies (1852). However, it was only in the post-war period that the archaeology of Roman and medieval Worcester began to be properly understood. Rescue work in the 1960s, notably at Lich Street and Broad Street (Barker 1969a, 1969b; see Fig. 2.1), produced important results and led to more extensive and better resourced work through the 1970s. This included major excavations at Sidbury (Carver 1980d; Darlington and Evans 1992) and a series of investigations along the line of the medieval walls during construction of City Walls Road (Bennett 1980; Hirst 1980; Wills 1980). A key achievement during this period was the completion of one of the first comprehensive urban archaeological assessments to be undertaken in Britain (Carver 1980b, 1980c), which then provided information for further excavations in the 1980s and 1990s, such as at Blackfriars (Mundy 1986). By far the largest of these was the major programme of excavation undertaken at Deansway in 1988–9 (Dalwood and Edwards 2004). This remains the most important excavation undertaken within the city, the publication of which reviewed earlier evidence and established a revised series of research themes for the archaeology of Worcester.

Since the completion of the Deansway excavations, the pace of development in Worcester has been relatively constant and a number of areas have been investigated (see Fig. 2.1), including Farrier Street (Dalwood *et al.* 1994); the Kardonia factory (CAS 1995); the Magistrates' Court (Jones and Vyce 2000); Warner Village Cinemas (Jackson *et al.* 2002); the Police Station (Edwards *et al.* 2002); 9–10 The Tything (Miller *et al.* 2004a); the Porcelain Works (Jacobs nd); 1, 8–12 and 14–24 The Butts (Butler and Cuttler 2011); City Arcade (Griffin *et al.* 2004); The Commandery (Miller *et al.* 2007); and 16–18 Sansome Street (Napthan 2006). Since completion of the Newport Street excavations further major programmes of investigation have also been completed on the site of the Castle Street University Campus (Sworn forthcoming) and the Hive on The Butts (WHEAS 2011), both of which have provided important new information about the Roman settlement. Of these the University Campus, the Hive, Magistrates' Court and Police Station sites comprised extensive excavation areas but all lay outside the City Walls. The Newport Street site, located in a low-lying riverside area which had seen very little previous investigation, had obvious potential for advancing knowledge of the origins and development of Worcester.

Information from this previous work, and from a wide range of other data, has enabled the development of a broad framework for the settlement history of the city, and contributed to the Research Framework document (WCC 2007), which is summarised below.

2.2 Archaeological and historical frameworks
Hal Dalwood and Robin Jackson

Settlement in the Worcester area appears to have its origins in the prehistoric period, with Late Bronze Age pottery and evidence for Iron Age activity having been recorded (Barker 1969a), the latter suggesting the possible presence of an Iron Age promontory fort and Late Iron Age political centre, probably located in the vicinity of the later castle and cathedral (Cunliffe 1991, 174). A small lithic assemblage (six tools and 33 pieces of debitage) was recovered from later deposits at Deansway, indicative of Bronze Age occupation of the gravel terrace (Dalwood 2004c, 36). There was also some evidence for late Iron Age occupation at Deansway, and there is a scatter of broadly contemporary evidence from the centre of the historic town (ibid., 39; WCC 2007). All evidence for prehistoric occupation in Worcester

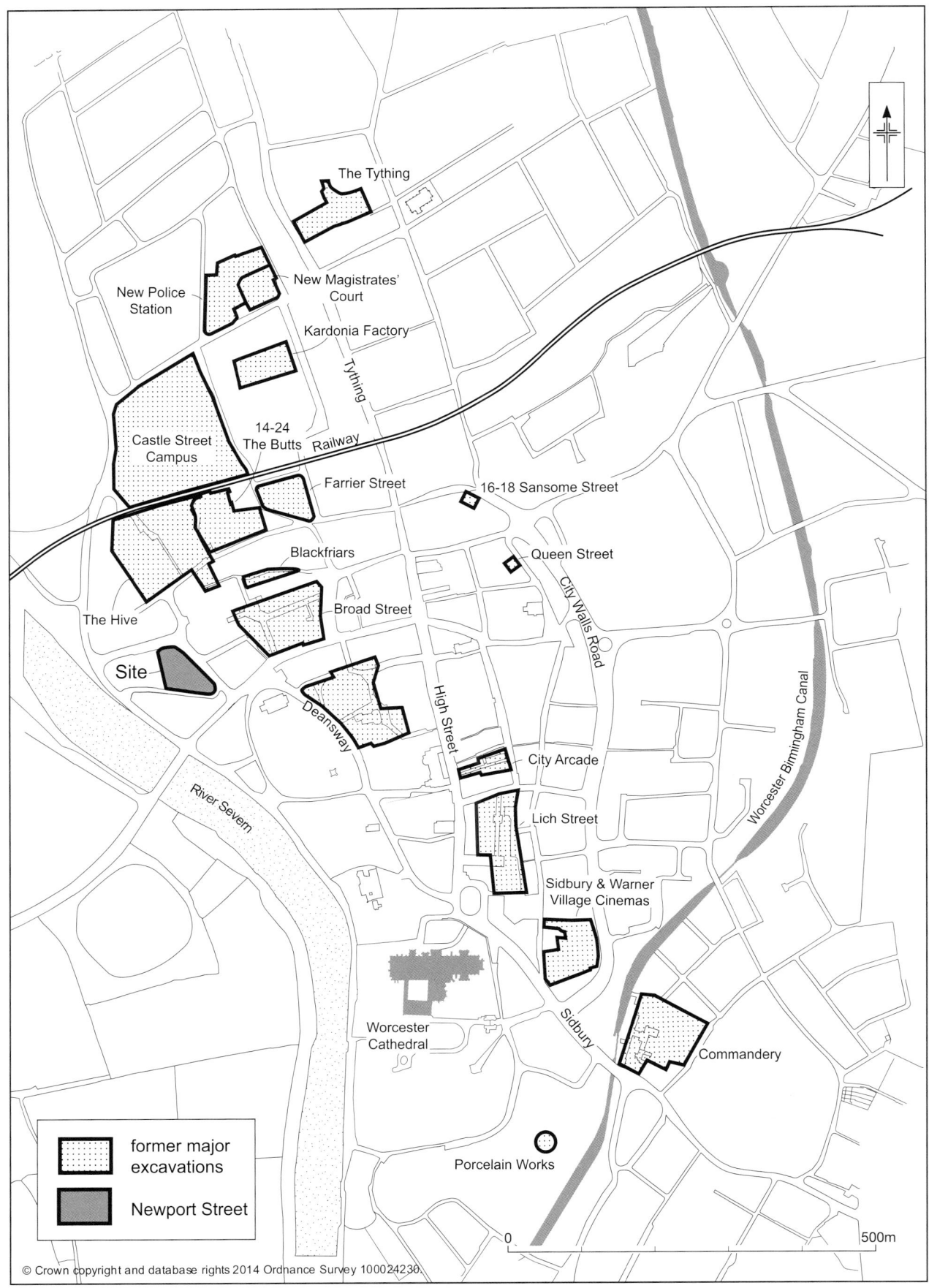

Fig. 2.1 The site in relation to other major excavations in Worcester. Scale 1:7500

has been recovered from the gravel terrace, above the floodplain. The form and character of prehistoric occupation remains unclear, but it seems to have been fairly widely dispersed.

The Roman conquest may have seen the establishment of a fort at Worcester (WCC 2007), but despite fairly extensive fieldwork within the historic city, no definitive archaeological evidence has been recorded, although a scatter of Roman artefacts with definite military associations have been recovered (Dalwood 2004c, 39). In contrast, the development of a Roman 'small town' at Worcester from the 2nd century AD onwards is fairly well established. Once seen as a defended 'core' area with a relatively small industrial 'suburb' to the north (Burnham and Wacher 1990, 232–4), the current picture is more complex and does not fit a simple model. In the late 1st to early 2nd century AD, the settlement was quite extensive and dispersed, and stretched at least 1km from south to north, including a large area to the north of the later medieval city (Fig. 2.2). The evidence is characteristic of rural settlement, and the intensive ironworking of the later Roman period (below) appears to be absent. The Deansway excavations found evidence for agricultural activity within large plots demarcated by boundary ditches and probably stockades, although elsewhere within the Roman settlement the remains of strip buildings have been located, but in general the late 1st to 2nd-century AD settlement remains poorly understood (Dalwood 2004c, 40–3, fig. 19).

Although the major road links to Gloucester and Droitwich were established at an early date, the evidence for roads within Roman Worcester does not form a coherent pattern (Dalwood and Edwards 2004, fig. 11). It has been inferred that there was a ford over the Severn where the medieval bridge later stood, to the west of the Newport Street site (Figs 2.2 and 2.3), and it has also been argued that the piers of the medieval bridge were of Roman origin (Carver 1980c, 19–21). The existence of a Roman bridge at Worcester would be significant in terms of the importance of the river crossing and contemporary routes to the west. Newport Street lies close to the site of the possible Roman ford or bridge, and this area has long been identified as being of high potential for Roman archaeology (ibid., 25–6).

In the 2nd to 3rd century AD the settlement expanded and developed an industrial character, with ironworking playing an important part in its economy. Occupation was not intensive or completely continuous, the settlement area being c. 1.5km from south to north, and up to 400m from west to east, with a defended area lying to the south (Dalwood and Edwards 2004, fig. 11; WCC 2007). It is clear that the later Roman iron industry was substantial, involving the smelting and primary smithing of blooms on a considerable scale. In contrast, evidence for secondary smithing to produce artefacts is surprisingly limited, suggesting that the focus of activity was firmly on iron production rather than the manufacture of finished objects (Jackson 2004). Soil micromorphology at Deansway indicated that areas were also used for penning livestock over a long period (Macphail 2004, 77). It has been argued that the Roman settlement at Worcester had a role in the trade of iron, cattle, salt and pottery from the local area (Dalwood 2004c, 47). In common with most Roman 'small towns', Worcester declined in size and intensity of occupation during the 4th century AD, and although occupation probably continued within the defences, many areas of the settlement were abandoned in the later 4th century (ibid., 51–2).

The question of post-Roman occupation at Worcester remains an unresolved issue, but it seems likely that the Roman defences remained a focus of occupation in the 5th and 6th centuries (summarised in Dalwood 2004c, 52–5). This defended settlement may have included a church (St Helen's) and may have formed the administrative and political centre for a small British Christian territory or 'sub-kingdom' (Bassett 1989). Although the episcopal see of Worcester was founded in AD 680, no firm evidence for significant re-occupation of Worcester emerges before the late 9th century, when the construction of burh defences is documented. These defences were identified at Deansway (Dalwood 2004c, 55–61, fig. 25) which, along with evidence from City Arcade (Griffin *et al.* 2004) and Sidbury (Carver 1980d; Jackson *et al.* 2002), showed that urban development within and beyond the burh defences from the late 9th century onwards was rapid and intensive. A street layout developed, lined with houses within plots and with backyards containing pits, within the area that became the core of the medieval city (Dalwood 2004c, 55–61).

The development of Worcester from the 11th century to the 16th century is fairly well documented (Stenton 1924), and more recently studies have looked at the social and economic life of its medieval inhabitants (Barron 1989) and the medieval landscape of the town (Baker and Holt 2004). The expansion and intensification of occupation within the medieval city is reflected by evidence that at least some elements of the burh defences had been levelled by the late 11th century, thus allowing occupation to spread over and beyond the former defensive circuit (ibid.).

Excavations at Deansway and other sites have revealed evidence for typical medieval urban occupation, with buildings occupying street frontages and back plots intensively used for urban industrial and craft activities, as well as for cess pits. The construction of houses on minor lanes and the sub-division of plots reflect the growing density of occupation and increasing land pressure within the city in the 13th to mid 14th century. The area surrounding the axial north/south road (the High Street) formed the commercial centre, a function which it retained throughout the post-medieval and later periods.

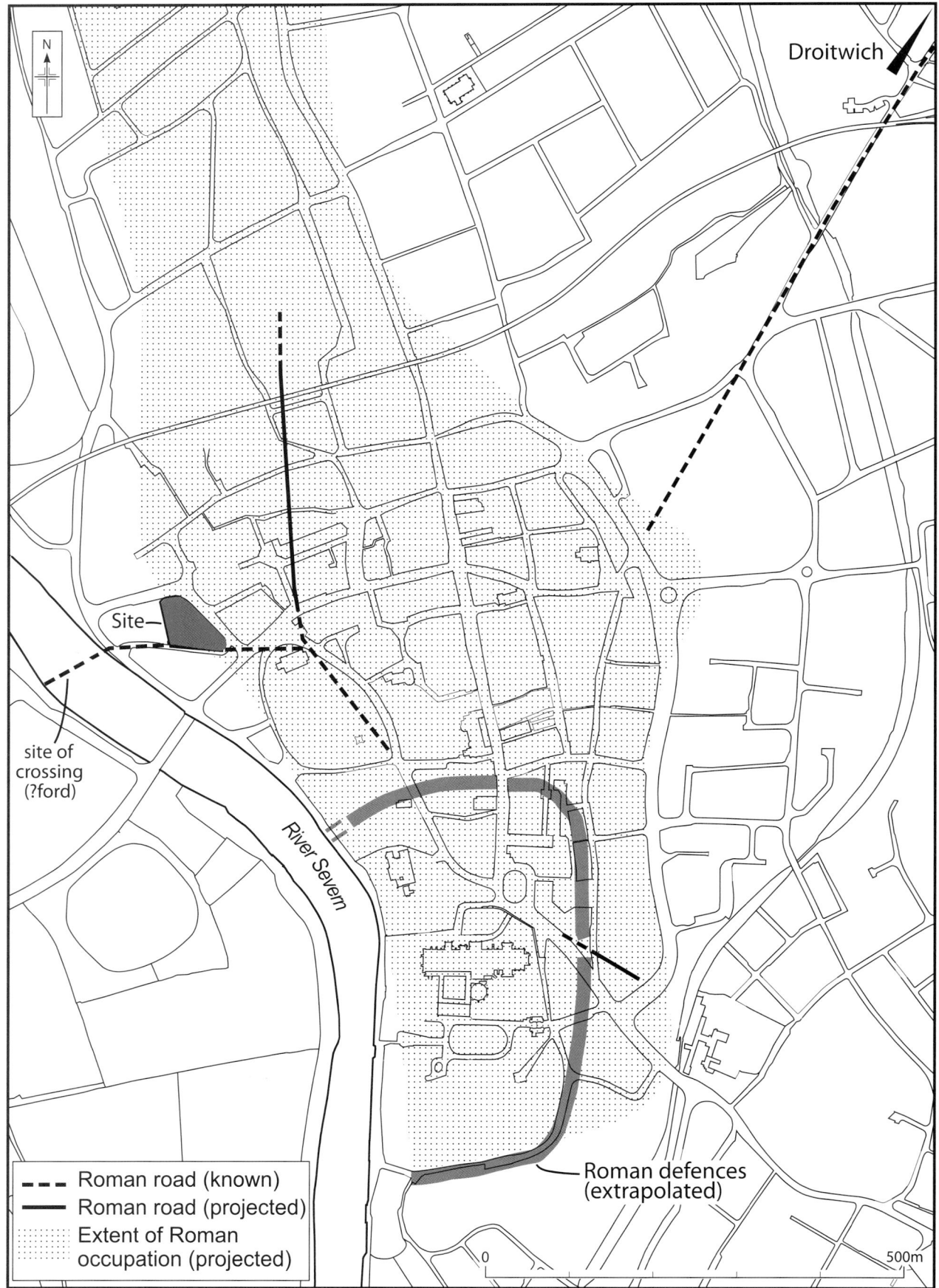

Fig. 2.2 The site in relation to Roman Worcester. Scale 1:6666

Archaeological and historical background 7

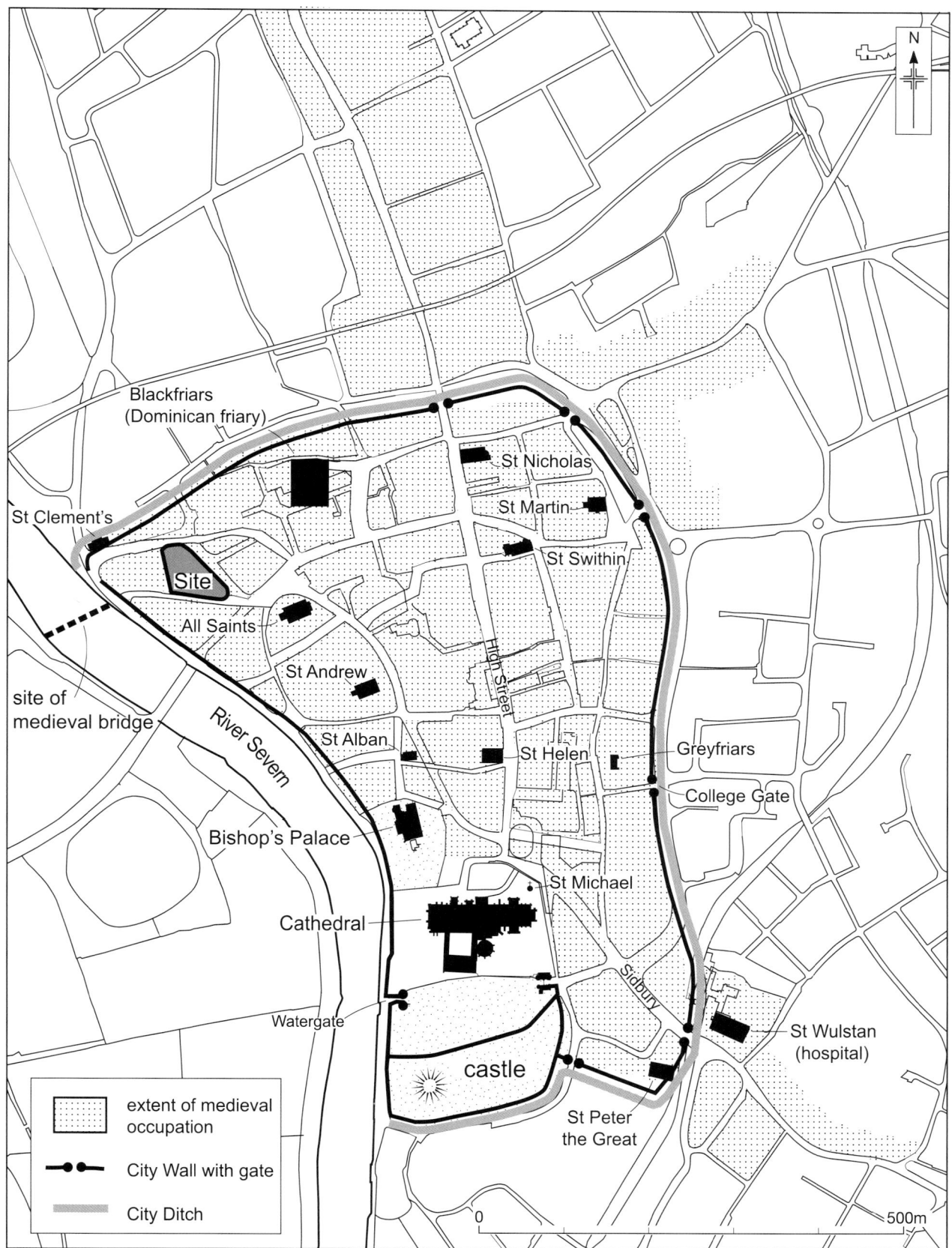

Fig. 2.3   The site in relation to Medieval Worcester. Scale 1:6666

Analysis of the medieval urban landscape of Worcester suggests that Newport Street and Dolday lay in an area of medieval reclamation of the floodplain, outside the Anglo-Saxon defences but inside the line of the city wall built by the late 12th century (Baker and Holt 2004, 178–80, figs 6.5–6.8; Fig. 2.3). The Newport Street site was in the parish of All Saints', which in the 14th century contained a relatively high proportion of craftsmen, particularly leatherworkers, tanners and textile workers (including dyers and fullers), and a relatively low proportion of mercantile occupations (Barron 1989, 12, table 5). Within the medieval urban landscape, Newport Street was of considerable importance as part of the route from the High Street to the medieval bridge. This was a major thoroughfare for goods entering and leaving the city, and the bridge was the focus of two major roads from the west, from south Wales and Hereford and from central Wales via Ludlow, which at Worcester connected to major roads to London, the Midlands, and the south (Dyer 1973, 57–60, fig. 11).

The dissolution of the religious houses in the early 16th century had a considerable effect on the urban landscape of Worcester, making new areas available for domestic occupation. However the most significant change in this period was rapid economic development and population growth. Cloth-making was the main industry by the late 15th century, and held a dominant role throughout the 16th century. The majority of the cloth was sold in London, and despite considerable fluctuations in demand and eventual decline at the end of the century, this industry had a dominant role in the town's economy, involving a wide range of specialised crafts (Dyer 1973, 93–119). This period of industrial growth saw the population doubling from around 4,000 in 1563 to around 8,000 in 1646 (ibid., 26–7). There was considerable rebuilding in the 16th to early 17th century as former church lands were redeveloped and this is reflected by the surviving timber-framed buildings in Friar Street and New Street (Hughes 1980; Brooks and Pevsner 2007, 742–6). The 18th century saw comprehensive rebuilding in brick, further population growth, and the development of the gloving industry as the mainstay of the urban economy to replace the traditional cloth industry (Whitehead 1989).

Until recent years, archaeological fieldwork has not made major contributions to the understanding of Worcester in the post-medieval period (WCC 2007). In the case of Deansway, analysis was only undertaken of remains dating to before *c.* 1600 (Edwards and Bryant 2004), although the recorded later stratigraphy and assemblages from that site have considerable potential.

2.3 The documentary history of Newport Street
Pat Hughes

A general account of the historical development of Newport Street is presented here; the documentary histories of individual properties can be found at the beginning of Chapter 5.

Newport Street, known in the medieval period as Eport Street or Ewport Street, is one of the oldest streets in the city. Leading from the site of the medieval bridge to the urban centre, its development has been shaped by the river, from the likely early crossing place in the Roman period (whether by ford or bridge) to the 19th and 20th centuries, when floods affected its future and its fortunes. There was an area still known as 'the Ford' in the 18th century, where the present bridge was built (WRO 496.5 BA 9360 Cab 16/11). Like Newport Street, Dolday ran from the river crossing to opposite All Saints' Church, but took a more circuitous route to the north (Figs 2.4 and 2.5). Unlike Newport Street, there is no direct evidence for its origin and the reason for its position is something of a mystery, although it clearly functioned as a back lane to plots on the north side of Newport Street in the medieval period (Baker and Holt 2004, 357). Dalwood (this volume, Chapter 6.2) has suggested that Dolday might pre-date the Roman road, or possibly originate in the post-Roman period. The sinuous shape of Dolday may perhaps have been to avoid a wet or muddy patch (in the same way as Severn Street in the south of Worcester curved round the millpond). Excavation showed that the north end of the plots close to Dolday was wet enough for the post-medieval structures to have to be built on piles, although foundation levels were not reached in excavation across the whole site, and this practice may have been more widespread.

The earliest known documentary evidence concerning the area is a rental of the priory from 1240. This refers to Amicus of Eport and Walter of Eport, presumably his son, and also mentions Marker and Martin, son of Marker, who gave a gift of 6/- to the priory, in perpetual alms for the salvation of his soul, from land in Eport in the holding of H. Flokesmud. There is no indication where these properties were sited. Early priory title deeds for the street are equally inconclusive as the names on the abuttals cannot be identified. However, properties between the south side of the medieval bridge and city wall can be traced through from the 14th to the 16th century. These formed a block of four dwellings and workshops in a triangle bounded on the north by an alley leading down to the quay, later known as Maddox slip. This area on both sides of the bridge was tenanted by cloth workers, particularly walkers and dyers. According to the Poll Tax of 1356, a dyer (John Dyer) and a walker (John Walker) lived in this area. These names also appear in 14th-century priory deeds and they may well be the same families. There were also tanners and shoemakers in the area. The effluent caused by these trades polluted the Severn and it is likely that following the prohibition, in the ordinances of 1466, of shaving 'flesh, skynnes or huydes' below the bridge, the leatherworkers moved away. They do not appear in the title deeds for the area, all of which relate to dyers

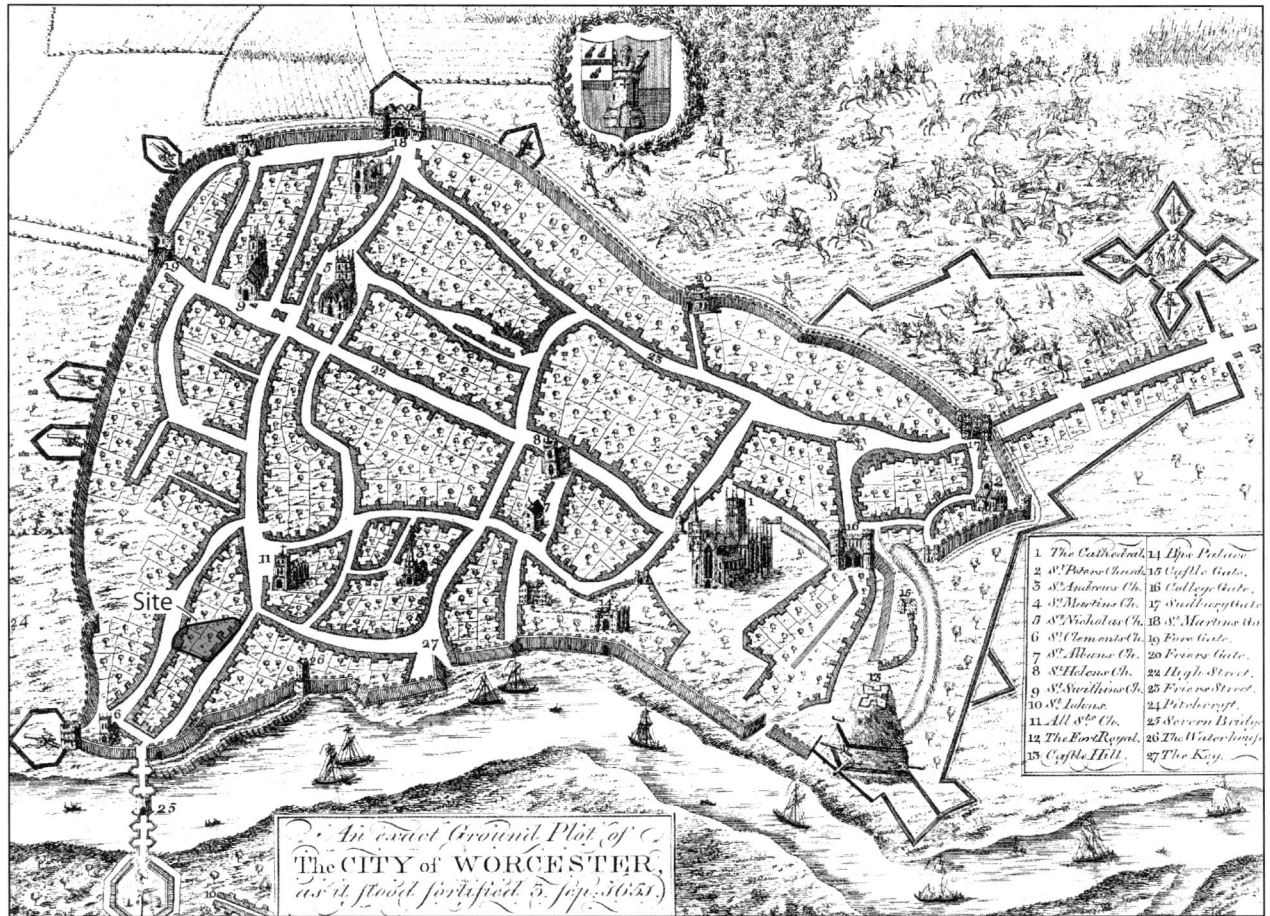

Fig. 2.4 Version of the 1660 map of Worcester as it stood fortified 3rd September 1651 (from an original plate re-engraved in 1723). © Worcestershire Record Office

(Baker and Holt 2004, 357). At this date dyers were not limited as to where they should dispose of their waste, but were enjoined only to empty their vats at night time.

At the end of the 14th century the area was still being developed. In 1394 Thomas Lekhulle agreed to build on a piece of land between William Newemon (a dyer) and the bridge (WCL B1117). In 1408 this property, then in the hands of William Newemon, consisted of a tenement with shops adjoining. To the east was Isabel Walker, whose property subsequently passed to David Dyer before 1461 (WCL B119a; 1421a). It is likely that Thomas the dyer (1337) and John le Deyzare (1356), had lived in the same property. East again in the 16th century were two other dyers, John Bach and William Maddox. Behind was land belonging to St Wulstan's Hospital. Other dyers lived on the north side of the bridgehead in a similar triangle of land, also priory property, in the angle of the bridge and wall and the lane leading to St Clement's Church which lay at the bottom end of Dolday (Fig. 2.6). This lane was little more than an alley and it appears that it ran under houses on the Newport Street frontage, since the abuttals imply that the houses on the west of the lane adjoined those on the east.

It appears that crosses were set up at most of the entrances to the town. The Newport Street cross is only known from one document, which refers to Humphrey Dedicott's house in Eport Street 'near the cross' (WCL B1113). This house was part of the triangle of dyers' houses on the south side of the bridge. A service trench dug in 2006 at the west end of Newport Street turned up a structure of dressed stone which may well have been the cross base. This area round the bridge is the only part of Newport Street that can be traced with certainty to the medieval period. Other parts cannot be identified before the 16th and 17th centuries, when title deeds and tax lists are a little more plentiful and Probate Records can be used establish the names of the occupants. In the 16th century the area round the bridge was still the preserve of dyers, while the available evidence suggests that the lower (western) end of Newport Street was populated by clothiers of all sorts, including weavers and walkers. In the mid 17th century a wealthy clothier, Anthony Careless, lived in the larger eastern part of no. 54 (see Fig. 5.1). He also owned the three houses immediately to the east and left money from the rents to supply two coats to two poor men of All Saints' parish.

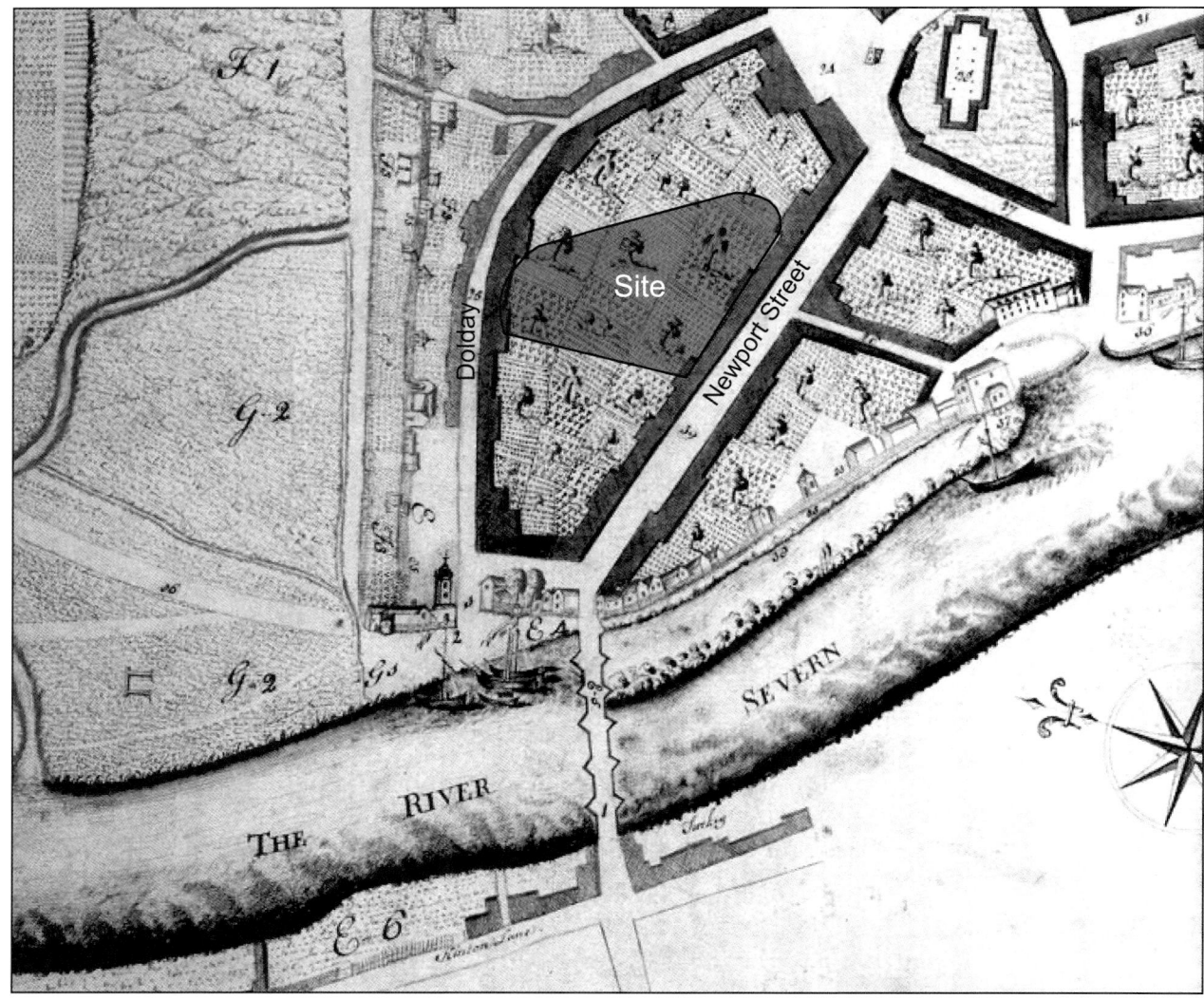

Fig. 2.5 Extract from Broad's map of Worcester (1768). Note the boats at the bottom of Dolday and the channel and waterhouse for the waterworks below the bridge. © National Archives

These houses may have been occupied by his weavers but there is evidence that one of them contained an oven, important enough to have been included as one of the assets. The houses have a confusing history, passing from one owner to another, with the back premises built up in a complicated pattern of tenures. A baker was among the 18th-century tenants (WRO 496.5 BA 9360 Cab 25/23). At no. 42/44 was The Green Dragon, an old established inn, which survived until the late 19th century and was quite possibly the hostelry of William Pelworth mentioned in the 1356 poll tax.

The next block of property also contained clothworkers. No. 32/34, one of the priory properties, was occupied by a walker, William Dodynge. He had a hemp house on his plot when he died in 1554, so may have been making linen cloth as well as processing wool cloth. Another clothworker, William Parker, weaver, lived at no. 26–30. He left ten yards of coloured broadcloth in his will (WRO Will William Parker 1624/201). The historical records for this block, later three separate houses, only make sense if it is regarded as being in one ownership. While most of the properties in Newport Street ran back to Dolday along the lines of the traditional burgage plots, this one was divided into two, one facing Dolday, before the end of the 17th century (and probably much earlier). In the 16th century this belonged to the Leddington family, a wealthy family well known in the city. Although the elder Robert Leddington lived in the High Street, it appears that the son Robert spent some years in All Saints' parish and probably lived in numbers 26, 28 and possibly 30 (see Fig. 5.1). The 16th/17th-century owner of no. 24 was Thomas Hill. He was probably a clothier, as was his father before him, and he left the property and loom equipment to his son-in-law in 1662 (WRO 899.82 BA 4893/7).

The upper (eastern) part of the street is not so well documented, but it appears that here the occupations were more mixed, with two public houses, a silk weaver

Fig. 2.6 St Clement's Church and the 'new key(e)' at the west end of Dolday (by H.B. Leigher; c. 1825). © Society of Antiquaries

and, at the far east end of the street (now under All Saints' Road), four butchers' shops. An order from the City Council in 1599 decreed that there should only be three sites for Shambles in the city: Sidbury, Baxter Street (where a new Shambles was built in 1600) and Newport Street. It is likely that the presence of butchers in Newport Street goes back to the 14th century and it may have been these tradesmen rather than the leatherworkers who washed their skins and hides in the Severn (WRO 496.5 BA 9360 A14; Barron 1989, 27).

On the south side of the street the plots were thoroughly disrupted in the 1770s by the cutting of Bridge Street through the back of the Newport Street premises. It appears that it looked towards the Lower Quay with back premises geared towards the water trade (Figs 2.5–2.7).

During the 17th century the focus of the street gradually changed. The building of a waterworks (on the site of the present bridge) and the construction of a 20ft wheel impinged on the plots on the south side of the bridge. The cutting of Bridge Street and construction of the new bridge in the 1770s considerably altered the layout of the area and passage of traffic into and through this part of the city (Figs 2.5–2.8). The presence of the dyers contributed considerably to the pollution of the water and various measures were put in place to mitigate this (WRO 496.5 BA 9360 A10 1624), although at the end of the century the area was still dedicated to dyeing. As late as 1763, a dyer, William Watton, was still renting five houses from the Dean and Chapter (WCL B3081). The herald, Thomas Vaulx, writing about the city gates in the last quarter of the 17th century stated:

> The third is St. Clements-Gate where the people doe loade and unload Barges and wash their Buckings, and fetch water; and walk into Pitchcroft a spacious meadow by the River side neere the city; their is another little gate opening also upon the river on the south side the Bridge; commonly called Maduckes Slip; where the dyers do wash and swill their coloured Cloth and the soile of the street runneth down. (WRO 989.9:16 BA 8306)

The reference to loading and unloading barges provides a clue as to the change of use to baking and brewing that occurred during the 17th century. There is some evidence that the increase in population in the 16th century and the demand for more in the way of bread and beer led to increased imports of grain from the county. It may have been in response to this that the Upper Quay, then called the 'New Keye', was built at the end of Dolday in the mid 16th century (Figs 2.5 and 2.6). In 1563 there is an entry for repairing the 'New

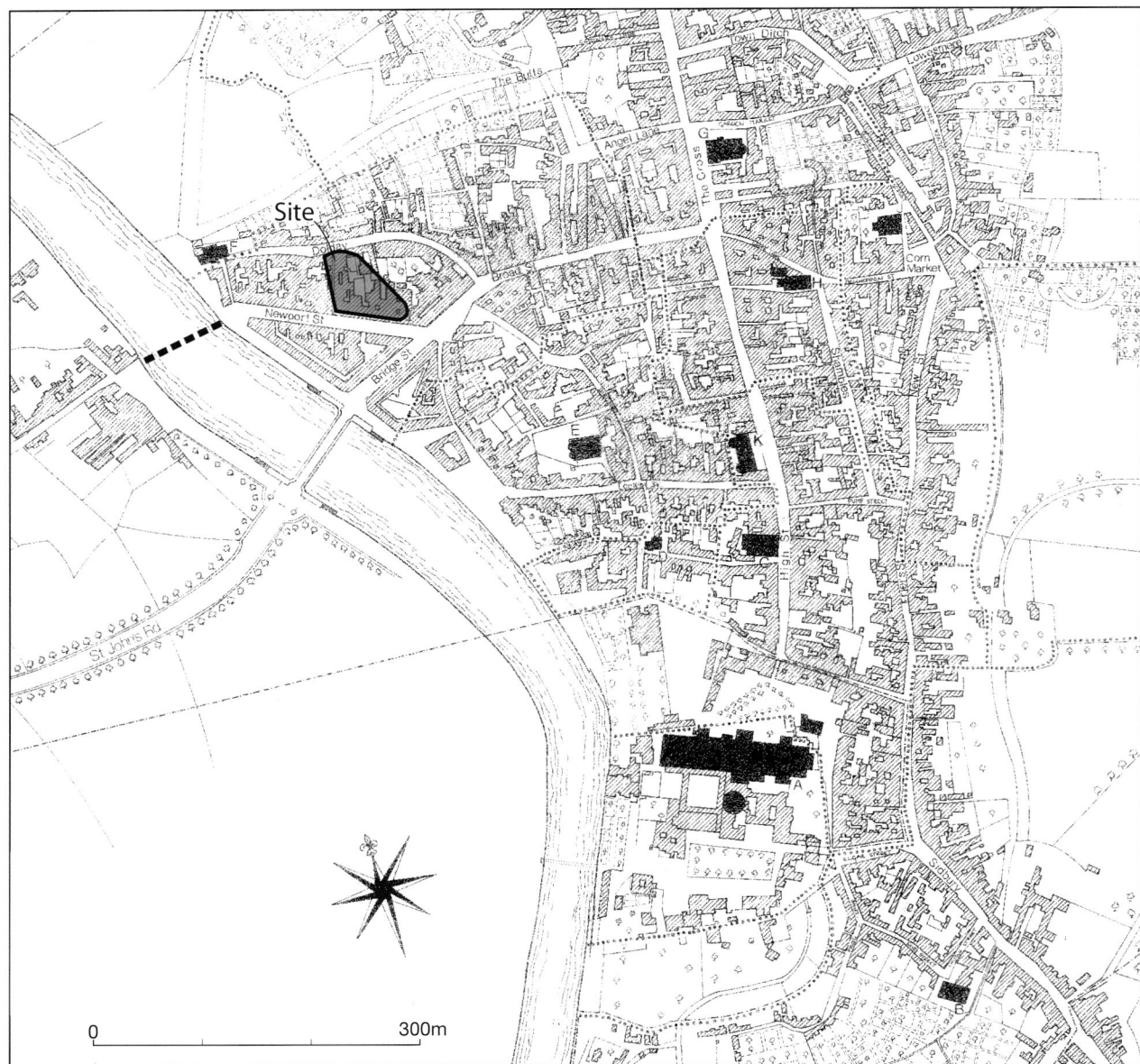

Fig. 2.7 Map of the city redrawn from Young's map of Worcester (1779). Note the insertion of Bridge Street and the site of the newly built bridge. © Worcestershire Record Office

Key' (WRO 496.5 BA 9360 A10 1563; A14 Chamber Ord. Bk I f. 158, 177). This facility allowed grain, shipped from the county farms, to be unloaded and taken directly to the warehouses which, during the 17th century, were springing up along the Dolday end of the Newport Street plots. At the end of the 17th century the cottages on no. 22 Newport Street were pulled down and a malthouse built in their place. By the end of the 18th century there were malthouses or warehouses on the back of nos 12, 16, 18 and 22. There was also a malthouse and an oven at the back of no. 54. Many of these buildings were speculative ventures, rented out to maltsters, rather than purpose-built. Nevertheless Newport Street attracted a number of tradesmen who used grain. John Writer (died 1601) moved into no. 32/34 (Fig. 5.1), traditionally a cloth merchant's house, and set up as a baker. In 1649, two corn chambers were recorded at the back of his family house, while there was a baker at nos 22, 24 and 36.

In the 18th century Abraham Lingham, maltster and oatmeal dealer, living at no. 20, rented three large malthouses on both sides of the street, and a distiller lived at no. 14 (WRO 496.5 BA 9360 Cab 25/23). The south side also had an enclave of bakers during the 18th century.

The area also must have attracted sailors, bargemen and travellers. Before the end of the 17th century the dyers' houses on the north side of the bridge gave place to a large inn, The King's Head, with stabling on the other side of the lane to St Clement's Church (Figs 2.8 and 2.9) (WRO 899.749 BA 87822/14). Another inn,

Archaeological and historical background 13

Fig. 2.8 Medieval bridge and houses built at the west end of Newport Street. The house at the end of the bridge was once the King's Head. The new bridge is visible through the arches (from the E.F. and T.F. Burney watercolour collection). © *Worcestershire Record Office*

Fig. 2.9 Demolition of the medieval bridge (c. 1780). Buildings visible at the end of Newport Street include the building now known as the Severn View and, to its left, the King's Head and St Clement's Church (from the E.F. and T.F. Burney watercolour collection). © *Worcestershire Record Office*

Fig. 2.10 The upper end of Newport Street (1930s; looking east). © Worcestershire Record Office

The Britannia, opened at the bottom of Dolday before 1770 (WRO BA 4600/1032). There was an alehouse at no. 36, The Drum, kept by John Singleton, and another (name unknown) at no. 18 kept by the Gibbes family. Moses Haden ran the Severn Galley, his father's bakery, later the Boar's Head, at no. 24, from the mid 18th century. To the west of the site, the Severn View public house can only be traced back to the mid 19th century, when it was known as the Hope and Anchor, but the Cookseys kept a pub or alehouse, the Anchor, on this or an adjoining site in the early 18th century (David Everett, pers. comm.; WRO Kidderminster Parish Settlement papers 3.2.1731). On the other side of the road, the Saracen's Head, Arnold Bean's old house, had become an inn by the middle of the 17th century.

It is not clear how the inhabitants of Newport Street were affected by the Civil War. They do not seem to have been in the direct line of fire in the 1646 siege, but their trade must have suffered from the curtailment of river traffic, and from the installation of the drawbridge in the central span of the bridge and fortification at its western end (Fig. 2.4). It would appear that the quays were damaged and that stones were dredged up from the riverbed in order to repair them (WRO 496.5 BA 9360 A14 Chamber Ord. Bk III 1656–1664 passim).

The area to the north, outside the city wall behind St Clement's Church, was fortified with a gun emplacement at the junction of the city wall and the river (Fig. 2.4). This was one of the places where Roman iron slag was found. Yarranton has always been associated with this find but, in fact, he was only one of a syndicate. It was a Richard Saunders who leased the site from the City Council on condition that he levelled the fortifications:

> That Richard Saunders shall have a lease of little Pritchcrofte for 21 yeares from the second of February paying £4 10s at out Lady day and Michaellmas in consideration of leavelling the workes raised upon the same. (WHS Bond, 429)

Saunders then complained about John Millard who dug in his patch and carted away 20 cartloads of 'scynders' (WRO 496.5 BA 9360 Shelf A2 Box 4 Court Books).

Until the end of the 18th century Newport Street seems to have been a thriving community, not as affluent as in the 16th-century Leddington era or in the 17th century when the dyers at the end of the bridge supplied the city with two mayors, Humphrey Dedicott and John Watts, but sufficiently prosperous to rebuild or at least re-front many of its houses in the current style, as can be seen from old photographs (Figs 2.10–2.12) and Phipson's painting of the street in 1905 (Fig. 2.13). The back end

Fig. 2.11 View from the top of Newport Street (c. 1967; looking west). © Worcestershire Record Office

Fig. 2.12 The central part of Newport Street (1930s; looking east). © Worcestershire Record Office

Fig. 2.13 The upper part of Newport Street in 1905 by Evacustes Phipson, showing from the left nos 32/34, 30 (with the creeper), 26/28, 24 (The Boar's Head), 22 and 20 (the tallest building). © Worcester City Museum Collection

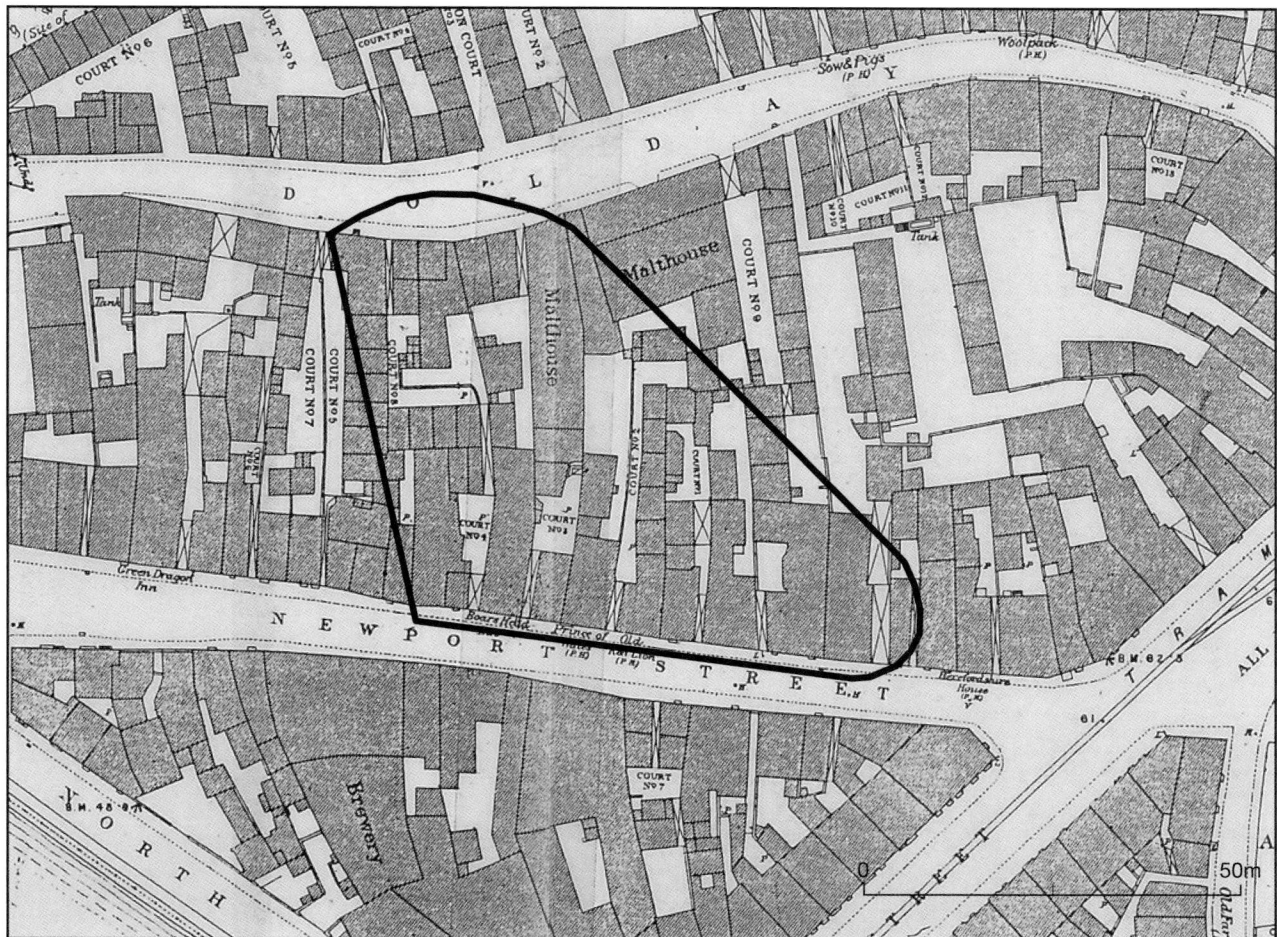

Fig. 2.14 Extract from the 1:500 1886 Ordnance Survey map of Worcester, showing the site location. Scale 1:1000

of the plots was less salubrious: the 18th-century City Leet records indicate that Dolday was used as a dump for muck of all kinds 'very offensive and unwholesome' (WRO 496.5 BA 9360 B10 City Leet Bk 1773–1776).

Many of the occupants were literate, with books in their houses and a strong political awareness. Of these, Clement Writer is the most well known but John and Jane Breynton at the bridge end of the street supported Parliament on the eve of the Civil War to the extent that Jane, in her will of 1640, left £20 'for ever the use of it given to 2 preachers the one for preaching the third day of November being the first day of the beginning of this happy Parliament 1640 The other to preach upon Ascension day.' This combination of religion and politics was typical of the period. The rise in literacy and the ability to read the Bible gave rise to a freedom of thinking in both matters, and the middling tradesmen of Newport Street were fertile ground. John Lilly and William Gibbes were among those whose inventories listed Bibles. The 17th-century Finchers and Daggets featured in the Quaker records, as did the Linghams, Lowes, Olivers and Southalls in the 18th century.

The 19th-century decline of Newport Street has been attributed to the re-siting of the bridge, but this seems an over simplification. It is more likely that the removal of the city wall which accompanied the bridge, alterations and the regular flooding that followed the demolition of this medieval flood barrier made Newport Street a less attractive place to trade. In addition, although the north side retained its link with the Upper Quay, much of the south side now merely served as back entrances to the houses in Bridge Street. A contributory cause was almost certainly the gradual decline in the number of prosperous tradesmen who lived 'over the shop' and their migration to the healthier suburbs of Foregate, St Clement's, St John's and London Road. Over the 17th and 18th centuries the Writer, Leddington, Haden, and Lilly families moved away in this fashion, leasing their property in the city to subtenants.

The closure of the old bridge also had an impact on the inns in the area. The King's Head disappeared almost immediately, the space being cleared for the North Parade. The Britannia was sold off in 1869 (WRO BA 4600/1032), but had already been replaced by The Hope and Anchor (Severn View). A number of small public houses flourished briefly towards the end of the century, all of them well above the area prone to flooding. They probably catered for the river trade which still flowed past the bottom of the street (Bridges and Mundy 1996).

By 1909 many of the houses at the bottom of the street had become slums. One by one these were condemned by Worcester City Council as unfit for human habitation and were demolished, making room first for the City Depot and then for the bus station. The top of the street disappeared under All Saints' Road in about 1967 and the final few surviving properties were pulled down about 2000.

Chapter 3
Project objectives and methodology

3.1 Project objectives and research priorities
Robin Jackson

Primary objectives for the project were established in the early stages of planning. These were:

- To undertake excavation and a watching brief, and ensure that a full and detailed record of the archaeological site was compiled;
- To analyse the primary data appropriately, and provide an interpretative synthesis of the data for dissemination (publication);
- To ensure dissemination was achieved and that the archive was deposited with the appropriate repository.

Site-specific objectives were also identified by taking into consideration national and regional research aims, and in particular the Research Priorities for the city (Worcester RP) as identified in the Worcester City research framework (WCC 2007). Additional site-specific project research aims that did not fit easily into the Worcester City research framework were also identified and included in the WSI (WHEAS/CA 2005). On completion of fieldwork, post-excavation assessment of the data gathered led to the production of an updated project design, which refined and updated these objectives in the light of the results of the excavation. These provided the framework within which post-excavation analysis and research was undertaken, and in particular framed the thematic sections of this report (Chapter 6). Eleven updated objectives were identified:

1. To collate data on the development of the area's topography, including information about possible palaeochannels of the River Severn and the deposition of alluvial layers associated with flooding episodes (WSI Objective 1; Worcester RP1.3, RP1.4, RP1.6, RP2.9, RP7.7);
2. To examine the environment of the site in the post-Roman and Anglo-Saxon period and the potential evidence for agriculture and other land use (WSI Objective 2; Worcester RP4.5, RP4.10, RP7.12, RP7.13);
3. To provide more information on the exploitation of the site in the Roman period, including further investigation of the substantial iron slag layer recorded during the borehole survey (WSI Objective 3, Worcester RP3.7, RP3.8); (Chapters 6.3, 6.4, 6.6);
4. To analyse the evidence for character and dating of the approach to the bridge, including the potential causeway, and to determine if there was any evidence relating to Roman and Anglo-Saxon river crossings (WSI Objective 4; Worcester RP3.9, RP4.18); (Chapter 6.3);
5. To investigate the evidence for industrial activity at the site, including the medieval cloth trade and the post-medieval glove and leather industries (WSI Objective 5; Worcester RP5.10, RP5.12, RP5.13); (Chapter 6.6);
6. To look at the establishment of medieval boundaries and land divisions and the development of these over time, including the post-medieval colonisation of back plot areas (WSI Objective 6; Worcester RP5.27, RP6.7); (Chapter 6.4);
7. To analyse the evidence for medieval and post-medieval buildings, including houses and workshops (Worcester RP5.6, RP5.9, RP6.3, RP6.4); (Chapter 6.5);
8. To analyse the evidence of medieval and post-medieval households and patterns of consumption, in the medieval and post-medieval period (Worcester RP6.7, RP7.19); (Chapters 6.5, 6.6, 6.7);
9. To examine the relationship between Newport Street and Dolday (WSI Objective 7; Worcester RP7.2); (Chapter 6.3);
10. To investigate the chronological sequence of activity, identifying any particular continuity of activity or periods of hiatus (WSI Objective 8; Worcester RP7.1); (Chapter 6.1);

11. To consider the site within its local and regional landscape, and to consider its national significance (WSI Objective 9; Chapter 6).

3.2 Methodologies

3.2.1 Excavation

Fieldwork was completed in accordance with an excavation strategy within the WSI as devised by WHEAS and CA, and approved by the Archaeological Officer for Worcester City Council. It also followed the *General Standards and Practices Appropriate for Archaeological Fieldwork in Worcester City* (Worcester City Council 1999), the *Standard and Guidance for Archaeological Excavation* (Institute for Archaeologists 1999), and the *Management of Archaeological Projects II* (English Heritage 1991). The excavation was monitored by regular visits from the Archaeological Consultant and City Archaeological Officer throughout its duration.

The site was excavated in a series of five discrete areas, defined by practicalities such as site access, storage of spoil and the presence of underground services (Fig. 3.1). Fieldwork commenced with the mechanical removal of modern surfaces and make-up deposits associated with the car park and recently demolished buildings, and of the majority of modern intrusions relating to the 20th-century development, such as fuel tanks associated with the bus station. This process took place under archaeological supervision.

The archaeological features thus exposed were hand-excavated to the formation level agreed for the development. Initially, this formation level was specified as 14m AOD and parts of the north-western and south-eastern areas of the site were taken down to this level; a subsequent redesign of the foundations of the new development resulted in a rise in formation level to 14.35m AOD for the remainder of the site. Pile caps which intruded slightly below formation level were also hand-excavated where masonry or other material that would potentially impede the piling operations was present. Within the excavation areas, where formation level permitted, each archaeological feature was fully excavated and recorded in accordance with standard CA practice (CA 1996). All heights were recorded as metres above Ordnance Datum (AOD).

Two deeper excavations (or 'sondages') were located within areas 2 and 3 along the southern limit of the site (Fig. 3.1). The East Sondage measured 7m by 5m in plan, while the West Sondage was smaller, at 3.5m by 2.5m. Both were excavated to as deep a level as was considered practical and informative (the maximum depth was at 12.2m AOD). The sondages were located to look for any evidence for a Roman road in this area. (One other feature, S113 in Plot 2, was investigated below formation level to its full depth, rather than leaving it partially excavated.)

The information from the sondages was supported by observations from the earlier borehole survey (Fig. 3.2; Table 3.1). A geoarchaeological borehole survey (6 boreholes: BH1–6) was also undertaken to investigate deep alluvial deposits lying beneath Roman horizons, which had potential to provide information on Holocene floodplain development and human impact on the area prior to the establishment of the Roman town (see Chapter 3.2.6). Geotechnical boreholes were also drilled, during both the design stages for the development (6 boreholes: DTS01–2, DTS04–5, BHE and BHF) and during the course of the excavation (16 boreholes; BH7–22). Problems of compaction, sample retention and contamination were encountered and little reliance can be placed on the integrity of the information recorded and the depths that observations were made at. Consequently, whilst this information has been of some use in making general observations about the depositional sequence, no great reliance is placed on information that was not substantiated by excavated evidence.

No buildings earlier than the 20th century survived; however, photographs of previous buildings had been taken at various times and these, in conjunction with historic maps and older topographical views, enabled an attempt to be made to relate the excavated remains to these records. Nos 16 and 18 Newport Street underwent salvage recording prior to their demolition in 1976 and these records were also integrated into the analysis.

Upon completion of excavation, and prior to commencement of construction works, unexcavated deposits were reburied and protected. Within deeper excavated areas such as the pile caps and the two sondages, a geotextile membrane (Terram) was laid over unexcavated deposits, and spoil was then used to backfill these areas to formation level, at either 14m or 14.35m AOD. The resultant levelled area of unexcavated deposits and infilled areas was covered with a protective geotextile membrane and a piling mat was constructed using graded brick and other recovered inert materials. This was completed under archaeological supervision.

3.2.2 Assessment and updated project design

Following the completion of the excavation an ordered, indexed, and internally consistent site archive was compiled in accordance with specifications presented in the *Management of Archaeological Projects II* (English Heritage 1991). A project database of all contextual and artefactual evidence and a site matrix were also compiled (using Microsoft Access) and cross-referenced to spot-dating. Evaluation records were tied into the matrix and considered alongside the records from the main excavation. All site plans were checked and digitised using AutoCAD. All categories of evidence (structural, artefactual, environmental and geoarchaeological) were assessed for their potential for further analysis and to contribute to meeting the identified project research objectives. The resulting post-excavation assessment was

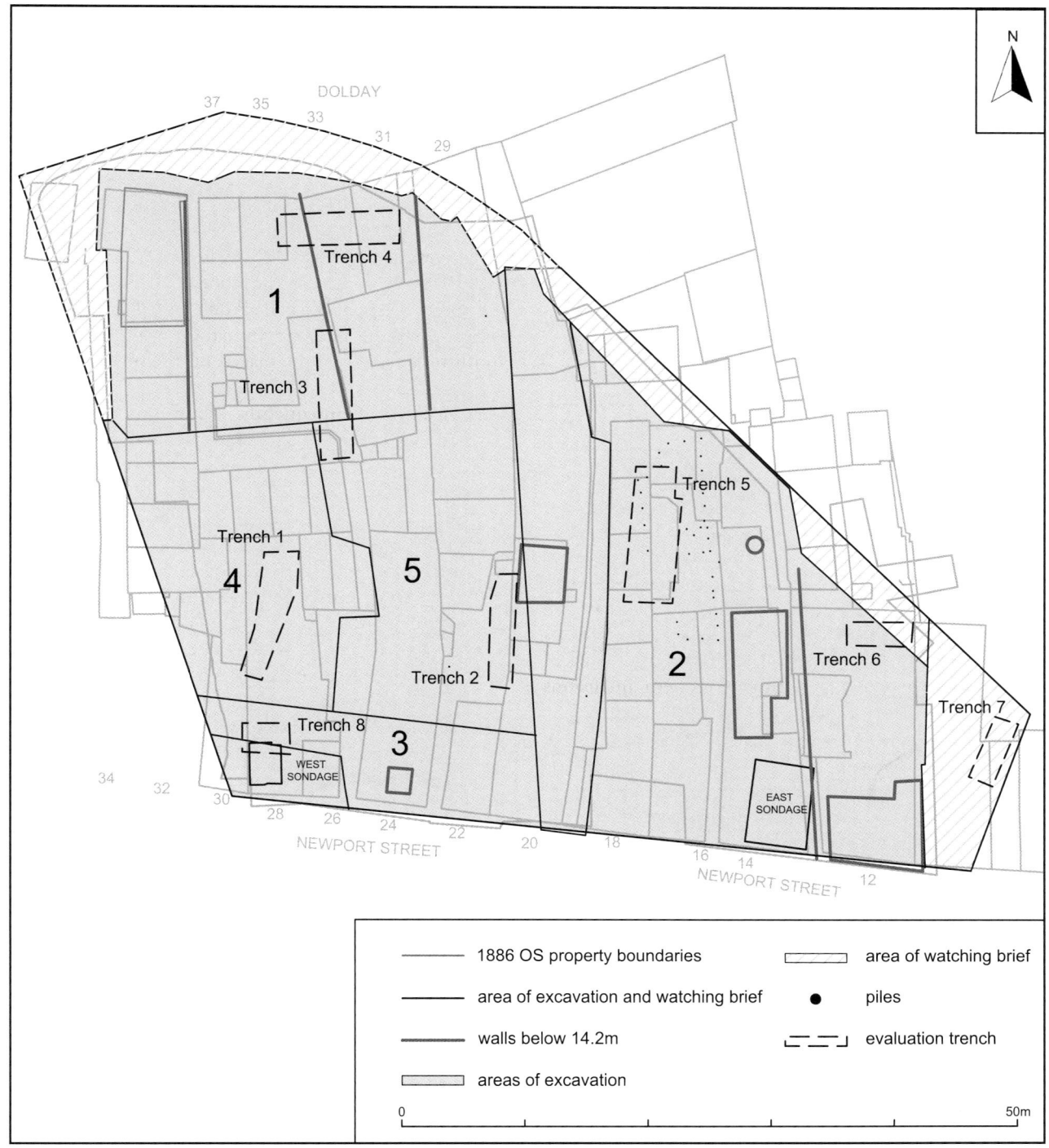

Fig. 3.1 Excavation areas and location of deeper excavations (West and East Sondages). Scale 1:500

compiled in association with production of an Updated Project Design, detailing the analyses recommended for fulfilling the research potential of the site archive (Evans *et al.* 2007).

3.2.3 Structural evidence

Analysis of the site record was led by CA, with specialist support deriving from artefactual and environmental specialists based at WHEAS. The latter also co-ordinated external specialist input for some classes of data including the historical research (Chapters 2.3 and 5.1). The database created at assessment was regularly updated throughout the analysis process, CA updating structural data and WHEAS other classes of information. Updated information was regularly exchanged and a number of meetings were held where ideas were discussed and problems resolved.

The principal tools used during structural analysis

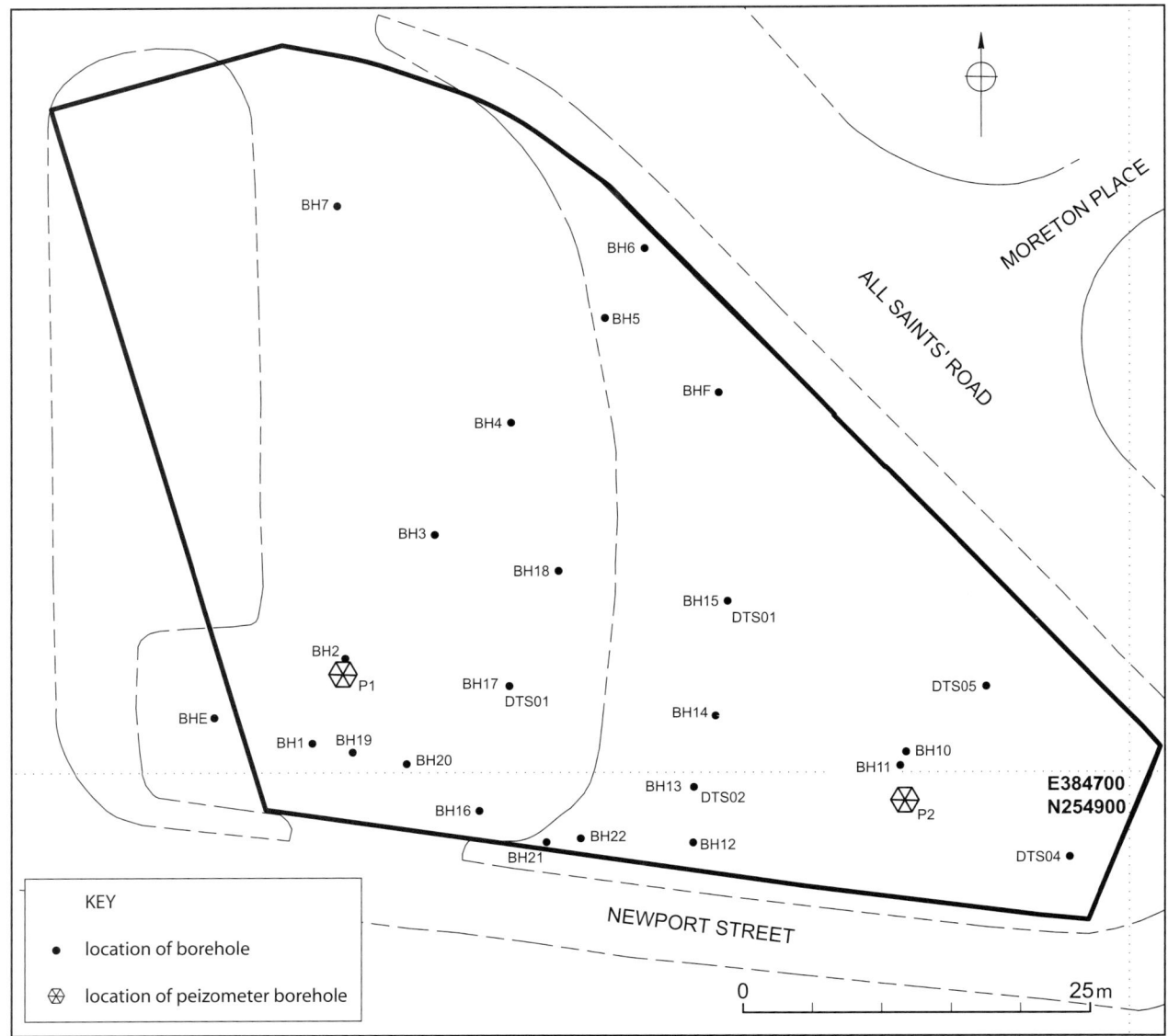

Fig. 3.2 Location of boreholes across the site. Scale 1:500

were the site matrix and the database. Site phasing was developed through use of structural and stratigraphic analysis combined with gradual refinement of dating evidence as specialist artefact analysis was undertaken. Interpretation of the structural sequence was built through gathering associated contexts into sets (directly associated elements, e.g. pit and primary fill) and then drawing the sets into groups (more broadly associated structural elements, such as groups of pits or a series of dumped deposits) or where possible into buildings. These were also represented as set and group matrices showing relationships between these higher-level interpretive units and allowing some elements to be dated more closely through associated assemblage groups.

Throughout analysis, a particular focus was placed upon the evidence derived from site plots. Fourteen of these were defined on the basis of the physical structures and boundaries identified by excavation. While some of these proved not to have been historic tenement boundaries, they had the advantage of being 'real' structures on the ground. A concordance was drawn up to link these plots to the historic properties identified through documentary research. The resultant structural narrative (Chapter 4) is ordered by, or directly referenced to, the individual plots defined. For each plot discussed, referencing within the text is to the highest level of interpretive unit relevant, this usually being a group (e.g. G123) or where the group clearly represents a coherent building (e.g. Building 10), although sets (e.g. S234) or individual contexts are referenced as appropriate.

Table 3.1: Summary of data recorded from boreholes

Borehole	Top of bore (m AOD)	East/West Roman road	Other slag surface	Estimated slag thickness (m)	Estimated top of slag (m AOD)	Notes
BH1	14.15	N/A	Not present	N/A	N/A	Archaeological horizons to 2.70m. Clay from 2.70m to 5.00m. Stopped
BH2	14.24	N/A	Not present	N/A	N/A	Sand at c. 6.00m
BH3	14.06	N/A	Not present	N/A	N/A	Sand at c. 5.80m
BH4	14.60	N/A	Not present	N/A	N/A	Sand at c. 6.80m
BH5	15.35	N/A	Not present	N/A	N/A	Sand and clay with some organic 6.80m–7.50m. Clear sand 7.50+
BH6	N/R	N/A	Not present	?	?	Hit brick obstruction at 1.00m. Abandoned
BH7	15.01	N/A	Not present	N/A	N/A	Sand at c. 6.40m
P1 (BH8)	14.41	N/A	Not present	N/A	N/A	Gravel and sand from c. 5.50m. Piezometer
P2 (BH9)	14.71	Present	N/A	1.00	13.11	Slag from 1.60m–2.60m then alluvium and clay to 6.00+. Piezometer
BH10	14.77	Not present	Not present	N/A	N/A	Organic clay 1.40m–3.00m then abandoned – no slag
BH11	14.72	Present	N/A	>0.50	?	Slag at 0.60m–1.00m. Nothing recovered 1.00m–2.00m. Slag 2.00m–2.50m, then alluvium
BH12	14.61	Present	N/A	1.20	13.01	Soil/organic over slag at 1.60m. Well defined slag to 2.80m. Alluvium below
BH13	14.67	Present	N/A	0.90	12.97	Clay over slag at 1.70m. Slag over alluvium at 2.60m
BH14	14.68	N/A	Present	?0.85	?12.73	?Slag at 1.95m. Void 2.00m–2.10m. Solid slag 2.10m–2.80m. Alluvium
BH15	14.79	N/A	Present	1.20	13.29	Organic over slag at 1.50m. slag to 2.70 then alluvium
BH16	14.83	Indeterminate	N/A	>0.30	?	Slag at 2.40m below brick and clay – probably truncated by late feature
BH17	14.56	N/A	Not present	N/A	N/A	Mixed deposits. No certain slag horizon. Organic from 2.00m–3.00m+
BH18	14.50	N/A	Present	?0.55	?12.80	Slag at 1.70m–2.00m. 2.00m–2.20m blank. Slag 2.20m–2.25m, then organic
BH19	14.25	Indeterminate	Indeterminate	0.10	11.95	Organic and clay horizons over thin slag 2.30m–2.40m. Over alluvium
BH20	14.70	Indeterminate	Indeterminate	0.20	12.40	Organic over slag at 2.30m. 0.20m slag. Organic alluvium at 2.50m
BH21	14.64	Present	N/A	>0.30	12.94	Dense compact slag from 1.70m. Not penetrated. Bore abandoned at 2.00m
BH22	14.64	Present	N/A	>0.50	13.14	Slag at 0.80m–1.00m. After 1.00m bore not retaining sample *in situ*. Very compact slag encountered at c. 1.50m and bore abandoned
DTS01	15.33	Not present	Indeterminate	N/A	N/A	?Roman lime mortar recorded at 12.33m AOD over slag and ash (0.30m in total). Over disturbed alluvial horizons to c. 11.63m AOD
DTS02	15.50	Indeterminate	N/A	0.15–0.50	?	Slag and ash deposit recorded but depth uncertain. AA 2003 records 0.15m but geotechnical log shows 0.50m. This overlaid a 'soft, riverine sand mixed with a dark brown silty soil with charcoal inclusions'. Waterlogged at 3.00m
DTS04	16.50	Indeterminate	N/A	?0.90	?13.90	Made ground over large void 'possibly a cellar'. AA 2003 records a dark alluvial silt at base (c. 13.00m AOD) but geotechnical log shows slag in soft dark soily matrix from 13.90m, then slag in dense matrix giving to compact and impenetrable horizon (?slag) at 13.00m AOD
DTS05	17.00	Not present	Indeterminate	N/A	N/A	Possible pit fill recorded from 14.50m to 12.20m AOD. Over compact slag rich layer then waterlogged (gleyed) alluvial silt and clay to 9.00m AOD. Slag remained sporadically present to near full depth (?contamination)
BH E	15.00	N/A	Present	1.50	11.50	Thick compact slag deposit over alluvium
BH F	15.80	N/A	Present	1.75	11.35	Thick compact slag deposit over alluvium

Notes

see Figure 3.1 for locations   BH1 - BH6 were completed for goeoarchaeological monitoring   BH7 - BH22 were completed for geotechnical investigation
DTS 1, 2, 4, and 5 and RO2 and BH E-F wre recorded by Archenfield Archaeology (AA 2003) during initial site investigations (some information recorded conflicts with geotechnical logs)
Slag thickness estimates cover the full accumulation of interleaved gravel, slag and clay deposits considered to relate to Roman activity (mostly road surface or make up horizons)
Slag thickness can only be estimated due to the very imprecise nature of archaeological deposits recorded from observation of boreholes
Compaction appears variable both across and through these deposits. Unless thick and/or compact slag deposits were present the results are considered indeterminate

3.2.4 Documentary evidence
Pat Hughes

The bulk of the documentary evidence examined relates to the late 17th and 18th centuries, as deeds and probate inventories are most prolific for this period. The 'evidence for individual properties' (Chapter 5.1) focuses on tracing the residents of Newport Street, and concentrates on the time from 1660 to 1800, while including earlier and later material where relevant.

The most obvious sources are title deeds. These are available for some properties: when the City Council bought up property in the street for slum clearance in the first half of the 20th century it acquired the property deeds and most of these are now stored in Worcestershire Record Office; some are still in the legal department in the Guildhall. There are also private collections relating to Newport Street. Few of these documents go back beyond the early 18th century. The earliest title deeds, for cathedral-owned property, go back to the 14th century and are in the library at Worcester Cathedral but these only concern one property in this part of Newport Street, no. 32/34. Such direct evidence, in listed deposits, covers perhaps half of the properties in Newport Street.

This evidence is augmented by abuttals, employed in some deeds as the pre-street numbering descriptions of a building, which identify properties by occupant. Tax lists, rates lists, lists of encroachment fines (purprestures) are also valuable sources, although these cannot be used without an extensive knowledge of the deeds which give fixed points from which to work.

Tax lists consulted include the hearth tax (there are three of these available for Worcester); poor rate, the Poll Tax (1660) and tax returns called lay subsidies. Only the Poll Tax and the Lay Subsidy lists, paid at the place of residence, name the inhabitant of the property. Other taxes, like hearth tax and poor rate might be paid by the landlord or even the mortgagee. These problems extend to other documents like title deeds and abuttals, where it is not always certain which is being named.

Purpresture records list the fines (rents) paid to the City Council for encroachments on the street frontage. They cover such matters as cellar openings, projecting windows and the posts set in the street to protect the house front from vehicles and cattle. In Newport Street many of the houses had projecting 'bulkes', stalls or shop fronts in front of the main building. These books present a range of information, with some gaps, from 1662 to 1760. However, many of the payments were made by the landlord, and the evidence is further complicated when the collectors moved from one side of the road to the other, a problem common with such lists. Only with the 1678 Hearth Tax can one be certain that the collectors worked down one side and then the other. Discrepancies in this list can be put down to the increasing building which was taking place on back plots, and to the recurring problem of who paid the tax.

More information was gained from probate records. Often a testator would cite his 'house in Newport Street' among his bequests and state the recipient. Witnesses are often a clue to the position in the street. When a man was suddenly 'taken bad' the nearest neighbours were often called in and they can often be recognised as living nearby. The probate papers sometimes refer to the lease; they also provide a social framework for the locality and sometimes a detailed understanding of the plot.

The close-knit historical community of Newport Street presents problems of its own. Families living in close proximity inter-married, borrowed money from each other, and witnessed each other's wills. Families such as the Bakers, Parkers, Lilleys, Southalls and Hinksmans persist for centuries. Rarely did they continue to live in the same house but moved up and down the street. Inherited property was often leased to a tenant, who might sublet it. Eventually, after several generations it might return to the original family. Only when the list of named occupants deduced from deeds, wills and lists connected up with the numbered street directories can the occupants' identities be traced with any certainty.

Mortgages are common and are not always differentiated clearly from sales and leases, and in lists of rents, rates, etc. the mortgagee is often cited as the owner. The Lilly family 'owned' mortgaged property up and down Newport Street and paid the purpresture charges for many of them during the first half of the 18th century. Mortgages were often passed from one lender to another as more money was needed. Eventually there might be four or five lenders with a stake in the house to be paid off when it was sold.

Both sides of the road were investigated during analysis, although research concentrated on the excavated areas. The houses outside the excavated area on the north side, are summarised in the gazetteer. The houses on the south side are touched on in the general history (Chapter 2.3). Transcripts of major sources and resumés of the main deeds and documents consulted can be found in the project archive.

3.2.5 Artefactual evidence
Robin Jackson

Finds recovery and processing followed the procedures of the Worcestershire Historic Environment and Archaeology Service Manual of Practice, Appendix 2: Finds recovery policy and Appendix 3: Guidelines on Finds Processing (1995 as amended). Specialist advice was available throughout on site, and site-specific guidelines were also produced. This determined that all post-medieval and earlier finds were hand-collected and retained, although procedures were established for sub-sampling of certain classes of bulk finds (ceramic building materials and ironworking residues). Material of modern 20th-century date was largely recorded and discarded on site with only a small sample and unusual objects being retained.

All hand-retrieved finds and those from processed environmental samples were identified, quantified and dated to period. A *terminus post quem* date was produced for each stratified context, and in conjunction with stratigraphic information this dating was used to determine site phasing. All information was recorded onto the project database to allow cross examination of structural, artefactual and ecofactual information. Pottery fabrics within this report are referenced to the fabric reference series maintained by WHEAS (Hurst and Rees 1992; Worcestershire On-line Ceramic Database).

3.2.6 Leather conservation
Ian Panter

Standard conservation techniques were applied to the waterlogged leather to ensure long-term preservation. The leather arrived wet-packed and was carefully cleaned using running tap water and a soft brush to remove adhering soil. Leather fragments recovered from context 1876, stained with iron corrosion products and other mineral deposits, were treated by immersion in a 5% w/v aqueous solution of EDTA (ethylene diamine tetra acetic acid) for 1 hour. The EDTA solution removed much of the iron staining and following immersion the leather was washed in running tap water. All pieces of leather were then consolidated by impregnation in a 25% v/v aqueous solution of glycerol for five days. After consolidation the leather was frozen in a domestic chest freezer and then freeze-dried in order to remove remaining water (using the small Heto machine, run number 299, 30/7/07 – 3/08/07). After drying the leather was allowed to equilibrate with ambient room conditions and then repacked into resealable pierced polythene bags containing inert foam inserts to provide physical protection..

Identification of species was carried out by hair follicle pattern using x10 and x20 magnification and comparison with reference images (Anon 1981). 'Bovine leather' is used where it was not possible to differentiate between immature cattle (calfskin) and mature cattle hides. The difference between sheep and goat is also difficult without recourse to thin sections, and therefore identification has been grouped as sheep/goat.

3.2.7 Bone and ivory conservation
M. Felter

Following assessment, several objects were recommended for further stabilisation treatment and repackaging. The three combs were treated by cleaning with 50:50 reverse osmosis water and Industrial Methylated Spirits on swabs and with small wooden implements. Where possible teeth were re-adhered using a commercially available cyanoacrylate adhesive (Loctite™ Super Glue) for strength and instant tack. For the more robust teeth of RF1302, HMG Paraloid B72 (methyl methacrylate co-polymer), a more reversible adhesive, was used. This was also used to adhere the larger pieces of the tooth plate of this object and the corner of SF32 (rec 1287).

The combs were packaged in crystal boxes with plastazote™ supports; the other objects were repackaged in finds bags with jiffy foam™ inserts. Digital images were taken of the combs before and after treatment and these can be found within the archive along with recommendations for storage.

3.2.8 Geoarchaeological survey
Keith Wilkinson

A borehole survey was undertaken following the completion of the primary fieldwork. A total of 22 boreholes were drilled by Global Probing and Sampling Limited (Fig. 3.2) using a Competitor tracked percussive auger. This collected continuous cores of *c.* 80–100mm in diameter and 1m length (Global Probing and Sampling Ltd 2004). The location and elevation of the boreholes was recorded.

Six of these boreholes (BH1–6) were drilled specifically to provide an archaeological cross-site transect, although all boreholes (plus boreholes drilled for the installation of piezometers) were recorded to the same standards and are therefore available for interpretation. The archaeological borehole survey was undertaken to investigate the geoarchaeological and palaeoenvironmental potential of deposits below the finish level of excavation, as well as to determine the extent of a Roman slag layer within the site, both for archaeological purposes and to inform subsequent piling operations during construction.

Retained sediments were cleaned and described according to standard geological criteria at the University of Winchester laboratories (Tucker 1982; Jones *et al.* 1999; Munsell Color 2000). The resultant lithological data was entered into a database of the geological utilities program Rockworks (RockWare 2005) and this was used to generate the single cross-section and surface models (for tabular data see Wilkinson 2007, appendix 1). Sediment retention in the cores was moderate in the uppermost 3m of sampled stratigraphy, as the weight used to drive the bore caused up to 15–20cm of compaction per metre. Sediment retention in cores obtained from >3m below ground surface was poor and high levels of sediment moisture content resulted in sediment loss from the gouge chamber of up to 0.60m per metre drilled. Despite these problems it was possible to reconstruct a reasonably reliable cross-section on a north/south alignment across the site. Geotechnical data from works preceding excavation did allow stratigraphic models to be developed for parts of the site located away from the BH1–BH6 transect, but their stratigraphic resolution was too low to enable the construction of high resolution models.

The objectives of the geoarchaeological borehole study were:

- To accurately model the topography of the archaeological stratigraphy beneath that exposed during the archaeological excavation together with that of the Roman iron slag layer and the underlying alluvial stratigraphy;
- To reconstruct the depositional environment in which each sediment unit accumulated;
- To provide a firm chronology for each depositional unit;
- To determine changes in river behaviour with time and its impact on human activity;
- To collect samples for palaeobiological and sedimentological study to reconstruct local and regional palaeoenvironments.

The archive resulting from the boreholes comprises a paper and digital record, which contains full core descriptions (Wilkinson 2007). The cores were discarded once they had been sub-sampled for palynological analysis and ^{14}C dating.

3.2.5.9 Pollen remains
Katie Head

The environmental sampling strategy conformed to standard WHEAS practice (CAS 1995, appendix 4). Two monoliths were taken from the East Sondage, encompassing the late prehistoric to medieval period. Between the two monoliths was a thick metalled layer of slag dating to the Romano-British period. Eighteen sub-samples were extracted from the monoliths for pollen analysis.

Eighteen pollen samples were selected from alluvial and organic deposits (depths 20, 36, 44, 56, 64, 72, 80, 88, 96, 106, 175, 184, 192, 200, 208, 216, 224, 227cm). Sediment samples of 2cm^3 were measured volumetrically and were subjected to standard chemical preparation including acetolysis and hydrofluoric acid digestion, the techniques of which are outlined in Barber (1976) and Moore *et al.* (1991).

Pollen grains were counted to a total of 250 to 500 land pollen grains (TLP) on a GS binocular polarising microscope at 400x magnification, and identification was aided by using the pollen reference collection maintained by WHEAS and reference manual by Moore *et al.* (1991). Nomenclature for pollen follows Stace (1991 and 1997) and Bennett (1994). The pollen diagram was constructed using TILIA, TILIA.GRAPH, and TGView 2.0.2 software (Grimm 1990; 2004) and the diagram divided into three pollen assemblage zones.

3.2.10 Sampling and plant macrofossils
Elizabeth Pearson

The environmental and residue sampling strategy was based on WHEAS and CA practice (CAS 1995, appendix 4; CA 2003). Amendments were made that allowed the sampling to be focused on the research aims of the project. Sampling strategy was also informed by the results of the extensive programme of sampling which had been undertaken over a large area during the nearby Deansway excavations (Moffett 2004b). Sampling of the following deposit types was prioritised:

- primary pit and ditch fills;
- selected secondary fills where deposits had obvious concentrations of material such as charcoal/charred plant remains, bone, organics, cess/phosphate concretions e.g. cess pits. All primary and all secondary fills were to be sampled once a complex sequence of specialised deposits within one pit emerged;
- hearths, especially those thought to be have been used in metalworking to retrieve hammerscale and other smithing waste;
- features with other possible industrial functions, such as tanning, dyeing and fulling.

Following assessment (Evans *et al.* 2007), processing of the recommended samples was carried out by flotation using a Siraf tank. The flot was collected on a 300μm sieve and the residue retained on a 1mm mesh. This allowed for the recovery of items such as small animal bones, molluscs and seeds. The residues were fully sorted by eye and the abundance of each category of environmental remains estimated. A number of flots were fully sorted (or a fraction of the flot/residue fully sorted), while some were scanned to estimate abundance of species. Where flots and residues were large, and it was necessary to sort a fraction, the quantified results were multiplied appropriately to show the number of items for the volume originally processed. These details are held in archive. A low power Meiji stereo light microscope was used and plant remains identified using modern reference collections maintained by WHEAS, and seed identification manual (Cappers *et al.* 2006). Nomenclature for the plant remains follows Stace (1997). A magnet was also used to test for the presence of hammerscale.

A number of the samples were taken from organic deposits (some partly mineralised). Assessment had demonstrated that these generally contained a significant component of domestic and industrial debris, and therefore it was considered that processing of large volumes using the flotation tank would be appropriate to recover these remains. Further processing of small subsamples by the conventional wash-over technique was not used as organic remains were well-preserved in the dried flots and residues.

During the processing and initial analysis the presence of plant remains of particular significance for the understanding of medieval environment and post-medieval economy were recognised, albeit in small quantities. The selection of samples made in the assessment was therefore amended to allow further work on the relevant samples.

3.2.11 Animal bone
Sylvia Warman

For each bone specimen the following details were recorded: element, species, size, sex, weight and parts present, using the Dobney and Reilly zonation system (1988). The age of specimens was estimated in two ways: the state of fusion of the ends of the long bones (epiphyseal fusion) and the state of eruption and wear of the mandibular (lower) teeth. Fusion follows Silver (1969), whilst mandibular tooth wear follows Grant (1982). The tooth-wear results are given as mandible wear scores (MWS). Fusion tables are available in the site archive. Bone specimens were also examined for pathology, burning, butchery and weathering following Behrensmeyer (1978). Whole long bones were measured following von den Driesch (1976) in order to enable the calculation of withers heights (von den Driesch and Boessneck 1974). The factors used were Kiesewalter (1888) for horse, Matolcsi (1970) for cattle, and Teichert (1975) for sheep. The number of live animals represented by the assemblage was estimated using both NISP (number of identified specimens) and MNI (minimum number of individuals). The minimum number of individuals was calculated on a context-by-context basis which was then summed by Period. The true values are likely to be lower, as any shared origin of material found in separate contexts will not have been identified (the problem of aggregation as defined by O'Connor (2000)). The assessment had identified sheep/goat bones were present within this assemblage; the criteria of Boessneck (1969) and Payne (1985) were used to separate sheep and goat. The fully analysed material is presented by species and element for each Period, hand-collected animal bone and that from processed samples being presented separately. In addition to this report the database is included within the site archive.

3.3 Retrospective view
Huw Sherlock and James Dinn

3.3.1 The consultant's perspective
Huw Sherlock

Archaeological projects frequently have long lead-in times and Newport Street was typical in this regard. I was originally engaged to give advice on the archaeological implications of developing this site in 2005. The proximity of the site to a major river crossing and thoroughfare into the city, its liminal nature on the riverine margins of the settlement, the possible preservation of deeply stratified environmentally rich deposits and the potential for Roman industrial activity and evidence relating to the existence of a long discussed Roman road, formed the framework into which my advice to my client was framed.

Archaeological monitoring of the earliest phases of intrusive work, in the form of a geotechnical borehole survey, revealed the presence of well-preserved beds of metalworking slag, with unusually well-defined stratigraphy and dating evidence in the form of Romano-British pottery found within some of the cores. The requirement for further evaluative work on the site to define the extent, nature and relative state of preservation of the archaeological resource on the site was identified as being crucial to allowing the details of the proposed development to be outlined at an early stage, and for the likely risk in terms of cost and time to be adequately forecast. Standing building assessment and documentary and archival research were combined to produce a detailed desk-based assessment which allowed the design of the subsequent evaluation to target key areas.

A collaborative approach to carrying out the fieldwork on the site was taken, with WHEAS being appointed to carry out the evaluation (WHEAS 2004). The results highlighted the excellent preservation immediately below the modern ground surfaces, and the remarkable nature of some of the structures and deposits exposed (a stone-lined medieval cellar, evidence of a metalled Roman surface formed of slag, medieval and post-medieval industrial hearths, etc.) was instrumental in a redesign of the finished structure, which was originally planned with underground parking.

Once the final planning was approved and the site had been acquired by Cabot Homes, a crucially important series of meetings ensured that the archaeological conditions attached to the planning permission could be achieved in a structured way that would not unnecessarily impede the progress of the development. This meant that finding the right team of archaeologists to be able to take on an excavation of this size (0.3ha) was critical to achieving a successful outcome. As consultant I had to balance the client's overriding concern, which was to have clarity about the programme and key delivery dates, with the need to combine depth of knowledge and experience of the local archaeology with sufficient resources to achieve the tight deadlines that were required. With these requirements in mind the joint bid by CA and WHEAS was adjudged to have the best balance of local knowledge, supervisory experience and resources.

Modern archaeological practice in the UK has adopted the mantra of 'preservation *in situ*' as its overriding precept and, to ensure minimum disruption to the archaeological resource, careful integration of the requirements for excavation into the detailed construction programme was necessary. At an early stage in the design process a piled foundation was adopted in preference to other potential designs as this allowed a defined zone of disturbance to be identified which could then be totally excavated. In addition a number of deeper areas of excavation were undertaken to provide a window through the entire depth of the stratigraphic sequence, targeted specifically at areas identified as being of high potential in the evaluation.

In consultation with the English Heritage Regional Scientific Adviser, a monitoring programme was designed to record the impact of the piling on the archaeological remains and in particular sealed environmentally rich deposits. This was to comprise groundwater monitoring both pre- and post-piling, to allow the effect of the insertion of piles on groundwater pH and redux values to be ascertained. The position of the monitoring wells was enshrined in the final design of the building and access issues and long term sampling strategies discussed. It is one of the few shortcomings of the project that this cutting-edge research for Worcester failed to proceed due to the inadequately drafted wording of the planning condition. This is something that in future projects will no doubt be more stringently addressed.

Overall the project was a very successful example of how early archaeological intervention and advice, and a collaborative approach between archaeological professionals, can help to achieve a good outcome for the preservation of the archaeological resource, both 'in situ' and 'by record', and also by the imaginative use of the 'percent for art' planning condition. For this the developer agreed to commission a series of panels from local artist Caroline Hands, reflecting the history and archaeology of the site, which have helped to retain a sense of place for Newport Street into the 21st century and have greatly added to the aesthetic, cultural and amenity value of the building.

3.3.2 The curatorial retrospective
James Dinn

The Newport Street excavation is the largest (by area) to have been carried out within the medieval walled city, and provided the first opportunity to examine in detail a large street-block including frontages and back plots.

The Newport Street area has long been recognised as having significant archaeological potential (Carver 1980a, fig. 7). Further detail was provided in a research paper for the St Clement's Gate Urban Design Campaign (Baker 1996). By 2003, early drafts of *An Outline Resource Assessment and Research Framework for the Archaeology of Worcester* (WCC 2007) were being produced. Baker's work on this document, which forms part of the English Heritage-funded *Worcester Urban Archaeological Strategy*, again drew attention to the potential of the Newport Street area for medieval industrial and domestic remains, as well as for Roman industry. However, very few opportunities were presented by development for archaeological fieldwork in this part of Worcester before 2003.

The western part of the site was identified in the 1996–2011 Local Plan as a mixed-use development site, part of the wider St Clement's Gate area. The 1996 Urban Design Campaign focussed on a large part of the north-western fringe of the city centre, both within and outside the medieval walls, as an area for regeneration and enhancement. The Newport Street site is at the southern end of this area, and was the first site within the city walls to be brought forward for development.

In mid 2003 borehole investigations took place, on behalf of Neil Grinnall Homes. No archaeological provision had initially been made, but the need for monitoring was raised by Worcester City Council. Archenfield Archaeology were then contracted to maintain a watching brief during the geotechnical work. Significant depths of archaeological deposits were recorded, as well as large deposits of iron slag, presumed to be Roman, and alluvium layers (AA 2003).

Land assembly by Neil Grinnall Homes had led to a wider area being proposed for development than that indicated in the Local Plan, taking in some buildings and their back plots at the eastern end of Newport Street. The results of field evaluation (WHEAS 2004) and a desk-based assessment (AA 2004a) were submitted with the planning application, and a conservation area consent application for demolition, in 2004. An assessment of the standing buildings was also produced (AA 2004b). Following the grant of planning permission the site was sold on to Cabot Homes, who undertook the development.

The excavation was designed alongside a strategy for the minimising of impact through foundation design. Significant archaeological remains occurred almost at current ground level over much of the site, so impact during development was unavoidable, especially as the design required variable ground level reduction to achieve a level floorplate. By far the greatest impact was from the ground level reduction, which affected nearly five times the volume of deposits impacted by all other groundworks. The new building is supported on around 400 piles; initially these were proposed to be continuous flight auger piles, but these were later replaced by smaller-bore driven piles, though with very little increase in estimated impact.

Materials from the demolished buildings were crushed and stored on site. This meant that only part of the site was available for excavation at any one time, raising significant recording issues for the excavators. It also meant that the site was unsuitable for extensive public access during the work, although one open day was held, and viewing windows and information displays on the site hoardings were well used. The nature of the development, and the decision to restrict the depth of excavation to the principal impact levels (on grounds of cost and impact), meant that the excavation addressed a 'diagonal slice' through the archaeological deposit sequence. This gave giving particular problems for interpretation in some periods, and means that the report cannot present a complete narrative history of the Newport Street and Dolday area.

Deeper excavation areas and the archaeological borehole survey were essential to make sense of the full sequence and provide a context for the extensive area excavation. More specifically they provided mitigation for the impact of the piles. However, it proved difficult to extend the conclusions of the small number of deeper excavations across the whole site. More flexibility in selecting these areas, with greater consideration of emerging results from the wider excavation, may have led to more useful results. Overall, in spite of the technical difficulties, a high quality record was achieved, which provided a suitable replacement for the deep deposits lost as a result of the development.

Following excavation and the completion of the development, up to 3m of cultural deposits remain on the site, with alluvium below this depth. These deposits form a significant reservoir of material for future research into the Roman, Anglo-Saxon and earlier medieval development of Worcester.

The failure of the deposit monitoring programme, due to the inaccurate drafting of a planning condition, which made it unenforceable, was a disappointment. However the extensive assessment of deeper deposits and groundwater on the subsequent Worcester Library and History Centre site, 100m to the north (The Hive), led to the conclusion that the groundwater there was in hydraulic connection with the River Severn (Panter 2009). These conditions are likely to extend across the floodplain in this area, and indicate that the impact of piling on the deposits should not be as significant as had been feared; indeed there may be an advantage in using driven piles, which would result in reduced migration of concrete into the deposits, at least in the short term.

The emerging results of the excavation at Newport Street had a direct impact on the detailed content of the research framework for the city, developed from 2004–7 (WCC 2007). The increased understanding of the nature and potential of floodplain and floodplain deposits in this area also informed the approaches taken to the subsequent University of Worcester (former Worcester Royal Infirmary) and Worcester Library and History Centre (The Hive) sites. Together these three sites cover over 200m of the floodplain edge, including much of the area which is believed to have been most intensively used during the Roman period. There is a strong case for a synthetic review of this area, which may lead to recommendations for further fieldwork, to build on the results of the development-related work.

3.4 Archive content and location

The excavation archive comprises the following records:

Context sheets	2929
Plans (1:20)	2767
Sections (1:10, 1:20)	55
Sample sheets	190
Monochrome films	63
Colour slide films	63
Matrices	28
Boxes of finds and environmental residues	165

The archive has been deposited at: Worcester City Museum and Art Gallery, Foregate Street, Worcester WR1 1DT (accession no. WSM 29964).

Chapter 4
Site narrative

4.1 Introduction
Peter Davenport

The excavations covered a large number of historic properties, running from the western edge of the former no. 10 Newport Street to the northern part of no. 32/34. Nos 24 to 28 Newport Street were uncovered in their entirety all the way to the Dolday frontage (Fig. 4.1). For the purposes of post-excavation analysis the site was divided into fourteen plots that largely reflect these historic properties, although some boundaries and land holdings changed over time, and some plot boundaries do not follow any historic ownership, particularly for the eastern part of the site (nos 12–18 Newport Street) where archaeological remains were sparser. Nevertheless, the plots defined during post-excavation analysis have been used as the basis for the description of the archaeological deposits. Their correlation to historic properties and 20th-century street numbers is clarified in both narrative and discussion as appropriate. In addition to plots, courts of low-status post-medieval housing are also used as reference points in the site narrative. Nine such courts were laid out in the 17th to early 19th centuries between Newport Street and Dolday (Figs 2.14 and 5.5), six of which fell into the area excavated: Court nos 1–4 and 8, and part of 5 (Fig. 4.1).

The site was excavated to the archaeologically arbitrary levels of 14.00m AOD and 14.35m AOD, the formation levels for the new development (Fig. 4.2). The borehole survey (Wilkinson, Chapter 4.2 below) indicated that up to 2.85m of archaeological deposits remained unexcavated below the higher formation level. The levels reached in each plot were not necessarily the same in date as those reached in neighbouring plots: each had their own history of development within property boundaries that changed rarely and hardly ever significantly. Some tenements had not been rebuilt since the 17th century. Medieval deposits and structures survived in some plots and not in others, and were encountered more often in the southern part of the site, as this was excavated to the lower of the two formation levels.

The archaeological evidence in each plot was recorded as single contexts. During post-excavation analysis these contexts were placed into sets of related events, and the sets into groups of related activities. It is the activity groups (prefixed G, e.g. G203) that form the basis of the narrative, with occasional reference, as appropriate, to sets (prefixed S, e.g. S413) and contexts (in parentheses, e.g. (2391)). Databases, matrices and text files in the site archive provide the connections between the members of this interpretative hierarchy and will allow further interrogation of the site data.

The archaeological sequence is divided into five broad periods, two of which are subdivided further. These are:

- Period 1: Roman
- Period 2: medieval, subdivided where appropriate into:
  - *Period 2.1*   10th to 11th centuries
  - *Period 2.2*   12th century
  - *Period 2.3*   13th to 14th centuries (subdivided further in some plots)
  - *Period 2.4*   14th to 15th centuries
  - *Period 2.5*   15th to 16th centuries
- Period 3: post-medieval, subdivided where appropriate into:
  - *Period 3.1*   16th to early 17th centuries
  - *Period 3.2*   mid 17th century
  - *Period 3.3*   late 17th century
- Period 4: 18th century
- Period 5: 19th and 20th centuries

Period 1 (Roman) was only recorded in the West and East Sondages, in the south-west corner of Plot 3 and the south-east corner of Plot 13. However, significant information on the Roman deposits was recovered from the borehole survey (Chapter 4.2) and this has been incorporated in the discussion of the Roman deposits in Plot 13. Period 2 was subdivided into five phases,

Fig. 4.1 Plan of structural features and courts superimposed on the OS 1886 map. Scale 1:500

not all of which were evident in all plots (due either to a real absence or because the evidence was unclear). The overlap in date ranges between phases reflects ceramic date ranges rather than uncertainty in the stratigraphic sequence. The same applies to Period 3, which has been subdivided into three phases.

Buildings identified from excavation were given Building numbers in sequence of recognition, therefore the numbers have no chronological or functional significance. Table 4.1 shows the concordance between Building number and plot.

4.2 Geoarchaeology
Keith Wilkinson

A total of six geoarchaeological boreholes (BH1–6) were drilled by geotechnical contractor during the excavation. A further 16 boreholes were drilled during the same interval for geotechnical purposes (Fig. 3.2). The results are summarised in Table 3.1.

4.2.1 Stratigraphy

The British Geological Survey (BGS 1993) maps the Newport Street site as lying on top of sediments

Table 4.1: Concordance of Buildings with land-use, Plots 1 to 7

Date (AD)	Period	Plot 1 Northern end 32-34 Newport St	Plot 2 Northern end 28 and 30 Newport St	30	28, 26 Newport St	Plot 3 Southern end 26-28 Newport St
1900	5	Countess of Huntingdon's school and footings				Buildings 6 and 7 in use
1800	5	Building 1b	Building 3 (on Dolday) — Building 3 in use to 1936; Building 36 (Court 8 1884); Building 37 (coal yard); 4 early 19th C cottages G2; Floors and dumps		Building 8	fragment of a cellar, G68; Building 8 uncertain date, at rear of plot next to Building 5
1700	4	19th C Industrial use: S17 machine base; Building 1 (alterations: G1)	Building 3 (on Dolday)		18th C rear yard activity	
late 17th	3.3	Building 1a	Building 3 (on Dolday); Cess pit G13		brick rebuild ?kitchen	
mid 17th	3.2	west wing: 1649 "Stable with yard" (doc)	Building 2 (on Dolday); pits G14	Building 7 (cellar)	Building 5; cobbler's shop? Building 6	G62/60 Hearths (Doc-Fincher tenant: 6 hearths); STORAGE (timber, wool, grain/flour)
16th to early 17th	3.1	HEMP PROCESSING; Building 1a: 1554 "Hemp House" (doc)	G11 (building 2 outhouse); Group 12 Spread layers is this S930?; Hearth S107: pitched tile, sq., (w circular tiled-lined pit)		Building 5 (kitchen/bakehouse)	cellar G54, 26 Newport St; Oven S256 and brick pit/bin; Cess pit S263
15th to early 16th	2.5				Building 4 (cellar)	Hearth (domestic) S?/2?706
14th to 15th	2.4					
later 13th to 14th	2.3					domestic? hearth seq. G56 in section; Dumping of material: G197 (preparatory to building)
12th	2.2				Open ground	ground consolidation
early medieval 10th-11th	2.1					Well S218
	1					?Roman road

Table 4.1: Concordance of Buildings with land-use, Plots 1 to 7

Site Narrative   33

Plot 4/5 No. 24 Newport St through to Dolday	Plot 6 29 Dolday, north 22 Newport St	Plot 7 22 Newport St
Building 13 (extension) / **Building 10** / **Building 12**: Buildings 12 and 13 remain in use to 1936; Outbuilding G35; Cess pit S129 / **Building 11: rebuild**	**Building 16**: subdivision of Buildings 15 and 16; Malthouse exists to 1936 / **Building 15 'The Malthouse'**; Building 16 Carpenter's workshop and store?	Court 3 / **Court 3**
Building 9 rebuild / **Building 11 (on Dolday)**	**Building 15 'The Malthouse'**: Well S337; **MALTING**; Brick pit S324; Well G84; Brick-lined pit S314; Drain and pier bases S321 and S323; Brick platform G80; Oven G90	
cess pit S128	**Building 14** / North of Building 14: Wall and brick piers; Structure S340/S341; Wells S337, S343; Oven (horseshoe-shaped) S353; Cess pit: S361 (replaces S361); S361 (Baker's?) Oven	**BAKERS**; Hearths E2020 and S202
Building 42: ALEHOUSE 'Severn Galley/Boar's Head' (doc)		
Clothier (doc), G45, G46 (and 50?) Fireplaces/hearths/ash boxes etc.		
Building 42		
Cess pit G50		**Building 39** / Side Alley
Building 9: Hearth S142		Hearths 291 and 294 / **Building 41** / ?Side Alley
		Pitched tile hearth/?oven S281 replaced by S280
Backyard to 24 Newport St — **DYEING** Oven G368 (keyhole with integral pit S148)		Pitched tile hearth S436
tile-base pit S141		
Oven G43 (post-dates G44); Oven G44 (beehive)		Hearth S275 open hearth; Hearth S276 cob walls; Hearth S277 pitched tile base
Dumping of material: G197 (preparatory to building)		Dumping of material: G97 (preparatory to building)

Table 4.1 (continued): Concordance of Buildings with land-use, Plots 8 to 17

Period	Date	Plot 8 central and north end 20 Newport St		Plot 9 South end 20 Newport St			Plot 10 Mostly north end 18 Newport St		
5	1900	**Building 18** Malthouse??					Air raid shelter in ruins of Building 23		
5	1800	Building 17	Building 17 demolished by 1886	Building 20 - rebuild		Building 21 brick cellar G95 at rear of plot ALEHOUSE 'The Prince of Wales'	Building 24	**Building 23** extended G362 Stables and yard north range to **Building 40**	Building 23
4	1700		Well G333 and walled yard at rear of Building 17					BREWING linked to **Building 27** cellar G308 Privy S429 G308 **Brewhouse?**	
3.3	late 17th		Brick tank (circular) G332 replaces oven G331 Oven base (oval) G331	Alleyway	Building 19 (kitchen/workshop)	(building 20?)	G107 part of unidentified building		
3.2	mid 17th						Building 22		
3.1	16th to early 17th			Building 20		Weaving (doc) Fireplace S371		Well and pits	
2.5	15th to early 16th C	Hearth G325: **Dyeing?**							
2.4	14th to 15th C					Oven G325			
2.3	later 13th to 14th C					Possible side alley between plots 9 and 7 Dumping of material: G97 (preparatory to building)			
2.2	12th C								
2.1	Early med. 10th-11th C								
1	Roman								

Plot 11 South end 18 and 16 Newport St		Plot 12 Northern end 14 Newport St	Plot 13 Southern end 14 Newport St		Plot 14 Southern end 12 Newport St		
		A few modern features		Building 30	Building 35	Building 34	
Building 27 (rebuild of the 'Old Red Lion')	Building 40	Building 40 rebuilt in brick			Cellar 17/18th C date (later incorporated into Building 35)		Oven G267
		A dump layer of this period is extensive		Building 29			
Building 26 'Old Red Lion'		ALEHOUSE Building 26 by 1717 (doc.)			Building 33 (rebuild)		
				occupation	Building 33		SMITHING hearths etc. Group 225/a oven and disuse
			Wall G142 Oven (pitched tile base) G146 Clay-lined pits Cordwainer's waste Oven (oval) G139 G132 Oven (demolished)				FORGE? Hearths G218, G220,G222-G235 G223 Anvil? and smithing hearth
			METALWORKING (smithing) Metalworking Workshop? G355, G361 BAKING Oven (keyhole) G357 Occupation: pits and a posthole	occupation	Building 32 (workshop)		METALWORKING Hearth G207 Oven (integral) G203: Dye-vat? Metalworking and pit G202/5
			ground consolidation G354 Alluvial silts Pit and posts G361 Alluvial silts METALWORKING Alluvium, slags G345-8, a pit Roman road G349	open ground			

Site Narrative 35

Fig. 4.2   General view of Plots 1, 2, 4 and 6 under excavation, looking south-west

attributable to the Mercia Mudstone Group (MMG), and immediately north and east of 'alluvium' deposited by the Severn. Rocks of the MMG date from Middle Triassic (*c.* 230 million years BP) and were formed in alluvial fan environments in an arid and semi-arid climate. 'Alluvium' is a catch-all title used by BGS to describe all recent (usually Holocene) fine-grained deposits forming in riverine and intertidal environments. Deposits of the Worcester Terrace (Pleistocene) are mapped as lying within 60m of the north-eastern boundary of the site.

The geoarchaeological investigation showed that the stratigraphy of Newport Street can conveniently be divided in two. The first division comprises 'made-ground' (including archaeological) deposits; the second is the underlying 'alluvium' (including deposits of the Pleistocene Worcester Terrace). No trace was found in the boreholes of sediments of the Mercia Mudstone Group.

Alluvium (Power House and Elmore Members)
Alluvial strata were found as the basal deposits in all boreholes except BH6 (Fig. 4.3). The alluvial strata were of two broad types: sands and gravels of the 'Worcester Terrace', which outcropped at below 8.5m AOD, and overlying alluvial silts and clays.

Coarse-grained deposits attributable to the Worcester Terrace (*sensu* Wills 1938; BGS 1993) were encountered at the base of BH2–5. These comprised matrix and clast-supported pebble gravels of quartzite, mudstone and sandstone clasts in a coarse sand matrix, together with occasional beds of coarse sands. The sorting and clast-shape properties of these deposits suggest that they were of fluvial origin. Maddy (1999) equates the 'Worcester Terrace' with the Power House Member which he suggests as being of Marine Isotope Stage 2 age (*c.* 24,000–11,500 BP). The presence of fluvial deposits of Pleistocene age at Newport Street is contrary to the BGS (1993) map of the area which suggests that the terrace outcrop is immediately to the north and east of the site, probably due to a lack of exposures and borehole data when the BGS mapped Worcester. Wilkinson and Marter (2006) also noted slight discrepancies between BGS maps and borehole data from The Butts, 150m to the north of Newport Street (Fig. 2.1).

Fine-grained alluvial strata unconformably overlay the sands and gravels of the 'Worcester Terrace' at *c.* 8.5m AOD and extended upwards to a contact with the archaeological beds at *c.* 11.5m AOD. These alluvial sediments comprised red-brown, well-sorted mineral silts and clays, although thin lenses of organic mud and even peat were also noted in BH3, BH4 and BH5. The latter layers were mostly concentrated towards the base

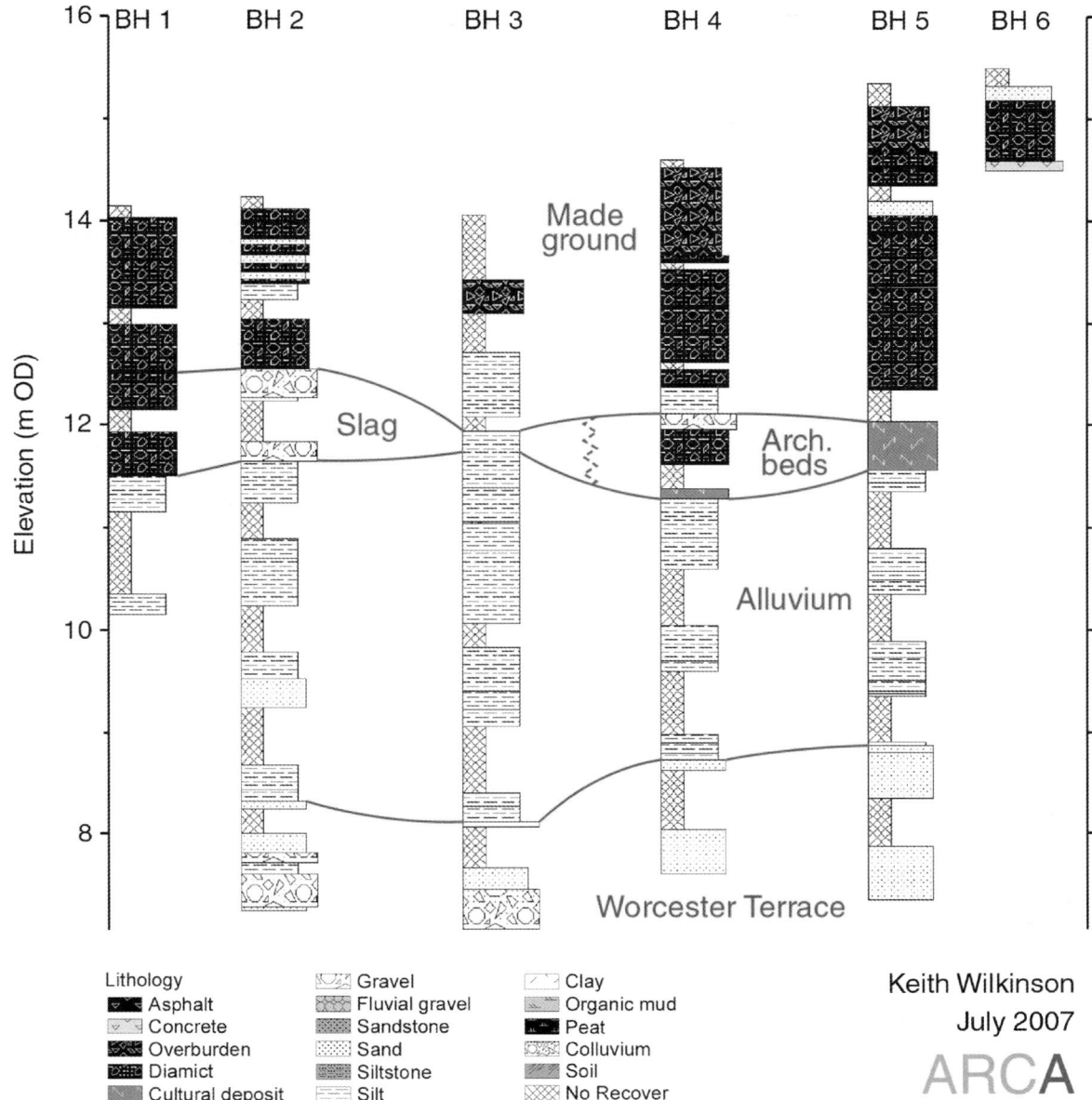

Fig. 4.3 Composite site section through Boreholes BH1–6

of the fine-grained alluvium and suggest that the site was located on the landward margins of a floodplain during deposition of this unit. Palynological assessment of samples from the organic strata suggests that they are of Holocene age (see Chapter 5.22), indicating that the fine-grained alluvium can be attributed to Maddy's (1999) Elmore Member. No detailed chronological data could be extracted from either the morphology of the deposits or their stratigraphy, but the presence of archaeological beds from the Roman period at the top of the Elmore Member suggests that accumulation was during the later prehistoric period.

Unlike Elmore Member deposits at The Butts (Wilkinson and Marter 2006), there were no notable topographic variations for this unit at Newport Street in either outcrop height or thickness. These data suggest that the site was relatively flat during deposition of these alluvial strata. It is, however, noteworthy that the elevation of the Elmore Member outcrop at Newport Street correlates with deposits interpreted as channel sediments at The Butts. If this correlation is correct it would suggest a facies relationship between alluvial units at the two sites.

Made ground

'Made ground' is a generic term used by BGS to encompass all deposits resulting from human action. In most instances the term is applied to deliberately deposited sediment of 19th to 21st-century date, but archaeological sediments are also included within the definition. At Newport Street, much of the 'made ground' was investigated by archaeological excavation. In the discussion below emphasis is placed on the lowest made-ground deposits, which were only occasionally reached by excavation.

Made-ground deposits tended to be thicker in the northern part of the site (e.g. 3.79m in BH5), and thinner to the south (e.g. 2.59m in BH2; Fig. 4.3). Archaeological strata also tended to thin to the south and change in their properties from occupational waste (e.g. in BH5), to concentrations of metalworking debris (e.g. BH2).

The base of the 'made ground' comprised cultural strata of Roman period date. As noted above, there was a broad trend for domestic debris to be found in relatively thick beds in the north of the site and concentrations of metalworking slag in the south (Fig. 4.3). These cultural layers outcropped at similar heights (12.0m to 12.5m AOD) in the archaeological boreholes but were noted at slightly higher elevations in the geotechnical boreholes (12.6m to 13.9m AOD). The latter is probably a reflection of the generalised descriptions produced by geotechnical engineers, and therefore the data is considered less reliable away from the transect through BH1–6. Indeed the cross section (Fig. 4.3) suggests that, just as was the case with the underlying Elmore Member, archaeological deposits outcropped at a similar height across the site. Modelled thicknesses of the archaeological deposits are also likely to have been impacted by generalised geotechnical data. The thickness of these deposits in the non-archaeological boreholes was up to 1m greater than in those drilled for archaeological purposes.

Cultural layers in BH4–5 comprised sands containing frequent burnt material, waterlogged plant macro-remains, brick, tile and mortar fragments, and moderate quantities of pebble-sized metalworking slag. It is probable that these deposits were derived from a mixture of domestic and industrial waste disposal, and demolition debris.

A dense layer of slag was found in BH2 between 1.69m and 1.97m below ground surface (*c.* 12.3m to 12.6m AOD). It comprised rounded and sub-rounded pebble and granular size slag 'droplets' in a fine sand matrix. Similar slag 'clasts' were present in the other geoarchaeological boreholes to the north of BH2 (and were recorded at The Butts at between 11.7m and 14.5m AOD (Wilkinson and Marter 2006)), but always as dispersed particles within an archaeological diamict.

Made ground of medieval and post-medieval date overlay the archaeological layers at 12.0m to 12.3m AOD. The later made ground comprised a complex of diamicts and poorly sorted sands, and is likely to have been deposited during construction and demolition activity. Slag particles present in the lowest of these layers suggests that some reworking of Roman period stratigraphy occurred.

4.2.2 Discussion

Topography of the archaeological stratigraphy

The composite cross section (Fig. 4.3) indicates that Roman period archaeological deposits exist across the site between 11.3m to 12.6m AOD. Whereas the ground surface prior to excavation sloped upwards across the site by 1.5m in a northerly direction, the ground surface in the Romano-British period was comparatively flat, and if anything may have dropped slightly in a northwards direction (Fig. 4.4). This is in contrast to conclusions reached from the study of stratigraphy at The Butts, where Roman deposits dipped southwards from 14.5m to 11.7m AOD, while the modern ground surface fell 1.7m across the same distance (Wilkinson and Marter 2006). It is clear from borehole studies of the type carried out at Newport Street and The Butts that the topography of this part of Worcester has changed considerably since the Roman period, and that the present topography of Worcester cannot be taken as a proxy for that of its Roman past.

The nature of the Roman period cultural deposits across the site changed from north to south. BH2 contained a dense layer of slag clasts, and it is also apparent from some geotechnical borehole data from the south of the site that slag gravels were present too. However, in the north of the site slag was present only as isolated particles in deposits that were otherwise dominated by Roman demolition debris. Excavation within Plots 3 and 13 (Chapter 4.3.3 and 4.3.8, below) showed the slag deposits at the south of the site to be the remains of a Roman road. The borehole data implies that, to the north, was an area of former Roman settlement, though no *in situ* structural remains were found.

Depositional environments

The sediment sequences exposed in the boreholes suggest that, until the Roman period, alluvial processes dominated the environment of the Newport Street area. Assuming that the correlation of the sand-and-gravel strata at the base of the stratigraphy with the Power House Member/Worcester Terrace is correct, the implication is that the site was on a braid plain of the River Severn during the Devensian Late Glacial. This would not have been a situation conducive to human activity, and it is unlikely that *in situ* archaeological remains exist within these deposits. There was then a probable hiatus until the second half of the Holocene when fine-grained alluvium of the Elmore Member was deposited. These latter deposits formed on the floodplain of a meandering river. The presence of organic mud and

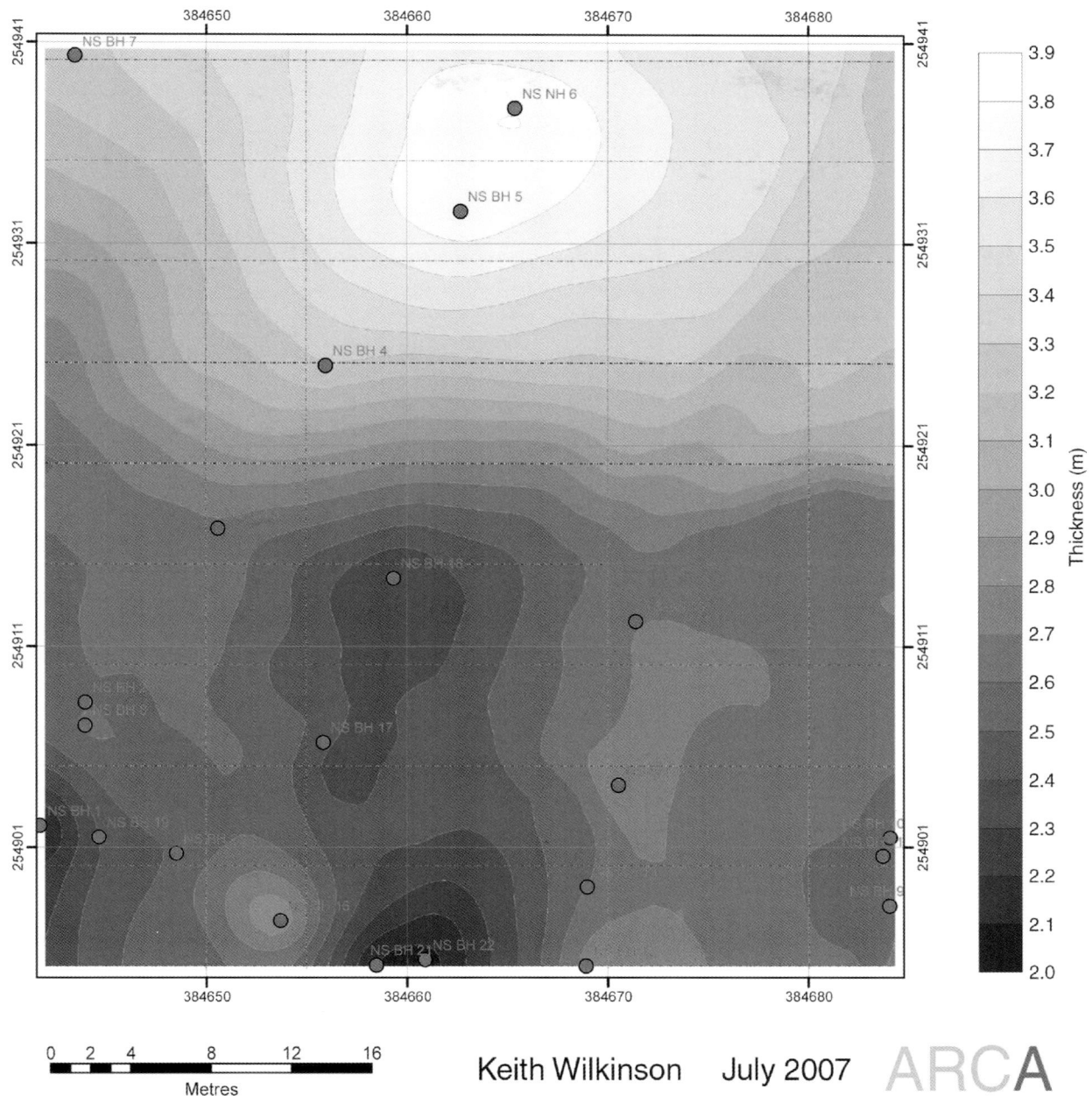

Fig. 4.4 Modelled thickness of made ground and archaeological beds (For borehole locations see Fig. 3.2)

peat bands within the fine-grained alluvial deposits suggests that during the later prehistoric period the site was located towards the edge of the floodplain adjacent to a backswamp environment. This situation appears to have persisted into the Roman period as the slag and cultural layers conformably overlay the fine-grained alluvium, whereas at The Butts Roman period strata were interbedded with alluvium (Wilkinson and Marter 2006). The upper made-ground deposits accumulated in a fully terrestrial environment.

Chronology

No new chronological information was obtained from the geoarchaeological investigations; however, the borehole data demonstrate that fine-grained floodplain deposits were forming immediately prior to Roman activity, while data from The Butts suggests that fluvial sedimentation continued through the period of Roman occupation (Wilkinson and Marter 2006).

River behaviour and its impact on human activity

There is no direct evidence for human activity in deposits of the Elmore Member but it is likely that humans were active in the surrounding environment during accretion of this layer. The Elmore Member on the site formed in a floodplain depositional environment. Floodplains are thought to have been brought into cultivation during the Bronze Age and Iron Age, when improved plough technology allowed heavier soils to be worked. Indeed Robinson (1992) has suggested that human cultivation in later prehistory caused the deposition of fine-grained floodplain deposits. It is therefore possible that indirect vestiges of human activity might be found within these deposits, for example as palynological evidence of cultivation.

The site is likely to have remained as a floodplain into the Roman period. A Roman road was constructed across the southern part of the site through the deposition of metal slag, raising ground levels above that of flood waters. To the north of this domestic and structural waste was deposited and this part of the site may have been occupied, though no *in situ* evidence for this was recovered.

4.2.3 Conclusions

The geoarchaeological borehole data obtained from Newport Street, although not of the highest quality, demonstrate that the earliest human activity recognised from these investigations took place in a floodplain margin environment. The Romano-British inhabitants of Worcester appear to have utilised the floodplain edge for the disposal of domestic and structural refuse. They also constructed a road by depositing metal slag further out on the floodplain.

Deposits post-dating the Roman period were investigated by archaeological excavation but it is worth noting that the borehole strata suggest that activities during the medieval and post-medieval environment appear to have taken place in a relatively dry environment. There is no evidence from the borehole descriptions for major floods. Deposits pre-dating human activity comprise sands and gravels of the Late Pleistocene Power House Member, and fine-grained alluvial deposits of the Elmore Member. Cores through these units did not contain cultural material.

4.3 The archaeological sequence
Peter Davenport

4.3.1 Plot 1: The northern part of no. 32/34 Newport Street

This plot comprised the northern end of the two tenements, no. 32/34 Newport Street, the majority of which fell outside the excavation area. Excavation uncovered the remains of 17th to 19th-century developments, including a large building, Building 1. This building is thought to have been a warehouse of the late 17th or very early 18th century, but it seems to have been built on the stone foundations of a building that may be of mid 16th-century date (Building 1a). The area to the rear of the building was developed as a court of single-cell cottages in the late 18th century, reached though a gateway from Dolday. Building 1 and the cottages were demolished in 1907 and a school was built over them. This survived until the late 20th century as part of the bus station (Pat Hughes, pers. comm.).

Plot 1: Period 3.1: 16th to early 17th centuries (Fig. 4.18)

The earliest features recorded were the remains of stone walls along the eastern boundary (G23 and G24) and of a stone building (Building 1a) fronting onto Dolday. The eastern side of Building 1a continued the line of the boundary northwards. Relationships were not clear but boundary wall (G23) appeared to abut Building 1a, but having been constructed from the same level it may not have been too different in date. Its construction was also different in character to Building 1a, and despite the use of relatively large blocks, its rather ramshackle nature suggested that it may have only have been intended to support a timber wall above. It is probable that boundary wall (G24) was earlier in the sequence, being set deeper and, relatively unusually, using lias stone in its construction. Its northern end turned very slightly to the west, suggesting that G23 was infilling between G24 and Building 1a. No evidence of earlier walls was discovered under G23 or G24, so these may have been the first masonry boundaries between these tenements. Excavation did not continue below Building 1a so any predecessors remain unknown. The construction of boundary wall G24 cut through a layer (646, not shown) that produced material from the late 15th to 16th centuries, which is consistent with a date in the 16th or early 17th century for this boundary wall.

The stone footings of Building 1a were laid in a shallow footing trench, through the base of which timber piles had been driven into the underlying layers (Fig. 4.5). The blocks were faced internally but were ragged externally, being packed with loose rubble and dirt against the edge of the foundation trench. This suggests that the wall was a retaining wall and the room was partially sunken. The footings did not look capable of having supported a stone wall of any height, having a typical (though varied) width of less than 0.30m, and the whole structure may well have been timber-framed on stone footings. No independent dating evidence for Building 1a was obtained, but a date earlier than the mid 17th century could be implied from a stone-and-timber construction. The will of William Dodynge in 1554 refers to a 'hemp house' at the rear of this property (Hughes, Chapter 5.1.3), for which Building 1a must be a strong candidate. If so, it would have pre-dated 1554, perhaps being of late 15th or early 16th-century date. William Dodynge was a walker or fuller and may have been trading in hemp (for both coarse and fine fabrics, as well as rope) as a sideline.

The remains of sandstone footings (G16a, 2912/2926) running westwards from Building 1a were probably for

Fig. 4.5 Plot 1, Period 3.1, piles under Building 1a, looking south

an associated western range, which had both internal and external stone surfaces (Fig. 4.18). This was probably a stable and yard, as described in a survey of no. 32/34 Newport Street from 1649/50 (and reflected in an earlier lease of 1615; Hughes, Chapter 5.1.4). The main area described in the 1649/50 survey was beyond the excavation area to the south: the Newport Street frontage of 29ft (8.84m) and depth of 116ft (35.36m) matches the tenement width shown on the 1886 OS map (Fig. 2.14) and the distance from Newport Street to the south wall of Building 1. The survey also describes, as an extra, a stable and yard, the stable 10ft (3.03m) wide and 15ft (4.57m) long, the yard 10ft (3.03m) by 20ft (6.06m), which fit the dimensions of the western range and yard. The survey excludes the main part of Building 1a, which it implies then belonged to the adjacent plot, the stable and yard 'lyeing next the Leddingtons land' (the Leddingtons held the adjacent Plots 2 and 3). The land is described in the same way in deeds of 1759 and 1773 (Hughes, 5.1.3 again), implying that Building 1 continued to be held separately. Cobble surface 347, which ran around the north-west corner of Building 1a, suggests that the floor of the stable was continuous with the external cobbling on Dolday, and suggests the same ambiguity about street frontages here as is indicated by Building 2 in Plot 2 (below).

From the later 16th century and throughout the 17th century the property was held by bakers (Hughes, Chapter 5.1.3). In 1601 John Writer left 'the house where I now dwell and the furnace used in my trade' to his son and the existence of a bakehouse is attested in the documents. The bakehouse was in the southern part of the main holding, and therefore beyond the excavated area. Cornlofts are also attested in the main building, making a grain or flour storage function for Building 1a unlikely.

Areas of substantial subsidence in the brick floor of subsequent Building 1b (below) indicated the presence of earlier pits, but these were not excavated. Given the degree of subsidence they must have been filled with organic material and were probably rubbish/cess pits and not much earlier than the construction of Building 1a.

Plot 1: Period 3.3: late 17th century (Fig. 4.22)

In the late 17th century, rectangular brick Building 1b (Fig. 4.6) was built directly over Building 1a (Period 3.1) reusing its stone footings. The east wall of Building 1b was a single skin of brick built against a pre-existing stone wall of the adjacent building in Plot 2 (Building 2, below), which overlay the edge of, and therefore post-dated, the stone footings of Building 1a. The building was a very substantial single room of 9.7m by 4m (*c.* 32ft by 13ft) with walls 0.36m to 0.4m (14" to 16") wide. It was floored in brick of similar date and followed exactly the plan of Building 1a. It seems to date from the later 17th century, based on the brick size and type, and from the irregular bonding that included random large stone blocks in the walls. There is a reference to Mr Southall building on the Dolday frontage of this property in or by 1705 and this may well be Building 1b (Hughes, Chapter 5.1.3).

A rectangular pit in the centre of Building 1b, with two brick walls lining either side of it and rising a little above the floor, looked like a machine base, although a central raised hearth or furnace is also a possibility (S17). It was too heavily damaged to be certain but the central pit and walls appeared to be of 17th/early 18th-century date.

Building 1b also had a short western range, again built off earlier stone footings, which also extended as far as the western plot boundary that had been refaced or rebuilt in brick (2906). A doorway with steps was recorded in the west wall of Building 1b, leading up into the western range that also featured brick floors, of which only fragments remained (G16b). Pottery indicated a 17th-century *terminus post quem* for these floors, but they could not be more closely dated. There were no remains of any masonry front wall to the western range onto Dolday, and if one had existed

Fig. 4.6   Plot 1, Period 3.3, Building 1b, looking south

evidence for it would have survived. This suggests that the north wall of this building was timber-framed with no stone footings, or if a stable it may have been a large door. Only a very limited investigation of the levels below the brick floor was possible and this provided no evidence of earlier floors. Layers pre-dating the floor and its make-up were excavated in Building 1b but were of the same date (i.e. 17th to 18th century).

Both ranges survived into the 20th century and therefore feature on the 1886 OS map (Fig. 2.14). The western range is shown to have risen to a second storey over a covered entry to a yard. This makes it very likely that the main range was of two storeys and there is other evidence to this effect on the eastern party wall. At the northern end, this wall was built in brick as a single skin against the stone wall of Building 2 on Plot 2 (G8/366, below). Both this wall and Building 1b were rebuilt in the early 19th and early 20th centuries respectively (Hughes, Chapter 5.1.3), but a photograph of 1936 (Fig. 4.7) shows the brick wall of Building 1 trapped between the rebuilds at eaves level, as they were built successively either side of it.

In the south-west corner of Building 1b was a square brick structure (G3). This was not excavated below floor level but it clearly pre-dated Building 1b, and featured two phases of brick flooring of 17th-century type. It did not survive to be mapped in 1886, although a set of steps is shown in its place (Fig. 2.14), suggesting it functioned as a porch. A similar, smaller room (G17) was later added on the south side of G3. Built against the south side of the south wall of Building 1b was a brick-lined pit (G18). This was clearly secondary to Building 1b and seems to have been a cess pit. It went out of use in the 18th century and the cottages in Court 5 (G21, below) were built over it.

Boundary wall G23/G24 was retained in Period 3.3 as footings, but otherwise replaced in brick (with some sandstone blocks, as in Building 1a) as G25 and G26 (north and south respectively). These respected the same section break and differed in thickness at either side of it. This section break coincides with a party wall between two of the 18th-century cottages in Court 5 (below), but it is hard to see how this is more than just coincidence. It more likely refers to some structure pre-dating the construction of the cottages. The southern brick section can be seen as a complex but single-phase construction, but this cannot be said of the northern element, which appeared to have a worn brick threshold to a blocked door, blocked windows and rebuilds.

Plot 1: Period 4: 18th century (Fig. 4.23)

The date of construction of the cottages G21 (Fig.

Fig. 4.7 Dolday, 1936 photograph. © Worcestershire Record Office

4.23) could not be determined from archaeological evidence, although their excavation produced pottery of the 17th and 18th centuries. They are not mentioned in a lease description of 1773, but appear in a lease of 1846. In 1870 they were described as 'brick, timber and tile built' and 'old and in indifferent repair' (Hughes, Chapter 5.1.3). They were cheap, one-cell and probably three-storey houses typical of those built in 'courts' in provincial towns up and down the country in the 18th and early 19th centuries, to house the urban poor (Alcock 2005).

It is clear that these cottages were built on the site of older structures, as a substantial wooden piling, S32, like that under Building 1a, was recorded under the early 20th-century walls of the Countess of Huntingdon's School (below), which partly reused the cottage footings. It does not seem at all probable that the builders of such jerry-built structures would take such care in foundation work.

Plot 1: Period 5: 19th and 20th centuries (Fig. 4.29)

The main element of Building 1b survived until 1907 when it and the cottages behind it in Court 5 were demolished (Hughes, Chapter 5.1.3). There was some evidence of alterations and the lifting and relaying of the brick floor in Building 1b to insert drains in the 19th century, associated with the installation of a sink or similar just north of the western doorway. In addition, the tops of vertical iron pins were seen in the make-up below the brick floor in areas where the floor was probably re-laid around them. These suggest heavy machinery was fixed to the floor. Pottery suggests a 19th-century date for these pins.

The site of Building 1 and all the six cottages provided the building footprint of the Countess of Huntingdon's School (in existence by 1909 at the latest), implying that the properties had been brought together by then. The Countess of Huntingdon's School was converted to a waiting room for the bus station in the 1950s and finally demolished sometime in the late 20th century (Pat Hughes, pers. comm.).

4.3.2 Plot 2: the northern part of nos 26 and 28 Newport Street (including nos 35 and 37 Dolday)

The properties in Plot 2 have a complicated history. It would appear that Plots 2 and 3 were in one ownership for much of the post-medieval period, if not earlier, with the properties in Plot 2 (originally the rear sections of Plot 3) let out separately at various times and eventually ending up in separate ownership. The earliest features uncovered were some hearths set on widespread accumulations of household/industrial waste and garden soil. The Dolday frontage was built up in the late 16th to early 17th centuries with structures that extended beyond the later building line. The frontage as historically recorded was established by 1719. Brick buildings were erected in the rear part of the plot in the 17th century. In the early 19th century, cheap brick cottages were erected around Court 8 at the southern end of Plot 2, and a coal store was built over the rear 17th-century building. Cess pits gave way to water closets and mains sewerage in the later 19th century, before the area succumbed to slum clearance in the 1930s. The boundary with Plot 4 is mentioned but is described below (Chapter 4.3.4).

Plot 2: Period 2: medieval (Fig. 4.14)

No medieval remains were uncovered in Plot 2 apart from a short length of wall (S52) projecting over 2m into the plot from the southern end of the eastern boundary wall (G5; Fig. 4.14). Wall S52 was broad and well built, and was presumably the remnant of a building against this boundary wall. It may have been part of a structure hinted at by the spreads and dumps (G4; not shown) covering the area of Period 5 Building 36 and the yard north of it (Fig. 4.29), but clearly pre-dated them. One layer in G4 was of white mortar, suggesting a floor, but no dating material was recovered.

Plot 2: Period 3.1: 16th to early 17th centuries (Fig. 4.18)

The lowest layers excavated in this plot were soil deposits G10 (not shown) at the southern end, the earliest of which, a mixed dump of ash and soils, post-dated the Period 2 boundary wall to Plot 4/5 (G5). The upper member of this group was a widespread garden soil. Dating was equivocal, layer 621 of S106 (not shown) containing potsherds no earlier than the early 18th century. However, this lay directly below intensive 18th and 19th-century activity, indicating the possibility of contamination, and the stratigraphic sequence and other dating evidence, none of it extensive, suggest that these garden soils were in place by the early 17th century.

Sitting on these soils on the other side of the plot, tucked against the boundary with Plot 1, a probable hearth, square in plan with pitched tiles (Fig. 4.8), was next to a brick-and-tile-lined shallow circular pit (S107). This combination was common on the site and in general a functional relationship seems certain, although here the pit partly truncated the hearth. The hearth dated to the late 16th to 17th centuries, and the bricks in the pit suggested a 17th-century date for that feature. Another hearth (or possible oven base) occurred at this level towards the centre of the plot (hearth 590) but this had been truncated on all sides. These provided evidence for processes of an unclear nature at the rear of the plot,

Fig. 4.8 Plot 2, Period 3.1, hearth S107, looking north

and seem to have been broadly contemporary with an interesting structure on the Dolday frontage: Building 2.

Building 2 was of stone and seems to have been a rectangular structure with substantial stone footings, although only the south-west corner survived (G8) with part of its northern and the eastern walls (G366), being heavily truncated by later drains and other disturbances. The remarkable feature of this building was that eastern wall G366 extended northwards into Dolday by more than 3.8m (12.5ft) forming a northern extension to the building that had well-laid cobbled surface 455 (Fig. 4.9). These were laid neatly up against the eastern and northern walls and had a parallel kerb on the west giving a width of 2.7m (or nearly 9ft). There was no evidence for a wall against this kerb, but this part of the site was only exposed during a watching brief for new drainage. The cobbles could be traced to the northern wall of Building 2, very close to the line of the Dolday frontage as it later became fixed. The building was at a slightly lower level to the later Building 3 (Period 3.3, below) that replaced it and seems to have had a pebbled floor, a section of which survived against the south wall G8. Internal arrangements were hinted at by a short length of wall running east/west near the centre of the building (728). This was truncated at both ends and its alignment largely removed by later intrusions.

The stratigraphic position and pottery dating indicate a 17th-century date for the building, but this is a *terminus ante quem* in most cases. The building was probably of earlier 17th-century date, and is of interest because it ignored what was assumed to be the line of the contemporary street frontage. Purpresture payments for the encroachment of Building 1a into Dolday (Hughes, Chapter 5.1.3) suggest it was classed as a highway. Purpresture payments usually covered small trespasses such as a projecting window or shop counter or, later, the underbuilding of jetties. Such a major intrusion appears to be unprecedented and suggests that the street was set back in the (later) 17th century, as does the large dump of animal bones found in the widespread silts S930 (not shown) excavated under Building 2 where it extended out across the later line of Dolday. This also suggests that there was something unusual about the street, as these were not typical street layers, and it was perhaps more of a waste tip. Building 2 is also of interest as its eastern wall bore no relation to the angled later boundary between Plots 2 and 4. This suggests that the angled boundary was later, and probably the result of the reallocation of Dolday frontage to the tenements running up from Newport Street. As the ownership of these plots was tangled and clearly sometimes unified (Hughes, Chapter 5.1.4), this is entirely feasible.

Fig. 4.9   Plot 2, Period 3.1, cobbling and kerb G366, looking south

To the south of Building 2, a series of shallow but wide pits or scoops were dug (G14), containing 17th to 18th-century pottery, and above them structure G11 was erected, still in the 17th century. This was a long thin brick structure, remarkably sinuous plan. It may simply have been a yard wall and outhouse at the back of Building 2. A small room was made at its west end, with a brick floor. At the eastern end it was associated with a cobble floor (S11) and was probably contemporary. A poorly surviving wall ran northwards from the north-west corner of structure G11 towards the south wall of Building 2. It is interesting that the east/west wall of structure G11 ended at a seemingly arbitrary point to the east that was in line with the east wall G366 of Building 2. This might have something to do with a change of the boundary of Plots 2 and 4, discussed below, but this area was heavily damaged by later drains and pits and was not excavated further. Cobble surface S11 seemed to respect the later Plot 2/4 boundary, although it may have pre-dated it, and structure G11 seems to have been extended to the later Plot 2/4 boundary over cobbles S11, when structure G11 was partially rebuilt but without a southern wall. It consisted of a set of linear mortar spreads with brick fragments. This rebuild has been placed in this phase but its stratigraphic relationships to Building 3 (Period 3.3) were unclear and it could have been later.

Plot 2: Period 3.2 to Period 4: mid 17th century to 18th century (Figs 4.21 to 4.23)

It is not possible to be more precise about the dating for this phase of activity. Building 2 was demolished and replaced by a pair of cottages (G6, Building 3), which are mentioned in 1719 as already existing, and by 1739 had become three (Hughes, Chapter 5.1.5). The title deed of 1719 states 'And all those two small tenements on the backer part thereof with the Appurtenances adjoining to Dolday'; by 1739, Beatrix Haden's will refers to 'and also all those three little Tenements'. The documents relating to these buildings are almost impossible to disentangle from those of Plot 4, but the change from two to three tenements between 1719 and 1739 is neatly shown in the archaeology of Building 3. (The references to numbers of tenements and the rebuild of cottages on Plot 4 is also clarified by the archaeology of Buildings 11 and 12 there.)

The Plot 2 cottages were L-shaped in plan together, with two (to the west and east) fronting Dolday and one to the rear of the west cottage (Figs 4.22 and 4.23). They are visible on a photograph of Dolday taken in the 1930s, where it is clear they had been refronted in the very late 18th or early 19th century (Fig. 4.10). The passageways either side leading to the rear courts are visible. The unified look from the refronting gives the appearance that the cottages on Dolday were the

Fig. 4.10 Plot 2, cottages (Building 3) leading to Court 8, 1930s photograph. © *Worcestershire Record Office*

original two, but this appears not to have been the case. All three cottages were built of brick but on footings of large sandstone blocks (G6; Fig. 4.22), presumably recycled from demolished buildings elsewhere. The recovery of medieval to 17th-century stonework from post-medieval layers and structures across the site suggests an ecclesiastical source (Guy, Chapter 5.11). It is clear that the western cottage on Dolday (no. 37) shared its footings with the cottage south of it (and also reused some Building 2 foundations) but not with the eastern cottage, whose footings were of smaller and more irregular sandstone blocks (Fig. 4.29). The eastern cottage could not have been built until a large stone-lined cess pit (S113) that occupied the central part of its footprint and which seemed to be contemporary with the two westerly cottages, went out of use (Figs 4.22 and 4.11).

Each cottage was of one room and presumably two floors. No evidence of internal arrangements survived except for a fireplace (166) in the east wall of the north-west cottage and another fireplace (509) in the north-east corner of the southern cottage (Fig. 4.22). The cottages were very economically built: despite massive footings, the base course of header bricks supported a single skin of stretchers placed centrally on the east and west walls, even for the fireplace back on the northern cottage. It seems possible that the later eastern cottage was built with notional nine-inch walls, as the second stretcher course was placed on the outside edge of the header course below, but not enough survived to be clear as to whether there was ever an inner skin. This might reflect a reduction in the price of bricks. Again no internal fittings survived, but fireplace (166) in no. 37 was converted to become a back-to-back. The single skin wall between it and the earlier one was not thickened.

The outer walls of the alleyways to either side of the cottages were also of brick. To the west the boundary wall had been completely removed, but to the east were the remains of a nine-inch wall (S122). It too had been built on a stone footing, but this has a complex history and is described as part of Plot 4.

Plot 2: Period 5: 19th and 20th centuries (Fig. 4.29)
Everything else that was excavated on this plot dated to the 19th and 20th centuries, although the four cottages erected along the southern perimeter of Plot 2 (Building 36), probably of early 19th-century date, were essentially part of the 18th-century development (Fig. 4.29). In 1804 there was no mention of these tenements, merely the three cottages on Dolday (Building 3), and they are not mentioned until 1856 (Hughes, Chapter 5.1.4). They seemed to have reused 17th-century bricks in

Fig. 4.11 Plot 2, Period 3.3, cess pit S113, looking north-west

some of the surviving walls and floors. Building 36 was part of the process, begun in the 18th and continued into the early 19th century, of building small cottages, generally one room in plan and back-to-back, in courts slotted into the backs of the tenements. This was Court 8 on the 1886 OS map (Fig. 2.14). As with the cottages fronting Dolday, these were built of nine-inch brick walls on stone footings (G2). The rear or south wall was mostly built on various earlier walls of Building 5 in Plot 3. At the south-west corner two short sandstone-and-brick walls (S83 and S86) acted as footings but were probably earlier than the brick wall above as there was a gap between them and Building 5 with no obvious footings. It appears that no new footings were built for the rear wall of Building 36, and all the wall fragments used as footings were earlier. This was certainly the case at the east side of Building 36 where the earlier walls of boundary walls G5 were reused. Building 36 comprised four cottages but almost no internal fittings or floors survived within them, apart from a few fragments of brick paving, both inside and out. Internal partitions were probably of stud timber construction. One length of stone footing (S60) suggested a partition between front room and entrance passage of the central cottage, which would presumably have been in brick.

Court 8 was separated from the rest of the plot by a brick wall, known from maps rather than archaeologically, although two areas of brick paving (S96) were separated by a gap where this wall had been removed (Fig. 4.29). These were of 17th-century brick and may have been from an earlier structure, cut by the wall. There was some 19th-century material below this surface, but it was not well sealed. Two brick cess pits were built against the front of the footings of Building 36 (S97, S98; Fig. 4.29), as was a well (S81) towards the east end of the court. These were paved over in brick, presumably in the late 19th or early 20th century when external WCs were provided in these courts (City of Worcester compulsory purchase surveys 1936). Context from the fill of well S81 (G53: S82) produced a good assemblage of redeposited 18th-century pottery.

The 1886 OS map (Fig. 2.14) shows that the first floor of the east end of Building 36 extended over a passageway that led from Newport Street. This gave no access to Court 8, but led through to Dolday via a coal yard (Building 37). Several more cess pits here and in Court 8 went out of use in this period, and one may be the ash pit mentioned in 1936 (City of Worcester compulsory purchase order). This yard area was paved in stone setts typical of the later 19th century.

4.3.3 Plot 3: the southern part of nos 26, 28 and 30 Newport Street

A medieval cellar under the frontage of no. 28 Newport Street provided the opportunity to excavate a sondage in the south-west corner of Plot 3 for the examination of Roman and early medieval layers. The West Sondage was 2.5m by 3.5m (more or less the size of the cellar) so the investigation of the lower levels was necessarily

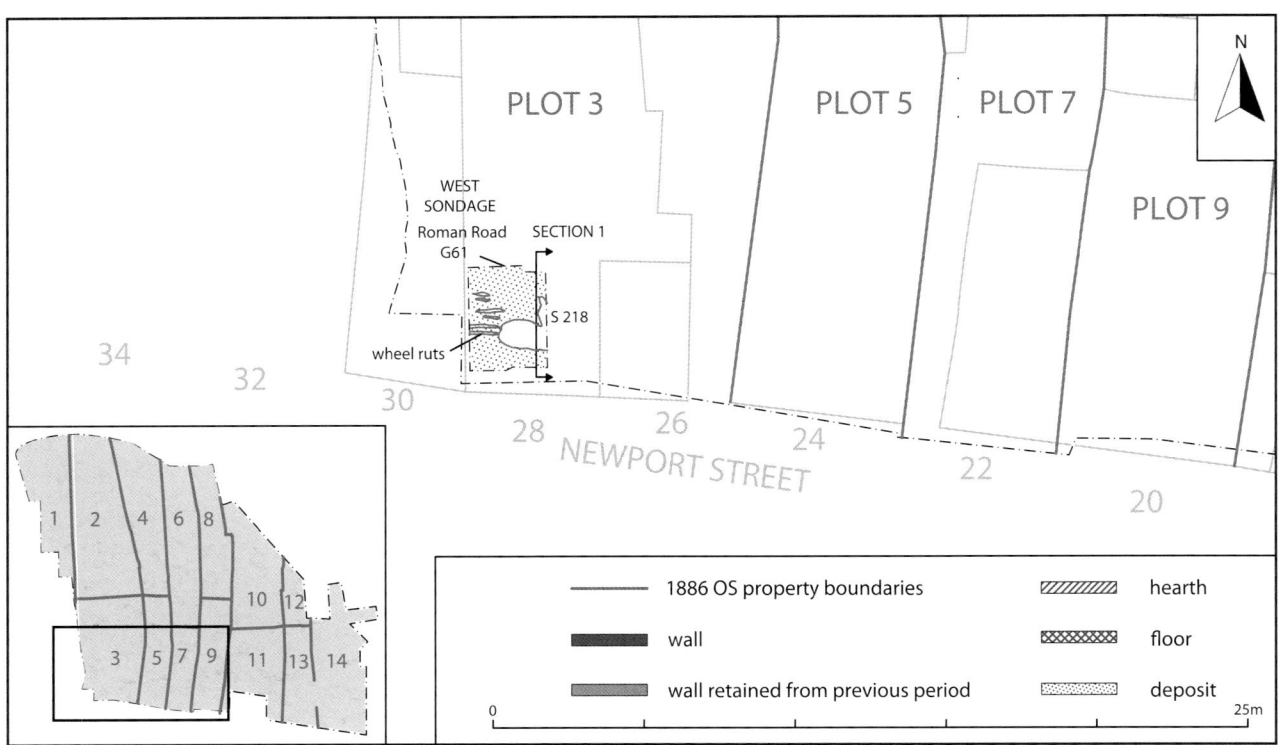

Fig. 4.12 Periods 1 and 2.1/2.2, west end. Scale 1:250

limited. The medieval cellar and associated layers were also investigated. The stone wall forming the boundary with no. 24 Newport Street (Plot 5) was of medieval origin. Against it, and incorporating parts of it, a large square building in the north-east corner of Plot 3 was dated to the later medieval period. It had been rebuilt twice, once in stone and once, in the 17th century, in brick. Map evidence suggests that it was replaced in the later 18th or 19th centuries, but no archaeological remains of this later period survived. The timber-framed and brick-panelled buildings fronting Newport Street were probably of early 17th-century date, and survived until the 1930s. A series of hearths to the rear of no. 28 suggests it was used for baking or some other activity in the period before these timber houses were built.

Plot 3: Period 1: Roman (Figs 4.12 and 4.13)

The earliest layers reached in the West Sondage were interleaved compacted layers of iron slag and alluvial clay (G61), the uppermost layer of slag having a series of wheel ruts indicating that this was a former road surface (Figs 4.12 and 4.13). It was not clear if the lower layers were part of the road structure interleaved with silts or some other structure, given the small area exposed and the apparent lack of ruts. The similarity of these layers in both character and level to those in the East Sondage (see Plot 13 below) strongly suggests that they were of Roman date, although the only dating recovered here was a sherd of 11th to 14th-century pottery, which was almost certainly intrusive from the early medieval layers immediately above. Indeed, it seems likely the road remained open, if disused, well into the early medieval period.

Plot 3: Period 2.1: 10th to 11th centuries (Figs 4.12 and 4.13)

The surface of the earlier Roman road was truncated by the construction of well S218 (Fig. 4.13, section 1),

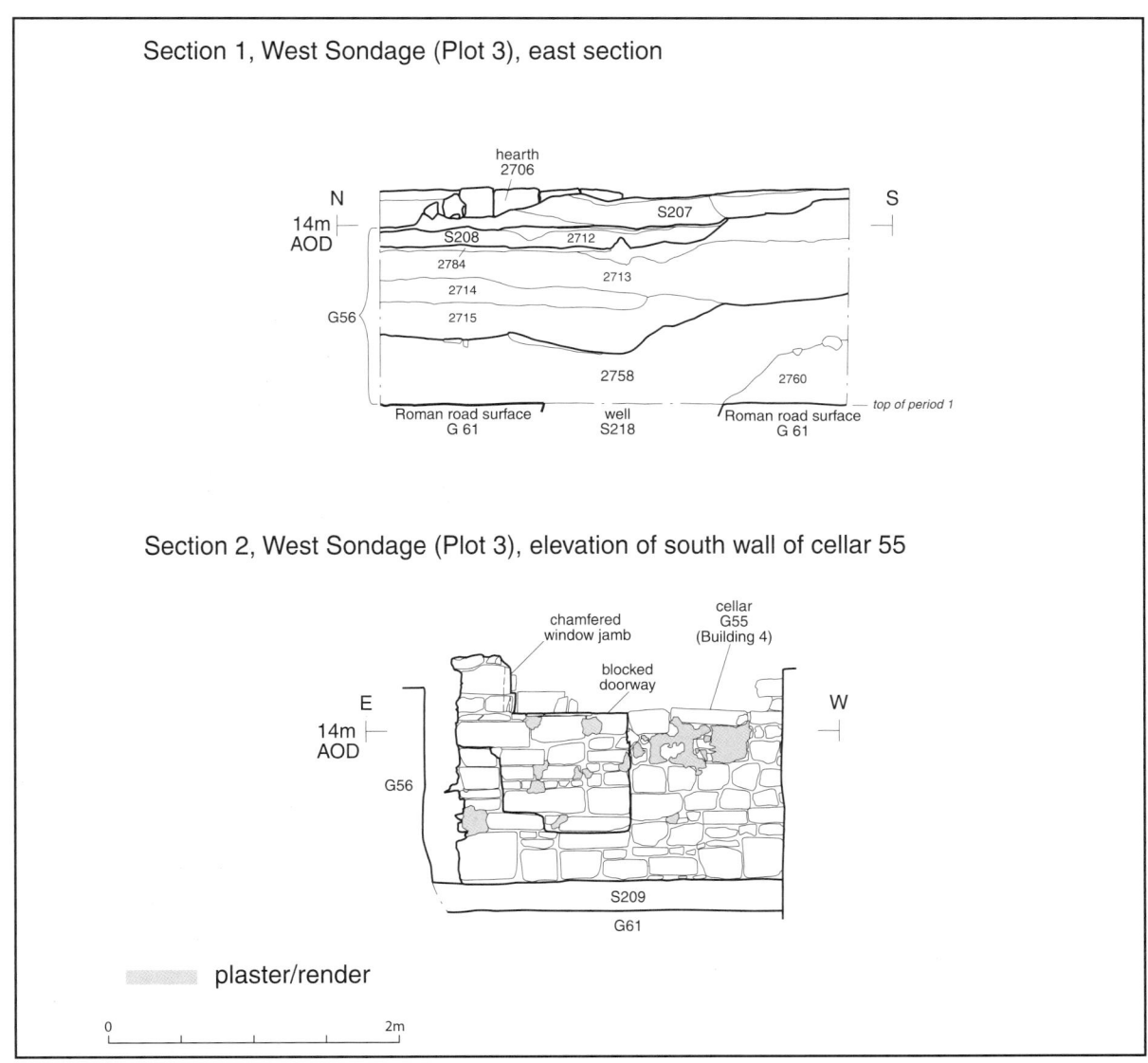

Fig. 4.13 Sections 1 and 2. Scale 1:50

the earliest activity in G56. Its fill contained Cotswolds ware dating from the 10th to 11th centuries. The well, which was circular with vertical sides, was excavated for 0.93m below the top of the Roman road surface but the base was not reached. There was no evidence for a masonry or timber lining, despite its waterlogged nature. The well seems most likely to be of late Anglo-Saxon date in origin, and abandoned during the currency of Cotswolds ware. A clayey deposit (2760) was recorded at the south end of the section, apparently truncated by the cone at the top of the well (Fig. 4.13, section 1). Elsewhere this layer had been removed by the construction of the cellar of G55 (see Period 2.4 to 2.5, below) but was sealed by the thick clay dump, 2758, the beginnings of Period 2.3.

Plot 3: Period 2.3: 13th to 14th centuries (Fig. 4.14)
This period saw an intensification of clearly urban activity on the site as a whole. In the West Sondage (Fig. 4.13, section 1), the layers above 2758 (from

Fig. 4.14 Period 2.3, west end. Scale 1:250

Period 2.1), S208 and S209, consisted of a series of silty clay deposits with thin lenses of burnt wood, the whole sequence suggesting a sequence of dirt floors and hearths (G56). Pottery gave a date range of the 13th to 14th centuries for this activity. An iron prick spur recovered from these layers was of late medieval type, suggesting a date towards the end of this range, although the spur may have been intrusive from the construction of a cellar in the following phase. To the north a series of silty soils (G66 and G67) were also dated to this period (Fig. 4.14), and probably represent the location of medieval gardens.

Plot 3: Period 2.4 to 2.5: 14th to 16th centuries (Fig. 4.15)

At the top of the recorded sequence in the West Sondage was a well-made and extensive hearth made of sandstone slabs (2706 of S207; Figs 4.15 and 4.16). It was truncated to the east by a 17th-century cellar (part of Building 6, Period 3.1 to 3.2, below). To the west

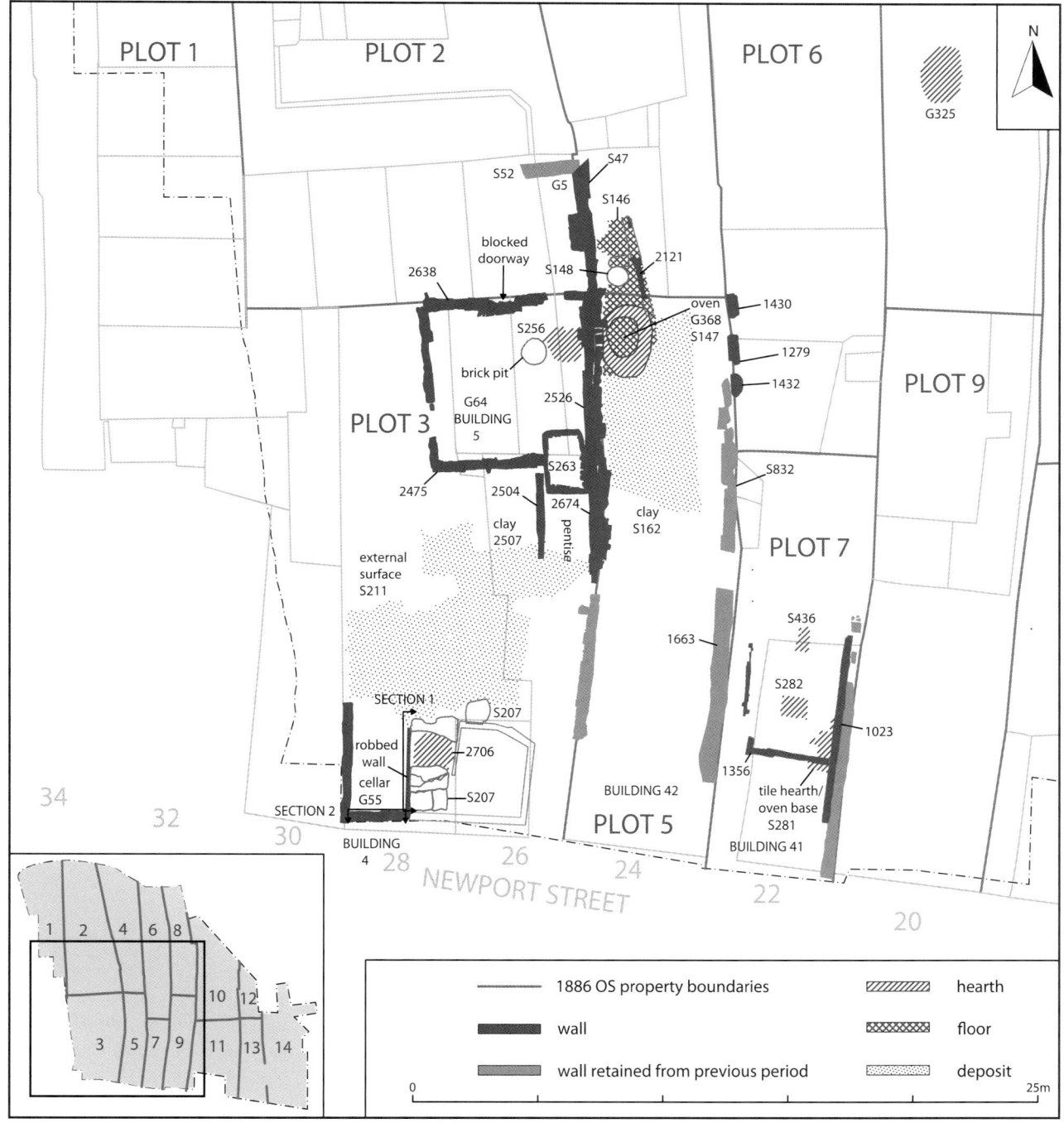

Fig. 4.15 Periods 2.4 and 2.5, west end. Scale 1:250

Fig. 4.16 Plot 3, Period 2.4/2.5, hearth 2706 and cellar G55, looking south-west

it clearly pre-dated the robbing of the G55 cellar wall, but was nonetheless largely intact on that side and to the north. Its dimensions were 1.2m by 2m and it was probably contemporary with the earlier cellar, being built against its eastern wall. Around it were extensive spreads of ashy material which in some cases were clearly rakings from it (S207). In one of these (layer 2754) was a well-made lias limestone spindle whorl of medieval type; another, less diagnostic in style but probably also medieval, was found in the same set of layers (Chapter 5.12.1, Fig. 5.27, 2 and 3). The character of the hearth was very like that of a domestic central hearth in an open hall, but the existence of a very slaggy layer (2622) associated with it suggests an industrial use. However, this could have originated from Roman layers dug up during cellar or well construction, as it was an isolated example in this group of layers. Abutting and partly overlying the hearth layers, but probably contemporary with the final use of the cellar, was a clay floor that extended northwards as much as 7.5m (2601 and 2694). This was most likely of 16th-century date and certainly pre-dated the infilling of the cellar, probably in the 17th century.

The cellar (Building 4; Figs 4.13, section 2; 4.32) was not very large (approximately 3.4m by 2.2m internally, later extended to 4.1m by 2.2m) and, assuming that layer 2758 was the floor, Building 4 may have had a ground floor at a level higher than the surviving excavation level to allow enough head room. A short length of wall was recorded set back on the top of the west wall which provided a shelf at about 1.6m above the floor. This may have been the ground floor wall set back to provide a rebate for the floor timbers which would give a very low room, or it may have been a later alteration. The minimum height for a ceiling on the west was given by the small cupboard recess with a lintel also at 1.6m (Fig. 4.17). On the south there was the chamfered jamb and cill of a window which implies either a ceiling at a much higher level, or a light well effect with the lintel sloping up in the thickness of the wall, or a partial cut-out in the ceiling. Below the window were discontinuities in the masonry which strongly suggest that there was at one time access into the cellar from the street (Fig. 4.13, section 2).

The wall of the original cellar was demolished and it was extended northwards. The original line was marked by a step in the floor, the survival of one squared block left in place at the east end, and the junction of the extension to the west wall (Fig. 4.17). The extension was minimal and may have been to provide access via a stairwell after the blocking of the door on the south. There was no surviving replacement north wall. This may have been robbed but there was little enough room

Fig. 4.17 Plot 3, Period 2.4/2.5, cellar G55 west wall, looking west

for it. All of these features and alterations pre-dated the plaster render on all the surviving walls.

The construction of the cellar was similar to known medieval cellars in Worcester. A comparable cellar, complete with recess and reached via an internal stair on the east was recorded in no. 16 Newport Street in 1978, under a 16th-century or earlier timber-framed building (Fig. 5.5). This, and its probable association with the hearth and clay floor to the east and north, suggests the cellar was built after the 14th century, but by the 16th century. Another, somewhat grander and earlier medieval stone undercroft was recorded during demolition work at nos 84–85 High Street, Worcester. This rectangular structure was set 15m back from the street frontage. It was sandstone and had stone vaulting, and dated to the 12th century. The building was estimated to be about 14m by 7.5m, and 2.5m high (Dalwood 1992). A late medieval date for cellar G55 is clearly indicated. The alterations to it suggest a long life, being infilled in the 17th century. The activities represented by the hearths and the cellar indicate development and occupation taking place along the Newport Street frontage.

Building 5 (G64) was constructed in stone against the permanent boundaries away from the street frontage. This was a square structure built in lias and sandstone, roughly 6m across internally (*c.* 20ft), with a central doorway on the north side. The east wall was built against the face of the boundary wall with Plot 5, with the other walls freestanding. The west wall was notably slighter than the others and may have had two openings in it. It may have butted up to the northern wall, but was carefully dogged into it as well. The southern wall had substantial footings and it is not clear whether the wall above (2475) was original or a rebuild; in plan it was out of alignment and the lower level was discontinuous. No floors survived, only the silty soils into which the walls were cut (G66 and G67 of Period 2.3.1). These were presumably garden soils and probably pre-dated the soil spread that cellar G55 was cut through, but the relationship was unclear. The step in the northern opening led upwards out of the building, reflecting the natural rise of the land surface. It may originally have been a garden wall with an opening in it. A potsherd from the northern wall (2638) suggests a date after a range of the 12th to the 14th century, and tiles from the southern wall (2475) give a *terminus post quem* of the 13th to the 15th century. A date in the 14th to 15th century for the structure seems reasonable, given that the walls are later than the G5 boundary walls. A 17th-century sherd was recorded from the eastern wall (2526) but this seems to be intrusive from the overlying post-medieval wall of G117 (below). Building 5 could have

Fig. 4.18 Period 3.1, west end. Scale 1:250

occupied, until demolition, by timber-framed buildings of probably late 16th to mid 17th-century date, the overlap of the demise of timber framing with the use of brick taking place over the second half of the 17th century in Worcester (Figs 2.12 and 2.13). A brick cellar (G54, Building 6) under no. 26 is of this phase, as is presumably, a similar cellar (G58, Building 7) under no. 30, of which only the north-east quadrant was exposed and not excavated. The medieval cellar, G55 in no. 28 Newport Street is recorded as having been filled in at this point. This seems a little unlikely at first glance, but the rear wall of the 16th/17th-century rebuild across the rear extension definitely cut through the backfill layers of this cellar, and it seems that no. 28 did not have a cellar from this point onwards.

It was at the rear of these properties, before this rebuilding, that a cobbled surface (G221) was laid over the later medieval layers of G55. This formed the basis for a series of hearth and oven bases, tightly packed into the north-east part of this area (G62; G60 on the east side of the plot may be an outlier). These hearths seem to represent an activity requiring largely rectangular hearths, built and rebuilt over a number of years. Stratigraphic relationships show a basic succession but with the possibility of two hearths occasionally together. On the east, running south from the south-west corner of Building 5, a lias stone wall (S222) post-dated the cobbled surface and may have formed the eastern side of an structure over the hearths (open-fronted to the south), along with the west boundary wall of Plot 3. In general, hearths with pitched-tile bases were replaced by hearths with brick ones, conforming with the increasing use of brick in the city during the 17th century. The boundary wall between nos 28 and 30 (G59) was a stone rubble structure, and appeared to be of 17th/18th-century date from pottery and from some of the hearths being built up closely against it.

A stub wall (S232) projected from the west boundary wall in line with the southern wall of Building 5, its alignment seeming to mark the northern end of the hearth complex, G62, and the make-up layers for the associated cobbled floor seemed to respect it. It appeared to represent the western jamb of a wide opening between the hearth area and the space to the west of Building 5, which may have been an open yard. Part of a pitched tile floor (S258) survived along the western edge of this yard, immediately north of the western jamb. This seemed to have been disturbed as a roughly square area of tips of ashy silts and clay occupied the space immediately east of it, which looked like the backfill of a robbed square structure (S265), perhaps a pitched or sett yard surface that was part of S258.

It seems probable that hearths G62 were in a building with a wide opening to the north into a yard, as well as an open south end. However, the enclosing structure suggested by wall S222 does not seem to be part of timber-framed Building 6 that covered much of the site in the early 20th-century photographs and is shown on the 1886 OS map (Fig. 2.14). This suggests that the hearths are earlier than that building and therefore earlier in the date range given by the pottery. Machine excavation removed the layers above these hearths and east of wall S222 so that nothing can be said about the sequence post-dating them. The only fragment of Building 6 that survived to be excavated seems to be wall S251 (Fig. 4.21), which closed the opening into the yard and was probably the north wall of Building 6.

Building 5 continued in use into this period, but was again largely rebuilt, this time in brick, (G117), probably at the same time as the construction of the timber-framed Building 6, nos 26 and 28 Newport Street. The south and east walls survived almost complete in plan, but only a few fragments of this rebuild survived on the west, one of which blocked the southern door in this wall. The east wall was moved slightly to the west (to the position of an earlier internal subdivision), providing the first clear evidence of the passageway through from Plot 3 to Plot 2, which remained in existence until 1936. A dark silty occupation layer (S253; not shown on plan) was found inside the building, but also seemed to spread to the south, beyond the outline of Building 5. It may be that the external layer was not the same layer as the internal. In the northern part of Building 5, a massive brick stack was built, with a brick floor and a brick ash box, positioned centrally and slightly in front of the stack base. It may be that the kitchen function tentatively ascribed to earlier phases is more supportable here. The ubiquitous use of brick implies a 17th-century date for this structure, but one where the medieval layout of buildings still dictated the property plan. A new cess pit (S233) may also have been part of this phase (Fig. 4.21).

Plot 3: Period 4 to 5: 18th century/early 19th century (Fig. 4.23)

The open yard west of Building 5 was built over during this period, creating Building 8. A brick wall on sandstone footings was built alongside the west wall of Building 5, against the blocked openings, and a cross wall was built halfway along. Only the eastern part of this wall was uncovered. At this point a set of brick steps descended into the northern room, which was not excavated further. Neither Building 8 nor 5 match those shown on the 1886 OS map, so it is assumed they were rebuilt before that date, but no evidence of such a rebuild survived.

To the west, part of the rear yard of no. 30 was uncovered and cess pits, a well, hearths and yard surfaces were recorded, providing a similar picture to other yards of this phase on the rest of the site. The limited dating evidence suggested an 18th-century date for the bulk of this activity. The plot was crossed by services of various types, all presumably of late 19th or early 20th-century origin.

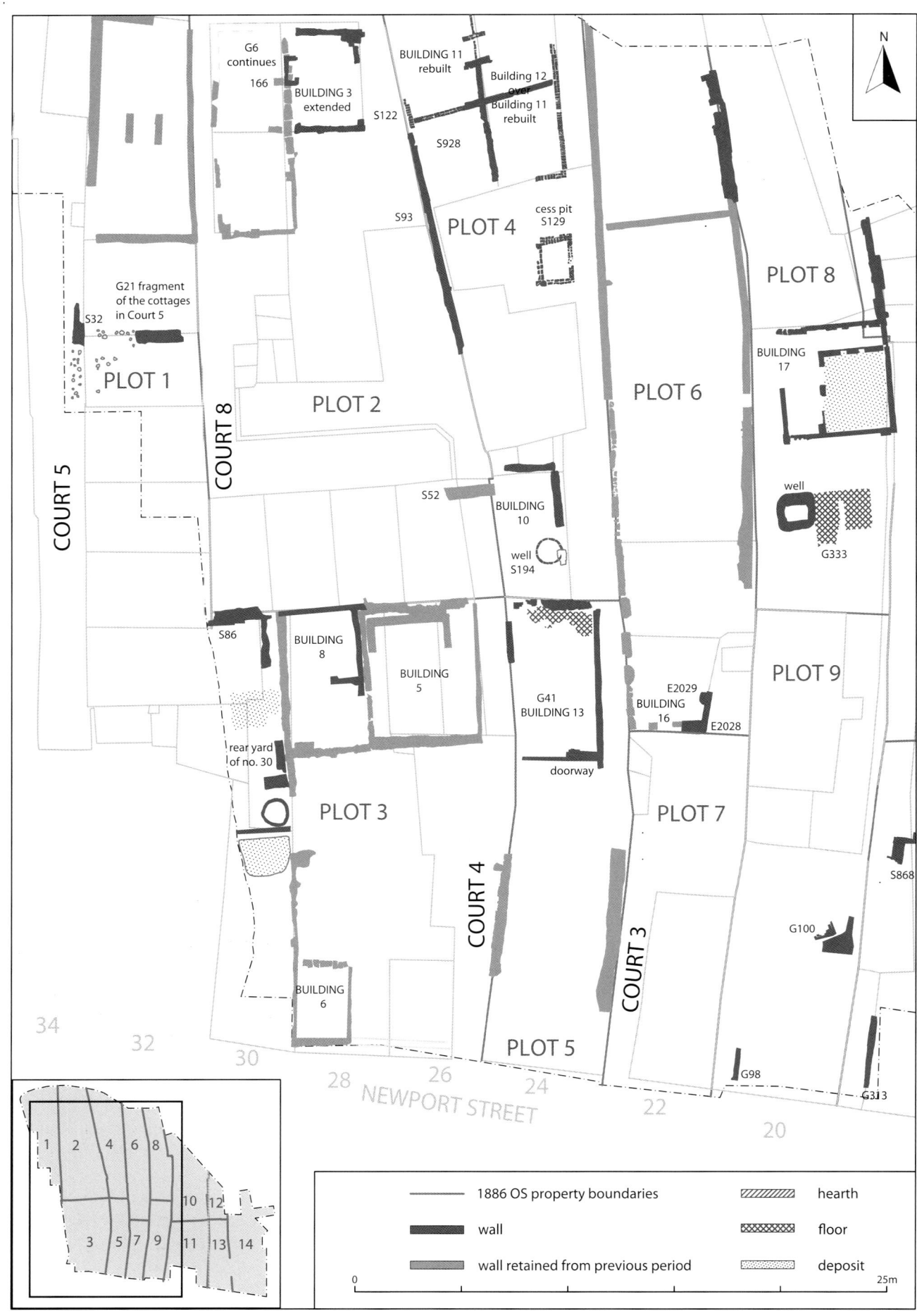

Fig. 4.23 Period 4, west end. Scale 1:250

The documentary evidence throws little light on the earlier activities in these properties. Nos 26 and 28 was in occupation by a cobbler in the later 17th century and there was a shop and a stall on the street. His widow was still there in the early 18th century. Plots 2 and 3 seem to have been practically separated by the mid 16th century, and finally passed into separate ownership in the early 18th century (Hughes, Chapter 5.1.4). It was only in the 19th century that the distinct identities of nos 26 to 30 Newport Street became reasonably clear.

4.3.4 Plots 4 and 5: no. 24 Newport Street

Most of the tenement boundaries of these plots, as depicted on the 18th and 19th-century maps, are shown to have been marked by substantial masonry walls by the 14th century, and probably by the 13th, but the boundary between Plots 2 and 4 seems to have only attained its mapped 19th-century form in the late 18th century. This ambiguity is also shown in the entrances from the alleyway between Plot 4/5 and Plot 6/7. Within these medieval boundaries, evidence for medieval buildings and hearths was also found. Ovens were a feature of this plot, and in the late medieval period a particularly grand example was built at the rear of the street-front building. Photographic evidence shows a (probably 16th to early 17th-century) timber-framed building occupying the street-front block, re-using the medieval boundary walls but with a brick rebuild of the front elevation. Some archaeological evidence for this building survived. To the rear, a stone cottage of 17th-century date completely disregarded the plot boundaries of the 1886 OS map (Fig. 4.1) and of later buildings, and seemed to be linked to a roughly contemporary cottage at the rear of Plot 2, which was rebuilt in brick in the early 19th century on a new alignment. The boundary wall between Plots 2 and 4 was built up to it in brick, supporting the map evidence of 1779 that this boundary was not in existence at that time. A large building in the centre of Plot 4 dated from the 19th century. Again, the change from cess pits to mains drainage is evident from the later 19th century.

Plots 4 and 5: Period 2.3: 13th to 14th centuries (Fig. 4.14)

The earliest excavated masonry walls (G5) were along the boundary between Plots 2/3 and 4/5. Their permanence is indicated by the fact that the boundary lines recorded by the OS in 1886 (Fig. 4.1) fall exactly on the centre line of these walls. The southern parts (walls 1650 and 2602) may have been one build on a massive footing of squared ashlar blocks, but it was not possible to show this from excavation. At the junction with the northern section of wall 2478 there was a slight indication that wall 2602 ended or turned eastwards, with wall 2478 built up against this corner. This was at the boundary between Plots 4 and 5, where a building line was established by the post-medieval period, but this seems never to have been a property boundary. These walls formed the western footings of a long-lived structure, Building 42. The wall footing S47 extended the boundary wall G5 another 5.4m northwards. Beyond this point the boundaries were represented only by post-medieval brick walls, with occasional sandstone footings, the line of which may not have been of medieval origin.

The walls of Building 42 were cut into layers at the lower limit of excavation, which were not directly dated. However, these layers were under ovens G43 and G44, which seemed to have been built into or against the lower part of wall 2602, and were most probably of 13th to 14th-century date. The substantial walls of Building 42 were therefore also of medieval origin, and quite probably of 13th to 14th-century date too. These walls were also under or butted by the late medieval Building 5 in Plot 3 (above).

The early boundary walls on the east side of Plot 4/5 were more complex. To the south, wall 1663 survived as a single-phase sandstone wall footing similar to wall 1650 and formed the eastern side of Building 42 (G51). It is clear that these two walls continued in use in Period 3 as the footings to the timber-framed Boar's Head (earlier Severn Galley) public house, the front part of which was rebuilt in brick in Period 4. They seem to be the first walls built here and were cut into layer 1746 (G97) that extended across Plots 3, 5, and 7. Both walls terminated to the north at about the same point as the timber frame is seen to give way to brick in a photograph of Court 4 of 1936 (Fig. 4.24), and that this was the north or rear wall of Building 42 is indicated by a change of alignment at this point. This wall position was also indicated in the complex of fragmentary medieval hearths and walls G47–G49 which evolved into a gable end stack in Period 3.1 or 3.2 (G45 and G46, Fig. 4.21). The eastern plot boundary continued northwards as wall S832, parallel to wall 2602 to the west and also built in sandstone but slightly narrower in width. The large blocks of the wall were set on a narrower bedding of smaller stones and tile levelling. Wall S832 came to a butt end at the Plot 4/5 boundary, this being the rear building line of the Boar's Head as recorded in 1886 (Fig. 2.14). There was no archaeological evidence for a wall continuing this alignment northwards but a drain, which was largely unexcavated, continued the alignment to Dolday.

The existence of a long-lived alley or passageway along the east side of Plot 4/5, running from Newport Street to Dolday, makes the existence of gaps in boundary wall S832 of some interest. These presumably represented entrances from the passageway into the rear of the tenement. Floor 1601 (not shown) appears to have been an early passageway surface between Plots 5 and 6, overlying the medieval layer S137 (not shown) and laid around two or three stone piers (1430, 1432 and 1279), the jambs of an entrance into Plot 6 (no. 22 Newport Street). The piers and threshold were later incorporated

Fig. 4.24 Plot 3, Court 4, 1936 photograph. © Worcestershire Record Office

into the walls of a late 17th-century malthouse built on Plot 6 (Building 15; see below). To the south was another entrance, between walls 1663 and S832, with a tiled threshold later blocked by sandstone walling. The passageway may have run more centrally along the plot boundary, moving as it were from side to side. The pre-Period 3.3 alignment seems to be shown archaeologically in Plot 6, whereas, historically, the passageway settled into Plot 4/5.

In Plot 4 there was evidence of medieval activity which seems best to fit into the period for the early boundaries discussed above. The lower limit of excavation was a widespread sandy clay layer (S137; not shown) on which was laid a cobbled surface (S140), now very fragmentary and of limited extent. This may have been for a yard to the rear of Building 42, which was contemporary with a truncated shallow pit (S144), a tile-lined cylindrical pit (S141) and broadly with other activity in Plot 5 (e.g. G43). Pit S141 is dated to the 12th to 14th centuries and had a flat tiled base. It was distinct from the ovens, which usually had pitched tile floors, and there was no evidence of burning or high temperatures in its fabric. It was bonded and lined with clay and as such could have held water. These pits were often found in association with ovens but no candidate survived in the vicinity.

In Plot 5, also tucked into the side of boundary wall 2602, was a very well-preserved small beehive oven (G44) built in tile set in clay (Fig. 4.25). This was just at the limit of excavation depth and was investigated in a small partial sondage. The layers it was cut into produced pottery dating to the 13th to 14th century. The tiles of which the oven was constructed, corbel fashion, were of 13th to 15th-century type and the oven was only 0.72m in diameter. The oven had been set slightly into its contemporary ground surface, and was buried up to its open apex by two later layers of soil. These layers were themselves sealed by a widespread silty ashy layer with much carbonised wood (S160, not shown), which covered nearly all the northern end of Plot 5, was seen in Plot 4, and formed the general limit of excavation. Onto this layer were built two more ovens. Oven G43 consisted of a pitched tile floor, a roughly rectangular patch which survived later truncation and damage, and the cut for the construction of the superstructure that reflected its original D-shape. Overall dimensions were approximately 2.5m by 1.5m. Again it was tucked into the boundary wall, but not as tightly as oven G44. A fragment of the tile superstructure wall survived on the south side, suggesting the oven mouth was to the north or north-east. The other oven is described below under Period 2.4 to 2.5.

Immediately south of this oven, but separated by a later drain which removed the connecting stratigraphy, was an island of stratified deposits, the lower parts of which also clearly belonged to Period 2.3. Dating, where present, was consistently 13th century. The lowest level, G49 (not shown), was at the limit of excavation and was similar and equivalent to layer S137 (not shown) further north. Into this layer was set a sandstone wall (S182), in a very poor state of preservation but running parallel to the plot boundary wall to the east. This seems to have been the west wall of an alleyway running northwards from Newport Street on the east side of the plot. It was short-lived, as all the succeeding layers covered it, but a much later brick wall followed its alignment, suggesting that the alleyway remained a significant feature, if not always structurally obvious to archaeological investigation. This alleyway is not evident on the 1886 OS map (Fig. 2.14) but it does appear on 19th and 20th-century lease plans, suggesting that its omission from the 1886 map was an oversight. It may have been part of an early and important route that may also have been represented later by G93 in Plot 6 (below). The area west of this wall was occupied by lenses of silt and clay interspersed with charcoal and carbon-stained soils (S187). This level was sealed by more similar lenses, S185, which also included the truncated tile floor of a hearth and a lens of clay silt with carbonised wood and bright orange clay pieces, the remnants of a less structured hearth. These lenses

Fig. 4.25 Plot 5, Period 2.3, small beehive oven G44, looking north

and hearths were covered over by a thin layer of clean sandy silt, S184, itself covered by a clay layer with 13th to 14th-century dating evidence, S168 (neither shown). This was equivalent to a widespread clay floor to the north (floor 1984; not shown) that post-dated burnt deposits from the oven G43.

Plots 4 and 5: Periods 2.4 and 2.5: 14th to 16th centuries (Fig. 4.15)
A very substantial oven (G368) and related structures was constructed at this period against the western boundary wall (Figs 4.26 and 4.27). The dating evidence is not strong but it is consistent with the stratigraphic sequence. A pitched tile floor (S146), more than 6m long and 1.8m wide, was constructed against the east side of Period 2.3 wall G5 and cut into soils at the lower limit of excavation. Towards its southern end, floor S146 featured a large oven of mortared tile (S147), with walls over 0.30m thick and with overall dimensions of 2.5m by 1.9m. The mouth of this keyhole-shaped oven was to the south. A low wall of similar tiles formed an edging to the eastern side of the pitched floor to the north (tile wall 2121). This may have been a later addition as it seemed to cut the tile edge and oversail the slight construction cut in which the tiles were laid, but clearly built as part of the continuing use of the structure. The tile wall appeared to join the oven wall to the south, which appeared to be thickened at this point to receive it, but the actual junction was truncated by later walls. A large sandstone block, 0.80m by 0.50m, was sunk into the tile floor towards its northern end, and north of it the tile floor was laid at a different angle, at about 20° to the rest. The tile floor within the oven was more elaborate, mostly of sandstone cobbles with areas of radiate and chordate tile pitching (S146). While this could be seen as a marking out the oven area, a small semicircular area to the north with angled pitching was hidden under the oven wall, giving the impression of infilling an earlier feature, quite possibly an earlier, smaller oven. A pit (S148) cut through the tiles to the north was on the central axis and may have been part of the structure. Its lowest fill contained a sherd of 13th to 14th-century pottery, and may have been contemporary with the large sandstone block adjacent. It appears that the oven S147 was a later structure than floor S146, but perhaps simply a replacement or improvement of an earlier structure continuing in use.

Apart from a layer of silty clay, S162, which sealed the earlier oven G43, little else survived to the southern side of the oven around its mouth. There were no spreads of ash or other evidence of burning. Layer S162 was extensive and was most probably truncated by tile floor S146. This, and the lack of burning or burnt debris, indicated that it was an earlier clay floor, or make-up

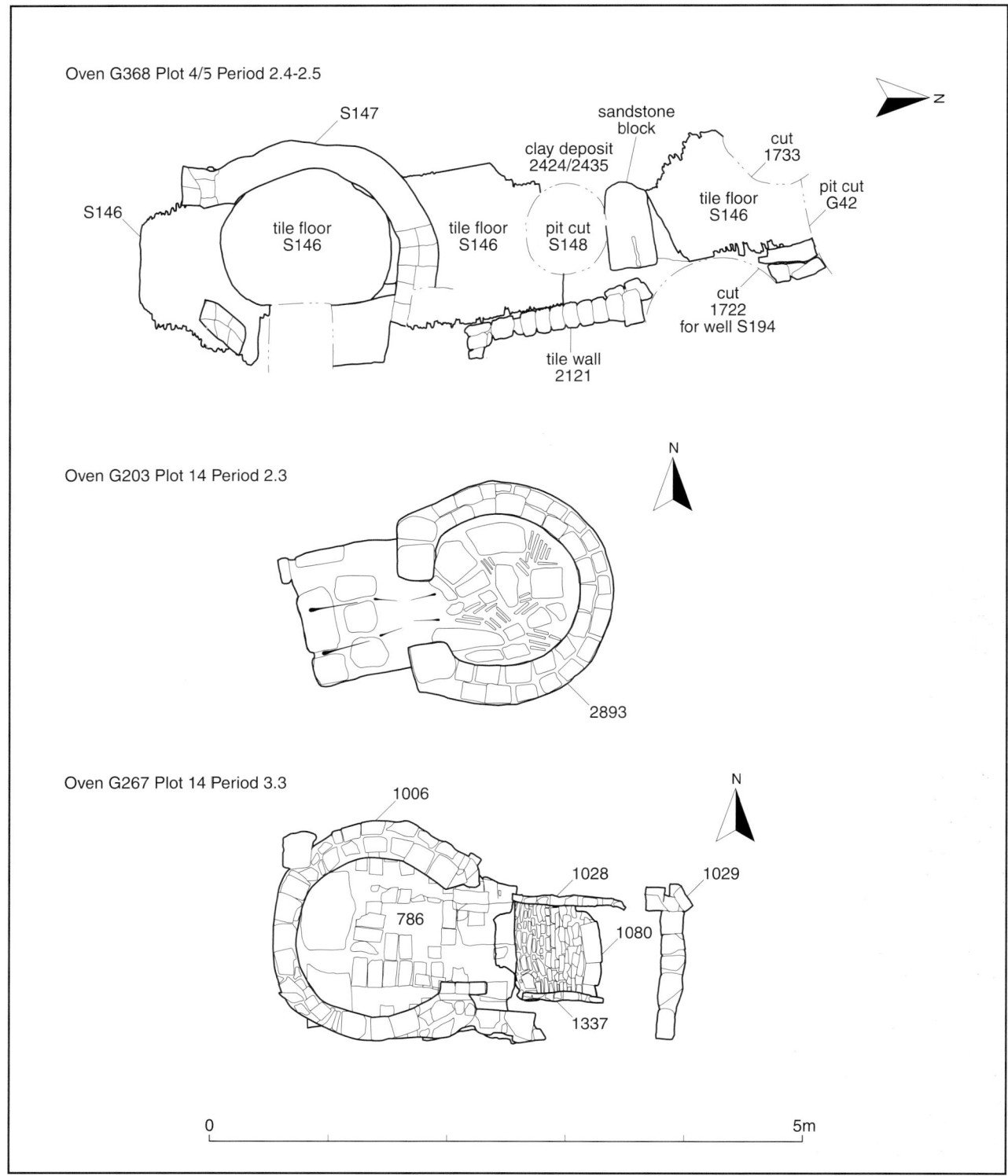

Fig. 4.26 Ovens G368, G203 and G267. Scale 1:50

deposit for one. There was a dump of ash (deposit 1542; not shown) to the north, directly on the pitched tile floor S146, which (apart from later intrusions) filled up the shallow area between by the low tile wall 2121 and the adjacent plot boundary. However, this was probably material from another hearth, as the rake-out from oven G368 could not have been deposited here easily as its mouth was to the south. A relatively small hearth or oven base, S142 occurred just east of the dump. This is described below as pottery supports a date for it and the associated group (Building 9) in the 16th century.

Fig. 4.27 Plot 4/5, Period 2.5, oven G368, looking north-east

Plots 4 and 5: Period 2.5 to Period 3.1: mid to late 16th century (Figs 4.15 and 4.18)

At what point the Period 2.4 oven G368 went out of use is unclear, but Building 9 was constructed adjacent to it, making use of and extending the low tile wall 2121 northwards for a short distance by a sandstone footing (1804). Building 9's north and east walls were built on a narrow footing of squared sandstone blocks in a narrow footing trench (S138), and may have supported a timber structure. The wall was cut into the lowest layer met with here, layer S137 (Period 2.3). Building 9 was of trapezoidal plan, partly a result of the property boundaries to either side, and may have been open on the south as no wall remains were apparent there. The room created was 5.6m long and 2.66m across at the north, narrowing to 1.74m on the south. Alleyways were left to either side of the building, the alley to the west passing over the site of the oven G368.

No floor was recognised to go with the building but some thick, flat-topped stones, S138 (not shown), at the south-east corner, may have been a remnant of a solid stone floor. A hearth, S142, was built into the south-west corner of the building. It seemed to incorporate part of the structure of the Period 2.3 tile-lined pit S141, which was otherwise sealed beneath wall 2121. This hearth produced a sherd of pottery dated to the 16th to mid 17th century. The thick layer of ash (1542) overlying Period 2.4 to 2.5 oven G368 (above) may well have derived from this hearth, as it was really not distinct from a similar layer (1543) which filled the site of Building 9. The spread of ash across the west wall of Building 9 indicates that this was an open-sided workshop to the west as well as to the south.

It has been suggested above that the front boundary walls supported a timber-framed building. This is plausibly of late 16th to early 17th-century date. A brick-lined cess pit near the Newport Street frontage is probably from this phase of building or perhaps a little later as it has extremely thin bricks, only just over 1.5" thick (0.04m) set in a greyish white mortar (G50).

Plots 4 and 5: Periods 3.2 and 3.3: late 16th century to late 17th century (Figs 4.21 and 4.22)

A new wall (G370) was built against the west face of the entrance in G134, seemingly blocking it (Fig. 4.21). However, it was only the footings of this later wall that continued across the openings, the wall proper respected them. The entrance was, at this later period, if not earlier, divided into two openings. A robbed length of wall in the centre of the opening suggests this division was primary, but if the robber trench represented the size of the original central pier, it left two extremely narrow openings. It seems more likely that the pier above was narrower. Later stone elements of wall G370 also seem to perpetuate these openings, the northern of which retained a brick threshold (1440) at about the level of the brick floor of Period 3.3 Building 15 in Plot 6 (below). By the mid 17th century there were seven small dwellings at the rear of no. 22. This passage and entrance would have given access to them or their predecessors. To the north of these entrances, the boundary continued as brick wall S333 built on stone footings S309 (Fig. 4.22) set on a double line of small piles (Fig. 4.28). The piling is characteristic of Building 15, and there is little doubt that this wall is all of that date. The wall continued in brick all the way to the Dolday frontage. The other side of the malthouse had a similar, piled wall but with slightly heavier stone footings.

The earliest contexts in the northern part of Plot 4 were probably of late 16th or early 17th-century date, based on pottery. The north wall of a building fronting Dolday, Building 11, was represented by a sandstone footing S116, and its south wall by a similar footing, S115 (Fig. 4.21). These did not share the alignment of the later 19th-century Building 12 that replaced Building 11 (Period 4, below), or of the frontage of Dolday as mapped in the 18th century, being rotated clockwise by several degrees. Neither were footings S115 and S116 parallel to each other, nor did they respect the later boundary between Plots 2 and 4, as footings S116 butted up to an early stone footing of Building 2 (Plot 2, Period 3.1, above). Its eastern end was not seen as it ran beyond the limit of excavation.

Footings S115 were of large sandstone blocks which ran roughly along the centre line of the later tenements. It too crossed the line of the later western boundary, also ending at the line of the east wall of Building 2 in Plot 2. Again, this indicates that the boundary had been re-aligned later, which might explain its odd appearance in plan. Given the apparently unified ownership of Plots 2 and 4, there may have been no permanent boundary here until the later 18th century or even the early 19th. Such a boundary is not apparent on Young's map of 1779 (Fig. 2.7). It may well have been fixed when the tenements represented by Building 12 were built shortly before 1811 (Hughes, Chapter 5.1.5).

A brick-built cess pit south of Building 11 (G36: S128) probably served this property, as it was backfilled some time before the late 18th century and the rear wall of Building 12 was built over it. However, the dating for its basal cess fill and the construction of the walls is late 17th century, and it may have belonged to the main house of no. 24 Newport Street (Building 42), rather than the lowly Building 11 fronting Dolday as the lowest fill was found to contain a variety of relatively high status foodstuffs, indicative of an affluent diet (Pearson, Chapter 5.23). As the property was occupied at this time by Edward Hurdman (obit 1682), who was in the distilling trade, it is also possible that the fruits may have been the waste from manufacturing spirits (Hughes, Chapter 5.1.5). The cess pit may have been in use until the 18th century, but the house was still in good status occupation in 1739 (ibid.).

Building 9 was probably demolished during Period 3.2 to 3.3, and a clay layer that cannot be dated more closely than to the 17th to 18th centuries was laid over its remains. Cut into this layer were various shallow scoop-like pits (S143; Fig. 4.21), and some short fragments of stone walling and cobbling G40 (not shown) that cannot be interpreted.

Plots 4 and 5: Period 4: 18th century (Fig. 4.23)

In the 18th century the rear wall of Building 11 subsided and fell: its lower courses were considerably slumped. It seemed to have been rebuilt as sandstone footing S928, running against the south side of the earlier south wall (S115). A new clay floor, 731 (not shown), covered wall S115 and butted the new wall; it also ran across the earlier north wall (S116) to a presumably rebuilt front wall, thus covering all of the area of the original Building 11. It also sealed a pit in the south-east corner that partly cut wall S115, confirming the sequence. It is possible that wall S122 was the west wall of this rebuilt Building 11, although it had no recorded relationship with clay floor 731. Wall S122 followed the later plot boundary, indicating that re-alignment of the building had occurred, although the boundary wall (S93) itself may have been later (see below). The brick walls of Building 12 used wall S122 as a footing but such stone footings were conspicuous by their absence elsewhere in this building.

Plots 4 and 5: Period 4 to Period 5: 19th century and 20th century (Figs 4.23 and 4.29)

The rebuilt Building 11 was itself demolished and replaced by Building 12. This was built of 9" (0.23m) brick walls, using the stone walls of Building 11 as footings where possible. It was roughly twice as big as its predecessor, effectively adding two rooms to the rear of the original plan, being designed as four one-up/one-down back-to-backs. Building 12 was 'new erected' in 1811 and presumably post-dated 1806, when only two tenements are mentioned in this plot on Dolday (Hughes, Chapter 5.1.5). Like the rebuilt Building 11, a passageway featured to the east, giving access to the rear properties. The properties were far from regular, having to fit within the diverging property boundaries and the Dolday frontage area, which was now the trapezoidal shape it had acquired from the late 18th century. The building had soil and clay make-up layers supporting mortar floors. The party wall of the two front tenements had back-to-back fireplaces, but no sign of such an arrangement was evident in the rear two houses. The Building 11 cess pit (S128) was replaced further south by cess pit S129, which presumably served the new tenements, and was slightly larger.

The layers over the demolished Building 9 were sealed by a clayey silty layer into which was cut a brick-lined well, S194; what may have been its enclosing building, Building 10; and another shallow scoop (G42; not shown). Building 10 was of brick on stone footings and is probably the small building on the 1886 map (Fig. 4.1) immediately south of Room G35 (below). Neither were mapped in 1779, and both may belong to Period 5.

In the 18th or early 19th century, a new brick range (Building 13) was added to the rear of Building 42 on the Newport Street frontage. This part of Plot 5 is shown built up in 1779 (Young's map; Fig. 2.7). However, any relationship Building 13 had with the front range was removed by drainage cut just south of the structure. Building 13 was a large brick rectangle, with 9" (0.23m) walls and a brick floor. At its north end it made use of a short length of stone wall footings (1889; not shown), which may have originated as part of a later alteration to the south end of Building 10. The new room was entered via a doorway in the south-east corner, and down at least one step. Whether this entry was from the outside or from the rear of the front range (Building 42) was unclear, but a short stub of wall continuing south alongside the doorway suggested an internal access from a lobby, as the end wall was only a single skin and the stub may have been a jamb of the side entry from the passageway.

It seems likely that the brick and sandstone boundary wall 575 (S93) between Plots 2 and 4, running northwards from Building 10 to the rear wall of Building 12, was new in this period. It had no recorded forebears, unlike practically all of the other remains of boundary walls that were investigated. The area behind Building 12 was not excavated to layers pre-dating it, the subsequent activities and structures taking place on a widespread dump or garden soil, S126 (not shown), which was of 18th-century date. Cess pit S129 of Building 12 was reduced and then completely abandoned when new drains were dug through its northern end. These served new WCs built against a large trapezoidal room (G35), against the boundary wall S93, which was also largely rebuilt at this time. Buildings 12 and 13 remained in use until 1936.

4.3.5 Plots 6 and 7: no. 22 Newport Street

This plot again demonstrated the medieval origin of its stone boundary walls, but also contained evidence of pre-wall activity in the form of ovens and hearths on widespread accumulations of mixed occupation soils. Under the frontage building there was evidence of clay floors and hearths of medieval date clearly belonging to the buildings on these walls. These were replaced by a 17th-century brick rebuild. At the rear of the property, nothing earlier than the mid 17th century was reached in excavation. Here, evidence of the seven dwellings mentioned in documents was found. Partially predating them but also continuing in the open space between them and the capital messuage, was a series of hearths. These dwellings were demolished for the construction of a large malthouse by or in 1698, but part of them was incorporated in its structure. This part, at the southern end, was then demolished and a separate building added in the early 18th century. This and the malthouse survived until 1936, when it, and the southern end of the malthouse, had been converted to slum dwellings (as had the frontage buildings).

Plots 6 and 7: Period 2.3 to 2.5: 13th to 16th centuries (Figs 4.14 and 4.15)

The central part of the development area was largely devoid of medieval deposits at the level reached during the excavation, but extensive deposits 1746/S197 (G97) were recorded at the southern end of Plots 3, 5, 7 and 9 that pre-dated the stone boundary walls. These deposits were not excavated so no finds were retrieved. It seems that these large dumps of material were brought to the site to consolidate and raise the level of low-lying, floodable ground before any masonry plot walls were built (but not necessarily before other boundary markers might have been in use). Boundary wall 1663 (G51) was of probable 13th to 14th-century date (see Plot 5, above) and a similar date is possible for deposits S197. This dating is supported by dump S97 (not shown), which was also of 13th to 14th-century date and was found to either side of boundary wall G52 between, Plots 7 and 9, providing that boundary wall with a similar *terminus post quem*.

These latter dumps also supported the remains of three hearths or ovens (S275, S276, S277). The northernmost, S275, was a simple rectangular clay pad, 1.8m by 1.2m, over a pebbly base with a darkened clay and ash deposit over it, and seemed to represent a simple open hearth. South of it was a roughly circular pitched tile base of an oven (S277) with remains of its sandstone and tile walls. To the east was a larger but less well defined semicircular oven base (S276) which being at the lower limit of excavation was not excavated but appeared to have been truncated by boundary wall S382. Its walls were of a clay cob rather than stone. All three of these features appeared to pre-date the earliest masonry boundary walls, though Plot 7 was probably already defined, as the east side of oven S276 did not project into the next plot.

Building 41 was constructed between boundary walls 1663 (G51) and S382 (G52) on the Newport Street frontage. Its remains comprised a sandstone wall (1023) built on top of the western edge of wall S382, and a similar cross wall (1356) was contemporary with it, dividing Building 41 into two rooms (Fig. 4.15). The cross wall had a return on its west end, suggested the early existence of the side passage known from much later maps (below). The setting of wall 1023 against the western side of the wide footings of S382 suggests that the footing was shared, and that it supported two separate party walls, the easterly one having been completely removed before excavation began. Within Building 41, a very mixed dark layer with much charcoal built up, which seemed to have been a dirt floor (S279, not shown) containing the trodden detritus from the activities that took place within this building, for which no evidence for a northern wall survived. In the northern room, dirt floor S279 contained two hearths: one a rectangular setting of pitched tiles (S436) set on the central axis of the building towards what must have been the northern part of the room; the other, which might have been an oven base (S281), nestled in the south-east corner of the room. The latter was not well preserved but the presence of stone blocks among its pitched tiles suggests an oven, as does its position.

Dirt floor S279 was covered with a paler silt, probably another an occupation floor (S280, not shown) and on this was a rectangular setting of pitched tiles (S282) forming another hearth, again on the central axis of the northern room but this time towards its southern end. The deposits beneath floor S280 contained pottery of 13th to 14th-century date, while the later floor and hearth contained pottery with a date range of 12th to 15th and 13th to 16th centuries, and tiles of medieval type.

Plots 6 and 7: Period 3.1: 16th to early 17th centuries (Fig. 4.18)

The hearths, clay floors and brick wall of the next phase on Plot 7 (G70) seem to have been of 16th to 17th-century in date, and may have been in use for all of this period. Building 39 replaced Building 41 at the street front of Plot 7, with a brick wall (S268) built on the line of the east boundary and across the north end. A clay floor probably united them but the relationships were uncertain (S272; not shown). The western wall to this north room was represented by a very slight construction of sandstone and brick (S269) that probably supported a timber partition, again marking out a passageway along the side of the plot. In general, the bricks suggested a 17th-century date, but the ones from this partition were of a very odd size (8" by 5" by 4", or 0.20m by 0.13m by 0.10m), which may suggest an early date in the range proposed.

Internally, clay floor (S272; not shown) was contemporary with a series of brick-and-stone walls and floors (S271) that were clearly fireplaces of some kind, but are difficult to interpret. The clay floor was laid against these structures, sealing medieval hearth S282. The eastern fireplace had quite substantial footings in brick and was set against the (robbed) wall S268. It occupied the position of the earlier oven S281, suggesting some kind of continuity, perhaps a brick rebuild after the demolition of the presumed timber-framed medieval building. Less than a metre to the west of this fireplace was a second one, slightly longer than the first and facing away from it. Between the two was a brick ash box, clearly a secondary addition. It would be reasonable to interpret this as a large, central stack with multiple fireplaces and ovens, but each element was structurally distinct, with its own construction trench.

This stack is of interest as it seems to have been an early use of brick in the city. The latest clay floor that abutted it (1247; not shown) contained a Nuremberg token dated to the 1550s–1580s, and the western part of the stack had another in its foundation trench, with a range of 1583–1601, so a late 16th or very early 17th-century date would seem to be indicated.

The date of the elements that formed the alley along the west side of the plot (perhaps originally identical with that on the east side of Plot 5) is uncertain. The gravel surface (G93) has been recorded in the southern part of Plot 6 and its existence is implied by the alignments of Building 14 (Period 3.2) and deposits dating from before Buildings 15 and 16 further north. A linear spread of bricks and cobbles at the north end of Plot 6 closely follow the alignment (G86). These latter elements are possibly earlier than the late 17th-century construction of Building 15, and are more probably contemporary with an early phase of that structure. A short length of solidly built sandstone flags and cobbles in the north of Plot 7 (S284) also lies on this alignment and pre-dates the 18th century. Parts of this alleyway survived as a side passage off Newport Street until the 1930s, but the northern part was sealed off when the malthouse, Building 15, was erected. It seems likely that the alleyway was of medieval origin, but this cannot be clearly demonstrated.

Plots 6 and 7: Period 3.1/3.2: mid 17th century (Figs 4.18 and 4.21)

It is known from the documentary sources (Hughes, Chapter 5.1.6) that by 1678 the rear plot of no. 22 Newport Street had seven small dwellings at the rear, which had been built after 1622 and by 1666. It is likely that the compacted sandy layer 1503 (not shown) along with the walls and possible oven (G91 and S361) Plot 6, related to these dwellings, as did the hearths that seemed to occupy a yard to the south (see below). In or by 1698, a large malthouse had been built on the site of these dwellings.

The known surfaces of the side alley, G93 in Plot 7, were buried under an extensive dark clayey soil layer S285 (not shown), probably garden soil. A few postholes were cut into this, probably supporting temporary garden features, before it was covered by another similar layer which covered the western part of this rear part of Plot 7 (S286; not shown). A similar layer was recorded in the evaluation trench as E2039. Dating evidence from these garden layers indicates they occupied a time span within the 17th and 18th centuries. Both of these spread layers pre-dated a long-lived (or fast-changing) succession of hearths in the northern part of Plot 7. The earlier of these (S293 and S294) pre-date the construction of a rectangular building on stone footings at the southern end of Plot 6, the structures of Building 14. The later of the hearths (S292 and E2020) post-dated the southern wall of Building 14. Brick occurs in the hearth structures both before and after the construction of the walls. Hearth S291 is cut by 2025. The brick and tile dating agrees with the pottery evidence in indicating a 17th or 18th-century date, and as these groups all pre-date the malthouse of 1698, a 17th-century date seems secure.

Despite its burial by garden soils, the structures and layers in Plot 6 still respected the line of the side alley. The earliest was a straightforward stone-built cess pit, S360 (Fig. 4.18), cut into the lowest level reached here. It had a layer of cess in the base. After this was deliberately backfilled in the 17th century it was reconstructed in brick and tile, as S361 (Fig. 4.21). This was slightly more complex and seems to have had a tile vault, the springing of which was recorded *in situ*. It may have been an oven, unlike any seen elsewhere on the site, but not unlike later baker's ovens. Its origins may make this seem unlikely, but the structural events are undeniable. Both phases of work respected the line of the alleyway, G93. The general dating for the backfilling of this structure seems to be mid 17th century, which might allow a construction date for the first element to be pushed back to the late 16th century. It obviously pre-dated the construction of the rectangular Building 14.

Plots 6 and 7: Period 3.2: mid 17th century (Fig. 4.21)

Broadly contemporary, but probably somewhat later and cut into S359 (not shown), a widespread dump or levelling layer, were the stone footings (S357) which represented the northern end of a rectangular building (Building 14). In strict stratigraphic terms Building 14 was erected after the cess pit/oven S361, but could have enclosed it. It was built against the eastern boundary wall to Plot 6/7, occupying a plot north of that occupied by the hearths and was certainly later than the earliest of that group. The west wall respected the line of the alleyway and aligned with the oven (rather than the underlying cess pit). The walls retained a sandy floor layer. A short length of north/south wall adjoining a cross wall at the south end of Building 14 lines up with the northern part of the west wall of the building and may be part of the same build, again alongside the alleyway. The cross wall, S306, seems to be stratigraphically later than other elements of Building 14, but if so, may be a rebuild of its southern wall. Pottery from the footings trench indicated a 17th-century date. Building 14 can, therefore, be seen as a long rectangular structure against the eastern side of Plot 6. Wall 1265 (and an unnumbered brick wall in the evaluation Trench 2) on the east side, probably belong to this phase of building and suggest a brick superstructure, distinguished from the later malthouse wall by being noticeably thinner. A construction of large sandstone blocks set near the centre of the east side of Building 14 seems to belong to this phase, but their function is unclear (S358). An extensive brick floor, much damaged by later works, occupied what is probably the interior of this southern part of Building 14 (S304). This building is not big enough to be all of the seven dwellings put up before 1666, but may be part of the presumed row (Hughes, Chapter 5.1.6).

North of Building 14 a few features may be of this period. They were cut into a widespread and thin sandy layer, 1573 (not shown) that also seems to have pre-dated Building 14. These included a length of brick wall running east/west from the Plot 4 boundary, just north of the building's north-west corner, and a few metres north, two brick pier bases and two enigmatic narrow piers of brick, all G90. They were all sealed by the late 17th-century brick floors of Building 15, Period 3.3.

The southern end of Building 14 underwent further changes, and if the building had originally been a dwelling, it certainly was not in this phase. A shallow horseshoe-shaped robbing trench (S353) showed the position of what was presumably a large oven cut through the brick floor S304. This had occupied most of the width of the building, being 3.6m wide externally. The base of the central area retained brick impressions. This was of a floor of the oven, post-dating 1166 (S304) and pre-dating the later brick floor (see below under Building 16). Some ash and burnt clay were all that remained of the activities and structure here, both inside the oven and outside it to the south. A circular brick tank (1486) is integral with the brick floor S304 so strictly pre-dates the oven. However, it is in a position where it could have been retained, as the brick floor seems to have been. If this is all a modification of the dwellings at the rear, it is probably after their construction in around 1650 (which can be suggested from documentary evidence) but prior to the construction of Building 15 in 1698 (Hughes, Chapter 5.1.6). The relationship of this oven phase of Building 14 to Building 15 (and 16) will be discussed further below.

Further structures pre-dating a later malthouse are found to the north of Building 14 but were either less well-preserved or below the limit of excavation. These included brick floors (S331), two brick-built wells, one backfilled by the mid 18th century (S337) and one not excavated (S343) but clearly earlier than all other features recorded to the north of Building 14. Another building (which may be another part of the 17th-century tenements) seems to be represented by sandstone rubble footings in foundation trenches (S340 and S341) that underlay the floors of the malthouse, Building 15. The north wall was missing, but the west wall again respected the alleyway alignment. The eastern wall alongside the boundary wall was particularly massive and may have contained a stack. Brick floors S331 may represent external areas or more structures to the north. S334 was a pitched tile surface originally recorded as part of an oven or hearth, but in plan looks more like an edging to brick path G86. This northern area, and these features, was covered by thin deposits of mortar, ash, clay and ceramic building material that probably represented demolition and clearance prior to the construction of Building 15.

Plots 6 and 7: Periods 3.3–4: late 17th to 18th century (Figs 4.22, 4.23 and 4.28)

Building 15 The Malthouse
After all these piecemeal changes it appears that the rear of no. 22 Newport Street was cleared and a new purpose-built malthouse constructed, Building 15. Documentary sources indicate that this had happened by 1698 when the dwellings had been cleared and the back of the plot was occupied by a malthouse and brewhouse. John Sowden, the occupier, was a baker (Hughes, Chapter 5.1.6). When he died in 1727, he was living in no. 20 and that plot apparently contained two furnaces, one in the 'upper backside' and one in the bakehouse. There was no clear reference to the malthouses, but it seems clear from the later 18th-century history of the malthouse that it was held separately from the rest of 22. The 'upper backside' may then have referred to the new malthouse, at the rear of the plot and the bakehouse to Building 14 incorporated into Building 15 as described below. The latter was replaced by Building 16 which was added on to the southern end of the malthouse and survived to be photographed in 1936 (Fig. 4.30). On this theory, Building 16 post-dates 1727 but probably not by very long. There seems to be a conflict of evidence, however, as no. 22 Newport Street was tenanted by a carpenter, John Kinsey, whose will and inventory of 1723 indicates only one furnace and a [work]shop (Hughes, Chapter 5.1.6). Building 16 would work very well as the replacement of one oven by a shop, but the dates obviously conflict here, and the confusions between nos 20 and 22 makes these interpretations difficult. It may be that Sowden's will refers only to no. 20 Newport Street.

The southern end of Building 14 was modified by extending it across the alleyway thereby blocking it (wall 1893). A new stone footing was added to the south-west corner and turned up alongside the west boundary wall to meet the overlapped wall S832. It was set on piles which distinguished it from the original wall of Building 14. It did not survive across the openings here but the piling continued, showing it had carried on across the gap. This piling indicated that the extension, and the boundary wall continuing its line northwards, also on piles, was of the same phase and represented the west wall of the malthouse, Building 15. This wall was a sandstone foundation which supported a brick

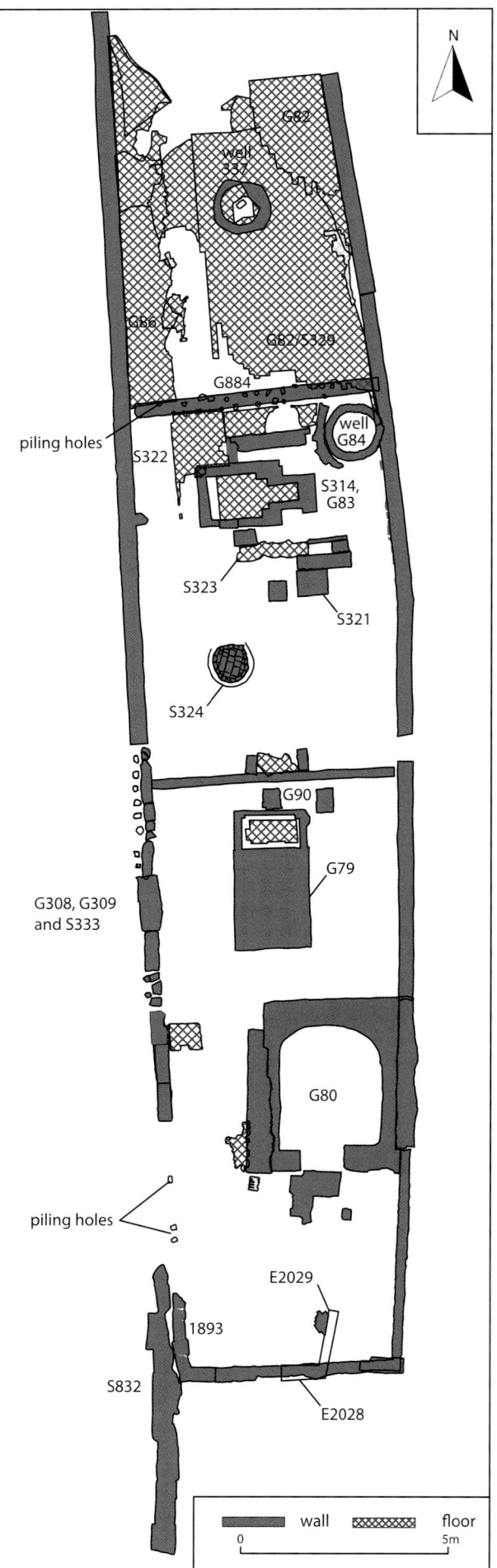

Fig. 4.28 The Malthouse, Plots 6/7. Scale 1:150

Fig. 4.29 Period 5. Scale 1:500

wall (S333/S309). The brick wall continued to Dolday but it was not clear that the sandstone foundation went any further north than the northernmost excavated cross wall of the malthouse, G884. The eastern wall incorporated parts of Building 14 at the southern end. It may be that the northernmost part of the malthouse is a later extension, but if so it was there by the later 18th century as it was mapped by Young in 1779 (Fig. 2.7). If so, the malthouse, built of brick almost exclusively, was originally a simple rectangle roughly 24m by 7m externally and was divided into three full width rooms, the southernmost being modified from Building 14.

The oven in Building 14 may have been retained until Building 16 was erected over it.

In the second room, immediately north of the oven S353 (Fig. 4.21), a similar large oven was constructed of brick, also on wooden piles, in the south-east corner of the middle room (G80). A complicated brick structure on its southern side, heavily robbed, may have been the flues leading to a stack, and one is shown in this position in the 1936 photograph (Fig. 4.30). Fragmentary brick floors survive to the west. The rest of the room is taken up with a raised brick platform in the centre (S298) surrounded by brick floors. This central part of the

Fig. 4.30 Plot 6/7, Court 3, Building 16, 1936 photograph. © Worcestershire Record Office

structure is a complex platform with a tank or tank base, a duct or channel and possible brick piers and walls seemingly supporting a vanished superstructure. This may have been a vat or tank of some sort, or perhaps a grinding mill.

The room to the north of oven G80 was completely repaved in brick in the 19th century (G82, Fig. 4.29), but below this a complex of brick and stone features seem to belong to the 18th-century use of the room (G83).

In the north-east corner of the room was a brick well capped with a millstone and some other blocks of stone, arranged with an opening in the top for a pumped extraction pipe (G84) (Fig. 4.31). A brick retaining wall held back the layers it cut through on the west. The floor of the room was essentially packed clay, but some small areas of brick flooring survived along the north side of the room (S322). Towards the north end of the room was a rectangular brick-lined pit S314. This had been re-paved (S315; not shown) but retained two settings for timber posts on either side. Despite the record of soot in a small dump at one end of this pit, no other evidence of burning was noted and the existence of the timber post settings seems to rule out a function as an oven. The east end of the pit narrowed to a small recess and at the west end a rendered step had been inserted. The whole structure seems to have been inserted into the west side of a pre-existing stone structure forming three sides of a room (S319), but the associated stratigraphy seems to show that these elements continued in existence and functioned alongside the brick pit. This suggests a modification of structures/equipment in the late 17th/18th century. Two brick pier bases and what seems to be a brick drain (S321 and S323) seem to be part of this structure south of the brick pit. The larger of the two piers was set on piles like the external wall. A circular brick pit, with its walls robbed, occurs at the south end of this room (S324). This and a robbed wall alongside it were cut into the clay floor of the room, S320, and must be contemporary with the use of the room. All these features were sealed by the 19th-century floors.

The area to the north of this northernmost room is separated from it by a brick wall on piles (G884) which may have been be the original north wall of the malthouse. This northern area was paved over in the 19th century but, before this, did not appear to have been built over, at least at first. Under this paving was a strip of 17th/18th-century brick paving (G82), against and broadly contemporary with the brick west boundary wall. The wall had slumped into the construction trench of a well which was structurally integral with the paving (S337). This paved path is most likely part of the activities in Period 3.1/2 but may have remained in use in Period 3.3, so is shown on both plans. This paving followed the alignment of the alleyway G93 very closely but it may simply be that it continued in use behind the malthouse as a rear access across an open yard.

Plots 6 and 7: Period 4: 18th century (Figs 4.23 and 4.28)

Changes occurred at the northern and southern ends of these plots. A photograph of 1936 shows a three-storey brick building against the south face of the malthouse with its stack as described above (Fig. 4.30). However, this is clearly not the southern room converted from Building 14 as it occupies only the western side of the plot leaving an access on the east to the malthouse house behind. Archaeologically this new building (Building 16) is represented by a brick wall E2028 in the evaluation trench (being the east wall of the building, and the upper brick floor E2029, an internal brick floor sealing the robbed oven S353. These clearly overlay all the elements of Building 14 and reused the south wall as extended to the west when it became part of Building 15. This rebuilding of the south end of the malthouse is presumably 18th century. It may have been John Kinsey's workshop and store and would therefore date to between 1706 and 1723, but as outlined above, this may conflict with the evidence of Sowden's will of 1727. This may be because it is not clear whether Sowden's will

Fig. 4.31 Plot 6, Period 3, millstone capping well G84 in Building 15, looking north-east

refers to both nos 20 and 22 Newport Street or just one of them (Hughes, Chapter 5.1.6).

By 1741 the malthouse was part of a group of malthouses occupying the northern end of no. 22, and nos 18–14, Newport Street. The latter were completely separated off from the Newport Street plots and reached from Dolday (Figs 4.7 and 4.32). These were all rented by a Quaker, Abraham Lingham, who was an oatmeal maker by trade. He lived in no. 20 Newport Street and in 1784 left 'all that dwelling house with the tenements behind it with the mills and implements of trade which I now occupy' (Hughes, Chapter 5.1.6).

Plots 6 and 7: Period 5: 19th century (Fig. 4.29)
In the 19th century a doorway existed in the north-east corner of the malthouse, Building 15. This was evidenced by the continuation through it of the extensive brick flooring S329 (same as G82 and covering the full width of the plot) although the doorway itself was not evident due to truncation. Excavation did not reach to Dolday in this part of the site, but the brick surface extended to the northern edge of the excavation and almost certainly to Dolday. Two earlier wells were retained in use via a pump.

The malthouses remained in the Linghams' hands into the 19th century and in use until the 20th century. No. 22 Newport Street was subdivided, presumably in the 19th century. In 1936 the frontage block had been divided into two back-to-backs, one facing the street, the other the court (Hughes, Chapter 5.1.6). The description from the report that led to their demolition in that year implies there were three further three-storey houses in the court. This could only be the case if Building 16 was one, and the furnace room of Building 15 had been converted into two tiny dwellings (as hinted at by the door into it from the courtyard) with the top floor in the roof. The 1886 OS mapping shows this marked off by a building line from the rest of the malthouse (Fig. 2.14). This perhaps makes sense in the light of the re-ordering of the rest of the malthouse in this period as represented by S329 and G82. The latter was a series of brick floors and slightly recessed areas, still clearly requiring access to the earlier wells.

4.3.6 Plots 8 and 9: no. 20 Newport Street

The earliest layers encountered pre-dated the stone boundary walls of this plot and were cross-boundary soil accumulations at the south end. The highest and lowest layer both produced pottery of the 13th to 14th centuries, reinforcing the similar story seen in the other plots. Little survived under the main Newport Street buildings later than this, apart from some fragments of

Fig. 4.32 Dolday 1930s photograph. © Worcestershire Record Office

stone and brick walls of 18th-century date. However a tiny piece of stratified deposit was recorded at the rear of the frontage building, including a wall on the line of its rear wall. An alleyway along the side of the plot has been suggested by these deposits and a wall at the northern end of the plot that must have gone out of use by the 17th century. The latter was a substantial stone footing. A large oval oven was built in what was presumably the yard alongside it, but was of medieval date. The lowest alley surface in the island of stratified deposits and a clay layer alongside were both renewed at an uncertain date and then built over in the early to mid 16th century. This probably reflects a rebuilding in timber similar to that seen at nos 18 and 16 Newport Street (see Chapter 4.3.7) at about this time. At the rear, along the eastern boundary wall, were the remains of a range of buildings with dirt and mortar floors, and timber partitions. The wall and building are of later 17th-century date. They are contemporary with ovens, one set into the boundary wall in the usual fashion. They presumably represent '...the tenements behind...' in Abraham Lingham's will of 1784 (Hughes, Chapter 5.1.6). This area is certainly built up on Young's map of 1779. The late 17th or 18th century is the most likely time frame for the construction of a hearth and later a brick-lined pit in the rear yard, replaced in the 18th century by a well on the edge of a cobbled, stone walled enclosure, possibly a well-building, if not simply a yard. Late in the 18th century, these were all demolished and buried by a deliberate clay dump. Above this a brick building was built to the north. This was itself demolished and replaced by a large brick building with a cellar in the early or mid 19th century, and the malthouses to the north (beyond the excavated area) were rebuilt from the ground up, probably a little later in the century.

Plots 8 and 9: Period 2: medieval (Figs 4.14 and 4.15)
A series of dumps and make-ups of 13th to 14th-century date were the earliest layers encountered in these plots (G97). The material, sparse though it was, was of the same date range throughout. It is therefore unclear whether the material was one episode or several. The deposits were about 0.30m thick so need not have taken long to accumulate. The western boundary wall (see Plots 6 and 7, Period 3) cut through this material. Little survived on the surface of these dumps before the 18th century, although a possible sandstone structure, S373, within the dumps, hints at a hiatus in the build-up.

An island of stratified deposits was recorded at the rear of the street-front building (as mapped up to 1936) close to the boundary with Plot 7. This little area was only 2.5m square but provided some interesting insights and covers more than one set of events. The earliest were two layers of gravel along the boundary, each flanked by a clay layer on its eastern side (S390, S392 and the lower part of S396; not shown). This may suggest a gravelled side alley. The earlier gravel layer seemed to have had small square pits cut into it, from the plan, but no records survived. These may have been for timber posts but the point cannot now be pursued. These were then sealed by a clay layer itself cut by a stone and tile foundation running east/west (S393 and S395, Period 3.1, Fig. 4.18). This wall was exactly on the line of the rear wall of no. 20 Newport Street as mapped in 1886 (and perhaps 1779, but the small scale and lack of clarity of the map in this area make such interpretation very uncertain). The second phase gravel has a 13th to 15th-century sherd associated with it, and a rubble dump over it has 16th-century pottery.

At the rear of the plot, what seemed to have been a similar series of soils to G97 formed the limit of excavation and was not excavated. However, cut into its surface was a large oval oven base of pitched tiles with a tile wall (G325; Fig. 4.15). This was isolated from other features and sealed by a layer containing 16th/17th-century pottery (G326). It may well be later medieval.

Plots 8 and 9: Period 3: post-medieval (Figs 4.18, 4.21 and 4.22)

The wall S393 (and S395) is dated 16th–17th century from the tile in it and post-dates the rubble dump with 16th-century pottery. It is likely to represent the rear wall of a 16th or early 17th-century timber-framed building (Building 20 early phase). Some internal wall fragments may belong to this building (G98) but their exact allocation to period is unclear. They could belong to a later rebuild. One element that probably belongs to this period is the base of a back-to-back fireplace, S371 set into a wall two thirds of the way back from Newport Street, (i.e. probably between the middle and rear rooms). As no trace of walls survived either side of the fireplace it was probably inserted into a timber frame in the 17th century. The timber building was later rebuilt or encased in brick in the early 18th century to judge from its facade as later recorded. This happened at nos 18 and 16 Newport Street, and of course, further west at nos 24–30. This rebuild has left remnants that will be discussed in Period 4.

In the rear plot, G330 was a wall footing made of large squared sandstone blocks (Fig. 4.21). It seems to mark off an alleyway or narrow yard on the west, but nothing survived at the excavation level to show what it might have enclosed on the east. The alleyway was surfaced with a pebbly sandy layer (2854; not shown) running up to the boundary with Plot 6. G330 was a solid foundation and it seems likely it supported a building, rather than just a garden wall. It post-dated layer G326 (not shown) which contained 16th to 17th-century pottery.

A mortar-flecked and -stained clay make-up layer and two associated rough rubble footings for partitions indicated a building to the north of Building 20 along the eastern boundary wall, Building 19, G96 and G102. It was divided into at least three sections by the partitions. The northern section had an oven set into it, S905, against the boundary wall. The building was 13.3m north/south and it survived to a maximum of 2.4m east/west. Pottery and clay pipe dating gives a later 17th-century date for this structure. Its southern end roughly aligned with the northern end of the frontage block, which it probably post-dated. However, two in-line lengths of sandstone footings, one against the boundary wall were recorded running east/west at the south end of Building 19 (S368). These may have been footings for a timber south wall of Building 19. As they post-date the late medieval layer and seem to be earlier than the frontage building that survived into the 20th century, they are probably best seen as fragments of an earlier building. They have been shown on Figs 4.18, 4.21, 4.22 and 4.43, as their stratigraphic position remains slightly uncertain.

At the rear of the plot (Plot 8) G330 was demolished, and an oven of the usual type constructed against its line, but overlying it (G331; Fig. 4.22). This in turn was replaced by a cylindrical brick tank, G332. This contained charcoal or burnt wood and may have been a fuel container. A water tank seems more likely, later filled with rubbish. No contemporary hearth or oven was found nearby. All this activity seems to be of 17th-century date and probably is broadly contemporary with Building 19.

Plots 8 and 9: Period 4: 18th century (Fig. 4.23)

Fragments of fireplaces and internal walls of the 18th-century rebuild of no. 20 Newport Street could be recognised in the excavated remains. These were a corner fireplace in a rear room (G100) which reused some large sandstone moulded blocks and had a brick ash box in front of it, and the brick wall of the front hallway behind the front door (G98, Building 20, later phase). Nothing further survived demolition and levelling.

At the rear, a square, brick-built well was set in one side of a small cobbled yard enclosed by a stone wall (G333). This superseded all the other features that had occupied this space (G330, G331, G332) but still respected the line established by the wall G330 in Period 3.

A brick outbuilding, Building 17 (G326/328), was then erected, coincidentally on the site of the late medieval oven G325. This had a square room on the south-east against the Plot 10 boundary, a smaller room to the west and what appeared to be a corridor or lean-to on the north. Overall it was 5.3m in each direction. It still maintained the passage or alley on its west, first marked out by the stone wall G330. This building does not appear to be mapped on the 1779 map, but the area to the north, known to be a malthouse, was. Building 17 presumably, therefore, post-dates 1779. The boundary wall on the east was rebuilt or reordered when Building 17 was constructed, as it was built off the corner of the building.

All these features were then sealed by a widespread clay layer S923 (not shown), which seems to be a deliberate sealing/levelling layer occupying most of the rear plot of no. 20 Newport Street. No dating evidence was recovered from it, but it may well be Period 5.

Plots 8 and 9: Period 5: 19th century (Fig. 4.29)
Building 17 had been demolished by 1886. The northern end of the eastern boundary wall was cut away when the large malthouse next door on the Dolday end of nos 18–14 Newport Street was rebuilt in the 19th century. A malthouse on that site is mentioned in the early 18th century (Hughes, Chapter 5.1.6), and on the same footprint as later on the 1779 map, so the 19th-century building was clearly a rebuild. The trapezoidal northern extremity of Plot 8 (also a malthouse) was also rebuilt in the later 19th century, based on the evidence of a short length of east/west wall finally cutting across the line of the western alleyway, butting Building 17 (S918; not shown), and a new section of brick wall (S928) in cement mortar, built on the western side, against the brick wall of Building 15 in Plot 6. Slightly earlier than this but within the 19th century, a large brick rear range (G95), Building 21 with cellar was added to the main Newport Street frontage, finally removing any hint of the side alley or passage in this part of the site.

4.3.7 Plots 10 and 11: nos 18 and 16 Newport Street

The Dolday frontages were separated from these holdings in the 17th or 18th centuries and the excavation area did not reach these rear properties. Plot 10/11 included both nos 18 and 16 Newport Street, but the street frontage buildings had only very partially survived (no. 18) or not at all (no. 16) within the excavation area. The wall taken during excavation to divide Plot 10 from Plot 11 to its south was of no property significance.

No. 18 Newport Street (western part of Plots 10 and 11)
No medieval deposits were reached in this plot, the earliest remains being of a stone building at the rear of the plot dating to the 16th or 17th centuries. This included a well and brick pavings and was clearly an outbuilding behind the main frontage. Two phases of frontage building were seen, but only fragments remained. The earlier of them probably referred to the timber-framed building found encased within the 18th-century rebuild before it was demolished in the 1980s (Hughes, Chapter 5.1.6). This is probably of 16th or early 17th-century date. A rear range of buildings was seen to be of two main phases, which matched the cartographic and documentary evidence, suggesting a date of before 1779 for the first phase and before 1851 for the second. This rear range is recorded as dwellings in the later 18th century but one or two of the elements at the south end are considered to have been part of the public house, possibly for brewing. An air raid shelter was contrived in a demolished part of the rear range in the Second World War.

No. 16 Newport Street (north-eastern corner of Plot 11)
Relatively little survived 20th-century clearance to be recorded here, although, paradoxically, the frontage building is the best recorded of any as its timber frame was recorded before final demolition in the 1980s (Hughes, Chapter 5.1.7). Behind it only some possible fragments of Period 3 buildings remained, with evidence for 18th-century rebuilds and 19th-century development of the rear of the plot.

Plots 10 and 11: Period 3: post-medieval (Figs 4.40, 4.42 and 4.43)

No. 18 Newport Street
The earliest events here belong to the 16th to 17th century and represent fragments of buildings robbed out in the 18th century. A compacted silt soil was the earliest feature, probably the top of one of the ubiquitous levelling or dump layers. It was not dated. Cut into it was a U-plan foundation trench containing a sandstone rubble footing (S407, Building 22; Fig. 4.40). This had been robbed by two 18th-century pits. The small structure it represented (Building 22, roughly 3.5m square) was in the back plot of no. 18 Newport Street, some distance back from the frontage buildings. South of the structure, fragmentary brick floors (S417), a well (S410), another small brick-lined pit (S414) and some unexcavated pits seem to be of the same period. Certainly, they are tucked up against its southern wall. Probably of this general date is the corner of a brick wall further north again, which was just picked up at the bottom of the excavation level under Building 23 (not shown), but otherwise isolated and uninvestigated (1101, not shown). It represents the north-west corner of a building against the eastern boundary of no. 18 Newport Street.

The frontage building of no. 18 Newport Street was mostly beyond the area of excavation. Two parallel east/west sandstone walls (G301, Building 26) probably represented an earlier version of the rear parts of this building as they were on an alignment that clearly pre-dated the Old Red Lion and its rear range (see below, G109 and G362, Building 27). They were parallel to Newport Street rather than at right angles to the rear plot, which came away at an angle to the frontage. They were cut into one of a series of clay and silt dumps (G300; not shown) which are all of 17th/18th-century date, and on stratigraphic grounds (being one phase older than the Old Red Lion, which is early to mid 18th century) are most likely to be Period 3.1/3.2. They are probably related to the timber-framed building, large elements of which were encased in no. 18 Newport Street and recorded in the 1970s (Fig. 4.40).

The well at the rear was backfilled and then the fill settled. The adjacent south wall of S407 probably settled too as it was demolished and a new wall (G107) was built over it (and over the well backfill) but turned south, so represented a different building on a plan distinct from Building 22. Only a fragment of this later wall survived, and the building of which it formed part remains unknown.

No. 16 Newport Street
Nothing of the frontage building here survived the large disturbance in this part of the site. Records made before it was demolished show a late 18th or early 19th-century three-storey facade, with windows arranged to take advantage of the window tax exemptions, so post 1790. A nearly complete timber-framed house of two storeys was recorded behind this facade in the 1970s, with a stone cellar very like Building 4 in Plot 3 (Fig. 4.40; Hughes, Chapter 5.1.7). The building was originally jettied and is probably of 16th-century or early 17th-century date, if not earlier. The jetty was underbuilt and the street facade replaced in brick in the very late 18th or early 19th centuries.

Plots 10 and 11: Period 3.2–3.3: mid to late 17th century (Figs 4.42 and 4.43)

No. 16 Newport Street
Two sandstone wall footings supporting sandstone walls G302, Building 40, (Fig. 4.42) have slight evidence of a 17th-century date (potsherd). They are rather scruffier, made of unshaped rubble rather than the larger blocks more typical of earlier phases. They fall on the north and east sides of a building marked on both the 1779 and 1886 maps (Figs 2.7 and 2.14). This rear building is most likely an addition to the building recorded on the street frontage, so a post 16th-century date is likely. A hearth of brick was built against the eastern wall in the yard outside and this must have been the source of the layers of ash and burnt sand dumped inside the north-east corner of the building. Four successive pits were dug alongside the hearth at about the same stratigraphic position (S855). There was much tile but little burnt material in them and on balance they may have been dug when the burnt material had been covered over, or otherwise unavailable for inclusion in the fill.

Plots 10 and 11: Period 4: 18th century (Fig. 4.44)

No. 18 Newport Street
The structure G107 was demolished and a thick layer of hard silty clay was spread over the rear of the site (G108). This was dated to 1720–50 from clay tobacco pipe and pottery and it is hard to resist the interpretation of it as part of the reorganisation of the site for the rebuilding of the Old Red Lion (Building 27). The description of the property in 1717 (Hughes, Chapter 5.1.7) implies that it had not yet been rebuilt and, with its brewhouse and back kitchen as well as a kitchen in the house, its barrels and pint measures, was in use as an alehouse by then. Little survived of the rebuilding in the excavation but the red-brick eastern wall of the passage along the side of no. 18 Newport Street to the rear yard was found (G313). A long rear range was constructed on stone footings, G109, Building 23. This appears on the 1779 map (Fig. 2.7). They were probably built as court cottages, as we have seen previously on other parts of the site. A cess pit, S429, probably reflecting a privy, was constructed on the end wall. A 'necessary' was recorded in the yard in 1804 (Hughes, Chapter 5.1.7).

The southern two 'cells' of the rear range probably belonged to the public house, and perhaps pre-date the rest of the range, as the west wall of the third cell north seems to butt the corner of the second. The cottages survived to appear on an aerial photograph of the 1960s, showing that they had two storeys and that the southernmost part, with its higher roofline, was indeed part of the pub, not the cottage row. The most southerly 'cell' was destroyed by a modern excavation prior to the archaeological dig, but the northern one was a well-preserved brick cellar with it own access down steps from the north (which would require space taken out of the cottage to the north), G308. It was built to include a well (S868) on its west side which fed a court pump, but to which it may also have had access from inside. A doorway leading directly to the court, next to the pump, had been blocked at some time. The south-east corner of the cellar had been removed by the same excavation that had destroyed the room to the south, but the beginnings of an angled return in the brickwork half way along the eastern wall suggests a major brick-built installation in this corner, and one must suspect boilers and other brewhouse equipment.

No. 16 Newport Street
The early 18th-century dump G108 (not shown) is implicitly extant over this area and this phase would post-date it, but its exact relationships in this area were not recorded. Building 40 seems to have been rebuilt in brick and both it and the yard to the east paved in brick (S858). These pavings buried the hearth activities. This is very probably to be dated to the same time as the casing of the frontage building in brick and the addition of a rear kitchen, i.e. the late 18th century.

Plots 10 and 11: Period 5: 19th and 20th centuries (Fig. 4.29)

No. 18 Newport Street
The rear range G109 of Period 4, is shown one room shorter in 1779 (Fig. 2.4) than on the 1886 OS map. This makes sense as a cess pit is incorporated in what would be the end wall. Archaeologically, the end room (G362) has clearly been added after the infilling of the

cess pit. This is likely to have taken place by 1851 as in that year there is reference to four tenements and a stable at the rear of the plot (Hughes, Chapter 5.1.7). The stable and the yard are represented by fragments of brick wall and floor in the north end of the plot (G113) and alongside the rear wing of Building 24 (G318). It, too, survived to be photographed from the air in the 1960s, showing it to be a two-storey building.

By 1936 one of the tenements in the rear range (the northernmost of the original range or the second 'cell' from the north) had been demolished and it was this blank space that was chosen for a Second World War 'Anderson' air raid shelter, utilising the brick and concrete floors of the cellar and the original brick steps to provide a better finish than most of these shelters had. The shelter was made of corrugated iron sheeting over a steel pipe frame, packed around with earth. The roof and upper covering had been removed before excavation began.

No. 16 Newport Street
A further detached rear range is marked on the OS map of 1886 but does not appear on the 1779 map. Its later date is supported by the fact that seems to have been built against the later brick version of Building 23. However, only a brick cess pit at the southern end, filled in with 19th and 20th-century debris (G112), and a brick room at the north end, given a concrete floor (G111), survived to be recorded archaeologically. It seems fairly clear that they were of 19th-century origin, and remained in use into the mid 20th. G111 was largely demolished when the 1960s aerial photograph was taken.

4.3.8 Plots 12 and 13: no. 14 Newport Street

A sondage similar to that in Plot 3 was dug into the deeper deposits in this plot (the East Sondage; Fig. 4.33), and Roman and medieval deposits were revealed in it. However, further medieval remains were also found in the general excavation area in these plots.

Plots 12 and 13: Period 1: Roman (Figs 4.33 and 4.34)
The earliest layer reached was alluvial clay, G345 (Fig. 4.34). This was more than 0.55m thick and contained sherds of samian ware dated to 160–200 AD (Jacobs, Chapter 5.2 for all pottery references in this paragraph). It also contained Severn Valley ware of late 2nd to 3rd-century date. This flood deposit stabilised for long enough for four small pits to be dug through it, G346. These contained pottery of 2nd to 4th-century type but stratigraphically, probably dated to the early to middle

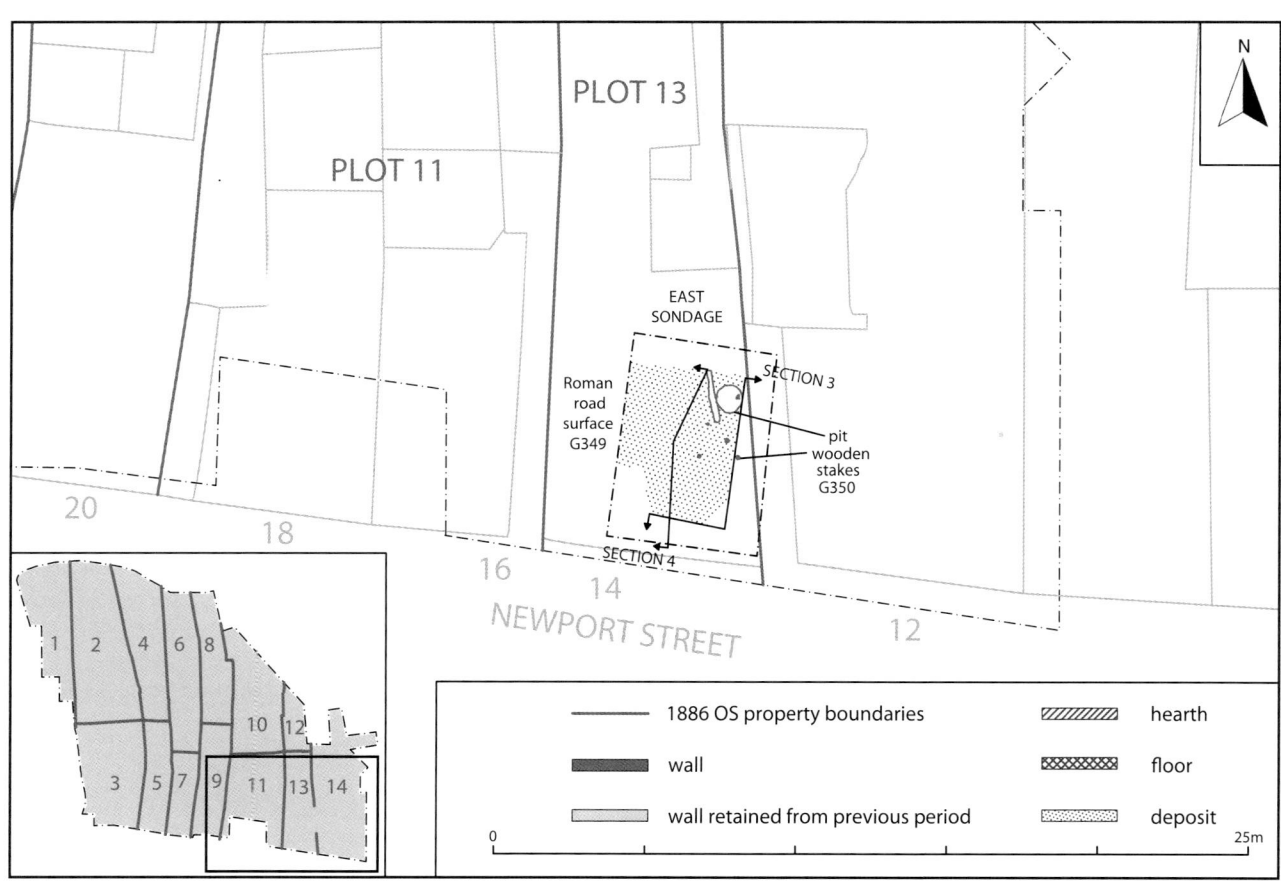

Fig. 4.33 Periods 1 and 2.1/2.2, east end. Scale 1:250

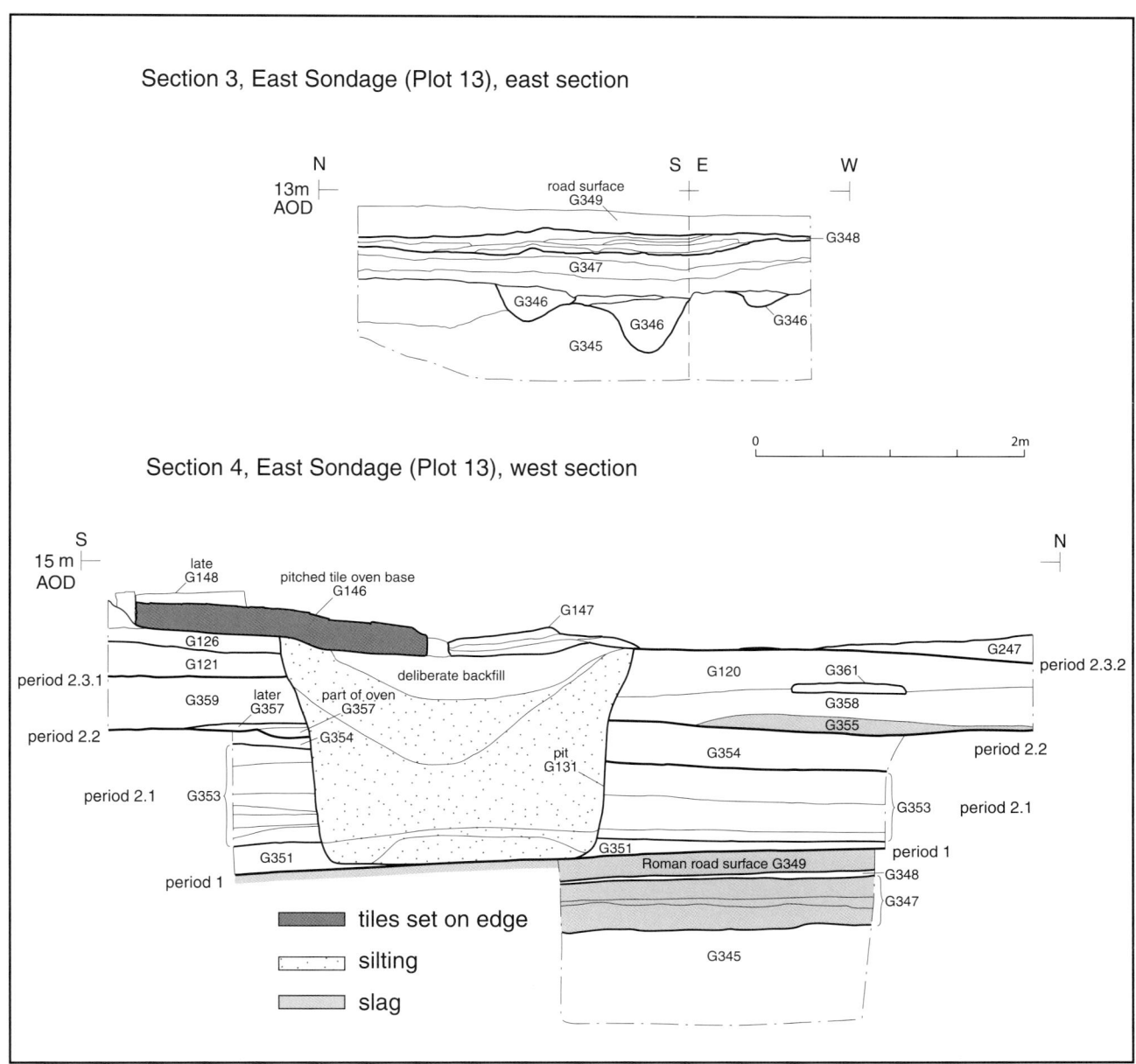

Fig. 4.34 Sections 3 and 4. Scale 1:50

part of this range. The pits each had different fills, clay, sandy silt and charcoal, sandy silt, and in one case, pure iron slag. They seem to have been filled in immediately before the deposition of layers of slag, G347, up to 0.55m thick. This contained similar material, but with one sherd of Malvernian metamorphic ware, suggesting a 4th-century date. These were covered by more alluvial clays but this time interleaved with lenses of charcoal, and dark silty layers G348. It seems unlikely that these layers are actually flood deposits, as they are much more typical of interleaved and irregularly shaped lenses of dumped material. This was immediately sealed by a dump of slag and cobbles, G349 (Figs 4.33, 4.34 and 4.35). This seems fairly clearly to be a road and lines up with that in the West Sondage in Plot 3, G61. It had a camber to the south, but its width could not be determined except that it was wider than the East Sondage, *c.* 5m. Pottery on the road surface was well-dated to the 4th century, but the large sherd size implies the road was already out of use when discarded.

The boreholes (Wilkinson, Chapter 4.2 above) confirmed the existence of anthropogenic deposits across the site at the depth comparable to the Roman deposits seen in the East and West Sondages. They rested conformably on the horizontal surface of the alluvial Elmore Member at 11.5m AOD, and were from 0.5 to 1.0m thick. The boreholes drilled specifically for archaeological research (BH1–6) suggested that 'archaeological strata also tended to thin to the south and change in their properties from occupational waste (e.g. in BH5), to concentrations of

Fig. 4.35 Plot 13, Period 1, road G349 and pit G350, looking south

metalworking debris (e.g. BH2)'. Along the southern side the Roman deposits were the more solid slag layers, whereas to the north the slag formed scattered lenses within occupation material. They supported the contention that that there was a strip of thicker and more compacted iron slag running parallel to Newport Street between the slag deposits interpreted as Roman road in the West and East Sondages. However, the boreholes drilled by the developers for geotechnical information (BH7–22) and by Archenfield Archaeology in 2003 (DTS01–05), indicated that the substantial slag deposits extended over the eastern end of the excavation area as well, suggesting a considerable area of hard standing north of the Roman street here. In addition, the borehole results can be interpreted as showing that there was occupation, or at least human activity resulting in the dumping of cultural material, directly on the floodplain alluvium alongside the slag-metalled road, as far north as the present All Saints' Road. This matches precisely the limited but more detailed picture drawn from the East Sondage, Plot 13.

Wilkinson points out that the geotechnical boreholes placed the upper level of the Roman deposits to 12.6 to 13m AOD (about 0.5m higher than BH1–6), and suggests this was the result of methodological biases, but the top of the Roman road in Plot 13 was recorded at 12.8m AOD suggesting a real rise of the top of the Roman deposits to the east and north-east, which these boreholes presumably reflect. This rise is very slight compared to the present rise in ground level in this direction, which is the result of medieval and post-medieval deposition.

Plots 12 and 13: Period 2.1: medieval (Figs 4.33, 4.34 and 4.35)
The earliest post-Roman activity consisted of a shallow, bowl-shaped pit, G350, cut into the upper surface of the Roman road G349, (Fig. 4.35), seven stakes driven into the road surface nearby and two more either into the pit fill or into its base while it was still open, the records are ambiguous. The pit fill was described as spongy peat with fine lenses of sand and gravel, which might suggest a long abandonment before the alluviation, but the lack of peat formation elsewhere suggests this is, rather, a deliberate organic fill that became peaty under the waterlogged conditions which also preserved the stakes. The stakes and pit (G350) are all essentially undated, but are sealed by an alluvial episode (similar to that sealing the Period 2.1 well in the West Sondage in Plot 3, G56) after the pit had been filled up (G351; Fig. 4.34).

The alluvial layer was only 0.20m thick and a thin strip of charcoal-rich clay was deposited on its surface before a succession of more silts (G353) was allowed

Fig. 4.36 Period 2.3, east end. Scale 1:250

to accumulate. Eleven layers and lenses were recorded, adding between 0.70m to 0.92m in thickness. These layers had the character of a washed-in silt, being a fine silty clay marl. The lowest member of this group, layer 1877, contained much bone including a bovid skull and horse and cattle limb bones (Warman, Chapter 5.24). This, with the pottery noted below and charcoal fragments, suggests this was an occupation layer, or rubbish derived from one. The other layers, although similar in character, contained no finds. They seem to be water-lain but the dark colour, rare charcoal and lenses of small stones recorded in them suggest that these deposits are best regarded as derived from adjacent occupation or rubbish deposits. Pottery from layer 1877 was early 11th-century Stafford-type ware and this dating of the episode was reinforced by the occurrence of 11th to 12th-century early Worcester/Stafford-type ware sherds in the extensive layer, G354, that sealed these layers (Griffin, Chapter 5.3) (Fig. 4.34, section 4).

Plots 12 and 13: Period 2.2: post-Conquest and 12th century (Fig. 4.34)

The layer G354, referred to above, seems to represent the first significant attempt to modify the alluvial flood plain, as the material appears to be a deliberate dump of soil to raise the ground level against flooding. It is not closely dated, but a date in the early 12th century seems very probable. It was only seen in the East Sondage in Plot 13 as it was below the general limit of excavation in the rest of the site. It was presumably made up of a very large number of tips, but this was only indicated by the recognition of a lens of not very distinct material in one corner of the sondage.

Plots 12 and 13: Period 2.3: medieval, 13th–14th centuries (Fig. 4.36)

Period 2.3 was dated by pottery and stratigraphy. The stratigraphic detail in this area, however, was such that subphases were more clearly distinguishable here than in most other areas of the site, although this was only generally reflected by the artefactual dating.

Plots 12 and 13: Period 2.3.1: earlier 13th century (Figs 4.34 and 4.36)

The dump of make-up, G354, sealing the last alluvial episode, had a spread of slag dumped on it (G355). This was probably derived from the Roman layers below, but may represent contemporary activity as nearby was a cobbled surface (G356; not shown), fragmentarily surviving and cut through on one side by a stone oven. This was a roughly circular, stone base on a broader clay layer which seems to represent the base of the clay superstructure (G357). The plan of this suggests a keyhole-shaped oven. It incorporated a rotary hand quern in what would have been the remains of its left-hand wing wall. Pottery suggested a 13th to 14th-century date.

This oven was demolished and layers of clay and ash were dumped over it and the other groups of this sub-phase (G358/359). On this surface and probably part of the dumping process, although it may derive from a structure, was a dump of stone on the east side of Plot 13: G119. This might suggest that the boundary between nos 14 and 12 Newport Street was already beginning to be established in this period, as they seem to respect it. Further activities apparently aligned with this boundary were represented by a series of intercutting scoops (G123 (not shown), G205 and G206) and another small patch of cobbles and metalworking waste, G202. Also recorded were two post pads of clay (G361), altogether suggesting some sort of workshop activity in a rough shed. A waste pit, G118 (not shown), was also recorded in this phase.

Plots 12 and 13: Period 2.3.2: later 13th century (Figs 4.34 and 4.36)

A series of tips and spreads of silts rich in ash, animal bone and pottery was spread over the earlier deposits to a depth of 0.14m. Six distinct episodes were recorded in this shallow sequence (G120, G121, G124, G125, G126, G128). Above the lowest and butted by the next in the sequence, was a bank of slag and an associated cobbled surface, G122. The slag bank lies alongside the Plot 13/14 boundary and may indicate it was in existence by this period. A short, isolated length of east/west wall (S541) was built at the same time, recorded in the north-east corner of the East Sondage, but its function could not be ascertained. At this same time, a group of pits (G123; not shown) was cut into the lower dumps. They contained a relatively large collection of animal bone and 13th to 14th-century pottery, suggesting occupation on the site or nearby. Their existence so near to the street frontage suggests that no permanent buildings were being erected at this point, although a single posthole (G125; not shown) may mean that a structure existed and a fragment of a rather ragged sandstone wall on the north side of the sondage (part of G122) suggests the same. The fragmentation of these deposits by later intrusions, and the small area covered by the sondage means that posthole structures, particularly, would be hard to spot or would not survive well. The spread of deposits continued above these features and while the pottery from them is mostly dated 13th to 14th century, a single sherd of Malvernian ware towards the upper levels suggests that these may date to the 14th century.

Plots 12 and 13: Period 2.4: 14th century (Fig. 4.37)

Deposits assigned to this period were dated on the quite substantial amount of 13th to 14th-century pottery and by their stratigraphic position above deposits in Period 2.3.2. A series of pits and ovens dominated this phase. Oven G132 had been fairly thoroughly demolished leaving a spread of sandstone rubble and burnt clay with a lot of charcoal mixed in and spread over, from which an iron arrowhead of late medieval type was retrieved. Little was intelligible of the oven plan and it does not seem to have had a tile base. A layer of silt separated it from the better-preserved oven, G139 (Fig. 4.38), that succeeded it, just nearby. This was an extended oval in plan, the base being of clay with sandstone lumps. Nothing *in situ* survived of its superstructure. A series of spreads of charcoal and burnt sandy deposits and a small amount of slag (G148) overlay it and lay around it and may be remains of the use of the oven. They were disturbed when the oven was demolished.

Earlier than the pits, but still in this phase, a pit was cut which was at first interpreted as a well, G131. It was 1.8m deep and round, with a diameter of 2.1m at the base. Its sides tapered outwards slightly but there was no sign of any lining. The pit was bottomed on the Roman road surface of G349 (Fig. 4.34, section 4). As this presumably was slightly more permeable than the alluvial clays through which the pit was largely cut, the pit would have collected water, as indeed it did during excavation. Otherwise it looked more like a rubbish pit and there was no sign of any lining, despite the waterlogged conditions. The fills of the lower three-quarters of its depth were largely undifferentiated silts, not deliberate backfills, though containing charcoal from the surrounding layers washed in, and contrasted both in this and in the quantity of finds, especially animal bone, with the upper fills which were a rapid backfill of many thin tips in the shallow cone left in the top of the silting. This might suggest a function as a well rather than a rubbish pit, which ought to contain rubbish from the early layers and have more backfills. There was an important collection of cordwainer's refuse in these layers but animal bone and pottery, though present, was quite scarce in these lower levels. As oven G146 (Period 2.5) was built immediately over the upper backfill, it might be that the upper layers were deliberate levelling to allow its construction.

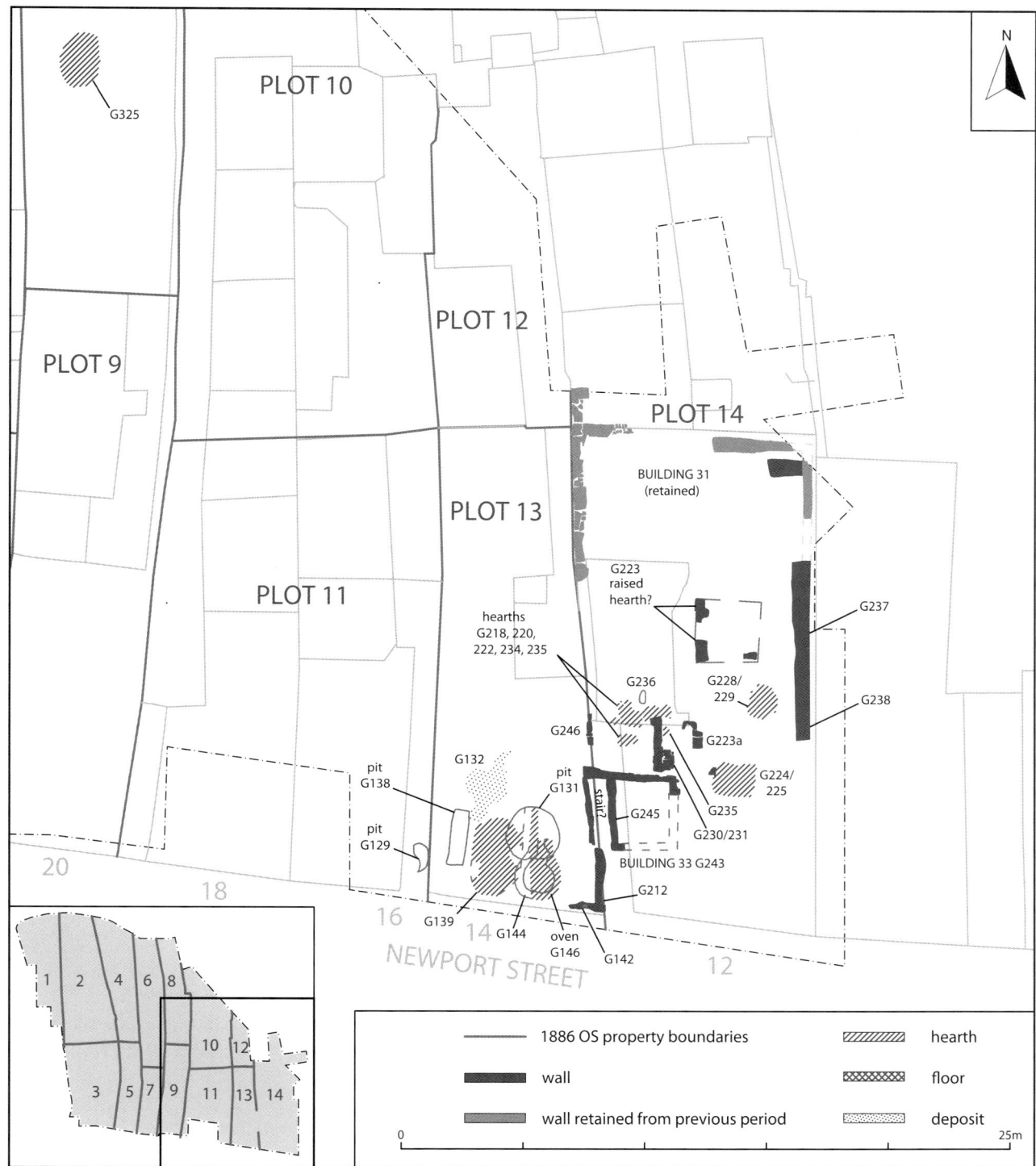

Fig. 4.37 Periods 2.4 and 2.5, east end. Scale 1:250

Seemingly contemporary with the use and replacement of the ovens, being cut into the same layers and in one case clearly post-dating them, were six pits, G129, G130, G134, G137 (not shown), G138 and G144. These all had very similar fills of clayey silts and some charcoal and sandstone rubble, but G138 was clay-lined with slag in its fill and G129 was also clay-lined with a higher proportion of charcoal than the others. This might indicate that these two pits were designed to hold water and were near some metalworking or hot process when filled in. In addition, G144 was also clay-lined.

One of these later pits is cut by the boundary wall with Plot 14, certainly indicating that this phase predates the stone walls on the tenement boundaries, but it is less clear what the nature of these boundary structures may have been at this time. A stone boundary on the

Fig. 4.38 Plot 13, Period 2.4, oven base G139, looking south-west

east, G212, is part of a building on Plot 14 and will be described there. A short length of stone wall, G142, was also recorded on the line of the Newport Street frontage of no. 14 against the east boundary that may also belong to this phase.

A sandstone foundation in a small square pit is recorded in this plot as a pillar base, but no further information on this exists. Pottery and stratigraphy dated it to this phase.

Plots 12 and 13: Period 2.5: late medieval (Fig. 4.37)
This phase is dated by its stratigraphic position over the preceding one and the characterisation of the pottery as 13th and 14th to 15th century in range. A dump layer G145 sealed the clay lined pit G144 of the preceding period and on it was constructed a keyhole-shaped oven, G146 (Fig. 4.39). The dump layer was rich in charcoal and slag and was not dissimilar to G140, which it overlapped. The base of the oven was pitched tiles set on a clay base, its wall was of tiles and sandstone rubble. The mouth of the oven faced north and seems to have been extended by a low wall of stone at least 1m long. It had been truncated by later intrusions, as had almost half of the oven to the west. Widespread lenses of burnt clays, charcoal and silts G151 (not shown), post-date this oven, and these probably represent general levelling and tidying up after the demolition of the oven. A single posthole was recorded cut through these deposits (G152; not shown).

Plots 12 and 13: Period 3.1: late 16th to early 17th centuries (Fig. 4.40)
The area of Plots 13 and 14 was covered by an extensive dump, G157, which sealed all the medieval layers. However it is of interest that this dump was laid against an early section of the eastern boundary wall, G155, and a short length of east/west wall, G158 at the rear of Plot 13 both of this period. This implies it is a deliberate make-up laid within the property of no. 14 Newport Street, Plot 13. However, as the dump also abuts G155 on the other side of the boundary, in Plot 14, it is either a joint redevelopment of the two properties, or perhaps more likely, an equivalent but not identical layer.

Be that as it may, the boundary walls on the east and north were rebuilt and/or modified after this make-up had been laid. Walls G161 and 160 seem to have been a rebuild against the earlier boundary wall (see G207 in Plot 14, Fig. 4.36). The east/west wall (G158), probably represented the footings of the rear wall of the frontage (Building 29), and a short length of stone footings running south from the west end of wall G158 may be

Fig. 4.39 Plot 13, Period 2.5, oven G146, looking south-east

an internal wall. Its relationship to the rest of the wall was removed by a modern conduit. G161 and G160 seem to be the footings of an added rear block as the southern end butts against G158 and G155. Dating evidence for these is not good and little survives. The rest of this boundary wall will be dealt with under Plot 14.

Plots 12 and 13: Periods 4 and 5: 18th and 19th centuries (Fig. 4.44)

The frontage building is known from old drawings and photographs to date from this period, probably mid to late 18th century, stylistically, but only a few clay dumps (G165 and G166) and short lengths of rebuilt brick and tile wall, G254 and G282, date from this period on the boundary between the plots. A large brick cellar, Building 30, was built at the rear, post-1779 from map evidence. This required the demolition of the earlier structure represented by G160 and G161 of Period 3.1. It is probably from the late 18th or early 19th century. It was not planned in detail and its outline is shown on Fig. 4.44. In the mapping of 1886 another building is shown to the north and this coincides with the planned outline of an area of garden soil, context 447. This preceded that building but showed its extent, as it was cut by the wall trenches. A well of unknown date was cut through this layer.

4.3.9 Plot 14: no. 12 and a small part of no. 10 Newport Street

In this plot were structures dated to Period 2 but not with clear stratigraphic subdivisions. Nonetheless, three medieval periods have been identified. As with Plot 13 some activity before the construction of boundary walls was confirmed. A date in the 13th century is indicated for their creation and a timber building on stone footings was built on the southern end of the plot. Hearths and an oven were built in the back side. The timber building may have existed into the early part of the next phase when hearths and ovens were built on its site, but was demolished by the time most of these were constructed, probably into the 14th century. There is good evidence for smithing at this time and some features may be related to this. A timber-framed building was erected on a stone cellar at the frontage, probably at this time or possibly as late as the 15th century. In the late 16th or early 17th century this building was rebuilt but the cellar retained. The ground level was raised and the boundary walls rebuilt. A new brick building was constructed at the rear of the plot, perhaps towards the end of the century and another oven was built in what may have been an open yard south of it. The frontage building may have been rebuilt at this time, as the brick

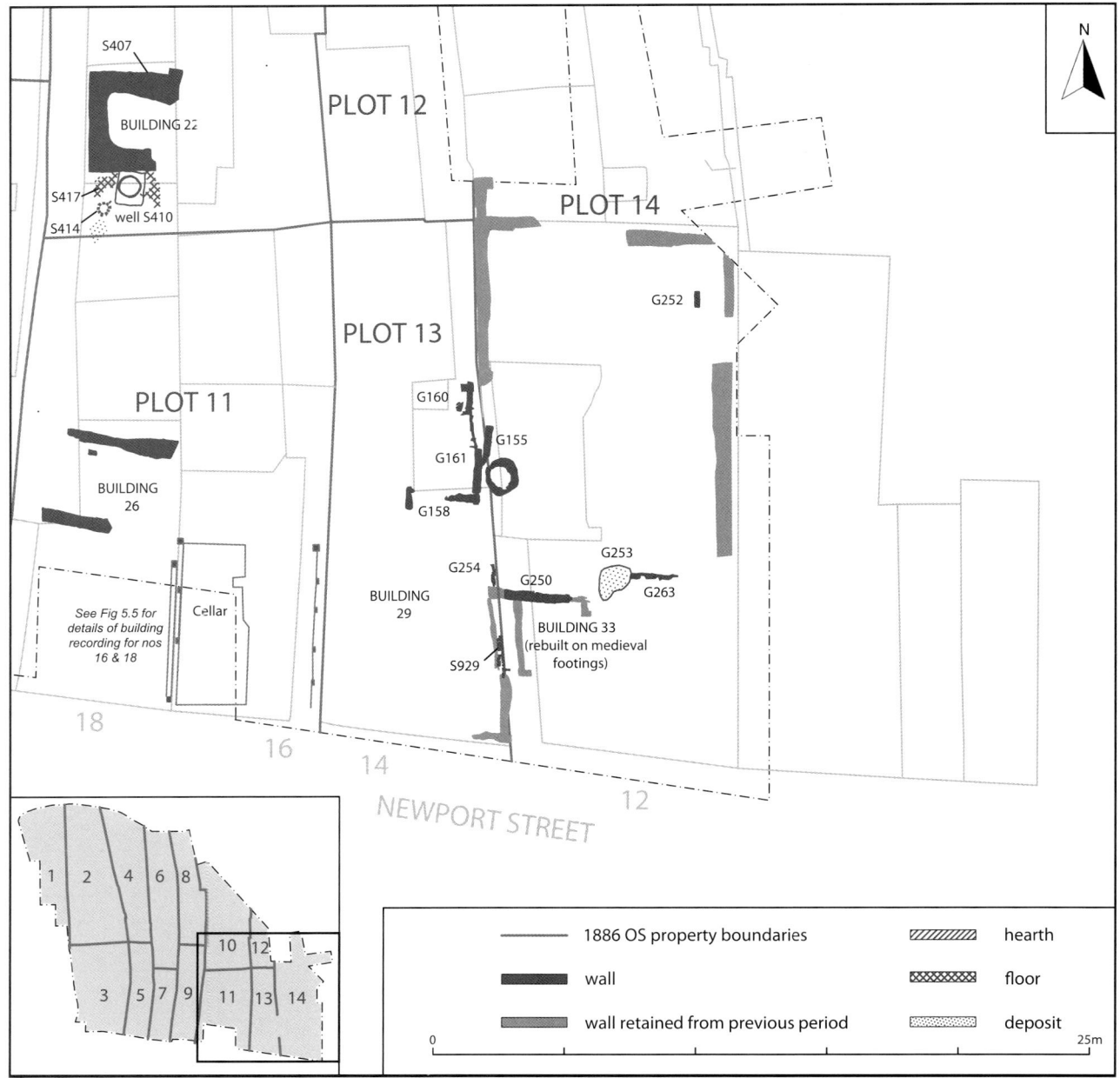

Fig. 4.40 Period 3.1, east end. Scale 1:250

cellar here, ostensibly of the 1920s, seems to include a 17th-century cellar whose construction required the demolition of the stone cellar and any superimposed building. The buildings on site were comprehensively rebuilt in the 1920s.

Plot 14: Period 2.3: 13th to 14th centuries (Fig. 4.36)
Widespread make-up dumps of dark clays and silts with charcoal, G200 and G201 (not shown), were dated to the 13th/14th centuries. A deposit of rubble, tile, gravel and sand, G208, overlay these and was probably a construction layer for the north, west and northern part of the east boundary walls of Building 31, G207, and what seems to have been an integral oven, G203,

respectively. The base of another wall, very similar in character to G207 was seen along the frontage, under the footings of the Period 5 cellar at the south end of the site. This was undated and stratigraphically isolated, but at an appropriate level to be of this date. As usual for this period the walls were made of substantial sandstone blocks and remained the foundations for successive rebuilds. At the south end of the west wall, near the Newport Street frontage, a cobble layer with metal slag (G202) was probably from broadly the same phase of activities as G122 from in Plot 13, and a layer of charcoal (G210) which reached under the boundary to overlie G126 in Plot 13 confirmed the industrial nature of the activity at these early Period 2.3 levels.

timber-framed building. A series of silty clay layers with tile and charcoal fragments and a patch of mortar lay in the bottom of this room (G244) and contained pottery of 13th to 14th-century date. These layers were cut by a north/south wall that was inserted on the western side of the room to subdivide Building 33, G245. This has a stub of a return on the south end (cut away by later disturbances) suggesting that the return divided the cellar into two equal rooms. The narrow space provided on the west by this wall may well have been for a stair, original access being simply a ladder or straight from the street.

Its western wall acted as the boundary wall to the plot and was the first clear masonry wall on the plot at this end, the southern end of G207 (wall 1290) coming to a clear stop some metres north. A short length of wall of narrow sandstone blocks (G246) occurs on the boundary just north of Building 32 and probably belongs to this phase, but no other boundary structure of the medieval period was recorded here.

Plot 14: Period 3: post-medieval
Apart from boundary walls, on the street frontage, nothing survived the construction of a large brick cellar. This was built in the 1920s but seems to have incorporated an earlier, probably an 18th or early 19th-century, cellar.

Plot 14: Period 3.1: 16th–17th centuries (Fig. 4.40)
The north of much of the plot was covered by a clayey dump G247 equivalent to the contemporary G157 in Plot 13. It was not as extensive, however. It did seem to seal off medieval layers where it existed and pre-date the activities of this period. These included the fragment of sandstone wall along the west boundary north of Building 32, G254. A pit, G253, was dug against the 'anvil stone' G223a and a short length of wall (G263) cut into the make-up G247. However, this wall may belong more comfortably with the later medieval layers. It is cut by the pit G253 and aligns nicely with the medieval ovens of period 2.4/5 and bears no spatial relationship to the later phase activities. It may well have been wrongly recorded cutting G247 and have been, rather, butted by it. Small scoops or pits were dug and lenses of clay and ash were deposited on the top of G247 and a short length of brick wall has been interpreted as the remains of an ash box (G252).

One significant activity dated to this period was the rebuilding or capping of the walls of the cellar of Building 33 in brick (S929, G250; a fragment, G251 was recorded as over the internal wall but does not appear on a plan). This probably indicates a rebuild of the house above, still quite possibly in timber, as the relatively slight cellar walls were reused without reinforcement.

Plot 14: Period 3.3/Period 4: later 17th to 18th century (Figs 4.43 and 4.44)
The plot boundary walls were rebuilt or refaced at this time (none shown), largely in brick, as G257 and

Fig. 4.45 Plot 14, Period 3.3, oven G267, looking west

G265 (on G207) and G255 (on G254). A possible clay floor, only a fragment truncated by later disturbance, was recorded against the rebuilt wall G257. Generally contemporary with these rebuilds and refacings was the laying of make-up layers: G249, G268 and G264; G268 being the main component, largely of clay (none shown).

A large keyhole plan oven was set on these dumps, G267 (Figs 4.26, 4.45), exactly but coincidentally over the 'smithing hearth' G223. Its base was built of brick and the superstructure of tile. Its mouth faced east and was rebuilt in two phases. A roughly square, tiled hearth was built over a clay layer that sealed the original floor. It had brick side walls and in a later phase, after charcoal had accumulated over this structure, a sandstone wall was built across its east end. Pottery associated with the oven gave it a 17th or 18th-century *floruit*.

North of this oven, which seems to have occupied an open yard, a new brick room was built on a sandstone foundation (G278/G279), Building 34. This occupied the whole width of the plot and survived to be plotted on the OS 1886 map. It was dated by pottery, tobacco pipe and brick to the mid–late 17th century. Its north, east and west walls were built on the old boundary walls and its southern side was a new construction cut into the dump layers. A corridor or passage ran around the west and north sides, and the room enclosed was floored in brick. G313 was a short length of isolated brick wall running parallel to the east boundary wall and about a metre from it. It may be analogous to the corridor wall on the west side.

An earlier yard surface here was indicated by cobbles G277, cut by the footing trenches but sitting on the earlier make-up layers, and a fragment of earlier sandstone wall running under the south side of Building 34 hints at earlier structures. Nothing more was seen of them, however.

Part of the cellar of Building 35 on the street frontage, in its latest form certainly of Period 5 (Fig. 4.29), probably reuses and modifies an older cellar of this period. The rebuilding proposal plans of the 1920s show a cellar only as big as the main room of the one found in excavation. The larger extent of the cellar as excavated seems likely to be the older one incorporated. For example there are relict fireplaces in narrow corridors and much of the brick in these areas was characterised as 17th to 18th century. Brick floors in these areas are cut through by the most recent brick cellar walls.

Plot 14: Period 5: 19th and 20th centuries (Fig. 4.29)

The entire plot was rebuilt in the 1920s and walls, floors and brick conduits from this period were everywhere on the plot, above and cutting through the earlier structures and deposits (G282–G292 inclusive). Building 35 on the Newport Street frontage, incorporated part of the earlier cellar (see above).

Chapter 5
Specialist reports

5.1 Documentary evidence for individual properties
Pat Hughes

5.1.1 Introduction

A general account of the historical development of Newport Street and Dolday, drawn from documentary sources, is presented in Chapter 2.3. The archaeologically-defined plots are discussed in the site narrative (Chapter 4); the documentary evidence for the history of individual properties, their owners, and their occupations is presented here. The evidence for properties along the whole of the north side of Newport Street, from no. 54 to no. 2 (i.e. not just the excavated area, from no. 10 to no. 34), is presented from west to east to facilitate cross-referencing to the plots discussed in the site narrative. Property ownerships have been tabulated and related to the available evidence for the buildings, mostly drawn from pictorial sources (Fig. 5.1).

5.1.2 Properties west of the excavated area (nos 54–36)

Hope and Anchor/Severn View (no. 54, with nos 52, 50, 48 and 46)

The property now called the Severn View was once two properties, of which the western one belonged first to the Priory, and later to the Dean and Chapter, of Worcester. It can be traced back at least to the 16th century. In the 17th century it was leased to John and Jane Breynton; John Breynton was a clothier. The larger house belonged to Anthony Careless, clothier, in the mid to late 17th century; he also owned the three houses to the east and rented the house which had been Breynton's to the west. His tenant there was Thomas Baldwin, baker; in 1671 an oven, built at the back of his house, was of sufficient importance to feature in the title deeds. The plot seems to have consisted of a large block of properties, with nos 52, 50 and 48 to the east forming an integral part of the property. In 1671 one of these dwellings was occupied by Vincent and Mary Philips, Careless's daughter and son-in-law, and contained a 'house of office' in the backyard. Such a mention is unusual. In the 18th century the property came to Thomas Bate, who rebuilt his own house in 1743 and agreed to rebuild the party wall with the adjoining house to the east. The sheer complication of the ownership and confusion of the premises is epitomised in a document in which two arbitrators had to decide on the ownership of part of the property:

> We the undersigned Francis James and John Rowlands haveing been called in in a matter of dispute between James Bristow of All Saints in the City of Worcester on one part and Ann Corker, Sarah Clarke and Richard Corker all of Bewdley on the other part and having carefully exhamined the premises and heard all matters in dispute Do award that the said James Bristow pay to the said Ann Corker, Sarah Clarke and Richard Corker or one of them the Sum of Twenty Pounds and also give up the present right enjoyed by him of a road to his stable, and brick up the door way next their yard and also for the purpose of emptying manure for his privy. And that the said Ann Corker, Sarah Clarke and Richard Corker do give up their claim to a Room formerly projecting over part of the premises of the said James Bristow and also grant to him the right of a horse road to his said Stable and to empty manure through another road now used by him as a back approach to his house and that the said Ann and others brick up the opening between their Stable and his premises giveing up their right to part of the dung hole. (WRO 496.5 BA 9360 Cab 25/23)

The three properties, nos 48, 50 and 52, were given to All Saints' Church in the 17th century as part of the Careless charity. An engraving from 1796 (Fig. 5.2) shows one narrow house (no. 52) adjoining the Severn View (no. 54; earlier the Hope and Anchor) and one building with two gables, which had obviously been subdivided into two separate units. When these three properties were bought for demolition in 1930 each had a sitting room, kitchen and two attics. No. 48 had two

94 *Excavations at Newport Street, Worcester, 2005*

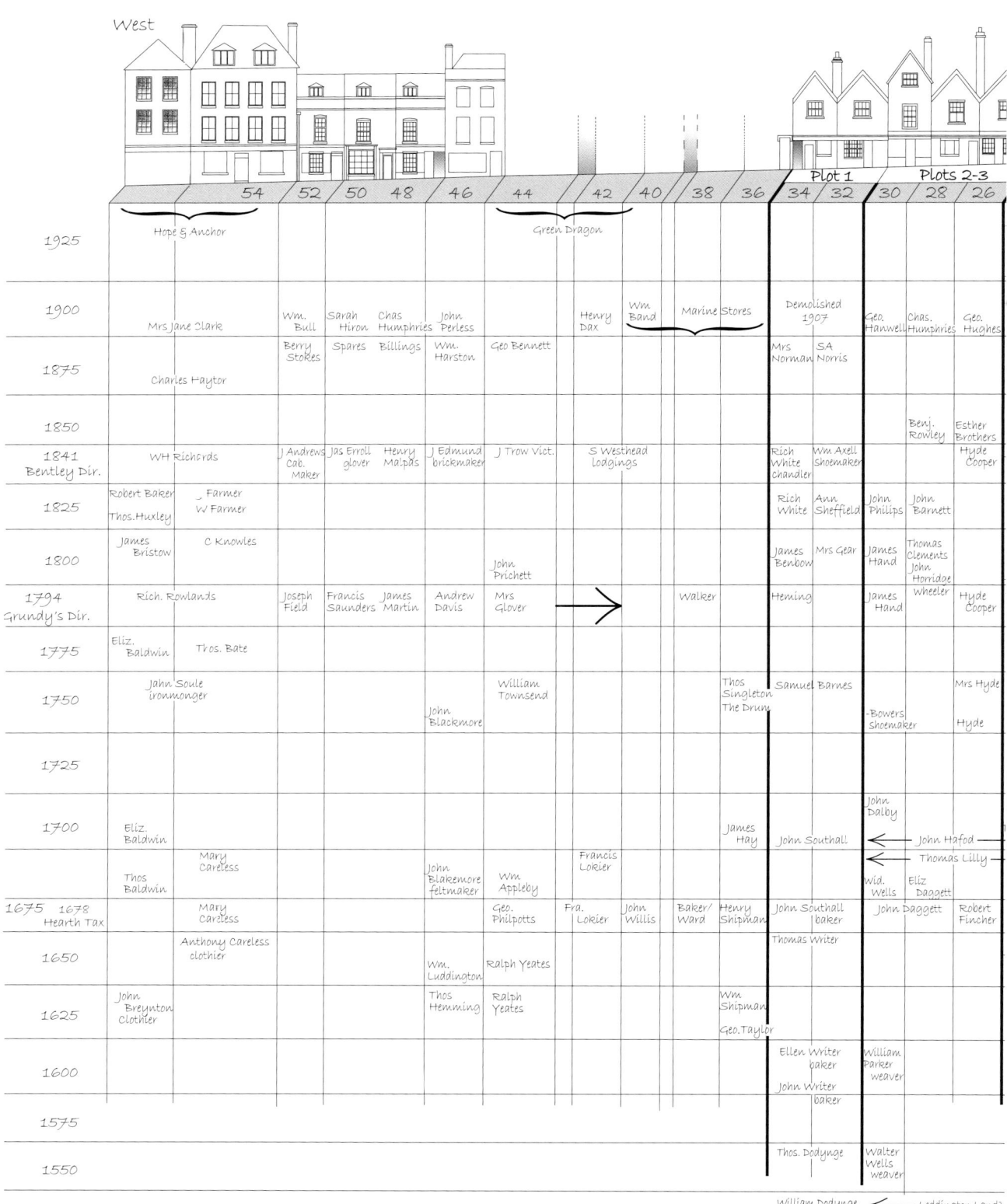

Fig. 5.1   Reconstructed street frontage and property ownership, c 1550 to 1925

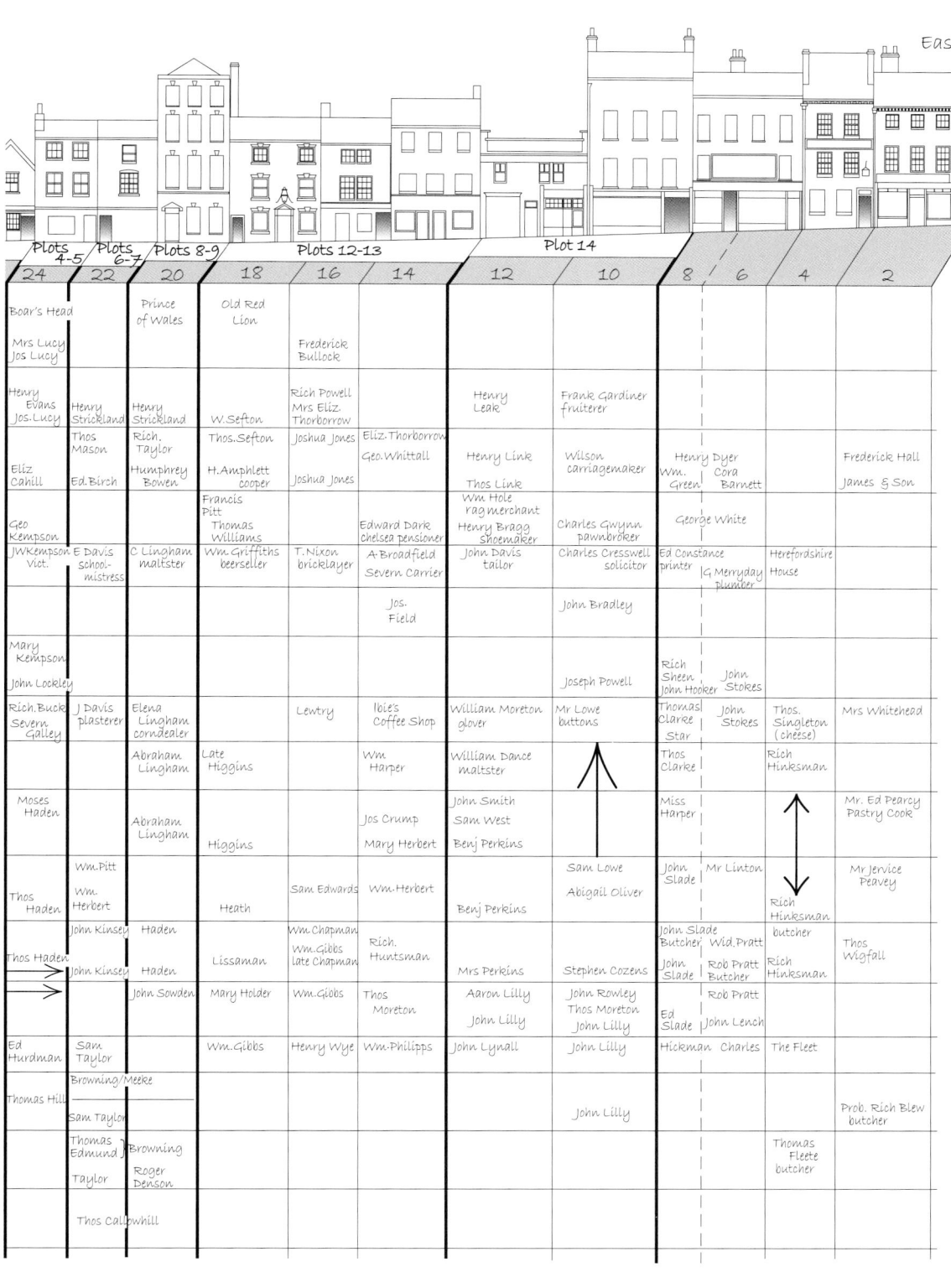

Fig. 5.2   'West View of the City of Worcester', engraving by J. Ross (from Green 1796)

bedrooms, while no. 50 had an additional bedroom and a cellar. Behind was a jointly held yard with wash-house and two WCs. No. 52 had a sitting room, kitchen and back kitchen, WC, coal store and ash place at the back, and two bedrooms and two attics. They were evidently in poor repair because they were bought up under the Public Health Act (Guildhall Newport St file 1/9).

There is some evidence to support the suggestion that these houses were the property of the Moule/Randle family in the 16th century. In 1576 Henry Randle also Moule left two houses in Newport Street to his children and the various lists place him in this position. He was a baker. The Randle family had a title to the property in the early 18th century.

The Green Dragon and associated buildings (Nos 40–44)

The Green Dragon in Newport Street was an ancient inn, with back premises that interlinked with the adjoining premises to the west. In the mid 17th century it was run by Ralph Yeates (or Yates) and his wife, although the Leddingtons were the landlords (WRO 899.81 BA 4893/7). It seems to have comprised both nos 42 and 44, though it is not clear when they were amalgamated into one property. Ralph Yeates kept a comfortable and well-furnished inn and seems to have done well out of his business, leaving over £122 when he died in 1671. He had six bedrooms, most with a main bed and a trundle bed, and a well-equipped kitchen. He was also something of a scholar; his study held not only four Bibles but also books in both English and Latin (WRO Will Ralph Yates 20th Oct. 1671). By 1687 part of the building had been rebuilt by Elizabeth Badland and in 1691 William Applebury rebuilt the rest (WRO 496.5 BA 9360 B10). A photograph suggests that the building was originally two properties. The Appleburys were associated with a number of houses in the area and had an interest in the King's Head by the bridge (Chapter 2.3).

John Pritchett was the landlord of the inn in the middle of the 18th century and also ran a carrier's business, which may explain the large driveway opening on the east side of the building which shows in the above photograph. James Glover took over at the end of the century. He combined his work as a publican with his hairdressing business. He eventually bought the property and left it to his four children (WRO 496.5 BA 9360 Cab 25/24).

During the 19th century the inn slipped down the social scale and eventually, in the 20th century, part of no. 42 was added to Band's Marine Store. The front building seems to have been gutted to provide covered access to the store (Guildhall Newport St file 1/3).

5.1.3 No. 32/34 Newport Street (Plot 1; Figs 5.3 and 5.4)

No. 32/34, which belonged first to Worcester Priory, and then after the Reformation to the Dean and Chapter of Worcester, is the best documented of all the houses in the excavated section of Newport Street.

The descriptions provided in title deeds and rentals not only clarify the use of the plot itself, but also shed light on adjoining properties. The earliest documents found for the site date from 1317, when William son of William le Horner quitclaimed to John de Braunesford a tenement between Robert de Hereford and John le Pynnare in Eport extending to Dolday (WCL B1114). If names attached to occupations mean anything at this date in the 14th century there were hornworkers and pinmakers on adjacent sites at this period. There are two candidates in the Cathedral deeds for a site extending to Dolday. One is at the west of the street, now part of the Severn View. The other Cathedral property that can answer to the description is no. 32/34. There is no way of telling which is which. There are other deeds in the collection for the 14th century but no others that can be

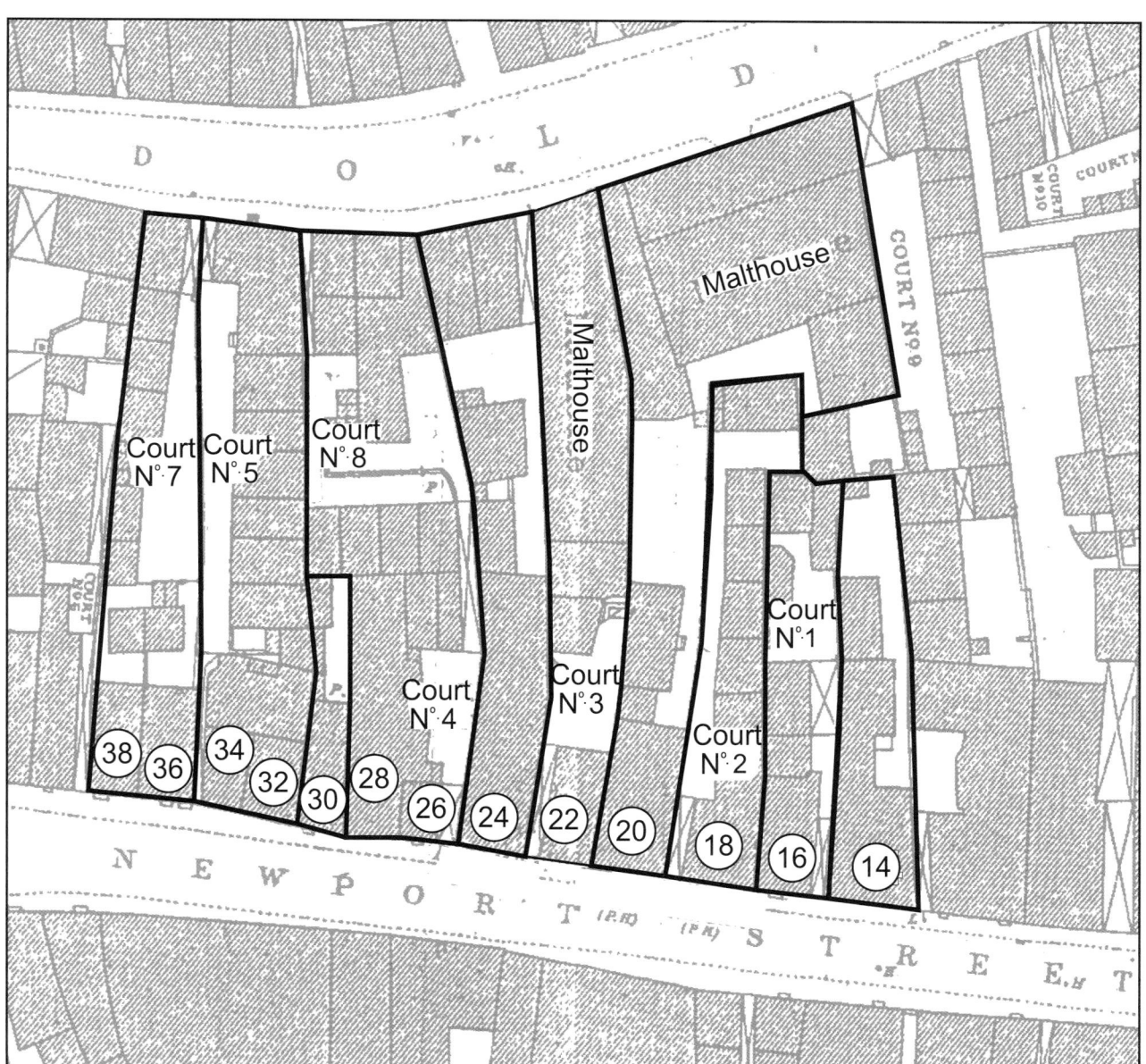

Fig. 5.3   Annotated extract from 1:500 1st Edition Ordnance Survey map (1886) showing nos 14–38 Newport Street

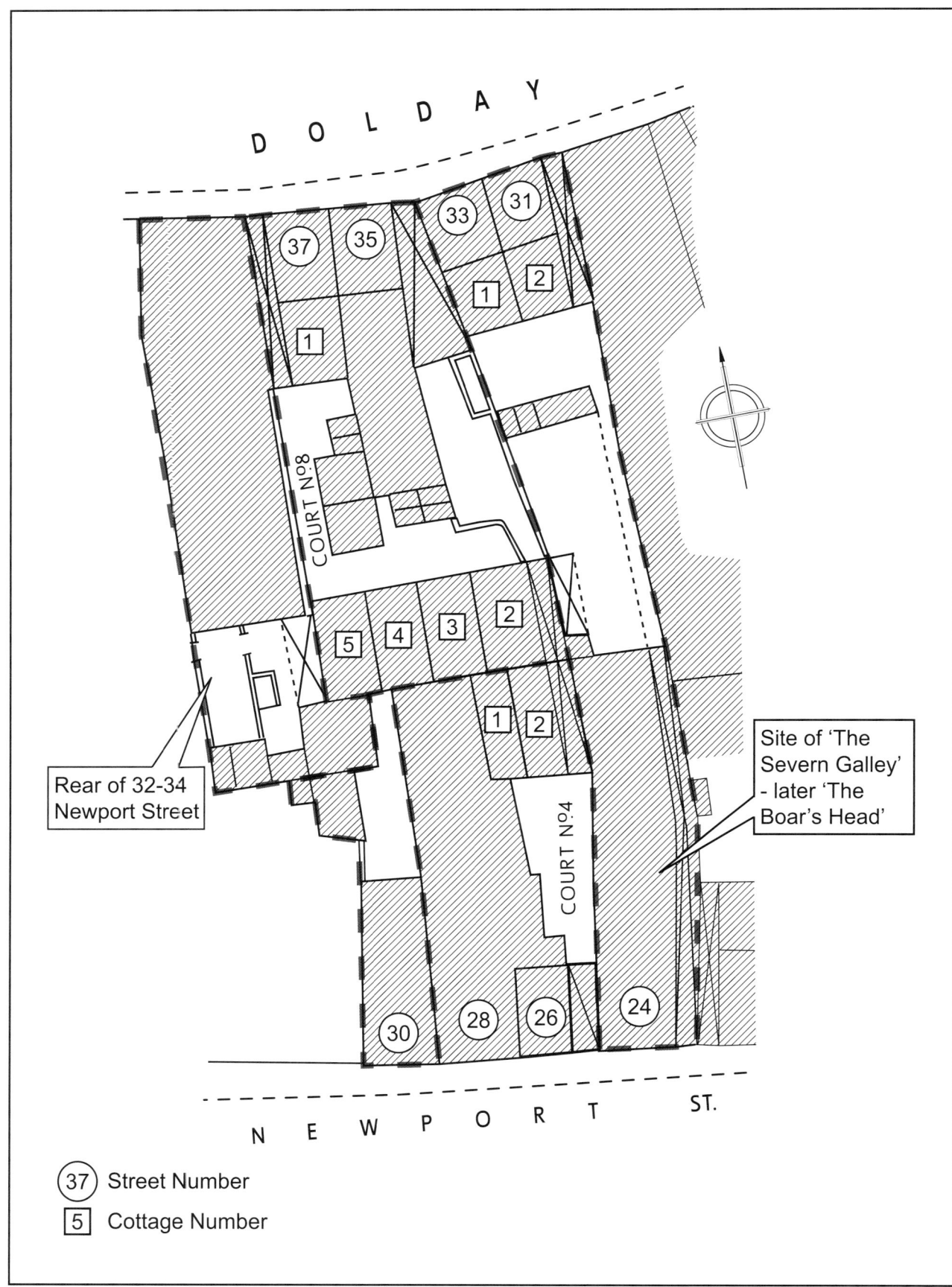

Fig. 5.4 Nos 24–37 Newport Street, as shown on plans accompanying sale documents of 1936

identified with this site, until 1534 when the property was leased to William Dodynge. The rent was quite high at 26s. 8d. but the cellarer was to provide timber for repairs from the woods of Crowle and Hymulton at the cost of felling and carrying (WCL B1124).

The back portion of no. 32/34 was excavated (Plot 1) and a building of early 18th-century brick on earlier stone footings, probably a warehouse, was identified. It is likely that the stone base relates to a 'hemp house', which, with a garden, William Dodynge left to his son Thomas in his will. According to the dimensions given in the various title deeds in the 17th century this plot was the yard, 20ft in length, and stable, 15ft in length, lying next to Leddington's land. On this plot, in 1705 John Southall erected a 'new building' which may account for the bricks.

In 1556 another lease was made to Thomas Dodynge, weaver of the tenements and howses with appurtenances in 'a street … called Newporte strete' late in the tenure or occupation of William Dodynge (WCL A7(ii)).

Twenty years later Thomas Dodynge had forfeited the property for non-payment of rent, but 'considering the great loss and decay that the said Thomas Dodynge hath susteyned sundry wayes having pitie on him his wyffe and many children' the Dean and Chapter granted him a further lease (WCL A7(iv) (1576)). Thomas Dodynge lived in St Helen's parish and let the property, probably to John Writer.

At this point the property changed from a weaver's shop to a baker's premises. In his will of 1601 John Writer, baker, left two houses to his wife Ellen and then his two sons Thomas and Clement 'a messuage in the parish of All Saints now Thomas Parker [see no. 26/28] and the house where I now dwell and the furnace used in my trade'.

Ellen Writer features in a lease for this property in March 1615 and Thomas renewed the lease in 1641/2 (WCL A7(xiii)). This is the lease quoted in the Parliamentary Survey of 1649 when the property is described:

> The house consists of a shopp, a haule, a parlour, a buttery and a bakehouse, a woodhouse, a cellar and a stable belowe, above stairs 3 lodging chambers, 2 corne chambers and a toploft. Worth above the rent £5. (Cave and Wilson 1924, 184)

This was the birthplace and family home of Clement Writer, one of the more colourful and controversial pamphleteers in the period of the Commonwealth. Clement's brother, Thomas, who had inherited the house, had moved to St John's by this time and the property had been sublet to a baker, William Shipman, when the Parliamentary Survey was made in 1649. In 1662 Thomas Writer paid for a window which encroached on the street (WRO 496.5 BA 9360 A17 Rent Roll).

Thomas Writer's lease was finally surrendered in 1674 and the next lease was made out to John Rea, clothier. His subtenants were Isaac White and Henry Steede (or one of them) (WCL A7(xvii) (1674)).

By 1678 the property, with 6 hearths had been leased to John Southall, baker whose family continued to hold it during much of the 18th century. John passed it on to Philip and eventually it became the property of Sarah Southall who had moved to London (WCL Dean And Chapter Houses All Saints p. 27). During that time it was sublet to a series of bakers, who sometimes 'sub-sublet' the property on their own account (WRO 496.5 BA 9360 B10). They paid an encroachment fine for an unspecified encroachment, a bread crib and a little shop, all of which projected into the street. One of these bakers was Samuel Barnes, baker and maltster, who left all his property to his 'loving wife Nancy' in 1776.

There is little information about the latter part of the 18th century. By the first half of the 19th century there were 8 houses or tenements lately demised as 7 houses and one yard formerly a stable (Fig. 5.3; mainly surrounding Court 5). The survey taken by the Ecclesiastical Commissioners in the 1860s described the site as 'two houses fronting the street and six up the passage each containing one room up and one room down, brick and timber and tile built and in indifferent repair. The situation is very bad one of the worst in the city' (CC FF8 33722 All Saints).

In 1907 'the said nine messuages having become ruinous had then been recently demolished and removed'. Before 1909 a schoolroom for the Countess of Huntingdon Chapel had been built on the back of the plot, using the foundations and footprint of William Dodynge's hemp house (the schoolroom can be seen on the far right of Fig. 4.7; Fig. 5.4).

5.1.4 Nos 26, 28 and 30 Newport Street (Plots 2 and 3; Figs 5.3 and 5.4)

It seems clear that nos 26, 28 and 30 were once one property and possibly originally one large house. Prior to 1719 they were in the same ownership as no. 24. Previous occupants can be deduced from the deeds of no. 32/34 (see above, 5.1.3) and the abuttals of no. 22/24.

The division of the plot

The back part of the plot was divided from the front by the mid 16th century (Fig. 5.4). The deeds of no. 32/34 imply that land to the east, the plot behind nos 26, 28 and 30, was in separate occupancy to the front range. For example in 1674 Widow Wells had no. 30 and behind was 'land now or late in the tenure of – Harvord gent' and a 'stable and yard heretofore Robert Luddington', while the Dolday end was 'late in the possession of Seabright Walshe'. This division is expressed in differing degrees of clarity from the 16th century onwards. The division seems to have taken place after 1534 when the description is quite different and is dealt with under no. 32/34.

Property in hands of the Leddington family
With the well-documented no. 32/34 providing a fixed point, a series of somewhat tenuous links makes it likely that nos 26, 28, and 30 were inhabited by the Leddington family in the mid 16th century. In 1563 John Leddington, clothier, left four messuages in Newport Street to his son Robert. Some of these overlap with the property leased by the Dodynge family from the Cathedral. One was 'where Walter Wells dwelleth'; one with a stable was in the occupation of Thomas Dodynge; two others were inhabited by Thomas Walsgrove and William Bissell and cannot be firmly identified.

William Bissell, his wife and seven children appear among those entitled to parish relief in 1555 (WRO 899.81 BA 1180; WRO 496.5 BA 9360 A6/4). A John Ibole/Ibull, who with his wife and three children lived near no. 36, was also in receipt of poor relief and so was Richard Woodsall, who according to William Dodynge's will, lived next to the Dodynge plot in a house owned by William. Woodsall had paid 20s. tax in the 1543 lay subsidy but had evidently fallen on bad times, perhaps due to an accident or possibly the temporary depression in the cloth trade (Dyer 1973, 166–7; NA E179/200/147). Dodynge also left a house in Dolday belonging to 'Newly' to his friend Hugh Gosling. 'Newly' is listed in neither the Poor Rate Assessment nor in the various Lay Subsidies for the 1550s nor among those who qualified for parish relief. He probably lived just above the poverty line.

Some houses probably built on Dolday
The presence of the 'poor' on or adjacent to nos 26 to 36 suggests that cottages had already been built on Dolday or elsewhere behind these plots, even though these dwellings do not appear in the deeds. Often the lessee was only interested in the ground rent. Tenants were expected to carry out repairs and development for subletting at their own expense. Only when the lease of the property changed hands completely were new developments noted and added to the description.

Cathedral deeds place Thomas Dodynge and his father, William, in no. 32/34 and several lists and subsidy rolls show Walter Wells as adjacent to Dodynge on the west side, that is at no. 36 (e.g. WRO 496.5 BA 9360 A6/4). It is likely that Leddington himself at one time lived in no. 26/28. The Leddington family were wealthy Worcester merchants with a strong trading relationship with London, where some of them had houses. Robert Leddington, who died in his 80s in 1563, had property in Newport Street and left it to his grandson, another Robert (WRO 899.81 BA 1180). He himself lived in the High Street. This second Robert had at least six children baptised in All Saints' Church, so he presumably lived, at least for part of his life, in the Newport Street house.

His memorial tablet in the Cathedral gives details of his journeys in Turkey and the Near East. These probably took place when he was a very young man (the regularity of the births of his children in the 1570s and 80s when he was in his twenties and thirties does not leave him much time for foreign travel!). As will be explained in the later text, it is likely that Leddington lived in no. 26/28 and let no. 30 to a tenant.

A comparison between the Lay Subsidy Roll for 1523 and the priory deed for 1534 places Richard Brassy west of no. 32/34 with John Leppynton (probably Leddington) two doors away to the east (WCL B1124; NA E179/200/131).

Later in the 16th century the tenant of nos 26, 28 and 30 was John Wylmington who left his house in Newport Street to his daughter Margery Parker (WRO 899.81 BA 4893/7). The upwardly mobile Leddingtons inherited a more prestigious site in the High Street and then moved out into the county.

In 1576 Humphrey Kings occupied the property, but by 1615 the Parker family were again the occupants; the abuttals for no. 32/34 place a William Parker in nos 26–30. Behind, Humphrey Kings had retained the use of the garden and Robert Leddington had kept 'a certain stable or yard'. The Dolday end was occupied by Thomas Dallow, chandler. By the beginning of the 17th century the property was therefore divided into four sections, with the dwelling house facing Newport Street, a garden behind leased to Humphrey Kings, and another building occupied separately facing Dolday. The Parliamentary Survey refers to this stable and yard in 1649, but there is no description of this building in the deeds before that mentioned above, as a stable and yard in 1674.

When the Cathedral property was valued by the Parliamentary assessors in 1649/50, William Parker and Luddington's land were still described as on the east (Cave and Wilson 1924, 184). In the 17th century the property was probably reunited to become a refuge for the Rev Robert Leddington (by this date calling himself Luddington) great-great-great grandson of the 16th-century Robert, when he was evicted from his living in Shrawley under the Commonwealth.

In 1719 the named tenant of the Newport Street frontage was 'Daggett widow'. The purpresture records for the late 17th century show that John Daggett was paying 'for an encroachment by a cobbler's stall' in 1687 (Table 5.1); Daggett appears to have occupied the premises since 1660 (Poll Tax) when he was assessed at £5. It is not clear how he fits in with Fincher, who also appears in this position paying the Poll Tax. It is probable that the premises were divided up in the mid 17th century with Daggett in the smaller house, no. 30, and Fincher in no. 26/28 with six hearths. In 1678 Daggett paid for two hearths, but by 1709 his widow Elizabeth and her three daughters were the occupants of no. 30. Her probate inventory is consistent with the

Table 5.1: Purprestures 1662 to c. 1780 with some additional information from deeds (D) and wills (W)

	= butchers		+ bakers			+ victuallers			

PURPRESTURES 1662 to c. 1780 with some additional information from deeds (D) and wills (W)

	1662	1687	1698	1708	1715	1721	1741	1750	1780s	Occupation/other
2	Prob. Rich. Blew					Tho. Wigfall	Mr Jervice Pearcy	Mr Jervice Pearcy	Mr Ed. Pearcy	
4	1643 Thomas Fleete	John Lench 1692	Rich. Hinksman	Rich. Hinksman	Rich. Hinksman	Rich. Hinksman	Rich. Hinksman	Rich. Hinksman	Rich. Hinksman	Butcher
6		John Lench	Ed. Slade	Robert Pratt	Robert Pratt		Widow Pratt		1769 Mr Linton	Butcher
8		Rich. Hill	Eliz Grove		John Slade	John Slade	John Slade	John Slade	John Slade	Butcher
10	John Lilly	Late John Lilley		Stephen Cozens	Mrs Abigail Oliver	Mr Lowe	Samuel Lowe	Samuel Lowe	Samuel Lowe	
12	Mr Sam. Roe (Lilly) late Bezar	Aaron Lilly	Mr Perkins	Mr Perkins	Mr Perkins	Mr Perkins	Mr Perkins	Mrs Perkins	Mr Sam West/ John Smith	Culvert D
14		Wm Philips	John Lissaman	John Lissaman	John Lissaman	John Lissaman	Mr Wm Herbert	Mr Wm Herbert Mary widow D	Mr Joseph Crump 1771 D; Wm Harper	Culvert W
16		William Philips; Rich Chance	Wm Gibbs	Wm Gibbs	Wm Gibbs W 1717	Thos Wilding	Sam. Edwards			
18	Henry Wye	Wm Gibbs	Mary Holder		Lissaman	Heath		Higgins D	Late Higgins	
20	Thos Browning	Browning/ Meeke Sam Taylor	John Sowden	Haden	Haden		Lingham	Lingham	Lingham	Malthouses Mills
22	Thos Browning	Rich. Agberrow	Joseph Pritchett/ John Pratt	John Kinsey	John Kinsey	John Kinsey	Mr Wm Pitt			
24	Edward Hurdman late Hills	1674 Mary Hurdman D		Thomas Haden D	Mr Moses Haden	Mr Moses Haden				Baker
26/28		John Hemmings for John Daggett, late Clempsons	Henry Fitzer; Thos Heath	Thos Lilly			Wanklin and Yarnold			
30										
32/34	Henry Shipman late Writers	John Southall	John Southall	John Southall	Philip Southall	Richard Baggett	James Whittall	Sam. Barnes	Sam. Barnes	Baker
36	Henry Shipman	Ed. Longmore/ Shipman	Seys (widow)	Rich. Wanklyn			Geo. Yarnold		Mr Herbert	Baker

hearth tax. It lists a kitchen with a heated room above, a shop with room over and top loft. Her inventory was taken by John Southall who was her landlord. Southall (who himself lived in St Helen's parish) left to his wife Margery 'my house in Newport Street wherein the widow Daggett now lives' (WRO Will, John Southall 27th Dec. 1709). As landlord, Southall was followed in quick succession by -- Needs and Thomas Heath. Henry Fitzer paid the purpresture fine in 1698 (Table 5.1), while Thomas Lilly, chapman, appears to have owned this house from 1703 (abuttals no. 30; WRO 496.5 BA 9360 Cab 25/18) until his death in 1732 when he left his property to his wife Margaret.

Cottages built at rear of no. 26/28

Before the 18th century (probably earlier) no. 26/28 had finally been separated from nos 24 and 30. During the second half of the 18th century and for much of the 19th century the Hyde family, father and son, occupied the property, first as tenants, paying the poor rate to the parish and later as owner occupiers. The Hydes were coopers. In 1804 John Hyde bought the Newport Street house and the three tenements in Dolday, but by the time he died in 1856 there were seven dwelling houses at the rear of the site, two in Dolday, later known as nos 35 and 37 Dolday (the cottages located second from the left and next to the Countess of Huntington's schoolroom, shown as Building 1 on Fig. 7), one behind, and another four built on the intervening land which had been garden (WRO 496.5 BA 9360 Cab 25/18). These became Court 8 Newport Street (Fig. 5.4; Cottages 1–5).

In 1919 the premises were described as messuage, shop and dwelling house with stable yard, coach-house and lofts, with three cottages in Court no. 4 immediately behind the Newport Street frontage. In 1936 when they were sold to the council there was a coal store and manure pit at the rear of no. 35 Dolday. The three cottages in Court No. 4 caused a certain amount of confusion as two of them faced Newport Street as shown by an answer to queries concerning the abstract of title of 1919:

> The premises have not been altered. Part of the building adjoining the shop faces Newport Street, though the actual entrance is the alleyway leading to court No. 4. Thus it is listed in conveyance as one of the cottages in Court No. 4 but the postal address is no 28, Newport Street. Both shop and house are occupied by the same tenant.

The entrance to no. 28 can be seen in a photograph (Fig. 2.12). The structure suggests that the building was erected in the first part of the 17th century and perhaps modified when it was split between Daggett and Fincher around 1660.

No. 30

By the beginning of the 19th century only the largest premises were owner-occupied. Houses in Newport Street were increasingly being purchased as an investment. No. 30 was one of these. It had been sold to John Featherstone, a barge owner, by James Glover, cabinet maker, who had inherited it from his father. James senior had been one time publican of the Green Dragon at no. 42/44. The property was described as:

> All that Messuage or tenement in Newport Street with the brewhouse Back Kitchen small shop over the kitchen Necessary small yard Pump and other outbuildings purchased by James Glover dcd from Thomas Willoughby Gent then John Featherstone now Thomas Clements.

The dwelling house was now permanently separated from the ground behind. Featherstone had a coal yard in Dolday.

In the first half of the 20th century no. 30 belonged to Harold William Haines. At this time it was described as a six roomed cottage. Downstairs was a parlour and living room. Upstairs were four bedrooms on two floors. In 1935 Haines and his wife had lived there for 20 years and had known the property, which had belonged to his aunt, since he was a child. In 1926 he had bought the premises from his aunt's brother for £100, taking out a £80 mortgage to do so. When the City Council offered him £40 for the property he was greatly incensed and bombarded the Town Clerk with a series of clearly written and articulate letters. He claimed that 'it was daylight robbery', that the price offered 'was not the price of a decent fowl house' … 'this after fighting at Mons, Aisne and Ypres … to be robbed by your committee under the Cloak of the government'. He further stated that since 'the ground is to be exploited by the City Council for … a business purpose I am entitled to a fair deal and compensation'. The Town Clerk countered with the claim that the council were only allowed to offer the price for the ground and finally placed a compulsory purchase order on the building, declaring it unfit for human habitation, with poor ventilation and lighting, defective plaster and walls, and the cellar subject to flooding. It is noteworthy that the western boundary of the new development runs just to the east of this property (WRO 496.5 BA 11241/b14).

5.1.5 No. 24 Newport Street (Plots 4 and 5; Fig. 5.4)

The earliest known occupant of no. 24 was Thomas Hill, clothier, who in his will left to his daughter Mary 'the use of the Messuage or Tenement and garden with the appurtenances now in the several occupations of myself, Edward Hurdman, Robert Lewes and others. Edward Hurdman shall have the Liberty to use the Loomes in the shop of the said house with the warping barr and starr and rath and the other implements thereto belonging freely without payinge anything for the same until my grandchild William Hill is twenty-four' (WRO 496.5 BA 9360 Cab 25/18). The implication is that Thomas

Hill had at least four dwellings on this site, probably including nos 26 and 28. He also had an interest in no. 22.

In 1662 Hurdman paid the City Council for a 'bulke' (a projecting stall) 'late Hills' (WRO Wills, All Saints' parish; WRO 899.81 BA 4893/7; WRO 496.5 BA 9360 A17/2, Rent Roll for 1662). In fact Edward Hurdman retained the use of no. 24 for which he left an inventory in 1682. The house consisted of a forestreet chamber, a middle chamber, comfortably furnished hall, kitchen, shop and middle shop and entry. It is not clear why Thomas Hill left him weaving equipment; he was a distiller with pewter measures and spirits in the shop and distilling and brewing furnaces on the site. He seems to have been a fisherman, for included in his goods are three fishing canes (WRO Will Edward Hurdman 6th July 1682).

There is other evidence that nos 24, 26, 28 and possibly 30 may have been one holding. The deeds for all three properties go back to a 'sale' for 1999 years from John Haford of Ombersley to Thomas Haden in 1719. The property was then described as in the hands of Thomas Lilly, chapman. Elsewhere he is described as 'a haberdasher of small wares'. John Lilly, Thomas' father, was a well-to-do silk weaver who acquired a number of properties up and down Newport Street and left them to his large family (WRO Will Richard Lilly 24th Jan. 1739). At that time the property on the east belonged to John Kinsey (no. 22) that on the west to -- Daggett (no. 30). An advertisement in Berrow's *Worcester Journal* shows that Thomas Lilly was not just an itinerant pedlar, but had a shop which he used as a base. His wife, Margaret continued to live in the house after Thomas died and the property had been sold to the Hafods and the Hadens (Will Thomas Lilly Prob 11/655; Berrow's *Worcester Journal* 22.6.1739) The advertisement reads:

> To be lett, a house, together with a good old accustom'd mercer's shop, in the Newport Street, next door to the Severn Galley, wherein Mrs Margaret Lilley lately dwelt. Also a small tenement of about 40/- a year, within the widow Pratt's, in the aforesaid street. Enquire of William Haden, baker, near All Saints church.

This is the first reference to the property being used as an inn.

The abuttals of no. 32/34, which was Cathedral land, tell the same story and imply that the land on the east of no. 32 had belonged first to the Leddington family in the 16th and early 17th centuries, and then to Thomas Lilly, before being bought by John Hafod. If the whole block of 24, 26, 28, and 30 was in single ownership (although divided among separate tenants) it would partly explain why the back buildings straddled several plots. Just where Thomas Hill fits into this sequence is obscure. He may have been a sub-tenant.

The land division is probably substantially the same as that shown on the plans on the sale documents of 1936 (Fig. 5.4). The presence of the names of both Wanklyn and George Yarnold, in the deed of 1741, and listed in the purpresture lists as having encroachments in 1741 (Table 5.1), suggests that, by that date, three separate tenants paid for encroachments on the frontage. With his own house and the two he had built in Dolday this would add up to the six tenements Thomas Haden's inventory states that he held at the time of his death. The hearth tax and other lists also indicate that the property was divided well before the end of the 17th century.

Buildings at rear of no. 24 in backyard and garden
The Hadens held the property for most of the 18th century, and all the evidence suggests that they were living in no. 24. The abuttals for no. 22 place Moses Haden in no. 24 in 1798 and the poor rate assessment lists show that he was already there in the 1750s. Analysis of Thomas Haden's detailed inventory shows that the furniture would fit into a three-storey house with two first floor front rooms (similar to the footprint of the 19th-century no. 24). The length of the inventory reflects the care with which it was taken rather than the size of the house. It provides details such as the presence of Dutch tiles in the surround to the grate in the parlour. It refers to the rear buildings and the survival of the garden. Clearly there was a malt kiln in the yard; there was also a stable and a malthouse and a separate bakehouse and brewhouse. Despite these buildings (the malthouse and brewhouse are cited in the title deeds) there was still room for a garden, a hen pen and four pigs. No wonder the garden was fenced with pales. His goods totalled £149. 10s. 8d., a large sum for a Worcester tradesman.

1719: Two houses built at the Dolday end of the site, later nos 31 and 33 Dolday (Fig. 5.4)
As early as 1719 the back part of the premises was built up. The first title deed states:

> And all those two small tenements on the backer part thereof with the Appurtennces adjoining to Dolday aforesaid and formerly in the several occupations of Francis Hart weaver and now in the several tenures or occupations of James Ruffe and Elizabeth Aberry.

Nos 31 and 33 Dolday can be seen on Figure 4.7 being the low building with a central chimney situated roughly central in the photograph.

1739: Three houses built at Dolday end of the site
Before Beatrix Haden died in 1739 these two dwellings had become three, one built behind the other two. To sons William and Moses she left:

> All that my message or tenement scituate and being … in Newport Street otherwise Eweport Street in the parish of All Saints aforesaid now void but late in the occupation of Mrs Margaret Lilly widdow and also all those three little Tenementes (at the end of the said Messuage and Premises) fronting a certain street called Dolday all of which were purchased by my late husband Mr Thomas Haden for a long term of years.

Moses shared the inheritance with his brother but it is clear that he lived at no. 24 and managed an inn (WRO 496.5 BA 9360 B10 Victuallers' Recognisances). It is likely that William, a city alderman, inherited the houses in Dolday and no. 26/28, which he leased to John Hyde. In the 1770s Alderman William was held responsible at the Court leet for not repairing the paving outside Mr Hyde's house in Newport Street and 'for placing rubbish in Dolday'. He was also fined 'for his soil in Dolday, encumbered with muck and a very offensive nuisance' (WRO 496.5 BA 9360 B10 Court Leet Book). Moses paid the poor rate to the parish. He features as the license holder in the City Victuallers' Recognisances when the inn was known as the Severn Galley, and he was fined for 'suffering his pavement to be out of repair' in Newport Street.

It appears that Moses Haden relinquished the inn before he died 1775, moving to St Clement's parish and that his brother took charge of the property. In his will William left the premises first to Moses' widow (who predeceased him) and then to the Smiths, relatives in Tenbury. During this period a series of publicans rented the inn: John Wormington, Benjamin and Hester Poole, Richard Buck and latterly John Hyde, the tenant and later owner of no. 26/28.

Boar's Head Yard houses built before 1811

In 1806 John Hyde bought no. 26/28 from the Smiths, while no. 24 was sold to John Lockley who took over the building, described as a 'Messuage, stables, yard, buildings, the Severn Galley, now the Boar's Head'; he also took over the license. Before 1811 he had capitalised on his purchase by building four 'new erected tenements or dwelling houses' in Dolday. These would later be known as the Boar's Head Yard. The name of the inn was changed to the Boar's Head in 1813. No. 24 remained in use as a pub under a series of publicans. In 1897 it was sold to Spreckley's Brewery, who leased it to Henry Evans:

> All these four tenements or dwellinghouses (4 cottages in Dolday). Lying at the back of the Boar's Head Inn premises and the yard, passage ashpit and water closet (Fig. 5.4; Nos 31 and 33 Dolday, and Cottages 1 and 2).

The Boar's Head remained open as a pub until 1907 when Henry Evans ceased to trade and subsequently became a private house, occupied by Evan's daughter Emily Lucy and her bricklayer husband.

5.1.6 No. 20 Newport Street (Plots 8 and 9) and No. 22 Newport Street (Plots 6 and 7; Fig. 5.3)

1622: One messuage and garden, probably nos 20 and 22

The earliest evidence for this plot is found in a schedule of deeds which pushes the ownership back to 1622 when the property was sold by Thomas Callowhill and his son Francis of Bristol to Edmund Browning. At this date it was described as 'Then in the tenure of Roger Denson with all gardens and garden ground' on which a fine was levied 'by the name of One Messuage & One garden which garden ground is since built upon' (WRO 496.5 BA 9360 Cab 25 All Sts/26). This appears to have been nos 20 and 22.

1678: House with four hearths and seven small dwellings behind

Edmund left it to his son Thomas in his will of 1652 and Thomas retained it until after 1666 (WRO BA 7996 Hearth Tax 1666 Microfilm). By this date he had carried out the building on the garden ground. He himself had a house with four hearths on the frontage in 1678, and a shop window and an encroachment in Dolday in the 1680s, (WHS Hearth Tax 1678; WRO 496.5 BA 9360 B10). The Purpresture Books suggest that the east side of the property, which became no. 22, was sublet for Denson had a projecting window which he paid for separately in 1662 (WRO 496.5 BA 9360 A17). Behind the frontage there were seven small dwellings, only one of which had more than one hearth (WHS Hearth Tax 1678). Samuel Taylor had taken over Thomas Browning's house by 1678 and continued for pay for the encroachments on the city's land (Table 5.1).

1698: Small dwellings at rear demolished. Malthouse 'newly built' 1703

A deed of 20th April 1703 transferring the property from Thomas Hill mercer to John Sowden explains that William Huntbach, on 7th/8th April 1687, bought the property from Daniel Hill whose wife Patience had inherited it from her first husband, Thomas Browning. Daniel was probably the father of Thomas Hill.

No. 22 Newport Street (Plots 6 and 7)

John Kinsey became tenant of no. 22 in 1706. He was a carpenter and his inventory lists timber and coffins. He left his house to his wife, Ann; the inventory (WRO Will and inventory John Kinsey 1722/3 1st March) details his possessions:

Imprimus his wearing apparel and Money in Purse	15 00 0
Kitchen one jack one dresser of drawers sixteen dishes of pewter	
Two dozen of Plates	05 00 0
Parlour Guns Flagons and other pewter	
For Irons of all Sorts	01 00 0
Brass of all Sorts	01 00 0
Table and Chaires and Skreene	00 10 0
In the parlour two Tables and Chaires	00 10 0
In the Cellar Ale and	40 00 0
In the Brewhouse One Furnace one Mash Fate and Coolers	04 00 0
In the Backside Two Piggs	00 10 0
Bacon an Cratch	02 00 0
Chamber over the Parlour One bed with Other furniture and one clock	05 00 0

At the Stairhead One bed	
Chamber over the Kitchen bed and Furniture	05 00 0
Back Roome Two beds and Furniture	02 00 0
In the Shopp, Working Tools	08 00 0
Linen of all sorts	05 00 0
Coffins Boards and lumber	02 00 0
One parcel of Hops	01 00 0
Good and bad debts	08 00 0
	106 10 0

The purpresture records and abuttals place William Pitt, an innkeeper and William Herbert, smith, in no. 22 after John Kinsey (Table 5.1), but by the 1780s it had come into the hands of the Davis family, father and son, who were plasterers (WRO Grundy Directories and Poor Rate Assessments). John was followed by Joseph, who was still there in 1841. His daughter Elizabeth Webb Davies, a schoolteacher, first mortgaged the property in 1847 and then sold it outright in 1854.

From this time both properties seem to have deteriorated into slums and it is hardly surprising that, during the first half of the 20th century Worcester City Council made plans to purchase the buildings for slum clearance.

Surveys of the buildings were made before purchase. Nos 20 and 22 Newport Street and Court no. 3, behind with three dwellings, formed one lot (Figs 4.30 and 5.3). No. 20 (earlier The Prince of Wales) was let out in rooms which failed to comply with regulations; there were only two water closets for three families living there, the east wall was bulging and the structure generally was in a dilapidated state. The ventilation and lighting were poor.

No. 22 was in a worse state, it lay back-to-back with the house in the adjoining court, with no means of food storage or cooking, no separate sanitary accommodation and little natural light. The three small three storey houses were in a worse state, damp dark and airless with no sanitary facilities. All were structurally dilapidated and no. 2 was bug infested (WRO 496.5 BA 11241/b14). They were declared unfit for human habitation and were pulled down in 1936.

No. 20 Newport Street (Plots 8 and 9)

At the end of the 17th century the property was tenanted by Joseph Pritchett, glover, son-in-law to John Southall at no. 32/34, and John Pratt, blacksmith. In fact the property appears to have changed hands quite rapidly between 1687 and 1700, moving from Thomas Browning, to Thomas Meeke, to Samuel Taylor (who paid the Hearth Tax) before Pritchett and Pratt took over in the 1690s.

John Sowden bought the whole plot from Joan, widow of William Huntbach, in 1698. By that time the two messuages cited in the 1703 deed had become one messuage, one brewhouse and malthouses. The passageway between nos 22 and 24 remained. It appears on Young's map of 1779 and can still be traced on the 1886 Ordnance Survey Map.

Newly erected malthouse

Another deed issued in 1703 says the premises had been divided into several dwellings. It appears that John Sowden mortgaged his property to a Cordelia Williams, perhaps to raise money for his redevelopment. In 1709 William Winsmore, Alderman, who lived in Quay Street and was related to the Hadens at no. 24, paid off the mortgage and advanced John Sowden £45. The property then consisted of two messuages and one 'newly erected malthouse'. Confusion in the deeds, abuttals and descriptions suggests that nos 20 and 22 were still in the same ownership at this point. The malthouse seems to have been built at the back of no. 22.

When John Sowden died in 1727 his plot contained two furnaces, one in the upper backside and one in the bakehouse. He also had a corn chamber, probably over the bakehouse. There was a cellar under the house. It is therefore likely that traces of furnaces survive in the 'upper backside' (WRO Will John Sowden 9th Nov. 1727). There is no mention of other property:

    Kitchen with jack and andirons
    Shop Goods
    Upper backside with furnace and ironwork
    Backhouse (bakehouse)
    Mill mouldingboard furnace troffs ironwork
    Cornchamber
    Beam scales weights
    Cellar
    Chamber over kitchen
    Toplofts

By 1741 Abraham Lingham, oatmealmaker, was living in no. 20 and rented the malthouse built by Sowden at the rear of no. 22 (Fig. 5.3). He had additional malthouses behind his own house and nos 18, 16 and 14 (see abuttals WRO 705.27 BA 385/44). When Abraham Lingham died in 1784 he left to his son Joseph the house he built in Bridge Street and to his son Thomas 'all that dwelling house with the tenements behind it with the mills and implements of trade which I now occupy' (WRO Will Abraham Lingham 1784). He left to his son Ephraim houses lying in Newport Street occupied by -- Kyte and widow Wanklyn (WRO Will Abraham Lingham 1784). The 18th-century Linghams were Quakers. The family continued there until the mid 19th century; Elena Lingham, corndealer, held no. 11 (20) in 1794 (WRO 496.5 BA 9360 B10; Bentley's 1841 Directory; Grundy's 1794 Directory).

According to the purpresture records the Wanklyns were at no. 18 in the 1760s. If this is so they did not pay poor rate. On the other hand another deed of 1741 (WRO 496.5 BA 9360 Cab 25/18) places them in no. 24.

5.1.7 Nos 14, 16 and 18 Newport Street (Plots 12 and 13; Fig. 5.3)

No deeds have been found for nos 14, 16 and 18 and any information has had to be put together from the abuttals listed in the deed of adjacent buildings, from the 1678 Hearth Tax, encroachment records in the city archives and from the list of those paying poor rate in All Saints' parish.

It does, however, appear that the back section of these plots was separated from the front in the 17th or early 18th centuries and that malthouses and, later, cottages were built on the back plots. A separate deed relating to Court no. 9 at the back of no. 12 refers to a plot with a 30-foot frontage to Dolday stretching 82ft towards Newport Street and with an additional 17ft towards the boundary with the Newport Street house. In 1776 this was built up with a warehouse and a dwelling house. To the west, behind nos 18 and 16, Abraham Lingham had built a malthouse.

No. 18 Newport Street: The Old Red Lion

According to the Hearth Tax and the encroachment records, this was in the hands of William Gibbs between 1678 and 1721. According to the Hearth Tax an adult son William Gibbs junior also lived on the site, paying for one hearth, while his father had two hearths. It is therefore likely that the probate inventory, taken in 1717, was for the son's belongings and that by this date he lived in the main house. It does not give an occupation, but the quantities of barrels and the 'earthen pints and quarts' imply that Gibbs junior kept an alehouse. The building had a cellar, a kitchen, back kitchen and brewhouse with two bedchambers over and a garret over the chambers. There is no mention of second house. The premises then passed to Samuel Edwards and then Mrs George Whittall, with Mrs Lissaman as landlady. However, between the 1750s and 1800 the landlord was James Glover, perukemaker, who was the innkeeper at the Green Dragon.

In the first decades of the 19th century Glover's children sold to a William Featherstone, a barge owner and coal merchant described as 'of Dolday'. William Featherstone, coal merchant, is listed as in Dolday in Grundy's directory for 1788 and it seems likely that he lived and had his coal yard in Dolday at the back of the Newport Street property before buying the Newport Street house. In 1804 the Newport Street property was described as having a 'brewhouse, back kitchen, small shop over the kitchen, Necessary, small yard, Pump and other outbuildings' (Guildhall Newport St file 1/9). The position of the shop suggests a basement kitchen, possibly the cellar of the early 18th-century house.

By 1842 it had become a pub, the Rose and Shamrock, but by 1851 it had changed its name to the more prosaic Red Lion and later became the Old Red Lion. By this date four tenements and a stable had been built behind the Newport Street frontage (Fig. 5.3: around Court 2) (Guildhall Newport St file 1/14). These had been reduced to three and a brewhouse and other buildings by the time the property was sold to Worcester City Council in 1944. After no. 20 had been demolished Mrs Sefton, the owner of the building, complained that the west wall of the Old Red Lion was unsupported and insisted that it should be shored up. However the surveyor maintained that there was a 'very perceptible gap between the two houses' and that the Old Red Lion was erected before no. 20 (WRO 496.5 BA 11241/b14).

No. 16 Newport Street

The 1678 Hearth Tax lists show that a Thomas Moreton paid for two hearths ('One conceled') at no. 18 in 1678. At the time Abraham Bowles was listed as the owner. The Hearth Tax implies that it had previously belonged to 'Mis Heming' who had moved to London. A butcher called Richard Heming had a shop in Newport Street in 1662. In 1687 a Thomas Marston, possibly the same man as Thomas Moreton, paid 9d. for an encroachment. The lists continue with a John Hurdman and a Mrs Lissaman, both of whom probably leased the property to tenants and they were followed by the Higgins family, Michael and his daughter Sarah who appear in both the encroachment books and the poor rate assessments. Ann (known as Nancy) Higgins left an inventory for the house, showing that she had a well-appointed kitchen, a store or wash-house and three rooms upstairs (WRO Will Ann Higgins 15th April 1771). In 1775 the house seems to have been occupied by Edmund Lewtry, china painter, and then in 1794 by John Lewtry, a carpenter (WRO 496.5 BA 9360 Enrolments 4 p. 189; Grundy's 1794 Directory). For most of the first half of the 19th century the premises were tenanted by Thomas Nixon, a bricklayer.

No. 16/18 stood until the 1980s and was surveyed by Nicholas Molyneux in 1978 (Fig. 5.5). No. 18 provided evidence for a jettied building, the jetty having been underbuilt in the 19th century. It was probably a single bay structure with a room below and a chamber above. No staircase position is recorded. No. 16 had a cellar of green sandstone and a three light window in the rear wall. A rear wing had been built behind which may have accommodated William Gibbs' kitchen and back kitchen, with chambers over and the front range as the 'shop', with cellar under and chamber over and a garret above.

No. 14 Newport Street

Like that of nos 16 and 18 the history of no. 14 can only be pieced together from the abuttals and encroachment records. As with nos 16 and 18 the Dolday end of the plot was taken up with Abraham Lingham's malthouse and a selection of outbuildings (Fig. 5.3).

In 1687 a Thomas Moreton paid the city 2s. for an 'incroachment & bulke and a cellar window' on this site. It seems to have been a substantial house with three hearths in 1678. By 1714 a Richard Hinksman was in occupation and he was still there six years later. In 1741 Mr William Herbert, smith, was the occupant and he and his widow continued to hold the house for 20

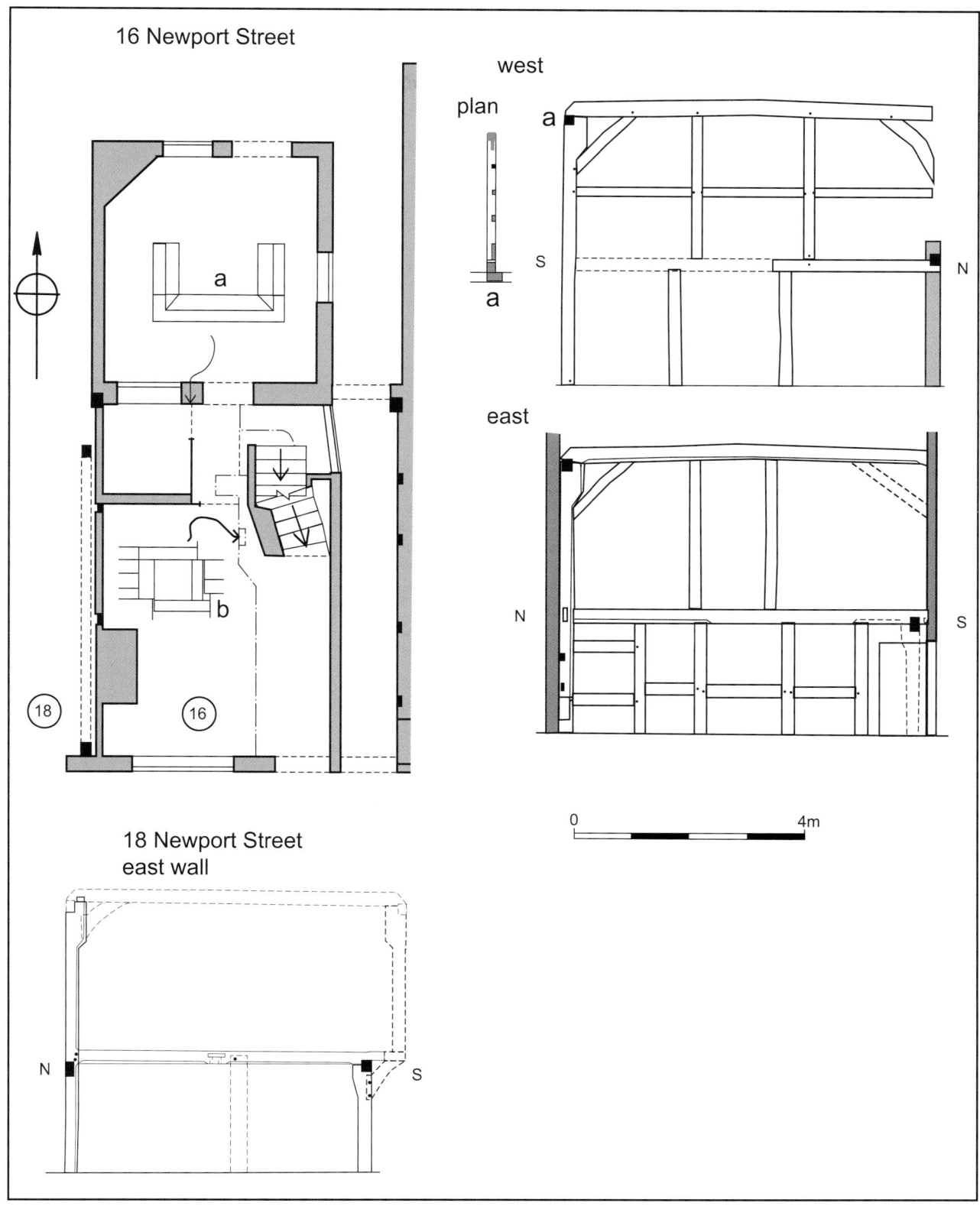

Fig. 5.5 Plan and Elevation survey of nos 16 and 18 Newport Street prior to demolition, as recorded by N.A.D. Molyneux, 1978. Scale 1:100

years. Herbert's brief inventory merely lists his rooms: kitchen chamber, chamber over the shop, back room, Buttery or Cellar ('four barrels and other lumber'), kitchen, and brewhouse. There is no indication in any of the documents that there was a smithy on the site. William Herbert died in 1744 and his wife Margaret in 1746 (WRO Will William Herbert 11th Dec 1744; Will Margaret Herbert 11th Nov 1747). Joseph Crump, who valued William's property and witnessed Margaret's will, was the next occupant, although a daughter, Mary, continued an interest in the property and features in the purpresture lists (Table 5.1). Joseph was paying the poor rate to All Saints' Church in 1755. By 1766 he was running the property as a coffee house. Joseph Crump's will gives no indication of his trade. It refers to 'All that my messuage with the appurtenances which I now live in the Newport Street … together with the partition wall which divides the same from another house adjoining to the said Messuage in the occupation of Mrs Higgins [no. 16] and also the water course which runs through the yard or backside of the last mentioned Messuage.' This may suggest that nos 14 and 16 were once one house. Joseph left the property to his son Joseph, who was to be allowed to buy his stock in trade at cost from his father's estate. Joseph seems to have declined the offer, for William Harper became the proprietor of the coffee house in 1776.

Grundy's Directory indicates that by 1792 John Stinton had taken over and the 1794 directory calls the premises 'Ibies Coffee House'. The property remained as a coffee house until after 1820 when Joseph Field was the proprietor (WRO 496.5 BA 9360 B9). Before 1841 it had become the property for A. Broadfield, Severn carrier.

5.1.8 Nos 10 and 12 Newport Street (Plot 14)

There is some indication that these two houses were in the same ownership in the 17th century, belonging to John Lynall and lived in by him and his tenant Philip Bezar or Beasons (John Lynall had five hearths while Philip Beason in the adjoining house and bracketed with Lynall had two hearths, recorded in the Hearth Tax 1678 (WHS Hearth Tax 1678). There is certainly some confusion in the numbering at the beginning of the 20th century when this property was no. 10.

At the end of the 17th century nos 10 and 12 belonged to John Lilly, who was an affluent silkweaver, worth £523 when he died. He had nine adult children living at the time of his death, six sons and three daughters. The daughters all seem to have married well-to-do local tradesmen and there were family links with the Winsmores, bakers, at the top of Quay Street, and with the Hadens at no. 24 Newport Street. His house contained three chambers and a large kitchen living room; there was a parlour, a shop and a little room by the shop. There was a furnace in the brewhouse (WRO Will John Lilly 4th Feb 1690; WHS Hearth Tax 1678).

It seems that even in John Lilly's time the house was divided into two; the abuttals to the west of no. 8 give both Richard Blew and John Lilly as occupants of the house to the west (WRO 496.5 BA 9360 Lib Rec. A2/1 1670). The purprestures also indicate that there were other tenants with street frontages on the site at the same time as Lilly. After their father died his sons (Moses and Aaron) inherited the property; one unit (no. 10) was leased to a John Rowley and the other (no. 12) to a Mr Benjamin Perkins. The Lillys owned property in other parts of Worcester.

No. 12 Newport Street

Hearth Tax and purpresture records indicate that no. 12 had a succession of occupiers/owners before John Lilly took the property, but by 1708 the occupant was Benjamin Perkins (WRO 496.5 BA 9360 B9). Aaron Lilly seems to have inherited the house from his father and before 1708, had sold the house to Benjamin Perkins, a distiller, about whom very little is known. It is clear however that he altered the building, adding more steps to the front of the house in 1741 and then removing them six years later (WRO 496.5 BA 9360 B10 purprestures).

Shortly after this the house was transferred as part of a marriage settlement (WRO 705:27BA 385/31). Samuel West seems to have been a trustee and in 1752 he was responsible for refronting the house 'building on the street'. This probably means that he underbuilt the jetty, modernising the facade, encroaching on the street and incurring a fine. At this time the whole plot was in the same ownership, extending from Newport Street to Dolday. Samuel West bought the site from Benjamin Perkins in 1760. According to a deed of 1772 when West, then living in Earl's Croome, mortgaged the property, the tenants were 'heretofore Benj. Perkins afterwards Samuel West now John Smith', and the premises extended to a stable, formerly a brewhouse in the possession of William Hall, brewer, now William Lewis (WRO 496.5 BA 9360 Enrolments 4 1772, p181). The sale included standards and fixtures and watercourses, 'particularly all watercourses running from the premises above granted through the said stable of the said Samuel West in Dolday'.

By 1778 this back plot contained a messuage fronting Dolday, with a warehouse behind and a malthouse adjoining. In 1776 this plot was leased to a maltster, William Dance. It then comprised a 'Messuage or Tenement with the Warehouse behind the same'. There was also a malthouse on the plot which adjoined Abraham Lingham's malthouse on the west.

During the next two years Pretty Mann and his wife acquired the property as an investment and leased it to William Moreton, glover, who was already the tenant (WRO 705.27 BA 385/44). He pulled down the warehouse and built a row of five cottages on the site. The malthouse remained and was rented out to William Holt. Measurements are provided on a 1772 mortgage document indicating that the Dolday plot extended 82 feet towards Newport Street and had a 30ft frontage to Dolday. The malthouse had a 63ft frontage to Dolday and from the back of the built-up court (Fig. 5.3; Court

9) to the boundary with the Newport Street frontage was an additional 17ft. On the east the five newly built messuages are bounded by the garden of Samuel Lowe. The measurements and boundaries can be traced on later maps and the footprint of the 18th-century development was retained until the City Council bought up the property for demolition in 1936.

No. 10 Newport Street

Before 1708 the occupant was another silk weaver, Stephen Cozens. Like John Lilly he had goods and furnishings worth more than £500 of which £200 were goods in his shop, presumably high quality silk material. He also had a brewhouse with furnace. In his will he stipulated that Abigail Oliver was to have first refusal of his goods at the value stated in the inventory. In fact Abigail Oliver appears in both the purpresture records (Table 5.1) and the deeds as the next tenant, holding the property from an Ann Trevett of Bristol who seems to have been the landlady. She had two houses, probably one behind the other, as they are described as adjoining together in Newport Street.

Abigail sold them in 1749 to Samuel Lowe, button maker, to whom she appears to have been related. Samuel's two younger children were called Abigail and Oliver. Both families were Quakers. In his will of 1769, Samuel left his house in Newport Street to his wife Mary. His elder son, another Samuel, continued to live in the house until his death in 1792, although the second house was leased out to Joseph Powell (WRO 496.5 BA 9630 Cab 25/26; Grundy's 1792 Directory). At this stage the house was still a high-class dwelling house with a garden behind, stabling and outbuildings. Lowe's heirs, a family called Eversleigh, Lowe's stepsister's children must have pulled down the second house because when they sold up (after bankruptcy) in 1831, the premises comprised: 'a tenement with buildings, stable, yard & premises formerly Samuel Lowe'. The property was bought by an attorney, William Parker and partner William Smith, who continued to pay the poor rate. In 1849 the house still had a garden behind the dwelling house and buildings (back kitchen, brewhouse, laundry, stable, buildings with garden ground beyond the same). In 1849 it was bought by another solicitor, Charles Creswell, but in 1853 it descended the social scale abruptly, becoming a pawnbroker's.

In 1888 the building was bought by a carriage builder, William Wilson, and in the 1920s, after the premises had been a fruiterer's shop, his successor Mr F. Gardiner rebuilt the premises.

5.1.9 Nos 2, 4, 6 and 8 Newport Street (to the east of excavated area)

In the 1960s the destruction of some of the houses at the east end of Newport Street to make way for All Saints' Road, and the subsequent renumbering of the remainder, has made the identification of some of these properties very difficult. The collection of Worcester Corporation documents housed in cabinet 25/41 purports to relate to the pub (no. 4) once called Herefordshire House. However the accompanying plan clearly shows that some of the deeds relate to no. 2.

No. 8 Newport Street

Very little is known of no. 8, which, at the end of the 17th century, was a butcher's shop in the holding of Edward Slade. It was later occupied by John Slade and then a Mr James Strickland. In the 1790s it was, briefly, a pub, The Star.

A deed of 1796 reads:

> 1796 27th December All those two Messuages or Tenements situate standing and being in … Newport Street one of which Messuage or Tenements lately was a public house and was known by the name or sign of the Star and was late in the possession of Henry Clarke now Judiah Flinn and the other adjoins thereto and was lately in the occupation of John Stokes Baker (WRO 496.5 BA 9360 Cab 25/25).

In the 1890s no. 8 together with no. 6 was part of George White's grocer's shop.

No. 6 Newport Street

John Lench, butcher, occupied no. 6 in the late 17th century and in the early 18th century it passed to Robert Pratt, another butcher. When he died in 1710, Pratt had a two storey house with garrets, he cured his own bacon, with four fletches weighing 44lb in his kitchen, he had a tripe house with a brass furnace and kept sheep and cattle at Broadheath and Cotheridge. He fattened pigs in his back yard. His widow continued to occupy the house until the middle of the century. The confusion with Edward Pearcy has already been mentioned. In 1794 John Stokes, pastry cook was the occupant.

No. 4 Newport Street: Herefordshire House

Richard Hinksman's family of butchers occupied and paid dues on no. 4 (Herefordshire House) from the early 18th century until the 1790s (WRO 496.5 BA 9360 B9 purpresture records 1708). He was one of the last of the butchers to occupy the 'shambles' area of Newport Street. He left to his 'dear wife Mary' the 'messuage or dwelling house with stable and buildings and app. in All Sts in my own possession' (WRO Will Richard Hinksman 1775). His parents, who had occupied the premises before him, were Robert and Judith.

There are no title deeds for this property before 1742 when a Mrs Sambach left it to Richard Mence in her will. The complications of the legal history and the multiplicity of owners, part owners and mortgage holders make it very difficult to trace. However, it appears that Richard Hincksman was the tenant in 1750, and that he bought the lease and left it to his son

Henry after Mary's death. When Henry died in 1790 and left it to Joseph Southall, the property was tenanted by a Joseph Brown. It was then described as a messuage in Newport Street with yard, garden and back buildings (WRO 496.5 BA 9360 Cab 25/41; most of the evidence for these houses comes from this box).

Before 1840 the building became a public house, the Herefordshire House; the landlady was a Mary Cauldwell. In 1842 the owner, Joseph Gummery, cut a window in the wall overlooking his neighbour on the west and had to agree to block it up if the neighbour wanted to put another storey on his house. This suggests that the Herefordshire House was already a tall three storey building, as it was latterly.

No. 2 Newport Street

Richard Blew appears to have occupied this property from the second half of the 17th century. He was a butcher and is listed in the purpresture records for 1662 (Table 5.1). He was still there in 1670 (WRO 496:5 BA9360 Liber Recordum A2/1; WHS Hearth Tax 1678) but had probably died or moved before the end of the century. There is no direct evidence of his immediate successor, but comparison with the 17th and 18th-century purpresture lists imply that Edward Pearcy, a pastry cook, was the tenant of no. 2 from the 1750s at least until 1773 (WRO 49.:5 BA 9360 Enrolments 4 p.189). He was probably followed by John Stokes, another pastry cook, who later moved to no. 6. This property is difficult to sort out as the deeds and poor rate lists imply that Edward Pearcy and John Stokes were always in no. 6.

In 1794 Grundy's Directory places two occupants on the plot. Mrs Whitehead, a grocer, probably had the front part, while Thomas Lane, barge owner, either had a house in the yard or else, more likely, he lodged with Mrs Whitehead. A plan made in 1851 shows a stable behind the house, with no indication of additional space. It appears that this plot did not extend to Dolday.

5.2 The Roman pottery
Alan J. Jacobs

5.2.1 Analysis

Roman pottery consisted of just 110 sherds weighing 2.169kg and in a limited range of fabrics. These were recovered and recorded according to the procedures described above (Chapter 3.2.5).

All securely stratified Roman material (Table 5.2) came from Plot 13, the only plot where Roman-dated deposits (Period 1) produced pottery (Period 1 deposits were also excavated in Plot 3 but produced no Roman material). Residual Roman material was also recovered from Plot 13 and 14 deposits (mainly within Period 2 contexts) and from machine-clearance horizons.

This small assemblage was dominated by Severn Valley ware (fabric 12), though the assemblage size

Table 5.2: Summary of stratified Roman pottery assemblage

Fabric	Type	Total	Weight
3	Malvernian	3	233
12	Oxidised Severn Valley ware	49	1073
12.1	Reduced Severn Valley ware	2	29
14	Fine greyware	1	4
15	Coarse greyware	1	2
17	Mudstone-tempered ware	1	8
22	Black-burnished ware	7	200
28	Nene Valley ware	3	4
29	Oxford red-brown colour coat	1	1
43	Samian	1	1
43.1	Samian South Gaulish	3	24
43.2	Samian Central Gaulish	13	222
43.3	Samian East Gaulish	2	42
Total		87	1843

meant that no statistical significance could be assigned to its quantification. The Severn Valley ware included a number of large storage jars (G347), narrow-mouthed jars of Webster types 1 and 3 (G345: context 2038) dating to the late 2nd to 3rd century, and a single example of a late wide-mouthed jar (Webster 1976, type 29; G349) of late 3rd to 4th-century date. A single example of a Webster (1976) type 43 tankard was also recovered (G346: context 2039), and dates from the late 2nd to 3rd century. Finally, a single example of a hemispherical bowl was recovered in a form similar to Webster 51/55, examples of which can be dated to the 2nd to 3rd century. Only a few sherds of the reduced Severn Valley ware fabric were recovered (fabric 12.1).

Greyware forms were only represented by two body sherds of small jars (fabrics 14 and 15), generally dating from the 1st to 2nd century. A single residual sherd of mudstone-tempered ware (fabric 17) was recovered from a modern context (896; Plot 14). Malvernian metamorphic ware (fabric 3) was under-represented in the overall assemblage; however, an example of the rim of one of the characteristic slab-built vessels, which occur in this fabric, was recovered (G347) and most probably dates to the 4th century. Fragments of cooking pot were more common but were all recovered as residual finds within the site clearance and machining horizon (G172) and are thus not located to any particular plot.

A total of three sherds of South Gaulish samian ware (fabric 43.1) were recovered. These were in the form of identifiable body sherds of a sizeable Dragendorff 30 cylindrical bowl dating from AD 50–110 (Webster 1996), but from a late Roman context (G349), and a decorated sherd of a Dragendorff 29 with a rope cordon and trifid above a base ring, dating from AD 50–85 and therefore residual within a medieval context (1787; G359; Plot 13).

The fine wares were dominated by Central Gaulish samian (fabric 43.2), of which 13 sherds were identified, making this ware more heavily represented within the assemblage than would normally be expected. Three rim fragments of Dragendorff 31 bowls were present in Roman-dated contexts (G346: context 2039; G347: context 2046) and as residual material (G202; Plot 14). All were probably of later 2nd-century date though use possibly continued into the early 3rd century. A further form 31 sherd was residual within a medieval feature (1487; Plot 14). Two examples of Dragendorff form 33 were also present, one as residual material (G353; Plot 13) but the other within a Period 1 context (G346: context 2039). These dated respectively from AD 120–200 and to the late 2nd century. Two fragments of Dragendorff 37 decorated bowls were also recovered along with a Dragendorff 31/31r bowl (G345: context 2038), and these date from AD 160–200.

East Gaulish samian (fabric 43.3) was represented by the rim of an unusual Dragendorff 40 cup dating from the late 2nd to early 3rd century, also from the modern site clearance (G172), while a Dragendorff 45 form of similar date was also present residually in a medieval context (Plot 13; G353). Three sherds of Nene Valley ware (fabric 28) were recovered (Perrin 1999: type 211); one was a very rare fragment of castor box lid in the form of the upper rim carination, and is closely dateable to the late 3rd to 4th century (G349). Lastly, a body sherd of Oxford ware (fabric 29) was also recovered from the modern clearance (G172).

5.2.2 Discussion

This is an unusual assemblage of Roman pottery, the small size making any conclusions tentative, but the balance of samian to other fabrics is unusual, as is the Castor box in Nene Valley ware. Interpretation must take into account the fact that pottery was incorporated into the construction levels of a Roman road, and may have been brought to the area from elsewhere in the settlement, possibly from higher status buildings to the east of the site.

A comparatively low level of residual material was recovered, with only about 20 sherds from post-Roman contexts, plus possibly some of those from the Roman road surface (G349, which is discussed below). This relative paucity of residual material probably reflects the thick accumulation of medieval alluvial deposits overlying Roman deposits as observed within the deep area of excavation on Plot 13 (G345–G349), which may indicate that, across much of the site, Roman horizons remain relatively undisturbed by later activity due to the protective effect of this deep alluvial accumulation.

The association of a metalled surface considered to represent a road (G349) with large fragments of distinctive 4th-century Roman pottery is also of considerable interest. Despite the presence of several probably intrusive sherds of medieval pottery, this 4th-century material may indicate disuse of the road at this period. Of similar interest is that the road sealed distinct late 2nd to 3rd-century contexts, providing a *terminus post quem* (earliest possible date) for the construction of the road. Together these provide an important indication of the potential for the survival of Roman occupation deposits of the late 2nd century onwards within this area of Worcester.

5.3 Medieval and medieval/early post-medieval pottery
Laura Griffin

A total of 2,428 sherds of medieval pottery (weighing 39.36kg) and 609 sherds of medieval/early post-medieval pottery (weighing 23.15kg) were recovered, accounting for 37% of the total pottery assemblage retrieved from the site. These were recovered and recorded according to the procedures described above (Chapter 3.2.5). Locally produced medieval and early post-medieval material was combined into one report due to a number of oxidised glazed Malvernian ware forms, which cross the two periods.

The largest proportion of the medieval and medieval/early post-medieval assemblage, totalling 1,799 sherds weighing 30.12kg, derived from Period 2 (medieval) deposits and dated to the 10th–15th century. A further 776 sherds were recovered from Period 3 deposits dating from the end of Period 2 through to about 1700. The remaining medieval material (251 sherds) was residual within Period 4 (18th-century) and Period 5 (19th and 20th-century) deposits, or was recovered either as unstratified sherds or from deposits which could not be securely phased. The level of preservation differed across the site, ranging from small, highly abraded residual fragments to well-preserved sizeable sherds. Identifiable sherds indicated a date range from the 10th–mid 17th centuries.

The assemblage was of a standard domestic nature with a varied and interesting range of forms and fabrics identified. As expected, the vast majority of the assemblage consisted of locally produced Worcester-type (fabrics 55 and 64.1) and Malvernian wares (fabrics 53, 56 and 69). However, a variety of other fabrics were represented in smaller number, including regional, non-regional and imported wares (Table 5.3).

5.3.1 Analysis

Locally and regionally produced wares

The assemblage was dominated by locally produced wares, primarily of Worcester-type and Malvernian fabrics. In total, 89% by count of the medieval and early post-medieval assemblage comprised five local

Table 5.3: Quantification of the medieval and early post-medieval pottery by fabric type (after Hurst and Rees 1992)

Fabric	Fabric common name	Total sherds	Weight (g)
46.2	Glazed Stamford-type ware	2	26
48	Stafford-type ware	7	95
53	Early glazed Malvernian ware	9	182
55	Unglazed Worcester-type ware	912	12042
56	Unglazed Malvernian ware	385	7321
57	Cotswolds unglazed ware	7	39
57.1	Cotswolds unglazed ware	71	788
58	Sandy limestone-tempered ware	2	58
62	Deritend-type ware	8	86
63	Brill/Boarstall ware	8	151
64.1	Glazed Worcester-type sandy ware	262	4631
64.2	Buff sandy ware	26	206
64.3	Green-glazed white ware	14	135
65	Minety-type ware	21	312
66	Herefordshire glazed fine micaceous ware	8	114
A7c	Herefordshire fine ware	1	19
A7d	Herefordshire ware	8	195
69	Oxidized glazed Malvernian ware	1141	32109
70.1	Tudor green ware	11	23
70.2	Southern border ware	3	5
71	Micaceous glazed ware	1	14
79	Merida-type ware	1	9
120	Saintonge ware	3	132
141	Oxfordshire Y-type ware	1	7
143	Ham Green ware	5	28
143.1	Ham Green type A	1	1
143.2	Ham Green type B	6	81
99	Miscellaneous medieval wares	113	3708
Totals		3037	62,517

fabric types (Table 5.3): unglazed Worcester-type ware (fabric 55), unglazed Malvernian ware (fabric 56), glazed Worcester-type sandy ware (fabric 64.1), early glazed Malvernian ware (fabric 53) and oxidised glazed Malvernian ware (fabric 69).

A further 3% of the assemblage consisted of sherds of three wares commonly categorised as regional: Cotswolds unglazed ware (fabrics 57 and 57.1), sandy limestone-tempered ware (fabric 58) and Ham Green ware (fabrics 143, 143.1 and 143.2). All of these fabric types have been described and dated by Hurst and Rees (1992) within the pottery report for the excavations at Upwich, Droitwich (Lentowicz 1997), and discussed at length by Bryant (2004) within the medieval pottery report for Deansway, Worcester. Comparison with these sites shows that Newport Street produced a standard range of forms within these fabric groups.

Other comparisons for this material can be made with the assemblages excavated from Friar Street and City Arcade, Worcester (Griffin 2002a; Griffin *et al.* 2004), with which many similarities in composition of the assemblage can be noted.

Sherds of Worcester-type cooking-pot fabric (fabric 55) formed the largest proportion of these sherds (30% by count) of the medieval/early post-medieval pottery. Although this fabric is most commonly reduced, a small number of oxidised sherds were also identified. The assemblage displayed a range of common cooking-pot forms dating from between the 12th–mid 14th centuries that could be paralleled with types 1, 2 and 3 from the Deansway assemblage (Bryant 2004). A large number of the sherds displayed sooting, carbonised fat deposits and blackening on the surfaces, and a small number had internal residues commonly associated with cooking pots. By far the most commonly identified form was type 3, everted-rim cooking pots with folded rims, which can be dated to between the 13th and mid 14th centuries. Three of these were decorated with roughly incised wavy lines running around the body. Three possible pitcher sherds (Deansway type 7) were also identified, although in general these were too small to make a definitive identification. A further two sherds with a very coarse and highly burnt appearance were tentatively identified as coming from a crucible form, although once more they were not big enough to be certain.

A total of 385 sherds of unglazed Malvernian ware cooking-pot fabric (fabric 56) was identified, forming 13% by count of the medieval/early post-medieval assemblage. Based on the proportions recovered from other similar assemblages in Worcester, this would appear to be quite high (Victoria Bryant, pers. comm.). However, due to the high level of residuality and the fact that in many parts of the site excavation was limited to later medieval and later contexts, it is likely that the relative proportions of earlier material are skewed. All rim sherds could be identified as deriving from cooking pots covering the range of commonly found forms, from everted upright rims to those with short everted folded rims (Deansway types 1, 2, 3 and 4). As with the Worcester-type cooking pots, the vast majority of sherds exhibited soot and carbonised deposits on the exterior surface, indicating use as cooking vessels. Just one sherd was decorated, with an applied, thumbed strip typical of this fabric type. Vessels of this fabric commonly date from the late 12th century onwards (Bryant 2004), peaking in the 13th century. This peak has also been observed in material from deposits in Droitwich where a high percentage of vessels of this fabric could be closely dated to between 1264–5 (Hurst 1992a). A similar pattern is clearly reflected in the assemblage from Newport Street.

Glazed Worcester-type sandy wares (fabric 64.1) formed 9% by count of the medieval assemblage, with a large proportion of the sherds being small, undiagnostic fragments. Of those sherds that were identifiable, there was a roughly equal division between tripod pitcher (Deansway types 1 and 3) and jug forms (Deansway type 4). The pitcher forms were of 12th to mid 13th-century date and pre-dated the jugs, which could all be dated to between the 13th and 14th centuries. Only two other forms were noted in this fabric and consisted of a dripping dish (Deansway type 7) and a bowl (Deansway type 8), both of 14th-century date. As at other assemblages of this date from Worcester, such as Friar Street (Griffin 2002a), City Arcade (Griffin *et al.* 2004) and Deansway (Bryant 2004), the occurrence of vessels of this fabric is far less frequent than those of unglazed Worcester-type (fabric 55). This is thought to be due in part to the specialised function of these fineware vessels and possibly that they were more expensive to purchase (Morris 1980, 224). All decorated sherds had a dark green glaze, in some cases speckled, characteristic of vessels in this fabric. Decorated sherds displayed stamped, roller-stamped, applied strips or rilling patterns, or various combinations of each. All handles were of strap form, the majority with stabbed decoration down the length.

Only nine sherds were identified as early glazed Malvernian ware (fabric 53). This is extremely uncommon in Worcester, with only a few sherds identified previously at Deansway (Bryant 2004) and City Arcade (Griffin *et al.* 2004). The only form known in this fabric is a tripod pitcher, which can be dated to between the late 12th and mid 13th centuries. All sherds were characteristic of this fabric type, being handmade with an orange-brown surface and thin, patchy yellow-green glaze. Four sherds (from contexts 935, 1897, 2755 and 2802) displayed decoration, including roller-stamped diamond patterns, incised diagonal lines and zig-zags.

Oxidised glazed Malvernian ware (fabric 69) accounted for 38% of the medieval/early medieval pottery assemblage but, as seen from other excavated sites in Worcester, formed the greater part of the late 15th to early 17th-century assemblage. The general date range for vessels of this fabric runs from the later 13th century until around the mid 17th century. A large proportion of sherds were diagnostic with a wide range of forms present (Fig. 5.6, 2–13), the most common being a large jar/bunghole jar form (Deansway type 8), which formed 26% of identified forms in this fabric type. A number of these examples were large with tripod feet and appear to have had two strap handles rather than the single handle noted on smaller jars of the same type. The majority were decorated with a thin, patchy glaze, sometimes to both surfaces but more commonly to one, and which ranged from dark green to green speckled to greenish brown in colour. Rim sherds were commonly decorated around the neck, often in the form of cow toe-bone impressions, as identified from the kiln site at Hanley Swan, Worcestershire (Hurst 1994, fig. 6). Other examples had fingertip impressions and five sherds had a 'rope' style similar to an example from Sidbury, Worcester (Morris 1980, fig. 76, TV 190). Further decoration was noted on a small number of sherds, including two strap handles with an 'X' stamped at the join to the vessel body (Plot 14; contexts 933 and 1273), three deep-finger impressions above a tripod foot (Plot 2; G14: context 19; Fig. 5.6, 7) and the most elaborate taking the form of a series of applied strips radiating from the bunghole itself (Plot 14: context 899).

In addition to the jar/bunghole jar examples, a further ten form types were present, spanning the whole production period of the ware. The earliest of these were jug forms, including baluster and rounded forms. The earliest of these (Deansway type 2) date from the mid 13th to 14th centuries, whilst the baluster and rounded forms (Deansway types 3 and 4) are of slightly later production, ranging from the 14th to 15th centuries. Remaining diagnostic sherds were of 15th-century date onwards and consisted of dripping-dish, pipkin/skillet, jar/pipkin, flared bowl, lid, cup and chafing dish forms (Deansway types 5, 7, 9, 10, 11 and 12). The dripping-dish sherds were of standard type, with the majority displaying heavy external sooting and/or evidence of burning, attesting to their function of collecting juices underneath a spit (Bryant 2004, 302). However, a small number (from contexts 936, 1045 and 2659) were sooted across breaks, perhaps indicating that they broke during use. This form is generally dated to the 15th to 16th centuries.

Many of the pipkin/skillet and jar/pipkin sherds also had heavy sooting/carbonised deposits on their external surfaces. Both forms performed a similar function, being most commonly used for cooking. All sherds were glazed internally, another characteristic of both form types. Almost identical forms were identified at the kiln site in Hanley Swan, Worcestershire (Hurst 1994, fig. 6).

Flared bowls accounted for 11% of identified forms within fabric 69. All were from types identified at Deansway (Bryant 2004, fig. 187) and Hanley Swan (Hurst 1994, fig. 6), and are generally thought to date between the late 15th and mid 17th centuries. The majority displayed internal glazing but a small number were also glazed externally. In contrast to the assemblage from Deansway, only a small number of sherds displayed evidence of external burning and/or sooting, and therefore it would appear that this type of vessel was not generally used in the cooking of foodstuffs at Newport Street. The level of sooting on flared bowls from other sites has prompted the suggestion that they may have been used to make cream (Vince 1984, vol. 2, 468).

Five lids were present within the assemblage, all of the flat-topped form identified at Deansway (Bryant 2004, fig. 188.3). One, a residual find, was complete and could feasibly have been used either as a lid or a small, shallow dish (Plot 4: context 755; Fig. 5.6, 9). Three were decorated with a thin greenish yellow glaze to the exterior, the remaining sherds were unglazed. It is thought that these lids were used to cover jars or cauldrons, and sooting/burning seen on three examples would appear to confirm this. All were residual except for one from context 899 (Plot 14; G268), which could be dated to the late 16th century, fitting into the established pattern seen at both Gloucester (Vince 1977, 272) and Deansway (Bryant 2004, 306).

A small but interesting group of cups was identified within the assemblage, including near-complete examples (Fig. 5.6, 10 and 11). All could be dated to between the late 15th and 16th centuries but once more, the majority were residual within contexts of later post-medieval date. All were wheelmade and copies of forms commonly seen in other fabrics. One such copy was that of a lobed cup (Plot 2; context 691), a form commonly associated with Tudor Green ware (fabric 70.1). Decoration commonly consisted of glaze to both surfaces and in some cases this was embellished with applied white-clay pellets in imitation of Cistercian-ware cups that were popular during this period. The best example is a near-complete vessel elaborately decorated with clay pellets in a zig-zag band running around the body and a further band of stamped pattern beneath it (Plot 14; G268: context 933; Fig. 5.6, 11).

The final form type recognised within this group was that of chafing dishes (Fig. 5.6, 12 and 13). All were glazed and some were decorated with frilled rims and/or flanges. This form type can be dated to the late 16th to 17th century.

In addition to the local wares, three fabric types considered to be of regional production were also identified, but in much smaller quantities. These were Cotswolds unglazed ware (fabrics 57 and 57.1), sandy limestone-tempered ware (fabric 58) and Ham Green ware (fabrics 143, 143.1 and 143.2).

A total of 78 sherds of Cotswolds unglazed ware was identified, seven of which were of the variant fabric containing ironstone. The majority of sherds were sooted, indicating use over the fire. Diagnostic sherds were all of this variant fabric and included a number which could be identified as coming from four rounded jars with an everted rim and convex base (Deansway type 1), dateable to between the 10th to early 11th century. Another 47 sherds were found to be from a single vessel of an unusual form which closely resembled that of unglazed Malvernian cooking pots commonly dated to between the 13th and 14th centuries (Plot 13; G122: context 1702; Fig. 5.6, 15). This challenges the currently accepted date range for the supply and use of vessels of Cotswolds manufacture in Worcestershire, which hitherto was thought to end in the early 12th century (Bryant 2004, 309).

Just two sherds of sandy limestone-tempered ware (fabric 58) were identified, one from a pit fill (Plot 13; G138: context 1425), the other unstratified. Both were undiagnostic but, when complete, these vessels are commonly of the same form as the Cotswolds unglazed ware cooking pots and therefore are thought to be similarly dated to the mid 11th to 12th century. Although the source of this fabric is unknown, the forms present and visual examination of the fabric suggests it was to the south-east of Worcester (Bryant 2004, 309).

Ham Green ware amounted to 12 sherds, one of which could be identified as being of type A (fabric 143.1) and six as of type B (fabric 143.2). The remaining sherds were too fragmentary to consign to a specific type. Identifiable forms consisted of jugs, indicating a date range of late 12th to mid 13th century for sherds of this fabric. All sherds were glazed, ranging in colour from dark green to a lighter yellowish green (Bryant 2004, 310), with three examples also having decoration in the form of applied strips.

Non-regional wares

Non-regional wares formed just 4% of the medieval pottery assemblage analysed (119 sherds; Table 5.3). These included 14 fabric types: glazed Stamford-type ware (fabric 46.2), Stafford-type ware (fabric 48), Deritend-type ware (fabric 62), Brill/Boarstall ware (fabric 63), Buff sandy wares (fabric 64.2), green-glazed white ware (fabric 64.3), Minety-type ware (fabric 65), Herefordshire glazed fine micaceous ware (fabric 66), Southern white wares, more commonly known as Tudor green (fabric 70.1) and Southern border ware (fabric 70.2), micaceous glazed ware (fabric 71), Oxfordshire Y-type ware (fabric 141) and Herefordshire fabrics A7c and d. The latter two fabrics have not previously been recorded within the Worcestershire fabric-type series and the Herefordshire fabric descriptions are used (Vince 1985).

Two sherds of glazed Stamford-type ware (fabric 46.2) were retrieved from the site, both were residual (Plot 14: contexts 837 and 1473). Both had a grey fabric and an external pale olive-green glaze characteristic of this ware type. One sherd was diagnostic (context 837; Fig. 5.6, 16) and could be identified as coming from the rim of a rounded jar similar in form to one found at Deansway which dated to the 10th to 11th century (Bryant 2004, fig. 193.3).

Other pottery of earlier medieval date consisted of seven sherds of Stafford-type ware (fabric 48; Plot 14: context 900; Plot 13: context 1841; and Plot 5: context 2210), which represented three rounded jars, the most common form type seen in on sites in Worcestershire. The sherds from context 1841 also displayed roller-stamped decoration in a diamond pattern around the shoulder, which is typical of this ware (Fig. 5.6, 17). Two of the vessels displayed sooting on the exterior, indicating use as cooking vessels. This form is generally considered to date between the early 10th and late 11th century in this area. However, evidence from Deansway indicated that vessels of this type might have been used from the late 9th century onwards (Bryant 2004, 316). Unfortunately the sherds from Newport Street cannot confirm this dating, due to all being residual in contexts of 11th to 12th-century date or later.

All remaining non-regional wares were of 13th-century date or later. A total of eight sherds of Deritend-type ware were identified amongst the assemblage (fabric 62). This type of pottery is thought to have been produced in the Deritend area of Birmingham, although it is not certain that material found there is actually kiln waste and therefore may have been made elsewhere (Bryant 2004, 317). Despite having a wide distribution covering most of the West Midlands, this type of pottery has only been previously identified in Worcester within the material from Deansway (ibid., 316). All material identified from both Newport Street and Deansway is from jug forms decorated with white painted and applied strips typical of this fabric type. Dating of non-residual sherds within the assemblage supported the 13th to 14th-century date range commonly given to this ware.

A total of eight sherds of Brill/Boarstall ware was identified (fabric 63; from Plot 2, G8: context 667 and G35: context 1522; from Plot 10, G108: context 1236; from Plot 13, G122: context 1225; and from Plot 14, G234: context 1251 and G201: context 1341). Decoration, which primarily consists of a green glaze with applied vertical strips of a lustrous reddish brown colour, suggests that all but one sherd comes from biconical jug forms, commonly dated to between the mid to late 13th century. The remaining sherd (context 1522) appears to be from a bunghole vessel dating to the 15th to 16th century. The presence of such a late sherd of this manufacture is unusual in Worcester but unfortunately, the sherd is residual within a context of 18th-century date and therefore the dating cannot be further tightened. This type of pottery was produced in Buckinghamshire. Although principally made for the Oxford market (McCarthy and Brooks 1988, 292–4), small numbers of vessels appear to have reached Worcestershire with sherds previously identified in Droitwich (Hurst 1992a), Evesham (Jones 2001) and the Deansway (Bryant 2004) and Friar Street (Griffin 2002a) sites in Worcester.

Twenty-five sherds of buff sandy ware (fabric 64.2) were identified, all with a patchy, green exterior glaze characteristic of this fabric. Other decoration is rare due to the small size of the majority of sherds, but includes incised lines, cordons and rilling. Evidence from Deansway (Bryant 2004, 316) and City Arcade (Griffin et al. 2004, 81), indicates that the vast majority of sherds of this fabric comes from jug forms and this is supported by the three diagnostic sherds identified within this group (Plot 2, G8: context 667; Plot 5, G44: context 2186; Plot 14, G247: context 900). Macroscopic comparison with sherds from sites within Staffordshire indicates that this fabric is most likely to have been produced within that region. More specifically, the products of a later medieval kiln site excavated in 2000 at the Burslem Art School, Stoke-on-Trent, appear to be of this fabric (J. Goodwin, pers. comm.) and may therefore provide a source for earlier material as well. Sherds of this fabric type have generally been dated to the 13th to 14th century and the non-residual sherds within this assemblage would appear to support that. No sherds of the unglazed version of this fabric were recovered from the site.

Fourteen sherds of green-glazed white ware (fabric 64.3) were identified. Diagnostic sherds were primarily from jug forms and included the base from a baluster jug (Plot 13; G148: context 1397; Fig. 5.6, 18) almost identical to one identified within the assemblage from Deansway (Bryant 2004, fig.198.6). In addition, a small sherd from a cup form, which appeared to be imitating that of Tudor Green ware, was retrieved from context 2659. Decoration in the form of a bright green glaze, occasionally speckled, was seen on all sherds. A small number of sherds also displayed incised wavy lines, applied thumbed strips and rilling. Very few sherds of this fabric have been identified from Worcester with just 24 sherds from the entire Deansway assemblage (ibid., 322). Its source is unknown but a date range of the 13th to 14th century has been indicated by stratified sherds from City Arcade (Griffin *et al.* 2004), Friar Street (Griffin 2002a) and Deansway (Bryant 2004). However, the presence of a cup sherd within this assemblage would push this range into at least the 15th or possibly early 16th century.

Minety-type ware (fabric 65) within the assemblage consisted of 21 sherds, none of which were residual. Sherds came from four contexts all within Plot 13 (G140: context 1304; G148: context 1362; G136: context 1372; and G131: context 1594). These appear to represent four individual vessels, all of which were identified as pitchers of early to mid 12th-century date. All displayed decoration typical of this ware type, having horizontal wavy combed lines covered by an olive-green glaze.

Four fabric types from Herefordshire (fabrics 66, 71 and A7c and A7d) were present within the medieval/early post-medieval assemblage. A total of eight sherds of Herefordshire glazed fine micaceous ware (fabric 66) were identified. This is a distinctive ware having a thick white slip underneath a clear or copper-flecked glaze. Additional decoration consisted of vertical applied strips fired to a brown colour. All are most likely to come from jugs, the most common form, accounting for 95% of forms identified in this fabric in Hereford where this fabric is abundant (Vince 1985, 43). This ware was produced between the 13th and 16th centuries, but as is the case at Deansway (Bryant 2004, 312), the material from this site appears to be of 14th to 15th-century date.

Just one sherd of micaceous glazed ware (fabric 71; context 1861) could be attributed to the late medieval/early post-medieval period and was identified as coming from a cup, which could be dated between the late 15th and 16th centuries. As typical of this fabric type, it was decorated with a dark brownish green mottled glaze to both surfaces. Small quantities of this fabric have previously been identified at Deansway (Bryant 2004, 313) and Droitwich (Hurst 1992a).

Herefordshire fabric A7c is very similar in composition to fabric 71, and is also mainly associated with cup forms (Vince 1985, 44). A single handle (Plot 11; G302: context 1221) was the only sherd of this fabric identified and is of the same late 15th to 16th-century date range as the micaceous glazed ware.

Eight sherds of Herefordshire fabric A7d were identified, all with diagnostic sherds from vessels of late medieval/early post-medieval date. These consisted of two conjoined sherds from a single chafing dish found in two different plots (contexts 2137 and 2626) and two flared bowls from Plot 2 deposits (G14: context 278; and G12: context 562). Both forms are generally dated between the 16th and 17th centuries, a range that fits well with that given to this fabric type in Hereford, where it forms around 1% of assemblages from the 16th century but becomes far more common in the 17th century (Vince 1985, 44). Decoration on all sherds consisted of a greenish brown glaze and the chafing dish was an extremely elaborate example with pierced holes and crosses, and a turreted rim with an incised zig-zag pattern running around the top (Fig. 5.7, 19). An almost identical example was found in oxidised glazed Malvernian ware at Deansway (Bryant 2004, fig. 188.12).

Southern white wares fell into two groups: Tudor Green ware (fabric 70.1) and Southern border ware (fabric 70.2). Eleven of these sherds were identified as being of the former, with diagnostic sherds coming from cup forms (Plot 14; G282: context 896 and G268: contexts 899 and 933; Plot 3, context 2601). Two of these were lobed cups characteristic of this fabric type and all had a fine, bright green glaze which could be dated to between the late 15th to 16th centuries. Just three sherds were identified as Southern border ware all small and undiagnostic (Plot 14, G233: context 1383; Plot 13, G131: context 1644). All are thought to have a similar date to the Tudor Green ware. Sherds of both fabrics are regularly identified in small quantities on sites in this region (Bryant 2004, 338).

A single body sherd of Oxford Y-type ware was identified within the assemblage (Plot 5; context 2093). It had a thin external yellowish green glaze typical of this fabric type and could be dated to the 12th to 13th centuries. Only one other sherd of this fabric has so far been identified in Worcestershire and this was residual within a 15th-century deposit at Deansway (Bryant 2004, 320).

Imported wares

Four sherds of imported pottery were identified, three of Saintonge ware (fabric 120) and one of Merida-type ware (fabric 79).

The Saintonge ware consisted of three sherds from two different vessels. The first was a small rim fragment from a bridge-spouted jug, typical of this ware type (Plot 13; G151: context 1188; Fig. 5.7, 20). It was decorated with painted copper and manganese lines covered with a thin amber glaze and is dated to the late 13th century, based on similar examples from Cuckoo Lane, Southampton (Platt and Coleman-Smith 1975, fig. 185.1022) The remaining two sherds were adjoining and from the handle of a chafing dish (Plot 3, context 2802; Fig. 5.7, 21). It was decorated with bright green and yellow glaze with lines of stabbed pattern just above the handle, and is dated to between the 16th and early 17th century based on an example found at Deansway (Type 120.4) and other parallels published by Hurst *et al.* (1986, figs 35–36). Saintonge ware has been identified in small amounts on a number of sites in Worcester and the surrounding county (Barton 1968; Morris 1980; Bryant 2004). It is thought to be the most widely distributed imported ware in medieval Britain (Brown 1999; Bryant 2004).

The single sherd of Merida-type ware (Plot 14; G247: context 900; Fig. 5.7, 22) came from the rim of a small jug of similar form to one found in Plymouth (Hurst *et al.* 1986, fig. 31.87) which is dated to between 1550 and 1650. Only a small number of sherds of this fabric have been previously found in Worcester. It is generally found at coastal ports and only occasionally further inland (Bryant 2004, 324).

Unidentified wares

A total of 113 sherds could not be paralleled with any of the fabric types within the type series and are thought to be regional imports from surrounding counties. These sherds have all been grouped as fabric 99, miscellaneous medieval wares. The majority are one-off body fragments but a small number are larger, adjoining and/or diagnostic and can be identified as being of particular vessel types and dated accordingly. In particular, sherds from four vessels are considered interesting enough to warrant illustration and description.

The first consisted of 23 sherds from an unusual form most resembling a frying pan (Plot 13; context 1567; Fig. 5.7, 23). It had a large, flat handle which joined at the rim, was of large diameter and was sooted on the underside, indicating use over a fire. The fabric was also of note being reduced to black in colour and containing a range of coarse inclusions including quartz and grog.

Two adjoining sherds from different contexts (Plot 14; context 900 and context 1064) and thought to be from a jug were of note, as it appeared to have been used for a purpose other than that intended (Fig. 5.7, 24). The vessel form is reminiscent of small jugs seen in stoneware fabrics, but this fabric is earthenware and very roughly formed with deep rills on the internal surface. There is a small patch of speckled green glaze towards the break and a crude handle scar, and there is external sooting around the foot and up one side. However, the most striking feature of this vessel is a large hole deliberately chipped out of the base. The purpose of this hole, and whether the sooting resulted from a secondary use relating to it, is unknown but it is possible that it may have been reused as an alembic (used in distilling). Associated pottery indicated a 15th to 16th-century date for this vessel.

Remaining sherds of note in this category consisted of the rim of a large jar/bunghole jar (Plot 13; context 1320; Fig. 5.7, 25) of late 15th to 16th-century date, and a body sherd of unknown medieval date, displaying distinctive decoration (Plot 14; context 1026; Fig. 5.7, 26). The rim sherd was highly fired and decorated with a distinctive dark green internal glaze with overlapping thumb impressions around the outside of the rim. The body sherd appeared handmade with a roughly finished, uneven interior surface and was highly decorated with an incised zig-zag and stamped 'scale-like' pattern covered by a dark green glaze.

Catalogue of the illustrated medieval pottery (Figs 5.6 and 5.7)

1 Cooking pot in unglazed Malvernian ware (fabric 56), cf Deansway type 56.3 (mid to late 13th century). Plot 13; G161: context 1072

2 Decoration from a jug in oxidised glazed Malvernian ware (fabric 69), no identified parallels (14th to 15th century). Plot 14; G282: context 823

3 Pipkin/skillet in oxidised glazed Malvernian ware (fabric 69), cf Deansway type 69.6 (15th to 16th century). Plot 14; G268: context 933

4 Jar/pipkin in oxidised glazed Malvernian ware (fabric 69), cf Deansway type 69.7 (Late 15th to 16th century). Plot 9; G101: context 1861

5 Jar/bunghole jar in oxidised glazed Malvernian ware (fabric 69), cf Morris 1980, TV 190 (15th to 16th century). Plot 5; G46: context 2133

6 Bunghole jar in oxidised glazed Malvernian ware (fabric 69), cf Deansway type 69.8 (late 15th to 16th century). Plot 14; G249: context 1273

7 Foot from a jar/bunghole jar in oxidised glazed Malvernian ware (fabric 69), cf Deansway 69.8 (Late 15th to 16th century). Plot 2; G14: context 19

8 Lid in oxidised glazed Malvernian ware (fabric 69), cf Deansway type 69.10, (15th to 16th century). All plots; G172 (machining horizon)

9 Lid or small dish in oxidised glazed Malvernian ware (fabric 69), cf Deansway type 69.10 (15th to 16th century). Plot 4; G36: context 755

10 Cup in oxidised glazed Malvernian ware (fabric 69), cf Deansway type 69.11 (Late 15th to 16th century). Plot 7; G70; context 1140

11 Cup in oxidised glazed Malvernian ware (fabric 69), cf Deansway type 69.11 (Late 15th to 16th century). Plot 14; G268: context 933

12 Chafing dish in oxidised glazed Malvernian ware (fabric 69), cf Deansway type 69.12 (Late 16th to 17th century). Plot 6; G90: context 1573

13 Chafing dish in oxidised glazed Malvernian ware (fabric 69), cf Deansway type 69.12 (Early 16th to 17th century). Plot 3; G63: context 2329

14 Jar in Cotswolds unglazed ware (fabric 57.1), cf Deansway type 57.1.1 (10th to early 11th century). Plot 3; G56: context 2770

15 Jar in Cotswolds unglazed ware (fabric 57.1), no identified parallels (?12th to early 13th century). Plot 13; G122: context 1702

16 Rounded jar in glazed Stamford-type ware (fabric 46.2), cf Deansway fig.193.3 (10th to 11th century). Plot 14; G268: context 837

17 Jar in Stafford-type ware (fabric 48), cf Deansway fig. 194.8 and 9 (Late 9th to 11th century). Plot 13; G354: context 1841

18 Baluster jug in green-glazed white ware (fabric 64.3), cf Deansway fig. 198.6 (13th to 14th century). Plot 13; G148: context 1397

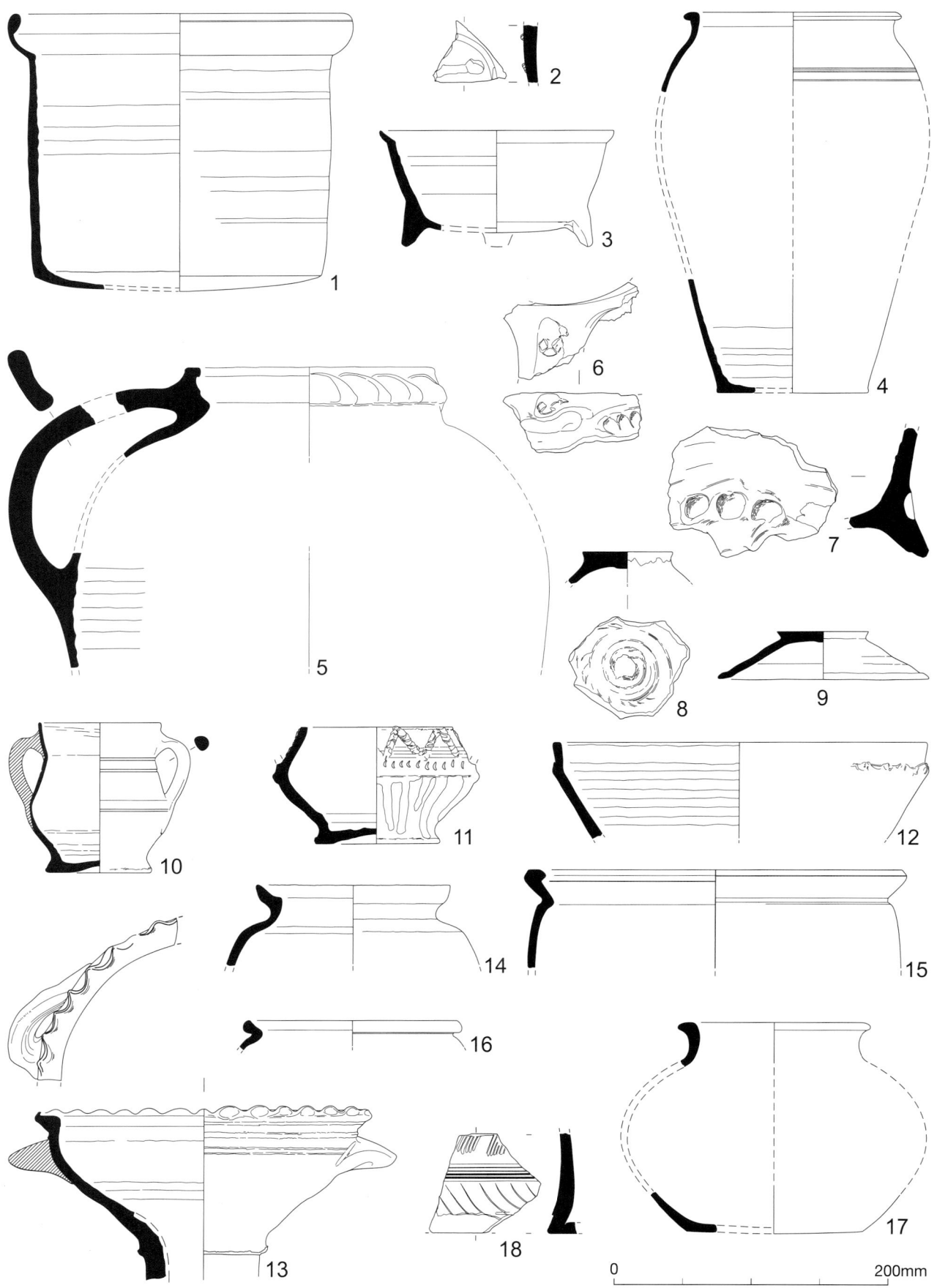

Fig. 5.6 Medieval pottery (Nos 1–18). Scale 1:4

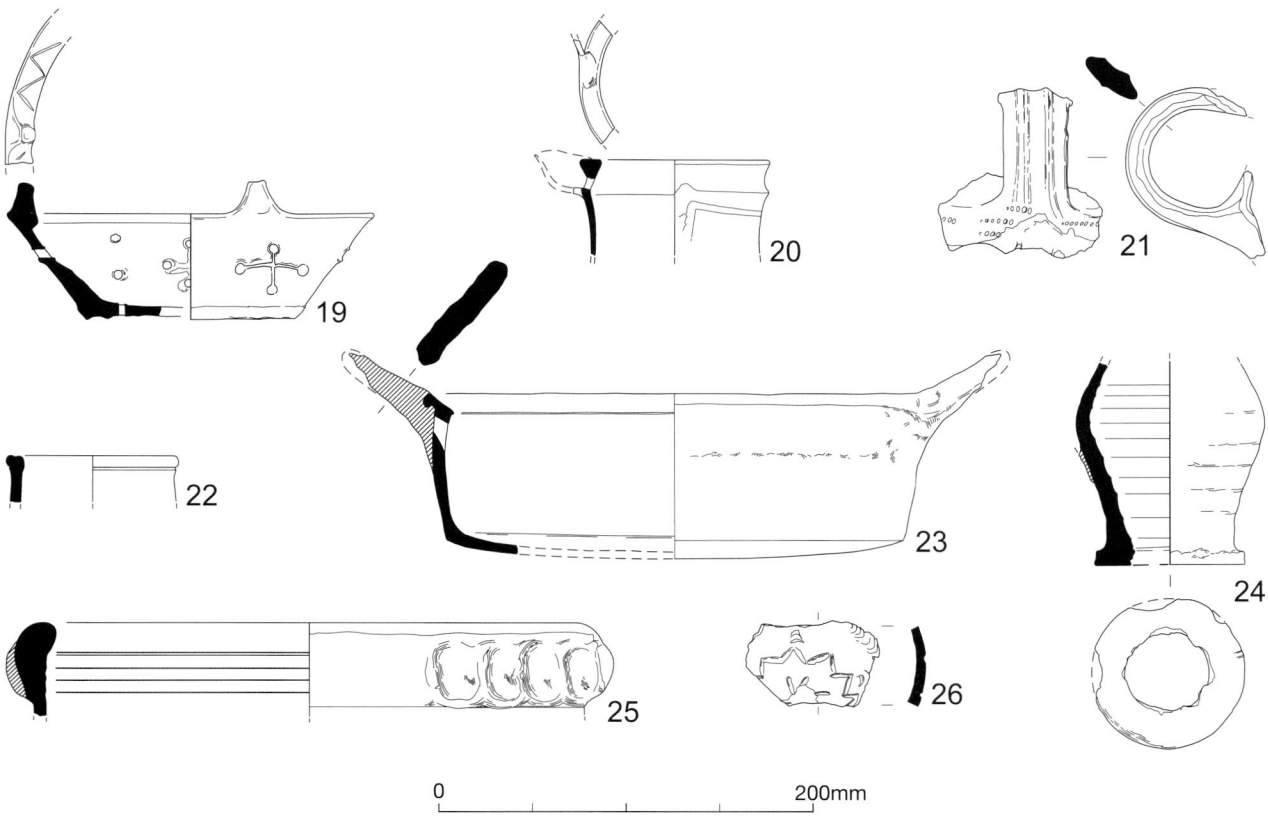

Fig. 5.7 Medieval pottery (Nos 19–26). Scale 1:4

19 Chafing dish in Herefordshire ware (fabric A7d), no identified parallels, cf Deansway fig. 188.12 (16th to 17th century). Plot 5; context 2137 (Unassigned)

20 Bridge-spouted jug in Saintonge ware (fabric 120), cf Platt and Coleman-Smith 1975, fig. 185.1022 (Late 13th century). Plot 13; G151: context 1188

21 Handle from a chafing dish in Saintonge ware (fabric 120), cf Deansway type 120.4 (16th to early 17th century). Plot 3; context 2802 (finds probably associated with cellar G55)

22 Jug in Merida-type ware (fabric 79), cf Hurst 1986, fig. 31.87 (1550–1650). Plot 14; G247: context 900

23 Frying pan in unidentified fabric type ('fabric 99'), no identified parallels (Late 11th to mid 14th century). Plot 13; G124: context 1567

24 Jar or jug in unidentified fabric type ('fabric 99'), no identified parallels (unknown date). Plot 14; G247: contexts 900 and 1064

25 Jar/bunghole jar in unidentified fabric type ('fabric 99'), cf Deansway type 69.8 (Late 15th to 16th century). Plot 13; G153: context 1320

26 Body sherd with green glaze and incised decoration of unidentified fabric type ('fabric 99'), no identified parallels (unknown date). Plot 14; G286: context 1026

5.3.2 Discussion (by period)

Period 1: Roman

A total of five sherds of medieval pottery were identified as intrusive within contexts of Roman date. These came from contexts 1897 (Plot 13) and 2744 (Plot 3) which were identified as a compact gravel surface and a road surface respectively. The most logical explanation for the presence of these sherds is that they originally came from the layers directly above these surfaces but over time had become embedded into the very top of them.

Period 2: medieval

The majority of medieval pottery came from contexts dated to this period, totalling 1667 sherds and weighing 26.3kg. Locally produced wares dominate, as would be expected between the 12th and 14th centuries, but are gradually joined by wares from further afield with the widest range identified from contexts dated between the late 14th and 15th centuries (Period 2.4).

Quantification of the unglazed Worcester-type ware (fabric 55) is of particular interest as it clearly illustrates the peak and demise of this industry between the later 11th and mid 14th centuries. Vessels of this ware can first be seen in small quantities in Period 2.2 but quickly rise in number to dominate the material from Periods 2.3.1 and 2.3.2, where it accounts for 95% and 73% of the assemblages respectively. However, by Period 2.4, which dates to the 14th century, sherds of this fabric form only 26% of the group, having been overtaken by unglazed Malvernian wares (fabric 56) which total 39% and continue to dominate at a similar frequency into Period 2.5, whilst the proportion of unglazed Worcester-type ware tails off to just 4%, signalling the end of the industry. A similar pattern can be seen amongst the glazed Worcester-type and Malvernian wares, although on a smaller scale due to fewer glazed than coarse vessels having been used during this period.

By far the largest proportion of medieval pottery came from Plot 13, with 1269 sherds recovered, including the earliest stratified material identified from contexts assigned to Period 2.2. These consisted of nine sherds from an extensive dumped deposit (G354: context 1841) and an alluvial deposit below it (G353: context 1877), which was dated to between the 11th and 12th centuries. Fabrics and forms present included those most commonly associated with early medieval assemblages in Worcester such as a Stafford-type jar and a Cotswolds unglazed jar (fabric 48; context 1841 and fabric 57.1; context 1877). In addition, two sherds of unglazed Worcester-type cooking pot (fabric 55; context 1841) and three of glazed Worcester-type sandy ware (fabric 64.1; context 1877) were also identified.

The 13th to 14th-century pottery from contexts from Plot 13 (Periods 2.3.1 and 2.3.2) is typical of that seen across the site at this date, with locally produced wares still dominating but a range of regional and non-local wares also making an appearance in small quantity. These included a small amount of Brill/Boarstall ware (fabric 63; G122: context 1225), Ham Green ware (fabric 143; G122: context 1702) and green-glazed white ware (fabric 64.3; G123: context 1532). A small amount of earlier wares such as Cotswolds unglazed (fabrics 57 and 57.1) and glazed Stamford-type ware (fabric 46.2) was residual within contexts of this date.

Forms commonly seen amongst the local wares included unglazed Worcester-type cooking pots, primarily of thickened, everted-rim form (Deansway form 55.3) and tripod pitcher forms amongst the glazed Worcester-type wares (Deansway forms 64.1.1 and 64.1.3). Perhaps the most unusual form within the material of 13th to 14th century from Plot 13 was the 'frying pan' of unidentified fabric described above (G124: context 1567; Fig. 5.7. 23).

Contexts of 14th-century date within Plot 13 (Period 2.4) displayed a similar range and proportion of wares as those above with only sherds of buff sandy ware not seen in contexts of earlier date (fabric 64.2; contexts 1248, 1278, 1304, 1478 and 1507; within G145, G144, G140, G148 and G139). Amongst the local wares, the start of the decrease in Worcester-type vessels and rise of Malvernian wares described above is clearly illustrated amongst this group. In addition, there are also a number of residual sherds of Minety-type ware which commonly dates to the early to mid 12th century (fabric 65; contexts 1304, 1362, 1372 and 1594; within G140, G148, G136 and G131). Other residual material includes two sherds of Cotswolds unglazed ware (fabrics 57 and 57.1; contexts 1304 and 1860; within G140 and G131).

The latest material of medieval date within Plot 13 (Period 2.4) showed oxidised glazed Malvernian ware to be dominating with vessels of this fabric accounting for 50% of the material from contexts of late 14th to 15th-century date, a pattern which is reflected in the relative proportions of the pottery across the site at this date. Other local wares found in much smaller numbers consisted of four sherds of glazed Worcester-type sandy ware (fabric 64.1; G151: contexts 1124, 1125 and 1188; and G70: context 1190) and unglazed Malvernian ware (fabric 56; G152: context 1033; G151: contexts 1188 and 1199), with the unglazed Worcester-type ware notably absent.

Non-local wares consisted of six sherds of buff sandy ware (fabric 64.2; context 1125), two of green-glazed white ware (fabric 64.3; context 1090) and a single sherd of Ham Green ware, type B (fabric 143.2; context 1090). All were recovered from a series of spreads and lenses of burnt clay, charcoal and silt (G151) associated with the demolition of an oven, and all are likely to be residual within this period with date ranges of the 13th to 14th century. Likewise a small sherd of a Saintonge ware bridge-spouted jug (fabric 120; context 1188) from the same group (G151) was also residual, dating to the late 13th century.

Period 3: post-medieval

Pottery from Period 3 consisted of 280 sherds of medieval and 188 sherds of late medieval/early post-medieval date. It is safe to say that all medieval sherds were residual within contexts of this period, whilst those of late medieval/early post-medieval date were predominantly of oxidised Malvernian ware forms bridging the late 15th to mid 17th centuries.

Contexts from the earlier part of this Period (3.1) were dated to the 16th to 17th century by 185 sherds of oxidised glazed Malvernian ware (fabric 69), two of Herefordshire fabric A7d and one of Merida-type ware (fabric 79). Identifiable forms present amongst the Malvernian wares were of types commonly seen within assemblages of this date including dripping dishes, pipkin/skillets, jar/pipkins, jar/bunghole jars, cups and flared bowls. A single sherd of the Herefordshire fabric was identified as coming from a flared bowl of similar form to the Malvernian vessels (Plot 7; G73: context 1270). The Merida-type ware was the only sherd of this fabric within the whole assemblage and was from a small jug dating between 1550 and 1650 (Plot 14; G247: context 900). Other fabrics of similar date found alongside these wares are discussed within the 'Post-medieval pottery' section below but included red sandy wares (fabrics 72 and 78), North Devon gravel-tempered ware (fabric 75), Midlands yellow ware (fabric 77), various stonewares (fabric 81), tin-glazed wares (fabric 82), orange wares (fabric 90) and buff wares (fabric 91).

Contexts of 17th-century date (Period 3.2) were the last within which non-residual pottery of late medieval/

early post-medieval fabrics and forms was identified, and within these was a notable decline in the number of residual medieval sherds. Once more, oxidised glazed Malvernian ware dominated with 169 non-residual sherds and Herefordshire fabric A7d was also present, albeit it just four sherds. The variety of forms within the Malvernian wares was much reduced by the 17th century with flared bowl, jar/bunghole jar and chafing dish forms the only types identified as non-residual. Likewise, a chafing dish and bowl were identified in the Herefordshire fabric (contexts 2626 and 278).

Periods 4 and 5: 18th to 20th centuries

All pottery of medieval and late medieval/early post-medieval date within contexts of Periods 4 and 5 was residual and in the light of the absence of any forms or fabrics of note does not warrant further discussion.

5.4 Post-medieval pottery
Alan J. Jacobs

The post-medieval assemblage comprised 2057 sherds weighing 61.55kg (Table 5.4), with preservation being variable. These were recovered and recorded according to the procedures described above (Chapter 3.2.5).

Only post-medieval pottery recovered from Period 3 (c. 1550–1700) and Period 4 (18th century) was analysed in detail, the focus of the analysis being on well-stratified material, especially from well-sealed groups of contexts. Residual material recovered from later contexts is omitted, except where objects of interest were identified.

This assemblage consists of distinct 17th and 18th-century groups with unusual elements, indicating continuous occupation in this area of Worcester from the middle of the 16th century until the end of the 18th century. Post-medieval assemblages have rarely been reported in detail in Worcester, and as such there is considerable scope for developing our knowledge of ceramic use, as well as patterns of trade and consumption in this period. Post-medieval red ware was by far the commonest type of ceramic in this period (58% by count).

5.4.1 Analysis

North Devon gravel-tempered and gravel-free wares (fabrics 75 and 75.1)

North Devon gravel-tempered and gravel-free wares are found within most post-medieval assemblages in Worcester in a limited range of forms, usually conical

Table 5.4: Quantification of the analysed later post-medieval pottery assemblage by fabric type

Fabric	Fabric common name	Total	Weight (g)
71	Micaceous glazed ware	1	43
72	Brown glazed speckled ware	104	1456
75	North Devon gravel-tempered ware	39	2085
75.1	North Devon gravel-free ware	1	2
77	Midlands yellow ware	191	4252
78	Post-medieval red ware	1193	42221
81	Stonewares	6	75
81.11	Frechen stoneware	2	28
81.2	Westerwald stoneware	13	200
81.3	Nottingham stoneware	20	395
81.5	White salt-glazed ware	75	741
81.7	Staffordshire stoneware	85	1294
82	Tin-glazed ware	87	757
84	Creamware	15	89
84.3	Whieldon-type tortoiseshell ware	7	14
89	Agate ware	11	40
90	Post-medieval orange ware	3	78
91	Post-medieval buff ware	186	6814
108	Midlands purple ware	10	377
100	Miscellaneous post-medieval wares	8	587
Totals		**2057**	**61548**

bowls and barrel-shaped jars but occasionally in more unusual forms. Most of this fabric was imported into Worcester during the late 16th to mid 18th century. Conical bowls have been recovered from Sidbury, dating to the 17th century (Morris 1980), while 16–18 Sansome Street (Napthan 2006) had both late 16th to 17th-century, and late 17th to early 18th-century forms. From The Commandery excavations only a single dateable form of late 16th century date was identified (Crawford 2007).

At Newport Street only 12 contexts contained North Devon gravel-tempered ware. A limited range of identifiable forms were present, including the rim of a conical bowl of 17th-century date recovered in Plot 6 (Period 3.3/4; G79: context 1466) and having a close parallel (cf Evans 1979, fig. 1.19). A barrel-shaped jar form of mid to late 17th-century date from Period 3.2 deposits (G89: context 1503) in the same plot could also be closely paralleled (ibid., fig. 2.59). The unusual form of a lid was also present (Plot 6; context 2021). The forms recovered were generally quite typical of the range produced in this fabric and imported into Worcestershire.

Midlands yellow ware (fabric 77)

Midlands yellow ware comprises a small but significant element of the post-medieval assemblage, and ranges in date from the late 16th to the early 18th century. A yellow glaze, usually with indications of crazing, and a pink-white underslip, characterises this fabric, which is found on most sites within Worcester in small amounts, usually in 17th-century contexts. For example, many forms were defined at Sidbury (Morris 1980) and mostly were attributed a 17th-century date. At the Porcelain Works excavation (Jacobs 2006) most of the material was residual in later contexts but two contexts were of late 16th to 17th and 17th-century date. There were few 17th-century contexts containing Midlands yellow ware from The Commandery excavation; however, several early to mid 18th-century contexts produced sherds of this fabric (Crawford 2007). As at 16–18 Sansome Street (Napthan 2006), Midlands yellow ware was recovered from late 17th and 18th-century contexts, supporting a later distribution date than is usually put forward for this ware. Older excavations within Worcester such as that at Queen Street (Whitehouse 1962) tend to describe this fabric within 17th-century date ranges although not always very clearly.

The amount of Midlands yellow ware, in proportion to later fabrics, indicates extensive 17th-century activity. A wide variety of forms were present within 17th-century contexts with substantial groups in some contexts (e.g. Plot 2; G10: context 621, G8: context 667, and context 723; Plot 10: G108: context 1026). Illustrated examples include a complete cup (Plot 2; G13: context 663; Fig. 5.8, 1), and a candlestick from the same plot (G8: context 667; Fig. 5.8, 2). A distinct group within the fill of a cess pit associated with Building 3 in Plot 2 (G6: contexts 668 and 773) contained several late forms including an example of a handled flared bowl (Fig. 5.8, 3), the rim of a cup (Fig. 5.8, 4), a handled jar (Fig. 5.8, 5) and a complete cup (Fig. 5.8, 6). This unusual group, dating to the first half of the 18th century, provides a clear indication of a later distribution of Midlands yellow ware in Worcester. Another important assemblage of this ware was recovered from make-up layers dumped in Plot 14 at the transition from Period 3 to 4 (G268: context 830). This included the rim of a flat ware plate (Fig. 5.8, 7) and an unusual candlestick (Fig. 5.8, 8).

More fragmentary examples of small hollow-ware vessels, cups, bowls or handled jars were also present in this fabric. Direct parallels are difficult to define within Worcester assemblages due to the lack of published forms, but parallels of several vessels recovered from make-up layers within Plot 10 (G108: context 1026) have been traced including a flared bowl (Woodfield 1964, F) and a jar with a flared rim (ibid., H), while a small cup and a straight-sided, handled jar from a pit fill within Plot 4 (context 1797) also have close parallels (ibid., GE and HH respectively).

Brown glazed speckled ware (fabric 72)

Brown glazed speckled ware (fabric 72) is a distinct variation of the commonly encountered post-medieval red ware (fabric 78). The body of the glaze has small sand fragments that have not fused, giving a very distinctive speckled look beneath the glaze. This fabric probably will have been often included within fabric 78 classifications, and as such is difficult to define through older reports. A more limited range of forms was recovered in fabric 72 and these are dominated by tygs (small drinking vessels) with smaller numbers of jugs and other forms.

The forms in brown glazed speckled ware are entirely of late 16th to 17th-century date and include a number of examples of globular tygs, some of which were recovered from the upper and lower fills of an early Period 3 cess pit excavated in Plot 3 (S263). The lower fill (context 2681) contained a fine example with very distinct white clay pads around the waist of the vessel with a reddish slip (Fig. 5.8, 9). Two further globular tygs were recovered from Plot 3, one from the upper fill of this cess pit (context 2659) and the other from a dumped deposit in the vicinity (G66: context 2590). Both can be paralleled with examples from the Sidbury site, Worcester (cf Morris 1980, TV193b and TV194b respectively). The upper fill of the cess pit (S263: context 2659) also produced a fine early example of a multi-handled cup with six handles spread evenly around the body (Fig. 5.8, 10). A good example of the rim of a small jug was also recovered from this context and is similar in form to one recovered from a site in Stoke-on-Trent (Greaves 1976, fig. 1.9).

Post-medieval red ware (fabric 78)

The easily identified post-medieval red ware (fabric 78) is commonly found on all post-medieval sites in Worcester, usually comprising 66–70% of individual assemblages. This was a widely used utilitarian ware with a broad date and a wide range of forms, and provides the largest single element of the analysed post-medieval assemblage (1193 sherds; 58% of the assemblage). It ranges in date from the late 16th to the late 18th or early 19th century, when more modern stonewares largely replaced it. Glaze can vary with an earlier metallic silver/black glaze giving way to a fabric with a dark brown/black glaze. Earlier examples, as with fabric 72, are largely smaller hollow-ware forms such as tygs of late 16th to 17th-century date, and by the later 17th century this fabric group had largely replaced earlier fabrics such as the late Malvernian and North Devon gravel-tempered wares (fabrics 69 and 75). Later forms include a number of press-moulded dishes dating broadly to the late 17th to 18th century, and press-moulded baking dishes or platters with a striped slip decoration, most often with a pie-crust rim. The latter forms display evidence of both combed and feathered decoration. Fragments of large storage jars or pancheons are also present. These predominantly date to the late 17th to 18th century and were extensively used in both domestic and dairying/industrial contexts.

A wide range of forms were recovered, with larger vessel forms including a pancheon or large storage jar with a brown streaky glaze, which clearly dates from the second quarter of the 18th century (Plot 10; G108: context 1026; Fig. 5.8, 11), and a 'butter pot' dated to 1650–1750, recovered from a pit fill in Plot 2 (G14: context 278; Fig. 5.8, 12). Further larger storage jar and pot forms came from Plot 2 deposits, two of which were recovered from structures associated with Building 3, a pair of cottages. These comprised a distinct late straight-sided jar (G6: context 536; Fig. 5.8, 13) and a distinct 'butter pot' of mid to late 17th-century date with a highly fired silver metallic looking glaze, recovered from a cess pit (G6: context 773; Fig. 5.8, 14). An early to mid 18th-century pit group (G14) in the same plot also contained another, less definitive, bowl form with a distinct internal black glaze (context 274; Fig. 5.8, 16) and a highly fired jar with purplish fabric and an irregular internal glaze dated to 1650–1750 (context 278; Fig. 5.8, 15). A chamber pot with a very distinct mid 18th-century form was recovered from Plot 2 but was clearly residual within a Period 5 well fill (G53: context 122; Fig. 5.8, 17). Lastly, an unusual example of a complete 'butter pot' was recovered from Plot 4 (context 1901; Fig. 5.9, 28).

Smaller hollow-ware forms in this fabric consisted of a variety of tygs/cups. These included an example with a silver metallic black glaze that can be dated to the early to mid 17th century, and derived from the same cess pit as a 'butter pot' described above (G6: context 773; Fig. 5.9, 18). Another good example of a tyg, with a black streaky glaze of 17th-century date, was associated with Building 40 in Plot 11 (G302: context 1314; Fig. 5.9, 19). The most distinct group of tygs comprised four examples recovered from deposits dumped into the top of a cess pit associated with Building 5 in Plot 3 (S263: context 2667). These included a multi-handled cup (Fig. 5.9, 20) and three two-handled cups (Fig. 5.9, 21–23), all with a distinct brown glaze and could be dated to the late 16th to 17th century. A lug from a costrel was also recovered in this ware from 17th-century dumped deposits in Plot 11 (G300: context 1123; Fig. 5.9, 24).

Flatware forms in this fabric were present in a number of different designs, for example several small yellow slip-trailed decorated bowls in a variety of designs with a red underslip (Plot 10, G108: context 1026; Plot 6, G89: context 1503, and G90: 1573; Fig. 5.9, 25–27 and 29). The latter of these (29), a shallow bowl, featured conjoining sherds in two separate contexts (1503 and 1573). These all date from the mid 17th to the mid 18th century. Further later forms included an example of a square baking dish recovered from a pit in Plot 2, from which a bowl and jar in this fabric have already been discussed (G14: context 278). This dish can be dated to between 1650–1750 and had a streaky black glaze (Fig. 5.10, 30).

Post-medieval stoneware (fabric 81)

A variety of stoneware was recovered, predominantly of late 17th to 18th-century date and mainly in the form of cups or tankards. Identifiable types include Frechen, Westerwald, Nottingham, White salt-glazed, and Staffordshire stonewares, but a number of fragments of stoneware for which the provenance was not more closely identifiable were also recovered (fabric 81). These consisted predominantly of tankard fragments of 17th to 18th-century date recovered from Plot 2 (G6: context 523; G12: context 562; and residually within G35: context 1522) and Plot 14 (G268: context 830). The only other form recovered consisted of two fragments of bottle, which are not closely dateable (Plot 2, G8: context 667; Plot 5, context 2033).

Westerwald stoneware (fabric 81.2)

This fabric originates in northern Germany on the east bank of the Rhine and is a distinctive part of the imported element of most post-medieval assemblages recovered in Worcestershire. It has a distinct manganese/purple glaze decoration over a light grey slip and was imported from the beginning of the 17th century to the middle of the 18th. Many examples have been recovered previously from sites in Worcester including at Queen Street (Whitehouse 1962), Sidbury (Morris 1980), 16–18 Sansome Street (Napthan 2006), the Porcelain Works (Jacobs 2006) and The Commandery (Crawford 2007). On most of these sites the fabric predominantly dates from the late 17th–18th century.

Westerwald stoneware was recovered from a number of post-medieval contexts, and predominantly comprised tankard fragments (contexts 19, 85, 274, 756, 1184 and 1221) with one possible example of a jar (G278: context 819). All of these contexts date from the late 17th to 18th century. Only two definable rim forms were recovered; one dating to the 18th century (G302: context 1221) was associated with Building 14 in Plot 11, while the other although closely dateable (1740–1760) was residual within a Period 5 context in Plot 2 (G53: context 122). The latter context contained a number of examples of wares of this date and appears to include a dump of redeposited middle 18th-century material.

Nottingham stoneware (fabric 81.3)
Nottingham stoneware was also present, primarily in 18th-century tankard forms with lustrous brown glaze and rills. This fabric appears to have been mostly brought into Worcester between 1690–1790. Many examples have been recovered as at Sidbury (Morris 1980), 16–18 Sansome Street (Napthan 2006), the Porcelain Works (Jacobs 2006) and The Commandery (Crawford 2007). On these sites the fabric predominantly dates from the late 17th–18th century. However, this fabric was not present at Queen Street (Whitehouse 1962), which was associated with a *terminus ante quem* of 1720 and this may be significant in terms of dating this fabric in Worcester.

Nottingham stoneware was recovered from four post-medieval contexts (contexts 19, 523, 731, and 2381) and two Period 5 contexts in Plot 2 (G9: context 18; G53: context 122), one of which has already been noted as containing redeposited 18th-century material. The assemblage was also dominated by tankard fragments broadly dated to the late 17th to 18th century. Two plate forms, one of them hexagonal, are more closely dateable to the mid 18th century but these were recovered among the residual material in the Period 5 context 122 noted above.

White salt-glazed stoneware (fabric 81.5)
This fabric was developed in the early 18th century as tea drinking developed and there was a need for heat-resistant ware. These forms generally date from 1720–1770 and were largely replaced by Creamware in the second half of the 18th century. Many examples have been recovered from previous excavations in Worcester, including those from Sidbury (Morris 1980), the Porcelain Works (Jacobs 2006) and The Commandery (Crawford 2007). On most of these sites this fabric predominantly dates from 1720–1760.

White salt-glazed stoneware was recovered from four closely dateable context assemblages, all from Plot 2. Two of these assemblages were recovered from pit fills (G14: contexts 19 and 274) while the other two derived from Period 5 deposits notable for containing significant quantities of redeposited mid 18th-century material (G53; contexts 121 and 122). Close dating of these pottery groups has been possible due to the presence of many forms and the size of the groups present, together with the mid 18th-century dating from associated tobacco pipe forms (Peacey, Chapter 5.15). A wide range of tea ware and tableware was present including examples of tea bowls (context 122; Fig. 5.10, 31–33), tankards, lids and a marble or knob from the top of a lid. A small eyebath (context 122; Fig. 5.10, 34) was an unusual item. Along with context 121 this group offers an unusual and closely dateable range of forms characterising a mid 18th-century domestic assemblage from Worcester.

Staffordshire stoneware (fabric 81.7)
This fabric developed at the start of the 18th century as part of a change in tastes, fed by German stoneware imports (see above). Forms are almost exclusively tankards and these are found on most 18th-century sites within Worcestershire. Many examples have been recovered previously within Worcester, including from Sidbury (Morris 1980), the Porcelain Works (Jacobs 2006) and The Commandery (Crawford 2007).

Staffordshire stoneware was recovered from twelve contexts (19, 65, 122, 274, 451, 461, 480, 497, 536, 562, 621 and 662), usually in fragmentary form (body sherds). There was only one good example of an 18th-century tankard and this was a residual item within a Period 5 context (Plot 2; G9: context 461; Fig. 5.10, 35). The limited range of fabric and forms make any conclusions on the use of this fabric difficult.

Tin-glazed ware (fabric 82)
Tin-glazed ware was imported into Britain from the late 1500s until around 1730. Initially predominantly in the form of Delft ware from Holland, Britain started to produce this fabric during the 17th century and these two types are very similar. As a result it can be difficult to sub-divide this fabric, which is found in small amounts on most post-medieval assemblages within Worcester. The range of forms is limited, usually consisting of small jars and bowls with occasional flatware (small plates and dishes). Mostly it was imported into Worcester during the 17th century (Derek Hurst, pers. comm.) but it can occasionally be of earlier or later date. This fabric was largely replaced by White salt-glazed stoneware in the 1720s. Tin-glazed ware has been previously recovered from Sidbury (17th century; Morris 1980), from 16–18 Sansome Street (late 17th century; Napthan 2006) and from Queen Street (early 18th century; Whitehouse 1962). A limited amount was also recovered in the excavation at The Commandery (Crawford 2007), dateable to the 17th to early 18th century.

A total of 23 contexts contained Tin-glazed ware. These were predominantly of late 17th to 18th-century date from Period 3 or early Period 4 (Plot 1, G17: context 382; Plot 2, G14: contexts 19, 31, 274, 278, G6: context 523, G8: context 602; Plot 6, G12: context

451, G89: context 1503, G92: contexts 1895 and 1922, and unassigned context 1835; Plot 10, G107: contexts 1206 and 1215). Many residual examples were also present in later Period 4 and Period 5 contexts (Plot 2: contexts 18, 121, 122, 261, 461, 585 and 596; Plot 4: contexts 273 and 755).

Small hollow-ware vessels dominate the forms recovered, with several examples of tea bowls from contexts within Plot 2 (contexts 31, 461 and 668) and Plot 6 (485), and a number of jars, including examples of small pharmaceutical or drug jars (context 122; Fig. 5.10, 36). A small lid was also recovered (context 1895).

Flatwares were present in the form of highly decorated plates or saucers (e.g. Plot 2; context 122; G14: context 278) but no individual form complete enough to allow closer dating was recovered. The latter example (from context 278) had evidence of repair work in the form of a hole drilled through it (Fig. 5.10, 37).

Creamware (fabric 84 and 84.3)

This fabric has a distinct cream glaze and is easily distinguishable from more modern china whitewares. It was a relatively short-lived fabric developed in Staffordshire during the early 1750s, becoming common from the very late 1750s when it largely replaced White salt-glazed stoneware. Forms include small tea bowls, cups, jars, plates and dishes. Distinct changes came over Creamware as the fabric developed over time, becoming whiter and more standardised in texture before being replaced by early mass-produced china in the 1790s. Within Worcester, Creamware has been recovered from most excavations but rarely has been fully reported or described. At the Porcelain Works, however, this period was covered and, although most of the material was residual, three contexts were dated from the late 18th century (Jacobs 2006). There are also several late 18th-century contexts containing Creamware from The Commandery (Crawford 2007).

Relatively few contexts contained Creamware; only one group could be dated by its presence (Plot 6; G79; contexts 1466 and 1513), other examples being recovered from unassigned contexts (2380) or as residual material from Period 5 contexts (18, 2412, and 2844). A limited range of forms was present, the rim of a mug or cup (context 1466), body sherds of small bowls or tea bowls (contexts 1513 and 2412) and a fragment of a flatware form (context 2380). The forms recovered were quite typical of the limited range of forms produced in this fabric and recovered from archaeological contexts elsewhere in Worcester. The relatively short time period that Creamware was produced mitigates against large amounts of material being recovered by modern excavation techniques.

Agate ware (fabric 89)

This very distinct fabric had a relatively short-lived period of distribution. The pottery was manufactured by layering clays of different colours for a marbling effect, and has been credited to Thomas Whieldon (1719–1795), who worked within the Staffordshire pottery industry at Stoke-on-Trent (Fisher 1970, 10). The major distribution of this pottery type dates between 1740 and 1775 (Noël-Hume 1969). It is usually rare on sites in Worcestershire, however, Agate ware has previously been recovered from a number of sites in Worcester including at 16–18 Sansome Street, where a tankard form was recovered in a mid-late 18th century context (Napthan 2006), and the Porcelain Works from a context dated to 1740–1800 (Jacobs 2006). Similar examples are mentioned in older excavations, in particular at Queen Street, just to the north of Sansome Street, where it was dated to 1740–1770 (Whitehouse 1962).

The only forms recovered were from Plot 2 and comprised a small fragment of the base of a hollow-ware vessel (context 121), rim and body sherds from a tankard or cup (context 122), and a body and rim sherd of a tankard or jar (Plot 2; G14; context 19). Although only the latter was in a post-medieval context, the Period 5 contexts from which the other sherds were recovered all produced redeposited mid 18th-century material. These can be closely dated to 1740–1760 by the presence of Agate ware and White salt-glazed stoneware, and the absence of Creamware, which as discussed previously appears in Worcester slightly later, during the late 1750s to early 1760s.

Post-medieval buff ware (fabric 91)

This fabric has a broad range of forms similar to those associated with post-medieval red wares (fabric 78), but with a late 17th to 18th-century date. Forms include jars, chamber pots and pancheons. Most sherds were glazed internally and externally with the exception of larger flat wares which were often glazed on the interior only. Fragments of press-moulded dishes or baking dishes with a striped slip decoration have a yellowish glaze and mostly have a pie-crust rim. These forms also display evidence of both combing and feathering and are a distinct feature of the 18th century. Other forms in this fabric include large storage jars or pancheons, predominantly dating to the late 17th to 18th century and extensively used in both domestic and dairying/industrial contexts. Hollow-ware forms include tankards, cups or small jars as well as chamber pots. Numerous examples of post-medieval buff ware have been recovered from Worcester, including those from Queen Street (Whitehouse 1962), Sidbury (Morris 1980), 16–18 Sansome Street (Napthan 2006), the Porcelain Works (Jacobs 2006) and The Commandery (Crawford 2007). On most of these sites the fabric predominantly dates from the 18th century.

Post-medieval buff ware was widely recovered from both late Period 3 and Period 4 deposits (Plot 1, G19: context 536; Plot 2, G14: contexts 19, 31 and 373, G6:

contexts 367 and 668, G8: context 602; Plot 6, G12: context 451, G79: contexts 1466 and 1513, G365: context 1638; Plot 9, G365: context 1723; Plot 10, G106: context 1226; Plot 11, G302: context 1221). Further examples were recovered as residual material from Period 5 contexts (Plot 2: contexts 71, 122, 461 and 596; Plot 6: context 2412; Plot 8: context 2844) and from an unassigned context (2380).

Forms recovered included large pancheons or storage jars (contexts 461 and 1226) and large straight-sided jars (context 19). A particularly good group came from Plot 2 within a Period 5 context, characterised by a significant assemblage of redeposited mid 18th-century material (G53, context 122). This included a chamber pot (Fig. 5.10, 38), a bunghole jar (Fig. 5.10, 39) and a small hollow-ware vessel (Fig. 5.10, 40), all of which are closely dateable to 1740–1760 by association with tobacco-pipe forms and other fabrics.

A number of examples of baking dishes with a variety of combed and feathered decorative styles were also recovered (contexts 19, 31, 122, 536, 1723 and 2332), these often having a laminated texture with white striations in the clay seen as indicative of 18th-century manufacture.

Midlands purple ware (fabric 108)
Relatively few examples of this fabric were recovered, only six contexts contained Midlands purple ware (19, 274, 278, 564, 668 and 1224). These were entirely in the form of large jars or 'butter pots' (e.g. Plot 2; G14: context 278; Fig. 5.10, 42). All examples were in 18th-century or later contexts, and were very highly fired.

Miscellaneous post-medieval ware (fabric 100)
This group included a very unusual object in the form of the neck and shoulders of an olive oil jar, with an irregular green glaze with darker brown patches (Plot 2; G12; context 564; Fig. 5.10, 41). This fabric has no specific parallel in the type series although it is similar to Merida-type ware (fabric 79), albeit a much finer oxidised fabric. The form and fabric would indicate a source of origin in southern Spain; the sherds were recovered from an early 18th-century context related to either Building 2 or 3.

Other fabrics
Very small quantities of micaceous glazed ware (fabric 71) and post-medieval orange ware (fabric 90) were also recorded.

5.4.2 General discussion

The post-medieval assemblage provides a large body of data, and includes a number of substantial assemblages recovered from pit groups of 17th and 18th-century date (Plot 2: G6 and G14). The pit groups are particularly significant as they can be used to more clearly date specific forms and fabrics within the context of Worcester. This importance is enhanced by the fact that no modern report has been undertaken within the city summarising the evidence for post-medieval pottery, a fact highlighted by work undertaken at Deansway, which did not include detailed quantification and analysis of material beyond the 16th century (Edwards and Bryant 2004). Thus the Newport Street material is of considerable importance in developing an understanding of ceramic supply in the city during the post-medieval period.

The extent of late 17th-century pottery could be taken as evidence for widespread dumping in this area of Worcester, possibly due to reconstruction following the Civil War. The overall assemblage does not indicate a particularly high status area, although the presence of the (probably) Spanish jar gives some indication of the use of Worcester as a river port. The Midlands yellow ware, in particular, is an unusual element in this assemblage, with many definable forms supporting evidence of activity of mainly the late 17th century, but also into the early 18th century. This fabric may well have been imported into Worcester to help fill up the gap left by the collapse of the Malvernian industry by the mid 17th century.

The distinct changes in vessel fabric and form clearly illustrate changing life-styles, eating habits and levels of personal wealth. Along with accompanying changes in other goods, such as glass and pewter, the distinct changes from tyg to tankard to teacup in the ceramic record help to illuminate the great cultural and social changes that occurred during the post-medieval period (to the end of the 18th century) prior to the high standardisation of the modern period, when basic fabrics and styles have not significantly changed in two centuries.

Catalogue of the illustrated post-medieval pottery (Figs 5.8 to 5.10)

1   Cup. Midlands yellow ware (Fabric 77; Plot 2; G13: context 663)
2   Candlestick. Midlands yellow ware (Fabric 77; Plot 2; G8: context 667)
3   Handled flared bowl. Midlands yellow ware (Fabric 77; Plot 2; G6: context 773)
4   Cup. Midlands yellow ware (Fabric 77; Plot 2; G6: context 668)
5   Handled jar. Midlands yellow ware (Fabric 77; Plot 2; G6: context 773)
6   Cup. Midlands yellow ware (Fabric 77; Plot 2; G6: context 773)
7   Plate or dish. Midlands yellow ware (Fabric 77; Plot 14; G268: context 830)
8   Candlestick. Midlands yellow ware (Fabric 77; Plot 14; G268: context 830)
9   Globular tyg. Brown glazed speckled ware (Fabric 72; Plot 3; S263; context 2681)
10   Multi-handled cup. Post-medieval red ware (Fabric 72; Plot 3; S263: context 2659)
11   Pancheon or large storage jar. Post-medieval red ware (Fabric 78; Plot 10; G108: context 1026)

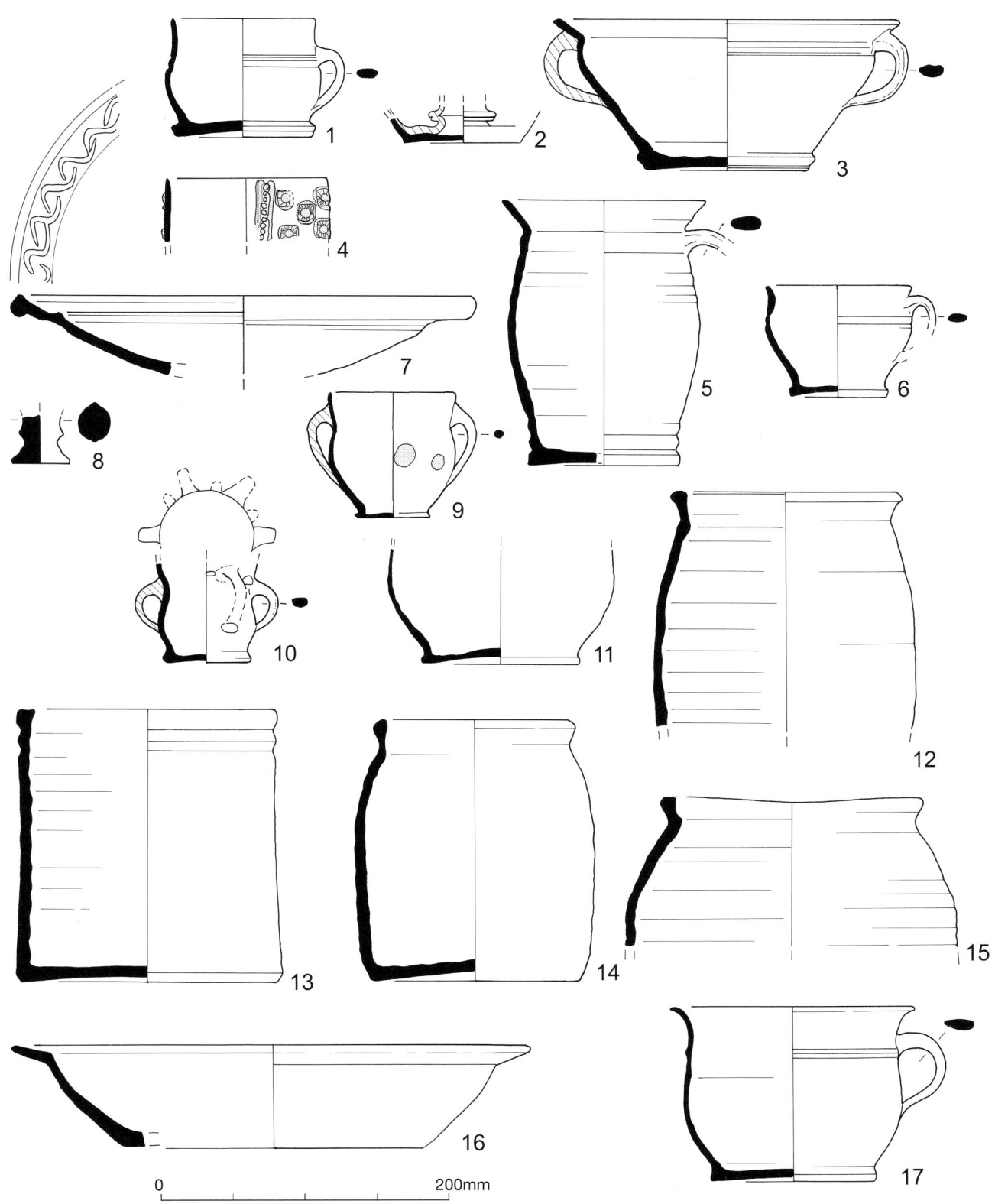

Fig. 5.8 Post-medieval pottery (Nos 1–17). Scale 1:4

12 Large 'butter pot'. Post-medieval red ware (Fabric 78; Plot 2; G14; context 278)

13 Straight-sided jar. Distinct late form. Post-medieval red ware (Fabric 78; Plot 1; G19: context 536)

14 'Butter pot'. Distinct form. Post-medieval red ware (Fabric 78; Plot 2; G6: context 773)

15 Jar. Highly fired with purplish fabric. Post-medieval red ware (Fabric 78; Plot 2; G14: context 278)

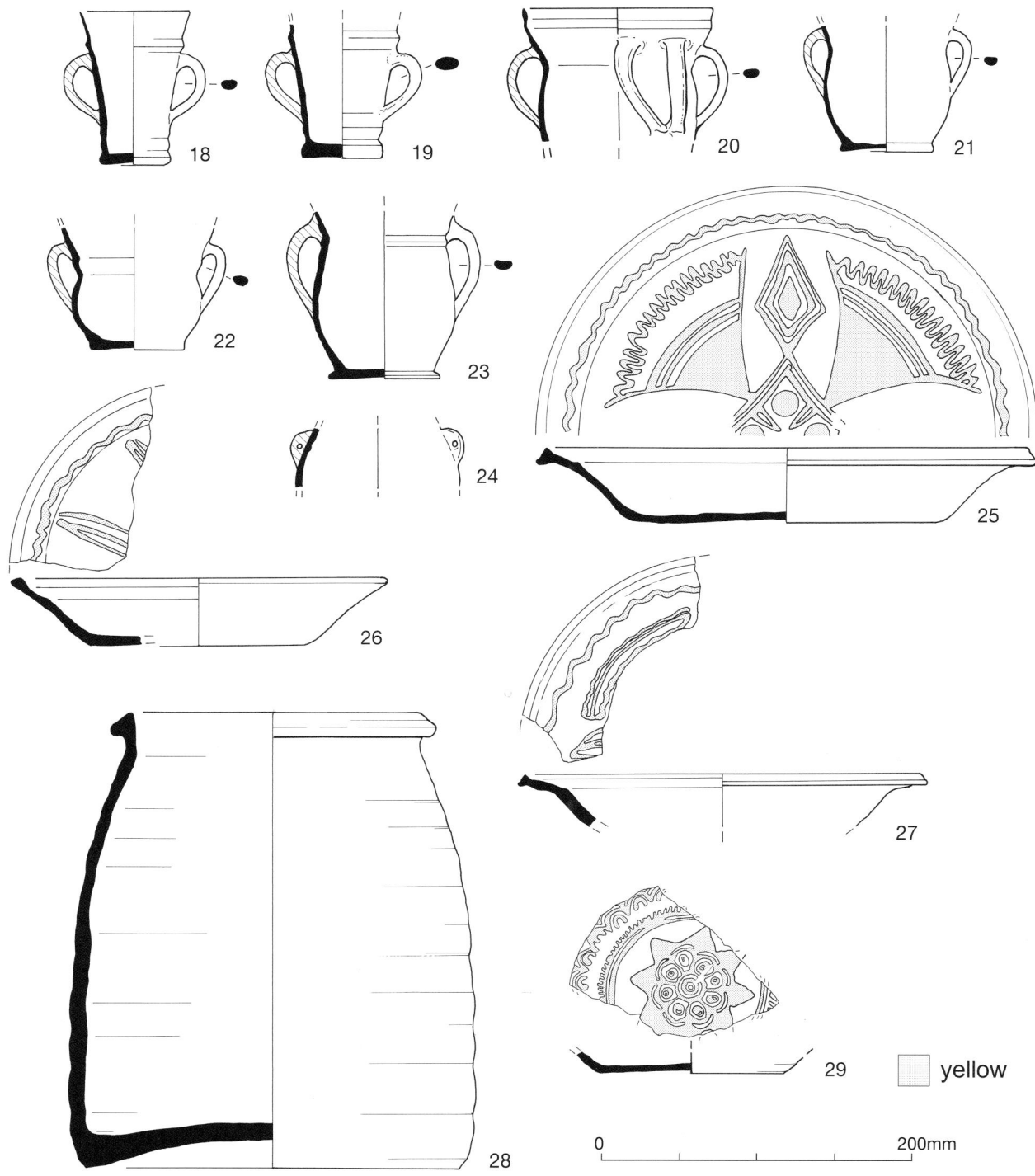

Fig. 5.9 Post-medieval pottery (Nos 18–29). Scale 1:4

16   Bowl. Post-medieval red ware (Fabric 78; context 274, S114, G14, Plot 2)

17   Chamber pot. Late form. Post-medieval red ware (Fabric 78; Plot 2; G53; context 122)

18   Tyg/cup. Post-medieval red ware (Fabric 78; Plot 2; G6: context 773)

19   Tyg. Post-medieval red ware (Fabric 78; Plot 11; G302: context 1314)

20   Multi-handled cup. Post-medieval red ware (Fabric 78; Plot 3; S263: context 2667)

21   Two-handled cup. Post-medieval red ware (Fabric 78; Plot 3; S263: context 2667)

22   Two-handled cup. Post-medieval red ware (Fabric 78; Plot 3; S263: context 2667)

23   Two-handled cup. Post-medieval red ware (Fabric 78; Plot 3; S263: context 2667)

Specialist Reports 129

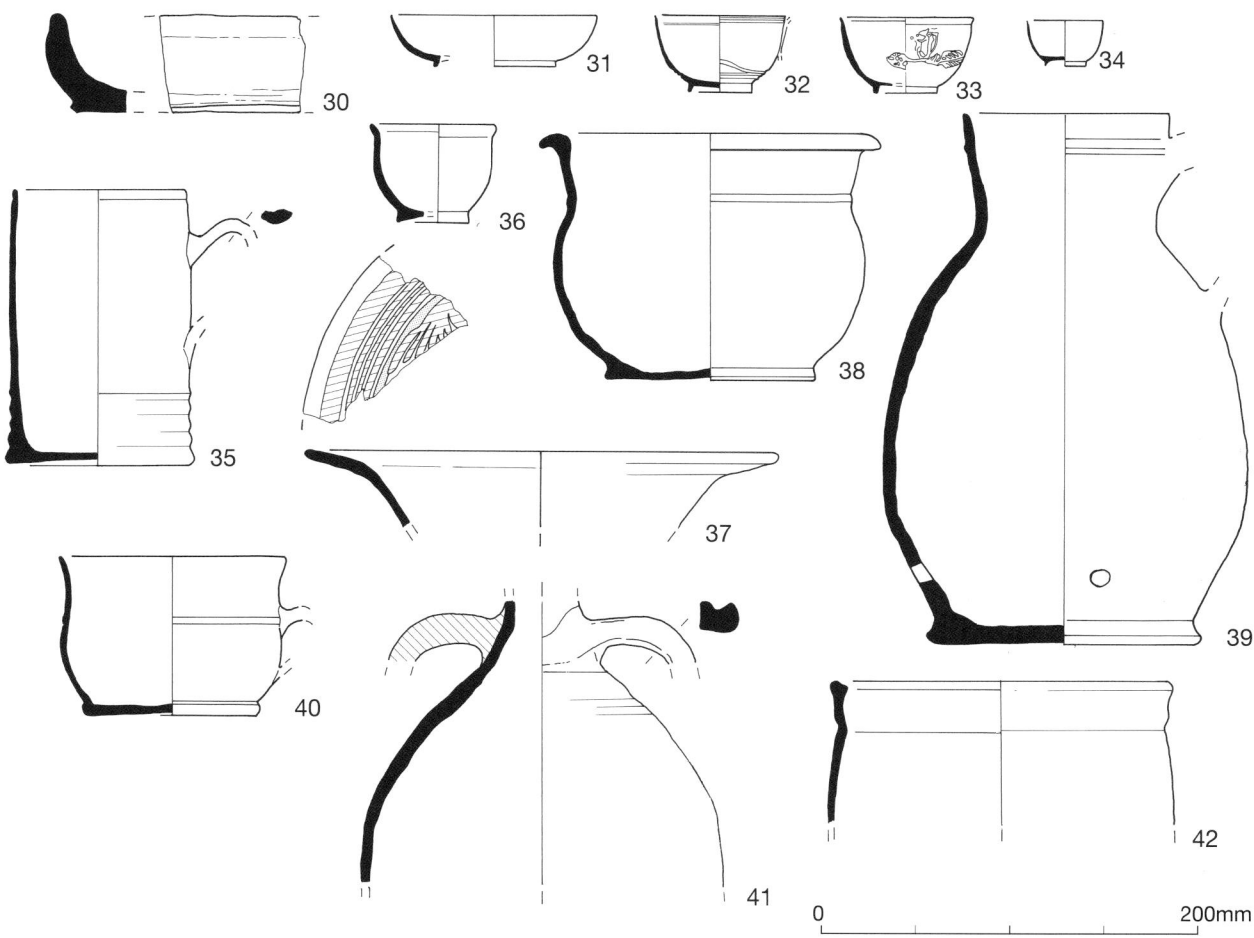

Fig. 5.10 Post-medieval pottery (Nos 30–42). Scale 1:4

24	Costrel. Post-medieval red ware (Fabric 78; Plot 11; G300: context 1123)	36.	Pharmaceutical or drug jar. Tin-glazed ware (Fabric 82; Plot 2; G53; context 122)
25	Slip-trailed decorated dish. Post-medieval red ware (Fabric 78; Plot 10, G108: context 1026)	37	Small plate or bowl. Tin-glazed ware (Fabric 82; Plot 2; G14: context 278)
26	Slip-trailed decorated dish. Post-medieval red ware (Fabric 78; Plot 10, G108: context 1026)	38	Chamber pot. Post-medieval buff ware (Fabric 91; Plot 2; G53: context 122)
27	Slip-trailed decorated dish. Post-medieval red ware (Fabric 78; Plot 10, G108: context 1026)	39	Bunghole jar. Post-medieval buff ware (Fabric 91; Plot 2; G53: context 122)
28	'Butter pot'. Distinct form. Post-medieval red ware (Fabric 78; Plot 4; context 1901)	40	Small cup or jug. Post-medieval buff ware (Fabric 91; Plot 2; G53: context 122)
29	Slip-trailed decorated dish. Post-medieval red ware (Fabric 78; Plot 6; conjoining sherds from G89 and G90: contexts 1503 and 1573)	41	Olive oil jar. Miscellaneous post-medieval ware (Fabric 100; Plot 2; G12: context 564)
30	Baking dish. Post-medieval red ware (Fabric 78; Plot 2; G14; context 278)	42	Large jar or 'butter pot'. Midlands purple ware (Fabric 108; Plot 2; G14: context 278)
31	Tea bowl or small bowl. White salt-glazed stoneware (Fabric 81.5; Plot 2; G53: context 122)		
32	Tea bowl or small bowl. White salt-glazed stoneware (Fabric 81.5; Plot 2; G53: context 122)		
33	Tea bowl or small bowl. White salt-glazed stoneware (Fabric 81.5; Plot 2; G53: context 122)		
34	Possible eyebath; small very fine vessel. White salt-glazed stoneware (Fabric 81.5; Plot 2; G53: context 122)		
35	Tankard. Staffordshire stoneware (Fabric 81.7; Plot 2; G9: context 461)		

5.5 The modern pottery
Alan J. Jacobs

Modern pottery was recovered and recorded according to the procedures described previously (Chapter 3.2.5). It was not analysed in detail but was used to support site phasing, while a basic summary of fabrics and forms recognised was also undertaken.

Table 5.5: Analysed modern pottery by fabric

Fabric	Name	Total	Weight (g)
81.4	Late miscellaneous Stoneware	30	1486
83	Porcelain	11	71
85	Modern china	5	118
85.1	White bone china	52	1495
85.2	Willow Pattern	42	794
85.3	Twig/Branched ware	5	14
85.4	Shell-edged ware	25	247
85.5	Brown-gold transfer pattern	4	119
85.6	Blue-white transfer pattern	10	43
85.7	Sponged ware	3	15
85.8	Flow Blue	8	112
85.9	Hand-painted china	1	3
85.10	Brown-white transfer pattern	8	975
101	Modern miscellaneous	16	1244
Totals		**220**	**6736**

5.5.1 Analysis

The modern (19th to 20th-century) pottery assemblage derived from Period 5 deposits and consisted of 220 sherds weighing 6.736kg (Table 5.5). This was recovered from contexts lacking distinct 20th-century material, although residual post-medieval pottery was also common in these deposits (181 sherds). The following is a broad characterisation of the assemblage with attention drawn to any individual examples of interest.

Most wares in this period are white, and there is a mixture of recognisable mass-produced types: Pearl ware (modern china; Noël Hume 2001), in the form of plates (contexts 15, 870 and 1791); Sponged ware, a distinct fabric that largely dates to the early 19th century, present only in small bowl or cup forms (contexts 426 and 1847); Flow Blue (Snyder 1992), common until around the middle of the 19th century, predominantly in the form of cups or bowls (contexts 15, 407, and 2255) but also as a small plate (context 2768); and unprovenanced porcelain (Fabric 83), largely in the form of small hollow-ware teacups (contexts 85, 407 and 470) and small sugar bowls (context 2895), but also as a hand-painted teacup (context 15), a style of decoration that became common in the first half of the 19th century.

Non-white wares of the period include late miscellaneous Stoneware (Fabric 81.4; e.g. a ginger beer or soda bottle stamped 'Packham and Co. Ltd. of Croydon' with a trademark from context 2768), brown kitchen-ware bowls (contexts 85, 1480 and 1837) and the ubiquitous brown teapot (context 2895).

Two fragments of biscuit-fired porcelain probably represent the sale of this material as hardcore from Worcester Porcelain works, and it is a common find around Worcester and beyond (Derek Hurst, pers. comm.).

5.5.2 Discussion

The ordinariness of the more modern assemblage was notable, providing some material evidence for the general social and economic decline of this district of Worcester during this period, though the size of the assemblage was too small for this conclusion to be confidently asserted based on this evidence alone.

5.6 Ceramic building material: medieval floor tiles
Laura Griffin

Ceramic building material was recovered and recorded according to the procedures described previously (Chapter 3.2.5). A small assemblage of 46 floor tiles and fragments was retrieved and consisted of decorated and plain tiles. These could be dated to the 13th to 15th centuries on basis of fabric, design and general appearance. A total of 12 individual designs could be identified from the 24 decorated tiles, whilst the 19 plain tiles displayed a variety of dark green, black, brown and yellow glazes (Table 5.6).

A narrow range of fabrics was identified and appears to correspond in part to design types present. These include tiles which are of definite Worcester-type fabric (some of which have been identified as being of a 'Worcestershire' type on the basis of design parallels), two thought to be of Malvern production, a small number of Bristol/Canynges type of the Malvern School, and one of

Table 5.6: Quantification of medieval plain floor tiles by glaze colour

Colour of glaze	Total tile frags
Plain with purplish black glaze	1
Plain with dark purplish brown glaze	2
Plain with brownish black glaze	1
Plain with dark brown glaze	2
Plain with dark greenish brown glaze	3
Plain with yellow glaze	7
Plain with yellow glaze and distinctive pinkish slip	2
Plain with yellow glaze streaked with green	1
Total	**19**

Westminster type. The body of the majority are well-made in the mould and bevelled slightly towards the base to allow the tiles to be set edge-to-edge without gaps or mortar showing from above. None of the tiles display keying on the underside, although all are sanded.

A full fabric description of floor tiles produced in Worcester has been published (Lewis 1999, 44–56, group 20). Those tiles identified within the assemblage as having designs and fabric of 'Canynges-pavement' type are also thought to have been produced in the vicinity of Worcester (ibid., 57, group 24). Although a kiln specifically for the production of floor tile has not been discovered in Worcester so far, the identification of a number of floor-tile wasters, and considerable documentary evidence, points towards Silver Street having been a production site for tiles of this fabric, and corresponding designs in the case of decorated examples (Brown 1990). The floor-tile industry in Worcester is thought to have begun in *c.* 1340 (Lewis 1999, 44), and dating based on associated finds from Silver Street, this site and parallel designs from the Cathedral Singing School pavement, which was laid in 1377 (Keen 1978), confirms a probable 14th-century date for the tiles within this group. In addition, a small number of both decorated and plain floor tiles were found during the excavation of a late 15th-century roof-tile kiln on The Tything, Worcester (Griffin 2004b, 12). It is almost certain that these were produced on the site due to the distinctive fabric but the small number found would suggest that they were almost a by-product of the production being undertaken here with roofing tile being the primary concern.

The assemblage consisted of two broad diagnostic groups of square pavement tiles and triangular edging tiles. As would be expected, square tiles dominated but the triangular examples indicate that the original pavements incorporated panels with diagonal designs, an assumption confirmed by a number of decorated tiles on which the design lies diagonally rather than square on. Tile came from a range of contexts spread across the site, the majority being residual within features and layers of late 16th-century date onwards.

5.6.1 Analysis

Decorated floor tiles

A total of 24 decorated tiles and fragments was retrieved, with 12 individual designs identified. A number of these can be paralleled with examples from elsewhere, both locally and from further afield, but others appear to be unique at this time (Fig. 5.11). A further four fragments are too small or worn to be assigned a specific design type and were recorded as unidentifiable. Where surviving, the dimensions of the decorated tiles mainly fall into a thickness range of 22–28mm, and length and width between 117–130mm. However, there is one notable exception which has dimensions of 95mm by 100mm, and is 37mm thick.

Just two designs can be paralleled with published examples from Worcester Cathedral Singing School (Keen 1978), with design 19 (context 2726) and a single tile from a multi-tile pattern either of designs 1–4 or 20–23 (unstratified). As was typical of the tiles identified at the Cathedral, the inlay on these examples is an extremely thin skim of less than 2mm deep, and the over-glaze is of poor quality. Both are highly abraded with some of the design missing due to the thin nature of the inlay.

A further fragment (Plot 14; G232: context 1258) and a tile with an unidentified design (Plot 9; G100: context 2753) also appear to have been of Worcester production, on the basis of fabric type. This latter tile (Fig. 5.11, 1) is thought to be later in date than parallels at the Cathedral, due to it being evenly fired throughout. In addition, it has a particularly unusual design in the form of a plant lying diagonally across the tile. Although highly abraded, again due to the extremely thin skim of inlay, the plant bears a striking resemblance to the banana plant, which would have been relatively new to the country during the 15th century, perhaps further evidence that this tile was also of later medieval production.

Two further tiles of unidentified design are also thought to be local products and include one complete example with a heraldic design (context 3; Fig. 5.11, 2) and one fragment with scrolling (Plot 3; context 2475; Fig. 5.11, 3). Both are well preserved but in both cases, the designs partially obscured by discoloured overglaze.

Other tiles thought to be of local production included two inscribed with '[AVE MA]RIA Q …' (Fig. 5.11, 4). The fabric, and the high quality slip and glaze (fired to a bright yellow and golden brown), would suggest that these were made in Great Malvern: no direct parallel has been found but they bear a striking resemblance to a design from St Albans Abbey (Eames 1980, cat. no. 1437).

A small number of other tiles are thought to have

been produced within Worcestershire, although the exact production sites are not known. These include one with a design which has been identified previously at Bordesley Abbey (context 3; Eames 1980, cat. no. 1608; Fig. 5.11, 5), and another two of a design which can be paralleled with a tile from Lilleshall Abbey, Shropshire (context 3; ibid., cat. no. 2799; Fig. 5.11, 6). There are also two tiles which have been identified as being of Bristol/Canynges type (contexts 2037 and 2821; ibid., cat. no. 2956; Fig. 5.11, 7) which are also thought to be Worcestershire products.

A single tile is identified as being of 'Westminster type', based on the design and dimensions, which at 95mm by 100mm and 37mm thick are noticeably smaller and thicker than the rest of the locally produced decorated assemblage (context 338; Eames 1980, cat. no. 2108; Fig. 5.11, 8). Such tiles are referred to as being of 'Westminster type' due to their first having been identified within the Muniment Room at Westminster Abbey and, in general, they date to the 14th century. Tiles of this type and design have previously been identified in Worcester from The Commandery (Griffin 2007) and, although not commonly seen in this area, have been found in small numbers across the West Midlands including at Leominster Priory (Laurence Keen, pers. comm.).

Just one edging tile is decorated. It is triangular in form and made from a square tile so only displays half of the original design (Plot 14; context 969; Fig. 5.11, 9). The design is closely paralleled at St Catherine's Hospital Chapel, Ledbury (Parker-Hore 2004, H517) which is dated to between the 13th and 15th centuries.

Catalogue of the illustrated decorated floor tile (Fig. 5.11)

1   Tile with unusual unidentified 'botanical' design, context 2753 (Plot 9; Period 3; G100), 15th–16th century
2   Tile of unidentified heraldic design, context 3 (machining horizon), ?15th–16th century
3   Tile of unidentified design, context 2475 (Plot 3; Period 2.4/5; G64), 13th–14th century
4   Tile from a multi-tile design bearing the words '[AVE MA]RIA Q …' (cf Eames 1980, cat. no. 1437), context 3 (machining horizon), earlier 14th century
5   Tile with heraldic design (cf Eames 1980, cat. no. 1608), context 3 (machining horizon), 13th–14th century
6   Tile from a multi-tile pattern (cf Eames 1980, cat. no. 2799), context 3 (machining horizon), 15th–16th century
7   Tile of Bristol/Canynges type (cf Eames 1980, cat. no. 2956), context 2821 (Plot 9; Period 3; G326), late 15th century
8   Tile of 'Westminster' type (cf Eames 1980, cat. no. 2108), context 338 (Plot 1; Period 3.1; G23), 14th century
9   Triangular edging tile (cf Parker-Hore 2004, H517), context 969 (Plot 14; Period 3.1; G262), 13th–15th century

Plain floor tiles

The plain floor tile assemblage bears many similarities to the decorated assemblage, although the majority are thicker than the decorated examples, between 22mm and 32mm. There are very few square tiles with whole dimensions intact but they appear to fall roughly into two size groups, with a small example measuring 79mm^2 and the larger tiles being approximately 126mm^2. The majority are highly worn and fragmentary, with even edging tiles displaying considerable surface abrasion.

There are eight glaze colour groups, all based around four main colours of yellow, green, brown and black (Table 5.6). As noted from other assemblages from Worcester, those with a yellow glaze dominate. In addition to the general yellow glazed group, there are a further two examples which could be described as yellow but are separated out due to a distinctive pinkish hue to the slip beneath the glaze. Both are of triangular edging form and of the sandy Worcester-type fabric, indicating them to be of 14th-century date. Tiles of this type have previously been identified at The Commandery (Griffin 2007) and were also all of triangular edging form. Another tile has a predominantly yellow glaze but with green streaking, and is of particular note as the fabric is of the type known to have been produced on The Tything during the late 15th century (Griffin 2004b).

Tiles with glazes based around the colour brown form the next largest group with variations in hue ranging from purplish to greenish. It is not known whether these differences in colour were actually intended or whether firing and glazing techniques have resulted in noticeable variations. Plain edging tiles consist of six triangular examples, all of which were clearly made for this purpose rather than cut down from larger tiles, as seen within the assemblage from The Commandery (Griffin 2007). One of the brown glazed square tiles (context 1209) is scored on the upper surface, the original intention being to split it into two triangular edge tiles post-firing.

5.6.2 Discussion

The floor tile assemblage is predominantly residual and was recovered from across the excavated area. Due to this, it is difficult to ascertain where the original pavement or pavements may have lain, but there are a small number of possibilities based on the remains of buildings and associated documentary evidence.

The first was identified on Plot 3 in Period 2.3 levels, and consisted of a stone-built cellar that must have originally belonged to a substantial building, which stood out from the other structural remains on the site. It is possible that a significant building such as this appears to have been would have had a tile pavement. The small number of tiles from contexts of Periods 2.4 and 2.5 on this plot, which relate to an apparent rebuilding programme, may have come from the removal of a pavement at this time. A similar floor was identified during at Friar Street, within what appeared

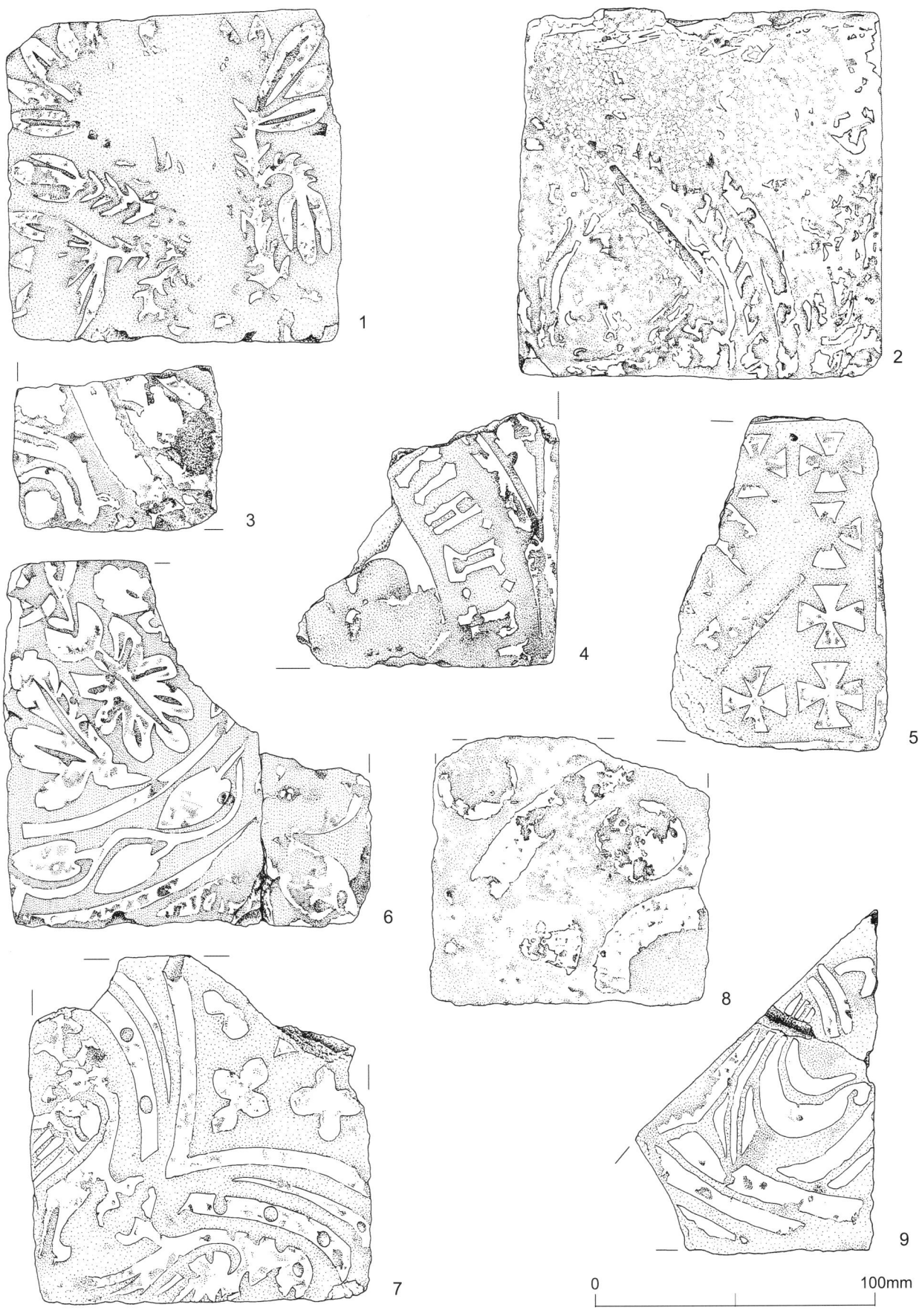

Fig. 5.11 Decorated floor tile (Nos 1–9). Scale 1:2

to be a high-status secular building, possibly belonging to a wealthy merchant (Griffin 2002b).

The remaining tiles from contexts of Period 3 or later and were found on Plots 2, 7, 9, 13 and 14, and those of Periods 4 and 5 were found on Plots 10 and 11, and the uppermost levels across the whole site. It is not clear where these tiles originally came from. It is possible that they were also from the rebuilding of the structure in Plot 3, or that they came onto the site as rubble resulting from the Dissolution in the 16th century. A likely source of such material would be Blackfriars Priory, which although a short distance from Newport Street, owned land on Dolday adjacent to the site (Baker and Holt 2004). Another possible source is the medieval church of All Saints', within whose parish Newport Street lies, which was almost totally demolished during the 18th century (Bridges 2000). During demolition, a large amount of medieval building material would have been removed from the site and most likely reused elsewhere within the parish.

This is the latest of a series of medieval floor tile assemblages excavated in Worcester in recent years. Although smaller in size than those from Friar Street (Griffin 2002b), The Commandery (Griffin 2007) and The Tything (Griffin 2004b), this assemblage is of interest due to the small number of designs which could be paralleled with those seen in the Cathedral, and the number which have not been recorded from the city previously.

5.7 Ceramic building material: Roman roof tile
Laura Griffin

Ceramic building material was recovered and recorded according to the procedures described previously (Chapter 3.2.5).

5.7.1 Analysis

A small assemblage of tile could be identified as Roman in date. This amounts to seven individual tiles or pieces of tiles, the majority deriving from a single tile (41 of 51 fragments). Three of these tiles or partial tiles were found within contexts excavated in Plot 13 and securely dated to Period 1 (G349: context 1897; G346: context 2039). The remainder were residual within Periods 2, 3 and 4.

The group includes a complete tegula formed from 41 adjoining fragments recovered from a pit fill (G346: context 2039; Fig. 5.12). The tile is oxidised throughout and of a fine, micaceous fabric with occasional soft, red mudstone-like inclusions. It is sizeable, measuring 440mm by 320mm and 500mm thick to the top of the top of the flange. The flanges are both poorly formed, being uneven and varying with the length of the tile, with a finger wipe where they adjoin the body of the tile.

Lower cutaways were identified at one end of the tile and took the form of Warry's type B, being a diagonal-type cut (Warry 2006, 44, fig. 3.13). Analysis of tegulae

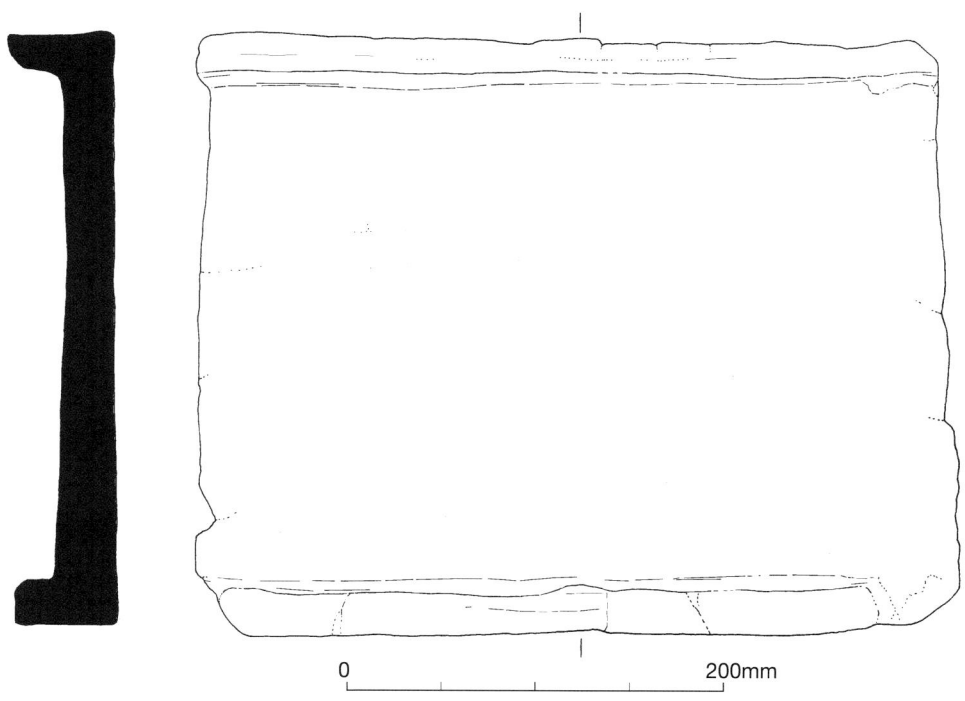

Fig. 5.12 Roman roof tile. Scale 1:4

from various sites across Britain has indicated a general date range of AD 100–180 for this form of cutaway, although this end date might extend a few years later on civilian sites (ibid., 64). This would fit well with the date range for this context, as indicated by associated pottery (Jacobs, Chapter 5.2). It is not clear if this tegula has deliberate upper cutaways. The end of the flange is missing on both sides at opposite ends of the tile to the lower examples, but this is certainly not a result of knife trimming, being very rough and having more the appearance of having been broken away post-firing. Due to surface abrasion, it is not clear whether this was deliberately done in the absence of intentional cutaways, or merely as a result of breakage following use.

Remaining non-residual material consisted of three fragments from a dump of iron slag and cobbles of late 4th-century AD date (G349). These were all from the same tile, being very roughly finished with large inclusions reminiscent of those seen in slab-built Malvernian-ware vessels of late Roman date (Fabric 3).

Residual material consists of a piece of tegula and two adjoining overfired fragments (Plot 3: context 2743), a small undiagnostic fragment of partially reduced, fine fabric (Plot 13: context 1620), a highly abraded fragment in a fine buff fabric (Plot 6: context 651) and a flanged piece of tegula similar in fabric to the complete example above (Plot 2: context 799).

5.7.2 Discussion

Although a small assemblage, the Roman tile forms an interesting group which supports the information provided by the Roman pottery assemblage. The assertion that this pottery may have come from higher status buildings to the east of the site, based on the range of forms and fabric present (Jacobs, Chapter 5.2.2), is further strengthened by the presence of tegulae.

5.8 Ceramic building material: medieval, post-medieval and modern roof tile
Laura Griffin

A substantial number of roof tiles of medieval, post-medieval and modern date was retrieved during the excavation, consisting of 1,047 pieces of tile weighing 205.45kg (Table 5.7). Just one complete tile is present with the remainder consisting of broken fragments. A small number are too small to be identified according to fabric type and were quantified by count and weight only. All tiles were quantified by fabric according to the type series held by WHEAS. Fabrics present within the assemblage are as follows:

1	Hard, modern type
2a	Common sandy type
2b	Coarse sandy type
2c	Grog/pellet sandy type
2d	Fine sandy type with buff banding

Table 5.7: Quantification of the ceramic roof tile by fabric and type

Fabric	Type	Total	Weight (g)
1	13	2	1408
1	19	5	256
2a	10	7	620
2a	12.1	1	53
2a	12.2	2	136
2a	12.3	4	480
2a	12.4	1	120
2a	13	14	6269
2a	14	11	3217
2a	19	95	23964
2a	20	3	917
2b	10	37	4982
2b	12	1	33
2b	12.1	13	2277
2b	12.2	12	1730
2b	12.3	3	597
2b	12.4	5	418
2b	13	16	2110
2b	14	24	11422
2b	19	347	29501
2b	20	11	3640
2c	10	4	454
2c	12.1	3	275
2c	12.4	1	158
2c	13	56	35405
2c	19	217	49827
2d	13	2	1252
2d	19	12	2332
3	10	83	7829
3	19	28	6302
3	20	1	511
5	10	1	687
5	13	10	3607
5	19	15	2663
Totals		**1047**	**205,452**

| 3 | Malvernian type |
| 5 | Slag and grog sandy type |

These fabrics were divided into tile types based on diagnostic attributes and appearance. These have been categorised as below:

10	Ridge tile
12.1	Pegged tile with round hole pierced
12.2	Pegged tile with square hole pierced

12.3	Pegged tile with round hole unpierced
12.4	Pegged tile with square hole unpierced
13	Nibbed tile
14	Nibbed and pegged tile
19	Undiagnostic flat tile
20	Other forms

A total of 65% of the assemblage consists of undiagnostic or unidentifiable tile fragments.

5.8.1 Analysis by fabric type

Fabric 1
Just seven tiles of this fabric type were retrieved; the small quantity recovered probably reflecting the removal of modern deposits by machine. All were high fired and of modern date.

Fabric 2a
A total of 138 tiles are identified as of fabric 2a and include ridge, nibbed, pegged and nibbed and pegged forms displaying both round, pierced, and square, unpierced holes. Other more unusual flanged, curved and valley forms are also present. The large proportion of tiles of this fabric within assemblages from Worcester suggests a local supply from the well-documented tile industry within the city (Hurst 1990). Tiles of this fabric are generally thought to date between the 13th and 15th centuries.

Flat tiles
A total of 95 undiagnostic flat tiles are present within this group, the majority being unglazed and sanded on the underside. Just 12 of these are glazed, all displaying green glaze to the upper surface. One tile from context 1842 has a maker's mark in the form of a circular stamp.

Nibbed tiles
There are 14 fragments of nibbed tiles. All are unglazed and two are stamped, one with two circles, one incomplete (context 1413) and the other with a segmented circle (context 2691). One tile is complete (context 1492) and another almost complete example could be made up from five adjoining fragments, and also displays a large paw print (context 2961).

Pegged tiles
A total of eight pegged tiles are identified within the fabric 2a assemblage. Holes of both square and circular form, both pierced and unpierced are present. Only three fragments from a single tile (context 1140) displays glaze and this appears to be accidental. Another piece displays sanding to both surfaces (context 1251). It is the only tile to have this feature and therefore, it is also assumed to be accidental.

Nibbed and pegged tiles
There are 11 nibbed and pegged tiles within this fabric group. Three of these stand out as all have broken lengthways down the centre of the nib. All are from the same context (1357) and it is likely that they were deliberately broken in this manner as the nib is the thickest part of a tile and therefore the most unlikely place for an accidental fracture to occur. If this breakage was indeed deliberate, it is possible that the tiles were intended to be reused for a specific purpose.

Ridge tiles
Seven ridge tiles are identified in this fabric group. Five are decorated with a thin streaked or speckled green glaze to the upper surface, a characteristic of this form type (contexts 19, 742, 1243 and 1341). The remaining two fragments are unglazed (context 396). None display any other decoration in the form of knobs or crests but one fragment (context 1243) has a dog paw print on the upper surface underneath the glaze.

Other forms
Two pieces appear to be of the Roman-style curved and flanged forms (contexts 1267 and 2737). Although not common, tiles of these forms have been previously found in small number within the assemblage from Deansway (Fagan 2004, 352).

The flanged or 'tegula-type' type (context 1267) was moulded to form a rectangular tile with a rounded curving at the edges. It displays a thin green glaze to the upper surface and was found within a Period 3.1 deposit. The curved tile (context 2737; Fig. 5.13, 4) is unglazed and very similar in form to a ridge tile but of slightly narrower diameter and with two round, pierced holes. The presence of peg holes enables tiles of this form to be distinguished from those of standard ridge types, and it is likely that fragments of curved tile that do not display this feature are commonly misidentified within assemblages of medieval date.

A further, unidentified form was retrieved from context 2660. This is slightly 'rhombic' in appearance but with one smooth, curved edge similar to the end of a ridge tile. Although incomplete, it is thought that this is an example of a 'valley' tile, which would have been used along the join where two pitched roofs met at an angle to each other.

Fabric 2b
A total of 469 tiles weighing 56.71kg are of this fabric type. It is the most common medieval fabric type identified, forming 42% of the total tile assemblage. The tiles are of a distinctive, highly sandy fabric, the majority buff or brown in colour at the surfaces with a dark grey, reduced core. As with fabric 2a, the large proportion of tiles of this fabric within assemblages from Worcester suggests a local production source.

Forms present within the group included ridge, nibbed, pegged and nibbed and pegged types, displaying both round, pierced, and square, unpierced holes. In addition, as seen within the tiles of fabric 2a, a small number of more unusual forms including flanged, curved and valley tiles are also present.

Tiles of this fabric are thought to have been produced between the 13th and 15th centuries and were most common within contexts of Period 2. However, smaller amounts of residual material were found within later periods.

Flat tiles
A total of 347 undiagnostic flat tiles are present within this group, the majority being unglazed and sanded on the underside. Just 33 of these sherds are glazed, all displaying green glaze to the upper surface. One tile from context 1271 has the paw print of a cat impressed into the upper surface. Another fragment has roller-stamped decoration on the upper surface (context 900; Fig. 5.13, 10). Decoration of this type has been identified previously on a small fragment of this fabric type from Deansway (Fagan 2004, 351). That fragment, although undiagnostic, was thought to have come from a ridge tile due to the presence of this decoration and a green glaze. However, the fragment from Newport Street is big enough to ascertain that it was from an unglazed flat tile, and therefore a rather rare find.

Nibbed tiles
There are 16 fragments from nibbed tiles. All are unglazed with no markings. The most interesting piece (context 1352) is overfired and warped. It is not clear whether this was a misfired waster from a local production site or the result of contact with fire.

Pegged tiles
There are 34 peg tiles within the assemblage. The most common types have pierced holes of either round or square form, with just eight with unpierced holes. Only one example (context 1262) has glaze and this runs over the break of the tile, suggesting it broke or cracked during firing. This piece also has a very small pierced hole next to a larger, more functional one. No fragments were stamped but one has two dog paw prints on the upper surface (context 1249). Another fragment (context 1299) is of interest due to it being overfired and warped. As with the nibbed example above, it is not clear whether this is a waster or due to accidental burning.

Nibbed and pegged tiles
A total of 24 pieces of tile in this fabric display both nibs and peg holes. Once more, the holes are a mixture of round and square, pierced and unpierced. No fragments are glazed. One tile (context 1249), in three pieces, is near complete and has a well-formed nib and round, pierced peg hole. A further fragment (context 1945) has a square peg hole with corroded nail still *in situ*, and a cat paw print on the upper surface.

Ridge tiles
There are 37 ridge tiles in this fabric type. All but four fragments are glazed and a number are crested, generally in a curved form (contexts 99, 231, 932, 1341 and 2393). Two fragments are particularly of note, one with stamped decoration in the form of small circles grouped in threes (context 1144) and the other with a point at the apex rather than being curved (context 667; Fig. 5.13, 5). Both also have a dark green glaze. Once more, a number of highly overfired and warped or waster tiles are found in this group, with 14 from context 2506 and one from context 1616.

Other forms
Six pieces appear to be of the Roman-style curved and flanged forms (contexts 3, 1052, 1610, 1727, 1777 and 1787; e.g. Fig. 5.13, 2). As with the example identified in fabric 2a, the flanged or 'tegula-type' types are moulded to form a rectangular tile with a rounded curving at the edges. Of these, three have an internal green glaze (contexts 3, 1052 and 1777) and two are glazed on both surfaces (contexts 1727 and 1787). The latter example also has a central round, pierced peg hole. Tiles of this form are known to have had peg holes but fragments with them surviving are rare in Worcester. One unglazed tile is of curved form (context 1610).

Three valley tile forms were recovered from context 1370, all unglazed, and a further tile thought to have been used in conjunction with these tiles was also retrieved from this context. This takes the form of a ridge-style tile, which tapers significantly towards one end, and has two round, pierced nail holes (Fig. 5.13, 6). No other tiles of this form were retrieved.

Fabric 2c
A total of 281 tiles weighing 86.12kg are of this fabric type, forming 26% of the total excavated tile assemblage. Forms present within the group include ridge, nibbed, pegged and undiagnostic flat tiles.

Results from previous excavations have indicated that tiles of this distinctive fabric type were produced from the later 15th century onwards, and this has been confirmed by the discovery of a roof-tile kiln on The Tything in Worcester (Miller *et al.* 2004a), which produced tile of this fabric type and was dated to between 1440 and 1480 by archaeomagnetic dating. As in the case of the assemblage from Deansway (Fagan 2004, 355), it would appear that tiles of this fabric were primarily used from the late medieval period and throughout the post-medieval period, being most common within contexts of Period 3 and later. The fabric is highly distinctive, containing clay pellets or grog and being significantly less sandy than either fabric 2a or 2b, and it has been suggested that tiles of fabric 2c may be representative of a new clay source for the production of flat roof tiles in Worcester from the late medieval period (ibid., 355).

Flat tiles
The majority of the assemblage, totalling 217 tiles, is made up of undiagnostic flat tile fragments. The vast

majority are plain, with only three fragments displaying a very thin green glaze to the upper surface (contexts 3 and 526), and another (context 2033) with what appears to be splatters of cream slip on the upper surface, perhaps indicating production and/or firing alongside decorated floor tiles. Floor tiles were identified amongst the kiln assemblage from The Tything (Griffin 2004b, 13) but the vast majority were plain being decorated only with a dark green glaze.

Three tiles have paw print impressions in the upper surface (contexts 451 and 233), including one from a small cat/kitten (context 233). Four fragments also display makers' stamps.

Nibbed tiles
A total of 56 nibbed tiles are of fabric 2c, all are unglazed fragments and very few display any unusual or distinguishing features. One large fragment is of note due to the nib appearing to have been removed prior to firing (context 233). It is not clear what such a tile would have been used for, as there do not appear to have been any peg holes that could have been employed as an alternative method of fixing this tile to the roof.

The only complete tile within the assemblage is of this fabric and form, with dimensions of 312mm by 165mm, and is 19mm thick (context 2992), making it slightly smaller in length and width but thicker than the complete examples identified at Deansway (Fagan 2004, 354). However, dimensions measured on examples from The Tything kiln assemblage indicate that there was a marked degree of variability in size of tiles of this fabric with width ranging between 140–180mm and thickness between 10–23mm, although the majority measured 15–18mm thick (Griffin 2004b, 11).

Other features of note consist of animal prints, with two small cat/kitten (contexts 523 and 621) and one dog (context 1005). Four fragments (contexts 233, 604, 621 and 863) also display makers' stamps.

Nibbed and pegged tiles
Just four tiles have peg holes, three with a round, pierced hole (contexts 2394 and 2691) and one with an square, unpierced hole (context 631). No tiles of this form in this fabric type were found at Deansway or from The Tything kiln assemblage, although a small number of nibbed and pegged examples were identified at both and therefore, despite the absence of nibs, it would seem likely that these fragments were originally from tiles of this type.

Makers' stamps
Eight tiles display makers' stamps (contexts 3, 143, 604, 621, 863, 969, 2669 and 2691). The increase in the proportion of stamps amongst this fabric type in comparison to the assemblages of fabric 2a and 2b coincides with the introduction of a city ordinance in 1467. This began the compulsory use of clay tiles for roofing due the threat of fire posed by wooden chimneys and thatched roofs. The ordinance also forbade tilers from forming any type of union or guild and as a result, tiles were to be stamped with a maker's mark (Fagan 2004, 342).

A number of the stamps have been identified previously on tiles from other assemblages in Worcester, primarily Deansway. These include four of segmented circle form (contexts 3, 143, 233 and 604; cf Fagan 2004, fig. 207, 11), one cross (context 2691; cf ibid., fig. 207, 15) and one which takes the form a circle divided into four segments to form the impression of a cross (context 2669; cf ibid., fig. 207, 6). An example of this latter type was also identified on a tile from The Tything kiln site (Griffin 2004b, 12). Parallels cannot be found for the remaining three, two of which take the form of a circle (contexts 696 and 863; Fig. 5.13, 8 and 9), the other a misshapen circle with a 'Y' form attached (context 621; Fig. 5.13, 7).

Fabric 2d
There are just 14 tiles of this fabric within the assemblage. A similarly small occurrence was also noted at Deansway where this was attributed to the tiles being of a later date than those of fabrics 2a, b and c. Evidence from Newport Street and other sites excavated since Deansway have confirmed this, and it is now thought that tiles of this fabric date from the late 16th to the 18th century.

Fragments all display the buff banding characteristic of this fabric and five fragments, probably from a single tile, also have fragmentary green glaze on the upper surfaces (context 772). Once again, two tiles show evidence of burning (contexts 130 and 593).

Fabric 3
A total of 112 fragments of roof tile are of Malvernian production. As expected, the predominant form type within this group is ridge tile, with the majority displaying green glaze to the upper surface and a substantial quantity also having decorative crests. The remaining tiles are of undiagnostic flat type, with the exception of one large piece which is similar to the flanged tiles in fabrics 2a and 2b.

The small proportion of flat tiles of Malvernian fabric is not unexpected when taking into account Worcester's large tile-making industry during the medieval period. Therefore, it appears that demand was for the more specialised ridge forms in this fabric, and it would not have been unusual for roofs to comprise locally produced flat tiles with Malvernian ridge tiles.

A characteristic of tiles of this fabric is that they are noticeably thinner than those of Worcester production, and the underside is commonly unsanded but left smooth and often displays a white patination, possibly the remains of a separating medium used to aid removal of tiles from the mould in the absence of sand (Fagan

2004, 356). Tiles of this fabric generally date to between the 13th and 16th centuries.

Flat tiles
Flat roofing tiles form only a very small proportion of this assemblage, amounting to just 28 pieces, 10 of which come from a single tile (context 2506). All are fragmentary and undiagnostic, with just three tiles displaying glaze to the upper surface.

Ridge tiles
Tile identified as being of definite ridge form amounts to 83 fragments. No tiles are complete, but 32 fragments from context 2506 adjoin to form a substantial proportion of one. All but four fragments are glazed and of the unglazed tile, one is burnt and warped (context 933) and the other three are highly abraded (context 590). Seven tiles were decorated with crests (contexts 3, 19, 140, 1273, 2440, 2821 and 2874). These are generally hand formed, very simple and low to the tile, but the near-complete tile from context 2506 displayed two such crests.

Roof furniture
A fragment of roof furniture of Malvernian fabric was recovered from context 2135 (Plot 5; G46; Fig. 5.13, 1). This takes the form of the top of a globular finial, almost mammiform in appearance and similar to an example identified in Southampton (Dunning 1975, fig. 212, no. 1394). The example from Newport Street is wheelmade and very fine, with a thin and patchy speckled green glaze to the external surface similar to that seen on vessels of oxidised glazed Malvernian ware (Fabric 69). The globular type is one of the more basic finial forms and as a result has a fairly wide distribution across the country (Dunning 1968, 224). Such finials are generally attached to the ridge tile by a shaft and, based on other simple finial forms identified in Worcestershire previously (Dunning 1967), this was also probably the case for the example excavated from this site.

Other forms
The only other form present within the Malvernian assemblage is similar to the flanged tiles identified in fabrics 2a and 2b (context 691; Fig. 5.13, 3). As with these, it takes the form of a rectangular tile with a rounded curving at the edges and is glazed on the interior surface. No flanged tiles have been found previously in this fabric type, although three adjoining tiles of a similar profile were identified at Deansway (Fagan 2004, 356). It was thought that these could have formed a gutter or have been used as valley tiles rather than as 'tegula'-type roofing tiles. Unfortunately, the small size of the fragment prevents a definitive identification or function.

Fabric 5
A total of 26 tiles are of fabric 5. Forms present consist of nibbed, ridge and undiagnostic flat tiles. This fabric type was first identified at Church Lane, Hallow, where it was thought to date between the 16th and 18th centuries (Griffin 2004c, 16). The assemblage from Newport Street has gone some way to confirming this date range. The fabric is distinctive, containing large inclusions of rounded slag and grog. It is thought that the rounded appearance of the slag suggests it was metalworking waste that had been incorporated into the clay used for the tiles, rather than having been deliberately added as temper. At Hallow, a small number of bricks also contained inclusions of the same type and it is likely that these were produced alongside the tiles.

Flat tiles
There are 15 undiagnostic flat tiles of this fabric type. All are unglazed and have no distinctive markings or features. Three are overfired and warped and once more, as in the case of similar tiles found across the site, it is not possible to say whether these are wasters or the result of contact with fire or extreme heat during use or post-depositionally.

Nibbed tiles
A total of 10 tiles are nibbed, the most complete examples being double nibbed (context 770).

Ridge tile
A single piece of ridge tile was retrieved from context 19. This is noticeably thicker than examples in fabrics of earlier date.

5.8.2 Discussion by period

Period 2: medieval (10th to 16th century)
A total of 410 pieces of roof tile weighing 63.54kg were recovered from contexts of medieval date. The tile falls into five main fabric groups; 2a, 2b, 2c, 3 and 5.

The form of the flat roof tile recovered from this period is a long-lived type produced between the 13th and 18th centuries. However, as a result of analysis undertaken in recent years on roof tile, it is now possible to date the tiles of locally produced fabric types far more closely and the results from this excavation have further supported the date ranges allocated. A significant proportion of tiles are diagnostic, displaying either nibs or holes, or in the case of 19 fragments (contexts 907, 932, 1249, 1306, 1317, 1340, 1357 and 1477), a combination of the two. Nibbed tiles and nibbed and pegged tiles are thought to have been the earliest form of flat roof tile, being produced from the 13th century onwards. These appear to have been superseded by pegged forms by the 14th century in some areas of England, becoming virtually universal by the end of the 15th century (Fagan 2004, 345; Drury 1981, 131).

The first occurrence of flat roof tile of this type is within Period 2.3 contexts (13th to 14th century), and different fabrics are present in varying amounts throughout the remainder of the period. Of the two local fabrics which dominate the medieval assemblage, fabric 2a is seen at a fairly constant low level throughout the period, whilst fabric 2b starts with similarly small amounts but increases substantially in Periods 2.4 and 2.5 (14th to 16th centuries). As would be expected from their production span, tiles of fabric 2c only really feature in Periods 2.4 and 2.5 but there is still very little material of this fabric type present. Likewise with tiles of fabric 3, which although known to have been produced from the 13th century, only seem to feature in any quantity after the 15th century. Only one tile each of fabrics 2d and 5 are present and these have both been categorised as intrusive.

Period 3: post-medieval (16th to 17th century)

A total of 331 roofing tiles were retrieved from Period 3 contexts. Fabric 2c dominates the assemblage, accounting for 40% of total fragments, with Fabric 2b forming the next most substantial group amounting to 22%. As would be expected, tiles of fabric 2c peak in contexts of Period 3.1 and gradually fall in number towards the end of the period, when production is thought to have been in decline.

Tiles of Fabric 2b were almost certainly residual by this date. However, the large quantity of tiles of this fabric found across the site accounts for the relatively high proportion found in contexts of 16th to 18th-century date, and most probably results from the re-roofing or demolition of earlier buildings during this period. This is also the case for tiles of fabric 2a, which although found in smaller quantity, are still present at a low level throughout the period. Malvernian tiles (fabric 3) are found at a similar level to those of fabric 2a throughout the period, despite tiles of this type still being in production during the 16th century. This would seem to back up the assumption that tiles from Malvern were only brought into Worcester in small numbers. The fact that those used in Worcester were primarily of ridge form would also account for the lower proportion in comparison to the locally produced flat tiles.

Tiles of fabric 2d are also present within contexts of this period, although the very small number of this fabric type as a whole makes it difficult to comment on any significance this may have for the dating of tiles of this type. Likewise, tiles of fabric 5 are identified in small numbers throughout the period.

Period 4: 18th century

Just 38 roof tiles were retrieved from contexts within Period 4. Once more, fabric 2c is dominant, accounting for 47% of the group, but by this time production of these tiles was nearing its end. Just two tiles of fabric 5, the other fabric thought to have still been in production during the 18th century, were present in contexts of this period but, as with fabric 2d in Period 3, tiles of this type are such a minor part of the assemblage as a whole that it is impossible to make any meaningful comment on the dating of this material.

Period 5: 19th and 20th centuries

Virtually all flat roof tile is residual by this period, with the exception of the seven fragments of fabric 1, which are known to have been produced from the 19th century onwards.

Catalogue of the illustrated ceramic roof tile (Fig. 5.13)

1   Wheelmade globular roof finial in oxidised glazed Malvernian ware (fabric 3). Plot 5; Period 2.3/4; G46: context 2135
2   Flanged 'tegula' form tile with glazed internal surface (fabric 2b). Plot 13; Period 2.3.1; G118: context 1777
3   Flanged 'tegula' form tile with glazed internal surface (fabric 3). Plot 2; Period 2/3.1; context 691 (Unassigned)
4   Curved 'imbrex' form tile with two round, pierced peg holes (fabric 2a). Plot 3; Period 2.4/5; G55: context 2737
5   Unusual ridge tile form coming to a point at the apex and covered with a dark green glaze (fabric 2b). Plot 2; Period 3.1; G8: context 667
6   Unusual form with two round, pierced peg holes (fabric 2b). Plot 14; Period 2.3; G227: context 1370
7   Nib tile with unusual maker's stamp and paw print impression (fabric 2c). Plot 2; Period 3.1; G10: context 621
8   Flat tile with circular maker's stamp (fabric 2c). Plot 6; Period 3.3; G83: context 696
9   Nib tile with circular maker's stamp (fabric 2c). Plot 14; Period 3.3; G278: context 863
10 Fragment of flat roof tile with roller-stamped decoration and thin green glaze (fabric 2b). Plot 14; Period 3.1; G247: context 900

5.9 Ceramic building material: bricks
Angus Crawford

Bricks were sampled from structural sequences across the site during excavation. A maximum of five bricks were retrieved from individual structures in an attempt to maintain a consistent sample of brick types present in surviving foundations and other structural remains. Provisional dates were allocated on site and where necessary these have been revised or refined during analysis. These can be compared within the catalogue presented as an appendix to this report (Appendix: Brick Catalogue). In retrospect, it is recognised that the sampling strategy had its limitations in the quantity retained (often only one was kept) and the non-prescriptive method of selection of bricks from single contexts (which may have resulted in selection for retention of those of 'more interesting and old' appearance). A more robust strategy aiming at retaining a larger and more certainly representative sample from each context would be recommended in the future.

During analysis all hand-retrieved bricks were examined, quantified and dated and a *terminus post quem* date produced for each stratified context where

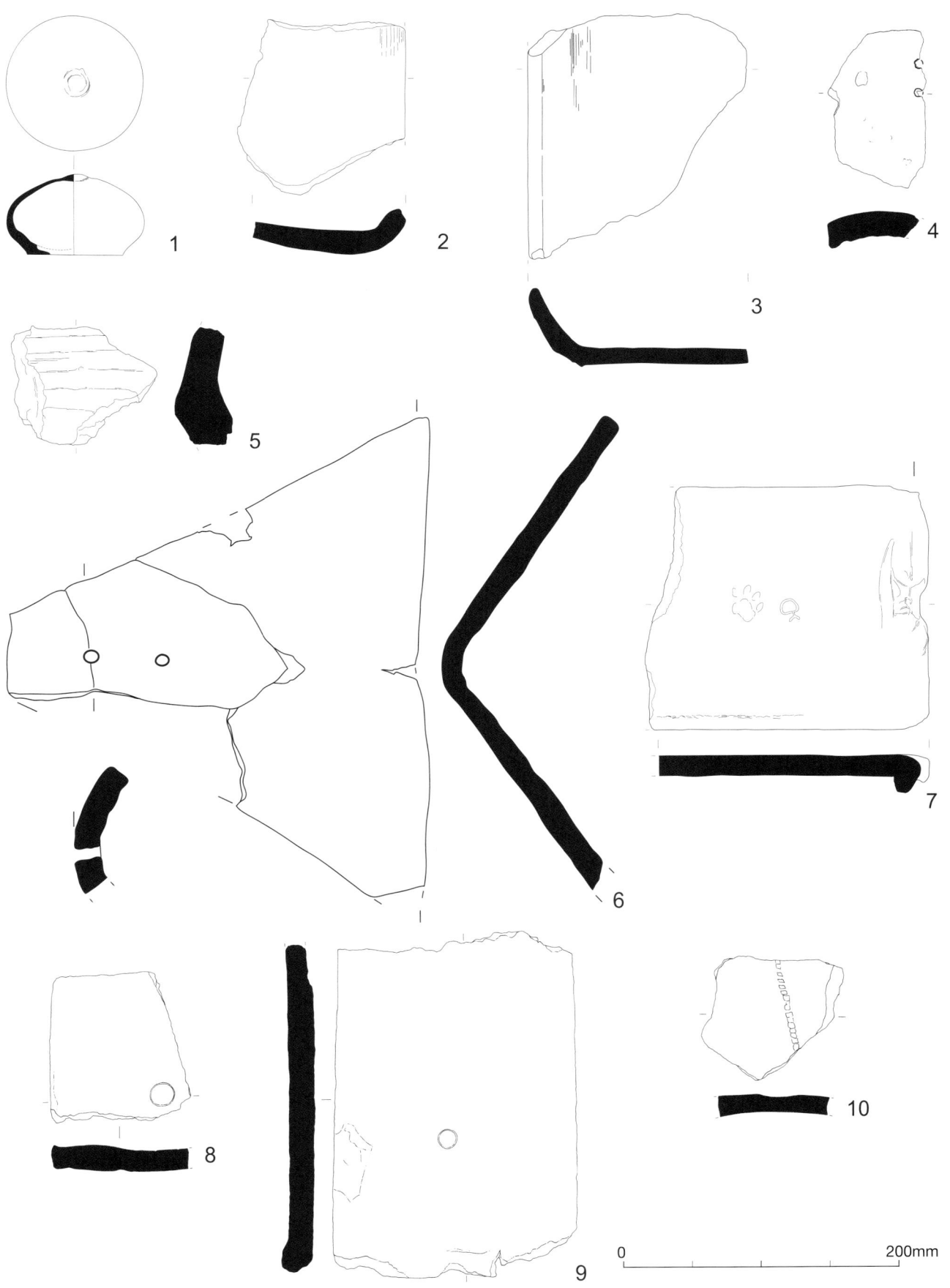

Fig. 5.13 Medieval and post-medieval roof tile (Nos 1–10). Scale 1:4

possible. Bricks were recorded by their dimensions in both millimetres and inches (the measurement on which they would have originally been based) and further identifiers recorded include fabric, colour, finish, method of manufacture, frogs (where present), and animal and human imprints. These details are summarised in the catalogue.

After recording and analysis the majority of the sampled bricks were discarded on site but a sub-sample has been retained, representative of the different fabrics and forms from broadly dateable structures. These form a potential core resource to support the development of a brick fabric and type series for Worcester.

5.9.1 Analysis

Introduction

The analysed assemblage consisted of a sample of 644 bricks. The group came from 212 stratified contexts dating from the late medieval/early post-medieval period onwards. A range of manufacturing techniques, including both handmade and mechanised, were identified within the assemblage, based on observations of fabric, size, finishes, etc., and several bricks designed, or used, for specific functions were also recognised. These are described below.

As noted above, there were limitations in the sampling strategy in terms of the quantity of bricks recovered from single contexts. In addition to this, the vast proportion of bricks recovered came from post-medieval and later deposits, with only a very small sample of medieval contexts being investigated. It was also evident that both the construction and repair of brick structures had partially, and in some cases completely, relied on the reuse of earlier bricks salvaged from demolished structures. This resulted in large numbers of bricks of early date being incorporated into structures of later date.

The large dataset created makes tabulation of the results difficult and only a summary is presented here and in the associated catalogue (Appendix: Brick Catalogue). A complete database of all of the bricks recorded is retained within the site archive, as is a type sub-sample series to support future research.

Late medieval to early post-medieval (16th to 17th century)

Initial examination failed to identify any medieval material that could be securely dated by context, though the assemblage does contain bricks of potential late medieval to early post-medieval date reused in later constructions, and these are discussed here.

Manufacture size was used as the classifying feature, while size and colour were also taken into consideration. A number of bricks were within the dimensional range recorded at the medieval kiln site at The Tything (Miller *et al.* 2004a) and similarity in size was noted (length 225–273mm, width 102–120mm and thickness 52–60mm), together with similarities in fabric and colour (sandy fabric in a range of orange to light brown colours). Examples were observed from several Period 3 contexts (e.g. contexts 41, 564, 1231, 1289 and 2335).

Close examination of the potential late medieval to early post-medieval brick assemblage has revealed three distinct and differing methods of production, which seems to indicate different production approaches, sites and/or kiln locations. The two main methods of production were pallet moulding and slop moulding. Pallet moulding results in a distinctive brick with sanded base, sides (header and stretcher surfaces) and a smooth upper surface. The distinctive features resulting from slop moulding include smooth upper, header and stretcher surfaces and a sanded base (see Hammond 1998 for a detailed analysis of both methods). Production anomalies were identified within the sampled bricks dating to this period, and included slop-moulded bricks that exhibited sanding to at least one stretcher surface. This most probably resulted from the bricks being stacked on their side on a sanded platform at some point prior to firing. A third and apparently entirely different process appeared to have been used in the manufacturing of five bricks from a Period 3-dated wall in Plot 13 (G162: context 908). Their size (230mm by 115–120mm; 55–60mm thick) indicated that these were potentially reused medieval bricks whose manufacture had involved crudely patting the clay into a brick shape on a bedding of straw creating an overall rough finish and external texture. These bricks, as with the other probable medieval material, appear to have been reused during the post-medieval period, making accurate dating of this manufacturing technique impossible from the currently available evidence.

Several bricks of potential late medieval to early post-medieval date featured prints from animals, including cat, dog and sheep (e.g. contexts 558, 589, 901 and 1269), and from light rain exposure (context 984) impressed into the upper surfaces (Fig. 5.14, 1). Similar observations were made on a range of the roof tiles within the assemblage (Griffin, Chapter 5.8). This indicates that during the curing process the bricks were stacked flat and probably under a roofed structure, at least partially open at the sides. Drury's examination of a brickmaker's will from 1646 revealed that 'the family must have been largely self-sufficient in food: cows, sheep, pigs and geese were kept. This has been used to suggest that brick and tile making was a seasonal and part-time occupation' (Drury 1975, 208). The bricks within the Newport Street assemblage exhibiting livestock prints support Drury's suggestion that production may have been a part-time occupation, combined with running a smallholding and occurring within a rural landscape rather than an urban industrial one. Further, given the seasonal nature of agriculture and Britain's highly seasonal climate (which would potentially render brick manufacture impractical during autumn and winter months), this may imply a seasonal cycle to brick manufacture.

A number of fingerprints have been observed in all surfaces of bricks imprinted after the moulding process and prior to firing (e.g. contexts 38, 159, 418, 1636 and 2335, all dating to the 17th century), indicating that some were individually carried (context 2335 has thumb and forefingers on upper and base surfaces) while others were carried supported at both ends leaving distinctive finger impressions at both header ends of the base. Again, similar observations were made on a range of the roof tiles recovered (Griffin, Chapter 5.8). Single bricks from contexts 158 and 2408 (dating from the 17th century) had distinctive finger imprints to the base, the size of the fingers indicating that children had carried these bricks during the moulding process (Fig. 5.14, 2). While Hammond refers to 'moulder's boys' working in the brick industry (1998, 11), there is the possibility that the finger indentations may be the result of family involvement in brick production rather than inherent child labour. Although discussing the industry at a somewhat later date, Stamp in *The Brick Children* records that in 1871 there would have been between 20,000 to 30,000 children ranging from 3 to 16 years working within the brick industry and employed mainly in the Midlands (Stamp 1988). The conditions within which they worked involved at least 13 hours' labour a day, and they were seen as a source of cheap labour and potential income generators for their families. George Smith wrote, as quoted by Daniell (1988, 43), that of brickyard conditions 'the uttermost abomination of immorality, prostitution, impurity and loathsome talk and cursing to be found … and precociousness of the things children ought not to know, much less to do, is one of the most terrible elements of the evil training'.

Bricks formed for specific functions were also identified within the assemblage and included bricks with chamfered ends (contexts 1137 and 2075) and curved bricks for well construction (contexts 1151 and 1591 dating from the late 17th to 18th century). Of particular interest and unusual form were 39 fragments of reddish-orange bricks recovered from Period 3.4 and Period 4 contexts in Plot 6, which appear to have been designed for use as mullion windows (G84: context 516; G79: contexts 1321 and 1398). Six complete examples were re-assembled from a number of fragments (from context 1321) and were of substantial size, averaging 600mm by 130mm by 63mm. Each appeared to have been cast as a single brick using the pallet method, with chamfers cut by knife or wire into both edges of a single stretcher surface. These cuts terminated in an upward curve, approximately 60mm from the header end, to form a plinth (Fig. 5.14, 3). There is no channel for taking a glass pane present and the exact method of their use remains uncertain. While all three contexts overlap in date from the 18th to early 19th century, these brick fragments (reused as foundation material in the construction of walls) appear to be of much earlier date, from the method of manufacture and their poor condition (potentially 16th or early 17th century). Locally, Pirton Church to the south of Worcester has been recorded as having had brick mullions and tracery added to the side windows of its chancel in the 15th century, while the north wall of the chancel had brick mullions added in the late 16th century (Willis-Bund 1924, 183).

Five bricks (including single bricks from contexts 564 and 1289, and three from context 1035) had drips and/or runs of dark green glaze along various surface faces. These all varied in size but were of the same pale to mid brown sandy fabric, suggesting that they originated from a single place of manufacture. The spacing between the glaze runs indicate that they were probably used as kiln furniture during the firing of glazed floor tiles or fired in a kiln of mixed products (Fig. 5.14, 4). While these bricks were recovered from contexts dating from the 16th through to the 18th century, they had been reused and the size and appearance of the bricks suggest a probable medieval date of manufacture. Quantities of green-glazed floor tiles along with roof tiles have previously been identified as being produced at The Tything in Worcester during the 15th century (Miller *et al.* 2004a), and this may tentatively be suggested as the point of origin for these bricks.

17th to 18th century

Bricks produced during the 17th to 18th century are also difficult to identify by dimensions alone, although those after the introduction of the brick tax of 1784 are more readily identifiable as this established the production of bricks of at least three-inch thickness (75mm) (Brunskill 1997, 192). Prior to this date, varying ranges of length and thickness were produced. Bricks are known to have been produced for the St Oswald's Almshouse in Worcester during the 1630s of 2½-inch thickness (65mm; Pat Hughes, pers. comm.), however there is evidence for the continuous production of 2-inch (approximately 50–55mm) thick bricks elsewhere. For instance, excavation of the brick-and-tile kiln at Runsell Green in Essex revealed that one kiln that went out of production in *c.* 1705–15 had been constructed of bricks of 220–230mm by 100–105mm by 55–60mm, and a second kiln was built during the 17th century from bricks 235mm by 110mm by 50–55mm. Further securely dated brick sizes, in this instance measuring 225mm by 105mm by 55mm, were recovered from a barge sunk in the Thames during the third quarter of the 17th century, which were probably bringing bricks to London for rebuilding after the Great Fire of 1666 (Marsden 1971).

A substantial number of the Newport Street bricks recovered from contexts dated to the 17th and 18th century were 9–9¾ inches long (230–250mm) and ranged in thickness from 2¼–2½ inches (57–65mm).

This appears to indicate an increase in brick thickness after the 16th century, a trend which may be related to the increasing demand for the product. Brunskill (1997, 140) notes that the 17th and early 18th century was typified by a more widespread use of bricks across the country and across the social scale. This general trend appears to evident within the Newport Street assemblage and correlates with Brunskill's research identifying 9-inch bricks of ½-inch thickness as a dimensional indicator for the period (ibid., 140). The 17th and 18th-century bricks also differ from earlier bricks in that the majority are of a darker red to purple colour, possibly due to a greater amount of iron oxide present in the clay. Quiney (1974, 111) states that given the organisation of the brick industry in the 17th and 18th century, it can be implied that brick clay was dug and fired locally.

Bricks from some contexts (e.g. 157, 499 and 537) also appear to have a rudimentary frog, consisting of a shallow impressed channel added during the moulding process. Brunskill (1997) records the use of frogs as being common by 1690, though there was little evidence for this within the Newport Street assemblage. The few rudimentary ones noted do not appear to be tally marks as there is no variation in style or position. The rudimentary nature of the frog would suggest a broad 17th-century date for the bricks, and all of the bricks recorded with this frog type were from contexts dated from the 17th to 18th century.

19th to 20th century

The bricks from the 19th and 20th centuries were the most readily identifiable due to substantial changes within the industry, with the mechanisation of the manufacturing process resulting in bricks of better quality and uniform appearance. Although 19th and 20th-century bricks were recorded with thickness below 75mm (such as context 512, with mechanically produced bricks ranging from 63mm to 71mm), physical characteristics such as darker reddish purple colourings and evidence for press-extruded and wire-cut bricks allowed for accurate dating. Further identifiers include the occasional presence of manufacturers' names or production areas placed within the frog recess (e.g. LBC: the London Brick Company, which distributed bricks in the West Midlands after the First World War), and an overall crisp appearance to the brick in comparison to the uneven finishes observed on bricks from earlier periods. No specific Worcestershire brick manufacturers were identified.

5.9.2 Discussion

Although a number of probable medieval bricks were identified within the assemblage, none were directly recovered from medieval dated contexts. There is, however, evidence for their use and production in Worcester during this period. In 1467 a Worcester City ordinance was passed specifying that 'for the prevention of fire neither wooden chimneys nor thatched roofs should be allowed thenceforward; by midsummer day next coming, the wooden chimneys should be replaced by brick or stone and the thatched roofs by tiles' (Stenton 1924, 387). After this ordinance there should have been an increase in the use of brick within the city; however, the Worcester City Corporation repeated the prohibition of thatched roofs and timber chimneys in 1496, suggesting that the prohibition was being only slowly acted upon, and may indicate that medieval brick use within Worcester may be rarer than documentary evidence might at first glance indicate (Fagan 2004, 342).

Apart from such documentary sources, direct evidence for the use of bricks during the medieval period within Worcester has been recorded during the excavations at 9–10 The Tything (Miller *et al.* 2004a), where kilns were recorded that had been specifically built for the manufacture of roof and floor tiles but which were partially constructed from brick. These were archaeomagnetically dated to the later 15th century, signifying the likelihood of at least some brick production occurring to the north of the town during the medieval period. Miller suggested that the demise of the kilns and the abandonment of the site during the 16th and 17th centuries may indicate a period of economic decline, though a relocation of the industry is also a possibility (ibid., 24).

Analysis of the probable medieval bricks identified that brick dimensions, while providing a good general dating guide, need to be considered against other general features such as the method of manufacture, fabric and overall colour. While the medieval bricks tended to be of irregular size there was some uniformity in thickness of around 50–55mm, with a variation either side of up to 7mm. The bricks were also predominantly manufactured using either the pallet or slop-moulded method, in a range of pale orange to light brown colours.

The post-medieval brick assemblage saw a general increase in bricks size with bricks of 65mm (2½ inch) thickness produced from the early to mid 17th century onwards. However, bricks of 2-inch thickness continued to be produced during the 17th century. Later 17th and 18th-century bricks tended to be of a red or purplish red colour, most probably reflecting the use of higher firing temperatures and the presence of iron oxide in the clay. The higher firing temperatures also resulted in quantities of partially vitrified and or substantially distorted bricks. While distorted, these bricks were still usable in structural applications where uniformity was not required.

The introduction of the brick tax in 1784 encouraged the manufacture of bricks with a thickness of 75mm (3 inches) and greater, though bricks of 63mm thickness were also recorded from the period. Evidence for the method of production, such as mechanical pressing, was used to more securely identify bricks made during the 19th and 20th century. Further identifiers for mid 19th-century production, as a result of increased industrialisation, include a greater consistency in sizes, specialised bricks (such as blue engineering bricks) and other distinct features such as brickmakers' names impressed within the frog.

Catalogue of illustrated brick (Fig. 5.14)

1. Bricks with animal prints:
   a) Unidentified hooves [1140]   b) Cat [1269]
   c) Sheep [558]   d) and e) Dog [901] and [589]
2. Bricks with children's finger prints [418] and [2335]
3. Brick mullions [1398]
4. Glaze runs [564]

Fig. 5.14 Bricks (Nos 1–4). Scale 1:5

5.10 Fired clay artefacts
Angus Crawford

A single counter produced from a body sherd of externally burnished Oxidised Severn Valley ware (fabric 12) was recovered from a medieval context in Plot 13 (Period 2.3.2; G124: context 1567; Fig. 5.15). The counter was roughly circular, having a maximum diameter of 22mm and thickness of 5.5mm. Oxidised Severn Valley wares were produced throughout the Roman period, however, the counter may have been produced from a residual sherd of Roman pottery during a later period.

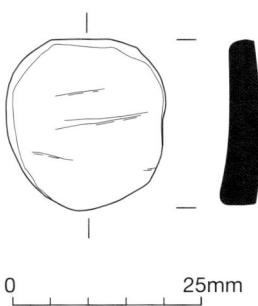

Fig. 5.15 Fired clay counter. Scale 1:1

5.11 Architectural stonework
Christopher Guy

5.11.1 Introduction

A substantial amount of stone was recorded in the surviving footings of many of the Period 3 and later buildings recorded across the site (e.g. Fig. 4.6). This included a number of apparently reused pieces of architectural stonework which were retained for analysis (see below). The majority of the stonework comprised roughly hewn ashlars, predominantly of green or red sandstone, but also included small quantities of limestone. Such stonework was recorded on site plans, context records and the accompanying photographic record.

The architectural stonework recovered was examined to identify the type of stone and form of moulding present. The stones were divided into groups representing structural fabric, such as shafts or window surrounds, and fragments thought to be from monuments. Within these groups the stones are arranged by approximate date order. Photographs and drawings of the mouldings have been compared with those present in Worcester Cathedral and with standard works (Forester 1972; Esdaile 1946). The website for the Corpus of Romanesque Sculpture in Britain and Ireland (2008) proved useful for finding a parallel for the chevron voussoir.

Catalogue of illustrated architectural stonework (Figs 5.16 to 5.26)

1. Short length of attached roll-moulding with keel; green sandstone. Diameter 100mm, height 140mm. Late 12th/early 13th century. Plot 4; G32: context 1528 (Period 5).

1a. Short length of attached roll-moulding with keel; green sandstone. Diameter 150mm, height 150mm. Late 12th/early 13th century. Plot 4; G32: context 1528 (Period 5).

1b. Short length of attached roll-moulding with no keel; green sandstone. Diameter 170mm. There is vertical tooling on the circumference. Probably 12th century. Unstratified.

2. Fragment of attached roll-moulding; green sandstone. Height 95mm, width 200mm, depth 200mm. It was probably part of the jamb of an opening. Possibly 12th or 13th century. Plot 14; G243: context 975 (Period 2.4).

3. Voussoir; limestone. Height 200mm, width 120–135mm, depth 250mm. This is a voussoir from an arch and carved with chevron decoration. Late 12th century. Plot 3; G64: context 2557 (Period 2.4/5).

4. Fragment of the base of a compound pier; green sandstone. Height 140mm, maximum width 400mm, maximum depth 250mm. There is a roll-moulding around the upper edge to define the shafts. The shafts set on this base would have had a curved cross-section, while the straight section of the roll-moulding may possibly have continued along the face of the wall to form a string course. Possibly 13th century. Plot 1; G23: context 338 (Period 3.1).

5. Fragment of door jamb; green sandstone. Height 210mm, width 310mm, depth 200mm. Flat vertical face with not quite symmetrical chamfered sides. This is probably a door jamb or could possibly have been the base for an attached shaft. Possibly 13th century. G172: context 3 (machining horizon).

6. Column base; red sandstone. Height 260mm, width 680mm, depth 390mm. Part of a compound pier or respond. Probably 14th century. Plot 6; G79: context 2868 (Period 3.4/4).

7. Window mullion; lias. In three sections (one section illustrated); total height 610mm, width 190mm, depth 375mm. This is part of the mullion between two lights of a window. There is a glazing slot 20mm wide on both sides. There is a possible mason's mark on the bed of one section. 14th century. Plot 13; G168: context 887 (Period 5).

8. Fragment of window tracery; green sandstone. Maximum height 270mm, maximum width 270mm, depth 360mm. This is the springer between two cusped window lights. There is an outer trapezoidal moulding following the line of the chamfer on the inner mouldings. The glazing slot is 15mm wide. 14th century. Plot 4; G282: context 409 (Period 5).

9. Possible fragment of window jamb; green sandstone. Height 280mm, width 320mm, depth 170mm. There are two rolls, one with a fillet, with deep hollow mouldings between them and to either side. There are traces of white limewash and possibly paint. Possibly 13th century. Plot 1; G1: context 348 (Period 3.1).

Fig. 5.16 Worked building stone (Nos 1–2). Scale 1:4

10. Possible fragment of jamb or arcade; limestone. Height 160mm, width 400mm, depth 235mm. This may be a reworked mullion with an attached chamfered shaft and a roll-moulding. Probably 14th or 15th century. Plot 6; G91: context 1413 (Period 3.2).

11. Possible fragment of door jamb; red sandstone. Height 190mm, width 310mm, depth 155mm. Small roll with shallow moulding to either side. This may have been part of a door jamb or possibly a tomb surround. Probably late 14th century. Plot 14; G278: context 842 (Period 3.3).

12. Possible fragment of door jamb; green sandstone. Height 175mm, width 280mm, depth 160mm. There are two slightly hollow mouldings but the moulding between (possibly a roll) has been hacked off. This may be part of a jamb but was possibly part of a monument. Probably late 14th century. Plot 1; G1: context 349 (Period 3.1).

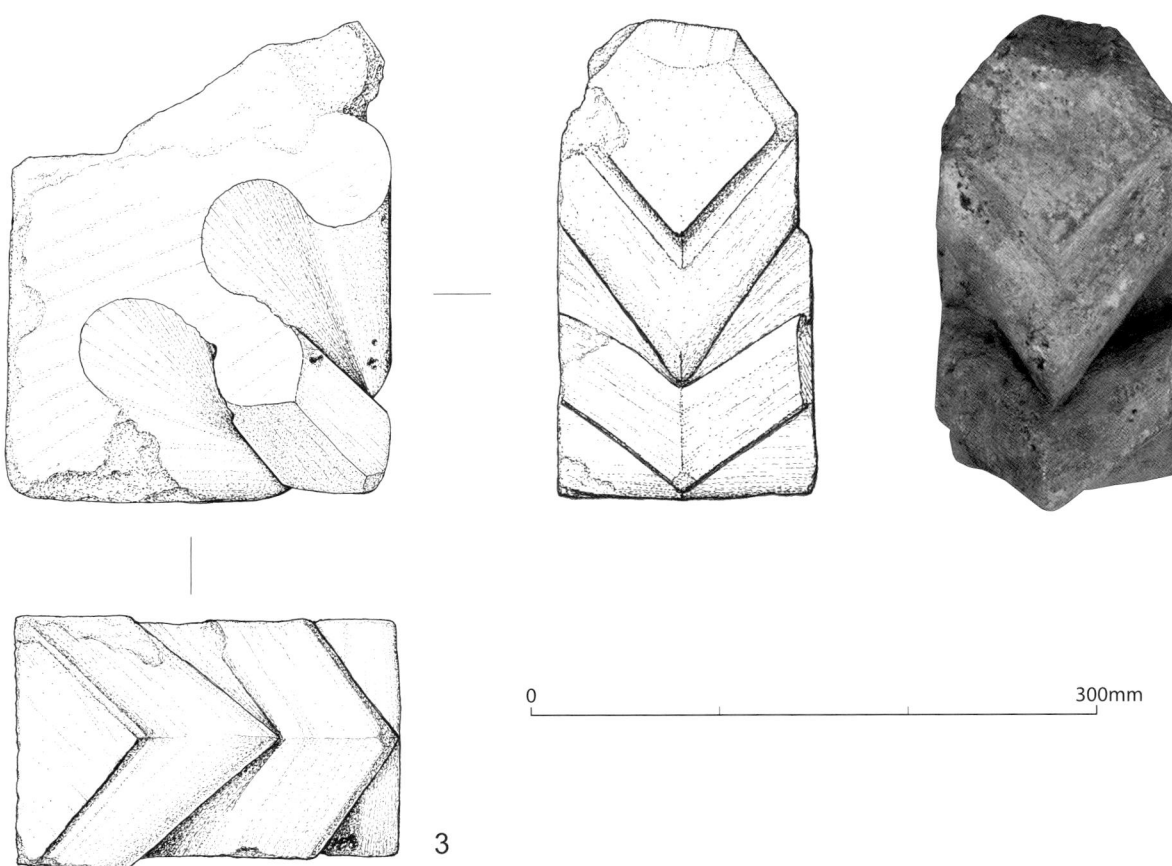

Fig. 5.17 Worked building stone (No. 3). Scale 1:4

13. Possible cusp from tracery; red sandstone. Height 170mm, width 210mm, depth 170mm. There is a flat 'nose' with a large cavetto moulding to one side and a smaller deeper hollow moulding to the other. There is no glazing slot so this is not from a glazed opening. It may be from a cloister. G172: context 3 (machining horizon).

14. Possibly weathered; red sandstone. Height 140mm, width 260mm, depth 240mm. One side of the block is chamfered with a quarter-round hollow beneath to form a drip moulding. Medieval. Plot 6; G79: context 1589 (Period 3.3/4).

15. Possible fragment of the top of a tomb; green sandstone. Height 150mm, width 610mm, depth 470mm. This is a corner of the upper slab of a tomb chest. It may have supported an effigy or had a brass attached or indented into it. The side of the slab has a compound moulding. Possibly 15th century. Plot 10; G111: context 963 (Period 5).

16. Possible fragment from a monument; red sandstone. Height 160mm, width 480mm, depth 200mm. There is a cavetto moulding below a step in the profile. This may be part of the edge of a slab from the top of a table tomb dating from the 16th or 17th century. The chamfer appears to represent a reworking of the block. G172: context 3 (machining horizon).

17. Fragment from the base of or for a monument; red sandstone. Height 200mm, width 340mm, depth 320mm. There is a series of mouldings on one side of the block: quarter-round over chamfer over hollow. There are traces of mortar on some of the surfaces. Probably 16th century. Plot 3: context 2568 (Unassigned; Period 3.2).

18. Possible fragment of a monument; green sandstone. Height 250mm, width 220mm, depth 150mm. It has a complex profile composed of a series of mouldings, very similar to those on No. 15. There are traces of mortar and limewash on the surface. This is probably part of the upper slab of a chest tomb base. Possibly 17th century. Unstratified.

19. Possible fragment of a monument; green sandstone. Height 135mm, width 340mm, depth 190mm. It has an ogee-moulding over two vertical steps. This may have been the corner of the base or top slab of a monument. Possibly 17th century. Unstratified.

20. Possible fragment from a monument; limestone. Height 235mm, width 160mm, depth 110mm. There is a raised chamfered border on two sides of the fragment which surrounds a flat panel. There are no clear tooling marks and the date of the fragment in uncertain. It may have been part of the surround for a panel on a tomb chest or wall monument. Possibly

Fig. 5.18 Worked building stone (Nos 4–6). Scale 1:8

late 16th century. Plot 5; G46: context 2187 (Period 3.1/3.2).

21. Fragment perhaps from the top of a screen or monument; green sandstone. Maximum height 240mm, maximum width 230mm, depth 120mm. There is a horizontal moulded band along the top with part of a small pointed arch recessed into the panel beneath. There is part of another arch to its right. Possibly 15th or 16th century. Plot 1; G21: context 25 (Period 4).

22. Possible fragment of monument or screen; green sandstone. Overall height 270mm, overall width 400mm, overall depth 170mm. On the right hand side there is a trefoil crocket on a chamfered background with the head of a cusped moulding below. To its left there is another trefoil crocket but the sides to the back are not chamfered. There is a plain panel above the top of the crockets. Possibly 15th century. Plot 1; G1: context 132 (Period 3.1).

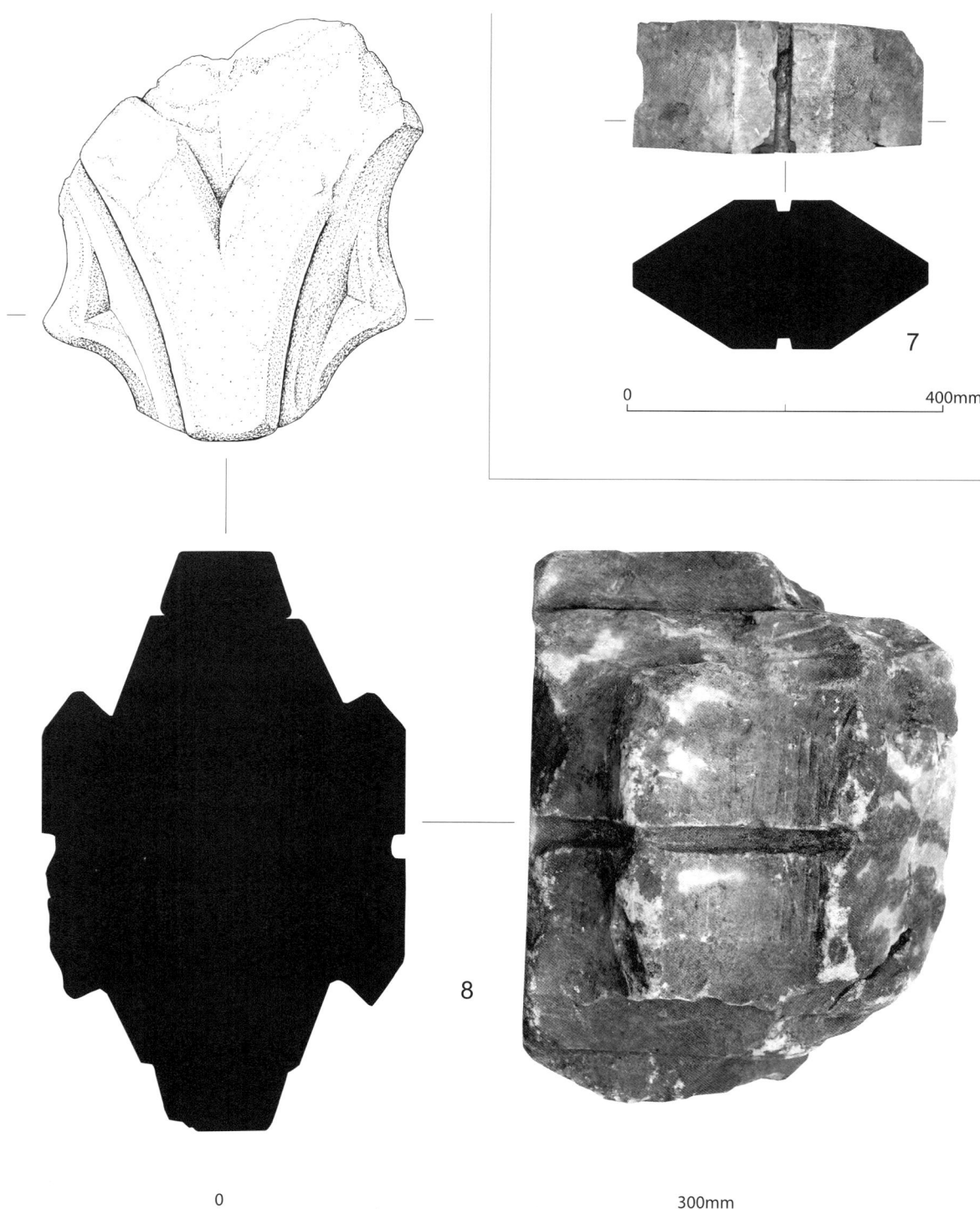

Fig. 5.19 Worked building stone (Nos 7– 8). Scales 1:4 and 1:8

23. Trefoil finial; limestone. Height 240mm, overall width 170mm, depth 90mm. This is a trefoil finial from the top of a screen or monument. All three arms are damaged so its proper shape is unclear. There are the remains of moulded decoration on either side of the base. There is also an incised central setting-out line running upwards from the base. Possibly 15th century. Plot 9; G101: context 1821 (Period 3).

24. Possible fragment of monument; green sandstone. Height 380mm, overall width 260mm, overall depth 260mm. In the centre there is a vertical quarter-round moulding which curves slightly towards the left at the top. To the right there is a cusped moulding with square decorative mouldings in the hollow. There is no evidence of a glazing slot to suggest that there was a window on this side. To the left of the upright

Fig. 5.20 Worked building stone (Nos 9–14). Scale 1:8

moulding there are the remains of carved foliage decoration or possibly swags of drapery which have eroded away to the left. Behind the decoration there is a panel running towards the left with two horizontal moulded bars. Probably 15th or 16th century. Plot 2; G9: context 22 (Period 5).

25. Possible fragment of column; unidentified stone. Diameter *c.* 260mm, depth 100mm. Slightly oval in plan, this may originally have been part of a column. There is a hole 80mm square the full depth of the fragment. This is slightly off-centre and may represent a reuse of the stone. The shape of the fragment and the location of the hole would suggest that this was not a grindstone. Also there are no clear grooves visible on the top or bed to channel the seed or flour. The face of the shaft is weathered. The hole may have been a socket. Plot 2; G6: context 687 (Period 3.2).

26. Voussoir; limestone. Height 80–155mm, width 130mm, depth 130mm. Oak-leaf decoration on front face and circular indentation 80mm in diameter and 1–2mm deep on bottom bed. Probably 14th century. Plot 2; G53: context 122 (Period 5).

5.11.2 Discussion

Twenty-eight fragments of worked architectural stone were recovered from the excavations. The majority appear to date from the medieval period and most have probably come from a church or associated building. They can be divided into two main groups: elements forming part of the building's structure and fragments from internal fittings.

The earliest structural fragments date from the late

Fig. 5.21 Worked building stone (Nos15–17). Scales 1:4 and 1:8

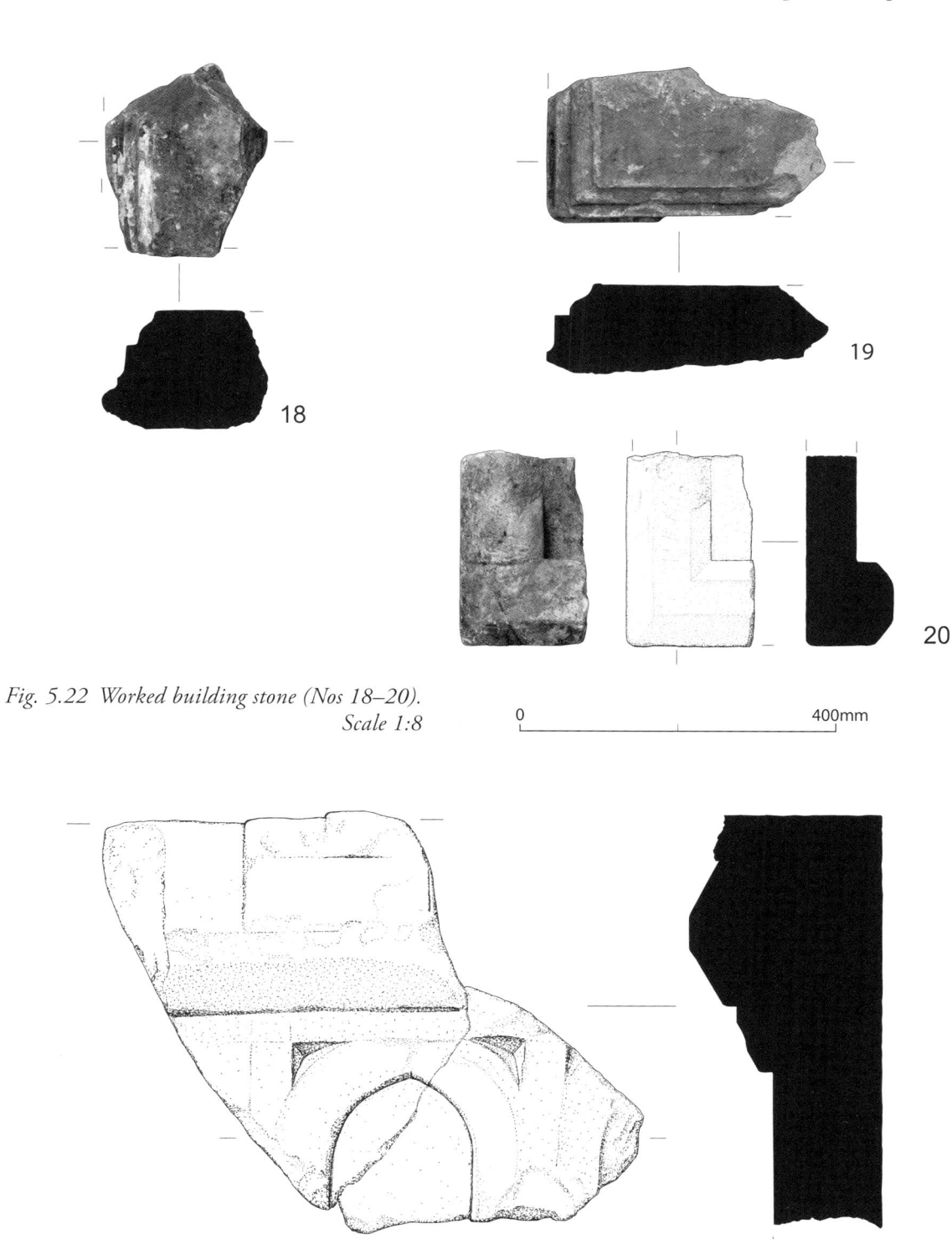

Fig. 5.22 Worked building stone (Nos 18–20). Scale 1:8

Fig. 5.23 Worked building stone (No. 21). Scale 1:4

154 *Excavations at Newport Street, Worcester, 2005*

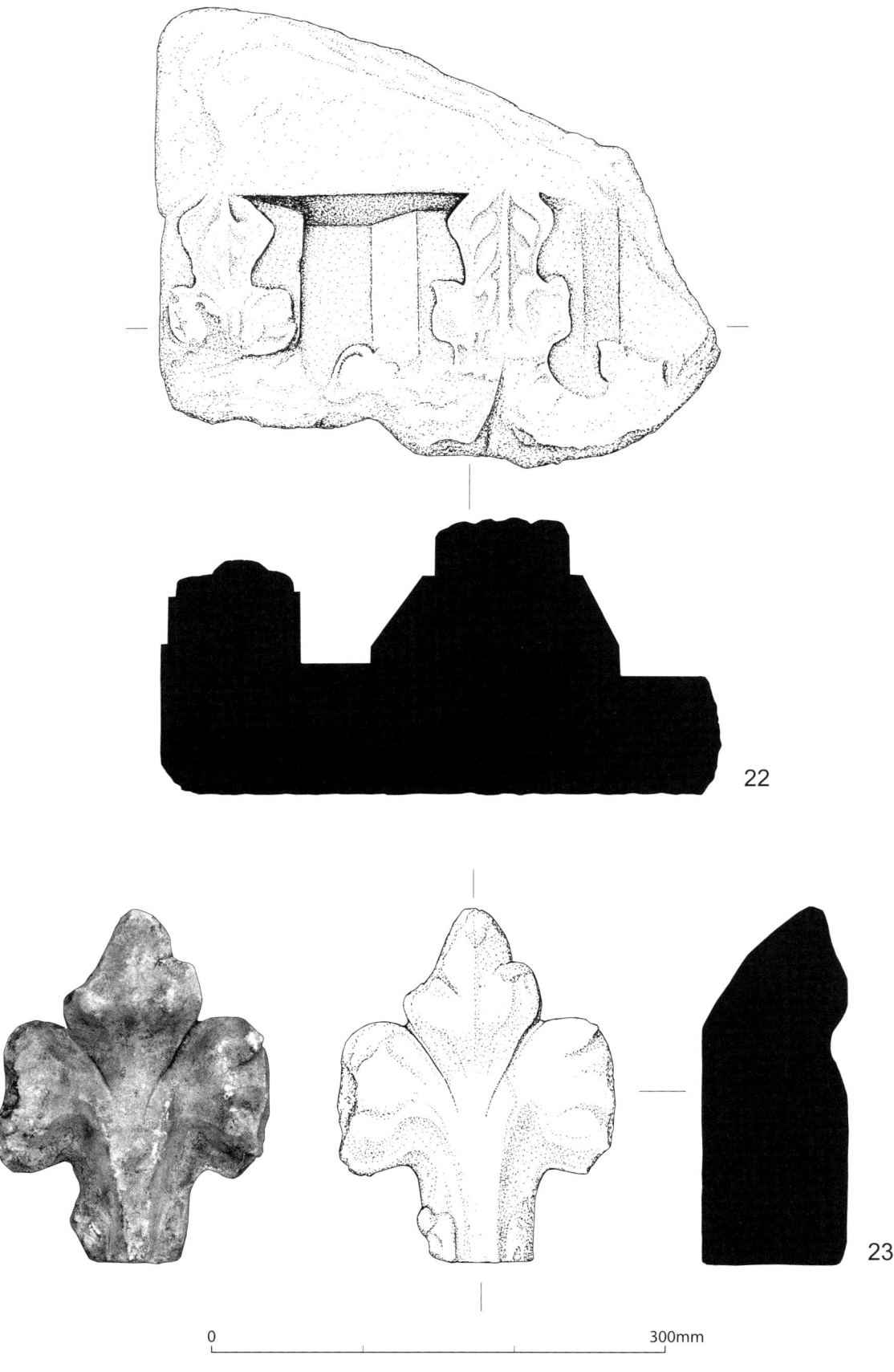

Fig. 5.24 Worked building stone (Nos 22–23). Scale 1:4

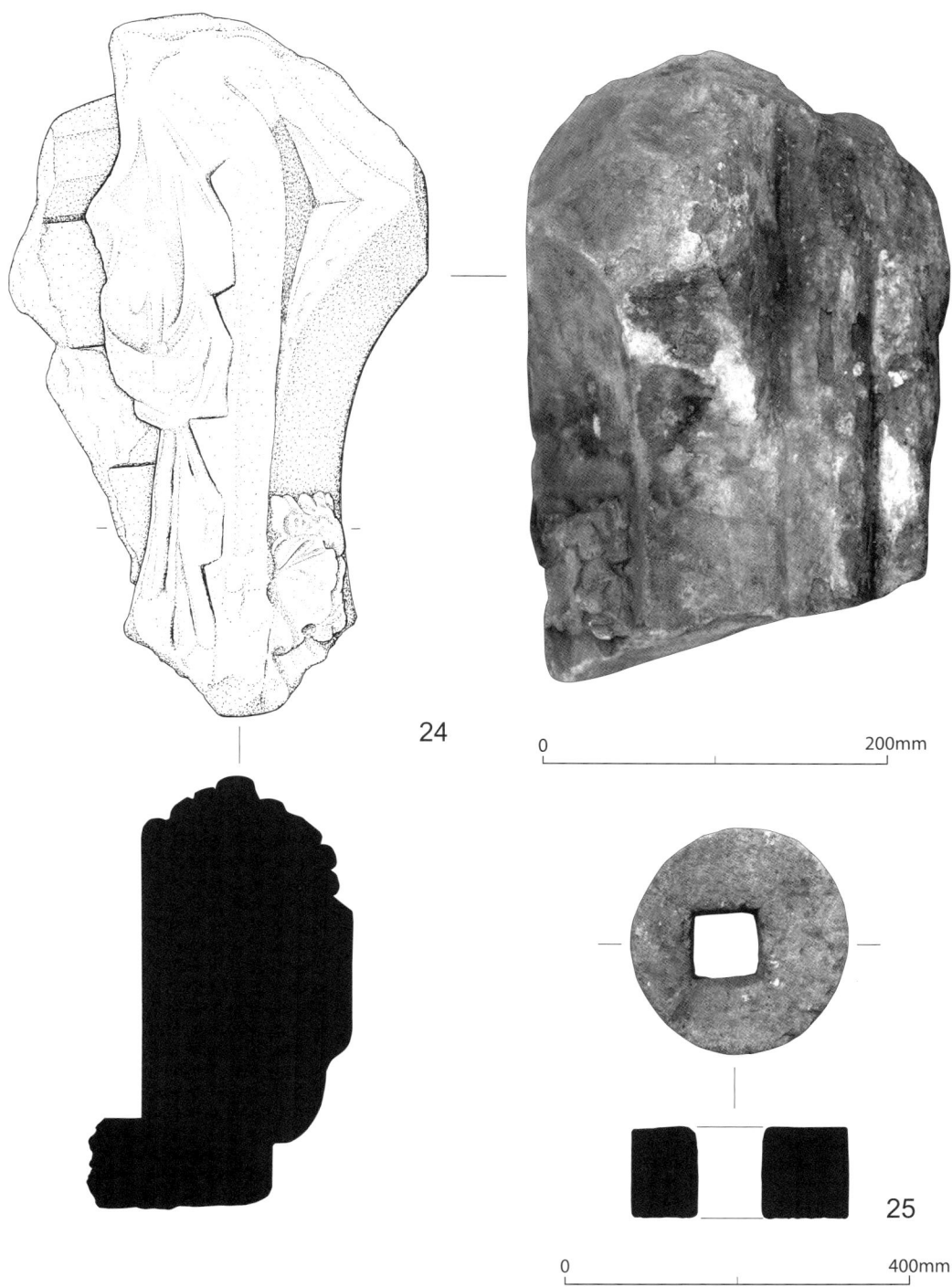

Fig. 5.25 Worked building stone (Nos 24–25). Scales 1:4 and 1:8

12th or early 13th century. Three (Nos 1, 1a and 1b) are short lengths of attached roll-moulding. The presence of a keel on the roll of mouldings 1 and 1a would suggest a date later in the 12th century or early in the 13th century, while the absence of a keel on fragment 1b would indicate an earlier date. The roll on No. 2 also has no keel but still retains much of the stone to which it was attached. This was probably part of the jamb of a window or possibly a door. All these fragments can be paralleled in Worcester Cathedral.

Another early piece is a voussoir from an arch, carved with chevron ornament (No. 3). The presence of chevron rolls on two adjacent faces, together with edge chevron carving, would suggest that this stone is from an arch of several orders. A similar style of decoration can be seen in the chancel arch at Garway, Herefordshire (Corpus of Romanesque Sculpture in Britain and Ireland, 2008).

Probably dating from slightly later in the 13th century are fragments of two piers (Nos 4 and 5). No. 5 is probably part of a door jamb and has vertical faces. The fact that the chamfered sides are not quite symmetrical would suggest that it was not part of an attached shaft. No. 4 may have formed part of the base of a compound pier to support a triple attached shaft. The roll may have been continued along the wall-face as a string course. Fragments similar to these (although not identical) can be seen in Worcester Cathedral, particularly in the 13th-century parts towards the east end.

No. 6 is another section of attached shaft or compound pier; however, this is probably of 14th-century date, although the moulding is very badly eroded. There are also fragments of window tracery dating from the 14th century. These include pieces of a plain chamfered mullion (No. 7), made of lias. This has glazing slots on both sides, showing that the window was of at least two lights. From a different window is a springer (No. 8) from between two lights. This has an outer roll moulding while the inner mouldings are slightly chamfered.

Other medieval mouldings that probably come from openings are Nos 9 to 13. No. 9 is probably part of the jamb of a window dating from the 13th century, while No. 10 may have been part of a door jamb, possibly dating from the 14th or 15th century. No. 11 may also have been part of a door jamb but could have come from the base of a tomb probably dating from the late 14th century. No. 12 could also have been either part of a door jamb or a monument and again may date from the late 14th century. No. 13 may have been part of a window reveal; the absence of a glazing slot would indicate that it is not from window tracery. It may come from a cloister.

No. 14 is a fragment of weathering from the exterior of a building. The chamfered upper surface and the hollow under it formed a drip moulding to stop water flowing down the face of the wall below.

A significant number of mouldings appear to have come from tombs or monuments. Some, such as Nos 15, 16 and 17, may have come from table tombs and been part of the slab to take a brass or effigy, while Nos 18 and 19 could have been parts of the base or pediment of a monument. Nos 15 and 17 probably date from the 15th or early 16th century but could be later. Similar mouldings can be found on tombs and monuments in Worcester Cathedral. No. 20 is possibly of similar date and may have formed part of the surround for a panel on a wall monument or chest tomb.

Some of the fragments have more detailed mouldings. No. 21 has what looks like a panel of blind arcading and could have come from the surround of a tomb recess. No. 22 could have come from a similar location and has the remains of a series of trefoil crockets, one of which is on a chamfered background. This fragment is probably

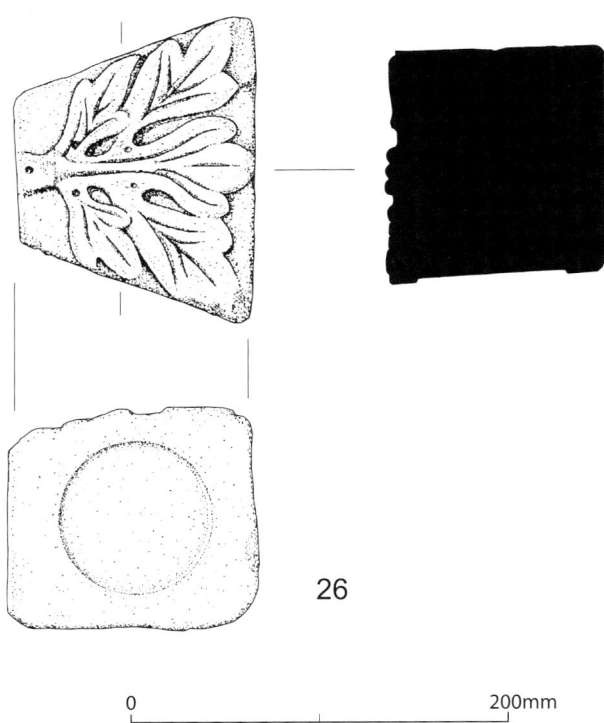

Fig. 5.26 Worked building stone (No. 26). Scale 1:4

15th century in date. Also possibly 15th century in date is No. 23, a trefoil finial from the top of a screen or monument.

The most elaborate piece is No. 24, which is carved on many of its surfaces and may have formed part of a freestanding tomb or a projection from a tomb recess. There are many different elements to the design, including foliage, decorative mouldings and chamfered bars. This again is possibly of 15th or 16th-century date. No. 26 is also elaborate and appears to be the lowest voussoir on the right-hand side of an archway or recess because of the circular indentation on the bottom bed. It may have been set on top of a shaft, although there would normally be an abacus or impost between a shaft and the arch. It is possible that the indentation was a form of keying to locate the stone and prevent it moving but it is very shallow.

One fragment that may not have come from a church or associated building is No. 25. Although originally it may have been part of a column, the stone is only 100mm in depth and therefore much shallower than might be expected. It is also slightly oval in shape, which again suggests that it is not from a column. It is possible that it may have been a grindstone, although the off-centre hole might indicate otherwise. It is also larger than might be expected for such an object (Hal Dalwood, pers. comm.).

The majority, if not all, of the fragments of worked stone described above appear to have come from a church. A possible source could be All Saints' Church, which lies close by to the south-east. This church was substantially rebuilt in the 18th century, although the medieval tower was retained (Bridges 2000). It is most likely that All Saints' was also the source of the material suggested as coming from tombs or monuments. However, it is possible that some of the other material, which formed part of the fabric of a building, may have come from a different, but still ecclesiastical source, for example Blackfriars to the north-east or St Clement's to the west.

Both All Saints' and St Clement's churches were probably founded before the Norman Conquest (Bridges 2000) and could thus have been the source of the earliest stonework described. All Saints' appears to have been rebuilt in the second half of the 15th century, as on 10 April 1450 an Indulgence of 40 days was granted to anyone who subscribed to its rebuilding. This might account for some of the masonry recovered from Period 2 or early Period 3 contexts (Nos 2, 3, 4 and 9). Both All Saints' and St Clement's churches were damaged during the Civil War and had to be repaired, possibly indicating a source for material deposited during the latter half of the 17th century. All Saints' was rebuilt *c*. 1740, and although St Clement's was also repaired again in the 18th century it was demolished in 1823 (Bridges 2000). A further possible source for some later medieval material would be Blackfriars, which was founded in 1347 and demolished in the 16th century following the Dissolution (Baker and Holt 2004), and can thus be regarded as a possible source for the later 14th and 15th-century fabric.

5.12 Other stone
Angus Crawford and Alan J. Jacobs

Apart from the architectural fragments discussed in the previous section (5.11), a number of worked-stone artefacts also were recovered, dated to the medieval period (Period 2) onwards. The majority are typical of types from urban assemblages within Worcester (Roe 2004) and comprise stone objects produced from local and regional sources. However there are several unusual forms and reuse practices as described below.

5.12.1 Spindle whorls
Alan J. Jacobs

Four examples of spindle whorls were recovered. One of these (from context 1860; No. 1; Fig. 5.27, 1), is a finely turned and decorated shale example derived from a medieval context but of a design and style indicative of a Roman origin. The remaining three examples are very well-made lathe-turned objects of blue lias decorated with concentric circles (Fig. 5.27, 2–4). Two of these (from contexts 2728 and 2754; Nos 2 and 3) were recovered from late medieval deposits associated with Building 4 within Plot 3, and it may be of note that documentary evidence indicates that during the early post-medieval period this property was occupied by a weaver (Hughes, Chapter 5.1). The final example (context 1576; No. 4) came from an unphased rubble spread in Plot 6; due to its remarkably similar form to the other two examples, it is also probably of medieval origin.

5.12.2 Rotary querns and millstones
Angus Crawford

Rotary querns (Fig. 5.28)
Five rotary querns were recovered. One near-complete example was recovered from context 1507 and is an upper stone of worked Gritstone (No. 5). The flat grinding surface of the stone (not shown) retains two small opposed square sockets to take a rynd, which would have been positioned on a spindle to facilitate the turning of the upper quern. A squared socket hole is present in the crudely finished upper surface, however a horizontal V-shaped socket is also present almost directly opposite, cut in from the edge of the stone. This appears to indicate two different methods for turning the quern, using either an upper vertical handle or a side mounted horizontal handle located in the V-shaped socket. The latter handle may have been constructed, presumably of wood, as a right angle also allowing for a vertical grip. Why there were two different methods for rotating the quern is difficult to discern, but the V-shaped socket is substantially damaged and the upper socket may indicate that the stone was modified to enable its continued use.

A morphologically similar quern of conglomerate stone was recovered from context 1840 (No. 6). The quern is partially reassembled from four substantial fragments and is wedge-shaped in section. This would indicate a variation in the distribution of stone size within the conglomerate matrix, resulting in uneven wear to the grinding surface. The hopper hole is of a maximum diameter of 80mm and, as with the quern (No. 5) there is a base socket for the rynd, a socket on the upper surface for the locating of a vertical handle and the probable remains of a V-shaped groove as discussed above. A further three sandstone rotary querns from the same context (1840; Nos 7, 8 and 9) were identified from seven conjoining fragments. The fragmentary nature of this material provides little diagnostic information, however three conjoining fragments appear to be from a lower stationary grindstone as the central hole has a maximum diameter of 35mm (No. 9). This indicates that it was designed for a spindle to be passed through to take the rynd of the upper stone rather than for use as a hopper. On this particular example the grinding surface has extensive wear with a raised lip around the outer edge, indicating that the upper rotating quern was of slightly smaller diameter.

Context 1507 had a *terminus post quem* of 14th-century date, while that of context 1840 is 13th century, suggesting that these reused quern stones are potentially of early medieval origin. While there was a 12th-century prohibition on the use of quern stones for the grinding of corn (Roe 2004, 472), there is evidence for continued quern use beyond this date. Langdon estimated that approximately 20% of early 14th-century English grain was still ground by hand mills (mainly for commercial purposes) and there is also documentary evidence for the granting of permission for their use (Watts 2002, 40–1). There is also the possibility that the quern stones were used to grind other materials such as malt grain. Both contexts 1507 and 1840 were associated with oven structures on Plot 13 (G139 and G357 respectively) with the quern stones used in their construction. Whether this represents the relocation or expansion of a previously established bakery within Worcester is not known, and the querns may simply represent the reuse of available stone for construction purposes.

Millstones (Fig. 5.29)
The remains of four substantial millstones were recovered, consisting of two near-complete stones and two individual halves. All display varying degrees of use wear. One of the near-complete stones (context 557; No. 10; Fig. 5.29, 10) had been worked from Forest of Dean quartz conglomerate (Devonian quartzite) with further cutting of furrows into the grinding surface in an arrangement that would indicate clockwise turning during milling. The stone had been reused as a well capping (contexts 589 and 650) dating from the late 17th to 18th century, with the shape of the rynd unable to be determined as the central eye had been filled with concrete, presumably when the well fell out of use.

The second near-complete millstone (No. 11; Fig. 5.29, 11) had also been reused as a well cap (context 294, dating from the late 17th to 18th century) and has extensive wear to the grinding surface. The amount of wear has removed any evidence for furrow cuts, if indeed any had been present. The stone is Cotswold conglomerate Gritstone, with curved sockets in the shape of two back-to-back letter Cs to take a rynd. This may be indicative of a late medieval date for this particular millstone (Watts 2002, 102), with reuse as a well cap during the later post-medieval period.

Two further millstones were cut from non-local granite (possibly from Shropshire) and consist of just under and over half of individual millstones (Nos 12 and 13; Fig. 5.29, 12–13). Both have furrows cut into the grinding surface with some evidence of use wear. The larger fragment (No. 13) retains its socket for the rynd, which is also of the form of back-to-back Cs. While the rynd form was again similar to those identified from medieval types, the quality of both the stone and the furrow carving suggests a post-medieval date of manufacture with later reuse to cap a well (context 1486 dating from the late 17th to early 19th century). The smaller millstone fragment (No. 12) recovered as unstratified material within context 3 is potentially of similar date.

The reuse of millstones to cap wells was identified in several instances at Newport Street, possibly reflecting a common practice within Worcester. One possibility is that, once placed over a well, a millstone provided not only a particularly strong and stable platform but that the eye of the stone would have provided a suitable aperture and mounting point for a hand pump (Robin Jackson, pers. comm.).

5.12.3 Other stone objects
Angus Crawford

Medieval stone mortar
Two conjoining fragments form half of a carved green sandstone mortar with a flat base and two remaining rounded lugs projecting from a flat rim (context 2560; No. 14; Fig. 5.30). Of the lugs, one has a runnel and narrows downwards, while the other runs down to form a tear-shaped rib. The interior is smooth with the exterior having traces of tooling. This includes an external beaded rim and hemispherical panel between the lugs. The mortar was retrieved from a context of 14th-century date and similar forms have been recorded from Deansway (Roe 2004, 472). The medieval catalogue from Salisbury has similar forms dated from the late 13th to 14th century (Drinkwater 1991, 176–7).

Carved stone candleholders
A stone candleholder turned from oolitic limestone was recovered (context 3; No. 15; Fig. 5.31, 15). The base is saucer-shaped with a remaining diameter of 100mm and an angled lip with a remaining height of approximately 18mm. The central shaft of the candleholder had a height of 130mm terminating in a flat, protruding and rounded lip with a slight undercut. The socket for the candle has a diameter of 17mm with an internal depth of 40mm. The body shaft has been divided into two segments by a raised and stepped band approximately one third up from the base. Both shaft segments are cylindrical with a gentle convex profile. While the object has been identified as a candleholder, attempts to identify parallel forms have proved unsuccessful. The uniqueness of the candleholder may indicate that it originates from a religious building and possibly from a visible static feature such as a memorial. Accurate dating of the object is problematic and it is only tentatively dated to the late medieval or post-medieval period.

A second possible turned oolitic limestone candleholder was also recovered (context 3; No. 16; Fig. 5.31, 16). This object has a partially turned foot ring forming a pedestal base. The diameter of the remaining base is 70mm and the overall remaining object height is 250mm. The body consists of ten concentric rings of saucer-shaped profile, regularly spaced and decreasing in diameter from the base up, with the overall appearance of the object best described as 'conifer-like'. The central recess for what was presumably the candle is 27mm in diameter, with a remaining internal depth of 107mm. As with the previous candleholder, no parallel objects have been found and there is the possibility that the object may be a decorative architectural object of unknown purpose but also probably originates from a religious building. The accurate dating of this object is again problematic and is only tentatively dated to the medieval or post medieval period.

Stone troughs

A large rectangular red sandstone trough (No. 17; Fig. 5.32, 17) was also recovered as an unstratified find. Cut from red sandstone, it is 1100mm long, 500mm wide with a height of 340mm. Two separate rectangular compartments have been cut into the upper surface. One is 400mm long, 310mm wide and 210mm deep, with a relatively flat base. The second is 430mm long, 300mm wide and has a maximum depth of 180mm, with a slightly concave base. The dividing section between the compartments is 80mm wide and is flush with the upper surface. Secondary stoneworking has been undertaken at the end of one compartment, with shallow, semicircular cuts into the upper surface of one end and both sides. These taper inwards and appear to facilitate the channelling, probably of liquid, into one end of the trough.

Another unstratified sandstone trough-like object consists of a large green sandstone block of rectangular shape with a single curved end (No. 18; Fig. 5.32, 18). The carved out interior of the 'trough' mirrors its exterior, with outer dimensions of 950mm long, 400mm wide and 250mm high and internal dimensions of 720mm long, 260mm wide and 170mm deep. There are extensive toolmarks to both the interior and exterior of the object creating a rough finished surface, and the upper surface is partly level with an irregular appearance. Laid flat, the object is reminiscent of a stone sarcophagus, though the period of manufacture and exact purpose are not known.

Catalogue of illustrated worked stone artefacts (Figs 5.27 to 5.32)

1. Kimmeridge shale spindle whorl. Possibly Roman. Annular plano-convex shape slightly damaged on top surface around central hole. The convex surface is decorated with two horizontal incised lines beneath and connecting a series of circles with a series of small semicircles framing the central hole. The base is decorated with an incised circular line with the base of the central hole framed by a rope-like pattern. Context 1860 (Period 2.4; Plot 13; G131; Fig. 5.27, 1)
2. Blue lias spindle whorl. Medieval. Annular globular or bun-shaped form, finely turned on a lathe with concentric circle decoration and red burnished surface. Context 2754 (Period 2.4/5; Plot 3; G55; Fig. 5.27, 2)
3. Blue lias spindle whorl. Medieval. Annular, plano-convex shaped form, finely turned on a lathe with concentric circle decoration and red burnished or tarnished surface. Context 2728 (Period 2.4/5; Plot 3; G55; Fig. 5.27, 3)
4. Blue lias spindle whorl. ?Medieval. Annular, plano-convex form, finely turned on a lathe with concentric circle decoration and red burnished or tarnished surface. Context 1576 (Plot 6; Unassigned; Fig. 5.27, 4)
5. Upper rotary quern stone. ?late Saxon to 14th century. Produced from Gritstone with possible modification

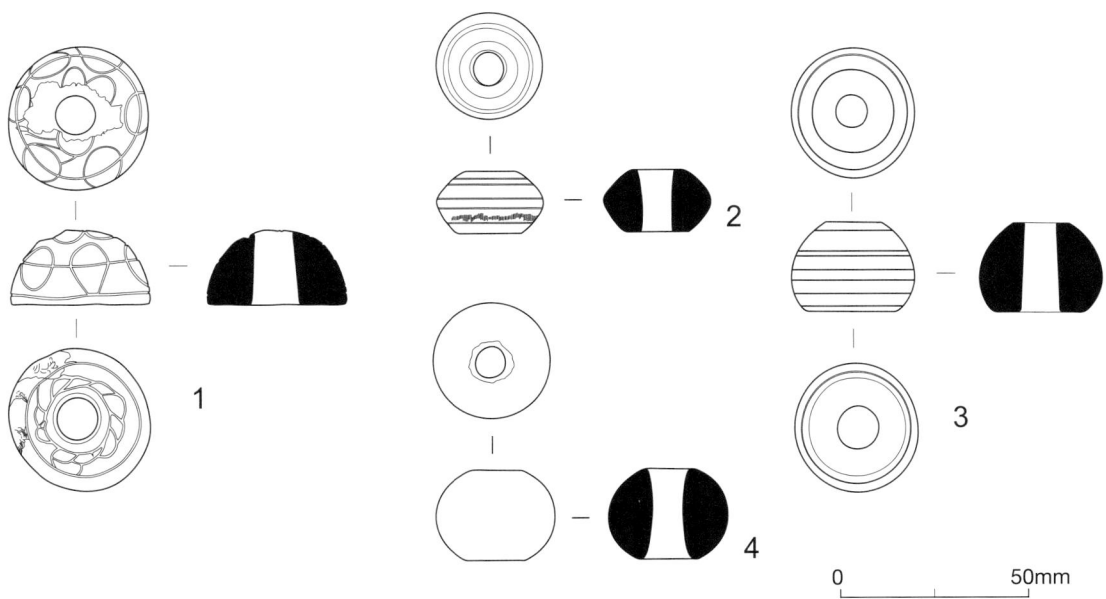

Fig. 5.27 Worked stone objects: spindle whorls (Nos 1–4). Scale 1:2

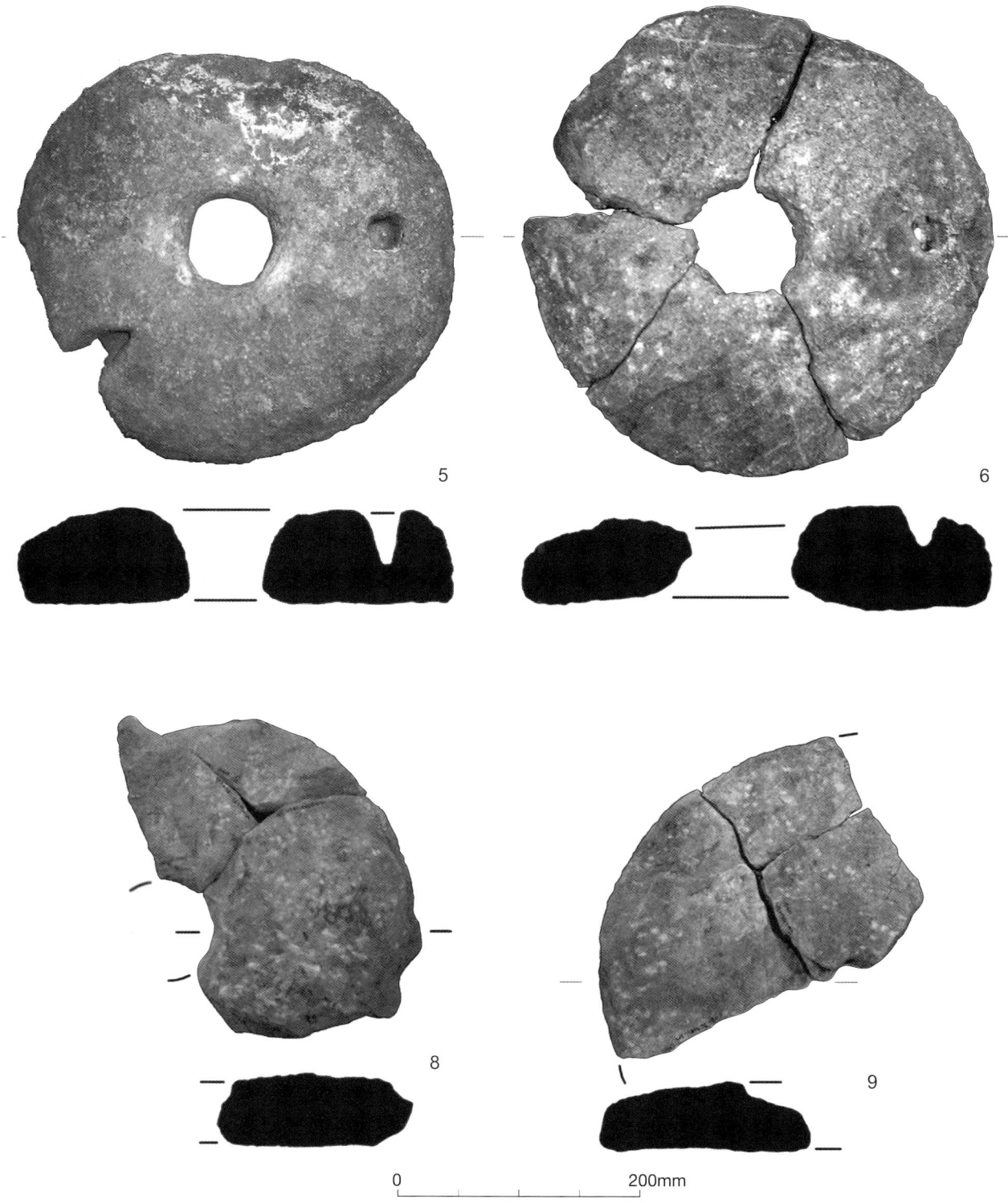

Fig. 5.28 Worked stone objects: querns (Nos 5, 6, 8 and 9). Scale 1:5

for continued usage, diameter of 370mm and maximum thickness of 80mm. The hopper hole has a maximum diameter of 75mm. Context 1507 (Plot 13; Period 2.4; G139; Fig. 5.28, 5)

6   Four conjoining rotary quern stone fragments. ?late Saxon to 12th century. Produced from conglomerate with possible later modification for continued usage. The quern had a maximum diameter of 390mm and thickness of 80mm. Context 1840 (Plot 13; Period 2.3.1; G357; Fig. 5.28, 6)

7   Rim fragment from rotary quern stone. ?late Saxon to 12th century. Produced from green sandstone. Has

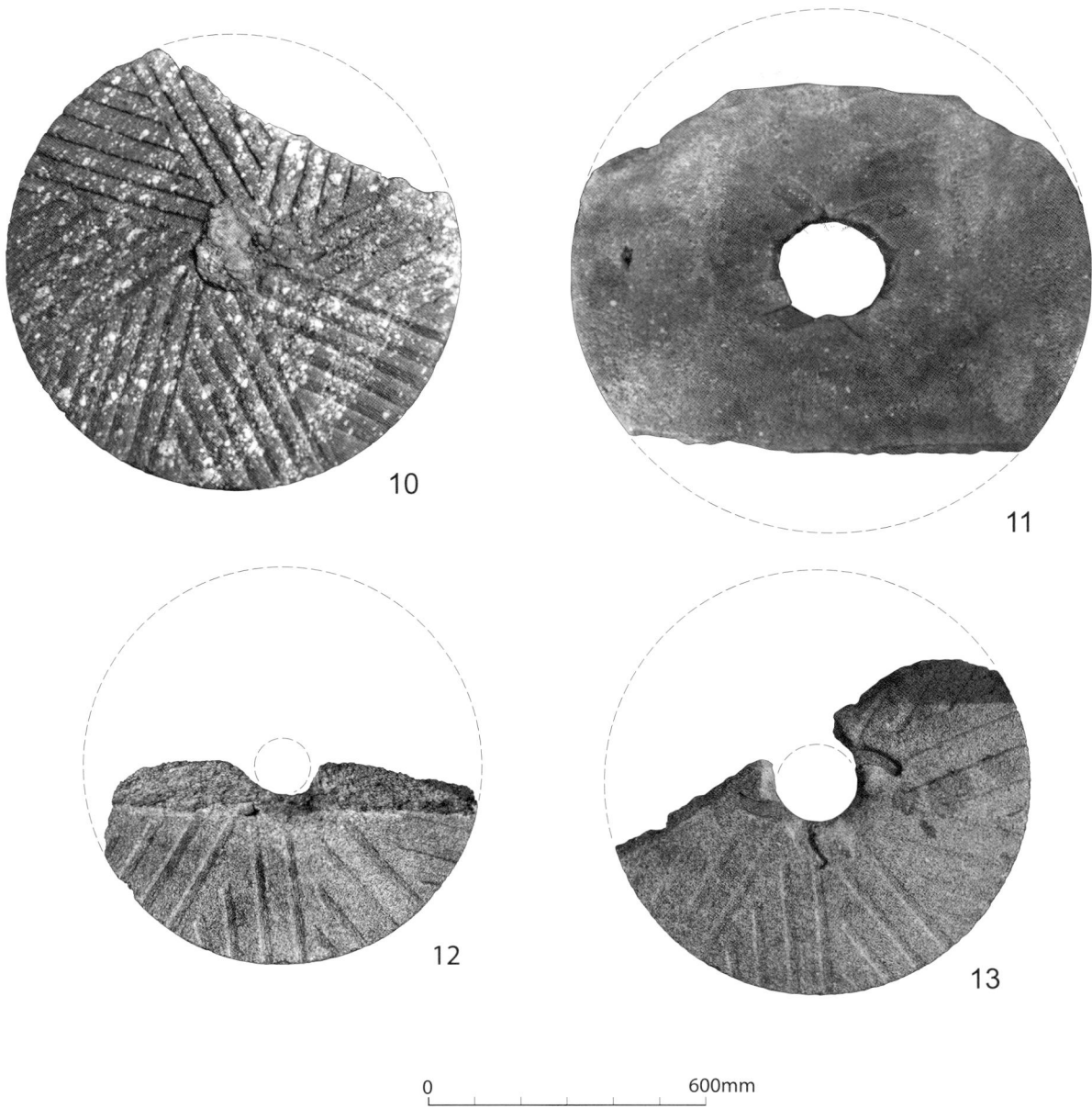

Fig. 5.29 Millstones (Nos 10–13). Scale 1:15

been subjected to heat and is pink in colour. Context 1840 (Plot 13; Period 2.3.1; G357; Fig. 5.28, 7)

8   Three conjoining fragments from an upper rotary quern stone. ?late Saxon to 12th century. Produced from pinkish sandstone. Extremely worn and damaged surfaces. Context 1840 (Plot 13; Period 2.3.1; G357; Fig. 5.28, 8)

9   Three conjoining fragments from a lower rotary quern stone. ?late Saxon to 12th century. Produced from pinkish sandstone with a diameter of 210mm. Heavily worn grinding surface with raised lip around the edge. Context 1840 (Plot 13; Period 2.3.1; G357; Fig. 5.28, 9)

10   Near-complete millstone of Forest of Dean quartz conglomerate. Probably of 17th to 18th-century date. Has cut furrows and recess for iron rynd. Overall diameter 980mm with the central eye of the stone having a diameter of 80mm. Thickness varied from 130mm at the edge to 260mm towards the centre. Context 557 (Plot 6; Period 4; G84; Fig. 5.29, 10)

11   Near-complete millstone of Cotswold conglomerate Gritstone. ?late medieval with reuse during the post-medieval period. Maximum diameter 1100mm. Edge thickness 80mm rising to 170mm towards the centre. The eye diameter is 240mm. Extensively worn grinding surface which retains the socketed recess for an iron rynd in the form of back-to-back letter 'C's. Context 294 (Plot 6; Period 3.3; G85; Fig. 5.29, 11)

12   Less than half of a millstone of non-local granite (possibly from Shropshire). Post-medieval. Has furrows

162   *Excavations at Newport Street, Worcester, 2005*

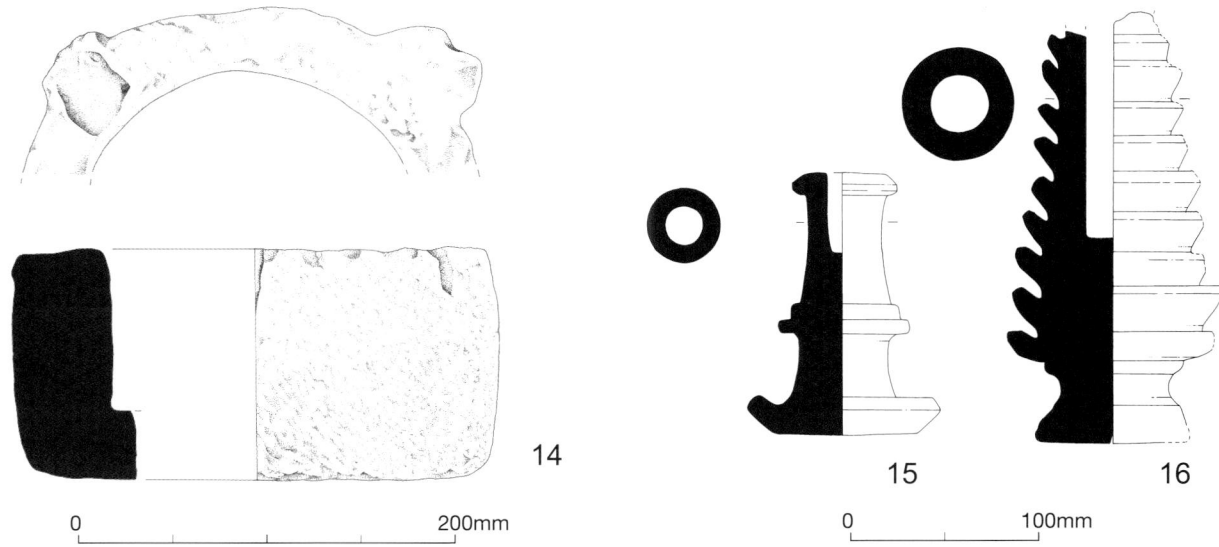

Fig. 5.30 Worked stone objects: mortar (No. 14). Scale 1:4

Fig. 5.31 Worked stone objects: candleholders (Nos 15–16). Scale 1:4

cut into the grinding surface. Diameter 900mm with an eye diameter of 180mm. Edge thickness is 80mm with a central thickness of 140mm. Context 3 (machining horizon; Fig. 5.29, 12)

13 Just over half of a millstone of non-local granite (possibly from Shropshire). Post-medieval date. Has furrows cut into the grinding surface and a socketed recess to take an iron rynd in the form of back-to-back letter 'C's. Diameter 900mm with an eye diameter of 180mm. Edge thickness is 80mm with a central thickness of 160mm. Context 1486 (Plot 6; Period 3.3/4; G79; Fig. 5.29, 13)

14 Partial medieval stone mortar. From a 14th-century context. Worked from green sandstone and approximately 280mm in diameter. Context 2560 (Plot 3; Period 2.4; G115; Fig. 5.30)

15 Oolitic limestone candleholder. Lathe-turned. Uncertain date but probably late medieval or post-medieval. Context 3 (machining horizon; Fig. 5.31, 15)

16 Probable oolitic limestone candleholder. Lathe-turned. Uncertain date but probably late medieval or post-medieval. Context 3 (machining horizon; Fig. 5.31, 16)

17 Large rectangular trough worked from red sandstone with two separate compartments. Unstratified. Uncertain date but probably late medieval or post-medieval (Fig. 5.32, 17)

18 Trough-like object worked from green sandstone with unusual sarcophagus shape. Unstratified. Uncertain date but probably late medieval or post-medieval (Fig. 5.32, 18)

Fig. 5.32 Stone troughs (Nos 17–18). Scale 1:15

5.13 Metal artefacts
Alan J. Jacobs

The metal objects include iron, copper alloy, lead and pewter artefacts. These are described below with the exception of coins, tokens and jettons, which are reported on separately (Chapter 5.14).

The assemblage consists of 541 objects weighing 13.239kg (Table 5.8), and predominantly comprises modern iron nails and a variety of bolts, tools, hooks and other modern objects. This material is very degraded, and many items were only identified following radiography, undertaken by York Archaeological Trust. Other generally smaller copper-alloy items such as thimbles are present, as well as several lead and pewter objects, including a complete pewter spoon. Only objects of significance are catalogued and discussed; further information and 21 radiographic plates being held in archive.

5.13.1 Period 2: medieval metal artefacts

A total of 87 iron objects were recovered from Period 2 contexts along with 28 copper-alloy objects or fragments, 26 lead fragments and a pewter spoon. A further probable medieval pewter spoon was also recovered as a residual find from a later context.

Apart from nails and unidentifiable objects, a number of iron objects of interest were recovered from Period 2 contexts. These include part of the handle of a small shovel or tool (context 1251; Fig. 5.33, 1), a prick spur (context 2758; Fig. 5.33, 2), a rowel spur (context 1251; Fig. 5.33, 3), and a heavily corroded arrowhead (context 1588; Fig. 5.33, 4). The iron finds all came from adjacent Plots 13 and 14, which during Periods 2.4 and 2.5 were associated with a number of hearths and metalworking residues indicative of smithing, suggesting that these objects may perhaps have been items for repair, or were beyond repair and intended for melting down as scrap.

An unusual find was a finely made copper-alloy object (context 2410; Fig. 5.33, 5). This appears to be a cap or lid, perhaps the top of a container of composite material, the body having been of leather. Another copper-alloy object of this period was a 15th-century buckle in the form of a rose (context 1899; Fig. 5.33, 6).

Pewter objects are represented by two spoons dating to the late 15th or 16th century, one of which is a complete example of a fine diamond-headed spoon, recovered from a cess pit, the other being the bowl of a spoon (contexts 2681 and 2451; Fig. 5.33, 7 and 8).

Catalogue of illustrated medieval metalwork (Fig. 5.33)

1   Iron. Possible handle of a small shovel or kitchen tool. ?Medieval. Plot 14; Period 2.4/5; G234: context 1251. (Record 1261/Plate 6647)
2   Iron. Prick spur. Late medieval. Plot 3; Period 2.3; G56: context 2758. (Record 1318/Plate 6642)
3   Iron. Rowel spur. Late medieval. Plot 14; Period 2.4/5; G234: context 1251. (Record 1215/Plate 6648)
4   Iron. Arrowhead. Heavily corroded. Late medieval. Plot 13; Period 2.4; G132: context 1588. (Record 1323/Plate 6640)
5   Copper alloy. Fine top or cap. Hinged. Possibly from a container of composite material (?leather bag with metal cap). Plot 3; Period 2.4/5; G64: context 2410. (Record 1167/Sheet 6651)
6   Copper alloy. Buckle in the form of a rose. Probably 15th century. Plot 5; Unassigned: context 1899. (Record 1165/Plate 6649)
7   Pewter. Diamond-headed spoon. Late 15th–16th century. Plot 3; Period 2.5/3.1; S263: context 2681. (Record 1117/Plate 6651)

Table 5.8: Metalwork assemblage (count and weight) by metal type and period

Material	Unassigned	Period 2	Period 3	Period 4	Period 5	Totals
Iron	23	87	71	20	156	357
	619g	3285g	2965g	304g	2649g	9822g
Copper alloy	9	28	50	12	24	123
	83g	185g	196g	130g	143.5g	737g
Lead	-	26	12	-	14	52
		2149g	47g		86g	2282g
Pewter	1	1	-	-	-	2
	25g	44g				69g
Composite	-	-	-	-	1	1
					117g	117g
Not identified	5	-	-	-	1	6
	20g				191g	211g
Totals						541
						13,239g

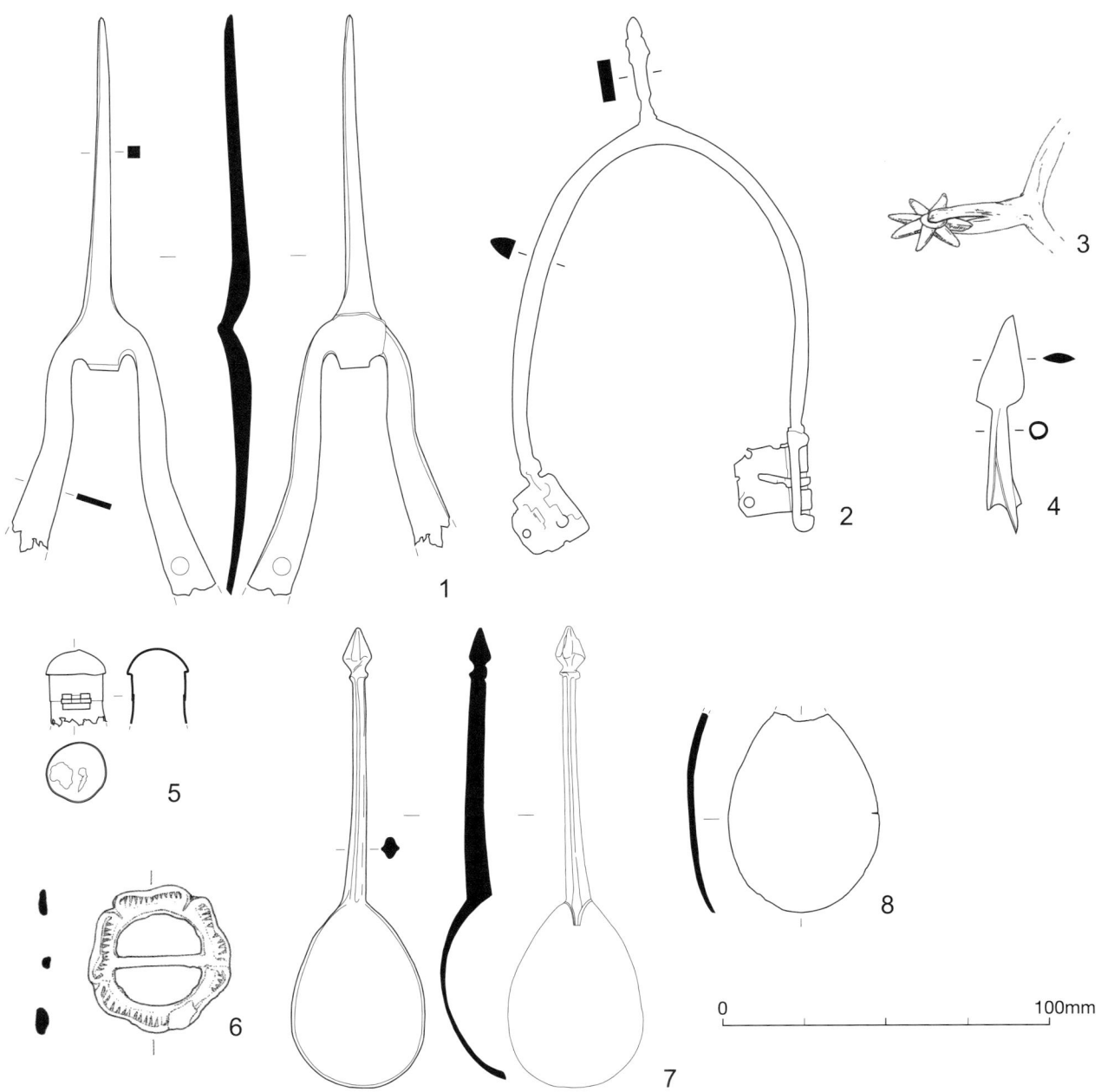

Fig. 5.33 Period 2: Metalwork (Nos 1–8). Scale 1:2

8 Pewter. Spoon bowl. 15th–16th century. Plot 3; Unassigned: context 2451. (Record 1116/Plate 6651)

5.13.2 Period 3: post-medieval metal artefacts

Post-medieval iron objects are consistent with urban assemblages from the West Midlands. Of the 71 iron objects recorded from post-medieval contexts, the most identifiable items are again nails, but domestic objects are also present. The assemblage comprises a typical range of personal dress fittings, household objects and small tools liable to be encountered in an urban domestic context of this period. These include examples of an iron boss, most likely a furniture or carriage fitting (context 2072; Fig. 5.34, 9), and a well-preserved iron key (context 373; Fig. 5.34, 10). An iron buckle was also recorded (not illustrated; Plot 2; Period 3.2; G6: context 523; Record 1343/Plate 6640).

Fifty copper-alloy objects were recovered from post-medieval contexts, and a number of additional distinctly late 16th to 18th-century objects of note were also recovered from unassigned contexts or as residual finds. Objects include buckles or strap fittings (contexts 523 and 1972; Fig. 5.34, 11 and 12) and a dress pin with reef knot top (context 2331; Fig. 5.34, 13). These could all date to the 17th to 18th century and reflect the variety and change in design of such items during the post-medieval period.

A small but distinct assemblage of copper-alloy thim-

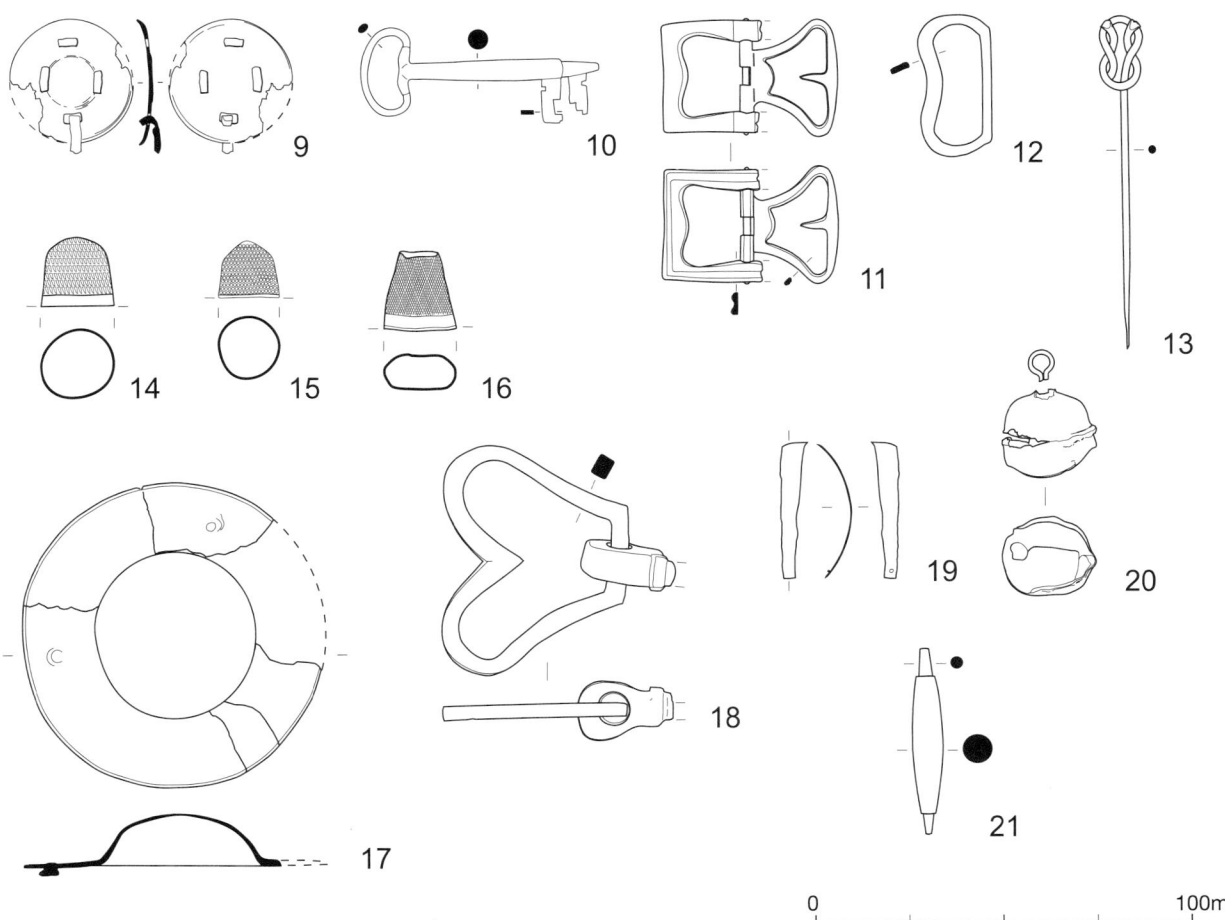

Fig. 5.34 Period 3: Metalwork (Nos 9–21). Scale 1:2

bles was also recovered. Two of the examples are beehive thimbles, one recovered during site machine clearance (context 3; Fig. 5.34, 14), the other from a late 16th to 17th-century context (899; Fig. 5.34, 15). The third example is a flat-topped conical thimble (context 2367; Fig. 5.34, 16). Other post-medieval copper-alloy objects include a boss or fitting (context 1232; Fig. 5.34, 17), a heart-shaped chafing-dish handle (context 2849; Fig. 5.34, 18), a small curved sheet of copper, part of a tool or fitting of probable 16th to 17th-century date (context 1273; Fig. 5.34, 19) and a well-preserved 16th to 17th-century rumbler bell (context 2601; Fig. 5.34, 20).

Amongst the 12 lead objects recorded was a lead plumb bob of 17th to 18th-century date (context 1576; Fig. 5.34, 21).

Catalogue of illustrated post-medieval metalwork (Fig. 5.34)

9   Iron. Boss or fitting. Post-medieval. Plot 5; Period 3.2; G41: context 2072. (Record 1229/Plate 6643)

10 Iron. Key. Post-medieval. Plot 2; Period 3.2; G14: context 373. (Record 1223/Plate 6643)

11 Copper alloy. Buckle. Post-medieval. Plot 2; Period 3.2; G6: context 523. (Record 1130/Plate 6649)

12 Copper alloy. Buckle or strap fitting. Post-medieval. Plot 7; Period 3.2; G75: context 1972. (Record 1132/Plate 6649)

13 Copper alloy. Dress pin with reef knot top. 17th–18th century. Plot 4; Period 2.4/5; G64: context 2331. (Record 1134/Plate 6650)

14 Copper alloy. Beehive thimble. Late 15th–17th century. Residual find from machine clearance G172: context 3. (Record 1151/Plate 6649)

15 Copper alloy. Beehive thimble. Late 16th–17th century. Plot 11; Period 3.2/3; G363: context 899. (Record 1152/Plate 6650)

16 Copper alloy. Flat-topped conical thimble. Late 16th–17th century. Plot 3; Period 3; Unassigned; context 2367. (Record 1122/Plate 6649)

17 Copper alloy. Boss or fitting. Medieval/early post-medieval. Plot 10; Period 3.1; G106: context 1232. (Record 1129/Plate 6650)

18 Copper alloy. Heart-shaped chafing dish handle. Post-medieval. Plot 9; Period 3; G96: context 2849. (Record 1126/Plate 6649)

19 Copper alloy. Small curved sheet. Part of a tool or fitting. 16th–17th century. Plot 14; Period 3.3; G249: context 1273. (Record 1184/Plate 6651)

20 Copper alloy. Rumbler bell. 16th–17th century. Plot 3; Unassigned; context 2601. (Record 1140/Plate 6650)

21 Lead. Plumb bob. 17th–18th century. Plot 6; Unassigned; context 1576. (Record 1118/Plate 6650)

5.13.3 Period 4: 18th-century metal artefacts

Period 4 metalwork includes 20 iron objects but little of note is present. The 12 copper-alloy objects include a buckle (context 1723; Fig. 5.35, 22) and a flat-topped conical thimble (context 2520; Fig. 5.35, 23), but more unusual was the base of a 17th to 18th-century skimmer or strainer with a rivet repair (context 1962; Fig. 5.35, 24). Skimmers were used for removing items from stew pots, and superseded the use of flesh hooks for this purpose from the end of the medieval period onwards (Egan 1998, 155–8). Again, as a group, these are typical finds within urban domestic assemblages of this date.

Catalogue of illustrated 18th-century metalwork (Fig. 5.35)

22 Copper alloy. Buckle. 18th century. Plot 9; Period 4; G365: context 1723. (Record 1324/Plate 6640)

23 Copper alloy. Flat-topped conical thimble. 18th century. Plot 3; Period 3.1/2 G62: context 2520. (Record 1123/Plate 6650)

24 Copper alloy. Base of skimmer or strainer with riveted repair. 18th century. Plot 7; Period 4; G76: context 1962. (Record 1131/Plate 6652)

5.13.4 Period 5 and unassigned metal artefacts

Some 156 iron, 24 copper-alloy, and 14 lead objects were recorded from Period 5 contexts, with a further 38 items recovered from unassigned contexts. The majority of these are modern objects of little or no note, however, a number of dateable residual items of interest were present and have been noted previously.

5.14 Coins, tokens and jettons
Alan J. Jacobs (identification by Martin Allen)

A total of 29 medieval, post-medieval and modern coins, tokens and jettons were recovered, and these are listed in Tables 5.9, 5.10 and 5.11. None of these objects are illustrated within this report. The catalogue was compiled by Dr Martin Allen of the Fitzwilliam Museum, Cambridge.

5.14.1 Analysis
Period 2: medieval

The medieval assemblage contains just one coin, a silver penny of Edward IV (Table 5.9; context 896), which was recovered as a residual find within a 20th-century context. Four definable jettons were recovered, although only one, a mid to late 15th-century example from Nuremberg, was from a medieval context (Table 5.9; context 2677). The remainder are less clearly identifiable but are of late medieval to early post-medieval date; one was recovered from a post-medieval context (1243), another residual within a 20th-century context (429). Taken together these might be indicative

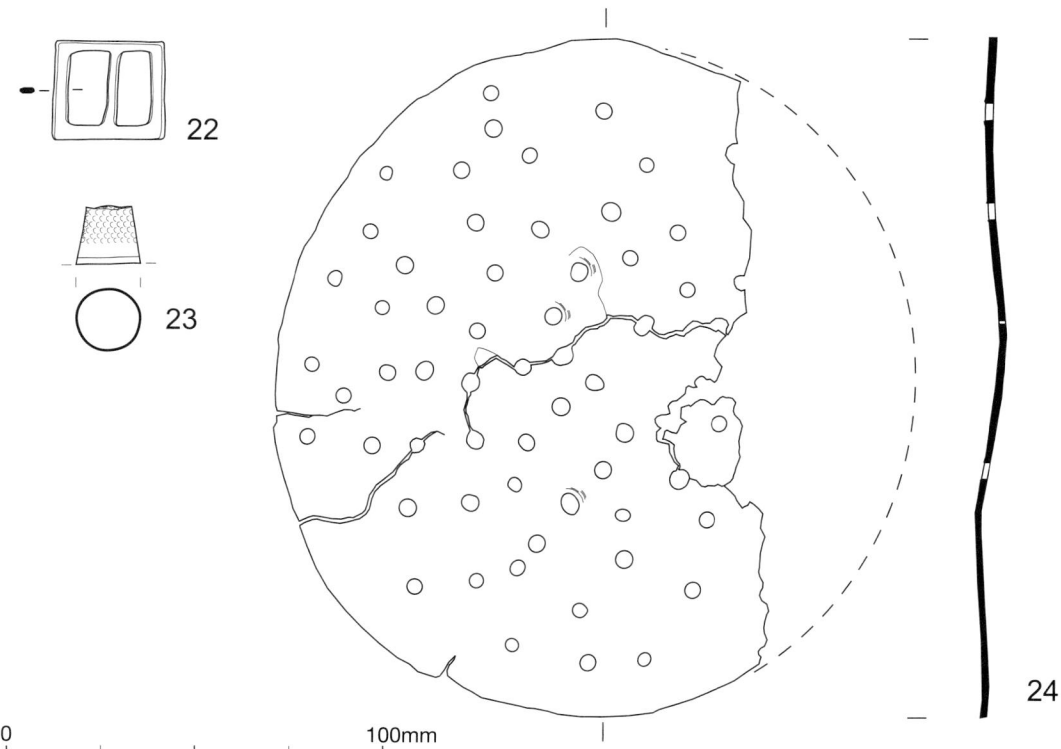

Fig. 5.35 Period 4: Metalwork (Nos 22–24). Scale 1:2

Table 5.9: Medieval coins, tokens and jettons

Context (Rec.no.)	Group	Plot	Period	Identification	Weight	Remarks
896 (1142)	282	14	5	Edward IV second reign (1471–83) or Richard III (1483–5), silver penny, Durham mint, D in centre of reverse. North 1991, nos 1658–66, 1687	0.72g	Coin was probably deposited no later than the removal of pre 1544 silver coins from circulation by the debasement of 1544–51
2677 (1125)	55	3	2.4/5	Copper-alloy jetton, Nuremberg, mid to late 15th century. Obverse: Rose in three-arched tressure. Reverse: Lozengy shield of Bavaria. Cf Mitchiner 1988, no. 997	1.27g	
654 (1157)	282	14	5	Copper-alloy jetton, Low Countries, c. 1490-1550s. 'Venus Penny' type. Cf Mitchiner 1988, nos 840–51	2.40g	
1763 (1247)	301	11	3.2	Copper-alloy jetton, Nuremberg, c. 1550s–1580s. Anonymous Rose/Orb type. Cf Mitchiner 1988, nos 1227-47	1.55g	Chipped
681 (1301)	10	2	3.1	Copper-alloy jetton, Nuremberg, Wolf Lauffer I (1554–1601), c. 1583-1601. Rose/Orb type. Same dies as Mitchiner 1988, no. 1672	0.95g	Chipped
429 (1180)	9	2	5	?Copper-alloy jetton, 15th to 17th century	0.37g	Fragment with outer circles missing
1243 (1188)	247	14	3.1	?Copper-alloy jetton, 15th to 17th century	0.42g	3 large and numerous small fragments

Table 5.10: Post-medieval coins and tokens

Context (Rec.no.)	Group	Plot	Period	Identification	Weight	Remarks
1982 (1154)	N/A	4	N/A	James I (1603–25), silver sixpence, third coinage, sixth bust, 1621, privy mark Rose. North 1991, no. 2126	3.01g	The recoinage of pre-1662 silver coins in 1696–8 is a probable *terminus ante quem* for this find
3 (1155)	172	N/A	5	Charles I (1625–49), silver half-groat, with bust, c. 1630–49. North 1991, 2250–60	0.94g	See above
1528 (1148)	32	4	5	Charles I (1625–49), copper royal farthing token, Rose type 1, 1636–44. North 1991, nos 2287–90	0.76g	
396 (1146)	N/A	2	5	Worcester, William Chetle, copper-alloy farthing token, 1666. Williamson 1891, Worcestershire nos 134–5	0.54g	Chipped, cracked and holed Williamson (1891, 1289–91) discusses the issuer of this token, and his merchant's mark on the obverse. It was probably deposited no later than the mid 1670s, as trade tokens were prohibited in 1672 and 1674.
2525 (1128)	64	3	2.4/5	Charles II (1660–85), silver shilling, 1668	6.04g	The light wear of this coin suggests that it is a late 17th-century or early 18th-century deposit

Table 5.11: Late post-medieval and modern coins and tokens

Context (Rec. no.)	Group	Plot	Period	Identification	Weight	Remarks
3 (1155)	172	N/A	5	Worcester, House of Industry, copper halfpenny token, 1811. Withers and Withers 1999, no. 1271	12.30g	Use of copper tokens was prohibited by Act of Parliament in 1817, but some remained in circulation until the early 1820s (Withers and Withers 1999, 18)
819 (1150)	278	14	3.3	Worcester, John Knapp Junior, copper halfpenny token, 1813, Withers and Withers 1999, nos 1280–4	9.01g	See above Intrusive in Period 3 deposit
3 (1155)	172	N/A	5	Victoria (1837–1901), copper-alloy (bronze) halfpenny, 1860	5.60g	Bronze halfpennies were withdrawn from circulation in 1969
3 (1155)	172	N/A	5	Victoria, copper-alloy (bronze) farthing, 186[0?]	2.82g	Bronze farthings were withdrawn in 1960
3 (1155)	172	N/A	5	Victoria, copper-alloy (bronze) penny, 1862	9.38g	Bronze pennies were withdrawn in 1971
2313 (1159)	4	2	4	Victoria, copper-alloy (bronze) halfpenny, 1875	5.13g	
3 (1176)	172	N/A	5	Victoria, copper-alloy (bronze) halfpenny, 1888	5.50g	
3 (1155)	172	N/A	5	Victoria, copper-alloy (bronze) penny, 1860–94	9.13g	
27 (1149)	9	2	5	Victoria, copper-alloy (bronze) halfpenny, 1860–94	4.93g	
3	172	N/A	5	Victoria, copper-alloy (bronze) halfpenny, 1895	5.31g	
3 (1155)	172	N/A	5	Edward VII (1901–10), copper-alloy (bronze) penny, 1902–10	9.43g	
149 (1145)	29	4	4	George V (1910–36), copper-alloy (bronze) halfpenny, 1921	5.37g	
1718 (1141)	N/A	5	N/A	Copper-alloy (bronze) farthing, 1895–1936	2.95g	
3 (1155)	172	N/A	5	Elizabeth II (1952–), cupro-nickel 10 pence, 1977	11.45g	10 pence pieces of this large size (28mm) were replaced by coins of the current size in 1992
3 (1136)	172	N/A	5	Copper-alloy token, 19th/20th century. Obverse: GARDNER BROS FRUITERERS around WORCESTER. Reverse: 6^D	6.21g	Broken into two pieces
526 (1124)	N/A	2	5	Copper-alloy coin or token, 18th–20th century, 26mm	7.98g	
2800 (1133)	58	3	3.3	Copper-alloy coin or token, 19th–20th century, 22mm	4.52g	Intrusive in Period 3 deposit

of mercantile activity within this area of Worcester during the medieval period. The jettons would indicate Continental trading connections not otherwise borne out by the pottery assemblage during this period.

Period 3: post-medieval

The post-medieval assemblage contains just four coins and a token. Two of the coins are from 17th-century contexts: a silver sixpence of James I (Table 5.10; context 1982); and a Charles II silver shilling (context 2525) of late 17th-century date (context 2525). Two coins of Charles I (a silver half-groat and a copper royal farthing; contexts 3 and 1528) were residual within modern contexts. The only token recovered dating from this period was again residual within a modern context (396). The small size of the assemblage again makes interpretation difficult beyond indicating activity within this area of Worcester during the 17th century. The lack of 18th-century coins along with the predominance of 17th-century activity on this site reflects a similar pattern observed within the pottery assemblage.

Periods 4 and 5: 18th to 20th centuries

The modern assemblage contains fourteen coins, a token, and two tokens/coins that are too worn for closer identification (Table 5.11). The majority of the modern coins were recovered during machining (context 3) and mainly range in date from the mid 19th to mid 20th century. The small size of the assemblage again makes interpretation difficult beyond indicating activity within this area of Worcester during the 19th and first half of the 20th century.

5.15 Clay tobacco pipes
Allan Peacey

An assemblage of 1,498 fragments of clay tobacco pipe was examined. These can be divided into 312 bowls, 50 bowl fragments, 43 mouthpieces and 1,093 stem fragments. These were recovered according to the procedures described previously (Chapter 3.2.5).

The stem fragments, mouthpieces and stem attached to pipes have a combined length of 5350cm (*c.* 17cm of stem for every bowl recovered). The bowl count is taken at confluence of stem, bowl and heel/spur regardless of the degree of completeness. If this point is not represented the material falls either into the stem or bowl fragment categories.

A total of 158 complete bowl profiles have been recorded; from these 114 have been selected for illustration (Table 5.12; Figs 5.36–44). This assemblage offers a fairly comprehensive corpus of the clay tobacco pipes used in Worcester from the second quarter of

Table 5.12: Illustrated clay pipe bowls

Cat. no.	Stamp no.	Context	Group	Plot	Period	Stamp/bowl date
1	117	279	14	2	3.2	1630–50
2	118	681	10	2	3.1	1630–50
3	119	441	6	2	3.2	1630–50
4	121	173	22	1	4	1630–50
5	120	273	32	4	5	1630–50
6	123	275	14	2	3.2	1630–50
7	-	447	N/A	12	3.3	1630–50
8	-	275	14	2	3.2	1630–50
9	-	1026	108	11	4	1630–50
10	-	1026	108	11	4	1630–50
11	124	98	53	2	5	1630–50
12	-	3	172	All	Machining	1630–50
13	-	3	172	All	Machining	1630–50
14	-	1797	N/A	4	N/A	1650–1730
15	-	1026	108	11	4	1650–1730
16	-	1026	108	11	4	1650–1730
17	-	1036	310	11	5	1650–1730
18	-	1121	108	10	4	1650–1730
19	-	275	14	2	3.2	1650–1730
20	-	98	53	2	5	1650–1730
21	-	447	N/A	12	3.3	1650–1730
22	-	1895	92	6	3.1	1650–1730
23	-	3	172	All	Machining	1650–1730
24	-	970	247	13	3.1	1650–1730
25	-	116	20	1	5	1650–1730
26	-	5	9	2	5	1650–1730

Table 5.12 (cont.): Illustrated clay pipe bowls

Cat. no.	Stamp no.	Context	Group	Plot	Period	Stamp/bowl date
27	131	0	U/S	N/A	N/A	1650–1730
28	-	1215	107	10	4	1650–1730
29	129	447	N/A	12	3.3	1650–1730
30	130	0	U/S	N/A	N/A	1650–1730
31	-	451	12	6	3.1	1650–1730
32	-	562	12	2	3.1	1650–1730
33	-	523	6	2	3.2	1650–1730
34	-	564	12	2	3.1	1650–1730
35	-	585	N/A	2	5	1650–1730
36	-	523	6	2	3.2	1650–1730
37	-	585	N/A	2	5	1650–1730
38	-	662	13	2	3.2	1650–1730
39	-	527	53	2	5	1650–1730
40	-	3	172	All	Machining	1650–1730
41	166	862	278	14	3.3	1670–90
42	149	1613	90	6	3.2	1670–90
43	163	1732	N/A	5	N/A	1670–90
44	145	1036	310	11	5	1660–80
45	165	1732	N/A	5	N/A	1670–90
46	147	3	172	All	Machining	1660–80
47	146	3	172	All	Machining	1660–80
48	144	3	172	All	Machining	1660–80
49	149	1714	N/A	4	N/A	1660–80
50	150	1797	N/A	4	N/A	1660–80
51	151	1797	N/A	4	N/A	1660–80
52	152	71	N/A	2	5	1660–80
53	153	1732	N/A	5	N/A	1660–80
54	154	3	172	All	Machining	1660–80
55	154	447	N/A	12	3.3	1660–80
56	156	1732	N/A	5	N/A	1660–80
57	158	273	32	4	5	1660–80
58	159	2768	105	9	5	1660–80
59	159	1797	N/A	4	N/A	1660–80
60	159	3	172	All	Machining	1660–80
61	-	3	172	All	Machining	1660–80
62	-	1797	N/A	4	N/A	1660–80
63	161	3	172	All	Machining	1660–80
64	-	3	172	All	Machining	1660–80
65	138	1732	N/A	5	N/A	1660–80
66	134	1732	N/A	5	N/A	1660–80
67	132	3	172	All	Machining	1660–80
68	143	3	172	All	Machining	1660–80
69	140	1121	108	10	4	1660–80
70	142	447	N/A	12	3.3	1660–80

Table 5.12 (cont.): Illustrated clay pipe bowls

Cat. no.	Stamp no.	Context	Group	Plot	Period	Stamp/bowl date
71	135	273	32	4	5	1660–80
72	-	1215	107	10	4	1660–80
73	-	1550	42	4	3.2	1660–80
74	-	1121	108	10	4	1660–80
75	-	1714	N/A	4	N/A	1660–80
76	-	1226	106	10	3.1	1660–80
77	-	273	32	4	5	up to 1730
78	173	756	36	4	3.2	1680–1730
79	171	3	172	All	Machining	1680–1730
80	174	636	N/A	2	N/A	1680–1730
81	169	3	172	All	Machining	1680–1730
82	172	1732	N/A	5	N/A	1680–1730
83	170	451	12	6	3.1	1680–1730
84	168	1732	N/A	5	N/A	1680–1730
85	167	1732	N/A	5	N/A	1680–1730
86	-	52	32	4	5	1730
87	-	1999	41	3	3.2	1730
88	177	97	32	4	5	1690–1720
89	178	564	12	2	3.1	1690–1720
90	-	585	N/A	2	5	1690–1720
91	176	536	19	1	4	1690–1720
92	-	631	87	6	3.2	1690–1720
93	-	3	172	All	Machining	1690–1720
94	-	523	6	2	3.2	1690–1720
95	--	3	172	All	Machining	1690–1720
96	-	3	172	All	Machining	1690–1720
97	-	3	172	All	Machining	1730–80
98	-	1121	108	10	4	1730–80
99	198	461	9	2	5	1730–80
100	-	121	53	2	5	1730–80
101	193	3	172	All	Machining	1730–80
102	-	99	53	2	5	1730–80
103	-	121	53	2	5	1730–80
104	-	121	53	2	5	1730–80
105	-	122	53	2	5	1730–80
106	-	122	53	2	5	1730–80
107	194/195	122	53	2	5	1730–80
108	-	3	172	All	Machining	1730–80
109	-	1083	74	7	4	1730–80
110	-	99	53	2	5	1730–80
111	-	1732	N/A	5	N/A	1730–80
112	-	122	53	2	5	1730–80
113	-	3	172	All	Machining	Mid 19th C
114	-	158	6	2	3.2	Mid 19th C

the 17th century until the end of the 18th century. Although substantial assemblages have been studied from Gloucester, Hereford and Worcester, there is little or no archaeological evidence for the use of clay pipes in the region prior to *c.* 1620. It would appear that smoking tobacco prior to this had not spread beyond a privileged few.

Worcester is situated on the River Severn, a major trade artery, between two major production centres: Bristol, 55 miles downstream, and Broseley, 35 miles upstream. There were more parochial producers at Cleobury Mortimer (15 miles) and Pipe Aston (30 miles) to the northwest, Leominster (20 miles) to the west and Gloucester (25 miles) to the south. It is not surprising therefore that some products from these and other sources are found in the city, and Worcester certainly had its own industry from 1657, and probably earlier, through to the latter part of the 19th century.

5.15.1 Analysis and discussion

Early forms (c. 1630–50)

The earliest forms (Fig. 5.36, 1–13) date from *c.* 1630–50. A little over half of these bear the stamp of a maker. Additional stamps dating from this period include Nos 115 and 116 (Fig. 5.45). Examples of these latter two have been recorded from a production site at Pipe Aston in North Herefordshire, provisionally dated *c.* 1620–40 (Peacey, forthcoming). Also from the same site are stamps very similar to No. 118. Forms 4 and 6 (Fig. 5.45: stamps 121, 122 and 123) are attributable to Bristol makers, both being commonly found in that city. Edward Lewis took his freedom in 1631 and is likely to have been deceased by 1652, as his widow Elizabeth was a founder member of the Bristol Guild (Price *et al.* 1981). Similar pipes marked with the incuse EL, widely distributed in Gloucestershire, are also recorded from Hereford. The I T stamp cannot be attributed with certainty to a particular maker. The origins of the remaining stamps from this phase are unknown.

Late 17th to early 18th-century forms

Figures 5.37 and 5.38 (14–26 and 27–40 respectively) illustrate the range of forms current in the region from *c.* 1650 to 1730 with the exception of the well-documented products of the Broseley/Much Wenlock school, which appear in later figures. Detailed study of production sites in and around Pipe Aston has shown that makers of this period produced pipes in a variety of forms and sizes so that while it is generally true that the majority of forms became larger as time progressed, it is now clear that smaller versions were also produced. A clear example is the tailed-heel form, generally accepted as making its first appearance *c.* 1680, miniature examples of which have been recorded that on size alone could be misplaced a generation earlier.

Pipes in this group all have flat heels, and all are milled round the bowl mouth as part of the finishing process. The size and shape of the heels is variable: round, sub round, oval and teardrop all feature. Few are stroke burnished, a practice common in south Shropshire but not exclusive to there. Forms 14 and 15 would not be out of place in Gloucester whilst forms 27, 29 and 30, with their distinctive wheel stamps, sit well with the products of the north Herefordshire makers. These wheel stamps are abundant in Hereford but rare in Gloucester and Worcester. No. 28 is a distinctive Pipe Aston form and together with the three wheel-stamped pipes is likely to have been made there. Another distinctive Pipe Aston form is represented by Nos 31–34. It appears in Phase VI of the Roy's Orchard site dated 1710–30 (Peacey, forthcoming). The heel is relatively small and stands well out from the stem. The bowl is more open and weighted towards its upper third. Forms 38–40 are variations on the hoofed or hammered heel. Although the source of these is not certain they are reminiscent of pipes from Cleobury Mortimer and might well have been made there.

The first certainly attributable Broseley/Much Wenlock form to make its appearance is the Type 2 (Atkinson 1975). Atkinson dates this form to *c.* 1660–80. It is easily recognised by its tall, narrow, elegant bowl. A high percentage of these pipes are stroke burnished. The milling is set much lower on the bowl and stamps are usually initials set in a round or heart-shaped ground. This form is unusually well represented in the assemblage (Figs 5.39 and 5.40, Nos 44, 46–64), its popularity underlined by its adoption by at least one local maker, marking his products FB (Fig. 5.41, 65–71). The unmarked pipes illustrated in this figure are also likely to be local products. Very few of these pipes are stroke burnished. The majority of the stamps are poorly impressed. At least seven different dies were used (Fig. 5.45, 132–43). It is likely that this maker served his apprenticeship with a Broseley/Much Wenlock maker. A clue to with whom may lie in the similarity between stamp 145, HB and 132, FB. The second initial is probably coincidental as HB is likely to be Henry Bradley of Benthall or Much Wenlock. Waste from this maker's kiln was excavated from a site in Benthall (Higgins 1987).

Pipes of Broseley Type 3, *c.* 1670–90, are less well represented (Fig. 5.39, 41–3, 45). The definitive feature of this form is a round heel large enough to take some early full name stamps. Several makers working at Much Wenlock made such pipes. Amongst these is found GRFE POVEL. Although a poor impression, Figure 5.39.43 is an example of this stamp which has been attributed to Griffith Powell of Much Wenlock, who died in 1673 (Higgins 1987).

The next Broseley form to make its appearance is the Type 5, instantly recognised by its large round tailed heel (Fig. 5.42, 78–87). The bowl form is more cup-shaped than that of previous forms; more open at the upper end. Milling and bottering of the bowl mouth

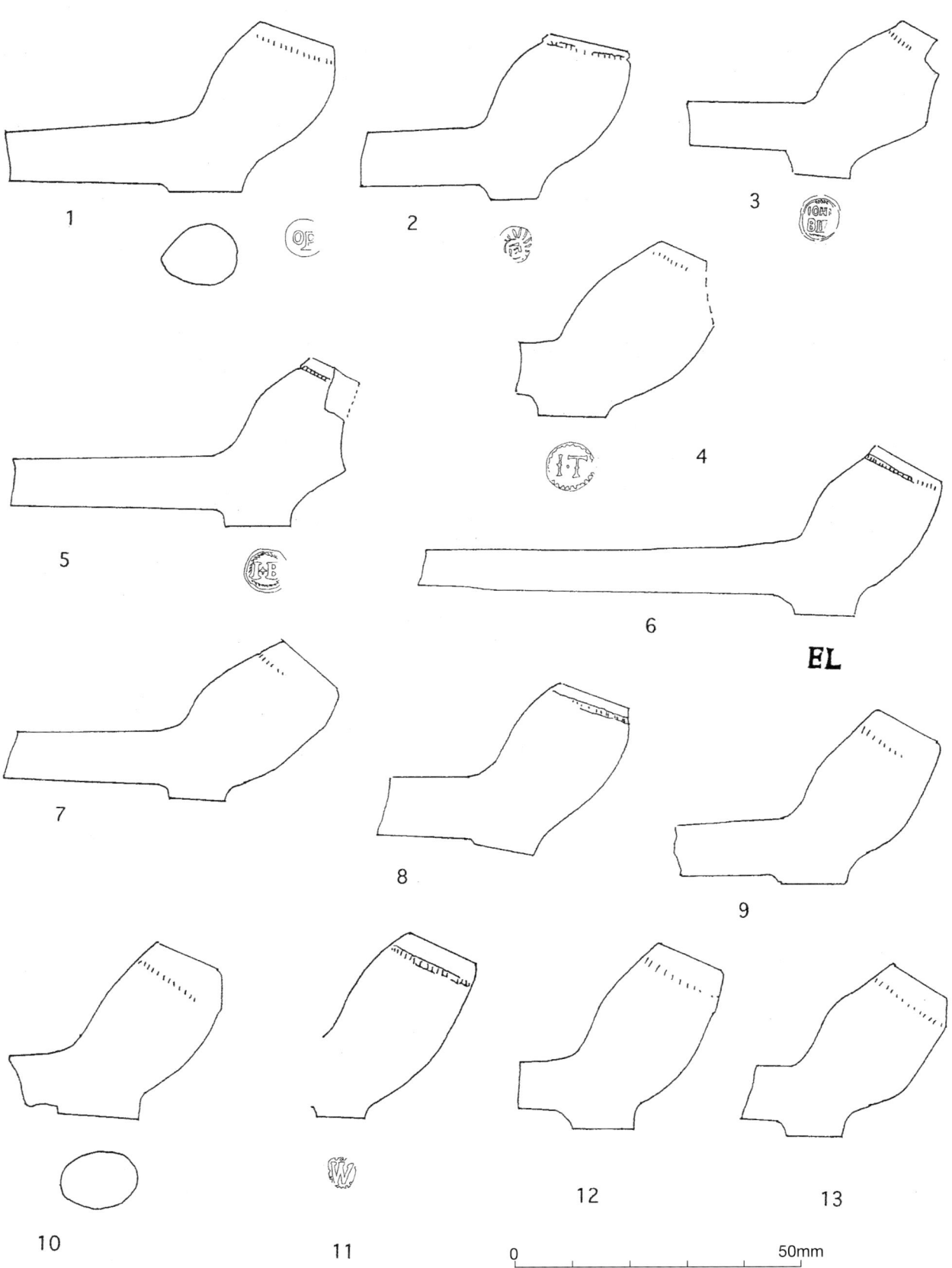

Fig. 5.36 Clay pipes (Nos 1–13). Scale 1:1

174 *Excavations at Newport Street, Worcester, 2005*

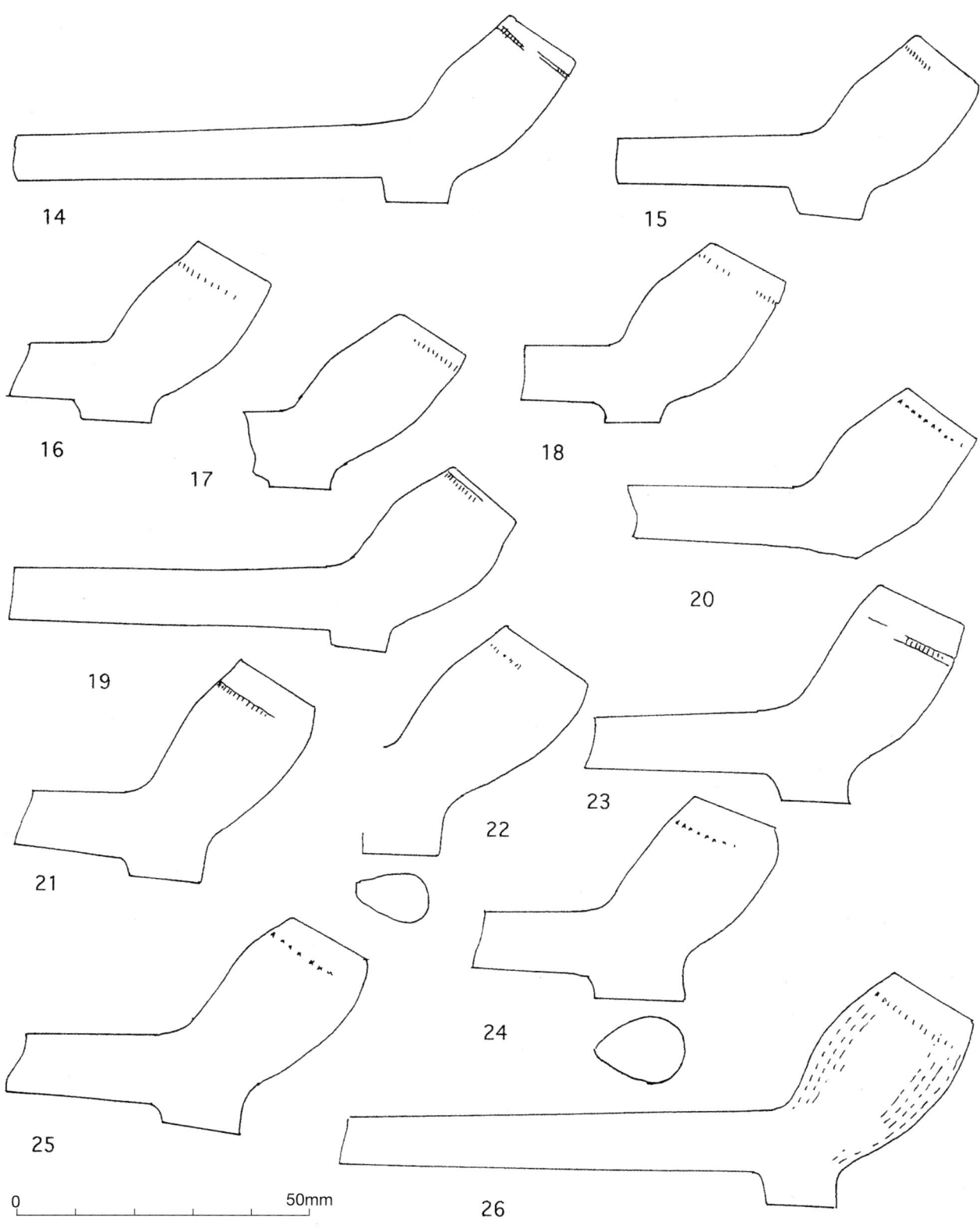

Fig. 5.37 *Clay pipes (Nos 14–26). Scale 1:1*

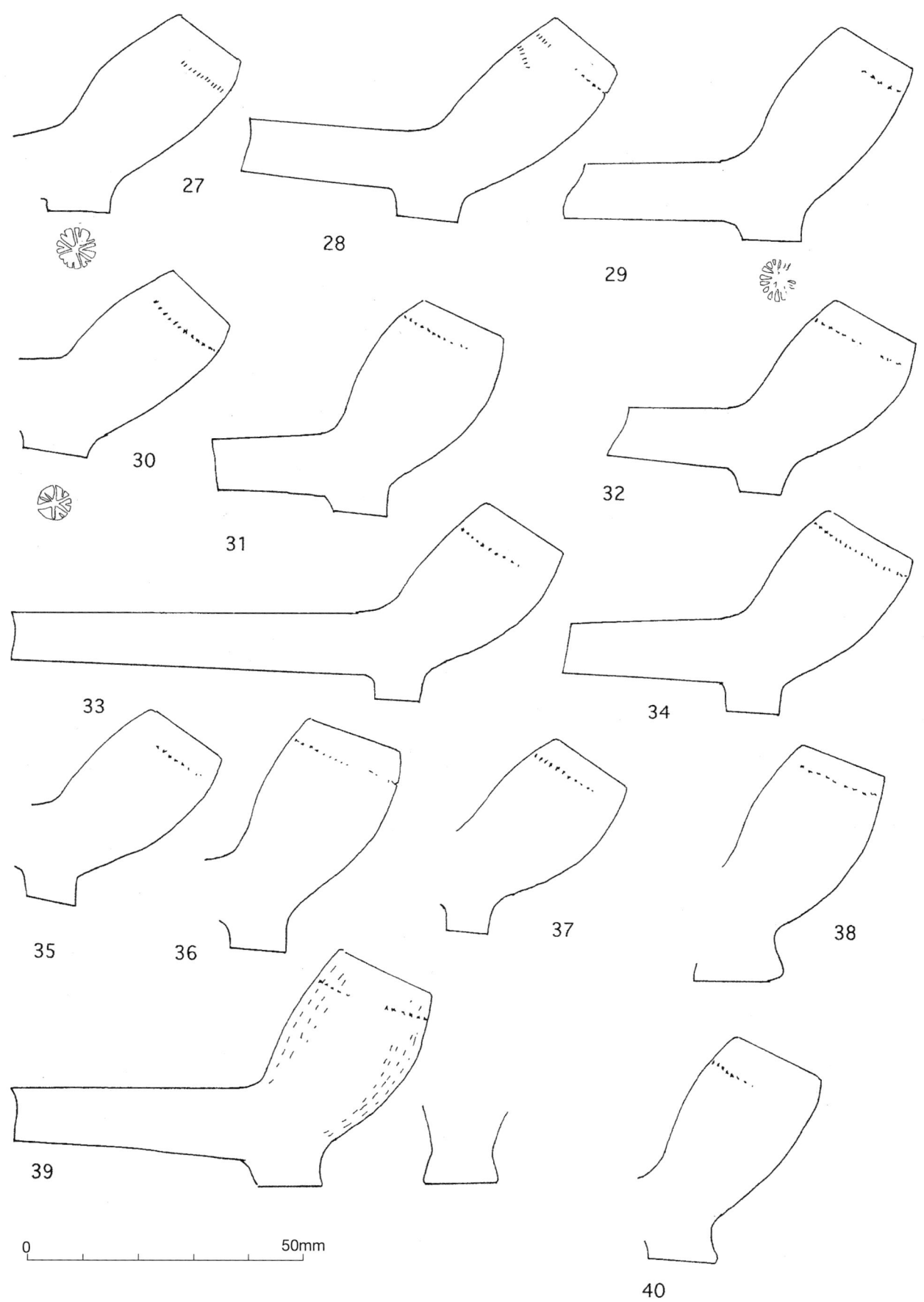

Fig. 5.38 Clay pipes (Nos 27–40). Scale 1:1

176 *Excavations at Newport Street, Worcester, 2005*

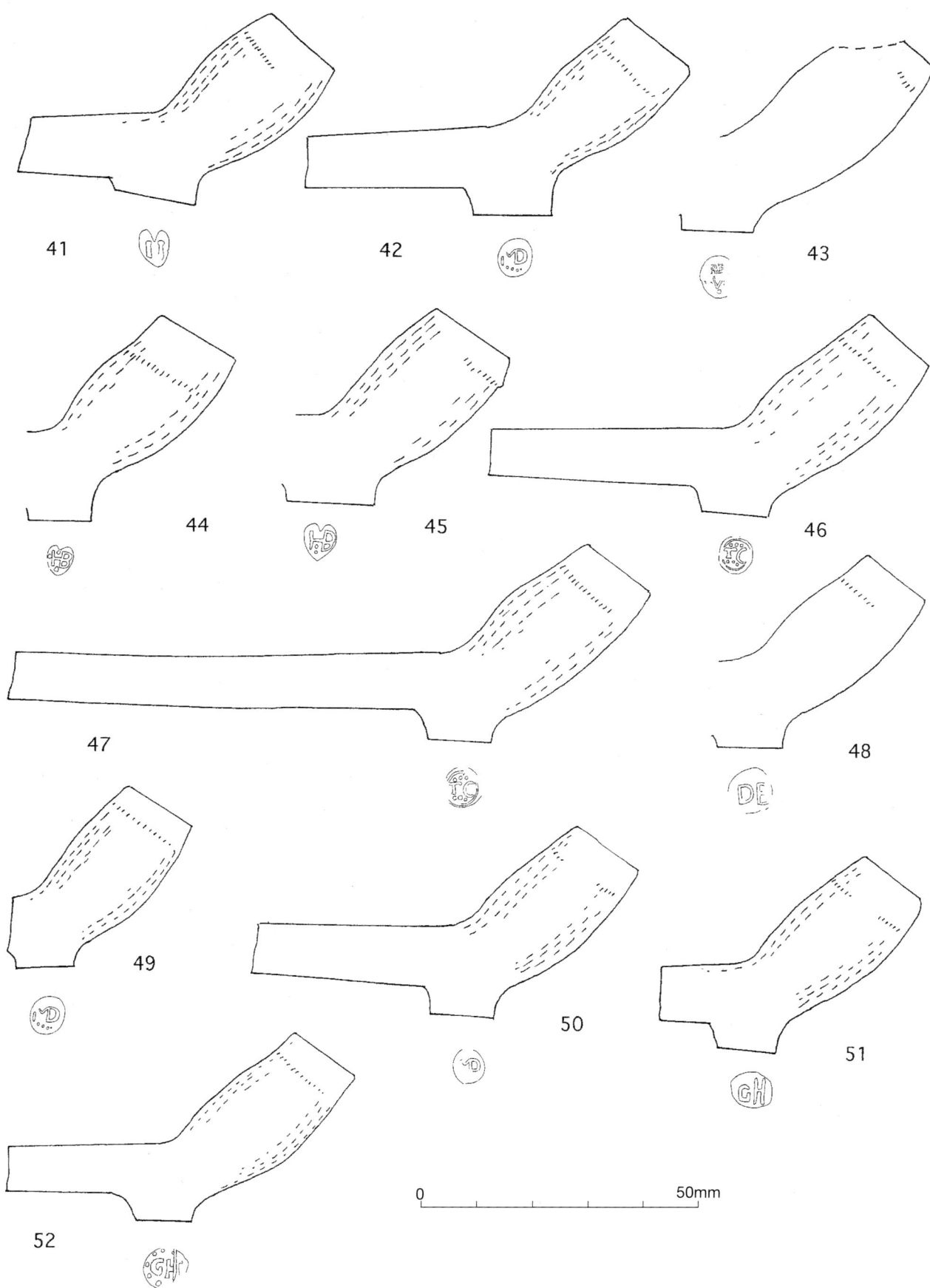

Fig. 5.39 Clay pipes (Nos 41–52). Scale 1:1

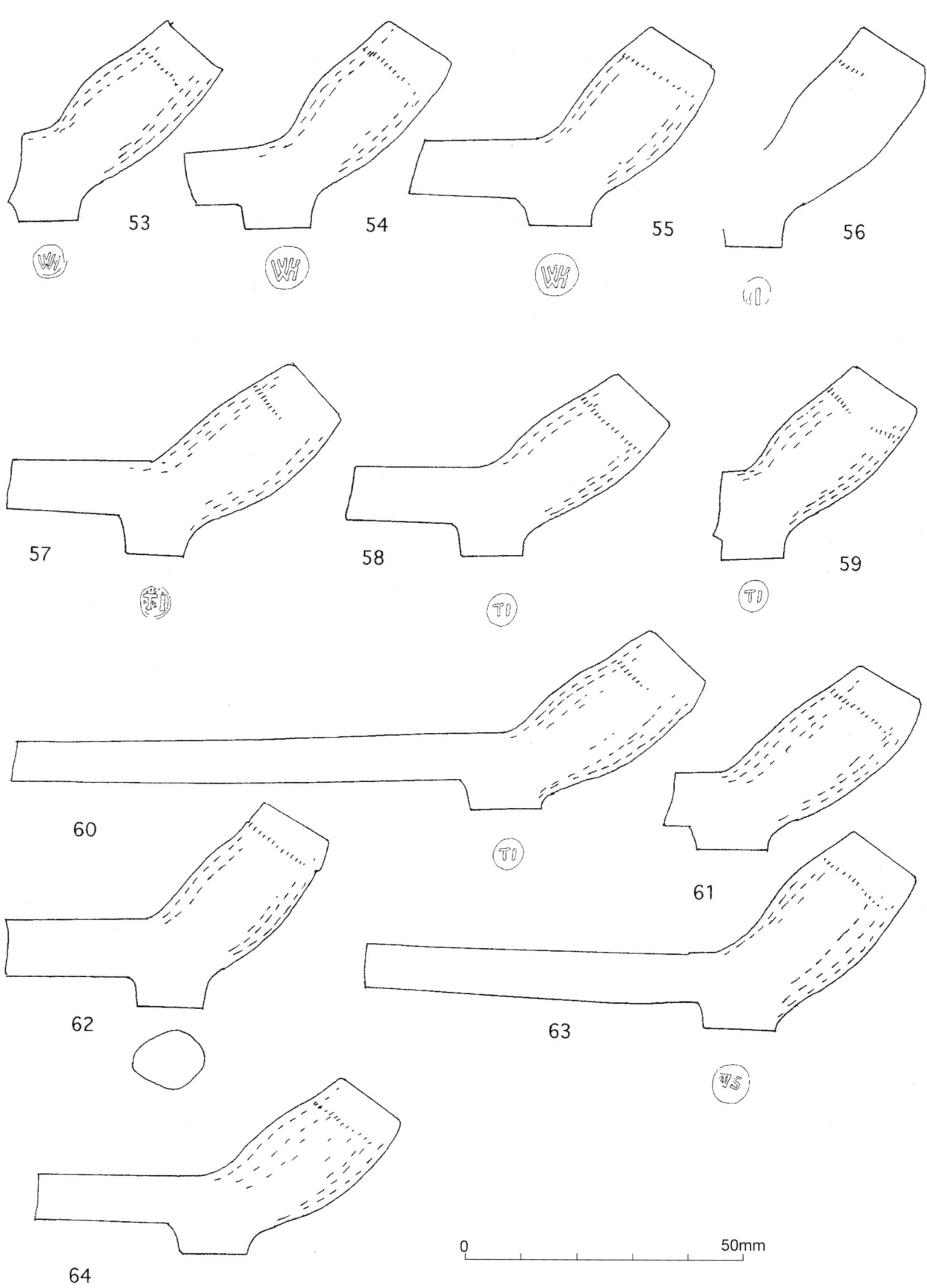

Fig. 5.40 Clay pipes (Nos 53–64). Scale 1:1

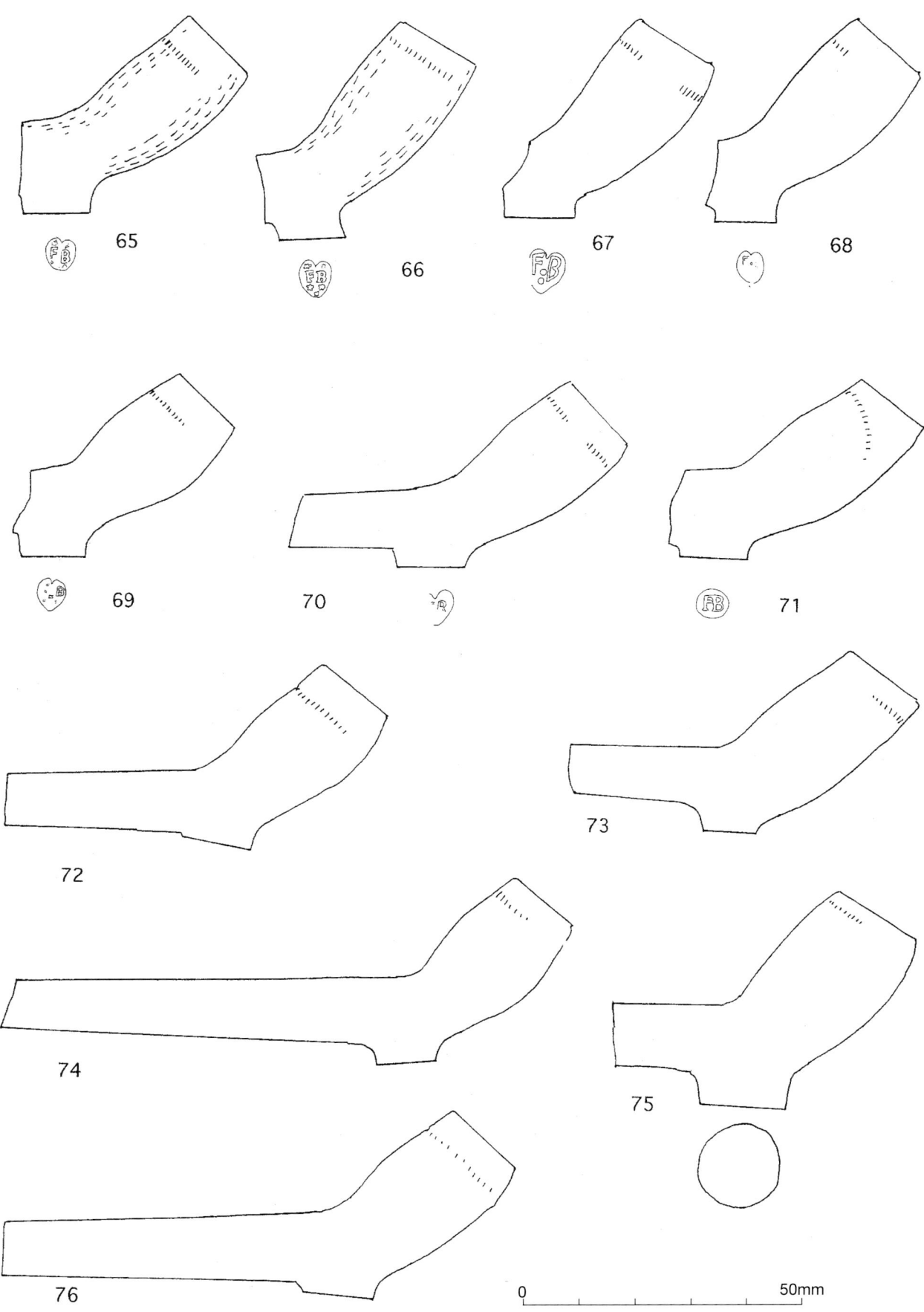

Fig. 5.41 Clay pipes (Nos 65–76). Scale 1:1

Specialist Reports 179

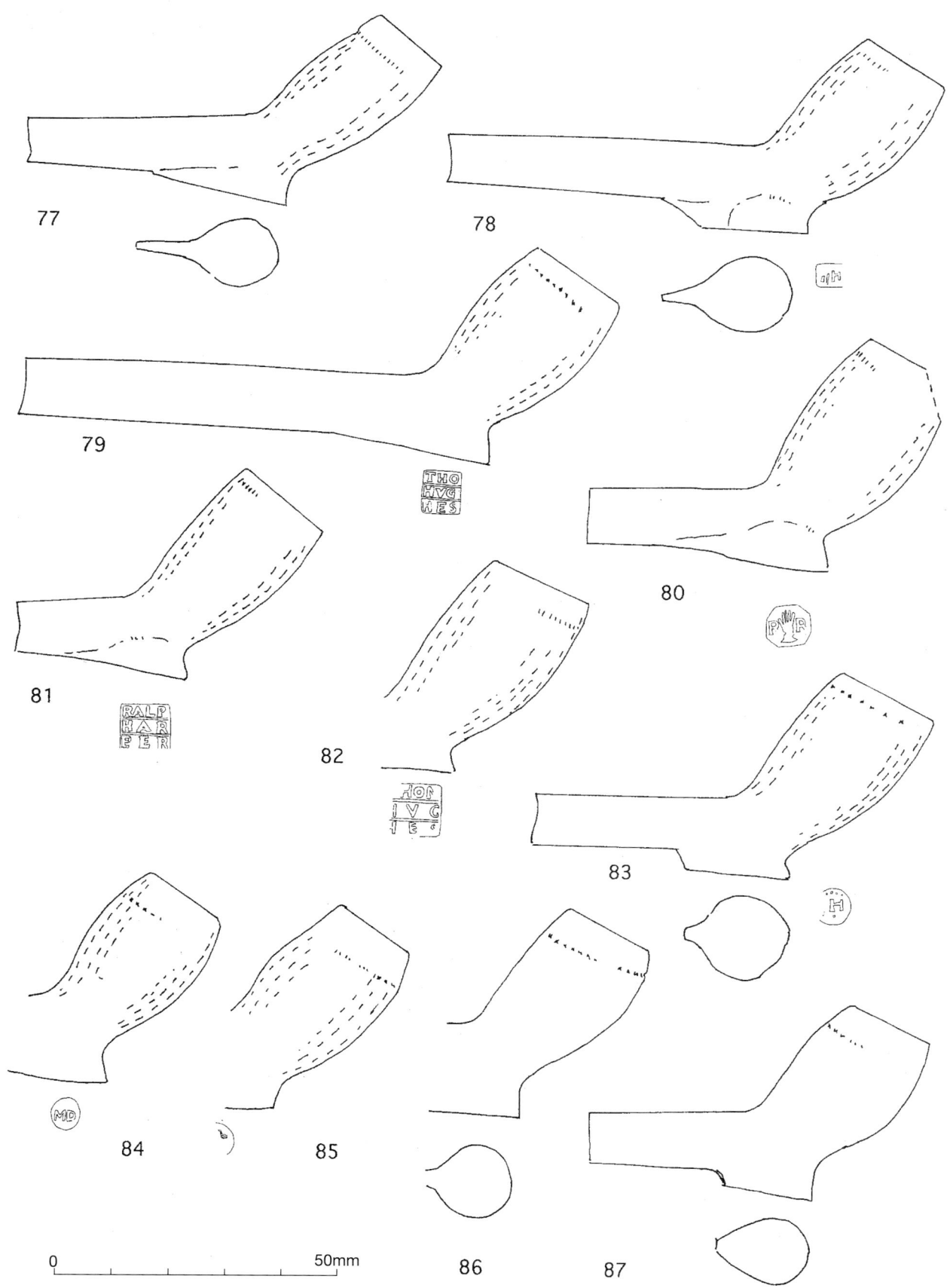

Fig. 5.42 Clay pipes (Nos 77–87). Scale 1:1

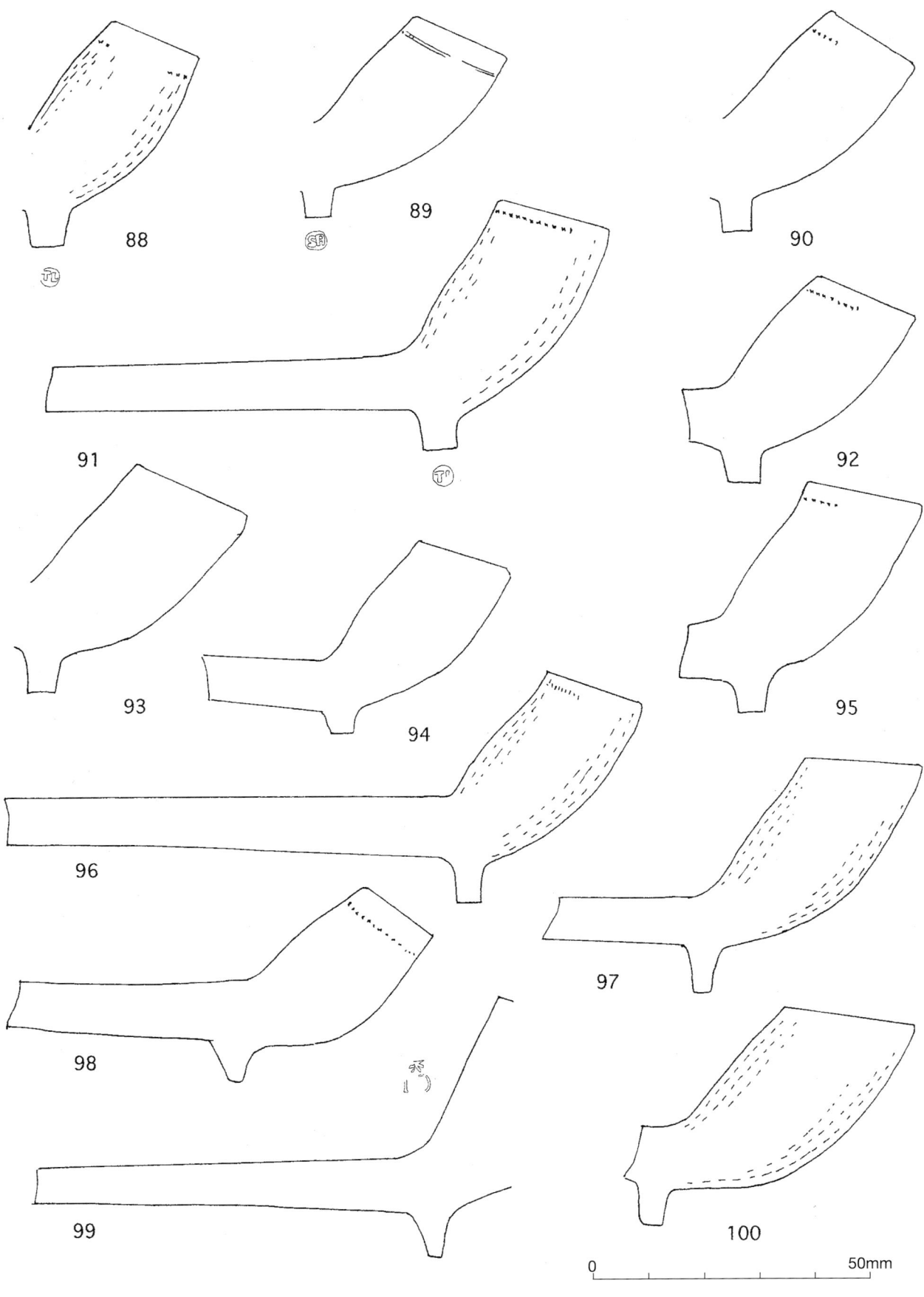

Fig. 5.43 Clay pipes (Nos 88–100). Scale 1:1

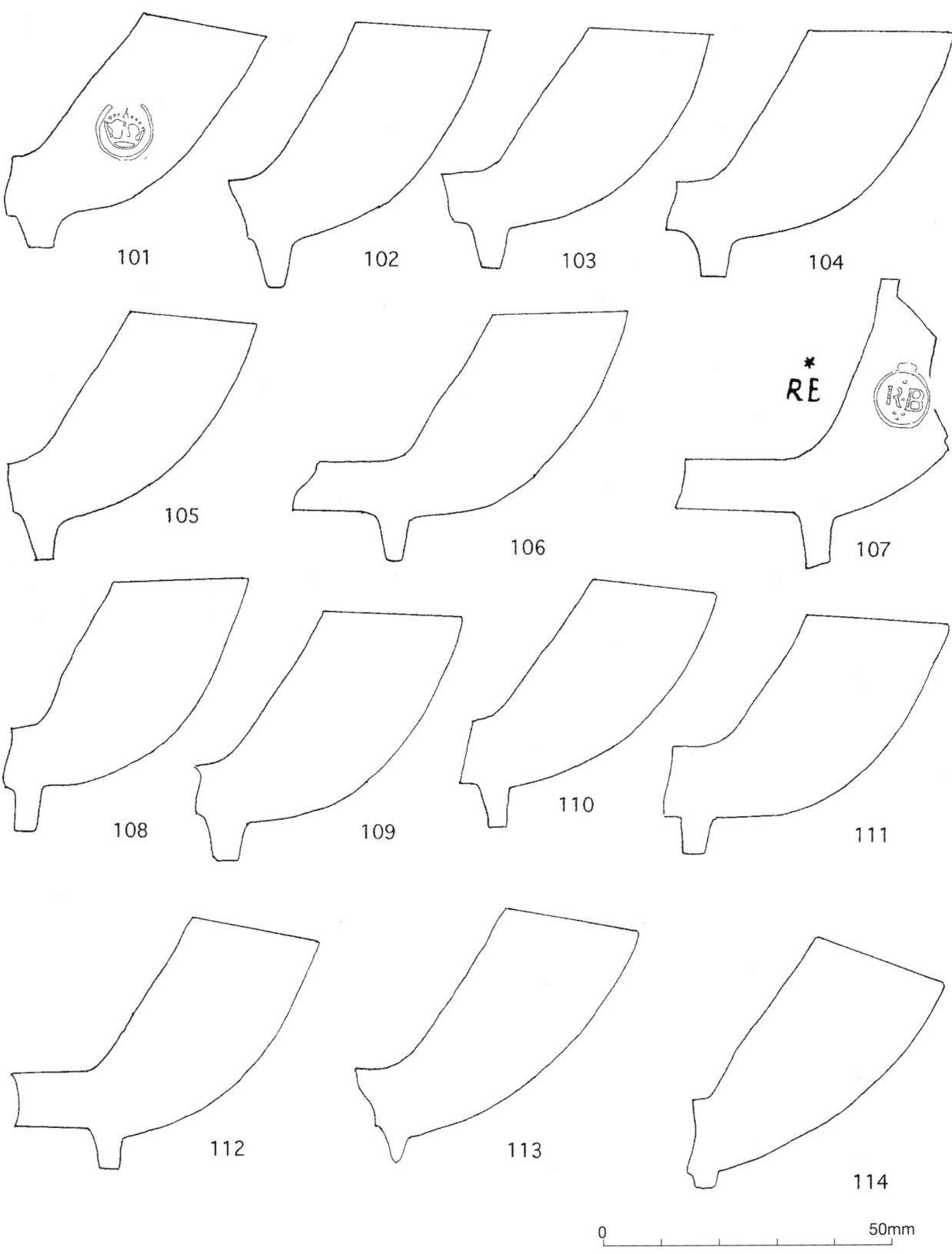

Fig. 5.44 Clay pipes (Nos 101–114). Scale 1:1

still features as the norm as does stroke burnishing. This form is distributed over a wider area and in greater numbers than the earlier forms. It was also made over a wider area, examples being at Pipe Aston, Buckley and Carmarthen. The examples from this assemblage appear to be all from the epicentre of the industry. Some of the more stunted tails might be the result of careless trimming (Fig. 5.42, 83, 86–7). There is an interesting hybrid form (Fig. 5.42, 77) which has the bowl of a Type 2 with a proportionately slender tailed heel. This single example is unmarked. Pipes of Broseley Type 5 form were still being made at Pipe Aston as late as 1730 and there is no reason to suppose that this was in any way unusual.

Next in the sequence is the Broseley Type 4, the most significant difference being that the tailed heel has given way to a cylindrical spur on which the makers frequently impressed a minute initial stamp. Atkinson gives the date range for this form as *c.* 1690–1720. Pipes of this form emanating from the Broseley area are less frequently stroke burnished than previous forms; not all are milled around the bowl mouth. Pipes illustrated in Figure 5.43 (88–96) reflect these variations. At Pipe Aston a derivative of this form was made in the final phase dated 1710–30, these are invariably without milling.

Figure 5.43.98 is of a form which is commonplace in Gloucester, but not recorded from Hereford, and with only two examples from Bromyard and one from Pipe Aston. It seems probable that all of these examples are products of Gloucester makers.

Mid to late 18th-century forms
Nos 97 and 100 (Fig. 5.43) are mid to late 18th-century forms, both examples are stroke burnished which is by this time unusual and may signify a Broseley origin. Figure 5.43.99 is a mid to late 18th-century form with an incuse mark on the back of the bowl, facing the smoker. The initials IO beneath a star might belong to a Bristol maker. A similar pipe is illustrated in *Bristol Clay Pipes* (Jackson and Price 1974, 105, no. 199).

From *c.* 1730 clay pipes become larger and finer; the line of the bowl mouth cut becomes parallel, or near parallel to the stem; milling and bottering of the bowl mouth no longer feature. Spurs become the norm and are longer and more pointed. Makers' marks from the 'Broseley school' are placed initially across the stem and later along the stem. Bristol makers adopted marks in a cartouche on the side of the bowl and incuse marks on the back of the bowl facing the smoker; sometimes both together on the same pipe. Gloucester makers borrowed from both schools. Stem stamps and moulded bowl marks feature on the products of that city (Peacey 1979, 54).

It seems likely that the pipes nos 101–12 illustrated in Figure 5.44 represent the whole of the 18th-century repertoire, when a single basic form held sway for as long as seven decades from *c.* 1730 to 1800. Both the cartouche and the incuse bowl marks were in use in Bristol from *c.* 1700, albeit on earlier bowl forms than those in this assemblage. Of the two illustrated (Fig. 5.44, 101 and 107), the first could date to *c.* 1720–40. A similar pipe is illustrated in *Bristol Clay Pipes Pipes* (Jackson and Price 1974, 124). The second, with both cartouche and back stamp, is later, possibly *c.* 1730–1800.

Richard Mathews of Gloucester, who died in 1800, used both Broseley-type stem stamps and Bristol-type cartouche marks. A pipe of this later 18th-century form, recorded from recent excavations in Hereford, is stamped on the stem with the mark of Richard Mathews. Lastly, those examples shown on Figure 5.44.113–4 have near parallels in the pipes of Robert Williams of Gloucester, working 1849–66.

Stamps
All of the stamps recorded are reproduced at twice actual size in Figures 5.45 and 5.46 (Table 5.13).

115–124	all date from *c.* 1630–50.
125–128	are all recorded from heel fragments so could date from between 1630 and 1700.
129–131	are all on north Herefordshire forms from the last quarter of the seventeenth century.
132–143	are locally made derivatives of 'Broseley Type 2'; 1660–80.
144–162	are all from 'Broseley Type 2' and its local derivatives; 1660–80.
163–166	are all from 'Broseley Type 3', 1670–90.
167–174	are on 'Broseley Type 5', 1680–1730.
175–179	are on 'Broseley Type 4', 1690–1720.
180	is stamped across the stem. The initials are RH. There are eleven examples from this assemblage. It is also recorded from Tewkesbury and could be a local Worcester product. 1690–1720.
181–186	are placed across the stem. All are recorded Broseley makers.
187–191	are placed across the stem.
192	is stamped across the stem.
193–194	are on a mould imparted side cartouche. Probably Bristol products.
195–198	are stamped incuse on the back of the bowl. Probably Bristol products.
199–201	are stamped along the stem and are products of Worcester manufacturers recorded in a Directory of 1850.
202	is stamped along the stem and is clearly a Broseley product.

Worcester pipemakers
There are a number of pipemakers recorded in Worcester in the second half of the 17th century, but there is some doubt as to how many. Between 1657 and 1676, the names Francis Brian, Francis Barber and Francis Baker appear as master pipemakers in apprentice indentures and a will. It seems unlikely that three men with the same christian name and the same surname initial

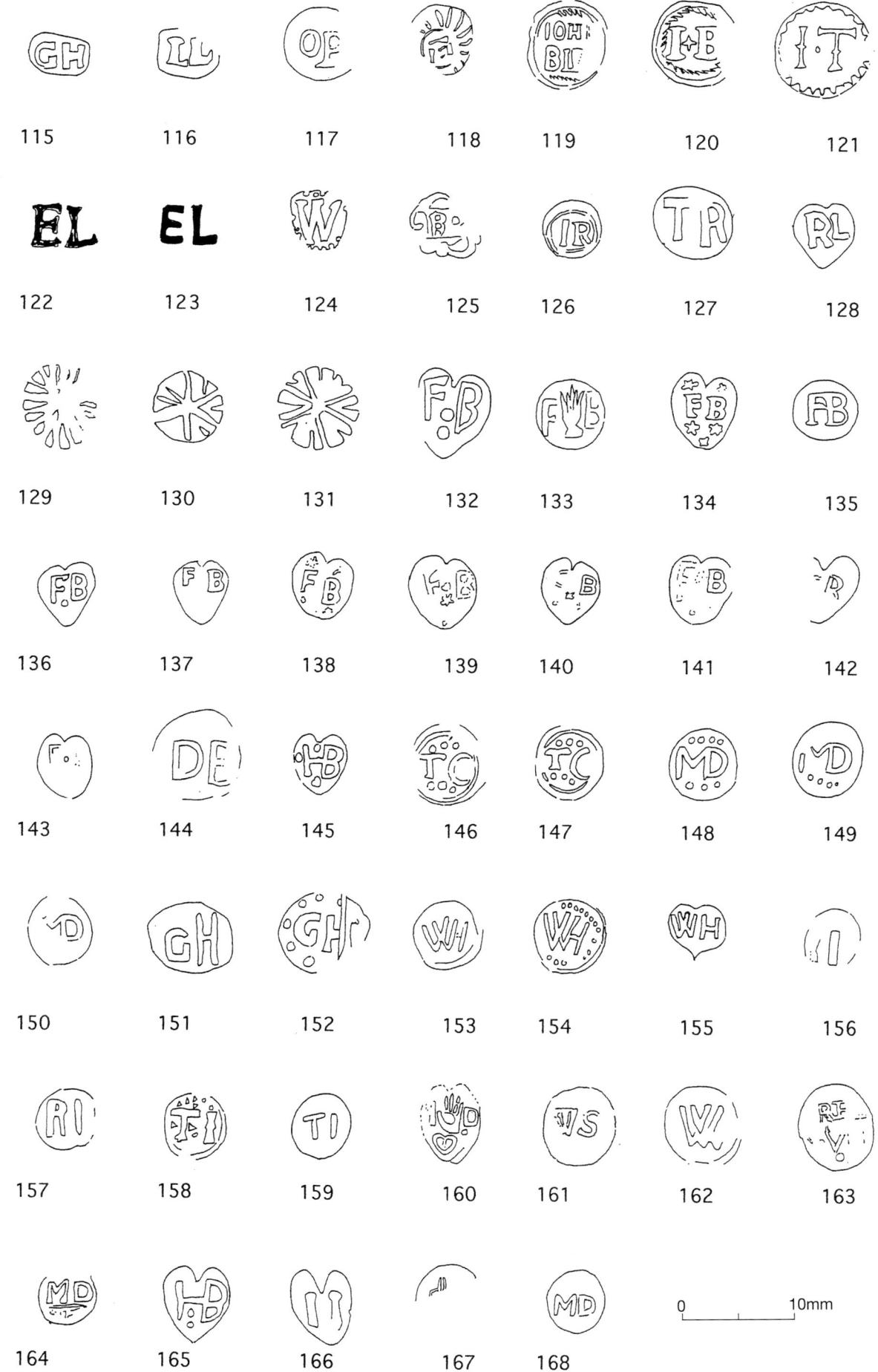

Fig. 5.45 Clay pipe stamps (Nos 115–168). Scale 2:1

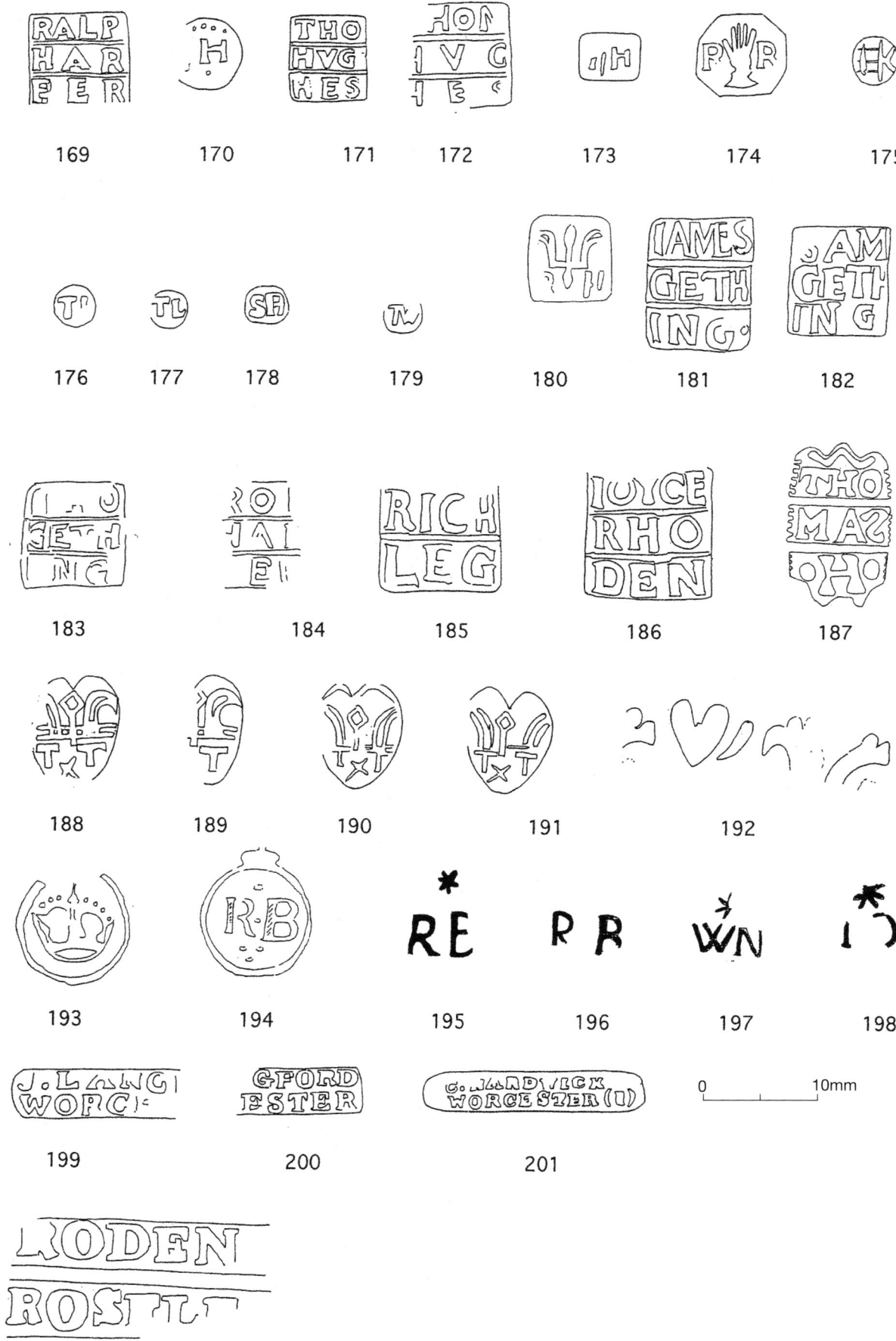

Fig. 5.46 Clay pipe stamps (Nos 169–202). Scale 2:1

Table 5.13: Illustrated clay pipe stamps

Cat. no.	Bowl no.	Context	Group	Plot	Period	Stamp date
115	-	277	14	2	3.2	1630–50
116	-	526	N/A	2	5	1630–50
117	1	278	14	2	3.2	1630–50
118	2	681	10	2	3.1	1630–50
119	3	447	N/A	12	3.3	1630–50
120	5	273	32	4	5	1630–50
121	4	273	32	4	5	1630–50
122	-	275	14	2	3.2	1630–50
123	6	3	172	All	Machining	1630–50
124	11	98	53	2	5	1630–50
125	-	1895	92	6	3.1	1630–70
126	-	275	14	2	3.2	1630–70
127	-	1121	108	10	4	1630–70
128	-	1215	107	10	4	1630–70
129	29	447	N/A	12	3.3	1650–1700
130	30	0	U/S	N/A	N/A	1650–1700
131	27	0	U/S	N/A	N/A	1650–1700
132	67	3	172	All	Machining	1660–80
133	-	1026	108	11	4	1660–80
134	66	3	172	All	Machining	1660–80
135	71	273	32	4	5	1660–80
136	-	1215	107	10	4	1660–80
137	-	1215	107	10	4	1660–80
138	65	3	172	All	Machining	1660–80
139	-	1215	107	10	4	1660–80
140	69	1121	108	10	4	1660–80
141	-	1206	107	10	4	1660–80
142	70	447	N/A	12	3.3	1660–80
143	68	3	172	All	Machining	1660–80
144	48	3	172	All	Machining	1660–80
145	44	1036	310	11	5	1660–80
146	47	19	14	2	3.2	1660–80
147	46	3	172	All	Machining	1660–80
148	-	1969	39	4	2	1660–80
149	42 49	1797	N/A	4	N/A	1660–80
150	50	1714	N/A	4	N/A	1660–80
151	51	1797	N/A	4	N/A	1660–80
152	52	71	N/A	2	5	1660–80
153	53	3	172	All	Machining	1660–80
154	54 55	447	N/A	12	3.3	1660–80
155	-	1613	90	6	3.2	1660–80
156	56	3	172	All	Machining	1660–80
157	-	273	32	4	5	1660–80

Table 5.13 (cont.): Illustrated clay pipe stamps

Cat. no.	Bowl no.	Context	Group	Plot	Period	Stamp date
158	57	15 273 2768	53 32 105	2 4 9	5 5 5	1660–80
159	58 59 60	273	32	4	5	1660–80
160	-	1121	108	10	4	1660–80
161	63	372	N/A	2	N/A	1660–80
162	-	273	32	4	5	1660–80
163	43	3	172	All	Machining	1670–90
164	-	18	9	2	5	1670–90
165	45	3	172	All	Machining	1670–90
166	41	862	278	14	3.3	1670–90
167	85	0	U/S	N/A	N/A	1680–1730
168	84	0	U/S	N/A	N/A	1680–1730
169	81	3	172	All	Machining	1680–1730
170	83	451	12	6	3.1	1680–1730
171	79	420	86	6	3.3	1680–1730
172	82	3	172	All	Machining	1680–1730
173	78	756	36	4	3.2	1680–1730
174	80	636	N/A	2	N/A	1680–1730
175	-	3	172	All	Machining	1690–1720
176	91	536	19	1	4	1690–1720
177	88	97	32	4	5	1690–1720
178	89	564	12	2	3.1	1690–1720
179	-	623	335	6	4	1690–1720
180	-	121 122	53 53	2 2	5 5	1690–1720
181	-	1923	N/A	7	N/A	-
182	-	122	53	2	5	-
183	-	122	53	2	5	-
184	-	122	53	2	5	-
185	-	99 122	53 53	2 2	5 5	-
186	-	121	53	2	5	-
187	-	99 121 122	53 53 53	2 2 2	5 5 5	-
188	-	99	53	2	5	-
189	-	99	53	2	5	-
190	-	99	53	2	5	-
191	-	99	53	2	5	-
192	-	13	N/A	2	5	-
193	101	372	N/A	2	N/A	1720–40
194	107	122	53	2	5	1730–80

Table 5.13 (cont.): Illustrated clay pipe stamps

Cat. no.	Bowl no.	Context	Group	Plot	Period	Stamp date
195	107	122	53	2	5	1730–80
196	-	122	53	2	5	-
197	-	122	53	2	5	-
198	99	461	9	2	5	1730–80
199	-	282	9	2	5	-
200	-	158	6	2	3.2	-
201	-	2181	44	5	2.3	-
202	-	689	N/A	2	5	-

should occupy the same time slot in the same city. All of the entries have been checked in the original documents and all are correctly transcribed, however, and all three men were illiterate, making a mark or shaky initials in witness to the relevant agreement. It is clear therefore that the name was spoken and then written by a scribe. The names Barker and Barber could easily be confused. In another document from a later period a maker's name is written variously as Brittain and Briton. With this *caveat* in place the documents will be quoted as they appear in the original.

In 1657 Francis Brian, pipemaker, took as his apprentice John Morley for the term of eight years. In 1667 he took Thomas Beardmore for the period of seven years. In 1670 he took Thomas Hopkins for eight years. At the time of these last two entries Francis Brian was living in the parish of St Swithin's (WRO BA 5234 and 1026).

In 1660 Francis Barker/Barber, pipemaker, took as his apprentice Richard Smith for the term of nine years (WRO BA 3696). The indenture of apprenticeship, Richard Smith to Francis Barker, is on a standard printed form. The master's name is written twice. In the first instance the central letter of the surname is obscured by the tail of the 'p' from the line above. It could be either Barker or Barber. At the foot of the document he makes his mark and the scribe has written his name, which is clearly Francis Barker. The document is twice folded and on the upper outside is written 'Richard Smith to Francis Barber 1660'. Although this is unquestionably Barber, it is in a different hand to that in the rest of the document and has clearly been added later and may be a misreading of Barker. In the will of 1676 and other documents relating to it the name appears clearly written several times as Barker. It seems likely, however, that the will and the indenture refer to the same person.

In 1676 Francis Baker died leaving a widow Mary and four sons, Francis, Richard, Joseph and Samuel (Guyatt 1994, 24). He left all of his tools and implements relating to the trade of pipemaking to his wife Mary, on the condition that she remain unmarried. In the event of her remarriage, the said tools etc. should be appropriated by two named friends for the benefit of his children (WRO wills). He was a man of substance. He left 13 pairs of moulds and other implements relating to the trade of pipemaking valued at £4 1s, plus clay and pipes valued at 10s 3d. Interestingly he applied a seal to his will in the shape of a lozenge with the initials F B either side of a pipe. As yet no pipe stamp similar to this has been recorded.

Of the four apprentices recorded above, nothing more is yet known of John Morley. The name Richard Smith appears as stem stamps recovered from Hereford and Pipe Aston, though it is unlikely that these date much before 1730 and therefore unlikely to be the product of the above named apprentice, who would have been free by 1669.

Thomas Beardmore, pipemaker of Worcester, is a witness on a document of 1676 relating to the probate of Francis Barker. He also took as his apprentice Thomas Laiton in 1691, for a period of seven years. Thomas Beardmore also features in the overseers' accounts for the parish of St Nicholas (WRO film 306/5). He is identified as a pipemaker in 1699. He is likely to be the same Thomas Beardmore that took apprentice Jos Middleton in 1695 (the overseers' accounts do not identify a trade) and may well be the same Beardmore whose family were to be taken care of during his absence from them, at the discretion of the churchwardens in 1698. Why he was away or where he was is not recorded. On 29 May 1699, it was ordered that the:

> churchwardens do provide tools and implements for Thomas Beardmore, pipe maker in the parish and lend them to him in the name of the parish goods and take a note of his hand for his redelivery of the same when demanded. All which time Mary Powell widow did promise that the said Tho Beardmore nor any of his family should be any way burdensome to the parish for one year in case he enjoy the use of the said implements. Always providing the churchwardens do not exceed forty shillings in buying such implements.

Thomas Hopkins could be the maker of the Thomas H stem stamps (Fig. 5.46, 187) although it is thought unlikely. He would have been free by 1678 and would have been in his mid seventies by 1730 when stem stamping was becoming fashionable in this region. As for Thomas Laiton, the apprentice of Thomas Beardmore, nothing more is known at present either from documents or pipe stamps.

In the accounts of the parish of St Nicholas it is recorded that one 'Browne pipe maker' received parish relief on at least seven occasions between 1691 and 1693 (WRO film 306/5). Two entries, one a payment for coals and the other for clay, are of particular interest in that they show that the overseers were trying to help him in practical ways to support himself and his family. It is unfortunate that these entries do not provide a christian name or initial to match against pipe stamps.

Although no apprentice pipemakers have been found in a complete search of the WRO slip index relating to 18th-century Worcester, the Newport Street site has furnished evidence of possible makers in the form of stem stamps No. 180 and Nos 187–91. These occurred in contexts 99, 121 and 122, together with bowl forms in use during the second half of the century. In this region, stamping across the stem became the norm from the second quarter of the 18th century. Amongst the products of Roy's Orchard, Pipe Aston, where work ceased *c.* 1730, no stem stamps were recorded.

Trade directories for the 19th century list clay tobacco-pipe manufacturers working in the city as: John Russell (1835); C. Hardwick (1850); J. Langford (1850); H. Shutter & Co. (1850); Joseph Andrews (1869); and William Shepherd & Co. (1869).

John Russell took apprentices William Philips and James Davis in 1820, and Thomas Heepox in 1826. It is clear that he was working from 1820 to 1835 and probably either side of these dates as well, though no longer by 1841. Numerous examples of pipes with marks impressed on the back of the bowl: 'Russell Worcester' circling a pair of dividers and a number (1 to 7), have been recorded from Cheltenham, Gloucester, Leominster and Ross-on-Wye. The numbers 1 to 7 probably indicate stamps held by seven individual workers as a recording mechanism for a piecework system.

Henry Shutter is listed in the 1841 census, aged 35, living in St Clement's, with wife Amelia aged 26 and daughter Amelia aged 2. Several other pipeworkers are listed living in St Clement's under different titles: Lewis Thomas, aged 50, not born in the county; Catherine Dovey, aged 28, born in Worcestershire; and Edward Okely, aged 35, not born in the county, are all listed as pipemakers. Elizabeth Price, aged 20; Richard Lee, aged 20; Charlotte Hewins/Harris, aged 35, all born in Worcestershire; and Robert Hewlett, aged 30, not born in the county, are all listed as J. (presumably journeymen) pipemakers. Charles Watkins, aged 15, and John Mayes, aged 55, neither one being born in the county, are listed as 'J Pipe M'. Elizabeth Hewlett, aged 30, is listed as a pipe trimmer. This cluster of workers is typical of the small pipe factories that sprang up in the 19th century, serviced by a motley band of journeymen moving from place to place in search of work. All of the work that they produced bore the stamp of their employer. Several incuse stamps along the stem, of 'H. Shutter & Co. Worcester', have been recorded from the Crystal Room site in Hereford (Hugh Sherlock, pers. comm.). It is clear that this factory was working from 1841 to 1850 and probably either side of these dates as well.

As work has yet to be done on the 1851 and later censuses we are left with bald spot dates for the remaining factories: C. Hardwick (1850), J. Langford (1850), Joseph Andrews (1869) and William Shepherd & Co. (1869). Stem stamps Nos 199–201 in relief along the stem are the products of J. Langford and G. Hardwick. Langford stamps have been recorded Tewkesbury and Gloucester (Peacey 1996), and a similarly styled stamp from Worcester porcelain factory appears to be that of Shepherd (Jacobs nd).

5.15.2 Conclusions

This assemblage underpins patterns emerging from previous work in Worcester. Notably scarce from Worcester assemblages are pipes of 'Broseley Type 5', the most usual of the Broseley types encountered elsewhere. Also scarce are any spurred forms dating from the 17th century, other than the 'Broseley Type 4'. Although it is tempting to explain the former in terms of a vibrant local industry covering the period of Type 5 production (*c.* 1680–1720), and excluding Broseley products from the city, there is as yet insufficient documentary evidence to support such a scenario.

The absence of 17th-century spurred forms is consistent with patterns elsewhere from north Herefordshire and Shropshire. A single example has been recorded from Pipe Aston and two from Bromyard. By contrast at Gloucester, the probable source, spurred pipes are made in equal numbers with heeled forms throughout the second half of the 17th century (Peacey 1996, 243–59).

Although no records are known of pipemakers working in Worcester in the 18th century, it seems likely that they did exist and that some at least of their products are present in this assemblage. There is clearly a need for further documentary research to prove the existence of and provide details of these suspected makers. Those documents that have been studied paint a varied picture of the social lives of pipemakers. In the late 17th century the records attest to successful operators such as Francis Baker leaving considerable assets to his family, and less fortunate men receiving help from the parish to survive. Clay tobacco pipes by virtue of the stamps placed on them can be attributed to particular makers through surviving contemporary records. It is this link that opens a window on the lives of the people involved creating a marriage between archaeology and social history, thus bringing the past to life.

5.16 Glass
Angus Crawford and Alan J. Jacobs

A total of 941 fragments of glass weighing 25.396kg were recovered (Table 5.14). This material was recovered according to the procedures described previously (Chapter 3.2.5) and dates from the medieval period onwards. The assemblage is dominated by examples of vessel glass (784 shards) and window glass (151 shards), although other objects such as modern glass beads (3), a marble and a rare example of a linen smoother were also recovered.

Most of the material is modern (Period 5) in date or from unassigned contexts (total 772 shards) consisting of a variety of beer and soda bottles, although examples of milk bottles and smaller condiment or sauce bottles were also recovered. Other vessel types were represented in the form of ash trays and beer or drinking glasses.

Much of this material is of little further interest beyond documenting social and economic change in the 19th and early 20th century, a period where glass became much more common. For the purposes of this report, glass from earlier periods is discussed in more detail, reporting on the modern material is limited to a short discussion of the complete bottles.

Table 5.14: Glass

Period	Type	Count	Weight (g)
Period 2	Vessel glass	2	4
	Other	1	1
Period 3	Vessel glass	93	5055.5
	Window glass	26	177
	Other	1	299
Period 4	Vessel glass	45	1519
	Window glass	1	1
Period 5	Vessel glass	559	14369.5
	Window glass	119	511
	Other	3	13
Unassigned	Vessel glass	85	3408
	Window glass	5	35
	Other	1	3
Total		941	25,396

5.16.1 Medieval and post-medieval glass
Alan J. Jacobs

Period 2: Medieval
A small quantity of glass was recorded from medieval contexts but most of it appears to be modern and, therefore, was either wrongly assigned or represents contamination so is omitted here (included in unassigned total). However, three tiny shards of vessel glass weighing 5g are present from more securely dated contexts and are considered to be of medieval origin.

Periods 3 and 4: Post-medieval (16th to 18th centuries)
A total of 166 fragments of glass (7.051kg) were recovered from Period 3 and 4 contexts, including 138 shards of vessel glass, 27 shards of window glass, and a linen smoother. The window glass is largely undiagnostic but includes a fragment with a pontil scar (Plot 11; Period 3.2; G302: context 1221).

Vessel glass
Post-medieval vessel glass was present in both Period 3 and 4 contexts, and was also recovered as residual finds from later contexts. A variety of bottles and other objects are present, the most unusual of which is the flat base and neck of a large costrel of late 17th to 18th-century date (Plot 4; context 1714; Fig. 5.47, 1). Another less commonly recorded object was a small phial or flask of late 17th to 18th-century date (Plot 6; Period 3.1; G12: context 451).

Several examples of onion bottle bases were recovered, some of which can be more closely dated by association with pottery. For instance, late 16th to 17th-century examples from Plots 4 and 6 (G42: context 1550; G89: context 1503) and an example dated 1740–1770 from Plot 2 (G14: context 19). Others have less certain dating associations (Plot 6; G87: context 683), or are residual in Period 5 contexts, including a near-complete example from context 527 (Plot 2, G6; Fig. 5.47, 2). All are still of broadly 17th to 18th-century date.

Of later date are the neck and shoulders of a greenish brown coloured cylindrical bottle recovered as a residual find from a Period 5 deposit (Plot 1; G27: context 20; Fig. 5.47, 3). This is similar in form to late 18th-century examples from Oyster Road in Portsmouth (Fox and Barton 1986, fig. 142.2). A fragmentary stamp from a late 17th to 18th-century brandy or spirits bottle was also recovered, with the lettering 'W[.]A' impressed into the seal (Plot 2; Period 3.2; G6: context 523).

A few examples of fine clear glass vessels were present within the assemblage, and included several fragments from Period 3, early post-medieval drinking glasses both as residual material (Period 5; context 461) and within stratified deposits (Plot 14; Period 3.3; G260: context 899; Plot 2; Period 3.2; G14: context 278), from which came the hollow stem of a bowl (context 278). Of slightly later date was the complete profile of an early 18th-century drinking goblet recovered from deposits associated with the cottages on Plot 1 (Period 4; G19: context 536; Fig. 5.47, 4).

Linen smoother
The linen smoother (Plot 6; Period 3.2; G90: context 1573) is formed from green translucent glass that has

been spun into an ellipsoid form (Fig. 5.47, 5). About two-thirds of it survives, with the handle apparently having snapped off, unless this was an unhandled form. Linen smoothers were used from the Anglo-Saxon period until the 19th century in the production of linen, with this example being of 17th to 18th-century date.

Catalogue of illustrated glass (Fig. 5.47)

1. Costrel. Late 17th to 18th century. Plot 4; Unassigned: context 1714
2. Bottle. Neck, large part of sides and part of base of onion bottle in dark greenish glass. 17th to 18th century. Residual within Period 5 deposit. Plot 2; G6: context 527
3. Bottle. Neck and shoulders of a greenish brown cylindrical bottle. Late 18th century. Residual within Period 5 deposit. Plot 1; G27: context 20
4. Goblet. Multiple-knop, baluster goblet with folded foot. Early 18th century. Plot 1; Period 4; G19: context 536
5. Linen smoother. Formed from green translucent glass spun into an ellipsoid form. 17th to 18th century. Plot 6; Period 3.2; G90: context 1573

5.16.2 The later bottle glass
Angus Crawford

A substantial quantity of glass bottle shards is present within the assemblage and includes general household types for sauce, medicines, carbonated drinks, beer, and wine. Bottles of these types are frequently encountered on urban sites, and are typically representative of various local and national industries of the later 19th century onwards. The Newport Street assemblage contains a number of soda water and beer bottles embossed with the details of Worcester suppliers, including Robert Allen and Co. Ltd, a brewery operating from *c.* 1900 to 1935, and Lewis Clarke & Co., which operated out of Angel Place in Worcester from *c.* 1895 to 1970 (Worcester City Museums). While the embossed bottles are of social interest for the range of small to medium suppliers operating within Worcester, the range of bottle production types also reflects the development of bottle production methods and the progress in designing improved closure types. All bottles described below date from the late 19th to early 20th century, when embossed bottles began to be superseded by mass-produced machine-made bottles with printed labels:

- Three complete ink bottles in varying bluish-green glass. Small square bodies with three ribbed sides and one plain/flat side. Visible three-piece mould seams both vertically and horizontally on shoulder. There are two depressions, one on either side of the neck for resting the quill/pen. All three have short necks with the mouth sheared. Probable late 19th to early 20th-century date.
- Six utilitarian bottles of almost colourless glass with a very pale green tinge, usually classified as 'sauce' bottles. All are mouth-blown in a two-piece mould,

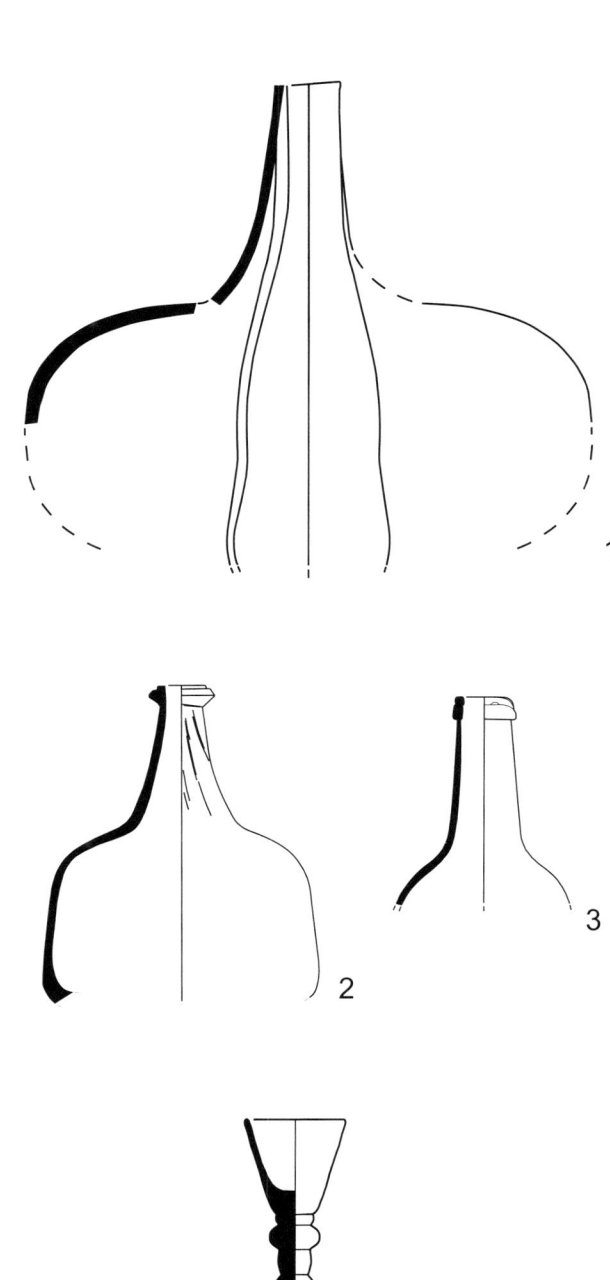

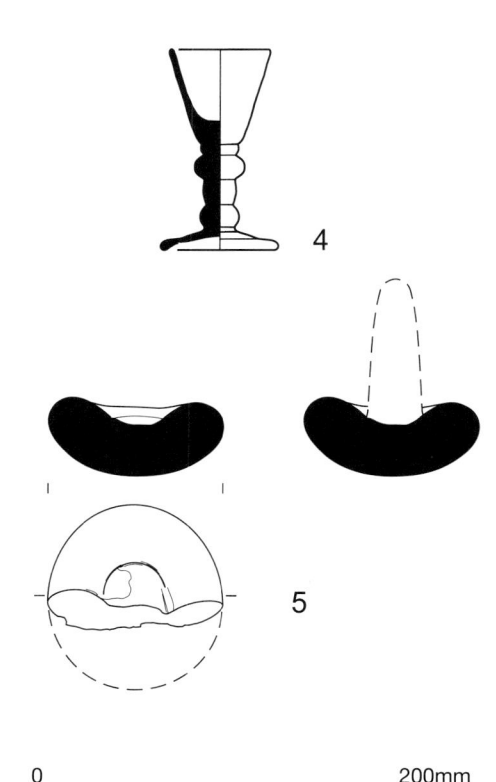

Fig. 5.47 Glass (Nos 1–5). Scale 1:4

with seams running from base to lip. They are of various standard sizes with four bottles 150mm high with neck diameters of 15–20mm and base diameters of 35mm. A further bottle has a height of 198mm, neck diameter of 20mm and base diameter of 52mm. The remaining bottle has a height of 115mm, neck diameter of 18mm and base diameter of 39mm, with an embossed panel of 'REEVE BROS, BIRMINGHAM'. All have sheared tops and date from the late 19th to early 20th century.

- Three moulded 'blob top' bottles, one of grass-green glass with an applied blob top onto a two-piece moulded body. Body embossed 'ROBERT ALLEN And Co Ltd WORCESTER'; base embossed with an arrow and '960'. Dark olive-green glass bottle with body embossed 'IMPERIAL' and 'LEWIS CLARKE & Co WORCESTER'. This bottle, with *in situ* remains of a lever-style closure, is of late 19th-century date. Bluish green moulded bottle embossed 'SPRECKLEY BROS WORCESTER', in an unusual form in that the blob top has been moulded with the body rather than applied after. Height 200mm with base diameter of 67mm. Probably of early 20th-century date.
- Five improved internal screw beer bottles with applied tops and moulded bodies. Two are grass-green glass bottles embossed 'SHOWELLS BREWERY COMPANY LIMITED' with bases stamped 'W 113' and 'W 105'; height 215mm, with a base diameter of 60mm. Another of deep green glass is embossed 'SPRECKLEY BROS WORCESTER', base embossed with 'C.S & Co Ltd 7684'; height 200mm, base diameter 64mm. The remaining bottle of this type is of olive-green glass embossed 'ALLSOPP'S Ltd TRADE MARK' surrounding a raised right hand with palm facing forward, and its base is embossed with the number 2956. Another embossed Spreckley Brothers bottle of olive-green glass is of large size being 245mm high with a base diameter of 76mm.
- Two machine-produced bottles in almost colourless glass with crown seal closures. One embossed 'BLAND & Co (BOTTLERS) Ltd' with the base embossed '8/20 949'. The other embossed 'CROCKETTS LIMITED WORCESTER', with the base embossed 'B& Co LD 2706'; both bottles 195mm high with a base diameter of 65mm and dating from the early 20th century.

5.17 Ironworking residues
Robin Jackson

The hand-collected ironworking residues comprise 440 fragments of slag weighing 27.878kg (Table 5.15). This was recovered and recorded according to the procedures described previously (Chapter 3.2.5). Hammerscale and further quantities of slag were also recovered from the processed residues of bulk soil samples. These were not quantified by count or weight but have been estimated according to frequency (occasional, moderate, frequent, and abundant). The residues were recorded from deposits of all periods but primarily comprise Roman redeposited and residual iron smelting waste. A quantity

Table 5.15: Summary of iron slag assemblage

Period	Count	Weight (g)
Unphased	24	1031
1	12	1306
2	135	11786
3	128	9374
4/5	4	108
5	137	4273
Total	440	27,878

of late medieval (Period 2) and post-medieval (Period 3) material was also recovered from the vicinity of a number of hearth/oven structures recorded in Plots 13 and 14.

In the light of the large quantities of ironworking residues examined from other sites in Worcester and the context and relatively small sample of material recovered from Newport Street, assessment indicated that this material did not have the potential to provide technical information on the organisation and character of ironworking during any period. However, it had some potential in defining a further area of Roman period iron slag dumping (to build up, and construct, a causeway/road (Plot 3; G61; Plot 13: G347 & G349), and later back plot activity including medieval and post-medieval smithing (Plots 13 and 14). Due to the limited potential for analysis, only basic quantification, identification, and distribution patterns have been undertaken to support interpretation of on-site activities and structures.

5.17.1 Analysis

Period 1: Roman

Only limited quantities of ironworking waste were recovered from stratified Roman deposits (Table 5.15). These primarily derived from deposits associated with the construction of a road (G61: context 2771) and from make-up horizons (G347) forming a postulated causeway on which the road was constructed. The road construction mirrored that seen elsewhere in Worcester, utilising a combination of coarse gravel and pebbles (presumably derived from local drift deposits) and iron slag waste. Observation of boreholes drilled for geotechnical and geoarchaeological purposes also recorded slag associated with these road construction deposits (Table 3.1; Fig. 3.2). This material was not retained but in several boreholes the deposit was in excess of 1.00m thick, and in three boreholes (BH21, BH22 and DTS04) the degree of compaction of the slag, pebble and gravel surface was so great that the boring equipment was unable to penetrate it.

Ironworking waste was also recovered from a 2nd to 3rd-century pit pre-dating the road (G346: context 2042) and slag deposits were also recorded to the north of the road in nearly half of the boreholes (9 out of 19) located in areas of the site where Roman deposits were not otherwise recorded (Table 3.1; Fig. 3.2), indicating widespread presence of this material across the site.

Periods 2 and 3: medieval and post-medieval
Ironworking residues recovered from medieval and early post-medieval contexts were more abundant than from Roman deposits, though this probably reflects the greater volume of deposits of this date excavated rather than greater quantities within the site (Table 5.15).

Material was particularly focussed around a sequence of hearths and associated features and spreads in Plots 13 and 14 dating to the medieval (Period 2) and early post-medieval periods (Period 3.1). Over a third of the total assemblage by count and nearly 45% of total weight (140 fragments weighing 12.562kg) derived from these contexts. Moderate to abundant quantities of both hammerscale and clinker/ash were also recovered from bulk samples taken from several medieval contexts (Plot 13; Period 2.3; G209: context 1365; Period 2.4; G137: context 1405, G131: context 1594; Plot 14; Period 2.4/5; G227: context 1378), and slag was also regularly present in samples from these deposits (Plot 13: G353, G133, G359, G126, G128, G129, G130 and G151; Plot 14: G210 and G233).

Beyond these deposits, ironworking residues were also recovered from bulk samples from deposits dating to these periods in Plot 5 (Period 2.5/3.1; G46: context 2098), where frequent ash, clinker and slag were recorded, and on Plot 11 (Period 3.2; G302: context 1314) where frequent hammerscale, ash and clinker were present.

Periods 4 and 5: 18th to 20th centuries
One later dated context (Plot 10; Period 4; G107: context 1215) produced a moderate quantity of iron slag and a moderate quantity of hammerscale from a bulk sample, but no associated structures were identified.

5.17.2 Discussion

Period 1: Roman
None of the Period 1 material is liable to have been in primary contexts and no evidence for on-site smelting activities was identified in the limited areas investigated. Redeposited Roman ironworking waste has been widely recorded in Worcester where it was regularly used in the construction of roads and yard surfaces and Newport Street seems to be no exception. The dating of the material and the location of the site suggest that it derived either from ironworking areas situated to the south-east, around Deansway, or those located along the river terrace to the north of the Deansway site and east and north-east of Newport Street (Jackson 2004).

Periods 2 and 3: medieval and post-medieval
Whilst some of the material recovered from medieval and post-medieval contexts is likely to be residual Roman (e.g. the 1.144kg of tap slag), the presence of hammerscale indicates that primary material is almost certainly present. Along with the presence of a few examples of smaller hearth bases (potentially from secondary processing: the smithing of blooms) and an association with a sequence of hearths, it can be suggested that a smithy was operating within Plots 13 and 14, throughout Period 2 and into early Period 3 (the 13th/14th century through to the 16th/earlier 17th century); though some of the later material could potentially be from disturbed Period 2 deposits. The presence of hammerscale in Plot 11 at a similar period implies localised smithing but in the absence of associated structures it seems likely that this was derived from the adjacent Plot 13.

Periods 4 and 5: 18th to 20th centuries
Although hammerscale and iron slag were present within Plot 10 deposits, no structural or documentary evidence was recovered to support the presence of a smithy and it is suggested that the material was residual, having been disturbed from an earlier, unexcavated part of the sequence in this plot.

5.18 Leather
Ian Panter

A small assemblage of waterlogged leatherworking debris and fragments of shoes was recovered from the excavation, providing evidence of leather manufacturing and repair work in the vicinity during the medieval period. Waterlogged leather was recovered from three contexts (1860, 1876 and 2681) and the largest group, from context 1860 represents primary, secondary and tertiary waste as well as fragments of shoe components.

Primary waste is the product of the initial trimming and cutting during hide preparation and tanning, and usually includes those areas of the hide or skin that cannot be used in the manufacture of shoes and other items. These often include fragments exhibiting hide edges, udders and areas around the head and legs. An example with an udder was recovered from context 1860, as were fragments of hide edges. A similar fragment of hide edge was recovered from context 1876. Several of the pieces have bristles still attached. Whilst the presence of primary waste could suggest that leather processing and tanning was occurring in the vicinity, it is more likely that the leatherworker was using untrimmed hides and skins. Tanning was (and still is) a very obnoxious activity which, by regulation, often had to be conducted away from habitation. Secondary waste results from the action of cutting out patterns from the hide or skin, with both triangular and elliptical-shaped forms being recovered from context 1860. Triangular offcuts, often known as intersectional cutting pieces (Mould *et al.* 2003), occur when a number of shoe soles are cut from one hide, and their presence is a good indication that shoe manufacture was occurring on the site. Tertiary waste is defined as the product of the final trimming of the cut-out patterns and usually consists of thin irregular-shaped strips of leather, and several hundred pieces (weighing approximately 250g) were recovered from context 1860.

The presence of both secondary and tertiary waste is evidence of leather manufacture, especially cordwaining, the production of shoes. There is also evidence for cobbling, or shoe repair, with several poor-quality clump soles recovered as well as a number of undiagnostic squares of leather showing evidence of cutting, possibly pieces being prepared for reuse. An incomplete shoe vamp (upper) recovered from context 1876 has had its upper edge trimmed off for reuse too.

Whilst no diagnostic shoe soles or uppers were recovered to independently date the assemblage, there is no reason to doubt the 14th-century date assigned to contexts 1860 and 1876, both of which were fills within a large pit on Plot 13 (G131). The presence of rands (thin strips of leather used in the construction of turn-shoes as an aid to waterproofing) were introduced in the 12th century and remained integral to turn-shoe construction until the development of the welted construction (welts are similar to rands but are wider and have double seams) much later.

A shoe upper from context 1876 is incomplete and is difficult to date on stylistic grounds. However the upper has been cut from bovine hide, the use of which becomes more common in the 14th century for shoe uppers (Grew and de Neergaard 1988). As the upper is incomplete it is impossible to say whether it represents a slip-on shoe or one that is fastened with a toggle or lace.

The clump sole (from contexts 1876 and 2681) is a typical repair patch commonly used on turn-shoes throughout the medieval period, whereby additional patches of leather were attached to the sole using a tunnel stitch after the original sole had worn through. During the later 16th century, when shoes were constructed with two or three sole components (outer, middle and inner soles) and with rands developing into welts, it was possible to attach a complete new outer sole rather than use small patches to cover the worn region.

Catalogue

- Large group of 13th to 14th-century leatherworking debris from Plot 13, context 1860, G131, Period 2.4. Comprises primary waste (11 pieces, bovine and sheep/goat); secondary waste (38 pieces, bovine and sheep/goat); and tertiary waste (several hundreds, weight approximately 250g, bovine and sheep/goat). Fragments of shoes include one sole, incomplete and torn with rounded toe; several rands; fragment of quarter (bovine) with flesh/grain lasting margin and whipped stitch seam; fragments of possible lace-hole binding strips with single flesh/grain seam; and also fragments of undiagnostic scraps, including bovine and sheep/goat but with many unidentified.

- Small group of 13th to 14th-century leather from Plot 13, context 1876, G131, Period 2.4. Includes an incomplete bovine-hide shoe vamp with elongated vamp wing, with flesh/grain seam along lasting margin, edge/flesh seam along throat, and edge/flesh side seams. The top edges are intentionally cut for reuse. It was probably part of a two-part upper, but the quarters are missing. Also includes a fragment of sheep/goat-hide primary waste, two fragments of clump sole (both for the forepart region of the sole and both with tunnel stitching): thickness suggests bovine hide, and one undiagnostic scrap, with no grain surface.

- A late 15th to 16th-century clump or repair patch with tunnel stitching for the seat region of the sole from Plot 3, context 2681, S263, Period 2.5/3.1. Length 96mm, maximum width 69mm. No grain pattern but thickness suggests bovine hide.

5.19 Cloth hose fragment
Penelope Walton Rogers

Remains of a cloth stocking or hose were recovered from a late medieval cess pit fill (Plot 3; Period 2.5/3.1; S263: context 2681). The surviving section would have covered the leg from knee to ankle, a distance of about 0.37m, and the calf circumference is 0.35m (Fig. 5.48). Most of the foot is missing, but the two curving slits at the torn lower edge mark where a triangular gusset would have been inserted on either side of the heel. There is a V-shaped reinforcement strip in association with one of the slits (Fig. 5.49). The side tabs form the back heel and the panel between the slits would have extended into a large tongue-shaped flap, forming the foot upper. A separately cut sole would have been stitched to the upper, and to the lower edge of the heel tabs. The cloth was cut 'on the bias' (diagonally across the fabric), so that there is a point at the top, but a triangular piece on one side (and probably originally on the other) marks where the stocking either continued above the knee, or had a fold-down top edge. The linen stitching has disintegrated but imprints of the thread indicate the types of seam used. The back seam is a standard 'open seam', with a seam allowance of 8–10mm held in place with a line of running stitch (18 stitches per 100mm), a feature seen in some of the London hose (Crowfoot *et al.* 1992, 187). All the other joins are flat seams, where the raw edges are overlapped by 6–7mm and stitched down with a spiral over-casting stitch (30 stitches per 100mm).

The fabric of the hose is a medium-weight wool tabby, 11–12 threads per cm in warp and weft, with Z-spun yarn in one direction (probably the warp) and S-spun in the other (the weft: for an explanation of technical terms, see Walton and Eastwood 1989). The wool is a relatively fine variant of the Hairy Medium fleece type in the Z-spun system and Generalised Medium in the S-spun: as such, they represent typical late medieval

Fig. 5.48 Fragments of cloth hose from cess pit S263. Scale 1:4

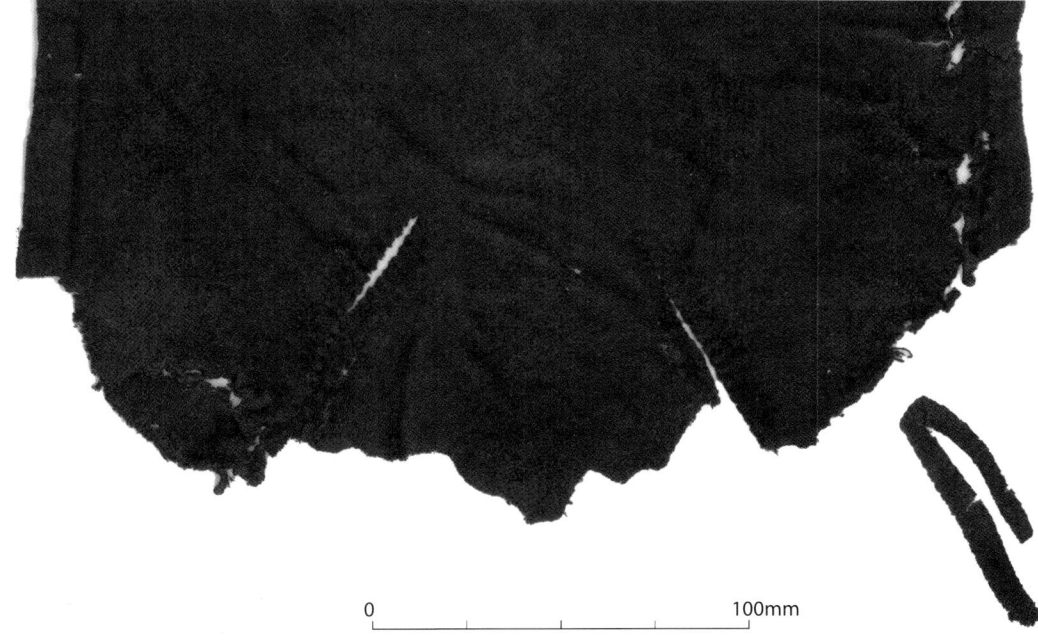

Fig. 5.49 The slits for the foot inserts and a reinforcement strip (Photo: The Anglo-Saxon Laboratory)

carding wools. The fleeces were originally white (non-pigmented), but traces of a tannin-based colorant detected by absorption spectrophotometry almost certainly indicate a reddish brown dye. The fabric may have had some soft-finishing (fulling and perhaps teaselling), but any nap originally present has mostly worn away. The fibres viewed at x400 magnification show numerous rounded ends, which indicate wear from rubbing (Cooke and Lomas 1990, 220–2, fig. 25.20), presumably caused by constant use.

Cloth hose was worn by men and women from Anglo-Saxon times onwards. Most surviving examples were cut on the bias, but there were several different methods of cutting and putting together the pattern pieces up until the 15th or 16th century, when they seem to have become more standardised (Nørlund 1924, 183–190; Crowfoot *et al.* 1992, 153–5, 186–190; Nockert 1997, 64–73, 105–8; Østergård 2004, 223–8). The pattern of this hose can be seen in 16th-century examples from London (Crowfoot *et al.* 1992, 189), and in some fragments from early to mid 16th-century Newcastle, originally identified as a shoe lining (Walton 1981, 202–3, T248–T253), and in a pair of hose on a body buried in about 1690 at Quintfall Hill, Wick, Scotland (Fig. 5.50; Orr 1922). The burial was of a man described as 'peasant class' and it probably represents the final stage of the wearing of cloth hose among poorer country people. By 1577 Queen Elizabeth had changed to knitted stockings (Arnold 1988, 206) and the rest of the population followed in due course: for example, a contemporary of the Quintfall Hill man, buried at Gunnister in Shetland, wore knitted wool stockings (Henshall and Maxwell 1952, 37–8).

The wool textile from which the hose has been made is a standard type in use from the later 14th century onwards (Crowfoot *et al.* 1992, 27; Walton 1981, 193–4) and offers little help with dating. The cut of the hose, however, suggests the 16th or 17th century and, since knitted goods probably reached English towns ahead of rural Scotland, an earlier rather than a later date seems likely.

Catalogue

The fabric is a tabby weave, 11–12/Z/0.8 x 11–12/S/0.8, slightly matted on inner face. Fleece types: Z is Hairy Medium, S is Generalised Medium. The wool is from a white fleece. Dye analysis (solvent extraction followed by absorption spectrophotometry) indicated the presence of a reddish brown tannin-based substance, probably dye. The fleece types were identified by measuring the diameters of 100 fibres in warp and weft (Z and S) and are quoted in microns:

- Z-spun: *range* 10–63, *mode* 25, *mean±S.D.* 25.7±9.1, *coefficient of skew* +0.58, skewed to positive, 5% fibres with medullas, 0% pigmented: Hairy Medium fleece type. Yarn spun in a counter-clockwise direction. The diagonal lines in the 'Z' suggests the direction of spin.
- S-spun: *range* 15–42, *mode* 20, *mean±S.D.* 25.6±6.4, *coefficient of skew* +0.93, skewed to positive, 1% fibres with medullas, 0% pigmented: Generalised Medium fleece type. Yarn spun in clockwise direction. The diagonal in the 'S' suggests the direction of spin.

5.20 Wooden small finds
Steven J. Allen

Four waterlogged wooden artefacts were recovered, all typical of medieval domestic assemblages. The objects from context 1860, a 13th to 14th-century pit fill in Plot 13 (G131) are the type of material caught up in the clearance of debris and the disposal of material which has no further value. Wooden artefacts do not always enter the archaeological record in a recognisable form: rubbish may be burnt as fuel, of which the small peg may be a reminder. This was probably from roofing material such as wooden shingles, slates or tiles, though other purposes cannot be entirely ruled out. The board offcut is the debris from the finishing or breaking up of a larger object.

The two most significant wooden artefacts are the remains of a comb and of a bowl, both recovered from context 2681, a cess pit fill from Plot 3 (S263) dated to the late medieval/early post medieval period. This context also included bark fragments, the debris from handling or working roundwood nearby, though no positive evidence of woodworking was present.

The comb is a good example of a double-sided comb with the usual biconvex cross section (Fig. 5.51, 1). Boxwood is frequently used for such objects, being tough and durable, and in this case a tangentially faced

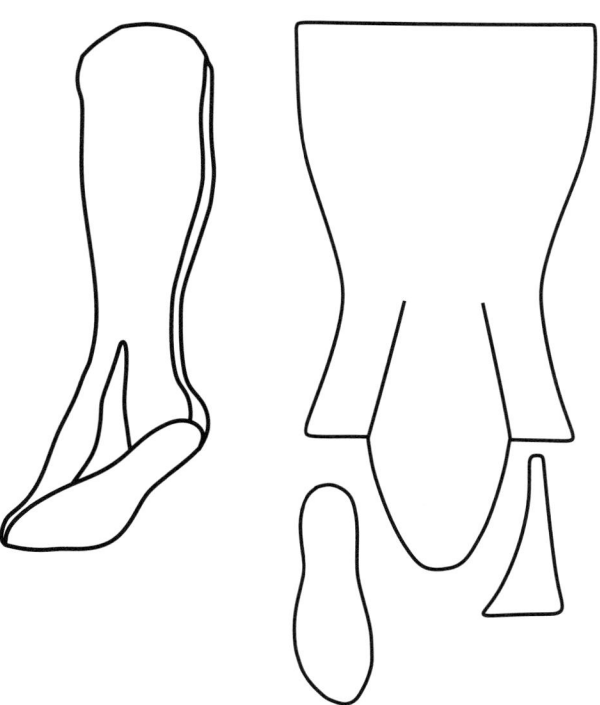

Fig. 5.50 The hose from Quintfall Hill, near Wick, and its pattern, after Orr 1922 (Illustration: The Anglo-Saxon Laboratory)

billet has been utilised. Assuming the comb blank was taken from a billet cut symmetrically about the centre of the parent log, it would have been at least 75mm long, not allowing for the guards at each end. The teeth of a comb are especially vulnerable to damage at the ends and so in comb production, solid wood, often shaped, is left at each end of the comb to act as a guard. One edge has widely spaced thick teeth, for coarse or rough combing, the other edge has fine, closely spaced teeth for more careful grooming. Manufacture of such a comb requires a significant investment in time and possibly specialist tools for accurate and even sawing of the fine teeth. This comb appears to have been a valued possession: at some point one end seems to have been broken away but rather than discard the object and replace it, the owner carefully trimmed the broken end for continued use. The fresh break at the other end, which is unworn, may have been the point at which this comb became unusable, resulting in its disposal. A similar fragment was recovered from the mid 16th-century fill of a pit at Sewer Lane, Hull (Armstrong 1977, 68, no. 133). Slightly more complete examples have been found in the fill of a 15th to 17th-century barrel-lined pit at Upwich (Hurst 1997b, 107), again of boxwood, and three more (one boxwood, two *Crataegus* spp) from 16th-century deposits in Exeter (Goldsmith Street and Trichay Street: Allan and Morris 1984, 309, nos W38–W40). The form and dating of these examples is very similar, and it may be tentatively suggested that this form of comb, with one set of very coarse teeth, one set of very fine teeth, plain and undecorated, is particular to this period.

The bowl is a standard medieval type: deep, thick walled, flat based and fairly plain with minimal decoration of three circumferential grooves around the exterior (Fig. 5.51, 2). The rim is slightly rounded and there is an internal carination approximately halfway up the height of the vessel. The bowl was face-turned on a lathe from a halved blank cut log at least 250mm in diameter. The object is quite badly fragmented and around one third is missing. Given that so much of the bowl, including some very small fragments, was recovered during the excavation, it seems that this bowl was already broken before it arrived in its burial context. There are no marks or obvious residues which would suggest what the bowl was used for or what caused it to break. The limescale deposits on the surface appear to be derived from precipitation within the burial context. The nearest parallel for this vessel is a *Fraxinus excelsior* L. bowl of similar form, reported from the late medieval fill of a garderobe from Lurk Lane, Beverley (Foreman 1991, 175, no. 950).

The parallels for these objects agree with the late medieval/early post-medieval date suggested for the fill of the feature from which they were derived. They are good examples of their type from this period and add to the few waterlogged wooden finds recovered from Worcester.

Catalogue

1   Part of a mid section from a double-sided comb from context 2681, S263, Period 2.5/3.1, Plot 3 (Fig. 5.51, No. 1). Species *Buxus sempervirens* L. Cut from tangentially faced blank, it has 5 coarse teeth on one edge, 36 fine teeth on the other edge, spaced at 8 teeth per 10mm. Tapers from mid point towards each edge. One end knife-trimmed, other end broken and missing. Length 49mm; width 72mm; thickness 9mm.

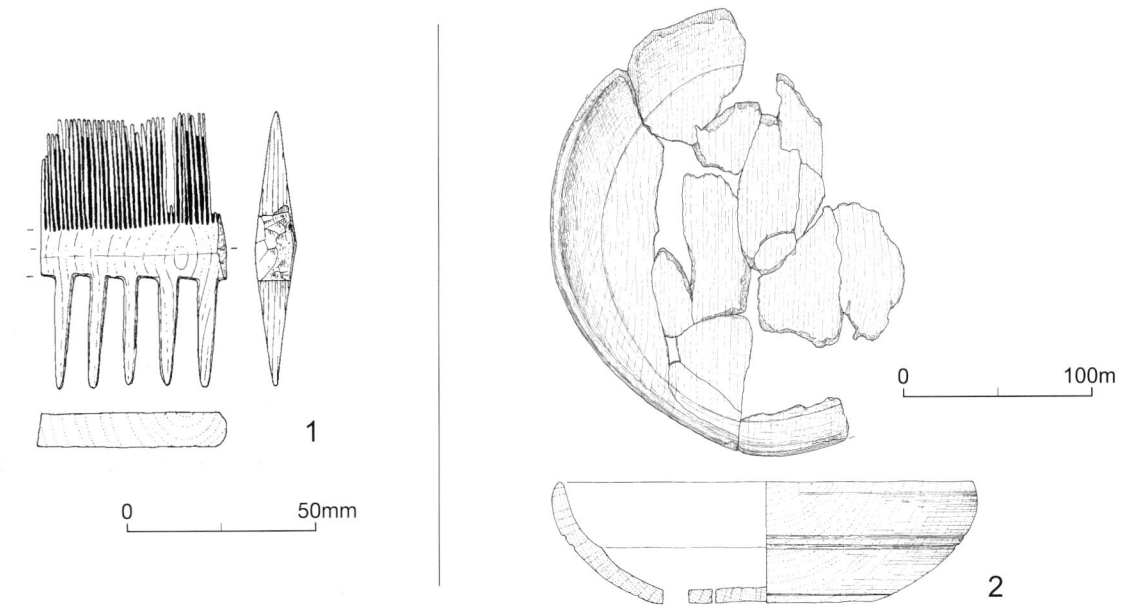

Fig. 5.51 Wooden objects: comb and bowl (Nos 1–2). Scales 1:2 and 1:4

2   Approximately 60% of a turned wooden bowl from context 2681, S263, Period 2.5/3.1, Plot 3 (Fig. 5.51, No. 2). Species *Acer campestre* L. The face is turned with the rim from towards centre of tree. There is a pair of prominent wide-turned grooves around exterior at mid height. It has a flat base and an internal shoulder *c.* 30mm above base, with limescale concretion on some interior surfaces. Very fragmented. Currently in 14 refitting and 5 non-refitting pieces. Diameter *c.* 230mm; height *c.* 60mm.

3   Charred peg fragment from context 1860, G131, Period 2.4, Plot 13. Species *Fraxinus excelsior* L. Cut from radially faced timber, with a circular cross section, tapering slightly towards trimmed end. Other end broken and missing. Length 20mm; diameter 8mm. Not illustrated.

4   Radially faced offcut from a board from context 1860, G131, Period 2.4, Plot 13. Species *Quercus* spp. Length 57mm; width 12mm; thickness 8mm. Not illustrated.

5.21 Bone and ivory objects
Nicola Rogers

Three ivory one-piece combs were found (contexts 3, 585 and 2377), and also a possible fragment of a bone comb of unknown form (context 372) (Fig. 5.52, 1–3). All were recovered as residual material. All three ivory combs are double-sided, with teeth of different gauges on each side, a form that is characteristic of the 16th and 17th centuries (Margeson 1993, 66). Numerous examples have been found previously, including several in Norwich (ibid., 66, 416–29), Winchester (Galloway 1990, 670, 2178–85), and London (Egan 2005, 65, 295–7). The sub-lentoid section of that from context 372 suggests it could have been a fragment of a comb but its form cannot be determined.

The bone pin from context 667 (Plot 2; Period 3.1; G8) appears to be from a pig fibula; and although recovered from an early post-medieval deposit this pin is likely to date from the Anglo-Saxon period (Fig. 5.53, 5). Whether these bone objects were pins rather than needles has been a matter of debate for some time (MacGregor 1985, 120–1), but a pin of this type was found with a leather thong in a grave at the Anglo-Saxon Castledyke cemetery at Barton-on-Humber, with its position in the grave suggesting that it was pinning together the front of a gown just below the throat (Walton Rogers 1998, 276).

A buzz bone from a metapodial which has been transversely perforated, but is otherwise unmodified, was found in a medieval context (Plot 13; Period 2.3.2; G121: context 1620) (Fig. 5.53, 6). Similar objects have been described as toggles or bobbins, but it is now thought that they are simple musical instruments. The bone would have been threaded on a string via its central perforation, and could then be made to hum by spinning the string rapidly (Brown and Lawson 1990, 589–90). Buzz bones are commonly found artefacts on sites of both pre-Conquest and medieval date.

A fragmentary bone handle appears to have been part of a socketed handle, probably for a whittle tang knife. The socket for the tang appears to have extended to the end of the handle, and may have been finished off with a metal end cap. It was recovered from a Period 3.1 deposit (Plot 14; G262: context 969), and an early post-medieval date for this handle is likely.

Four other finds, all from Period 5 deposits, are probably 19th–20th century in date. These comprise a probable button (context 654), a cutlery handle (context 98), a possible textile tool or handle, with a possible spindle fragment and a further possible spindle (context 3).

Catalogue of bone and ivory objects

1   Double-sided one piece ivory comb, with teeth of differing gauges on each side, some broken away on each side. Of lentoid section, with slightly shorter teeth in the centre than at ends, producing concave edge. Finer teeth 15 per cm, coarser teeth approx. 11 per cm. Length 79mm; width 51mm; thickness 3mm (Rec. No. 1287; Plot 3; Unassigned: context 2377; Fig. 5.52, 1)

2   Double-sided one piece ivory comb, incomplete, in two fragments, of rectangular section. Teeth of differing gauges on each side, finer teeth all broken

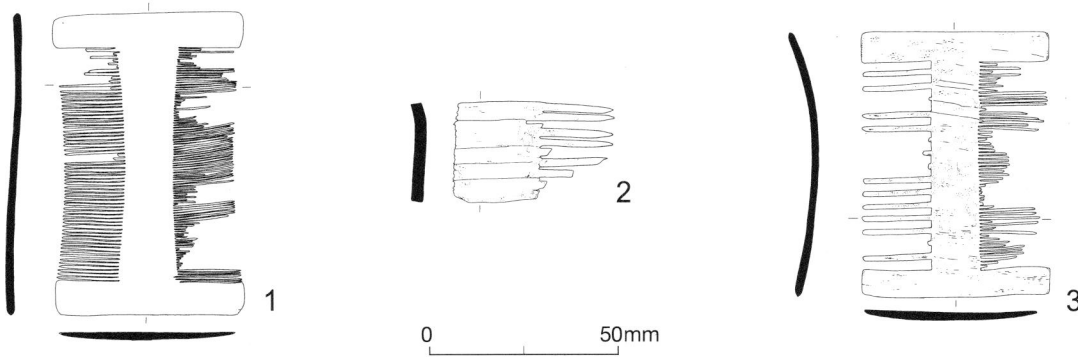

Fig. 5.52 Ivory combs (Nos 1–3). Scale 1:2

off, fragmentary survival of coarser teeth. Finer teeth approx. 8 per cm, coarser teeth 4 per cm. Largest fragment length 42.5mm; width 21.5mm; thickness 3.5mm (Rec. No. 1302; Plot 2; Period 5; Unassigned: context 585; Fig. 5.52, 2)

3   Double-sided one piece ivory comb, in 4 fragments, with teeth of differing gauges on each side, some broken away on each side. Of lentoid section, largest fragment distorted into convex profile. Coarse teeth 3–4 per cm, finer teeth 11 per cm. Largest fragment length 56.5mm; width 49mm; thickness 2mm (Rec. No. 1309; Machine clearance; G172: context 3; Fig. 5.52, 3)

4   Fragment of unfinished bone comb, or possible offcut, rectangular, of sub-lentoid section. Length 41mm; width 11.5mm; thickness 1.5mm (Rec. No. 1232; Plot 2; Unassigned: context 372; not illustrated).

5   Bone pin, with circular perforation in head naturally flattened with trimmed rounded top, tip of shank broken off. Probably a pig fibula, possibly early medieval. Length 82mm; width 9mm; thickness 4mm (Rec. No. 1922; Plot 2; Period 3.1; G8: context 667; Fig. 5.53, 5)

6   Buzz bone, made from a metapodial which is unmodified apart from perforation. Length 75mm; width 19mm; thickness 17.5mm (Rec. No. 1310; Plot 2; Period 2.3.2; G121: context 1620; Fig. 5.53, 6)

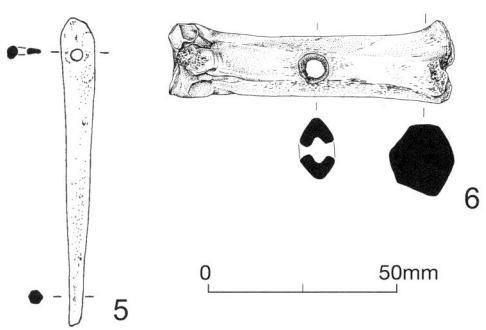

Fig. 5.53 Bone pin and buzz bone (Nos 5–6). Scale 1:2

7   Bone fragment, probably of socketed handle, of rectangular section, both ends broken. Length 37mm; width 11mm; thickness 8mm (Rec. No. 1303; Plot 14; Period 3.1; G262: context 969; not illustrated)

8   Socketed bone handle, from piece of cutlery, iron tang within handle, rounded terminal, tapering slightly to other end. Length 47.5mm; width 15.5m; thickness 10.5mm (Rec. No. 1291; Plot 2; Period 5; G53: context 98; not illustrated)

9   Possible bone button, discoidal, with central perforation. Diameter 27mm; thickness 2.5mm (Rec. No. 1290; Plot 14; Period 5; G282: context 654; not illustrated)

10 Possible bone spindle, complete apart from fragment broken off one end, lathe turned with bands of concentric circles at each end. Length 86mm; diameter 6mm (Rec. No. 1293; Machine clearance; G172: context 3; not illustrated)

11 Possible bone brush handle or textile tool, turned, upper end hollow with two pairs of opposed perforations, other end socketed with turned decoration. Also possible spindle fragment, both ends broken. Length 103mm; diameter 13mm (Rec. No. 1313; Machine clearance; G172; not illustrated)

5.22 Pollen
Katie Head

5.22.1 Results

Following sample selection and analysis as described previously (Chapter 3.2.9), a pollen diagram was constructed and divided into three pollen zones (Fig. 5.54). The lower monolith (NP1) sampled the thick alluvium pre-dating the Roman slag surfaces (G345). The overlying part of the section was left unsampled as it comprised either Roman slag surfaces, or was missing due to sampling difficulties in the field. Overlying the Roman surfaces, two later sequences were sampled (NP2, NP3); one of which (NP2) included alluvial deposits (G353).

Newport Street Zone 1 (NP1): 229–168cm

The base of the sequence was dominated by Poaceae undiff. (grasses), making up approximately 75% of total land pollen (TLP), and remaining fairly constant throughout NP1. Other herbs primarily consisted of Lactuceae *cichorium intybus*-type such as *Taraxacum officinale* (dandelion), making up around 15% TLP, as well as the Rosaceae family including *Filipendula* (meadowsweet), both of which fell in number towards the top of the zone. The Apiaceae family and *Plantago lanceolata* (ribwort plantain), started to rise towards the top of the zone. There were occasional herbs present, including Chenopodiaceae, Caryophyllaceae, and *Helleborus viridis* (green hellebore). Trees and shrubs were in low numbers, being dominated by *Alnus* (alder) and *Corylus* (hazel), both of which rose towards the top of this zone. Spores, primarily *Pteropsida* (monolete) indet (ferns), as well as *Pteridium* (bracken) and *Selaginella selaginoides* (lesser clubmoss), were also present.

This early part of the sequence comprised the alluvium located below a Roman metalled layer (G347), and the uppermost part of the sampled alluvial sequence (G345) contained Romano-British pottery (late 2nd to 3rd century). The pollen evidence indicates a cleared landscape, most probably originating in the late Bronze Age or early Iron Age.

Newport Street Zone 2 (NP2): 112–63cm

This second zone was similar to NP1, dominated by Poaceae undiff. (grasses), which peaked towards the middle of NP2. Other herbs were in similar numbers and species composition to NP1, although there were a number of new introductions, which included weeds typical of arable ground. These included *Rubus chamaemorus* (cloudberry), *Sorbus* type (whitebeam/sloe/cherry), *Vicia* undiff. (vetch), *Ononis* type (restharrow), *Cirsium* type (thistle), and *Centaurea cyanus* (cornflower). This zone saw the appearance of *Cerealia* (cereals) including occasional *Secale cereale* (rye). There was also an isolated, but notable peak in *Ranunculus acris*-type (meadow buttercup). *Alnus* (alder) fell in number compared with NP1, while *Corylus* (hazel) remained constant and *Quercus* (oak) began to rise towards the middle of the zone. Spores had now fallen to very low numbers compared with NP1.

NP2 spanned the section situated directly above a metalled surface (G349) and also reflected a fully cleared landscape, which now included the cultivation of cereals, probably grown in the surrounding countryside. This part of the sequence was broadly post-Roman, but it contained pottery dating to the 12th century at the base of the sequence (G351) and throughout the alluvium (G345).

Newport Street Zone 3 (NP3): 63–19cm

The final zone continued to be dominated by Poaceae undiff. (grasses), although there was a slight fall in numbers from the beginning of this zone. Other herbs were comparable to NP2 but included a notable rise in Lactuceae *cichorium intybus*-type (e.g. *Taraxacum officinale* (dandelion)) early on, as well as a later rise in *Filipendula* (meadowsweet). Trees and shrubs remained low but constant, and included occasional examples of *Ligustrum vulgare* (common privet), *Fraxinus* (ash), and *Viburnum opulus* (guelder rose).

This final zone sampled a thick dump deposit (G354) which is dated to the 12th century. The vegetational history reflects a cleared landscape with the cultivation of cereals in the surrounding countryside.

5.22.2 Discussion

Late Prehistoric to Romano-British

The upper part of the alluvial deposit (G345) below the Roman metalled/slag layer was dated to the late 2nd to early 3rd century AD. The vegetation sequence suggests there was a fairly cleared landscape, probably originating in the later Bronze Age/Iron Age. There was a dominance of grasses as well as meadowland herbs, particularly dandelion vegetation. Rather than reflecting cultivation (no cereals were recorded this early on in the sequence), this type of vegetation tends to suggest general meadowland immediately around the site in the floodplain. The dominance of alder and hazel within the arboreal population reflects vegetation growing in a riverside area. This wetland/riverside environment is further supported by water-loving *Sagittaria sagittifolia* (arrow-head) and *Polygonum persicaria* (red shank/persicaria), as well as the marshland herb *Bidens* type (bur-marigold), and Cyperaceae (sedge). Later in the sequence, around the late Iron Age/earlier Romano-British period, the landscape seems to have seen

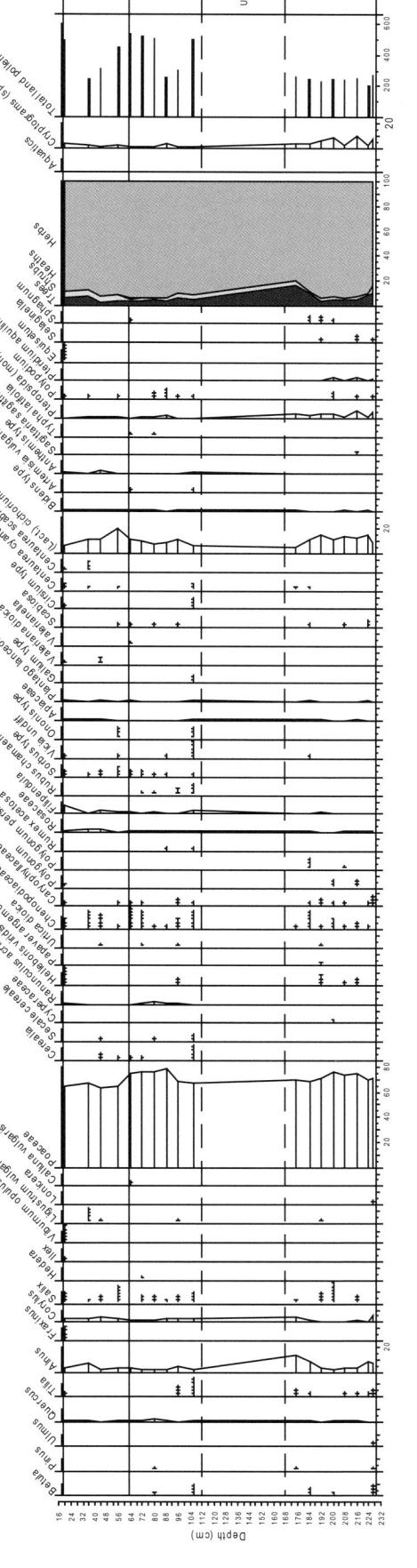

Fig. 5.54 Pollen percentage diagram for Monolith 1 spanning above and below the Romano-British metalled layer in the East Sondage

regeneration in alder and hazel. This could indicate coppicing beside the river, although the peak is not that significant and may merely reflect localised flooding. In the surrounding countryside, where the soils were better drained, mixed woodland of oak and lime seems to have prevailed, although this would have been very open, with a patchy distribution situated within a relatively cleared grassland landscape.

There is a lack of late prehistoric/early Romano-British pollen sequences in Worcester that can be used in comparison. However, at urban sites in Droitwich, including Old Bowling Green (Colledge and Greig 1992), Saltway (Head 2005a), and Bay's Meadow Villa (Greig 1991), weed flora dominated both the pollen and plant macrofossil record. The Old Bowling Green site had seen saltworking in the Romano-British period and the vegetation was generally sparse and open, presumably from the constant activity of trampling and burning. As areas of the site became disused, weeds of wasteland were then able to colonise. There is some evidence for wasteland at Newport Street, highlighted by herbs such as Caryophyllaceae, Chenopodiaceae, and ribwort plantain, suggesting direct human activity. Further afield, in Leominster, Herefordshire (Pearson *et al.* 2005), the Romano-British site of Mill Street, which is also comparable to Newport Street, provided an insight into the vegetation of the area, with alder or mixed alder/hazel woodland colonising the river's edge and with evidence of seasonal flooding. This would have been combined with a mosaic of damp and drier grassland, characterised by meadow and wetland herbs, similar to those found at Newport Street.

Medieval

Progressing up through the sequence to above the metalled layer, herbs increased in diversity, possibly reflecting the development of managed meadow, while alder continued to dominate the wetter areas of the site. The lower values in alder/hazel seem to indicate that the riverside was relatively open with human populations occasionally using these trees for firewood, etc. This period, still within Romano-British times, saw the cultivation of cereals around the site. Cereal pollen was only occasionally recorded, suggesting that small-scale arable cultivation was occurring in the surrounding countryside. The dominance of grassland may partially represent pasture for grazing livestock, some of which would have been close to the river area where arable cultivation would not have been possible.

Within the upper part of the sequence, dating to the high medieval period, the herbaceous community increased still further in diversity. Scrubland may also have developed, indicated by guelder rose, whitebeam, and common privet. Continuing evidence of arable cultivation during the medieval period is indicated by herbs such as *Anthemis* type (chamomile), cornflower, ribwort plantain, and *Valerianella* (lamb's lettuce/corn salad). Wetland or marshy areas also continued beside the river, indicated by herbs such as *Valeriana dioica* (marsh valerian) and bur-marigold, and the spore *Equisetum* (horsetail).

At nearby Deansway there was pollen evidence of 10th-century date, comprising a mosaic of open grassy land and mixed alder/oak/hazel woodland, some growing along the river (Greig 2004). Evidence of arable cultivation was also found in the form of cereals such as rye but also hemp, suggesting that the processing of crops or even cultivation was occurring. It appears that at Newport Street, cereal cultivation was not being undertaken near the site but in the surrounding countryside, as so few grains were recorded.

The West Midlands in general has provided much pollen evidence for the early medieval period. Palaeochannel sites in Coventry such as Far Gosford Street (Head and Wilkinson 2006) and Coventry Transport Museum (Head and Wilkinson 2005) provide comparable sequences. The land beside the River Sherbourne at Coventry represented a swath of marshland, again including a mosaic of landscape types. The site was used for dumping waste, collecting firewood, etc., with the pollen being derived from foodstuffs, building materials and animal bedding. There was little evidence for cereal cultivation compared with Newport Street, most probably because both the Coventry sites were much more marginal to the settled urban centre.

In Birmingham, pollen sequences at Bourn Brook in Selly Oak, dating to the 15th and 16th centuries (Goad *et al.* 2004), and at the early medieval site of Longbridge (Head 2006), reflected a typical floodplain landscape. This was characterised by wetland or meadowland-type herbs such as dandelion, suggestive of an open damp grassland environment, with the river edge colonised by alder, or a mixture of alder and hazel. At Longbridge, the riverine landscape was more wooded than at Bourn Brook and Newport Street, although there were comparable meadowland herbs apparent. The woodland at Longbridge was eventually cleared and replaced by grassland. There was also evidence of arable agriculture, with cornflower present, indicative of a medieval agricultural flora (Colledge and Greig 1992). During the Anglo-Saxon and medieval periods, pollen evidence from Newport Street and other sites in the West Midlands suggest that the landscape was a complex mosaic of wetland/meadowland herbs and mixed alder/hazel woodland beside the river, as well as having pasture nearby. Arable land existed on varying scales, together with open mixed woodland of oak and lime on drier slopes in surrounding areas.

5.23 Plant remains
Elizabeth Pearson

Sampling strategies, processing and analysis were undertaken according to the procedures described above (Chapter 3.2.10). A total of 192 samples of up to 40 litres were taken from a wide range of feature and deposit types of Roman to post-medieval date. The following contexts were selected for full quantification of plant remains recovered:

- Period 2 (medieval): 1876, 1877, 1918, 2016, 2004, 2005, 2007
- Period 3 (post-medieval): 737, 756, 765, 2678, 2681

Estimates of abundance of plant remains are presented from the following samples:

- Period 1 (Roman): 2046, 2054
- Period 2 (medieval): 1239, 1285, 1288,1401, 1425, 1421, 1483, 1533, 1684, 2785

Table 5.16 shows all bulk samples included in the full analysis of macrofossil plant remains. Table 5.17 shows a summary of the environmental remains recovered. The plant remains recovered are summarised in Tables 5.18 to 5.22.

5.23.1 Results

Period 1: Roman (Table 5.18)

Only small quantities of charred cereal crop remains, including emmer or spelt wheat (*Triticum dicoccum/spelta*) and hulled barley grain (*Hordeum vulgare*) were recovered in association with occasional chaff fragments and weed seeds from a pit cut into the alluvium (G346:

Table 5.16: List of environmental samples from bulk samples

Context	Sample no.	Sample type	Context type	Period	Plot	Sample vol./ processed (litres)	Residue scanned/ sorted (s/c)	Flot volume/ Flot sorted
0737	21	bulk	layer	2/3	1	30/30	3.7ltrs - c	680mls/85mls
0756	20	bulk	fill of cess pit 733	3.2	4	40/30	4.9ltrs - c	600mls/75mls
0757	17	bulk	fill of cess pit 1130	3.2	2	40/40	? ltrs	-
0765	18/22	bulk	layer	3.1	2	20/20	3.9ltrs - c	170mls/170mls
0765	18	bulk	layer	3.1	2	2020l	3.9ltrs - c	-
0765	22	bulk	layer	3.1	2	20/10	2.5ltrs - c	-
1072	38	bulk	deposit	2.4	13	10/10	1.2ltrs - s	-
1090	40	bulk	dark silty layer	2.5	13	20/20	1.3ltrs - s	-
1239	60	bulk	red clay	2.5	13	20/20	2100ml - s	55mls/55mls
1285	66	bulk	charcoal fill of 1284	2.4/5	14	5/5	250mls - s	600mls/150mls
1288	67	bulk	charcoal rich deposit	2.4	13	10/10	100mls - s	50mls/50mls
1401	79	bulk	charcoal rich deposit	2.4	13	20/20	-	-
1421	82	bulk	charcoal rich deposit	2.4	13	20/20	900mls - s	425mls/425mls
1425	85	bulk	fill of clay pit	undated	13	40/40	4ltrs - s	-
1483	89	bulk	charcoal rich deposit	2.4	13	40/40	1.2ltrs - s	465mls/465mls
1490	91	bulk	charcoal/clay deposit	2.3.2	13	20/10	3ltrs - s	100mls/100mls
1533	94	bulk	charcoal rich deposit	2.3.2	13	20/20	3.3ltrs - s	150mls/150mls
1668	104	bulk	charcoal/mortar deposit	2.3.2	13	40/40	1ltr - s	-
1684	106	bulk	deposit	2.3.2	13	10/10	1000mls - s	100mls/100mls
1785	111	bulk	burnt deposit	2.3.1	13	10/10	800mls - s	200mls
1844/1877	121	60–70cm	organic layer	2.2	13	10/10	2.7ltrs	-
1844/1877	121	70–80cm	organic layer	2.2	13	10/10	700ml	-
1844/1877	121	30–40cm	organic layer	2.2	13	10/10	1ltr	-
1844/1877	121	50–60cm	organic layer	2.2	13	10/10	1ltr	-
1844/1877	121	0–10cm	organic layer	2.2	13	10/10	1.1ltrs	-
1844/1877	121	40–50cm	organic layer	2.2	13	10/10	675ml	-

Table 5.16 (cont.): List of environmental samples from bulk samples

Context	Sample no.	Sample type	Context type	Period	Plot	Sample vol./ processed (litres)	Residue scanned/ sorted (s/c)	Flot volume/ Flot sorted
1844/1877	121	20–30cm	organic layer	2.2	13	10/10	1.3ltrs	-
1844/1877	121	10–20cm	organic layer	2.2	13	10/10	1ltr	-
1844/1877	121	70–80cm	organic layer	2.2	13	10/10	-	-
1844/1877	121	30–40cm	organic layer	2.2	13	10/10	1.2ltrs	-
1876	119	bulk	charcoal deposit	2.4	13	30/30	4.75ltrs - c	1.5ltrs/145mls
1877	121	bulk	organic layer	2.2	13	10/1	1ltr - c	20–40mls
1877	122	bulk	soil horizon	2.2	13	40/40	7.6ltrs - c	1500mls/375mls
1895	124	bulk	charcoal/ash deposit	3.1	6	15/15	? Ltrs	-
1918	123	bulk	woody brown pit fill	2.1	13	40/30	6.8ltrs - c	440mls/110mls
2004	155	bulk	green-grey deposit	2.2	13	5/5	1ltr - s	1.8ltrs
2004	129	bulk	alluvial layer	2.2	13	10/10	7ltrs - s	1800mls/450mls
2005	156	bulk	grey deposit	2.2	13	10/10	3ltrs - s	300mls
2005	130	bulk	alluvial layer	2.2	13	10/10	3.8ltrs - s	300mls/300mls
2006	133	bulk	alluvial layer	2.2	13	10/10	1.1ltrs	-
2007	161	bulk	organic deposit	2.2	13	20/20	1300mls - c	600mls/300mls
2007	136	bulk	buried soil layer	2.2	13	10/10	300mls - c	300mls
2016	160	bulk	grey deposit	2.2	13	7/7	2ltrs - c	150mls/150mls
2016	135	bulk	buried soil layer	2.2	13	10/10	-	-
2046	141	bulk	red slag layer	1	13	10/10	8ltrs - c	150mls
2054	150	bulk	fill of pit 2055	1	13	10/10	3.3 ltrs -s	190mls
2678	171	bulk	cess deposit	3.2	3	40/40	1.6ltrs - c	?/100mls
2681	172	bulk	waterlogged deposit	3.2	3	40/40	10.4 ltrs - c	?/50mls
2713	186	bulk	green clay	2	3	40/20	3.4 ltrs - s	100mls/100mls
2785	188	bulk	charcoal deposit	2	3	25/2.5	150mls - s	300mls/300mls

context 2054) and a layer within the slag surface (G347: context 2046). The presence of only occasional robust, non-charred seeds of elderberry (*Sambucus nigra*) and bramble/blackberry (*Rubus* sect. *Glandulosus*) suggest that these deposits were not permanently waterlogged at the time of deposition.

Period 2: medieval (Tables 5.19 and 5.20)

Plot 13

The medieval deposits (11th to 12th century) overlying a compact surface of Roman date were highly organic. Context 1918 (G350) was predominantly made up of unidentified herbaceous material but included a low level of identifiable seed remains that reflect vegetation largely growing along the edge of the river. Celery-leaved crowfoot (*Ranunculus sceleratus*) and wild celery (*Apium graveolens*) would have colonised the muddy edges, while bramble scrub or hedgerow and herbaceous vegetation such as common nettle (*Urtica dioica*), self-heal (*Prunella vulgaris*), white horehound (*Marrubium vulgare*) and common hemp-nettle (*Galeopsis tetrahit*) would have existed nearby. The presence of wild celery is of interest as it is usually found near the coast or along estuaries, but has also been known as a culinary herb since the Roman period. Sloe (*Prunus spinosa*), would have grown amongst the scrub or hedgerow vegetation but could have been collected for food, and likewise the apple (*Malus sylvestris/domestica*) may represent crab apple growing in a similar environment, or cultivated apple grown in orchards. The only definite evidence of waste from occupation of the area was a low level of charred cereal grains and hazelnut fragments, with occasional stones of possible domesticated plum (*Prunus domestica* spp *domestica*) and fig seed (*Ficus carica*).

An assemblage of plant remains (seeds) from an organic layer (G351: context 2007) overlying this was considerably more species diverse. Bramble scrub vegetation predominated with other herbs which may have grown along riverbanks in meadows, although weeds of cultivated and waste ground were more evident.

Table 5.17: Summary of environmental remains from bulk samples
occ = occasional; mod = moderate; abt = abundant; frq = frequent

Context	Sample	large mammal	small mammal	fish	frog/toad	bird	mollusc	insect	eggshell	charcoal	charred plant	mineralized plant	waterlog plant	Comment
0690	14	mod	-	occ	-	occ	-	-	-	-	-	-	occ	
0737	21	occ-mod	occ	occ	-	occ?	occ*1	mod*2	occ	mod-abt	occ	-	abt	*1-oyster, *2-incl pupae
0756	20	occ	occ	occ	-	occ	-	Occ	-	-	-	occ	abt	frq plant detritus/phosphate
0765	18	occ	occ	occ	-	-	-	-	-	mod	occ	occ	abt	occ plant detritus, phosphate, hammerscale
1239	60	occ	-	occ	-	-	-	-	occ	abt	abt	-	-	mod slag, occ hammerscale
1285	66	occ	-	occ	-	-	-	-	-	abt	occ	-	occ	
1288	67	occ	-	occ	-	-	-	-	-	occ	mod	-	-	
1401	79	occ	occ	occ	occ	occ	-	-	-	-	occ	-	occ	occ flake hammerscale
1421	82	occ	occ	occ	-	occ	occ	-	-	abt	mod-abt	-	-	abt clinker
1425	85	mod	occ	occ	-	occ?	-	-	-	-	occ	-	occ	occ hammerscale
1533	94	mod-abt	occ	occ	-	-	-	-	-	abt	mod	-	mod	
1684	106	occ	-	occ	-	-	-	-	-	abt	mod	-	occ	
1877	122	occ	-	occ	-	occ	occ*1	abt*2	occ	occ	occ	-	mod	occ hammerscale, *1-tiny frag, *2-mostly pupae
1918	123	occ	-	occ	-	occ	-	occ	-	-	occ	-	abt	occ hammerscale
2004	129	occ-mod	-	occ	-	-	-	-	-	abt	abt	-	mod	
2005	130	occ-mod	-	occ	-	occ?	-	-	-	-	abt	-	mod	occ-mod hammerscale
2007	161	occ	-	occ	-	-	-	abt*	occ	-	-	-	abt	* mostly pupae
2046	141	occ	-	-	-	-	-	-	-	-	occ-mod	-	occ	frq slag
2054	150	occ	-	occ	-	-	-	-	-	abt	-	-	mod	occ hammerscale
2678	171	occ	occ	mod-abt	-	occ	-	-	-	occ	-	occ	abt	frq phosphate
2681	172	abt	occ	mod	-	occ	abt*	abt	-	-	-	-	abt	*- oyster frags, frq phosphate/plant detritus
2785	188	mod	-	occ	-	-	-	-	-	-	occ	-	-	

Table 5.18: Plant remains from Period 1 (Roman)

Latin name	Family	Common name	Habitat	2046	2054
Charred plant remains					
Triticum dicoccum/spelta glume base	Poaceae	emmer/spelt wheat	F	11	-
Poaceae sp indet. grain	Poaceae	grass	AF	6	-
unidentified seed	unidentified			2	-
Waterlogged plant remains					
Urtica dioica	Urticaeae	common nettle	ABD	-	+
Rubus sect *Glandulosus*	Rosaceae	bramble	CD	-	+
Conium maculatum	Apiaceae	hemlock	AB	-	+
Hyoscyamus niger	Solanaceae	henbane	AB	-	+
Lamiaceae sp indet.	Lamiaceae	dead-nettle	ABCDEF	-	+
Sambucus nigra	Caprifoliaceae	elderberry	BC	3	++
Carex sp	Cyperaceae	sedge	CDE	1	-
Carex spp	Cyperaceae	sedge	CDE	-	+

Key:

Category of remains
A = cultivated ground
B = disturbed ground
C = woodlands, hedgerows, scrub etc.
D = grasslands, meadows and heathland
E = aquatic/wet habitats
F = cultivar

Quantity
+ = 1–10
++ = 11–50
+++ = 51–100
++++ = 101+

Table 5.19: Plant remains from Period 2 (medieval): quantified data.
N.B. Counts from fraction of flot or residue have been multiplied to provide counts per whole sample (details in archive)

Latin name	Family	Common name	Habitat	1876	1877	1918	2007	2016
Charred plant remains								
Triticum sp (free-threshing) grain	Poaceae	free-threshing wheat	F	1	84	7	19	1
Triticum sp tail grain	Poaceae	wheat	F	-	-	1	1	-
Triticum/Secale sp grain	Poaceae	wheat/rye	F	-	8	-	-	-
Hordeum vulgare grain (hulled)	Poaceae	barley	F	4	3	1	2	-
cf *Hordeum vulgare* grain (hulled)	Poaceae	barley	F	-	4	-	-	-
Cereal sp indet. grain	Poaceae	cereal	F	-	-	-	2	-
Avena sp grain	Poaceae	oat	AF	-	1	-	-	-
Poaceae sp indet. grain	Poaceae	grass	AF	1	4	-	-	-
Corylus avellana shell fragment	Betulaceae	hazelnut	C	-	-	-	19	-
Vicia/Lathyrus sp	Fabaceae	vetch/pea	ABCD	-	4	-	-	-
Mineralised plant remains								
Poaceae sp indet. grain	Poaceae	grass	AF	-	-	1	-	-
Prunus sp	Rosaceae	sloe/damson/plum/cherry	CF	-	-	1	-	-
Waterlogged plant remains								
Ranunculus acris/repens/bulbosus	Ranunculaceae	buttercup	CD	599	168	12	163	19
Ranunculus arvensis	Ranunculaceae	corn buttercup	A	64	4	-	-	-
Ranunculus sceleratus	Ranunculaceae	celery-leaved buttercup	E	4	88	40	192	43

Table 5.19 (cont.): Plant remains from Period 2 (medieval): quantified data.

Latin name	Family	Common name	Habitat	1876	1877	1918	2007	2016
Ranunculus sp	Ranunculaceae	buttercup	ABCDE	-	-	-	4	1
Fumaria sp	Fumariaceae	fumitory	ABC	8	-	-	2	-
Ficus carica	Moraceae	fig	F	-	-	4	-	-
Urtica dioica	Urticaeae	common nettle	ABD	24	136	1	428	16
Urtica urens	Urticaeae	small nettle	AB	32	92	36	86	-
Alnus glutinosa	Betulaceae	alder	CE	-	4	4	10	-
Corylus avellana shell fragment	Betulaceae	hazelnut	C	167	57	64	-	-
Chenopodium glaucum/rubrum	Chenopodiaceae	oak-leaved/red goosefoot	AB	-	20	-	-	-
Chenopodium album	Chenopodiaceae	fat hen	AB	8	96	12	252	20
Atriplex sp	Chenopodiaceae	orache	AB	8	20	-	12	1
Chenopodium/Atriplex sp	Chenopodiaceae	goosefoot/orache	AB	-	-	28	4	-
Montia fontana ssp *chondrosperma*	Portulaceae	blinks	AE	-	4	-	-	-
Stellaria media	Caryophyllaceae	common chickweed	AB	40	8	-	10	-
Stellaria graminea	Caryophyllaceae	lesser stitchwort	D	-	-	-	8	-
Spergula arvensis	Caryophyllaceae	corn spurrey	AD	-	12	-	2	4
Agrostemma githago	Caryophyllaceae	corn cockle	AB	-	12	4	4	-
Agrostemma githago fragments	Caryophyllaceae	corn cockle	AB	28	-	-	-	-
Silene sp	Carypohyllaceae	campion	AB	-	-	-	2	1
Persicaria maculosa	Polygonaceae	redshank	AB	-	-	-	8	11
Polygonum aviculare	Polygonaceae	knotgrass	AB	8	20	-	52	-
Fallopia convolvulus	Polygonaceae	black bindweed	AB	-	12	1	14	-
Rumex acetosella	Polygonaceae	sheep's sorrel	ABD	12	40	4	34	8
Rumex sp	Polygonaceae	dock	ABCD	8	40	8	2	3
Viola sp	Violaceae	violet	DF	-	4	-	8	1
Thlaspi arvense	Brassicaceae	field penny-cress	AB	-	4	-	2	-
Brassica sp	Brassicaeae	cabbages	ABDF	4	4	-	-	-
cf *Sinapis alba*	Brassicaceae	white mustard	ABDF	-	-	-	4	-
Brassica/Sinapis fruit	Brassicaceae	cabbage/mustard	ABDF	-	-	-	-	1
Reseda luteola	Resedaceae	dyer's rocket, weld	ABDF	-	-	-	4	1
Lysimachia sp	Primulaceae	loosestrife	CDE	-	4	-	-	-
Rubus cf *idaeus*	Rosaceae	raspberry	CD	8	-	-	-	-
Rubus sect *Glandulosus*	Rosaceae	bramble	CD	68	1261	129	1336	230
Rubus sp	Rosaceae	raspberry/bramble/dewberry	BC	-	56	4	26	-
Potentilla erecta	Rosaceae	tormentil	D	-	-	-	14	
Potentilla sp	Rosaceae	cinquefoil	BCDE	-	12	-		
Frageria vesca	Rosaceae	wild strawberry	C	-	20	4	34	19
Rosa cf *arvensis*	Rosaceae	rose	CF	-	4	-	-	-
Prunus spinosa	Rosaceae	sloe	C	-	5	129	27	2
Prunus domestica	Rosaceae	plum/bullace/damson	CF	-	2	-	-	-
Prunus domestica ssp *domestica*	Rosaceae	plum	F	-	-	4	-	-
Prunus sp	Rosaceae	sloe/damson/plum/cherry	CF	-	4	-	-	-
Malus sylvestris/domestica	Rosaceae	crab apple/apple	CF	-	2	45	-	-
cf. *Crataegus monogyna*	Rosaceae	hawthorn	C	-	4	-	-	-
Onobrychis viciifolia	Fabaceae	sainfoin	D	4	-	-	-	-
Vicia/Lathyrus sp	Fabaceae	vetch/pea	ABCD	-	4	-	-	-

Table 5.19 (cont.): Plant remains from Period 2 (medieval): quantified data.

Latin name	Family	Common name	Habitat	1876	1877	1918	2007	2016
Linum usitatissimum seed	Linaceae	flax	AF	16	-	-	2	-
Linum usitatissimum capsule segment	Linaceae	flax	AF	8	-	-	-	-
Aethusa cynapium	Apiaceae	fool's parsley	AB	-	28	-	10	1
Conium maculatum	Apiaceae	hemlock	AB	-	-	4	2	-
Apium graveolens	Apiaceae	wild celery	E	-	144	32	32	-
Torilis japonica	Apiaceae	upright hedge-parsley	CD	-	20	-	-	-
Daucus carota	Apiaceae	carrot	DF	-	20	-	14	-
cf *Daucus carota*	Apiaceae	carrot	DF	-	-	12	-	-
Apiaceae sp indet.	Apiaceae	carrot family	ABCDEF	-	-	4	-	-
Hyoscyamus niger	Solanaceae	henbane	AB	-	8	4	4	2
Solanum nigrum	Solanaceae	black nightshade	AB	-	-	4	26	4
Solanum dulcemara	Solanaceae	bittersweet	CDE	-	8	-	-	-
Stachys sylvatica	Lamiaceae	hedge woundwort	CD	-	4	-	2	1
Lamium sp	Lamiaceae	dead-nettle	ABF	-	4	-	-	-
Galeopsis tetrahit	Lamiaceae	common hemp-nettle	AB	-	16	4	18	-
Marrubium vulgare	Lamiaceae	white horehound	ABD	-	4	4	6	-
Prunella vulgaris	Lamiaceae	self-heal	D	16	24	12	16	-
Satureja hortensis	Lamiaceae	summer savory	AF	-	20	-	8	-
Lycopus europaeus	Lamiaceae	gypsywort	E	-	8	8	42	-
Mentha sp	Lamiaceae	mint	ABDEF	-	-	-	2	-
Sambucus nigra	Caprifoliaceae	elderberry	BC	16	24	-	14	4
Valerianella dentata	Valerianaceae	narrow-fruited cornsalad	AB	-	-	-	4	-
Carduus sp	Asteraceae	thistle	BCD	-	12	-	2	1
Carduus/Cirsium sp	Asteraceae	thistle	ABDE	-	-	-	2	-
Centaurea sp	Asteraceae	knapweed/cornflower	ABD	4	-	-	-	-
Lapsana communis	Asteraceae	nipplewort	BCD	8	8	4	12	-
Sonchus arvensis	Asteraceae	perennial sow-thistle	AB	-	-	-	2	-
Sonchus asper	Asteraceae	prickly sow-thistle	ABD	-	32	8	28	-
Taraxacum sp	Asteraceae	dandelion	BDE	-	4	-	-	-
Anthemis cotula	Asteraceae	stinking chamomile	AB	-	8	-	2	-
cf *Anthemis cotula*	Asteraceae	stinking chamomile	AB	4	-	-	-	-
Chrysanthemum segetum	Asteraceae	corn marigold	AB	12	4	8	-	-
Leucanthemum sp	Asteraceae	ox-eye daisy	BD	-	-	-	2	-
Bidens sp	Asteraceae	bur-marigold	ABE	4	-	-	-	-
Lemna sp	Lemnaceae	duckweed	E	-	4	-	2	-
Juncus sp	Juncaceae	rush	DE	-	-	-	2	-
Eleocharis sp	Cyperaceae	spike-rush	E	16	56	8	56	9
Schoenoplectus lacustris	Cyperaceae	common club-rush	E	-	4	-	2	-
Carex spp (2-sided)	Cyperaceae	sedge	CDE	28	16	4	24	2
Carex spp (3-sided)	Cyperaceae	sedge	CDE	24	13	4	35	12
unidentified seed	unidentified	-	-	-	-	4	-	1
unidentified thorn	unidentified	-	-	-	-	1	-	-
unidentified nutshell frag	unidentified	-	C	-	-	-	-	1

Table 5.20: Plant remains from Period 2 (medieval): scanned results

Latin name	Family	Common name	Habitat	1239	1285	1288	1401	1421	1483	1490	1533	1684	2004	2005	2713	2785
Charred plant remains																
Triticum aestivo-compactum grain	Poaceae	club wheat	F	-	-	-	-	-	-	-	-	-	-	-	-	-
Triticum sp (free-threshing) grain	Poaceae	free-threshing wheat	F	++	+	+	+	+	++	++	++	+++	+++	+++	+	-
Triticum sp grain	Poaceae	wheat	F	-	-	-	-	-	-	-	-	-	-	-	-	-
Triticum/Secale sp grain	Poaceae	wheat/rye	F	-	-	-	-	-	-	-	-	+	-	-	-	-
Hordeum vulgare grain (hulled)	Poaceae	barley	F	-	-	+	+	+	+	+	+	+	+	+	-	-
Secale cereale grain	Poaceae	rye	F	+	-	-	-	-	-	-	+	-	-	-	-	-
Cereal sp indet. grain	Poaceae	cereal	F	-	-	++	-	+	-	-	-	-	-	-	-	-
Cereal sp indet. grain (fragments)	Poaceae	cereal	F	+++	-	-	-	-	-	-	-	-	-	-	-	-
Cereal sp indet. culm node	Poaceae	cereal	F	+	-	-	-	-	-	-	-	-	-	-	-	-
Festuca/Lolium sp grain	Poaceae	fescue/rye grass	A	-	-	-	-	-	-	-	+	-	-	+	-	-
Bromus sp grain	Poaceae	brome grass	AF	-	-	-	-	-	-	-	-	-	-	-	+	-
Avena sp grain	Poaceae	oat	AF	+	+	+	+	++	+	+	+	+	+	+	+	+
cf *Avena* sp grain	Poaceae	oat	AF	-	-	-	-	-	-	-	-	-	-	++	-	-
Poaceae sp indet. grain	Poaceae	grass	AF	++	+	-	-	+	+	+	+	++	+	+	+	+
Poaceae sp indet. culm node	Poaceae	grasses	AF	-	-	-	-	-	-	-	-	-	-	-	-	+
Ranunculus acris/repens/bulbosus	Ranunculaceae	buttercup	CD	+	-	-	-	-	-	-	-	-	-	-	-	-
Corylus avellana shell fragment	Betulaceae	hazelnut	C	-	-	++	-	++	++	-	-	-	-	+	-	+
Agrostemma githago	Caryophyllaceae	corn cockle	AB	+	-	-	-	-	-	-	+	-	-	+	-	-
Persicaria/Fallopia sp	Polygonaceae	knotweed/bindweed	ABE	-	+	-	-	-	-	-	-	-	-	-	-	-
Rumex acetosella	Polygonaceae	sheep's sorrel	ABD	-	-	-	-	-	+	-	-	-	-	-	-	-
Rumex sp	Polygonaceae	dock	ABCD	+	+	-	-	-	-	-	-	-	-	-	-	-

Table 5.20 (cont.): Plant remains from Period 2 (medieval): scanned results

Latin name	Family	Common name	Habitat	1239	1285	1288	1401	1421	1483	1490	1533	1684	2004	2005	2713	2785
Prunus cf *spinosa*	Rosaceae	sloe/blackthorn	C	-	-	-	-	-	-	-	-	-	-	+	-	-
Vicia sativa	Fabaceae	common vetch	AB	+	-	+	-	-	+	-	+	++	-	+	-	-
Vicia sp	Fabaceae	vetch	ABD	+	-	+/++	-	+	+	-	+	-	-	+	+	-
Vicia/Lathyrus sp	Fabaceae	vetch/pea	ABCD	-	-	-	+	-	-	-	-	-	-	-	-	-
cf *Pisum sativum*	Fabaceae	garden pea	AF	+	-	-	-	-	-	-	-	-	-	-	-	-
Asperula/Galium sp	Rubiaceae	woodruff/cleavers	ABC	-	-	-	-	-	-	-	-	-	+	+	-	-
Sambucus nigra	Caprifoliaceae	elderberry	BC	-	-	-	-	-	+	-	+	-	-	+	-	-
Centaurea sp	Asteraceae	knapweed/cornflower	ABD	-	-	-	-	-	+	+	+	-	-	-	-	-
Anthemis cotula	Asteraceae	stinking chamomile	AB	+	-	-	-	-	-	-	-	-	-	-	-	-
Chrysanthemum segetum	Asteraceae	corn marigold	AB	-	-	-	-	+	-	-	-	-	-	-	-	-
Waterlogged plant remains																
Urtica dioica	Urticaceae	common nettle	ABD	-	+	-	-	-	-	-	-	-	-	-	-	-
Atriplex sp	Chenopodiaceae	orache	AB	-	+	-	-	-	-	-	-	-	-	-	-	-
Rumex sp	Polygonaceae	dock	ABCD	-	+	-	-	-	-	-	-	-	-	-	-	-
Rubus sect *Glandulosus*	Rosaceae	bramble	CD	-	+	-	-	-	-	-	-	-	-	-	-	-
Conium maculatum	Apiaceae	hemlock	AB	-	-	-	+	-	-	-	-	-	-	-	-	-
Stachys sylvatica	Lamiaceae	hedge woundwort	CD	-	-	-	-	-	-	-	-	-	-	+	-	-
Galeopsis retrahit	Lamiaceae	common hemp-nettle	AB	-	+	-	-	-	-	-	-	-	-	-	-	-
Sambucus nigra	Caprifoliaceae	elderberry	BC	-	-	-	-	-	+	+	++	+	++	++	+	-
Sonchus asper	Asteraceae	prickly sow-thistle	ABD	-	+	-	-	-	-	-	-	-	-	-	-	-
Carex spp (3-sided)	Cyperaceae	sedge	CDE	-	-	-	-	-	-	-	-	-	-	+	-	-
Carex sp	Cyperaceae	sedge	CDE	-	-	-	-	-	-	-	-	-	-	+	-	-

Key

Category of remains
- A = cultivated ground
- B = disturbed ground
- C = woodlands, hedgerows, scrub etc
- D = grasslands, meadows and heathland
- E = aquatic/wet habitats
- F = cultivar

Quantity
- + = 1–10
- ++ = 11–50
- +++ = 51–100
- ++++ = 101+

There was slight indication of aquatic vegetation such as duckweed (*Lemna* sp) and marsh vegetation such as sedges (*Carex* spp), alder carr (*Alnus glutinosa*), wild celery (*Apium graveolens*) and spike-rush (*Eleocharis* spp), for example. Wild strawberry (*Frageria vesca*) and wild carrot (*Daucus carota*) may have been part of the local flora, or in the case of carrot may have been a cultivar or casual escape from gardens. Both could also represent food waste as other evidence for occupation debris was found, although only in low levels. Seeds of summer savory (*Satureja hortensis*) were found which was a plant used as a culinary herb, and also of particular interest is the presence of dyer's rocket (*Reseda luteola*) and cultivated flax (*Linum usitatissimum*). The former was commonly used as a yellow dye, and the latter for producing linen from the fibres or linseed oil from the seeds.

An assemblage from an overlying layer (G353: context 1877) was equally species diverse, indicating similar environmental conditions, with a small number of seeds of herbs and vegetables such as summer savory (*Satureja hortensis*), carrot (*Daucus carota*) and a Brassica, which may be a cultivar such as cabbage or turnip/swede. Occasional fruit stones from sloes (*Prunus spinosa*) or plum/damson/bullace (*Prunus domestica*) were also recovered which may have been collected for food, while a small assemblage of charred plant remains indicate the presence of domestic or occupation waste. Other contexts, for example, G353: context 2016, were also highly organic, showing similar environmental conditions to the other samples but no evidence of crop or food waste.

Later layers, also of 11th to 12th century date, were less obviously organic in nature and included, for example, dumps of waste consisting of charred cereal remains (G353: context 2005 and G354: context 2004). These were predominantly made up of grains of a free-threshing wheat or (*Triticum aestivum* or *Triticum turgidum*), most likely to be bread wheat or club wheat, and grasses such as wild or cultivated oat (*Avena* sp). Occasional common weeds of cultivation included corn cockle (*Agrostemma githago*) and vetch (*Vicia sativa*). The presence of occasional uncharred elderberry (*Sambucus nigra*), sedge (*Carex* spp) and bramble (*Rubus* sect. *Glandulosus*) seeds suggest limited waterlogging or anoxic (oxygen-reduced) conditions at this time as they are relatively hardy.

Cutting all the above deposits in Plot 13 was a pit or well. At its base, context 1876 (G130) of 12th to 13th-century date, was rich in waterlogged plant remains of similar composition to contexts 2007 and 1877 described above. Similar environmental conditions were indicated, and flax seeds and capsule fragments were also recovered.

Other plots
Scanned results from several other contexts (such as 2004 and 2005) showed a similar composition to the later 11th to 12th-century layers in Plot 13, but also in Plots 3 and 14. Possible pea (cf *Pisum sativum*) in charred form was also identified in context 1239 (Plot 13; G151).

Period 2/3: 15th to 16th century (Table 5.21)
An assemblage of waterlogged plant remains from layer 737 in Plot 1 (G15) of 16th to 17th-century date was similar to that described for contexts 2678 and 2681 below (a cess pit and underlying organic layer respectively). Possible raspberry (*Rubus* cf *idaeus*) was also recorded which would have grown in grassland locally or cultivated in gardens. Occasional eggshell fragments were found along with fragmented large mammal bone, small mammal, possible bird and fish bone. The presence of a component of edible plant remains and large mammal, bird and fish bone suggests that this layer consisted of dumped domestic refuse containing kitchen waste.

Period 3: post-medieval (Table 5.22)
Early post-medieval deposits of 16th to 17th-century date were well preserved as a result of waterlogging and mineralisation, being dominated by food remains, predominantly fruit. An organic layer (G8: context 765) in Plot 2 contained plant remains preserved by waterlogging. The assemblage included many of the fruit remains common on this site, although in this case, elderberry seeds (*Sambucus nigra*) were most abundant along with fig, while grape was only present in low levels. Of interest was the presence of black pepper (*Piper nigrum*) and the culinary herb fennel (*Foeniculum vulgare*).

In Plot 4 (G36: S128, context 756), a lower fill of cess pit 733 of 17th-century date, was rich in mineralised concretions, although the plant remains were largely preserved by waterlogging with a smaller proportion being mineralised. The latter included relatively abundant seeds, fruit and fruit stalk fragments of currant/gooseberry (*Ribes* sp), and fennel (*Foeniculum vulgare*) with occasional grains of barley (*Hordeum vulgare*), ryegrass (*Lolium temulentum*), unidentified grasses (Poaceae sp Indet.) and unidentified fruit fragments. Amongst the waterlogged remains, grape pips (*Vitis vinifera*) were most abundant in association with fig (*Ficus carica*), dwarf cherry (*Prunus cerasus*), plum (*Prunus domestica* ssp *domestica)* and other *Prunus* species, rose (*Rosa* sp), apple (*Malus sylvestris/domestica*) and raspberry (*Rubus idaeus*). Medlar (*Mespilus germanica*), a rare orchard cultivar, was also recorded while exotics included cucumber (*Cucumis sativa*) and from the New World, pumpkin/squash/marrow (*Cucurbita maxima*). Herbs and spices included coriander (*Coriandrum sativum*) and black mustard (*Brassica nigra*) while buckwheat (*Fagopyrum esculentum*) and possible hop (cf *Humulus lupulus*) were also useful crops; the former as animal feed (particularly for pheasants or for medicinal purposes;

Table 5.21: Plant remains from Period 2/3 (medieval to post-medieval). N.B. Counts from a 1/8 fraction of the flot have been multiplied to provide counts per whole samples (details in archive)

Latin name	Family	Common name	Habitat	0737
Charred plant remains				
Triticum/Secale sp grain	Poaceae	wheat/rye	F	8
Waterlogged plant remains				
Ranunculus acris/repens/bulbosus	Ranunculaceae	buttercup	CD	584
Ficus carica	Moraceae	fig	F	560
Corylus avellana shell fragment	Betulaceae	hazelnut	C	52
Atriplex sp	Chenopodiaceae	orache	AB	16
Chenopodium/Atriplex sp	Chenopodiaceae	goosefoot/orache	AB	8
Stellaria media	Caryophyllaceae	common chickweed	AB	8
Stellaria graminea	Caryophyllaceae	lesser stitchwort	D	32
Agrostemma githago	Caryophyllaceae	corn cockle	AB	1
Persicaria maculosa	Polygonaceae	redshank	AB	16
Polygonum aviculare	Polygonaceae	knotgrass	AB	16
Fallopia convolvulus	Polygonaceae	black bindweed	AB	24
Rumex spp	Polygonaceae	dock	ABCD	168
Thlaspi arvense	Brassicaceae	field penny-cress	AB	8
Brassica oleracea/napus/rapa	Brassicaceae	cultivated Brassica	ABF	16
Brassica nigra	Brassicaceae	black mustard	ABF	16
Lysimachia sp	Primulaceae	loosestrife	CDE	8
Rubus cf *idaeus*	Rosaceae	raspberry	CD	8
Rubus sect *Glandulosus*	Rosaceae	bramble	CD	16
Rubus sp	Rosaceae	raspberry/bramble/dewberry	BC	72
Frageria vesca	Rosaceae	wild strawberry	C	16
Prunus spinosa	Rosaceae	sloe	C	2
Prunus cerasus	Rosaceae	dwarf cherry	CF	2
Prunus sp	Rosaceae	sloe/damson/plum/cherry etc.	CF	8
Malus sylvestris/domestica	Rosaceae	crab apple/apple	CF	16
Vitis vinifera	Vitaceae	grape-vine	F	8
Stachys sylvatica	Lamiaceae	hedge woundwort	CD	8
Carduus sp	Asteraceae	thistle	BCD	16
Lapsana communis	Asteraceae	nipplewort	BCD	8
Sonchus sp	Asteraceae	thistle	ABD	8
Chrysanthemum segetum	Asteraceae	corn marigold	AB	16
Eleocharis sp	Cyperaceae	spike-rush	E	8
Carex spp (2-sided)	Cyperaceae	sedge	CDE	80
Carex spp (3-sided)	Cyperaceae	sedge	CDE	224
unidentified seed	unidentified	-	-	4
unidentified bud	unidentified	-	-	1

Key: **Category of remains**

A = cultivated ground
B = disturbed ground
C = woodlands, hedgerows, scrub etc
D = grasslands, meadows and heathland
E = aquatic/wet habitats
F = cultivar

Table 5.22: Plant remains from Period 3 (post-medieval): quantified results.
N.B. counts from fractions of flot or residue have been multiplied to provide count per whole sample (details in archive)

Latin name	Family	Common name	Habitat	0756	0765	2678	2681
Charred plant remains							
Triticum dicoccum/spelta grain	Poaceae	emmer/spelt wheat	F	-	1	-	-
Triticum sp (free-threshing) grain	Poaceae	free-threshing wheat	F	-	4	-	-
Hordeum vulgare grain (hulled)	Poaceae	barley	F	-	2	-	-
cf *Secale cereale* grain	Poaceae	rye	F	-	1	-	-
Avena sp grain	Poaceae	oat	AF	-	1	-	-
cf *Avena* sp grain	Poaceae	oat	AF	-	1	-	-
Poaceae sp indet. grain	Poaceae	grass	AF	-	11	-	-
Corylus avellana shell fragment	Betulaceae	hazelnut	C	-	3	-	-
Vicia sp	Fabaceae	vetch	ABD	-	1	-	-
Vitis vinifera	Vitaceae	grape-vine	F	-	1	-	-
Mineralised plant remains							
Triticum sp (free-threshing) grain	Poaceae	free-threshing wheat	F	1	-	-	-
Triticum sp grain	Poaceae	wheat	F	-	-	-	1
Triticum/Secale sp grain	Poaceae	wheat/rye	F	1	-	-	-
Hordeum vulgare grain (hulled)	Poaceae	barley	F	6	-	1	-
Cereal sp indet. grain	Poaceae	cereal	F	1	-	3	-
Festuca/Lolium sp grain	Poaceae	fescue/rye grass	A	-	-	2	-
cf *Bromus* sp grain	Poaceae	brome grass	AF	1	-	-	-
cf *Avena* sp grain	Poaceae	oat	AF	-	-	-	4
Poaceae sp indet. grain	Poaceae	grass	AF	98	1	-	160
Poaceae sp indet. culm node	Poaceae	grass	AF	-	-	-	32
cf Cucurbitaceae sp indet.	Cucurbitaceae	cucumber/melon/pumpkin etc.	F	-	-	2	-
Ribes sp seed	Grossulariaceae	currant/gooseberry	BF	2257	-	-	-
Ribes sp fruit	Grossulariaceae	currant/gooseberry	BF	141	-	-	-
Ribes sp fruit stalk	Grossulariaceae	currant/gooseberry	BF	32	-	-	-
cf *Ribes* sp seed	Grossulariaceae	currant/gooseberry	BF	-	-	1	-
Vicia sativa var *nigra*	Fabaceae	common vetch	BD	1	-	-	-
Foeniculum vulgare	Apiaceae	fennel	ABF	48	-	-	448
unidentified seed	unidentified	-	-	2	1	-	-
unidentified berry	unidentified	-	-	-	-	26	-
unidentified bud	unidentified	-	-	1	-	-	-
unidentified fruit fragments	unidentified	-	-	336	-	-	-
Waterlogged plant remains							
Lolium temulentum ear	Poaceae	darnel	AB	1	-	-	-
Poaceae sp indet. grain	Poaceae	grass	AF	112	-	24	-
Piper nigrum	Piperaceae	black pepper	F	-	1	-	1
Ranunculus acris/repens/bulbosus	Ranunculaceae	buttercup	CD	16	-	5	64
cf *Humulus lupulus*	Cannabaceae	hop	CE	16	-	-	-
Ficus carica	Moraceae	fig	F	5088	106	16,181	25,408

Table 5.22 (cont.): *Plant remains from Period 3 (post-medieval): quantified results.*

Latin name	Family	Common name	Habitat	0756	0765	2678	2681
Juglans regia	Juglandaceae	walnut	F	-	-	-	8
Corylus avellana shell fragment	Betulaceae	hazelnut	C	10	-	1	56
Corylus avellana whole nut	Betulaceae	hazelnut	C	-	-	-	3
Chenopodium album	Chenopodiaceae	fat hen	AB	16	-	1	64
Agrostemma githago fragments	Caryophyllaceae	corn cockle	AB	-	-	96	272
Silene latifolia	Caryophyllaceae	white campion	AB	16	-	-	-
Persicaria maculosa	Polygonaceae	redshank	AB	16	-	2	-
Persicaria hydropiper	Polygonaceae	water-pepper	E	-	-	2	-
Fagopyrum esculentum	Polygonaceae	buckwheat	ABF	70	-	-	-
Polygonum aviculare	Polygonaceae	knotgrass	AB	16	-	1	32
Fallopia convolvulus	Polygonaceae	black bindweed	AB	-	-	1	32
Rumex sp	Polygonaceae	dock	ABCD	16	-	35	32
Cucumis sativa	Cucurbitaceae	cucumber	AF	19	-	-	-
Cucurbita maxima	Cucurbitaceae	pumpkin	AF	16	-	-	-
Brassica nigra	Brassicaceae	black mustard	ABF	80	-	8	240
Rubus idaeus	Rosaceae	raspberry	CD	1626	-	-	-
Rubus cf *idaeus*	Rosaceae	raspberry	CD	-	3	-	-
Rubus sect *Glandulosus*	Rosaceae	bramble	CD	1535	7	928	1522
Rubus sp	Rosaceae	raspberry/bramble/dewberry	BC	1712	-	207	-
Frageria vesca	Rosaceae	wild strawberry	C	192	5	224	64
Rosa cf *arvensis*	Rosaceae	rose	CF	-	-	1	-
Rosa sp	Rosaceae	rose	CF	-	-	146	129
cf *Rosa* sp	Rosaceae	rose	CF	49	-	-	-
Prunus spinosa	Rosaceae	sloe	C	36	-	196	854
Prunus domestica ssp *insititia* bullace type	Rosaceae	damson/bullace	CF	3	-	-	-
Prunus domestica ssp *insititia* damson type	Rosaceae	plum	F	231	-	4	7
Prunis domestica *ssp* insititia	Rosaceae	bullace/damson	CF	-	-	-	4
Prunus domestica *ssp* domestica	Rosaceae	plum	F	-	-	7	7
Prunus domestica	Rosaceae	plum/bullace/damson	CF	-	1	-	-
Prunus cf *avium*	Rosaceae	wild cherry	C	6	-	-	-
Prunus cerasus	Rosaceae	dwarf cherry	CF	425	-	10	149
Prunus cf *cerasus*	Rosaceae	dwarf cherry	CF	-	-	1	-
Prunus sp	Rosaceae	sloe/damson/plum/cherry etc.	CF	-	-	2	24
cf *Prunus* sp	Rosaceae	sloe/damson/plum/cherry etc.	CF	-	-	2	16
Malus sylvestris/domestica	Rosaceae	crab apple/apple	CF	588	4	1243	2908
Mespilus germanica	Rosaceae	medlar	F	17	-	-	-
Vicia sativa	Fabaceae	common vetch	AB	-	-	1	-
Vicia/Lathyrus sp	Fabaceae	vetch/pea	AB	-	-	-	32
Vitis vinifera	Vitaceae	grape-vine	F	4794	1	523	245
Coriandrum sativum	Apiaceae	coriander	ABF	16	-	-	-
Foeniculum vulgare	Apiaceae	fennel	ABF	-	1	97	-

Table 5.22 (cont.): Plant remains from Period 3 (post-medieval): quantified results.

Latin name	Family	Common name	Habitat	0756	0765	2678	2681
cf *Foeniculum vulgare*	Apiaceae	fennel	ABF	-	2	-	-
Conium maculatum	Apiaceae	hemlock	AB	-	4	-	-
Daucus carota	Apiaceae	carrot	DF	-	1	-	-
cf *Daucus carota*	Apiaceae	carrot	DF	-	-	1	-
Hyoscyamus niger	Solanaceae	henbane	AB	-	1	-	-
Stachys sylvatica	Lamiaceae	hedge woundwort	CD	-	1	-	-
Galeopsis tetrahit	Lamiaceae	common hemp-nettle	AB	16	-	-	-
cf *Galeopsis* sp	Lamiaceae	hemp-nettle	ABCD	-	-	3	-
Prunella vulgaris	Lamiaceae	selfheal	D	-	-	-	16
Sambucus nigra	Caprifoliaceae	elderberry	BC	-	361	-	-
Lapsana communis	Asteraceae	nipplewort	BCD	-	-	37	48
Sonchus oleraceus	Asteraceae	smooth sow-thistle	ABD	-	-	-	16
Sonchus asper	Asteraceae	prickly sow-thistle	ABD	-	-	32	-
Sonchus sp	Asteraceae	thistle	ABD	-	-	-	32
Chrysanthemum segetum	Asteraceae	corn marigold	AB	32	-	-	48
Carex spp	Cyperaceae	sedge	CDE	-	1	-	-
Aframomum granum-paradisi	Zingiberaceae	grains of paradise	F	-	-	112	-
unidentified seed	unidentified	-	-	-	-	-	16
unidentified bud	unidentified	-	-	16	-	-	-

Grieve 1931) and the latter a common flavouring for beer from around the 16th century onwards. Of these, the currant/gooseberry, medlar, rose, cucumber, pumpkin and buckwheat are unusual. The combination of mineralised and waterlogged remains may reflect either material from different sources (including cess pits), or merely that certain seeds, grains and fruit (mericarp) fragments are more readily mineralised.

In Plot 3 (Period 2.5/3.1; S263: context 2681), an assemblage of plant remains in a waterlogged organic deposit of 16th/17th-century date was rich in seeds of plants which have culinary uses. Exotic cultivars included fig (*Ficus carica*), which was exceptionally abundant, grape and walnut (*Juglans regia*). Plum (*Prunus domestica* ssp *domestica*) was a common orchard cultivar, while other fruit or possible food remains, such as dwarf cherry (*Prunus cerasus*), bullace/damson (*Prunus domestica* ssp *insititia*) apple (*Malus Sylvestris/domestica* sp) and rose (*Rosa* sp) may have included either wild or cultivated varieties. Sloe/blackthorn (*Prunus spinosa*), hazelnut (*Corylus avellana*), wild strawberry (*Fragaria vesca*) and blackberry/bramble (*Rubus* sect *Glandulosus*), could all have been collected from woods and hedgerows locally. Black mustard (*Brassica nigra*) is native, but more common in coastal or estuarine areas. Its presence may, like celery have extended up river into Worcestershire or could have been a cultivar locally. Other remains included seeds of buttercup (*Ranunculus acris/repens/bulbosus*) and self-heal (*Prunella vulgaris*) which may have grown in meadowland or other disturbed grassland/woodland. Corn cockle (*Agrostemma githago*), nipplewort (*Lapsana communis*) and corn marigold (*Chrysanthemum segetum*) were common on cultivated or disturbed ground, but may have derived from crop products used on site.

An overlying cess deposit (Period 2.5/3.1; S263: context 2678) was rich in phosphate concretions, although the plant remains appear to have been largely preserved by waterlogging or anoxic (oxygen-reduced) conditions. Fig (*Ficus carica*) was overwhelmingly abundant, in association with many of the fruit remains described above. Occasional herbs, that is, fennel (*Foeniculum vulgare*), possible carrot (cf *Daucus carota*) and black mustard (*Brassica nigra*) were recovered, while other remains of significance include grains of paradise (*Aframomum granum-paradisi*), rose (*Rosa* sp), unidentified berries and a possible mineralised cucurbit (cucumber/melon/pumpkin etc.). Abundant eggshell with moderate quantities of fish bone and large mammal bone also indicate the disposal of kitchen waste. A similar assemblage of weed seeds described in the Period 3 contexts above, deriving from plants common on cultivated or disturbed ground, were also present, but formed only a small proportion of the assemblage.

5.23.2 Discussion

Period 1: Roman

As only two samples were available for analysis, only limited information is available for this phase. Sparse quantities of charred cereal crop waste were noted, and it appears that these deposits were not affected by flooding. In the case of the layer within the slag surface (2046) this may be because it had been artificially raised above the level of flooding.

Period 2: medieval

Deposits of 11th to 12th-century date in Plot 13 vary from the base to the upper part of the sequence. Plant remains from the lower deposits (G350: context 1918; G351: context 2007; G353: contexts 2016 and 1877) represent a mosaic of bramble scrub and vegetation common in relatively undisturbed grassland or wooded areas which were either present on Plot 13 at this time, or had been brought in with floodwater inundating the plot periodically. If from floodwater, it seems unlikely that the plant material had been carried from far upstream as the assemblage is remarkably diverse and well preserved (at least from contexts 2007 and 1877), and hence it is most likely that it derived from vegetation on the riverbanks close to the site. The presence of heavier material such as animal bone and artefacts in these deposits suggests they were not likely to have been carried far in floodwater. Some dumping is evident, but the good preservation of delicate seed remains in the lower waterlogged deposits seems unusual for dumped material, hence much of the deposits appear to be made of waterlain debris.

The presence of wild celery indicates that the river at this point was brackish during this phase, as it is generally found along coastlines and estuaries (Stace 1997) or in areas where there are saline springs. The lower reaches of the Severn are brackish today due to tidal flow but historical sources indicate that tidal effects in the past were significant as far north as Upton upon Severn (Richardson 1964, 4). The Botanical Society of the British Isles database shows the distribution of this species extends up the River Severn from Avonmouth, and partly along the River Avon, while the Botany of Worcestershire (Amphlett and Rea 1909) describes this as being particularly abundant at the time along the Droitwich Canal, an area of extensive brine deposits, and in some areas along the River Avon and at Longdon Marsh where there are brackish conditions. Although wild celery can be cultivated and used as a culinary herb, in this context it seems more likely that it was part of the natural flora.

The seed remains of dyer's rocket and flax in these deposits (G353: context 1877 and G130: context 1876) is not unexpected, as these remains are archaeologically more common in urban waterfront deposits, and also because there is documentary evidence for tanning and cloth dyeing on the site. Dyer's rocket and flax fragments have been recorded locally from Bridge Street, Hereford (Pearson 2003), and flax from the Hop Pole Inn, Leominster (Buteux *et al.* 1994). Dyeing and flax-retting activities were often carried out on the outskirts of urban areas along watercourses or beside pools and marshy areas. This type of location may have fulfilled the conditions necessary for flax retting: slow-flowing water from a canalised small stream (Higham 1989) and, because of the noxious nature of this process, a location outside of an urban centre. These remains are found in an 11th/12th-century deposit (context 1877) and in the base of a pit (context 1876) of 13th to 14th-century date, which cuts the former layer. However, the contamination of the lower layers of the pit by material from the underlying layer during its construction is a possibility.

Where the fruit or berry remains (blackberry, wild strawberry, sloe, bullace, damson/plum) from 11th to 12th-century contexts are concerned, their provenance is uncertain. Blackberry, strawberry, sloe and bullace would have been growing wild and not cultivated, while damsons and plum would have been cultivated orchard fruit (Roach 1985). Strawberries were not cultivated until the 16th century (ibid.). Although it is known that fruit and berries were collected or cultivated and sold at markets in the medieval period, these remains may not necessarily all be food waste. For example, much of the sloe, blackberry and wild strawberry may have come from the riverbanks (deposited with floodwater), while summer savory and sloe could be escapees from cultivation. It is interesting that grape is not present in early medieval deposits at a time when they were being cultivated locally (ibid.). This may simply be because the component deriving from food waste was small and therefore the chance of it being recovered is low.

Overlying deposits of this date (contexts 2004 and 2005) are more consistent with dumping (probably to raise the land above the level at risk of flooding) and appear to have been little affected by waterlogging at this depth. The plant assemblages from these contexts predominantly consist of charred cereal grain. The condition of this is good, and hence it is most likely to have been dumped directly on the site, rather than deriving from secondary dumping.

Period 3: post-medieval

Evidence for food remains, particularly fruit, is predominant in the contexts examined from this period. Grape and currants or gooseberry are present for the first time, and there is a greater concentration of exotic cultivars. Grape pips are plentiful in a couple of contexts despite the fact that by this time vineyards in the British Isles were failing because of climatic decline. The grapes are therefore likely to have derived from imported dried fruit, although some vines were grown in gardens or in small vineyards around the country and were being used to make a wine vinegar or 'verjuice'.

Mineralised currant/gooseberry remains are abundant in the primary fill of a cess pit of 17th-century date (G36: S128, context 756). Although there are red and white currant species native to the British Isles, in this context they are likely to be cultivars. At this time, cultivated varieties of red and white currants, and to a lesser extent blackcurrants, became popular for making wines and jellies; particularly (in the case of winemaking) as the keeping of vineyards in the British Isles had declined (Roach 1985). These wines were sometimes distilled to produce brandies. Spirits had become popular by the 16th century although more commonly for medicinal use (Sim 1977). It seems likely, by comparing dating and documentary evidence (Hughes, Chapter 5.1), that the cess pit in which these remains were found belonged to Edward Hurdman, a distiller, and by extension that the currants recovered from this cess pit were waste from winemaking or spirit distilling rather than food waste. Locally, red currant has been identified from a cistern of 18th-century date at Worcester Cathedral (Pearson 1995) and gooseberry at Sidbury, Worcester (Greig 1981).

Medlar stones were also found in this cess pit (G36: S128, context 756). This is a fruit which has been grown since the early medieval period, but which never became particularly popular. Medlars become edible after they have partially rotted (known as 'bletting'). In England, one tradition was to serve them after a meal accompanied by port (Roach 1985, 208), presumably a tradition of the moderately well-off at least. It is interesting that this was found in a context with other relatively rare fruits of the period such as currants/gooseberry, raspberry and vegetables such as cucumber and pumpkin. They have also been recorded from a 17th-century latrine deposit at Dudley Castle (Moffett 1992), where an equally diverse range of edible cultivars was found. Cherries were also common in this context and at the base of another slightly earlier cess pit S263 (Period 2.5/3.1; contexts 2678 and 2681). These are largely identifiable as dwarf cherry, a sour cherry which would have been used in cooking rather than as a fresh fruit (unlike the sweet cherry, which are a group of cultivars of *Prunus avium*). Although sour cherry may have been growing wild locally, cultivated varieties were widely available and popular from the medieval period onwards. These seem to have been widely available locally as William Langland of Malvern in 1362 describes in *Piers Plowman* the housewives of the poorer classes using 'many ripe cherries as well as peas, beans and baking apples' (Roach 1985, 165). It is interesting that the cultivated varieties of *Prunus domestica* (damson and plum) were found at Newport Street as it has been commented on that these varieties were absent from other deposits of a similar nature and date, such as from the 15th-century barrel latrine at Sidbury, Worcester (Greig 1981), Deansway, Worcester (Moffett 2004b, 553), the 17th-century latrine at Dudley Castle (Moffett 1992) and at the Tudor Merchant's House, Tenby (Nye 1989).

The rose seeds identified in context 756 could be from either wild or cultivated species. However, these have not been found in archaeological contexts locally (except small numbers from one medieval context on this site), so it seems unlikely that they derive from the local flora. They are found in a context with the greatest range of edible fruit remains, as discussed above, and hence it is likely that they had a culinary or medicinal use. The fruits were frequently used to make rose-hip syrup. Dorothy Hartley (1954) quotes a passage describing this, dating to 1730. They may also be a by-product of using rose petals to make rose-water, which was used in a wide variety of products including flavouring wines, spirits, and cordials in the production of medicines and perfumes, and in jams and jellies. Rose seeds were also found in a 15th-century barrel latrine at Sidbury, Worcester (Greig 1981, 270, 273).

Other vegetables of interest are the seeds of cucumber and pumpkin/squash/marrow found in context 756. Cucumber (thought to have been domesticated in the Himalayan region of India; Vaughan and Geissler 1997, 124) is likely to have been grown locally. This is also likely for pumpkin, squash or marrow, species native to the New World. Cultivation of the latter was common in Europe from at least the 17th century and they appeared in 16th and 17th-century Dutch paintings (Moffett 1995). At the time these were deposited in this cess pit (G36: S128, context 756; late 17th to early 18th century), local cultivation and availability in markets of both vegetable types is likely.

Peppercorn (G8: context 765 and S263: context 2681) and grains of paradise (S263: context 2678) are rare and are evidence of the long-distance trade in exotic spices that became increasingly common from the late medieval period onwards. Peppercorn and grains of paradise are both known from Sidbury, Worcester (Greig 1996, 226), the latter having been recovered from a 15th-century barrel latrine but identified post-publication of the site (Greig 1981). Both have also been identified at Fore Street in Taunton, Somerset, and in 18th-century deposits at Shrewsbury Abbey (Greig 1996, 227). Peppercorn has been identified on several sites of this date from London (Giorgi 1999) while grains of paradise were recently identified from an evaluation at Mary-le-Port, Bristol (Pearson 2006). It is from here that they were most likely to have been distributed to Worcester via the River Severn. Grains of paradise were imported from West Africa and as Bristol was one of the key ports involved with the slave trade with Africa, they are likely to have come into the country through this route. The seeds, which were used as a pepper for flavouring drinks and as a cattle medicine, are however known historically in Britain from the 13th century onwards. Greig (1996, 227), however, states that they seem to have gone out of use in the 17th century. Their presence in 16th/17th and 17th-century deposits at Newport Street is therefore of interest. Both grains of paradise and melegueta pepper seem to have been used as pepper, and are related to cardamom and ginger, all members of the ginger family.

During the post-medieval period, Bristol was also probably importing peppercorn from India, and was particularly known for its trade contacts with the East India Company (PortCities Bristol undated), formed in 1600. The peppercorn found at Newport Street is likely to have been imported from India and may well have been imported through Bristol via the East India Company.

The variety of food remains in these deposits, and in some cases the rarity, implies a reasonable level of wealth. The contexts where this evidence has been found are 16th to 17th-century in date, and suggest that wealthy inhabitants were living on the site at this time, in an area of commerce where traded goods were readily available. A particular case is the cess pit (S263) from Plot 3 (no. 26/28 Newport Street). This dates to the 16th century and may have belonged to the Leddington family, who were wealthy merchants. Later in the 17th century, documentary evidence suggests that the area suffered a decline, with tenements being subdivided (Hughes, Chapter 5.1). Nevertheless, the river trade at Worcester was still important through much of the 17th century and into the early 18th century, as boats of Worcester, Bewdley and Shrewsbury were still dominating the carrying trade from Bristol. These were the main urban centres on the Severn and the main ports ferrying goods to Bristol. It was from 1713 that trade in Worcester boats with Bristol declined (Hussey 2000).

5.24 Animal bone
Sylvia Warman

Hand-collected animal bone was recovered from all deposits with the exception of those known to be of 20th-century date. Environmental samples were taken of deposits rich in organic material, often waterlogged plant remains, wood or leather (Chapter 3.2.10). These samples also yielded substantial quantities of animal bone (5,226 fragments weighing 3kg). The animal bone assemblage, comprising 5,190 fragments of hand-collected bone weighing almost 100kg, and bone identified from processed samples, was assessed (Warman 2007a). A total of 525 fragments from 505 bones weighing 16.7kg identifiable to species from secure contexts dating to Periods 2 and 3 were subject to full analysis.

Period 1 (Roman) material was too weathered and fragmented to require further analysis but the results obtained during the assessment are discussed, particularly in relation to assemblages of a similar date from Deansway (Dalwood and Edwards 2004). The data collected during the assessment was sufficient for this, with the additional scanning of two processed samples (141 and 150) and the measurement of the complete cattle metatarsal.

The well-preserved material from selected deposits assigned to Periods 2 (medieval) and 3 (post-medieval) was subject to full analysis. Processing and analysis were undertaken according to the procedures described above (Chapter 3.2.11).

5.24.1 Results

Period 1: Roman (Tables 5.23 and 5.24)
Animal bone was recovered from the Roman deposits in the two areas of deeper excavation, mostly within Plot 13 and a single deposit within Plot 3. The species identified are cattle, sheep/goat and pig. Additional fragmented material is classified by size as cow-sized, sheep-sized, cat-sized, mouse-sized and chicken-sized.

From deposit 2744 (G61) within Plot 3, a probable road surface, fragmented cow-sized long bones were recovered which showed signs of butchery and weathering. Animal bone from Plot 13 is more numerous and cattle bone is predominant, although sheep, pig, chicken, cat and mouse are also represented. Notable from this assemblage is the cattle bone from deposit 2046 (G347), which shows signs of butchery and weathering. A complete measurable metatarsal was recovered from deposit 1897 (G349), a compacted gravel road surface which also produced a number of cattle limb bones. Pit fill 2054 (G346) was the only context from which species other than cattle were recovered.

Period 2: medieval (Tables 5.25 and 5.26)
Animal bone from Periods 2.1–2.2 was only encountered in Plot 13, as this contained one of the smaller areas of deep excavation and thus encountered earlier deposits. Bone from Periods 2.3–2.5 was recovered from deposits in Plots 3, 5, 13 and 14, although the majority of the animal bones from deposits assigned to Period 2 are from Plot 13.

Periods 2.1–2.2: 10th/11th century to 12th century
Animal bone from Plot 13 was recovered two deposits, pit fill 1918 (G350), and layer 1877 (G353). The species identified are horse, cattle, sheep, sheep/goat and chicken. The cattle bone is predominantly skull and foot bones.

Period 2.3: 13th/14th century
Deposits within Plots 3 and 5 contained small quantities of cattle and pig bones.

Periods 2.3–2.5: 13th/14th century to 15th/16th century
Plot 13
The species identified from Plot 13 deposits from the latter half of Period 2 include cattle, goat, sheep, sheep/goat, pig, cat, goose, chicken and *Gadidae* (cod family).

Pit 1667 (G131) is notable for a wide range of

Table 5.23: Animal bone from Period 1 (Roman): hand-collected material

Plot	Context	Description	No of frags	No of bones	Identified to species	Weight (g)	Mandibles	Epiphyses	Whole long bones	Species identified
13	1897	Compact gravel surface	8	7	4	474	-	5	1	cattle, cow-sized
13	2038	Alluvial clay with evidence of anthropogenic actions	1	1	0	16	-	-	-	cow-sized
13	2039	Fill of 2112	1	1	1	14	-	1	-	cattle
13	2042	Slag deposit in pit 2043	1	1	0	18	-	-	-	cow-sized
13	2046	Dump of slag	9	9	3	326	-	3	-	cattle, cow-sized, sheep-sized
13	2053	Industrial dump deposit	2	1	1	170	1	-	-	cattle
3	2744	Probable road surface	2	1	0	82	-	-	-	cow-sized
Totals			**24**	**21**	**9**	**1100**				

Table 5.24: Animal bone from Period 1 (Roman): sieved assemblage

Plot	Context	Description	Sample number	No of frags	No of bones	Identified to species	Weight (g)	Species identified
13	2046	Dump of slag	141	29	29	0	40	cow-sized, sheep-sized
13	2054	Fill of pit 2055	150	61	61	0	28.2	cattle, sheep/goat, pig, cow-sized, cat-sized, small mammal, chicken-sized unidentified mammal, unidentified fish
Totals				**90**	**90**	**0**	**68.2**	

species. Relatively high quantities of cattle, sheep/goat are present with some sheep and pig bone. A single fish bone identified as *cleithrum* from a Gadid (cod family) was recovered from deposit 1876, a charcoal-rich dump within 1667. The pit also contained single bones identified as goose, chicken and cat.

Oven-associated deposit 1840 (G357) and occupation layer 1877 (G353) produced prolific assemblages from the processed samples. The animal bone comprises mainly cattle, represented mostly by teeth and skull fragments. Sheep/goat is also present, represented by limb bones. Pig bones include skull, teeth, and limb bones including meat-bearing ones. A single goose tibia is also present. The cattle bones are largely foot bones (metapodials and phalanges) and some skull fragments with very few meat-bearing bones. Sheep and sheep/goat include foot, head and limb bones.

The animal bone from deposit 1304 (G140), a dump of hearth waste, comprises predominantly cattle skull, teeth and toes. This deposit also contained a sheep horncore, with a depression in it similar to that described by Albarella (1995), and a cat mandible.

The deposits associated with oven 890 (G151) contained mostly cattle bones, often head parts such as skull fragments, jaws and teeth, although pig and sheep/goat bones are also present.

Plot 14
Two deposits from Plot 14 produced animal bone, cattle, sheep and pig. Deposit 1409 (G222), a grey ashy deposit overlying hearth 1404, included three complete sheep metacarpals and one metatarsal. In addition, a bottle-nosed dolphin metatarsal was recovered from context 1162, a fill between two walls (Plot 14; G154) assigned to Period 2.4.

Period 3: post-medieval (Tables 5.27 and 5.28)
Animal bone was analysed from deposits within Plots 1, 2, 3 and 4. Other than the distinctive deposit 2919 (Plot 1/2), the analysed material was derived predominantly from cess or rubbish pits.

Table 5.25: Animal bone from Period 2 (medieval): hand-collected material

Taxon/element	Horse	Cattle	Sheep	Sheep/goat	Goat	Pig	Cat	Goose	Gadid
Skull	-	16	2	3	-	5	-	-	-
Skull and horncore	-	1	1	-	-	-	-	-	-
Horn core	-	3	2	-	-	-	-	-	-
Maxillary tooth	-	-	-	2	-	-	-	-	-
Deciduous maxillary tooth	-	2	-	-	-	-	-	-	-
Hyoid	-	1	-	-	-	-	-	-	-
Mandible	-	8	1	5	-	3	1	-	-
Mandibular tooth	-	7	-	1	-	2	-	-	-
Atlas	-	3	-	1	-	-	-	-	-
Sternum	-	-	-	1	-	-	-	-	-
Cleithrum	-	-	-	-	-	-	-	-	1
Scapula	-	-	-	3	-	2	-	-	-
Humerus	-	3	-	4	-	2	1	1	-
Radius	-	6	-	9	-	3	-	-	-
Ulna	-	2	-	3	-	-	-	-	-
Carpal	-	2	-	-	-	-	-	-	-
Metacarpal	-	2	4	6	2	1	-	-	-
Pelvis	-	1	1	6	-	-	-	-	-
Femur	-	1	-	4	-	-	-	-	-
Tibia	1	2	-	4	-	1	-	2	-
Fibula	-	-	-	-	-	2	-	-	-
Tarsal	-	1	-	-	-	-	-	-	-
Metatarsal	-	-	-	3	-	2	-	-	-
Metapodial	-	-	-	-	-	1	-	-	-
Astragalus	-	2	-	-	-	-	-	-	-
Proximal phalange	-	2	1	-	2	-	-	-	-
Intermediate phalange	-	-	-	1	-	-	-	-	-
Terminal phalange	-	1	-	-	1	-	-	-	-
Total NISP	1	103	14	56	5	22	2	3	1
Total weight (g)	155	4315.3	173	789	36	374	5	13	7
% by NISP	0.5	50	7	27	2	11	1	1	0.5
% by weight	3	72.2	3	13.2	0.6	6.3	0.1	0.2	0.1
MNI	1	21	10	14	1	13	2	3	1

Plots 1 and 2
Deposit 2919, which was black and organic, and extended across Plots 1 and 2, produced a rich assemblage. The bone almost entirely comprises cattle metapodials with some skull fragments including horncore and teeth. Sheep and sheep/goat limb bones are also present. Most of the bones from this deposit are broken but appear to be smashed (as if they had been dropped from a considerable height rather than deliberately chopped).

Period 3.2: mid 17th century

Plot 2
The 17th-century deposits contained horse, cattle, sheep, sheep/goat, pig, goose and chicken. Measurable long bones from horse and sheep are present. Deposit 31 (G14), the fill of pit 32, included a cattle pelvis, radius, ulna and tarsal. The pelvis shows pathological changes consistent with a lame animal. Cut and chop marks are also visible.

Plot 3
The species identified are cattle, sheep, sheep/goat, pig and chicken. The only fish bone is a dermal denticle from a ray (*Raja* sp) from deposit 2681 (S263).

Plot 4
Animal bone was recovered from two deposits and

Table 5.26: Animal bone from Period 2 (medieval): sieved assemblage

Taxon/element	Cattle	Sheep	Sheep/goat	Pig	Goose	Chicken
Skull	3	1	-	1	-	-
Maxillary tooth	1	-	-	-	-	-
Mandible	1	-	-	1	-	-
Mandibular tooth	4	-	3	2	-	-
Mandibular deciduous tooth	1	-	-	2	-	-
Tooth	1	-	-	-	-	-
Atlas	-	-	-	1	-	-
Scapula	-	-	1	2	-	1
Humerus	-	-	-	-	-	-
Radius	-	-	1	-	-	-
Ulna	-	-	-	-	-	1
Carpal	1	-	-	-	-	-
Metacarpal	1	-	-	-	-	-
Pelvis	-	-	-	-	-	-
Femur	-	-	-	-	-	-
Patella	-	-	1	-	-	-
Tibia	1	-	1	-	1	-
Fibula	-	-	-	-	-	-
Tarsal	1	-	-	-	-	-
Metatarsal	-	1	1	-	-	-
Metapodial	1	-	-	2	-	-
Calcaneus	-	-	1	-	-	-
Astragalus	-	-	-	-	-	-
Proximal phalange	2	-	1	1	-	-
Intermediate phalange	-	-	-	-	-	-
Terminal phalange	1	-	-	1	-	-
Total NISP	20	2	10	13	1	2
Total weight (g)	520	55	16.7	92.6	0.8	0.8
% by NISP	42	4	21	27	2	4
% by weight	76	8	2	14	0.1	0.1
MNI	4	1	3	2	1	2

almost entirely comprised cattle bones, including a mandible and hind limb bones, showing extensive butchery marks. The only other species identified is a chicken skull from fill 756 (G36: S128) of cess pit 733.

5.24.2 Analysis

Age at death

For Period 1, the unfused cattle distal metacarpal from context 1897 indicates an age at death of 2 years or less. For Period 2, there are some sheep represented which are under 1.5 years, some under 2.5 years, and only a small proportion in excess of 3.5 years. This greater proportion of younger specimens seems to be reflected in the tooth wear data (see below). Most cattle represented are older than 1.5 years and a significant proportion are over 2.5 and 3.5 years. Again the upper end of the age range is confirmed by the tooth wear data. Many of the pigs present are probably under a year old and only a few are over three years old.

For Period 3, sheep show a similar pattern from the fusion data as observed in Period 2. For sheep/goat all of the animals present are over 1.5 years and many are older than 2.5 years, but a relatively small proportion are over 3.5 years. Almost all of the cattle represented are not only over 1.5 years old, but also over 2.5 years old and many are fully mature at over 3.5 years old. The fusion

Table 5.27: Animal bone from Period 3 (post-medieval): hand-collected material

Taxon/element	Horse	Cattle	Sheep	Sheep/goat	Pig	Goose	Chicken
Skull	-	12	-	-	5	-	1
Skull and horncore	-	5	2	-	-	-	-
Horncore	-	-	-	-	-	-	-
Maxillary tooth	-	3	-	-	-	-	-
Deciduous maxillary tooth	-	-	-	-	-	-	-
Upper third molar	-	-	-	-	-	-	-
Upper canine	-	-	-	-	1	-	-
Mandible	-	11	-	-	5	-	-
Lower canine	-	-	-	-	-	-	-
Third molar	-	-	-	-	-	-	-
Mandibular tooth	-	-	-	-	1	-	-
Tooth	-	-	-	-	-	-	-
Atlas	-	-	-	-	-	-	-
Furcula	-	-	-	-	-	-	2
Coracoid	-	-	-	-	-	-	1
Sternum	-	-	-	-	-	-	2
Scapula	-	2	1	5	-	-	-
Humerus	-	2	1	1	-	-	3
Radius	-	7	3	-	-	-	-
Ulna	-	6	-	-	1	1	-
Metacarpal	1	8	13	6	3	1	-
Pelvis	-	3	-	3	-	-	2
Femur	-	7	-	1	-	-	3
Tibia	1	6	-	4	1	-	8
Tarsal	-	3	-	-	-	-	-
Metatarsal	-	12	11	9	3	-	-
Metapodial	-	3	-	-	1	-	-
Calcaneus	-	4	-	-	-	-	-
Astragalus	-	-	-	-	1	-	-
Proximal phalange	-	4	1	-	1	-	-
Intermediate phalange	-	2	-	-	-	-	-
Total NISP	2	101	32	29	23	2	22
Total weight (g)	637	7745	556	439	407.1	10	78.4
% by NISP	1.1	55.5	17.6	16	12.6	1.1	1.1
% by weight	6	81	6	4	4	1	0.8
MNI	2	21	16	14	6	2	9

data for pig reveals that they are all less than 2 years old. The sample of tooth wear data for cattle, sheep, sheep/goat and pig is too small to offer firm interpretation; however, the presence of MWS (Mandible Wear Scores) of 40 and above in the cattle and sheep data indicates the presence of older adult animals, possibly kept for dairy products, breeding or, in the case of the sheep, for wool production. The MWS for pig indicate mostly sub-adult and younger adult specimens the upper end of the age range indicated by the fusion evidence.

Size of livestock
Only four cattle bones were complete and could be used to calculate withers height, although the apparent trend in size is roughly consistent with the much greater sample from Deansway (Nicholson and Scott 2004a).

Table 5.28: Animal bone from Period 3 (post-medieval): sieved assemblage

Taxon/element	Cattle	Sheep	Sheep/goat	Pig	Chicken	*Raja* sp
Skull	1	2	-	4	-	-
Horncore	1	-	-	-	-	-
Maxillary tooth	-	-	1	1	-	-
Deciduous maxillary tooth	2	-	-	-	-	-
Mandible	-	-	-	2	-	-
Lower first molar	-	-	-	1	-	-
Mandibular tooth	-	-	1	-	-	-
Dermal denticle	-	-	-	-	-	1
Atlas	-	-	-	-	-	-
Sternum	1	-	-	-	-	-
Coracoid	-	-	-	-	1	-
Scapula	-	-	-	-	-	-
Humerus	-	-	-	-	-	-
Radius	1	-	-	-	3	-
Ulna	1	-	-	-	4	-
Carpal	-	-	-	4	-	-
Metacarpal	-	1	-	2	1	-
Pelvis	-	-	-	-	1	-
Femur	-	-	-	-	2	-
Patella	1	-	-	-	-	-
Tibia	-	-	1	-	3	-
Fibula	-	-	-	-	2	-
Tarsal	-	-	-	1	-	-
Metatarsal	-	1	-	-	1	-
Metapodial	-	-	-	3	-	-
Calcaneus	-	-	-	-	-	-
Astragalus	-	-	-	-	-	-
Proximal phalange	-	-	-	1	-	1
Terminal phalange	2	-	-	-	1	-
Phalange	-	-	-	-	1	-
Total NISP	**10**	**4**	**3**	**17**	**20**	**1**
Total weight (g)	**318.1**	**42.4**	**4**	**79.1**	**46**	**0.04**
% by NISP	**18**	**7**	**5**	**31**	**36**	**2**
% by weight	**65**	**9**	**0.8**	**16**	**9.4**	**0.01**
MNI	**3**	**3**	**2**	**3**	**4**	**1**

The complete cattle metatarsal from context 1897 (Period 1) suggests a withers height of 1030mm. The Period 2 cattle show an increase; the metatarsal from context 1877 has a withers height of 1134mm, whilst a radius from context 1867 has a withers height of 1097mm. The Period 3 metatarsal from context 434 has a withers height of 1308mm; again an increase is seen.

For Period 2, the two complete sheep metatarsals have a withers height range of 550mm to 613mm. The sheep metacarpal has a withers height of 616mm. The Period 3 sheep metacarpals have withers heights ranging from of 533mm to 611mm. The sheep metatarsals have a withers height range of 499mm to 622mm. These ranges are similar to those seen in Period 2.

Measurable horse bones were only present in the Period 3 assemblage. A tibia with a withers height of 1421mm, or just below 14 hands, is equivalent to a large modern breed such as a Dales or Highland pony. The horse metacarpal has a withers height of 1282mm, or 12 hands 2 inches, representing a considerably smaller individual, similar to a smaller modern breed such as an Exmoor pony.

Bone modification: weathering

In general the animal bone is in good condition but some specimens showed erosion to the bone surface from exposure to the elements prior to deposition or redeposition. A total of 78 of the 505 specimens show signs of weathering. The majority are scored as 1 on Behrensmeyer's scale; only 19 specimens have scores of 2 or higher (Behrensmeyer 1978). The generally good condition meant that other modifications to the bone surfaces, such as pathological changes, butchery and gnawing, could be observed.

Pathology

Of the identifiable animal bone from the selected deposits, 3 of the 505 specimens show some sign of pathology, equating to less than 1% of the assemblage. One of the pathologies noted is a depression in a sheep horncore from context 1304 (Period 2). The form is unusual as the depression is located anterior to posterior rather than medial to lateral. This condition may have been caused by dietary or other stress, and has been observed in lactating and pregnant ewes (Albarella 1995). It was also noted in the assemblage from Cabot Circus in Bristol (Warman 2007b). In the sheep/goat mandible from context 1617 (G131) a milk tooth (fourth deciduous premolar) was broken whilst it was being shed, and a small fragment of it remains in the jaw trapped between the fourth permanent premolar and the first molar. The most severe pathology noted was the cattle pelvis fragment from deposit 31 (G14), which showed joint disease, the acetabulum (hip socket) having additional porotic bone within and around it, and the muscle attachment ridges on the ischium are overdeveloped with additional new bone, possibly the result of the animal being lame and carrying its own weight awkwardly. Also inside the acetabulum are some signs of polishing or eburnation, which occurs when the cartilage is so damaged that bone moves against bone. It is very likely that this specimen had osteoarthritis as several of the signs for identification of this condition are present (Baker and Brothwell 1980). The area around the acetabulum has some areas of disorganised new bone which were possibly abscesses. The infection was active at the time of death and is probably linked to its arthritic condition.

The only non-metric trait is the supra-trochlea fossa present in both the pig humeri identified (context 1409 (G222) and context 1610 (G131)). This trait is not mentioned in the Deansway animal bone report (Nicholson and Scott 2004a) but can be common in some pig populations.

Butchery

Of the 505 specimens examined, a total of 102 have some signs of butchery. The most common form is on long bones where the shaft had been chopped right through, dividing the bone into two pieces. A variation on this is the splitting of long bones longitudinally, commonly seen with cattle and sheep/goat metapodials. This practice is usually interpreted as being for the removal of the marrow from the bones. Chop marks are also present on bones where the blow had failed to go all the way through the bone and simply left an indentation. A small number of specimens exhibit finer incisions into the surface of the bone, which appear to be from the disarticulation of specific parts of the carcass. For example, a sheep/goat atlas (first vertebra) from deposit 1644 has several cut marks across the lateral surface, consistent with the separation of the head from the body by means of severing the neck muscles. A cattle horncore and skull fragment from context 434 (G107, Plot 2) has a cut mark on the posterior close to the base of the horncore, which may be the result of levering off the horn sheath for hornworking. The cattle pelvis from deposit 31 (G14) has a cut mark just above the acetabulum, and the shaft of the ischium has been chopped through. This specimen has quite severe joint disease (above), and possibly the reason for this individual's slaughter was its lameness. The cut and chop marks indicate that the carcass was butchered so it can be assumed the meat was used, but whether this was for human consumption cannot be determined.

Many of the bones from deposit 2919 (Plots 1 and 2) exhibit interesting breakage but sharp edges to the breaks do not indicate that these were chopped through. There are no obvious points of impact from a chopping tool. A possible explanation is that the bones incurred this damage on impact with other bones and at the point of deposition. If so, it is likely that a considerable quantity of animal bone was discarded in a relatively short space of time. The animal bone from this deposit is in every other respect very well preserved, although stained dark brown in colour as if preserved in a damp pit fill or by waterlogging.

Gnawing

The gnawing of bone by either dogs or rodents is taken as evidence that the material was not immediately deposited and was either made available (in the case of dogs) or found by vermin (in the case of rodents). Gnawing indicates the presence of the taxa doing the gnawing on site, even if skeletal remains are not present. A total of 21 specimens show signs of gnawing, predominantly by dogs. The gnawed bones come from cattle, sheep/goat and pigs and a range of skeletal parts is seen both skull and post-cranial. Two specimens show signs of gnawing by other species: a goose humerus from context 1390 (G130) has a puncture mark consistent with a cat tooth, and a cattle metacarpal from context

1877 (G357) seems to have been gnawed but the nature of the tooth marks is not consistent with dog, and may be an example of herbivore gnawing. This has been observed amongst sheep, particularly during periods of malnutrition (Brothwell 1976).

Burning

Burnt bone is relatively rare with only six examples, two of which are from deposits associated with hearths and ovens. The colour of the bone may give some indication of the temperatures reached during burning. Most are burnt white or grey, indicating that a high temperature of over 700° Celsius was reached (Lyman 1994).

5.24.3 Discussion

Period 1: Roman

Within the small Period 1 assemblage, cattle are the dominant species; sheep/goat and pig are also present. The assemblage shows some similarities with that from the Roman deposits at Deansway where cattle was also the dominant taxon (Nicholson and Scott 2004b). The Deansway Roman assemblage had a greater range of species and included red deer, horse, goat, dog, cat, shrew, field vole, house mouse, chicken, goose, raven, frog, herring, eel and tope (shark). In terms of age at death, most specimens are adult or subadult. The cattle metatarsal withers height of 1030mm is slightly smaller than those from Deansway, which ranged from 1087–1096mm (ibid.).

There is no evidence for stock pens as suggested at Deansway. The interpretation at Deansway of the animal bone as being largely domestic waste rather than from butchers' or other trades seems appropriate for Newport Street as well. The nature of the butchery evidence is such that it follows the general Romanised pattern. The association of animal bone with possible road surfaces was also noted at Deansway and the animal bone (mostly cattle) may have been deliberately selected in order to repair the surfaces as a sort of hardcore. This is supported by the observation of some weathering to the bone surfaces from these deposits in the Newport Street assemblage.

Period 2: medieval

From the hand-collected material (Table 5.25), cattle is the most numerous species by both count and weight. Sheep/goat is the next most numerous taxon, then pig and sheep. Other species are represented by just a few individuals. The same hierarchy is seen in the animal bone recovered from the processed samples (Table 5.26). In terms of body parts, cattle shows the widest range including both meat-bearing and non-meat-bearing ones. Sheep/goat also has a wide range, but pig is more restricted. The sieved material shows a greater proportion of smaller items such as teeth and toes as would be expected. The Deansway animal bone, particularly that from periods 8 (11th to 13th century) and 9 (13th to 15th century), showed a greater proportion of sheep than at Newport Street (Nicholson and Scott 2004b). Goat bone was recovered from both sites, but only in very small numbers (ibid.). The Deansway assemblage also had a much wider range of species from these periods with hare, rabbit and two species of deer, as well as small mammals and amphibians. At Newport Street, other than domestic stock, only cat, goose, dolphin and Gadid have been identified. During the assessment some of the more fragmented material was identified as cat-sized, which includes cat, rabbit and hare, but none could be identified to species. This difference may be due in part to the much larger size of the assemblage from Deansway, and the difference in sampling strategies adopted.

The dental evidence for the age-at-death for sheep is generally adult, which conforms to the pattern from Deansway. The evidence for pig is less clear; fusion data suggests that younger animals were killed, whilst the dental data shows older individuals are present. This was also a problem at Deansway (Nicholson and Scott 2004a). The withers height data enables further comparisons with Deansway: the cattle metatarsal from context 1877, with a height of 1134mm, is within the range seen at Deansway, and the sheep metatarsal withers heights ranges from 550mm to 613mm, also similar to that seen at Deansway. The metacarpal, at 616mm, is at the upper end of range as compared with Deansway.

Period 3: post-medieval

The animal bone from Period 3 shows an even greater proportion of cattle than Period 2. Sheep are more numerous than sheep/goat followed by pig. The other species present in the hand-collected material are goose and chicken. The sieved bone has a very different composition. Although cattle is again the most numerous species by weight, chicken is the most numerous by number of specimens, followed by pig and then cattle. A single fish specimen was identified as a dermal denticle from a ray. Cattle show the widest range of body parts, particularly of postcranial elements, but there is a smaller proportion of skull and particularly tooth fragments. Pig shows the next widest range of body parts, with skull, teeth and limb bones. The sheep assemblage is largely limb bones apart from the presence of horncore, and sheep/goat is represented entirely by limb bones. Chicken bones are predominantly postcranial meat-bearing ones.

The assemblage from context 2919 (Plots 1 and 2) is rich in cattle bones, with damage consistent with being dropped or smashed rather than butchered. The bones are also dark brown in colour as if from a cess or rubbish pit, or from waterlogging. Given that this deposit extended across Plots 1 and 2, and was beneath Dolday, it may be that waste/rubbish was cleared up and deposited prior to the construction of the road surface and subsequent development along the frontage. The fact that all the bones have a similar dark brown staining supports the suggestion that, although they may be redeposited within context 2919, they are derived from a single source.

Comparison with the large assemblage from Deansway is limited by the fact that the post-medieval animal bone, although archived, was not examined in detail. In the Deansway period 10 (15th to 16th-century) assemblage, cattle are dominant followed sheep/goat and pig, and there is also an increased reliance on domestic birds in this period. This is interesting considering the large proportion of chicken in the Newport Street Period 3 assemblage. The Deansway assemblage also included goose, which was only represented by a single bone at Newport Street. Ray is the only fish taxon to be found in this period at Newport Street, which is absent from the range of fish bone in the Deansway assemblage (comprising herring, eel, cod and ling). The thornback ray is a species regularly seen in Bristol where the estuary provides the opportunity to catch it from both shore and boat. It would not have been available in the upper Severn so its presence suggests it was imported, possibly from Bristol.

In terms of the age structure of the main domestic species, cattle are almost all adult; a similar pattern is observed at Deansway. In terms of age-at-death, sheep and sheep/goat are mostly adult (although the fact that sheep are more easily identified when bones are fully fused must be taken into account). The dental evidence confirms that the sheep and sheep/goat are generally adult. A similar pattern was observed at Deansway. The pig fusion data places all specimens at under 2 years whilst the dental data indicates some adult and sub-adult individuals. At Deansway there was a move towards fewer pigs being retained into adulthood and although the assemblage from Newport Street is much smaller, a similar trend is apparent.

The withers heights from Period 3 equate to those from Deansway period 10 (15th to 16th century) and 11 (17th to 18th century). The cattle metatarsal from deposit 434 produced a withers height of 1308mm, which is significantly larger than those from Deansway. The horses have no comparable data from Deansway. The sheep metacarpals from Newport Street give a withers height range of 533mm to 611mm, which is very similar to that seen at Deansway, although the measured sheep metatarsals suggest a wider range.

Correlation of results with documentary data
The documentary research carried out focuses on the period 1660–1800, which falls within Periods 3 and 4 The animal bone from this period was examined with reference to properties in which trades or activities were indicated by the documentary data, but no correlations were identified. Plot 3 equates to the southern end of nos 26, 28 and 30 Newport Street, properties that were owned for a time by the Leddingtons. The samples from deposit 2678 and 2681 were very rich in chicken bone, possibly a reflection of a more affluent diet.

5.24.4 Conclusions

The small Roman assemblage, although of variable preservation, has added further evidence to that from the Deansway excavations for the use of cattle bones within (road) surfaces as hardcore. The single withers height estimation, based on the complete metacarpal, is similar to the values from Deansway for this period. Cattle appear to have been an important part of the Roman economy in Worcester. A larger proportion of cattle is often taken to be a sign of military presence (Dobney 2001), however sheep/goat and pig were also present, and thus the interpretation of the Deansway species composition, as being part way between urban and military in character, holds true for Newport Street. But results from such a small assemblage should be viewed cautiously.

The medieval assemblage also shows some similarities with Deansway, although the numbers of sheep are proportionately less. It also lacks the wide range of wild species recorded at Deansway, which may in part be due to its smaller size.

The post-medieval assemblage, compared with the medieval one, shows a significant increase in the presence of domestic fowl, which was also noted at Deansway, and which may reflect changing patterns of consumption (Nicholson and Scott 2004b). Another trend identified at both sites, which may reflect changing patterns of consumption, is the shift to fewer pigs reaching adulthood in the post-medieval period. There were also some general trends in terms of species present that seem to reflect the relative wealth of the Newport Street, when contrasted with the poorer Dolday dwellings.

The size of the specimens from all periods at Newport Street generally falls within the ranges seen for the larger quantities of measurable bones from Deansway; the only exception being the very large cattle metatarsal from Period 3 deposit 434. The animals represented appear to have been relatively healthy with only three examples of pathology. Pathology was also noted at Deansway at a low level of occurrence.

The analysis of the animal bone has made a limited contribution to the investigation of medieval and post-medieval economic activity and the processes of industrial activity (Davenport, Chapter 6.6). The medieval and post-medieval (Period 2 and 3) assemblages are not clearly derived from domestic waste, butchery waste or industrial waste, but appear to have some contribution from each. This is not dissimilar to the situation at Deansway, where little evidence for specialised butchery was found (Nicholson and Scott 2004a). The animal bone offers little in terms of the identification of workshops: no evidence was found for the leatherworking or glovemaking industry. The very small numbers of cattle, sheep and goat horncores at Newport Street contrasts with Deansway, where a large quantity of horncores were recovered, many being sufficiently complete for measurements to be taken.

In terms of long-term processes (Dalwood, Chapter 6.7), the animal bone from Periods 2 and 3 shows a very similar range of species and it is the only the relative proportions that change. In terms of the local and regional significance (Davenport, Chapter 6.8), the animal bone is of greatest use when viewed alongside that from Deansway. The much larger Deansway assemblages show a number of trends such as increased reliance on birds in the late medieval and post-medieval period, which can also be tentatively identified in the Newport Street assemblage.

5.25 Synthesis of environmental evidence
Elizabeth Pearson and Sylvia Warman

5.25.1 Early deposits, build-up of alluvium and phases of flooding, and the site over time

At the base of the sequences revealed on site by the borehole survey were deposits interpreted as Worcester Terrace material, which is likely to have built up between c. 24,000–11,500 BP. Overlying these were alluvial layers, identified during the borehole survey and in the base of the deeper excavation trenches. These suggest flooding of the site and correspond to upper Elmore Member deposits (Wilkinson, Chapter 4.2) which are fine-grained alluvium layers with some lenses of organic mud and peat, mostly concentrated towards the base of the layer in the boreholes. These suggest that the site was located on the landward margins of a floodplain during deposition of this unit (ibid.). They are likely to have built up during the Holocene until the Romano-British period, and during this time the topography was relatively flat.

Pollen evidence indicates that the landscape was relatively open and cleared of woodland during the late prehistoric period. The upper part of this alluvial sequence exposed during excavation contained pottery dating to the 1st to 2nd centuries AD. Cutting into these alluvial deposits were a small number of pits and then a phase of dumping occurred which is dated to the 3rd to 4th century, probably to raise the ground level.

The botanical evidence from the latter deposits shows limited evidence of waterlogging, and therefore the raising of the ground level above flooding levels was presumably successful. Further alluviation occurred, and then a metalled surface was laid down which formed a road. During the early medieval period, botanical evidence suggests that clay layers overlying the slag surface contained flood debris and may have been partially waterlain, although some dumping from riverside activities may have been a component of their make-up. Much of the flood debris has been interpreted as being largely from the adjacent waterfront on the basis of the condition of the botanical remains. Flooding resulted in a significant depth of alluvium during this time, but alluviation appears to have subsided by the 13th to 14th centuries.

5.25.2 Environment of the site during the medieval period

Both plant macrofossil and pollen evidence from early medieval (11th to 12th-century) deposits indicate that there was a mosaic of scrub or hedgerow vegetation, cultivated or disturbed ground, and grassland, the latter most likely including neglected, overgrown waste ground and meadowland to the north of the city. Cultivation of cereals (including rye) in the area is apparent for the first time in the pollen sequence. The pollen evidence also suggests that there was a low cover of trees and shrubs in the general area, although plant macrofossil remains indicate significant localised bramble growth on waste ground on the site.

The river appears to have been slightly brackish, allowing the growth of wild celery. Although historically wild celery was grown as a vegetable or herb, evidence for primary disposal of food waste was lacking and hence, in this context, it is more likely to have been part of the local flora. The presence of significant levels of whitebeam/sloe/cherry pollen suggests that even sloe stones, which were present as food waste in later contexts, are likely to have originated from vegetation nearby.

5.25.3 Medieval industry on the riverside

The evidence for dyeing and flax retting from the early medieval deposits from Plot 13, although limited, is consistent with the documented development of dyeing, in association with other industries such as tanning. The results compare with other urban waterfront sites such as at Bridge Street, Hereford (Pearson 2003; Pearson 1999). The animal bone shows a lack of convincing evidence for tanning or whittawing (the making of white leather goods), common medieval and post-medieval urban trades. However, this is not surprising given that such trades moved away by the 14th century, following concern over the pollution of the Severn (Hughes, Chapter 2.3). Following this, the area became a focus for the dyeing industry, to which the animal remains are unlikely to relate to directly.

5.25.4 Introduction of new crops, crop varieties and animal breeds

The 17th century was an important period for the development of the certain varieties of fruit cultivated in this country, such as the plum, damson and currants recorded on this site. In particular, fruit growing was a regional speciality of Worcestershire and Herefordshire.

Other vegetables such as cucumber and pumpkin/marrow/squash were also becoming part of the market garden economy nationally, and may have been grown in the Vale of Evesham. Market gardening became a flourishing economy at this time, and it is likely with the proximity of the Vale of Evesham and fruit growing areas in Worcester and Herefordshire, the diversity of produce sold in Worcester would have increased considerably. A significant proportion of this would have arrived in Worcester by river as the town (along with Bewdley and Shrewsbury) served as a collection point for the agrarian economies of the Severn valley (Hussey 2000, 67).

Walnut and medlar, both recovered from post-medieval deposits, were established crops but are rarely found archaeologically. Their recovery here is likely to reflect both good conditions for survival (a combination of waterlogging and mineralisation) and the availability of a diverse range of food goods.

The Period 3 (16th to 17th-century) animal bone assemblage shows a significant increase in the presence of domestic fowl, which was also noted at Deansway. This may reflect a change in taste, fashion or affluence. Although the sample size is very small, some tentative comments on the sizes of domestic species can be made. The withers heights calculated for cattle show an increase from Period 2 into Period 3, as would be expected; and the cattle metatarsal from context 434 is larger than comparable specimens from Deansway. The horse withers heights for Period 3 are comparable to one medium-sized and one large pony, suggesting a diversity of types or breeds for different tasks. Sheep withers heights show a wider range but do not show an increase from Period 2 to Period 3. The pathology seen in a sheep horncore from Period 2 may relate to stress or malnutrition in lactating or pregnant ewes. The bone with signs of gnawing by sheep in Period 3 indicates that malnutrition may have occurred during this period as well. If a large number of horncores were present and a significant proportion showed this condition then it may be possible to comment on the health of the population, but in this case the sample size is too small to do so.

5.25.5 Trade and imported exotics

The botanical evidence demonstrates trade in new varieties, rare cultivars and/or imported exotics from the post-medieval period, and suggests that Newport Street had a number of wealthy inhabitants at this time. Its position on the Severn meant that Worcester was well placed to engage in trade through Bristol, bringing in peppercorn and cucumber via the spice routes, and grains of paradise possibly via the slave trade with Africa. Although pumpkin or squash, for example, may have been grown locally at this time, their introduction was originally as a result of contact with the New World. Bristol in particular was a key port for New World contact, and Worcester one of the main urban centres receiving up-river trade along the Severn.

The only fish bone identified from Period 2 is *Gadidae* (cod family), which being a marine species must have been caught further afield and traded, possibly via Bristol. Another interesting and uncommon specimen is the bottle-nosed dolphin vertebra from context 1162 (Period 2.4) in Plot 14. From deposit 2681 (Period 3), a ray spine is probably from a thornback ray, which is a sea and estuarine species and a relatively common find in Bristol, probably caught in tidal/estuarine parts of the Severn. It is would not naturally occur this far up a river and is likely to be traded, with Bristol the most likely source.

5.25.6 Information on specific documented households

For some of the cess deposits of post-medieval date, it is possible to tentatively relate these with the ownership or occupation by specific individuals or families identified from the documentary evidence. In one case, the deposits are most likely to relate to the occupation of part of Plot 3 by a distiller, Edward Hurdman. Components of the botanical assemblage may relate to distilling spirits, wines or medicines, although generally these components were also well known as food commodities. Deposits in a brick-lined cess pit on the frontage of Plot 3 may have accumulated during the occupation of no. 26/28 Newport Street by the Leddington family in the 16th century. The diversity of food remains, including exotics, correlates well with the occupation by this wealthy merchant family. For the animal bone, general trends in terms of species present are evident, that seem to reflect the relative wealth of the Newport Street frontage when contrasted with the poorer Dolday dwellings.

5.25.7 Comparison with similar sites, locally, regionally and nationally

The excavation of deep deposits has refined the dating of phases of Roman to early-medieval flooding and alluviation, and the cessation of alluviation, that has been seen elsewhere along the Severn. Information has been recovered previously from boreholes with limited radiocarbon dating, but at Newport Street the excavation and exposure of archaeological features and the recovery of artefactual data has shed new light on this sequence (Dalwood, Chapter 6.2).

New botanical data has also come from post-medieval samples, which begin to address some issues raised in Regional Research Frameworks for the period for the West Midlands (Pearson 2001) and East Midlands (Monckton 2006). In particular, the data have provided new information on the introduction of new crop species, varieties and imported exotics, particularly from the New World. In addition to the information already known from documentary records, this provides more specific information on their local use, and is particularly useful where the data can be correlated with detailed historical records, as at Newport Street, and may provide a reference point for similar assemblages in other urban locations. It also strengthens the argument that, although this type of evidence is rare, the screening of large numbers of samples from sites such as Newport Street can produce valuable results. At Deansway, two New World exotics, tomato (*Lycopersicon esculentum*) and pumpkin/marrow/squash (*Cucurbita* cf *maxima*), were found in late medieval/post-medieval deposits (Moffett 2004b, 554), but the range of cultivars and exotics was smaller. Deposits of the same date at Newport Street showed more evidence of cultivation of new species and varieties or trade in exotics, and is more comparable with the Sidbury barrel latrine in Worcester (Greig 1981), and other urban sites nationally.

The Period 2 animal bone assemblage shows some similarities with Deansway but the elevated levels of sheep seen at Deansway are not apparent at Newport Street. The Newport Street assemblage also lacks the wide range of wild species recorded from Deansway, which may in part be due to its smaller size. The Period 3 assemblage shows a significant increase in the presence of domestic fowl, which was also noted at Deansway.

Chapter 6
Thematic Discussion

6.1 Chronological overview
Peter Davenport

It is clear that, leaving aside detailed consideration of the activities in each plot over time, there are some clear and broad conclusions than can be drawn from the analysis of the excavation records.

Lying on the floodplain of the Severn, the site was subject to periodic inundation and the deposition of fertile alluvial clays, and was already a cleared agricultural/pastoral landscape by the Late Bronze Age or Early Iron Age (Head, Chapter 5.22, dating based on pollen spectra). Alluviation continued into the Roman period, when massive amounts of ironworking slag were deposited onto the floodplain, with thin lenses of alluvial clay interleaved, and a road made largely of slag was laid across the deposits. The interleaved layers were quite mixed, with charcoal and small pieces of slag, indicating that the alluvial clays were collecting other materials of anthropogenic origin before deposition. The road ran parallel and very close to the line of medieval Newport Street, suggesting that there was a Roman river crossing at the same point as the medieval bridge, on which the later street was aligned. The road seems to have been primarily used in the late 2nd and 3rd centuries AD, falling out of use (or was very rarely used) in the 4th century AD. The limited investigations into this period did not allow anything to be discovered about the nature or even presence of any Roman occupation alongside the street, although clearly the massive quantities of dumped ironworking debris implies ironworking on an industrial scale in the vicinity.

Alluviation continued after the Roman period with a further 0.2–0.3m of silts laid down before direct evidence for human activity was again attested. The pollen results from this layer showed the continued existence of the cleared landscape in the vicinity, with evidence for both cereal cultivation and for meadow, which is not very surprising given its location. This continued until alluviation ceased, a result of more intense occupation of the site in the medieval period.

At the west end of the site, a well dug through these post-Roman alluvial layers and then filled in, probably in the 11th century, probably represents the earliest attempt at settling the area. At the east end of the site, similar activity was represented by shallow pit digging and the driving of several posts into the ground. Both of these episodes were sealed by yet more alluviation. In Plot 13 at the east end of the site, at least 0.2m of water-lain silt accumulated over the Roman road before occupation started. The earliest occupation layers contained large pieces of animal bone and 11th-century pottery, and were covered by a series of layers and lenses that were probably a result of localised flooding of occupied areas. Other pottery evidence indicates that these episodes of flooding had ceased by the later 11th or 12th century. This suggests that the first attempts to settle this piece of ground were tentative and sporadic, perhaps affected and discouraged by the flooding.

The first determined attempt to permanently settle the area seems to date from the 12th or 13th century. Extensive dumps of soil were imported and spread around with the clear intent to raise the area above flood level. In this it appears to have been successful, as no further flood silts were recorded. Dating evidence for these layers, which were generally at the lower limit of excavation, was not prolific but was consistently of 12th or 13th-century, date, and we might conclude that the first serious attempts to colonise the area are of that period, with major engineering taking place in the 13th century. Quite intense occupation of the plots was evident from this period onwards, wherever excavation was deep enough to encounter relevant deposits. It is clear that the dumps of material were a communal effort, not an individual one, as the dumps quite clearly extended across subsequent tenement boundaries. Evidence for tenement boundaries prior to the building of substantial masonry walls was rare but the occurrence of short rows of pits and some gullies on the line of (and under) boundary walls, as well as truncation of earlier features by the boundary walls, shows that the plots had been properly subdivided and demarcated before major building works took place. Again the dating evidence for these early plot boundary walls is not overwhelming but consistently shows that these masonry boundary walls were first created in the 13th and 14th centuries. There is also evidence that timber buildings with masonry cellars were erected on the site from the late 13th or 14th century, and the earliest known documentary evidence for the site shows a tenement extending from Newport Street to Dolday by 1317.

The earliest archaeological evidence for buildings on the Dolday frontage was from the 16th century and building seems to have become common there by the 17th century. However, the development of the actual frontage was probably considerably earlier, but it does not seem to have become fixed until the later 17th or even 18th century, judging by the projection of Building 2 beyond the frontage mapped from 1779. The boundary between Plots 2 and 4 was also not fixed in its present position until after 1779, which reflects the fluid property-holding position revealed by the documentary sources for these plots (Hughes, Chapter 5.1.4). By contrast, the frontages on Newport Street seem to have developed with substantial buildings, presumably houses, from the 13th or 14th century onwards, paralleling the evidence for the first masonry boundary walls. Ovens, hearths and further raising of the ground level shows the exploitation of their rear yards, presumably for a mix of craft and domestic activities. None of the ovens had evidence for specialised processes, apart from smithing evidence from Plot 14, although the concentration of hearths there was probably for other processes and the ovens in its vicinity were almost certainly for baking. There was little evidence for building in the rear yards, although this was as much a result of the limited depths of excavation as anything else. The exception was Building 5, which, with rebuilds, seems to have lasted for two or three hundred years behind the frontage of no. 24 Newport Street.

Both archaeological and cartographic evidence indicates that the density of occupation and use of the rear yards increased in the 17th century, and was very well developed by the late 18th century. The economic growth this implies was also reflected in the rebuilding of many of the Newport Street frontages during the 18th century. This seems to have often left large elements of earlier timber-framed houses within the later work. In particular, the increased accommodation for workers provided by the almost exclusively single-celled and often back-to-back cottages in courts laid out over the gardens and yards in the 18th and 19th centuries suggests that this economic growth led to an increased working population, and segregation of the workers from the middle classes in the main houses along the frontages. After the middle of the 19th century, the houses on Newport Street themselves became lower status in multiple and split occupation, with the owners (or head lessees) living elsewhere. Newport Street headed downhill socially, and by the early 20th century it was largely slum, overcrowded and insanitary. It was this that led to its almost total demolition in the mid 20th century.

6.2 The river, the floodplain and its transformation
Hal Dalwood

The Newport Street excavations provided the first opportunity to carry out an extensive archaeological excavation in the floodplain area of the north-west part of the historic city, close to the river and the medieval bridgehead. This area had long been seen as having archaeological research potential, on the basis of historical and topographical rather than archaeological evidence (Carver 1980c, 19–21, fig. 7). The majority of archaeological fieldwork within the historic core of Worcester (Fig. 2.1) has taken place on sites where the underlying geology is the gravel terrace (Worcester Terrace). The riverside and the area of Newport Street and Dolday had seen little archaeological fieldwork previously, but the research potential was considered high because it is an area where waterlogged deposits could be anticipated (WCC 2007, 12–14). An archaeological evaluation on the north side of Dolday in 1985 (the site of the present bus station) showed that deposits in this area were up to 5m deep, although difficult recording conditions precluded the establishment of a well-dated stratigraphic sequence (Mundy 1985, 3–5: Trench 1/5).

The channel of the River Severn at Worcester is on the eastern side of its floodplain, which here is *c.* 0.5km wide. The geomorphology of the area has been described and related to the development of settlement (Morris 1974): the present river channel is likely to have been stable throughout prehistoric and historic periods, and the relationship between the channel and the adjacent gravel terrace has been a key factor in the history of settlement at Worcester. The surface of the gravel terrace is level at 20m to 22m AOD and is covered with varying thicknesses of archaeological deposits. The floodplain conforms to the wide braided channel of Late Glacial Devensian date and contains up to 5m of fine-grained alluvium; the present-day surface is relatively low-lying at around 14m AOD (ibid.).

The historic core of Worcester mostly lies on gravel (which in turn overlies Mercia Mudstone) but the Newport Street/Dolday area is an exception as it forms a narrow band of floodplain within the medieval city wall, between the river channel to the west and the gravel ridge to the east. The geoarchaeological investigations at Newport Street have shown that the alluvial silts and clays within the site are *c.* 3m thick, overlying sands and gravels of the Worcester Terrace (outcropping at <8.5m AOD, Chapter 5.22), and that a significant thickness of archaeological deposits overlay the floodplain alluvium.

The character of the Severn was transformed by engineering works to improve navigation in the mid

19th century, with the aim of maintaining consistent water levels between weirs and locks along the middle reach of the river, and providing a reliable connection to the important canals which joined the Severn at Worcester and Stourport. Historical sources allow the natural state of the river prior to this development to be understood (Richardson 1964). The river was always difficult to navigate due to generally low water levels and numerous rock bars and gravel shoals, although navigation was aided by tidal rises in the water level as far north as Upton upon Severn, and particularly by high spring tides that held back the river flow and caused a rise of 0.45m at Worcester a few times a year. Much more common were the rapid rises of short duration, called 'freshes', from rain falling in the catchment. River navigation depended on shallow-draughted river boats and an understanding of the character of the river, and consequently groups of skilled watermen were to be found in all riverside settlements. The river was canalised from 1842: weirs and locks were constructed at both Diglis and Bevere near Worcester (and further downriver) and there was extensive dredging both above and below the city. These works maintained a consistent depth of water in the river and considerably improved navigation, but the historic character of the river was permanently changed.

Newport Street and Dolday both slope down to the river, broadly following the natural topography as it slopes down from the gravel terrace to the east, and reflecting the slope of the river bluff where it cuts into the underlying Mercia Mudstone. The 1985 evaluation work to the north of Dolday revealed the slope of the Mercia Mudstone overlain by Roman and later deposits that dipped to the west (Mundy 1985, 3–4, fig. 4). North of the city wall, the low-lying area of Pitchcroft remains subject to annual flooding, as does the broad western floodplain, and these areas remained largely unoccupied up to the 19th century. The Newport Street/Dolday area lies on the east bank of the Severn, but it was not previously known when and how this area was reclaimed for occupation. The stratigraphic evidence and borehole data from the Newport Street site has provided the first comprehensive archaeological evidence for both historic flooding and reclamation in this area.

The sand and gravel deposits over which the Newport Street site lies were encountered in boreholes between *c.* 8.3m AOD on the south side of the site and 8.8m AOD on the north side. These correlate to the Worcester Terrace and have been interpreted as alluvial strata deposited within the Devensian braided river channel (Wilkinson, Chapter 4.2.2). The 1985 evaluation trench, next to Dolday, recorded sand at 10.85m AOD (Mundy 1985, 4, fig. 4). The sand and gravel at Newport Street is overlain by over 3m of fine-grained alluvium (Elmore Member), which was also recorded in the borehole survey (Wilkinson, Chapter 4.2.2) and partly excavated in the East Sondage in Plot 13. The upper part of the alluvial sequence (G345) contained late 2nd to 3rd-century AD pottery and was cut by contemporary features. A borehole survey of a site to the north of The Butts has provided further evidence of the alluvial sequence in the floodplain: here the fine-grained alluvium was similar in thickness to Newport Street, and the upper levels also contained Roman artefacts and iron slag (Wilkinson and Marter 2006).

The alluvium at Newport Street produced a pollen sequence that could only be dated by stratigraphic evidence, as radiocarbon dating was not possible (Head, Chapter 5.22). Pollen analysis showed that the prehistoric environment was dominated by grasses, meadowland herbs and marshland plants. The floodplain was clearly utilised as meadowland, with alder and hazel probably restricted to the river banks, and there was no evidence for cereal cultivation. There was evidence for some regeneration of floodplain woodland in the Late Iron Age to Roman period.

Geoarchaeological research in the Severn Valley has indicated a consistent pattern of Holocene alluviation, with a considerable increase in deposition beginning in the Late Bronze Age/Early Iron Age, which has been interpreted as a consequence of an increase in arable cultivation together with climatic deterioration (Brown 1997, 223–5). More recent research has indicated that increases in flooding in river valleys can be detected across Britain, with consistent episodes of flooding in *c.* 2730bp (780 BC), *c.* 2550bp (600 BC), *c.* 2280bp (330 BC) and *c.* 1950bp (AD 1), attributed principally to worsening climatic conditions but exacerbated to an extent by changes in agriculture and land-use (Macklin *et al.* 2005, 939–42, table 1). The alluvium at Newport Street is consistent with this broad pattern of alluvium accumulation from the Late Bronze Age to the Late Iron Age, although the lack of dating evidence for the sequence precludes detailed discussion. However, the archaeologically-dated upper part of the sequence shows that the alluvium continued to be deposited up to the later 2nd century AD, when there was limited occupation on the floodplain, with features cut into the surface of the alluvium. The recorded top of the alluvium was at *c.* 11.5m at the west end of the site (borehole data) and at 12.3m AOD at the east end (excavated sequence). There was very extensive dumping of iron slag across the southern part of the site which raised the ground level by between 0.5m (to the east) and 1.0m (to the west), over which a road was constructed (surface at 12.85m AOD at the eastern edge of the site). The borehole survey indicated that the slag dumping was concentrated in the southern part of the site, and that there were layers containing domestic debris in the northern part of the site up to 0.5m thick (Wilkinson, Chapter 4.2.1). The surface of the Roman road appeared to have been unaffected by flood deposits and it seems likely that the roadway was built at a level to avoid any risk of flooding, at least in Roman times.

An evaluation trench at The Hive site to the north of The Butts exposed the buried soils and a linear ditch dated to the mid 2nd to 3rd century AD, indicating a ground surface at 13.3m AOD, overlying a thick alluvial sequence (Trench 6: Sworn and Phear 2007, 9, fig. 9). The associated borehole survey at this site revealed topographical variation in the upper part of the alluvium, but showed a pattern of Roman activity and dumping across the contemporary floodplain surface (Wilkinson and Marter 2006). Although it has been stated that most lowland river valleys saw considerable flooding and alluviation during the Roman period (Brown 1997, 225–6), other research has indicated that there is little evidence for widespread flooding during the period (Macklin et al. 2005, table 1). The Newport Street evidence seems to indicate that there was continued alluviation in the earlier Roman period, which ceased in the late 2nd to early 3rd century AD.

The Roman road provided a dry ground surface in the post-Roman period, when some undated small pits were dug into its surface, and a well was dug through it probably in the 11th century (Plot 3). This indicates a much reduced use of the road in the post-Roman period, but it probably continued to provide foot passage to the river. During the post-Conquest period there was a considerable build-up of alluvial deposits, dating to the 11th to 12th century. These deposits (recorded as 0.55m thick at the eastern end of the site in Plot 13) buried the Roman road surface and the metalled roadway certainly became unusable during this period. The date for the beginning and duration of this alluvial sequence is not closely defined, but can be dated between the 11th and 12th century. There was no parallel evidence for alluvial deposits of this date from evaluation trenches in the historic floodplain at The Hive site (Sworn and Phear 2007).

Pollen from the alluvium sequence post-dating the Roman road showed that the immediate area was meadowland in the 11th to 12th century, and that it was probably more intensively managed than earlier (Head, Chapter 5.22). There was also evidence for arable cultivation nearby and perhaps some scrubland. The plant macrofossils from the medieval alluvium also indicated vegetation growing alongside the river and bramble scrub (Pearson, Chapter 5.23). This area was immediately adjacent to the developing town, and was certainly crossed by an approach road to the bridge.

There is little evidence for widespread flooding episodes due to a worsening climate in the medieval period prior to the late 13th century (Macklin et al. 2005, table 1). The alluviation at Worcester in this period can probably be interpreted as a local phenomenon. However the alluviation is certainly significant, and can provisionally be interpreted as the result of an expansion in arable cultivation in the town's hinterland, leading to increased soil erosion. There is some documentary evidence for growth in rural settlement and for intensification of agriculture in the 11th to 13th century in the local area, for example at the bishop's estate of Whitsones, north of Worcester (Dyer 1980, 90–1) and in Ombersley (D. Miller, pers. comm.). In Hanbury, however, significant expansion in population and farming did not take place before the late 12th century and the 13th century (Dyer 1991, 27–43). The evidence for medieval alluviation at Newport Street is certainly significant as it suggests that there was considerable aggradation of the Severn floodplain in this period, which should be detectable over a significant area. At Clifton Quarry (Severn Stoke), archaeological fieldwork has recently recorded 9th-century features that were overlain by an alluvial sequence which could potentially be of 11th to 12th-century date (A. Mann, pers. comm.). Otherwise the Newport Street evidence remains rather isolated, and further investigation and dating of the alluvium in the Severn floodplain remains an important research question. Dated alluvial sequences from the Severn Valley provide a source of evidence which, when combined with landscape archaeology and historical research, provide a means of investigating widespread changes in the medieval landscape.

In the late 12th to early 13th century there was an episode of deliberate reclamation of the floodplain at Worcester, when an extensive soil layer 0.3m thick was dumped over the 11th to 12th-century flood deposits, raising the ground level to 13.8m AOD at the eastern end of the site. This provided the basis for the layout of a new street (Eport Street, later Newport Street; see Chapter 6.3). Nevertheless this area of Worcester remained subject to flooding, although probably only during the highest floods.

The present surface topography of the Newport Street area is the result of the long-term accumulation of fine-grained alluvium in the prehistoric period and the 11th to 12th centuries, short-term episodes of large-scale dumping of deposits to raise the ground level in the Roman period and in the 13th century, and the subsequent gradual deposition of occupation deposits up to the 20th century.

6.3 The development of the street system and medieval town planning
Hal Dalwood

Recent intensive study of the medieval urban landscape of Worcester has included detailed consideration of the origins and development of the medieval street pattern (Baker and Holt 2004, 147–54, fig. 6.6). The development of the street system within the north-western part of the walled city has been the subject of some debate, based on rather limited evidence, and the results of the excavation have refocused the research questions. This area of the medieval town saw extensive replanning and change in later centuries, including the construction of Bridge Street in 1771–80, and much of the medieval street and plot pattern can only be traced from cartographic sources, and for the area erased by Bridge Street even this is not possible.

The Newport Street site lies in the historic parish of All Saints' (Baker and Holt 2004, fig. 7.1). All Saints' Church was probably founded in the late 9th century, close to or on a gate that formed part of the defences of the burh (ibid., 178–80). The parish lay outside the burh defences but by the early 13th century had been enclosed within the medieval city walls (ibid., 206–7; Fig. 2.2). North of the church there was an open space, All Hallows' Square, which was the medieval cattle market (ibid., 207). From here, Broad Street led east to The Cross, and Newport Street and Dolday led west towards the river crossing. Newport Street was first documented in the 12th century as *Eport*, meaning 'river gate' (the form 'Newport' is a 16th-century corruption), whereas the etymology of Dolday is unknown (Mawer and Stenton 1927, 21). Newport Street was aligned directly on the medieval bridge and was clearly the direct route to the bridge. Dolday followed a more sinuous course to the north and led to the Upper (or North) Quay, immediately north of the bridge, opposite St Clement's Church, a probable mid 11th-century foundation (Baker and Holt 2004, 207–10). The North Quay was secondary to the principal medieval quay (the Lower Quay) at the western end of Copenhagen Street. The Lower Quay was an area of open space which was probably reclaimed from low-lying land next to the river bank during the medieval period, and probably developed from a length of the riverbank that was used for beaching ships in the 10th century (ibid., 176–7), and a similar process of reclamation would have been required for the Upper Quay. St Clement's Church lay inside the city wall, but the majority of its parish lay on the west side of the river, and the dedication probably reflects a medieval association with maritime occupations, including boatmen who were concentrated in the parish west of the river (ibid., 207–10, fig. 9.1). The expansion of settlement into the area north-west of the burh defences could be broadly dated on this evidence to the period between the early 10th century (after the establishment of the burh defences) and the mid 11th century (the probable foundation date of St Clement's Church). The earliest documentary sources to the rent of land in this area date from the 13th century (Hughes, Chapter 2.3).

There has been considerable debate about the origin and development of river crossings at Worcester. An artificial causeway crossed the wide floodplain on the western side of the river in the medieval period, which carried a road (later called Tybridge Street) aligned on the medieval bridge (Hughes 1980, 290; Baker and Holt 2004, 193–4). The bridge was first documented in 1088 and was rebuilt in stone in 1313–28 (Beardsmore 1980, 61–2), and it could be inferred that the approach roads, comprising the western causeway and Newport Street, were in existence from at least the later 11th century. This bridge location continued as the primary river crossing at Worcester until its demolition in the 18th century.

The earlier history of a river crossing at this point is more circumstantial. Carver (1980c, 19–20) argued that the piers of the medieval bridge were elements of a Roman bridge, constructed using iron slag in their cores. The existence of a Roman bridge at Worcester remains an untested hypothesis, but there is documentary evidence for a ford close to the Newport Street bridge (ibid., 19; Baker and Holt 2004, 180). This ford could not have been used when the river was in flood and during high tides, but the existence of a natural ford at this position seems uncontroversial, and a ford, supplemented with boats, may have been the principal crossing point of the river prior to the 11th century (Dalwood and Edwards 2004, figs 11 and 13).

Research drawing on town-plan analysis has defined Newport Street, Dolday and the associated tenement plots as a single plan-unit, a town-planning event that defined the local topography of the historic town up to the 18th century (Baker and Holt 2004, 178–80, fig. 6.8). This analysis identified the two streets as representing 'the most eccentric element in the medieval intra-mural site plan' (ibid., 178). The possibility that Dolday was the earlier main route to the river crossing, later replaced by Newport Street, was considered but not favoured and it was concluded that Dolday originated as a service lane for Newport Street (ibid.,180); it has been suggested that Newport Street was probably an expansion of the burh in the 10th or early 11th century (ibid., 357). The excavation at Newport Street has allowed these various hypotheses to be evaluated against new archaeological evidence.

The Roman road that preceded Newport Street is a significant discovery and an important addition to our knowledge of the Roman street system in Worcester. Dumps of slag and gravel on the floodplain, interspersed with thin bands of alluvium, formed the base for the road (*c*. 0.6m thick; surface at 12.85m AOD at the eastern edge of the site). The southern edge of the excavated road surface was cambered, and dipped beneath the southern edge of the excavated area, indicating that the Roman road lay parallel but to the north of the medieval road alignment. It seems certain that the Roman road was aligned on a river crossing that was close to the site of the medieval bridge. The hypothesis that there was a Roman crossing at this point is thereby strengthened, as is the suggestion that Tybridge Street is on the same alignment as a Roman road across the floodplain on the west bank.

Judging by the alignment of the excavated road, the crossing point lay to the north of the abutment of the medieval stone bridge, which suggests that the piers of this bridge were not originally from a Roman structure. Furthermore, the Roman road appears to have been constructed on the top of the floodplain, whereas it might be expected that the approach road to a bridge would be on a causeway, to prevent transport being disrupted by flooding. There is also no evidence that an important Roman road ran west from Worcester, which might be expected if there was a bridge. It is relevant in this context that the crossing over the Severn at Wroxeter was a ford rather than a bridge, despite the size and status of that city and its demonstrable importance as a crossing over the Severn in the road network of the West Midlands (White and Barker 1998, figs 28 and 39). The question of the nature of the Roman river crossing at Worcester remains an open one, but it appears to be more likely that it was a ford and ferry rather than a bridge.

The excavated road was constructed relatively late in the development of the settlement, as it was constructed over features dated to the late 2nd century AD. Its alignment can be extrapolated eastwards to form a T-junction with a previously identified Roman road that follows a broadly north/south alignment (Dalwood and Edwards 2004, fig. 11; Fig. 2.2). It had a relatively short period of use, as refuse deposits were dumped on the road surface in the 4th century AD. This late date seems somewhat anomalous as it is likely that an established river crossing would have been important from shortly after the Conquest. It is possible that the excavated road was the reconstruction of an earlier roadway that may have been narrower and so not observed in the excavations. A sequence of road rebuilding was observed at the Farrier Street site in Worcester, where a narrower cobbled road surface was replaced by wider slag road surfaces from the 3rd century AD onwards (Dalwood *et al.* 1994, 80–2, fig. 5). Another possibility is that Dolday followed the line of a prehistoric and early Roman route to the river crossing, and was replaced by the metalled road on the Newport Street alignment as the settlement developed.

In the post-Roman period the excavated road surface was cut by a number of features, but it could have continued to function as a causeway to the river crossing up to the onset of alluviation in the 11th to 12th century (Chapter 6.1). The construction of the burh in the late 9th century was undertaken with military considerations, but the area enclosed by the ditch and rampart did not include the ford, perhaps suggesting that its control was not considered to be essential strategically. This observation underlines the argument that the medieval bridge did not have Roman origins: the strategic potential of a bridge would have been too great to have been left out of the Anglo-Saxon defensive circuit.

The documented early medieval routeways to Worcester from the south-west, west and north-west (Hooke 1980, fig. 12) show that there was an early medieval river crossing at Worcester, and this is likely to have been the Roman crossing point at the 'Newport Ford'. Any route across the floodplain in the early medieval period would only need to be a track, and would probably follow the line of the Roman approach roads on either side to the river. A well was cut through the road surface and backfilled, probably in the 11th century, but there was no evidence for intensive use of the floodplain in this period.

The excavation showed that the Roman road was buried by up to 0.6m of alluvium during the 11th to 12th century (Chapter 6.1). This would have clearly disrupted traffic along the route to the crossing point; however, the documentary evidence clearly indicates that a bridge (and therefore certainly an approach road) was in existence in 1088, and it has also been argued that St Clement's Church was founded in the late 11th century. The medieval alluvium is only broadly dated and it is not possible to definitely reconcile the archaeological evidence within a coherent narrative. If the Roman road was used to some extent in the early medieval period, the construction of the bridge and the foundation of St Clement's Church near the bridgehead would appear to be important suburban developments of the 11th century that might be expected to be rapidly followed by the laying out and occupation of tenement plots along the approach road to the bridge (Newport Street). However this is not what occurred as the archaeological evidence shows that intensive occupation of this area did not begin until later. There is evidence that the area was affected by an increase in flooding, but it is probable that there was also little pressure to reclaim the area for occupation. The route to the bridge could have been maintained at this time by a brushwood causeway across the floodplain.

The origin of Dolday remains an open question. An early origin as a trackway across the floodplain has been suggested above but, once the Roman road was constructed, there would have been no need for this parallel route if the direct route remained in use or could be maintained by a brushwood causeway. However, the fact that Dolday was incorporated into the town plan suggests that it was the route used to the river crossing following post-Conquest alluviation and the demise of the Roman road, and remained in use up to when Dolday was incorporated as the rear access lane following the laying out of Newport Street in the late 12th or early 13th century.

There was no opportunity to examine deposits beneath Newport Street itself, but excavation showed that tenement plots aligned on the street were laid out in the early 13th century, following extensive dumping of soil deposits on this part of the floodplain. The earliest property rentals from this area also date from the mid 13th century (Hughes, Chapter 2.3). It is now clear that it was at this relatively late date that intensive urban occupation of the western part of All Saints' parish began, following organised reclamation of the floodplain and the construction of the city defences in the late 12th century, which ran across the floodplain on an alignment that enclosed St Clement's Church.

6.4 Colonisation and property division
Peter Davenport

The floodplain of the Severn was clearly under some form of cultivation or management in pre-Roman times (Pearson, Chapter 5.23), but was also subject to seasonal inundation and alluviation. Information from the two sondages and the borehole logs show that large amounts of metalworking slag were deposited over the flood silts in the later 2nd to early 3rd century AD. While the floodplain may have been at first a convenient tip, it is likely that some form of reclamation was being implemented by this large-scale dumping. To the south of the site, thick and dense deposits of slag were used to create a road, although it is not clear if the earliest slag deposits formed a foundation or an earlier surface, or were just pre-road dumping. They were separated from the later slag road surface by tips and spreads of clay, charcoal and less compact slag, which may be evidence of industrial activity or just the accumulation of dirt and rubbish on the earlier surface.

Borehole evidence suggests that Roman-dated layers to the north of the road comprise a mixture of domestic and industrial waste disposal, and demolition debris (Wilkinson 2007, 11). While slag continues to be a high proportion of the material in these layers, they are otherwise dominated by domestic and structural remains (Wilkinson, Chapter 4.2.2). There is no sign of this material thinning further from the road line and the area appears to have been not only reclaimed but occupied in the Roman period, although details of that occupation were not retrievable. Little more can be said about the nature of the occupation, although the mortar, stone and brick debris indicates Romanised construction techniques, but it seems that there was some kind of Roman settlement on a reclaimed area alongside the road that led to a presumed crossing point on the Severn.

Dateable occupation ceases in the 4th century AD and it is after this point that alluviation seems to resume. The laying down of these deposits was presumably gentle and episodic as they are interleaved with evidence for human activity, including the digging of pits and the inserting of posts into the top surface of the road. It also seems that alluviation did not reach these levels for some centuries as 11th-century pottery (at the earliest) was found in the earliest layers of this activity. The deposition of up to 0.3m of alluvial deposits was perhaps as a result of an increased silt burden in the river in the 11th century, which may have been the result of the construction of the medieval bridge, which was certainly there by 1088 (Baker and Holt 2004, 142).

It is in the 11th or 12th century (probably the latter), that there is evidence of renewed reclamation and occupation of the site. Layers of clayey silts up to 0.7m thick were dumped on the site, at least on its south side, over the old Roman road. By this stage, over 2.3m of both man-made and natural material had accumulated over the pre-Roman floodplain. These layers were only reached in the two sondages, but the continued extensive dumping of soils in the 13th century was also in evidence where excavation levels reached this depth across the southern part of the site (deposits of this date were not generally reached in the northern part). These extensive dumps do not appear to have been occupation layers, although they may have derived in part from urban refuse, but the slight evidence for hiatuses in the process suggests that some activities may have represented settlement. The digging of a well in this period in Plot 3 indicates occupation of the area, as opposed to casual exploitation. The dating is sparse but consistent, both from finds and stratigraphically, and it seems that the whole of the Newport Street site was artificially raised ready for organised occupation in the 13th century.

That this process of dumping and ground raising was communal rather than individual is suggested by two things: the considerable scale of the operation, and the fact that the dumped deposits extended across property boundaries. The layout of these boundaries follows very soon after the dumping. The short time gap implied from the archaeological dating between the final episodes of ground raising and the establishing of property boundaries seems to indicate that these were carried out as essentially one operation, in concept at least. In addition, the relatively short time scale implied by the consistency of the dating evidence from the first clear medieval occupation levels above them, might also indicate a communal decision to colonise the area, however implemented. Yet the lack of obvious uniformity of plot width or of a planning module in laying out the tenements suggests a more *ad hoc* approach to actual land apportionment. The relationship between the establishment of property boundaries and the extension of the defended area of the town to include this area remains uncertain, but it raises interesting questions.

The Newport Street and Dolday area has been identified as a 'plan unit', i.e. an element of town topography that implies at the least a self-contained phase of development, and at most an entire planned quarter (Baker and Holt 2004, 188). It may very well have been a planned extension to the city, and the building up of the ground levels over several plots at a time may be an example of the kind of civil engineering that is often overlooked but was an important element of town planning, and the responsibility of the landlord. The latter would have been the king, acting through his sheriff and bailiffs, as there was no City Corporation at this time, but who actually organised, carried out, and paid for the work remains unknown. That corporate development of riverside areas was undertaken in other areas at this time is indicated by the works at Bristol in the early 13th century when the River Frome was diverted although, as befitting a much larger port, the works were on a considerably larger scale (Lobel and Carus-Wilson 1975, 1–27), and at Shrewsbury, where the medieval market hall was built on reclaimed wetlands (Baker *et al.* 2006).

The depth of excavation dictated by the formation level for the new development largely precluded the investigation of layers beneath the masonry property divisions of the 13th to 14th century. However, earlier divisions are hinted at by the hearths and oven in Plot 7 that pre-dated the walls but seemed to respect their alignment, and the way that various elements of the Period 2.3 layers in Plots 13 and 14 also seem to have followed the boundary that was not, literally, set in stone until Period 2.4. It is interesting to note that some of these elements seem not to have been completely restrained by the apparent boundary, with slag deposits spilling to either side of the Plot 13/14 boundary, for example. Despite the lack of direct evidence, it is probable that property boundaries were initially marked out with fences or hedges, and only later fixed in masonry.

The earliest masonry boundaries recorded during excavation were not just boundary walls but often were also part of the foundations of buildings. This was apparent from the walls generally not extending beyond the footprint of the buildings. At the greatest extent the foundation/boundary wall in Plot 14 was 71ft (21.68m) long, but more typically these were around 35ft (10.5m) e.g. in Plot 5. Nonetheless, the medieval boundary wall between Plots 3 and 5 appears to have extended as far as 90ft (27.4m) from the highway (although the northern 12.5m were probably not primary and may have been another fragment of a building). These walls provided the basic framework for the main property boundaries which remained in use into the 20th century.

The plots were presumably laid out by the landowner, which in one case was certainly the Church, but other landowners are unknown. There was no standard width to the frontages, which measured 16ft, 18ft 6in, 18ft 9in, 20ft, 24ft (twice), 28 or 29ft and 42ft. The plots were clearly laid out from the Newport Street frontage and ran back to Dolday as urban strip tenements, which implies that both streets were already in existence. The evidence of medieval walls along Newport Street at no. 28 and (probably) no. 12 indicates that, allowing for minor purpresture, the Newport Street frontage hardly moved between the 13th/14th century and the late 20th century. Dolday is more of a puzzle, not being an obvious back lane, and possibly pre-dating the property layout (see Chapter 6.3 above). The considerable projection of Building 2 into the later street alignment in the 16th century, and the changing alignment of Buildings 11 and 12, implies that this frontage was not fixed until after that time, and only confirmed by the conformity of Building 1a to the later street frontage.

Once established, the plots were leased out for a ground rent and fine, presumably with a clause to build. The use of substantial masonry blocks in the footings is surprising, as sandstone was expensive. Perhaps it was recycled from Roman buildings nearby, or acquired as poorer quality stone rejected from large-scale building projects such as the construction of the city wall or major churches. In at least one case, walls were built as party foundations to support independent non-party walls of buildings on both sides of the line. This occurred most clearly in Period 2.3 in Plots 7 and 9. The thickness of the walls to Plot 5 suggests a similar intention, which was certainly acted on with the construction of Building 5. This co-operative use of footings and the foresight it implies again suggests an overall organising body or at least joint development of several plots.

Access to the rear yards was also organised from the beginning, via side alleys. One of these, known later as Browning's Passage, provided access from Newport Street to Dolday between nos 22 and 24 Newport Street. There is evidence of its existence in Period 2.3 and it remained in use until the 20th century. Other routes to Dolday were maintained through the tenements in nos 26 and 32 Newport Street, the former of which was post-medieval in origin, but others were blocked by more intensive development of the rear yards and the creation of separate holdings at the rear of nos 12 to 22 Newport Street in the post-medieval period.

On the whole, the major physical plot boundaries changed little, but ownership and holdings were much more complex and variable. For example, where multiple tenements were in single ownership in later years, it is not clear whether this had medieval origins or was the result of later amalgamation. The interpretation of Building 4 on Plot 3 suggests that nos 26 to 30 Newport Street were one plot in the 15th century. Changes cannot easily be traced in the medieval period, and it is clear that in the 17th and 18th centuries, legal boundaries were not reflected in any simple way by physical ones. Documents show that nos 26 to 30 Newport Street were probably in one ownership well into the 18th century, but in three or more occupations, and this is one plot where the northern end was eventually legally separated off from the southern part. Part of no. 32/34 Newport Street was legally part of no. 30. Nos 20 and 22 Newport Street were held together in the late 17th and early 18th century, and nos 14 to 18 seem to have lost their northern ends when the malthouses were built fronting Dolday in the late 17th century and later. By the later 18th century these northern properties also had a separate legal existence (Hughes, Chapter 5.1.4). No. 12 Newport Street remained as one holding but the northern end was redeveloped and occupied separately from the southern end.

The only boundary to have been realigned seems to be that at the northern end of Plots 2 and 4. This was altered after 1779, and probably between 1806 and 1811, when the cottages on Dolday were rebuilt.

No earlier boundary was found, although hints of its alignment were noted, which suggests an insubstantial structure in the earlier period, such as a fence.

The rear of the properties was always intended for use and not merely for gardens. The process of building up the rear yards probably began early, but excavation at the northern side of the site generally did not go deep enough to investigate any levels earlier than the 16th century. The open areas would have been used for storage and those processes that were too unpleasant or dangerous to be undertaken in the houses, or that required more space. There is evidence for ovens (probably bakers') and hearths, smithing workshops and cordwaining from Period 2, but, apart from Building 5 and the northern part of Building 41, there was little evidence of substantial building in the rear yards during the medieval period. The late medieval oven in Plot 8 is a rare example of evidence for the utilitarian exploitation of the rear yard, well back from the frontage. This and the other ovens and hearths in the rear of nos 12, 20 and 24 Newport Street are unlikely to have been completely in the open air, and timber lean-tos and sheds are very likely to have provided shelter from the elements. As well as buildings for craft and industry, stables, pig sties, fowl houses and even cow houses are all possibilities, leaving little large-scale open space at the rear of the tenements. Stables are certainly mentioned in some post-medieval documents.

The combination of documentary and archaeological evidence available for the 16th century makes it clear that both frontages were built up by then, and that little of the rear yards has escaped development. Early post-medieval inventories do not suggest that this was large-scale warehousing, except for a hemp house at no. 32 Newport Street that was almost certainly Building 1a, a large timber hall on stone footings, probably erected in the early to mid 16th century. The house was then owned by a fuller and it may be that he had branched out into hemp processing as an adjunct to the usual woollen fabrics. Next door at nos 26–30, Jone (sic) Parker distinguishes a workhouse, with timber in it, from his house, with wool, in his will of 1558. Storage for grain or flour, as well as wool, seems to have been accommodated within the main buildings, in cornlofts for the workhouse.

Apart from back kitchens and bakehouses, which tended to be close to the house or attached to its rear, the earliest documented developments are the provision of 'tenements', i.e. houses, located at the rear of the plots in the 17th century. Building 14 appears to have been part of a row of tenements built around 1650 in the garden of no. 22 Newport Street, and Building 19 at no. 20 was probably a similar development. The terrace formed by these cottages was conditioned by the shape of the plots and their boundaries and, at least in Building 19's case, led to the building of new stone boundary walls where none were available from earlier periods. By the end of the 18th century, rows of single-cell cottages had been erected at the rear of nos 12, 18 and 32 Newport Street. Brick outbuildings created from the 17th century onwards (notably the big malthouse, Building 15) led to boundary walls in brick, but no changes in position.

By the time of the Young map of 1779, the western part of the site was as built up as it would be in 1884. Only no. 16 Newport Street on the east saw significant infill between these dates, although there was some small-scale replacement and rebuilding elsewhere. Even when the first phase of the bus station was built in the early 20th century on the site of no. 32/34 Newport Street (which had been demolished in 1907), the old property divisions were respected, and the Countess of Huntingdon's School building at the rear of the plot fronting Dolday remained. It was not until the slum clearances of 1936 and the extension of the bus station that historic property boundaries started to disappear. Even so, the new area, covering all of nos 20–30 Newport Street, followed the western boundary of no. 18, with only a minor change to the south of the surviving Dolday malthouse. In 1960, property was purchased to allow the construction of All Saints' Road and the widening and realignment of Dolday, all of which completely ignored historical boundaries: removing nos 2–10 Newport Street, slicing away the northern ends of nos 12–22 and completely replacing the Dolday malthouse behind nos 14–18. Further clearance of properties at the east end of the site took place from 1978. The cleared area became a car park and then, after this excavation in 2005, was developed into flats. Little of the properties laid out in the 12th and 13th centuries now survives except possibly at the river end of Newport Street, although this has not been investigated archaeologically, and the area underwent significant change between the mappings of 1779 and 1884.

6.5 Buildings and houses
Peter Davenport

In this section an attempt is made to characterise the buildings on the site over the periods covered by the excavation. Dimensions are given first in feet and inches, with metric equivalents following, as if there is any significance in the dimensions they are more likely to be apparent in imperial measurements.

6.5.1 Period 1: Roman

There was no clear evidence for buildings in Period 1 due to the limited extent of excavation. However, fragments of masonry found in one of the northern boreholes and the general run of demolition debris in the borehole cores suggest that Roman masonry buildings may have stood here. Should the area north of the Roman street be excavated at depth, the remains of a mix of masonry and timber Roman structures may be revealed, but the present state of knowledge prevents this view from being more than a hypothesis.

6.5.2 Period 2: medieval

Structures of various kinds were found almost wherever excavation reached the relevant deposits. Little evidence for medieval timber buildings was found, but this is almost certainly because of the depth of excavation, leaving the great majority of pre-13th century levels unexplored. The areas investigated in the deeper sondages were too small to make general assumptions but suggest that building was sparse. Masonry buildings were on every plot where the relevant depths were reached, but it is very likely that the majority of the walls recorded in this period were no more than the dwarf support walls for timber frames.

Period 2.1: 10th to 11th centuries

The first structural evidence occurs as a set of earth-fast posts, none of a size to suggest more than a shed or temporary shelter, and in no coherent pattern. That actual timber survived in the waterlogged conditions indicates the considerable potential for the survival of early medieval timber structures that remains elsewhere within the site.

Period 2.3: 13th to 14th centuries

The ovens, spreads of iron slag, fragmentary cobbled surfaces and occasional isolated posthole or pad close to the street frontage suggest that in places, industry/craft processes were taking place on the plots before any substantive building was begun (or as considered below, that the earliest buildings were not necessarily on the frontage).

Plot 13, where these processes were most evident, may have been part of Plot 14 at this early period. While there is some evidence that the boundary between them was present in some form at this time, there are also indications that the same layers occurred to either side of and across this divide. Building 31 is only clearly evident away from the street frontage and is most easily interpreted as a rectangular building set back from the street, possibly with Building 32 as part of its southern end. There is no evidence that it continued to the street frontage and the existence of Building 33 in Period 2.4 seems to preclude this possibility. This suggests that activity in Plot 13 may have taken place in a yard in front of Building 31 and perhaps 32, which extended across into Plot 13. The boundary hinted at between them may at this point have been merely functional. If so, then these early buildings could have been entirely industrial, with ovens, hearths and smithing taking place both inside and in front of the structures. Therefore, Building 31 may have been built as a large workshop, 32ft wide by 20ft 9in (9.75m by 6.32m), with a substantial keyhole oven built into its eastern side and possibly open to the south. The inclusion of an oven in the east wall implies that this wall was of masonry, even if the rest may have been of timber on the stone footings. If Building 32 was also part of this building, then its combination of rough dwarf walls, drains and cobbled surfaces indicates a workshop rather than 13th or early 14th-century accommodation. The apparent intensification of smithing and a possible blacksmith shop here in Period 2.4 (below) only strengthens this interpretation. The interpretation of this group of 13th-century buildings as industrial makes it all the more surprising to note the massive use of sandstone blocks in the footings, a characteristic that, while not exclusive to these periods, seems to have been a common feature of the earliest medieval boundaries/buildings.

The other buildings of this period consist of little more than the wide stone party foundations in Plots 5 to 9. However, deposits at the north end of Building 42 in Plot 5 (no. 24 Newport Street) seem to represent the rear of a building with a narrow stone wall that probably supported a timber wall on the east, with tile and clay hearths with burnt spreads inside. The area was much truncated and dissected, but there was also some indication of an end or cross wall. If so, then the building would have been about 39ft (11.89m) long from the frontage and about 13ft (3.96m) wide. It is probably coincidence that this is a proportion of 3:1. A passage about 4ft (1.22m) wide to the east was the precursor to the post-medieval Browning's Passage.

In Plot 7, narrow stone walls were built over the wide footings and across the plot, forming the east and central cross-walls of a building that again was probably timber-framed above (Building 41), and may not have been significantly later than the broad stone foundations. A dirt floor was laid inside with a pitched-tile hearth in the northern room, on the centre line but to the north. It seems that this room was a hall at right angles to the street, probably set behind a shop on the frontage. A tile-and-stone structure in the corner was possibly an oven base but could have been a remnant of a partial floor. It probably pre-dated a re-flooring in clay and the moving of the hearth to what was a more central position. As with Building 42, Building 41 had a side passage, but this time to the west.

Period 2.4: 14th to 15th centuries

This period saw the first construction of cellars or undercrofts. Building 4 had a stone cellar built against the street frontage (Fig. 4.7). Later alterations obscured the original access but there appeared to be a blocked door from the street. The original floor seems to have been dirt. It occupied what was later part of the south end of no. 28 Newport Street, but seems likely to have been part of a building running across the whole frontage of nos 26 to 30 (Plot 3) as well as a stone hearth was laid hard against the east wall of the cellar at ground floor level. Assuming the cellar was covered over with thick clay or slabs as fireproofing over the boarding (there was no hint of vaulting), the hearth could have been central to a hall that was full width to the combined plots, with a parlour on the west and screens passage to the east, i.e. a parallel hall-house. Again, it is most probable that the building above ground level was timber-framed. No more of the building survived (but see Building 5 below) but later clay floors to the north appeared to show its extent.

At the other end of the frontage in Plot 14 was another stone building, Building 33, which certainly post-dated Buildings 31 and 32 (Fig. 4.16). It may have been a semi-sunken room, quite probably with access from the street, although this part of the building was missing. A wall of stone blocks recorded underneath the frontage of the subsequent Building 35 may have been the front wall of this phase, but was undated. The structure would have been 10ft 10in by 17ft 10in (3.30m by 5.46m) internally, and occupied half of the plot width. A wall inserted in Period 2.5 created a narrow passage on the west side, which might well have held a wooden stair, and the room also seems to have been subdivided by an east/west cross wall at this later date. The cellar was similar to and, if full length, slightly larger than Building 4's. Like Building 4, an area to one side was not cellared. An oven/hearth occupied the northern end of where the ground floor of an adjacent room might have been expected, but it seems more probable that the structure was external. Most of the rest of this area was destroyed by a later cellar. The southern extension of the west wall of Building 31 was also allocated to this period. It would have continued to the frontage and enclosed both a side and a rear yard, in which late medieval smithing took place. The side yard area was removed by the later cellar, but can be inferred.

In Plot 3, Building 5 was constructed to the rear of Building 4 (Fig. 4.7). It was slightly later in construction than Building 4 but was of contemporary use. It was a roughly square building, just under 20ft (6.10m) across internally. The stone walls were rough rubble, and, apart from the north wall that appeared to have been an earlier boundary incorporated, were rather narrow, suggesting once again that the building was timber-framed. When it was rebuilt (or repaired) the walls were raised in similar fashion, which implies the rebuild was a similar structure to the original. In the first phase, the room had three (or perhaps four) doors but no clues to function remained. When rebuilt, a pentise was added to the south door, suggesting it was a detached part of the medieval building on the plot. Its position and the late insertion of a probable bread oven strongly suggest that this was a kitchen/bakehouse, and the inclusion of a massive brick fireplace/stack in its post-medieval rebuilding strengthens the argument. It would be entirely appropriate for such a building to exist at the back of a plot that, by placing its hall parallel to the street, was making some statement of status. The bakehouse can be imagined as a large open room, at first with a central hearth, the smoke escaping up into and out of a pyramidal or heavily hipped roof. The added pentise may have lined up with a screens passage at the service end of the hall, turning the usual rural arrangement through ninety degrees to fit the constricted urban space.

The insertion of a well-built cess pit into the junction of the main room and pentise of Building 5 at the end of Period 2.5 or early 3.1 might suggest a change of use, but not necessarily, and it seems to have been a useful rubbish disposal. The contents of the last of the cess fills (as opposed to the upper backfills) seem to have been indicative of kitchen waste, especially animal bones, as well as more generally domestic material.

Period 2 Discussion
Despite the relatively uniform works of initial reclamation and boundary allocation, from the limited information available the way properties developed was much more varied and individual. Building 41 was a fully urban linear plan of a hall-behind-shop, probably with a chamber over the shop and possibly a kitchen or parlour behind the hall: a commercial design, maximising space behind a narrow frontage (Fig. 4.6). The fragments of Building 42 next door were probably from a similar building. Buildings 4 and 5, however, were an attempt to fit a full-hall plan (with separate services) across a plot: a conservative, status-claiming design, wasteful of space that may explain why this wide plot was later subdivided. The cellar was also indicative of wealth, both in its construction and in the fact that it would have been used for storing stock or valuables. It was not very large but more than respectable enough in Worcester, rather than in comparison with Southampton, Chester or Norwich.

By contrast, Building 31/32 was completely industrial in its earlier phases and may not have had any residential accommodation, although we do not know what was at the rear of the plot. Like Plot 3, Plot 14 was wide and, although not as extravagant, the amount of effort put into the construction of its buildings was no less remarkable. The structural investment speaks of wealth, and the presence of Saintonge ware in late medieval rubbish dumps in Plot 13 indicates access to imported goods.

The above-ground parts of these buildings were most likely timber-framed, and probably of two storeys, while the halls, however small, would have been open and essentially of one floor. Later rebuilds visible in topographic views and old photographs were also mostly two-storey, even if the documentation usually refers to lofts as well.

6.5.3 Period 3: post-medieval (*c.* 1550–1700)

Period 3.1/3.2: 16th to mid 17th century
The only substantive buildings certainly of this phase

were along Dolday: Buildings 1, 2 and 11. Building 19, at the rear of no. 20 Newport Street, was probably a little later, but was not well-dated. The fragmentary remains of Building 22 (Plot 10) also may belong to this phase. The building techniques had changed little from the previous period and brick, which might have been expected to have made an appearance, was still absent.

The buildings on Dolday were uncertain as to purpose. Building 1a (Fig. 4.8) may well have been the 'hemp house' referred to in 1554 and therefore was a warehouse or storehouse. Its stone walls were slightly sunk into the contemporary surface and again almost certainly supported a timber superstructure. They were, in the small area investigated, set on deeply driven timber piles. The lack of any surviving superstructure or floor means that the function of the building is unclear, but loading from the yard to the side seems possible and a storage loft on an upper floor seems likely. Clearly, this property was in the hands of an affluent businessman. William Dodynge was a walker, or fuller, who held the tenement from at least 1534 until his death in 1554. His will shows that his house, on the Newport Street frontage (beyond the excavated area) had a hall with a hearth and a parlour with a chimney. A shop with 'sheres, handells and presse' also existed. By the standards of the time, the house was well furnished with 'cubords, tabulls & hangyns … and rownde tabulls'. There was a garden, which must have been between the house and the hemp house. The property descended to his nephew, Thomas Dodynge, who was not such a good businessman. By 1576 he had forfeited his lease for non-payment of rent but was allowed to renew 'considering the great loss and decay that the said Thomas Dodynge hath susteyned sundry ways, [the landlord] having pitie on him his wyffe and many children'.

Buildings 2 and 11 (Figs 4.8 and 4.9) were similar in that their footings were built of sandstone blocks. There was no evidence of a stone or brick superstructure, and the buildings were probably timber-framed. Building 2 had a pebble floor in the south side and a solid cobbled floor on the part that projected into Dolday. It is tempting to think that this was a loading hardstanding, but equally could have been part of a stable floor or workshop. The building was just over 30ft (9.14m) wide and more than that north to south (its northern limit was not seen). It would have worked well as a cart house and stable, but there was no direct evidence for this. Building 11 was smaller and its clay floors perhaps more indicative of low-status housing. The rear wall subsided, which suggests a heavier load than a timber wall, unless there was a soft patch under the wall. It was not excavated, but doubts about the bearing capacity of the ground here are indicated by the piling under Building 1a. Hughes (Chapter 2.3) suggests that this part of the plot was in low-status occupation in the late 16th and early 17th centuries, having already been separated from the southern half of the holding.

In 1978, nos 16 and 18 Newport Street were inspected by N. Molyneux prior to their demolition and substantial elements of probable 16th-century timber framing were found and recorded (Hughes, Chapter 5.1.7, Fig. 5.5). Other timber-framed buildings in Newport Street, photographed in the 1930s, were also likely to have been of this period (Figs 2.10–2.12). Nos 16 and 18 Newport Street were traditional, oak-framed, jettied houses, but relatively economical in the use of timber. Their side walls were panelled rather than close-studded. No. 16 was certainly only two-storeyed and no. 18 probably was as well. Both presumably had a gabled loft but wall-plates from both were missing, which would have indicated whether there had been another floor. No. 18 was clearly a two-chamber over kitchen-and-parlour plan, with no sign of an original rear wing in the recorded standing fabric, though a low one could have existed on footings recorded during excavation as Building 26 (Fig. 4.17). There is what may be a description of this house in a probate inventory from 1717 before it was rebuilt as a Georgian house (Hughes, Chapter 5.1.7). This gives us, on the ground floor, a kitchen, hall and a 'hawl' and parlour and a new parlour, plus an enigmatic reference to a shop ('the little house in the shop', which may mean a rear workshop with accommodation), and a stable. On the first floor there was a forestreet chamber, a middle chamber and a chamber over the kitchen, indicating that the kitchen was at the rear, then there was an upper loft. Leaving aside the 'hawl', which may be a mistaken repeat, this gives four rooms on the ground floor. The hall was, by this stage, probably a single storey room under the middle chamber. The new parlour would have been an addition to the rear, the shop to the front (unless it was a rear workshop, as suggested above). Archaeologically, the rear part of the house may be represented by Building 26, the southern stone wall of which seems to have been the footings for the rear wall of the timber frame, so the northern one could have been part of one or more rooms to the rear. This is a clear example of a stone footing supporting a timber frame, as has been suggested for numerous other buildings on site where only the footing remained. Here the stone footing was clearly all below ground level, and the same can be inferred for no. 24 Newport Street. No. 16 was a similar building, being slightly longer but narrower. No evidence for this building was found during excavation, but the cellar recorded in the inspection of 1978 was very similar to Building 4's, as excavated in Plot 3 (Hughes, Chapter 5.1.7; Fig. 5.5).

Nos 24, 26 and 28 Newport Street were either entirely or partly timber-framed, and all of the same style. No. 24 sat on earlier (Period 2.3) stone footings, which again remained entirely subterranean, while nos 26 and 28 (and presumably no. 30, from what little could be seen in the excavation) used some of the old footings, but used brick for new cellars and presumably for the footings of completely new rear wings, for which there was no evidence. Photographs of these buildings taken in the 1930s show coursed brick panel infill in the majority of the walls. However, there are also hints of wattle and daub infill, suggesting that may have been the original fill, and implying that brick infill was a later replacement.

All these buildings were aligned and roofed at right angles to the street frontage. The three buildings of nos 26–30 Newport Street occupied the site of earlier Building 4, showing that by this stage Plot 3 was now three separate holdings running back from the street (Fig. 4.9). Despite their superficial similarities evident from old photographs and records, these buildings were all rather different, as can be seen clearly in the plans drawn up by the city surveyor prior to purchase for demolition in the 1930s (Hughes, Chapter 5.1.7). No. 26 was a small, square structure on the frontage with no rear wing, and a large part of its tiny footprint was taken up with a passage to a rear court. At the rear of this plot, the old kitchen (Building 5) was completely rebuilt in brick with a huge fireplace in its north-west corner. By this stage it must have been a freestanding bakery or brewhouse rather than a kitchen (Table 4.1). The passageway along its eastern side was arched. No. 28 was a rather large house with a rear wing running right back to the north end of the plot (although the final extension to the northern end of the plot may well belong to Period 4 or 5). It had cross-gables fronting on to the court and was jettied (Hughes Chapter 2.3, Figs 2.10–2.12). There is even a hint in the photographs of cusped bracing. This all suggests a fairly high-status design, at least in the context of Newport Street. This house must have overlain the hearths attributed to Period 3.1/3.2, and therefore a 17th rather than a 16th-century date seems appropriate, but surely no later than 1650. No. 30 Newport Street had three storeys on the frontage, which may have been compensation for being on a narrower tenement that continued to narrow to the rear. In the mid 17th century, this house was occupied by a cobbler whose widow was still in occupation in 1719. The probate inventory does not refer to a third storey beyond a top loft, which is puzzling. Otherwise, a shop and kitchen on the ground floor, and a room over each, fit well with the size and appearance of the structure. It is most unlikely that the upper floor (if an addition) was added after about 1670. Sash windows and under-built shop fronts on all three of these buildings date from the 18th century. Illustrations of no. 32/34 Newport Street, which was not excavated, show identical houses, suggesting they were rebuilt at the same time as no. 30, possibly as part of the same development (Figs 2.12, 5.1, 5.4)

Fragments of wall foundation and a back-to-back fireplace in what would have been an internal timber cross-wall, represent Building 20, another rebuilt house of this period at no. 20 Newport Street (Fig. 4.8). This was almost certainly another timber-framed structure. The position of the fireplace is typical of the experimental nature of urban house planning in the early to mid 17th century, party-wall and corner fireplaces being more usual by late 17th and 18th centuries. At the eastern end of the excavation in Plot 14, Buildings 31 and 33 were also rebuilt in brick at this time (or possibly, as Building 34, in Period 3.3), confirming this phase as a period of widespread rebuilding in Newport Street.

Period 3.3: late 17th century

With the exception of Building 22 at the rear of no. 18 Newport Street, the infilling of the rear areas with buildings seems to have started in this period, or at least, evidence does not survive from earlier.

Building 22 (Fig. 4.17) is enigmatic. Its wide rubble footings suggest a masonry superstructure. Building 14 at the rear of no. 22 Newport Street (Fig. 4.9) probably represents the cottages built in the 1650s, only one of which had more than one hearth in 1678, indicating their lowly (and residential) status. Previously the land had been garden, showing that this was the beginnings of infill at the rear of the plot. The character of Building 19, to the rear of No. 20 Newport Street (Fig. 4.10), is less clear, the rear oven suggesting a kitchen or workshop, but nevertheless it is another example of infilling on an open rear area, the limited evidence allowing the reconstruction of three small compartments against the eastern boundary wall. In Plot 1, Building 1b was rebuilt in brick in the late 17th century or early 18th, using the lower walls of Building 1a as footings, and was clearly used for storage or as some kind of workshop. Photographic evidence shows it was of two full storeys, but its appearance is otherwise unknown (Hughes, Chapter 2.3; Figs 2.10–2.12).

The major development of this phase was Building 15, a purpose-built, industrial-scale malthouse to the rear of no. 22 Newport Street, along with the probably slightly later Building 16. The former was in existence by 1698, and was probably then new. It was a very considerable investment and mortgages seem to have been raised to pay for it. It was of two storeys plus a roof space (it survived into the 1930s) and built of brick but was raised on new stone footings set over timber piles. It extended over the whole of the rear of the tenement, with access from Dolday, although there is a possibility that it was at first shorter, and was later extended to the Dolday frontage. The large brick oven at the southern end of the building was also set on a piled foundation, and presumably sent warm air across the sprouting floors at first and possibly attic levels. The ground floor was extensively paved in brick (like Building 1b). Part of the ground floor was presumably used for grinding the malted grain, and large brick platforms may have been the bases for mills. Two malt-grinding mills are mentioned in a will of 1719 for this property (Hughes, Chapter 5.1.6). Large millstones of the kind used in powered mills were found capping Period 3 to 5 wells (e.g. Fig. 4.39) but it is not clear how they could have been used in the narrow confines of Building 15 before steam power. There was no room for animal gins in the malthouse. A smaller structure may have been an oven for roasting the germinated barley. A house seems to have been intended at the southern end from the beginning, and Building 16 was added to this probably in the early 18th century (Fig. 4.11). This integral building was set under the same roof, and was probably for the malthouse 'manager', the actual owner living in the frontage houses.

Period 3 Discussion

Whatever the exact arrangements were of the medieval buildings of Period 2, and we have seen that they were probably varied, post-medieval Period 3 saw widespread rebuilding of the frontage properties and the increased development of their rear areas, it seems the former followed by the latter. The frontages still contained commercial premises, with the owners living over and behind the shop (e.g. Thomas Hill, clothier, with looms in his house at no. 24 Newport Street in the mid 17th century; and Thomas Writer, baker, with bakehouse and cornlofts as well as well-appointed accommodation, at no. 32/34), but it is clear that some owners were living in wholly residential property with the commercial elements banished to the rear, the malthouse at no. 22 Newport Street being the clearest example, and late in the sequence. Poorer occupants held the tenements to the rear: details of these are elusive but are hardly likely to have been better than the courts built in the following century. One heated room was the norm, and one room altogether may have been common for the poorest. Brick was being used increasingly, probably exclusively by 1700, but was rare in cheap housing before that date.

6.5.4 Period 4: 18th century

This is the period when Newport Street acquired the appearance and to some extent the character that is known from old photographs and other topographical sources. All of the houses to the east of no. 26 were rebuilt or refronted in brick, and rear ranges added or extended. For example, no. 18 (Fig. 4.20) was rebuilt in brick, leaving much of the timber frame of its predecessor in place, and with an extra storey and a long rear wing added, in the first half of the century (after 1717). This was in part to provide a new brewhouse for the tavern business and a small number of one-up one-down cottages. The brewhouse replaced one described in 1717 (when the house was still the Period 3.1 structure) with a shop, presumably with the 'bar', at the front. At the rear of the plot was a stable, with access only via the side passage. The stable was big enough for two horses and had a hayloft, but no vehicle could have been taken into the back yard. Another stable and a coach-house is mentioned behind no. 26 Newport Street in Court 4 (Fig. 4.11), which must have been on the site of the then demolished Building 5, and while vehicular access would have been possible, it would also have been extremely tight. No. 16 Newport Street was simply refronted and a new brick kitchen built on the rear. The Prince of Wales public house (no. 20 Newport Street) was completely rebuilt in brick, probably a little earlier, to four storeys, with a large, brick-cellared range at the rear. A similar process took place later in the century at no. 14. In fact, the only houses in the whole of Newport Street that were not rebuilt or refronted in the 18th century were nos 26–34. The reasons for rebuilding were various, but a desire for more room must have been one of them. The descriptions of earlier period houses show that they had an adequate number of rooms, but the Georgian fashion was for larger and airier rooms and the rebuilt houses certainly provided this. The local brick Georgian vernacular was the style chosen everywhere, but up-to-date nuances were followed.

At the rear of the properties, development largely took the form of cramming as many small, cheap houses as possible into the space available, forming the courts. Although the tenements at the back of no. 22 Newport Street were demolished to allow the construction of the malthouse, at least 20 small, brick, single-cell cottages of up to three-storeys were erected in the rear of properties during this period, and six more were erected in the early years of the 19th century. These were of low quality, with shared wash-houses and privies, and often reached from Dolday. They feature on the 1884 OS maps and in early 20th-century photographs. Examples from the excavation were Buildings 3, 12, 23 and 36, but none survived well enough to enable a study of their interiors. Building 16 was a multipurpose structure in the early 18th century, being both a house but with a workshop on the ground floor.

Period 4 Discussion

Period 4 was characterised by a change to the almost exclusive use of brick and the adoption of Georgian style and proportions. The rear areas of the properties were heavily exploited for cheap housing and industry, and there was a noticeable concentration on malting. This was the last significant structural change until the demolitions of the 20th century.

6.5.5 Period 5: 19th to mid 20th century

Replacement of buildings in this period, until the creation of the Bus Station from 1922, was rare. To the north of the excavation area, a malthouse was built in 1770 behind nos 14–18 Newport Street on a strip between Dolday and the 17th-century warehouse of Abraham Lingham (Fig. 5.3). The older building was removed between 1884 and 1922, but the Dolday block remained into the 1970s. Photographs suggest a construction date around 1860–80, so it must have been rebuilt in Period 5. No. 12 Newport Street was completely rebuilt in the 1920s. Building 1b and the cottages in Court 6 behind it were replaced by the Countess of Huntingdon's School in 1907–9, and this remained until the late 20th century.

However, the buildings that survived changed considerably in use and status. Nos 20 and 22 Newport Street are good examples. In the early 18th century, no. 20 was occupied by John Sowden, a considerable businessman, who also owned no. 22. In the earlier 19th century until 1841, the latter was occupied by small businessmen/traders. It was inherited by a daughter, Elizabeth Webb, school teacher, who sold it in 1854. By 1936, when it was compulsorily purchased and demolished, the house was divided into two back-to-backs, no. 20 was let out to three families and the two houses in Court 3 (Building 16 and the house at the south end of Building 15) were unfit for human habitation and bug-ridden. Nos 24–32 seem to have undergone similar declines, although these had never had the improvements of the 18th century. Building 5 was replaced by a stable before 1884. No. 30 was in private owner-occupation in the 1920s, and had been since the late 19th century at least, but was in such poor condition that it was compulsorily purchased by the corporation as unfit for human occupation (Hughes, Chapter 5.1.4). Other properties along the frontage were in a similarly poor structural condition, evidence of the lack of maintenance flowing from their low values at this time (Hughes, Chapter 5.1.6).

One set of changes that was evident in both the archaeology and the documents was the attempt to improve sanitation in the later 19th and early 20th century. No clear signs of mains water supply were evident, although the provision of mains sewage and WCs in this period rather assumes a good supply. Pumped well water was still common in 1884, but had probably largely vanished by 1936 when no reference to it is made: the compulsory purchase maps of 1936 show a good provision of (outdoor) WCs and wash-houses to the tenements in the rear courts, and where they are absent, in Courts 3 and 4 for example, were presumably internal to the houses. Differences in plan between 1884 and 1936 suggest, as might reasonably be suspected, that this was the period in which most sanitary improvements were made, following on from the establishment of local boards of sanitation and the improved arrangements for local government, especially under the Acts of 1875 and 1894.

The low property values and poor condition of the buildings made the purchase of parts of the site for a new bus station, from 1922 and its extension in the late 1930s, all the easier. Urban design philosophies of the 1960s facilitated the creation of All Saints' Road, and the remaining historic properties were cleared in the early 1980s for the creation of a car park.

6.6 Industry and craft
Peter Davenport

The information on trade and industry from the Roman period is fairly one-dimensional, with vast dumps of ironworking slag implying a sort of monoculture. Evidence from other sites in the vicinity suggests these were the result of a widespread iron-smelting industry and detailed discussion of the evidence of iron production and ironworking in Roman Worcester can be found elsewhere (e.g. McDonnell and Swiss 2004). There is little evidence for smithing and the majority of the evidence is for the dumping of smelting slags in the later Roman period, which corresponds with the limited evidence from Newport Street. Unlike other Roman excavations in Worcester there is no evidence for other late Roman industries in the immediate vicinity, although this might change should more extensive excavation take place.

6.6.1 Period 2: medieval

For the medieval period, it is reasonable to assume that the colonisation of the Newport Street suburb was an economically-driven decision, and that properties were laid out on the reclaimed floodplain with the aim of making a living for the occupants and owners. However, unlike in the Roman period, where iron smelting seems to have formed the basis of the economy, it is not immediately obvious exactly what the 'business plan' was. It simply may have been the desire to collect an enhanced income from the land on the part of the landowners.

Post-medieval records make it clear that the river was a convenient source of water for dyers and fullers (as well as a useful sewer), and it was probably these trades that were uppermost in the minds of medieval developers, and which certainly became the economic engine for the area. The earliest references to dyers, walkers (fullers) and tanners are in the 1356 tax returns, and there are also references to shoemakers, presumably taking advantage of the ready supply of leather. Positioning them in the street is not easy, but fullers were certainly down at the river end on the south side of Newport Street by the later 14th century (Hughes, Chapter 2.3). Later information suggests that dyers clustered down by the river, and the same must be true for fullers who needed a good supply of clean water. The presence of the tanners is inferred from the fact that they were banned from the area in 1466, because of the filth and stench. There are references to clothiers in the 16th century but there is no known medieval documentation of occupations for the properties further away from the river, unless William le Horner and John le Pynnare, lessees mentioned in a document of 1317 for no. 32/34 Newport Street, were a hornworker and pinmaker respectively (WCL. B1114), although they need not have occupied the land themselves nor carried on their trade there. For the properties investigated archaeologically the only evidence for medieval trade comes from the excavation itself, which is rather limited but more varied than the documentary evidence implies.

In view of the later evidence for dyers, it is intriguing to see that dyer's rocket (a plant used to provide a yellow dye) occurred in the 10th or 11th century (Period 2.1). It was identified from an alluvial deposit that contained a large variety of plants of mixed origin, some river-margin/boggy-land plants and others more suggestive of gardens and orchards, perhaps indicating flood deposits that had incorporated material from either a midden or a garden. Thus, dyers' rocket may well have been cultivated and could have been grown in a garden. However flax was also present in this deposit and, if cultivated for linen, requires a larger area, the crop not being an urban one. Its association in this deposit, and in a 14th or 15th-century pit (Period 2.4), with cereal seeds and weeds of cultivation suggests that it arrived as a crop rather than as a local product. Alternatively, the presence of flax seeds in these deposits may be a by-product of flax retting (to separate the fibres prior to processing for cloth) in the river or in ponds or pits, or perhaps the seeds were for oil production. In any case, dyeing materials were available in the 11th to 12th centuries, and it is probable that either linen or linseed oil was being produced. These plant remains were introduced to the site before the area was properly colonised, and so may be hinting as to how the area was used before it was formally developed.

Medieval animal bone (particularly cattle bone from a pit in Plot 13) was predominantly skull and foot fragments, suggesting that the tanning was already underway in the 11th to 12th centuries, although the quantity and proportion of these bones is not enough to show conclusively that tanning took place here (Warman, Chapter 5.24). The majority of other bone recovered (humerus) seems to represent a particular, good quality cut of beef. There were no recognisable structural features or other evidence from the excavation to indicate tanning, and the presence of this industry on the site cannot be confirmed with any certainty.

Period 2.3: 13th to 14th centuries

The earliest ovens and hearths are attributed to this period, although these functions are plausible rather than proved. Only one oven was complete enough to make its identification certain, rather than the base for a structure such as a dye vat, which was the small beehive oven G44 Plot 5 (Fig. 4.6). It was only large enough to cook a couple of loaves at a time so could not have been a baker's commercial oven. The much larger but less well-preserved oven G43 was set up to replace this. With an inside dimension of about 1m either way, this could well have been for commercial use. Similar-sized ovens were built in Period 2.3 in Plot 7, along with two broadly contemporary hearths, one of which could have been an oven base. To the east (Fig. 4.15), further Period 2.3 oven-like structures were built in Plot 14 (oven G203, built against the plot boundary like the others) and in Plot 13 (oven G357, which occupied the plot frontage and seems to have been replaced twice over in Periods 2.4 and 2.5).

Such a large number of ovens, built in the earliest stages of the built occupation of the area, seems too great to have simply supplied bread or other baked or roasted food commercially. The structures make more sense if interpreted as dye-vat hearths. However, for a ring-wall around a hearth to have supported a large hemispherical metal vat with enough water in it to dye broad cloth, about a tonne in weight, it would had to have been very well made. The 0.3m-thick rough rubble-and-clay circular wall around oven base G146 (one of the rebuilds of oven G357 in Plot 13) is unlikely to have been able to take such a load, but could easily have been the base of a clay-domed oven. Among the better preserved examples from this period, only oven G203 in Plot 14 was sturdy enough to support such a weight. It is also possible that hearths for this process might have been less robust than the later designs, or smaller and more abundant. Tanks for the cold-water fixing process using a mordant were not recognised. Such is the interpretation of a 12th-century wooden vat at Beverley, which had arrangements for channelling liquid into it and no hearth under it (Evans and Tomlinson 1992). A more likely possibility at Newport Street is that these ovens were used to roast malted barley for beer; a few waterlogged barley grains were found in a pit dug both physically and temporally between the ovens in Plot 13. A stone quern (Fig. 5.28, 5) found built into the 14th-century wall of oven 1507 (G139) in Plot 13, although redundant at that point, might indicate the preparation of malt flour or bread flour, the former slightly more likely as handmilling corn was outlawed in the 12th century (Roe 2004, 472). A similar quern was found in an exactly similar context of 13th-century date (1840; G357). In the post-medieval period, malting was carried on at both industrial and domestic scales. Another possibility, given the presence of horncore and skull fragments, is that horns were being heated in ovens to facilitate the removal of the keratin sheath (Wenham 1965). However, no horn-shaving residues or other evidence of hornworking was noted during excavation.

Period 2.4: 14th to 15th centuries

An activity for which there is plenty of evidence in Period 2.4, at least in Plots 13 and 14, is smithing (Fig. 4.16). In Plot 14, Building 31 was converted to a forge in Period 2.4, with hammerscale and smithing hearth bottoms present. These were also present in rather unstructured Period 2.3 spreads, suggesting an earlier phase of smithing activity before the forge was built. No coal was recorded so charcoal is assumed to have been the fuel, and carbonised wood was very common in the clay spreads and floors close by. As well as a (probable) raised hearth, a number of floor-level hearths were recorded in the forge. These may represent subsidiary hearths or furnaces for tempering, heating water for quenching, or for assistants to finish forged work. It is possible that they were used for preparing fuel, but the absence of any large concentrations of charcoal waste makes this unlikely. Raised hearths are known from at least the 14th century (Geddes 1991, 175). Evidence for a smithy and smithing was identified slightly earlier at Deansway Site 2 (periods 8.2 and 8.3: 12th to 13th century), with yard/floor surfaces and hearths with hammerscale, and pit fills and dumps with waste products such as hearth bottoms (Dalwood and Edwards 2004, 63–6, 139–47). The remains of oven G224/225 in poor condition, suggest that the area to the east of Building 33 was used for other purposes. This oven was different to the others, being rectangular externally and circular internally, but there were no clues as to its function.

Ovens continued to be built and renewed in this period, but still without clear evidence of their function. One craft that was apparent in the archaeological remains was cordwaining, or shoe manufacture. Specific cuts of waste leather and part of a shoe from a pit in Plot 13 provided good evidence for shoe manufacture in the vicinity. The remains are typical of later medieval shoe-manufacturing techniques, and suggest that a shoemaker was in residence at no. 14 Newport Street in the 14th to 15th century. The rubbish pit in which the waste was found and the continuing presence of ovens at the front of the plot, suggest that a permanent building still had not been erected on this part of the plot at this date. A repaired late medieval shoe fragment was also found in the late medieval cess pit at Building 5 at no. 26 (Plot 3), but this was evidence of no more than professional shoe repair, not manufacture.

Period 2.5: 15th to 16th centuries

Two large 'ovens' were built in this period, both of which may have been dye-vat hearths. Oven G368 in Plot 5 was well enough built to have supported a dye vat (Fig. 4.7). This had solidly built tile walls over 1ft thick and was reinforced by its position against a boundary wall: a subsidiary side wall and its slightly oval plan resulting in a buttressing effect to the north and south. It was provided with an extensive pitched tile apron, flooring the area to the north. There was no direct evidence for its function, but the complete absence of seeds of any kind from its fills and associated deposits makes its use as an industrial-scale bread oven seem improbable. Plot 5 (no. 24 Newport Street) was in the occupation of the clothiers (the Hills) in the first two-thirds of the 17th century, but there is no known documentary evidence surviving earlier than this. The other candidate is structure G325 in Plot 8 (no. 20 Newport Street), which was much less well preserved and only partly excavated as it was at the lowest limit of excavation. Nonetheless, it seemed substantial enough to be considered as a possible dye-vat base. Its broadly circular or keyhole shape (for the stokehole) with a pitched stone or tile base seems to have been a 14th-century invention (Newman 2001, 144). These are the first such bases found in excavation in Worcester (Hal Dalwood, pers. comm.) but the type is widely distributed, with examples, *inter alia*, being found in London, Bristol, East Anglia and the north (Walton 1991, 337). A series of keyhole-shaped stone hearths was uncovered at the Courage Brewery site in Bristol (Jackson 2006, 20–5) and their backfills contained 13th to 14th-century pottery. The excavator considered them to be of 14th-century date, but the sequence could have begun quite early in the possible date range. They were considered to be probably dye-vat hearths, as post-medieval dyeing is attested on the site. Further well-preserved examples were found at nos 1–2 Redcliff Street and no. 3 Redcliff Street, Bristol, in an area known to have been occupied by dyers in the middle ages (Hart forthcoming; Davenport forthcoming). A late medieval hearth of slightly different design was recorded in a dyehouse with a brick-paved working area in front of the hearth at Westwick Street, Norwich (Walton 1991, fig. 174). Again there is no known documentary evidence other than that clothiers (who were definitely weavers) were in occupation at no. 20 Newport Street in the late 16th century. Clothiers were certainly in occupation in the area when documents start to survive for this part of Newport Street in the 16th century, but no dyers *per se*. It may be that in the late middle ages, the dyers had moved nearer to the river, where they seem to have concentrated (Hughes, Chapter 2.3), and weavers and fullers occupied the tenements further away. The recovery of medieval-style spindle whorls from hand distaffs from Period 2.4 and 2.5 contexts (both associated with Building 4 in Plot 3), and another unstratified, provides evidence for the spinning of yarn for weaving. This is hardly an unexpected activity in a medieval household under any circumstances but ties in with the later, 16th-century references to cloth being stored in clothiers' houses and the occupation of Building 4 by a weaver in the mid 16th century (Hughes, Chapter 2.3).

The recovery of a turned wooden bowl from Period 2.5 cess pit S263 provides evidence of wood turning, and the early post-medieval probate inventories often mention treen (wooden household implements), but there was no other evidence of wood turning or other carpentry skills from the site in the middle ages, outside of those implied by the existence of timber-framed buildings. Neither was there any evidence for medieval pottery manufacture from the site, but the pattern of supply of pottery over this period has some implications for the local pottery industry and trade. In Periods 2.1 to 2.3, local Worcester-type pottery was predominant, but was gradually supplanted by Malvernian wares and had all but vanished by the end of Period 2.5. Obviously a local industry had died off, but there must also have been a business in transporting and marketing the pottery from the new kilns.

6.6.2 Period 3: post-medieval (*c.* 1550–1700)

For the post-medieval period there is documentary evidence for trades but there was not a lot more archaeological evidence. It is clear that clothiers were predominant in the 16th century. The Parkers, described as weavers, were known at nos 26–30 Newport Street from 1558; the same family were there back to 1534 and almost certainly in the same business, and remained at the property until 1624 or so. Thomas Hill was at no. 20 Newport Street until 1596, where his looms are specifically mentioned, and his son or grandson Thomas was a weaver at no. 24 Newport Street until 1662. This later Thomas was the last known clothier in Newport Street. He had a shop, projecting into the street, and also owned large amounts of other property along the street, suggesting other income when the cloth trade was declining. Another clothworker was William Dodynge, a fuller whose success in the mid 16th century may have been due to having more than one iron in the fire. It was he who was, in some sense, trading in or working hemp, with his large 'hemp house' on Dolday (Building 1a). As well as rope and sacking, hemp cloth was a good substitute for linen or cotton and there are references to 29 hemp sheets in John Lilly's inventory of 1690 at no. 12 Newport Street (Plot 14). Jone Parker also had timber in his 'work house' in 1558, as well as wool in the house on Plot 3, perhaps exemplifying the need for diversification as the cloth trade became less profitable.

William Dodynge's nephew, Thomas, who inherited the house and business at no. 32/34 Newport Street in 1576, was a less successful clothier, this time a weaver. By 1601 this property was leased to Thomas Writer, a baker. Baking and brewing seem to have been the trades of the 17th century, and traditional clothiers had all but vanished from this part of Newport Street, appearing in documents as owners from time to time but in only one case as occupants running their trade from the address (the second Thomas Hill, above). For example, the clothier John Rea acquired Writer's plot (no. 32/34 Newport Street, Plot 1) in 1674 but it remained leased to a baker. Indeed this particular property remained a baker's until the end of the 18th century at least. By the mid 17th century, bakers were also at nos 22 and 24 Newport Street, as well as further down the street at no. 36. While no archaeological evidence for bakers' ovens or other indications of their presence were found at no. 32/34 Newport Street, the group of well-made pitched-tile bases of ovens at the rear of no. 22 are most likely to refer to this activity at this time (Fig. 4.9). It is probable that more than one was in existence at any time, but there was also evidence for replacement. Only fragments survived but the two largest were at least 1.9m long and over 0.8m wide internally. Unlike the earlier oval or keyhole-shaped ovens, these appear to have been rectangular in plan, better fitted to use in bakehouses. Just to the north of these ovens, structure S361 was a well-preserved tile construction that appears to be a large, early 17th-century square oven, with hints of a tile-vaulted roof, but was rather enigmatic. Bakehouses are referred to in documents for no. 32/34 Newport Street in the mid 17th century, but most references are from the 18th century. Building 9, at the rear of no. 24 Newport Street, was another possible early post-medieval bakehouse (Fig. 4.8) but was too truncated by later disturbance for the evidence to be conclusive.

One clothier who did spectacularly well in the 17th century was the silk weaver, John Lilly. He owned nos 10–12 Newport Street and left over £500 when he died in 1690. His property included a brewhouse, in which was 'a furnace with lead about him'. A lead-wrapped oven sounds unlikely and may refer to associated lead-lined troughs and trays. Kettles and testing equipment are also mentioned. A keyhole-plan oven (G267; Fig. 4.19) built of brick was found at the rear of this property during excavation, dated to the 17th or 18th century. It sat adjacent to brick Building 34, also of this period, and probably sat in a southern part of this building which was not represented archaeologically but was mapped in 1779 and 1886 (Figs 2.7 and 2.14). The only other circular oven of this period was G331 at the rear of no. 20 Newport Street (Fig. 4.19), but this was isolated from any contemporary structures.

Malting is something that came to the fore archaeologically at the end of 17th century (Period 3.3) with construction of the malthouse (Building 15) at the rear of no. 22 Newport Street, which occupied more than half of the plot (Fig. 4.10). In the following decades the northern side of the properties to the east of Building 15 were also given over to malthouses, and this became the predominant industry here until the early 20th century. That these malthouses included breweries to complete the process is an example of the intensification of capitalistic investment at this time. A brewhouse was part of Building 15 and the equally extensive malthouses built on Dolday, east of Building 15, also had an associated brewhouse along the Dolday frontage. The scale of the process is apparent from the size of the (coal-fired) oven installed in the malthouse at no. 22. With an internal measurement of 2.5m by 3m, it probably warmed a first-floor malting floor of either around 84m² or an additional 70m², depending on how the first floor is interpreted. Thomas Haden took over the malthouse at the beginning of the 18th century. His probate inventory also gives an idea of the scale of the operation: he had in store over a ton and a quarter of hops, 39 bushels of barley and over £172 worth of malt. He also had two malt mills and hoppers. Worn out millstones (of a size to require mechanical or animal power) were used to cap wells in the malthouse in succeeding periods (Crawford, Chapter 5.12.2). He also had £133 worth of wheat, and over £26 worth of meal and coarse corn from his continuing bakery business. His sons continued the public house into the late 18th century and it continued as such until 1907 (Hughes, Chapter 5.1.5).

Rather stronger alcoholic drinks were also being prepared at this time in Newport Street by Edward Hurdman, who inherited Thomas Hill's looms in 1662 but set up as a distiller at no. 24. He had a shop and a distilling furnace as well as a brewing furnace. Another distiller set up at no. 12 in the 18th century (Period 4). Spirits and 'waters' also had medicinal and prophylactic uses. A 17th-century cess pit at the rear of no. 24 contained seed remains of currants, and other fruits and rose (Pearson, Chapter 5.23.1), all possible ingredients in Hurdman's products. The general level of wealth implied by the variety of relatively unusual fruits from this cess pit is high, or at least very comfortable and, if they were not waste from the distillery, fit well with the status of the successful tradesmen who were the occupiers of this plot in the 17th and early 18th century.

An important industry that began in the 17th century was the production of clay tobacco pipes, after the introduction of tobacco smoking in the late 16th century. There is no evidence that pipes were made on the site, nor reason to think they may have been, but the products of the industry were common among the finds of Periods 3 and 4. It is clear that, in common with the rest of the county, smoking tobacco only became at all common during the second quarter of the 17th century (Peacey, Chapter 5.15). Worcester clay pipe manufacturers are not noted until after 1650 but pipemakers are known in the town for the rest of the century, and again in the 19th century. There seems to be a gap in the documentation in the 18th century, when no named pipemakers are currently known from Worcester. If this represents a real absence of 18th-century Worcester pipemakers, then the city must have been supplied from the known nearby manufacturing centres such as Broseley, Pipe Aston and Gloucester, and even from Bristol, whose products were found in the excavation. However, some forms found suggest an (as yet) unknown production site in the city or nearby at this period (Peacey, Chapter 15.15.1) and the complete disappearance of the industry from the city, only to reappear in the 1820s, seems unlikely.

6.6.3 Period 4: 18th century

Benjamin Perkins, distiller, succeeded Hurdman at no. 12 Newport Street from 1708 to before 1747. Little is known of him or his activities, although he made various alterations to the frontage which required purpresture payments (Hughes, Chapter 5.1.8).

A brewhouse was something that most houses in Newport Street seemed to have in the 18th century, and their active use is obvious by occasional references to hops, hogsheads of beer or brewing vessels. Copper furnaces are referred to on several occasions, and once an iron boiler. It is likely that most of these brewhouses were for production of beer for private consumption, so not actually for trade. Nonetheless, the quantities of beer in some of the probate inventories rival those of the public houses. The Red Lion had 235 gallons of ale in its brewhouse in 1717, and the Hope and Anchor had 270 (some spoiled) in 1671. Compared to this John Lilly, silk weaver and owner of nos 10–12 Newport Street in 1690, had 189 gallons. Stead the baker, at no. 32, had 180 gallons in 1709 and Cozens, the successor to Lilly at no. 12 and also a wealthy silk merchant, had 90 gallons in 1727. At first these seem large amounts, but these were for a whole household and constituted the staple drink. It did not keep well (hence the spoiled beer at the Hope and Anchor) and it is likely that these volumes represented no more than a month or two's consumption. If we assume that Stead's supply was for two months for the whole household, three gallons a day (total) is not so high for domestic consumption. On the other hand, carpenter John Kinsey had £40 worth of ale in his cellar at no. 22 in 1722, which is a huge stock. If he was running an alehouse it was as an adjunct to his active joinery and coffin-making business. Nevertheless, brewing was an important and regular activity, even for those who made no income from it.

Nothing certain remained archaeologically of these brewing activities, although it is likely that Buildings 13, 17, 21, 23, 30, 34 and 40 were among the structures erected or adapted to house them. The enclosed well yard at the rear of no. 20 Newport Street may also have been created to serve this function.

Building 1b in Plot 1 (Fig. 4.10) was late 17th or 18th century (Periods 3.3 or 4) but its function remains mysterious. Stratigraphically below the floor, but not actually sealed by surviving elements, was set a group of upright iron bars. In the centre of the room was a pit with two stout brick walls lining it that rose above the floor, probably an addition but not later than Period 4. These fittings suggest the installation of machinery, boilers or something similar, but there were no other clues to their nature.

Large-scale malting and brewing required outlets and one feature of the 18th century was the growth in alehouses. Newport Street had six alehouses and one inn, apart from undocumented possible ale houses such as suggested by Kinsey's stock of ale at no. 22. Perhaps the coffee house that flourished from 1766 to around 1840 at no. 14 Newport Street did so as a welcome contrast.

6.6.4 Period 5: 19th and 20th centuries

Towards the end of the 18th and into the 19th century, the houses on Newport Street become the bases for smaller businesses. The public houses continued but the other houses generally became the residences and offices of tradesmen, such as plasterers (no. 22), carpenters then bricklayers (no. 16), or coopers (no. 26/28). The rear of no. 35 Dolday became a coal merchant's yard. After the mid 19th century, the properties became more residential, and some were divided up into multiple occupation. Some pubs such as the Boar's Head closed (in 1907). Malting continued in the buildings established in the late 17th and early 18th centuries, but changes were evident in the demolition of the large maltings on Dolday behind nos 14–18 Newport Street after 1884, and the rebuild of what had been a brewhouse as a maltings next to it on Dolday at around that date.

The creation of the bus station in the 1920s to 30s meant the end of any other businesses on the station site, and reduced the buildings to the east to small shops, pubs and housing, and these disappeared under All Saints' Road and the later car park. The site has been redeveloped again after the completion of the excavation, and is now mostly given over to residential occupation.

6.7 Consumption and urban households
Hal Dalwood

The Newport Street excavation produced assemblages of artefacts and ecofactual evidence that have considerably expanded our knowledge of the goods consumed by households in Worcester between the medieval and the late post-medieval period, and which indicate changes in the nature of river trade. In the report on the Deansway excavations, an attempt was made to define the characteristics of domestic consumption over time from a variety of standpoints (Dalwood and Bryant 2004; Moffett 2004a; Nicholson and Scott 2004b; Bryant and Dalwood 2004). The specialist reports on the evidence from Newport Street make explicit comparisons with the Deansway site, but there are some more general points to be made about household consumption and trade, focusing on the medieval (Period 2) and post-medieval (Period 3) evidence. The analysis of material from Deansway had a cut-off date of the late 16th century, so the Newport Street site provides an opportunity to frame the broad outlines of changes in everyday patterns of consumption that occurred in Worcester in the 17th to 18th centuries. In contrast, the small size of the Roman material culture assemblage has precluded detailed discussion and comparisons.

The study of documentary sources relating to individual properties has provided detailed evidence for Newport Street households in the 16th to 18th century (Hughes, Chapters 2.3 and 5.1). Some of the inhabitants in the 16th century were fairly prosperous, including clothiers, innkeepers, and rentiers, but alongside their houses were the cottages of poor families, some of whom received parish relief. From the 17th century onwards there is clear evidence, from both documentary sources and structural evidence, for a denser occupation of back plot areas, where small houses were built alongside new malthouses and warehouses.

6.7.1 Period 2: medieval urban households and trade

The medieval (and earlier post-medieval) pottery assemblage showed strong similarities to the contemporary pottery assemblages from Deansway, with a preponderance of cooking pots up to the 14th century, after which a much greater range of ceramic kitchenwares and tablewares was used in urban households, reflecting a rise in living standards in the late medieval period (Griffin, Chapter 5.3; Dalwood and Bryant 2004, 90). A single turned wooden bowl was recovered, a standard form and common type of artefact in the period, but a rather rare survival (Allen, Chapter 5.20). Other medieval domestic artefacts, such as the iron and copper-alloy objects, are all consistent with urban domestic assemblages.

The rather small size of the medieval animal bone assemblage precludes detailed comparisons with the larger contemporary assemblage from Deansway, but broadly similar patterns can be traced once the scale of the two excavations and differing sampling methods are considered (Warman, Chapter 5.24). The animal bone assemblage from Deansway indicated few changes in the range of meat and fish consumed over a long period, from the late 11th to the late 16th century, although poultry and fish had become more widely available by the 16th century (Nicholson and Scott 2004b). The range of evidence for cereals, cultivated orchard fruit (plum and bullace), and wild fruit (blackberry, wild strawberry, and sloe) is characteristic of medieval urban sites (Pearson, Chapter 5.23), and comparable to the medieval material from Deansway (Moffett 2004a, 2004b). The evidence for food waste indicates that the local farming landscape supplied the majority of the food requirements of medieval urban households.

The medieval river trade was certainly important for the economy of Worcester, with the principal import being wine, as well as other luxury goods; and salt from Droitwich was shipped downriver. Coventry was particularly important as a destination for trans-shipped goods (Whitehead 1976, 27, 30). The medieval inhabitants of Worcester included those who depended on regional and long-distance trade, ranging from merchants to carters and boatmen. However, this is not reflected in the archaeological evidence from domestic households, either due to the nature of the goods (such as salt) or to their relatively high cost (such as wine). Everyday needs were supplied by the production of Worcester craftsmen and raw materials from the town's hinterland, brought by road over relatively short distances.

Medieval pottery serves as a reliable proxy for the

relative unimportance of long-distance trade for medieval domestic households and the foodstuffs consumed daily. The medieval pottery assemblage was dominated by locally-produced wares of Worcester-type and Malvernian fabrics (Griffin, Chapter 5.3). The assemblage bears out the evidence from other excavations in Worcester, in the range of forms and sources of supply. Medieval imported pottery was insignificant, and regional products were not very important either. This reflects what has been found throughout excavations in Worcester, where the local pottery kilns supplied most of the needs of domestic households up to the end of the 16th century, even when demand changed (Bryant and Dalwood 2004, 100).

6.7.2 Period 3: post-medieval households and trade

The artefacts and ecofactual assemblages from Newport Street reflect the profound changes that took place in the post-medieval period in terms of the range of goods and foodstuffs available to a wide range of households. At the broadest level, changes in material culture reflected the breaking down of the parameters of traditional medieval society, and a new reliance on the expression of social status through material goods (Howard-Davis 2001, 211).

The differences in the character of the pottery assemblages between the 16th century and the 17th century are significant (Griffin, Chapter 5.3; Jacobs, Chapter 5.4), particularly as the substantial assemblage of later post-medieval pottery from Deansway has not been analysed in detail (Edwards and Bryant 2004), although a better understanding of household assemblages is anticipated from ongoing research into this assemblage (V. Bryant, pers. comm.). From the early 17th century onwards, a range of different wares were widely used in the Newport Street households, reflecting considerable changes in dining and drinking across the social spectrum. The use of tygs, tankards and drinking cups reflects long-lived cultural traditions in the consumption of alcoholic drink in the household by all of its members, as does the small number of drinking glasses (Jacobs, Chapter 5.16). The new form of material culture can be characterised by the widespread use of individual drinking vessels and flat plates for the serving of food that were quite distinct from cooking vessels. There is considerable evidence from Britain for changes in material culture associated with food preparation and serving at this time, that reflected wider changes in social behaviour, placing greater emphasis on the individual rather than the communal household (Howard-Davis 2001, 221–2). Rather than being rapidly taken up as social emulation of the wealthy, new ideas relating to food preparation and serving spread throughout the population. The adoption of tea drinking in the 18th century is reflected in new types of ceramics being imported to Worcester, including White salt-glazed stoneware and Creamware tea bowls (Jacobs, Chapter 5.4).

These changes were also reflected in the adoption of new food ingredients, and 17th-century deposits at Newport Street included imported food ingredients such as raisins, figs, black pepper and grains of paradise, as well as new domestic cultivars such as cucumbers and pumpkins, reflecting significant changes in diet (Pearson, Chapter 5.23). Although only small quantities of these foods were recovered, their presence at Newport Street suggests that they were quite widely available in Worcester, as they were in 17th-century London (Giorgi 1997). Tobacco smoking in the region does not appear to have been widespread before c. 1620, as is reflected by the dating of the clay pipes from Newport Street, which is the first substantial assemblage to be analysed from Worcester (Peacey, Chapter 5.15).

The post-medieval animal bone assemblage shows a reliance on cattle but with a notable increase in the consumption of poultry (chicken and geese) compared to the medieval period (Warman, Chapter 5.24). The sample size was too small to reveal the timing and impact of stock improvements in the local area, which has been highlighted as an important research question for archaeozoological studies in Worcester (Nicholson and Scott 2004b, 96).

Worcester had an important role as a river port in the post-medieval period, and both the nature of the traded goods as well as their origin and destinations differed from the medieval period. The documentary evidence is good (Whitehead 1976, 27–31; Trinder 2005) and, as would be expected, is much more detailed than for the medieval period. From the 17th century, coal and iron were the most important goods transported on the river, and Worcester was the chief coal port on the river from 1695 (Whitehead 1976, 28).

The Severn grew in importance as a trade route for a wide range of goods from the 17th century onwards (Trinder 2005). In the early 18th century, pottery was a significant element of this trade, with crates of pottery from Staffordshire and Ironbridge transported down river, and North Devon pottery carried upstream (ibid., 83–4). The demand for clay pipes only arose when tobacco smoking became widely popular in the regions, which was not before a relatively late date, c. 1620 (Peacey, Chapter 5.15). Broseley clay pipes came to dominate the supply to the Severn Valley, Bristol Channel and South Wales; in 1722, the consignments of clay pipes carried downriver totalled half a million items (Trinder 2005, 83).

The post-medieval pottery assemblage was dominated by non-local pottery, including North Devon gravel-tempered Ware, Midlands yellow ware, and Nottingham and Staffordshire stonewares (Jacobs, Chapter 5.4). Apart from the porcelain produced in the second half of the 18th century, as far as is known, none of the pottery used in Worcester in the later 17th to 18th century was produced locally, and the Newport Street assemblage indicates the importance of centres of pottery production in South-West England and the Midlands that emerged in the 17th century and developed as a significant element of international exports (Barker and Majewski 2006, 223–4).

From the 17th century, trade upstream on the Severn was based on the supply of a wide range of goods to retailers in river ports and market towns in their hinterlands, including textiles, grocery, wine, spirits, tobacco, books, and stationery, and a very considerable range of goods was carried: 'currants, raisins, figs, prunes, walnuts, rice, ginger, herrings, sugar, molasses, treacle, olives, olive oil, vinegar, brown paper, Jamaica pepper [allspice], whalebone, soap, wine, rum and brandy' (Trinder 2005, 78). The documentary evidence shows that Worcester was involved in very long-distance trade via the port of Bristol, with trade routes to the Mediterranean, West Africa, the East Indies and the New World. The presence of evidence for exotic spices and foods within post-medieval cess pits at Newport Street was due to Worcester's role within this growing trade network. Such goods were available to domestic households in Worcester, as well as being widely distributed across the urban hinterland.

6.8 Patterns of wealth and social change
Peter Davenport

Elements of this theme have, of necessity, appeared in the sections on colonisation (Chapter 6.4), buildings (Chapter 6.5) and craft and industry (Chapter 6.6), so some duplication is unavoidable.

6.8.1 Period 1: Roman

Little can be said on this theme from the evidence from Newport Street for the Roman period. Fragments of demolition debris suggested the former presence of Roman buildings in the area. Very large-scale ironworking was clearly underway but its impact on wealth and social change cannot be ascertained. The construction of the Roman road shows that funds were available for such investment, but the source and nature of this funding remains unknown. The small pottery assemblage was dominated by large storage jars, hinting at a commercial or service element to the activity here.

6.8.2 Period 2: medieval

The basic trajectory inferred from the evidence is of trade and craft-based wealth reaching a high point around the 16th to early 17th centuries (Periods 2.5 to 3.1), a plateau of varying character from the 17th into the 18th century (Period 4) and then a decline into the 20th century (Period 5). Within this overall picture, the individual scenes are, as might be expected, more variable.

The earliest medieval occupants of the site were presumably people of substance, able to invest the time and resources establishing themselves and their businesses on the new properties that were laid out (or those of their lessees: the church in the 16th century was clearly responsible for repairing its properties at no. 32/34 Newport Street; Hughes, Chapter 5.1.3). The building of timber structures, iron forging and eventually the creation of masonry-founded buildings indicates that there was a command of resources and a continuing ability to fund the operation of the businesses.

The historical documentation of the excavated plots is almost non-existent for the medieval period so we must rely predominantly on the archaeological evidence, which itself is not extensive. The evidence for buildings on the site generally suggests average wealth: the houses that can be inferred were generally not of the highest mercantile size and type, neither were they poor hovels. The provision of cellars seems to have been rare, perhaps related to the risk of flooding, but the size of the houses and their substantial nature shows that they were nonetheless the homes and headquarters of reasonably wealthy individuals. One house, Building 4 on the Plot 3 frontage at no. 28 Newport Street, was arguably evidence for an individual who had enough wealth to wish to flaunt it, or whose wealth was not primarily from trade. The plan, of a hall laid alongside the street rather than a long, thin building running back from it (and the disregard of the commercial value of the frontage it implies), betrays social aspiration (or achievement) to a status above that of mere trade. On the other hand, it was not at all uncommon for successful burgesses elsewhere to be proud of their success and conduct their affairs from a grand town house. Animal bone evidence generally shows a diet containing good cuts of beef, mutton and pork, with beef predominating, another indication of a higher status. There is little evidence of wild animals, venison or other game, but cod and ray were imported, presumably via Bristol and the Severn, and goose occurs, which would, of course, be available locally.

Of the various plant remains found, there was little in earlier medieval deposits to reflect status or wealth. In the late medieval phases the cess pit in Building 5, on Plot 3, possibly associated with Building 4, was alone in providing a rich source of information. In the deposits from this pit more exotic or higher-status food stuffs were represented: fig, dwarf cherry, sloe, wild strawberry and blackberry show the consumption of wild, locally cultivated, and imported fruit. Black mustard is also present. This deposit also yielded a large amount of chicken bone (and eggshell) as well as pig, sheep and cattle bone, evidence of a sophisticated and varied diet in the late 15th to early 16th centuries. In the overlying fills (probably of post-medieval date), evidence for the grape and plum family was recovered, along with fennel, mustard, cucumber and grains of paradise, but here mixed with more bone debris from non-meat-bearing bone, but which must still have come from the immediate vicinity.

There was little recovered from the excavation to show the standard of medieval living beyond these finds. The wooden bowl, pewter spoons, and wooden and ivory combs recovered from this period from Plot 3 are very middle-of-the-road, and there was no exotic glass or pottery beyond a few sherds of Saintonge ware from western France. The households represented by these remains would have contained servants and workers as well as the relations of the head of the family, and there was, therefore, no sign at this period of the habitations of the poor. In this area they lived as part of the master's *familia*.

6.8.3 Periods 3 and 4: post-medieval and 18th century

It is at the beginning of this period that individuals and an intimation of their wealth become known. In the mid 16th century, Parker the weaver (living in Plot 3) and Dodynge the fuller (and owner of the hemp house, living in Plot 1) were clearly men of wealth. The fickleness of such wealth is shown by Dodynge's heir, a weaver, who was unable to pay his rent twenty years after inheriting a successful and, it seems, multifaceted business. This shows how the retention of wealth depended on individual skills, which in some cases were passed on: the Parkers were still in possession of their plot and business well into the 17th century, as were the Hills, also weavers, although the latter moved from no. 20 to no. 24 Newport Street in the early 17th century. The Linghams also retained their position from the early 18th to the mid 19th century. It was presumably people such as these who rebuilt most of the houses on the Newport Street frontage in the late 16th to 17th centuries.

The descriptions of houses in early post-medieval inventories show that the houses were generally very similar, with a shop, hall and/or parlour and kitchen, with chambers over and often a top loft. The latter was used both for storage and occasionally as a bedroom. Brewhouses, bakehouses and the occasional cellar are mentioned. It is hard to judge wealth from their contents as the comprehensiveness and detail of the inventories varies, for example, the two silk weavers, Lilly in 1690 and Cozens in 1722, were worth very nearly the same, but the inventories are vastly different in length. However, an impression of what kind of possessions people had, and how they changed, can be gained by comparing the longer late 17th and early 18th-century inventories with the longer ones from earlier in the period (e.g. Dodynge of 1556, Lilly of 1690, and Haden in 1730; Hughes, Chapter 5.1). The main impression is that there was much more in the way of furniture and furnishings at the later date, as opposed to the practical implements of business and household, an impression that is not at odds with the known general increase in such possessions in this period. That there was a major variation in wealth among the occupants of Newport Street and Dolday is evident nonetheless. Some inhabitants, such as Thomas Haden in the early 18th century, were the owners of much property and businessmen with many interests. Others were simply tenants and owned nothing else. Haden was worth over £1500 when he died; Lilly was worth £523; whereas John Kinsey, living next door to Haden, left £106 worth of goods and William Gibbs, probably an innkeeper at the Old Red Lion, left just £22.

The late middle ages to the early 18th century was a high point in the prosperity of Newport Street. Many wealthy men, mostly successful businessmen, lived in the street. The cloth industry was the source of much of this wealth in the earlier part of the period but it is noticeable, as far as it is possible to compare the values, that the wealthy men of the later 17th to early 18th centuries were richer than the clothiers of a hundred and more years earlier, for example William Parker the weaver was worth only £14. 6s. 3d. in 1624.

It seems to be in the later 18th century that the decline in the fortunes of Newport Street began. There were very few big businessmen in residence and this may have been connected to the increase in smaller cottages being crammed into the back lots, and an increasing fashion to live away from the shop. The development of the malthouses must have led to a considerable increase in the smell, also making the street less attractive. By the later 18th century, the Newport Street houses were increasingly occupied by small tradesmen: a painter, a carpenter, plasterers, and in the case of no. 18, poor relatives of the wealthier owners. These changes may have resulted, at least in part, from the new bridge over the Severn, which opened in 1781 and rapidly relegated Newport Street from a main thoroughfare to a side street. However, the Linghams, rich maltsters in the mid 18th century and later corn dealers, bucked this trend by occupying no. 20 until the mid 19th century. When they sold up, however, the house rapidly went into multiple occupancy, and declined into a slum, and a similar process took place at no. 22. Three houses within the excavation area became public houses, this trend beginning in the earlier 18th century, in addition to the longer-established inn and alehouses nearer the river. In 1841 the coffee house at no. 14 became the offices of a Severn Carrier, in keeping with the decline in character of the street.

Whatever its true origins, Dolday had mostly functioned as the back lane for the Newport Street properties, but all of them lost untrammelled access during the 18th century as properties were *de facto*, and sometimes *de jure*, split up into smaller units. It became exclusively a frontage for small cottages or access to rear courts or the maltings. A coal merchant had premises in Dolday in 1788, and bought property on Newport Street in the early 19th century. A coal merchant, possibly the same business, occupied the rear of no. 35 Dolday (Building 37) in 1936 and was probably there in the later 19th century as there is reference to a coal merchant having retired by 1911. It is possible a coal merchant was there from soon after the rebuilding of nos 35 and 37 Dolday in 1806–11.

From being a thriving business district in the late medieval period, the site moved from an apparent dependence on the cloth industry and leatherworking (specifically cordwaining) into a more service-based economy, with baking, brewing and a short episode with distilling coming to the fore in the 17th and 18th centuries. Malting and brewing became the dominant industries in the 18th and 19th centuries, with what appears to have been a growth in separate workers' housing, increasing the amount of poor quality accommodation. The report of the General Board of Health in 1849 (pursuant to the acts of 1847 and 1848) makes it clear just how poor the housing was in the worst areas, of which Dolday was noted as one. The provision of this separate housing may just reflect the separation of workers from the households of their employers following the social and economic changes of the Industrial Revolution, and may also simply be a reflection of the national increase in population at this period (see Alcock 2005, 49–51 for a short general consideration). By the late 19th to early 20th century, the area was largely one of poor workers' housing, although some of it (e.g. no. 30 Newport Street) was still in private if hardly affluent owner-occupation. The impact of social legislation and the increasing effect of the state on the fabric of the area was first apparent by the provision of improved sanitation, and later the compulsory purchase and demolition of substandard housing.

The rebuilding of no. 12 Newport Street in the 1920s shows that there was no clear view that the street was economically beyond recovery at that time, although the opening of a carriage builder's in that decade seems to reflect a misplaced optimism, unless for the automobile trade. Otherwise, there had been no significant rebuilding of the frontage buildings since the period 1750–1820, and that was often only refronting or partial replacement of existing structures. The earlier 16th to 17th-century (Periods 3.1 to 3.2) rebuilding phase was possibly more thorough-going. It is hardly surprising that both these phases of improvement coincided with periods of economic improvement. The survival of buildings and improvements from these phases until 20th-century demolition equally indicates a period of economic stagnation, if not decline, in the 19th and early 20th centuries (Period 5).

Chapter 7
Conclusions

Hal Dalwood

The results of the Newport Street excavations have made a considerable contribution to our understanding of the archaeology of Worcester. The large excavation area provided a rare opportunity to study a broad swathe of the urban landscape across a long chronological span, and identified a coherent pattern of plots and an extensive range of buildings and backyard areas.

Newport Street has been the first substantial excavation in Worcester to have paid regard to the full excavation and analysis of post-medieval deposits, artefacts and environmental remains. The interpretation of the archaeological evidence has been related to a detailed analysis of the known documentary evidence for individual land holdings and houses, as well as their owners and their occupations. The project has helped to advance the development of historical archaeology in Worcester along research directions which have considerable potential, but had been rather neglected due to limitations of resources (WCC 2007, 80–90). It was also the first opportunity to investigate in detail the floodplain adjacent to the River Severn, and the results demonstrate that the area contains important geoarchaeological and palaeoenvironmental evidence, as well as waterlogged deposits containing a range of organic artefacts that are rarely recovered from sites in Worcester on the well-drained gravel terrace. The high research potential of the riverside areas of Worcester had been identified previously, on the basis of topography and limited direct evidence (WCC 2007, 108–12), and the good preservation conditions of this area have now been confirmed.

The post-excavation analysis addressed a range of research goals that were related to current archaeological research priorities for Worcester (Jackson, Chapter 3.1). The excavation provided the first significant evidence for past land-use and environments of the floodplain. Pollen and plant macrofossils showed that, as far as can be ascertained, the area was wet meadowland throughout the prehistoric period and up to the 13th century, and was affected by considerable alluviation in the prehistoric period and again in the 11th to 12th century (Dalwood, Chapter 6.2). The medieval alluviation is a phenomenon which deserves further investigation and research in the context of changes in settlement pattern and agriculture in the Severn Valley.

It is now clear that the origins of Newport Street were as an approach road across the floodplain to a river crossing from the later 2nd century AD, but that occupation of the floodplain was not intensive in the Roman, Anglo-Saxon or post-Conquest periods (Dalwood, Chapter 6.3). It was only following determined reclamation of the floodplain in the 13th century that the area was laid out into tenement plots along Newport Street, and became part of the urban landscape. The reclamation of land from rivers has been widely studied in medieval towns and is a complex historical process, as has been discussed in the case of York (Hall and Hunter-Mann 2002, 856–8, 860). The evidence from Newport Street is an important step in understanding the process of reclamation of the riverside areas of Worcester, and the identification of the relatively late date for this reclamation underlines the importance of archaeological excavation in establishing the chronology of change in the urban landscape.

The excavation revealed a pattern of long, narrow medieval tenement plots, laid out along the north side of Newport Street and stretching back to Dolday, which served as the back access lane (Davenport, Chapter 6.4). The plots were irregular in width from the outset, confirming that this part of the medieval town was indeed 'unplanned', in contrast to the Foregate Street suburb which has been identified as a planned urban addition (Baker and Holt 2004, 371–2, fig. 15.1). The laying out of plots along Newport Street may have been undertaken in a piecemeal fashion. Excavation showed that, once laid out, the framework of medieval tenement plot boundaries was long lived, although documentary evidence revealed a complex pattern of changing property ownership and rentals from the 16th century onwards, with new houses built on back plot areas and warehouses later built along Dolday. Although the plan of medieval Worcester has been reconstructed and used to develop a model of its planning history (ibid., 2004), the Newport Street excavation provided the first opportunity to comprehensively examine part of its medieval urban landscape. Thus the results of this excavation are a contribution to wider research into the nature of medieval urban planning (e.g. Lilley 2002, 138–77).

The excavation produced an extensive body of archaeological evidence for medieval and post-medieval buildings (Davenport, Chapter 6.5). There was good survival of building foundations and associated remains close to the street frontage, with little truncation by 19th-century cellars or deep 20th-century foundations as found at Deansway (Dalwood and Edwards 2004). The plots laid out in the 13th century were not built on in any consistent pattern, and the range of buildings on the street frontage included narrow shops with halls to the rear, parallel halls occupying wide plots, and open industrial workshops. The high and late medieval buildings were timber-framed, with extensive use of stone for the foundations of timber-framed buildings as well as for the (rare) stone-walled cellars. There was extensive rebuilding in the 16th to 17th century, during which timber construction was gradually replaced by brick, followed by further rebuilding in brick in the 18th century, utilising the Georgian architectural style for the frontage buildings, while the back plots were built on with workshops and smaller houses for the poor (Davenport, Chapter 6.5). The physical evidence for the development of the buildings on individual plots has, where possible, been related to the documentary evidence, which revealed details of the owners' families, their occupations and their household goods (Hughes, Chapter 5.1). The Newport Street site has produced an important body of evidence for buildings, expanding current knowledge of urban vernacular building traditions prior to the 18th century (WCC 2007, 63–4, 83–4).

The excavation produced a range of evidence for crafts and industries (Davenport, Chapter 6.6). Medieval ovens and hearths included smithing hearths as well as structures interpreted as bread ovens, hearths for roasting barley and dye-vat bases, and there was also evidence for shoemaking (cordwaining). This evidence is in line with a study of the 14th-century poll tax returns, which highlighted the 'industrial' character of All Saints' parish in the medieval period, where tanners, leatherworkers, dyers and fullers were concentrated (Barron 1989, 12). The availability of more comprehensive documentary evidence for the post-medieval period has provided more detailed insights into the range of economic activities practised by the inhabitants of Newport Street. Documentary and archaeological evidence are complementary in the identification of a bakery and malthouses, though in some cases it is the documentary evidence alone that has provided the telling evidence, such as for the identification of a hemp warehouse. Medieval craft production was largely organised on the basis of households, sometimes employing a small number of servants (ibid., 7–9), but from the 16th century onwards there was a change to a more 'industrialised' economy, though production was still organised around fairly small workshops (Dyer 1973), and the documentary and archaeological evidence for Newport Street reflects this pattern.

The material culture from the excavations has provided evidence for differences in household consumption between the later medieval period and the early modern period (Dalwood, Chapter 6.7). A wider range of foodstuffs and a new culture of dining and drinking (and smoking) in ordinary households are measures of change, but the most significant difference lies in the evidence for Worcester's role in long-distance river trade in commodities and its links to developing worldwide trade routes. Newport Street itself saw an increase in wealth of individual households between the late medieval period and the later 16th to 17th century, with a decline in the later 18th century (Dalwood, Chapter 6.8).

The nature and quality of the buried archaeological deposits at Newport Street have built on earlier work within the historic city in allowing the form of buildings and the activities in back plots to be identified and studied over time. The availability of detailed documentary evidence for individual plots from the 16th century onwards has greatly enhanced our understanding of the archaeological evidence and driven its interpretation forwards. Interpretation of the results has addressed a number of research priorities identified in the recent archaeological research framework for Worcester (WCC 2007).

The excavation project was undertaken with similar goals to the earlier Deansway excavation, but importantly it has established a baseline for the study of post-medieval structural evidence and material culture in Worcester. There has been no legitimate reason for ignoring post-medieval archaeological deposits for some time, so it is expected that this knowledge will be built on in the future. The Newport Street excavation represents an important step in the application of urban historical archaeology to the buildings and backyards of Worcester. This project has engaged with the developing research that has an international scope, revealing both 'the constant process of change that is a fact of urban life' and 'above all … people, both remembered and not remembered, and connect[ing] them to the present' (O'Keeffe and Yamin 2006, 102).

Appendix 1
Brick Catalogue

Context	Count	Dimensions (mm)	Dimensions (inches)	Fabric description	Method of manufacture and specific features	Date of manufacture?	Period dating	Period
37	1	240x120x60	9 7/16x 4 3/4 x 2 3/8	Mid to dark reddish brown sandy fabric. Frequent inclusions of small iron like particles and small voids. Occasional buff clay inclusions. One large stone inclusion.	Mortar encrusted.	17th	17th	3.2
38	1	240x110x60	9 7/16x 4 3/8 x 2 3/8	Retained as intact sample.	Mould made brick. No section done as has fingerprints on both base ends	(?) 17th	17th	3.2
39	1	202x115x50	8x 4 1/2x 2	Mid orange, sandy fabric with occasional voids. Occasional small stones and frquent small maganese/iron particles	Pallet moulded.	Mid 15th – 16th (?)	17th	3.2
39	1	220x115x50	8 5/8x 4 1/2 x 2	Mid orange sandy fabric with occasional voids. Occasional small stones and frquent small maganese or iron particles.	Pallet moulded.	(?) Late 15th – 16th	17th	3.2
39	1	225x110x50	8 7/8x 4 3/8 x 2	Dark reddish brown and very fine fabric. Frequent inclusions of small quartz/ sand particles and (?)Iron. Large voids in fabric and has glossy appearance (overfired?).	Pallet moulded	16th – 17th	17th	3.2
39	2	240x120x50	9 7/16x 4 3/4 x 2	Mid orange sandy fabric with occasional voids. Occasional small stones and frequent small maganese/iron particles	Pallet moulded.	16th – mid 17th	17th	3.2
40	1	232x110x65	9 1/8x 4 3/8 x 2 1/2	Mid to dark reddish/orange brown. Frequent small voids and well sorted manganese or iron inclusions. Swirls of buff clay.	Pallet moulded.	17th – 18th	17th	3.2
40	1	235x110x52	9 1/4x 4 3/8 x 2 1/16	Mid to dark reddish/orange brown. Fabric. Frequent small voids and well sorted manganese(Fe?) inclusions. Swirls of buff clay.	Pallet moulded.	17th – 18th	17th	3.2
40	3	235x110x65	9 1/4x 4 3/8 x 2 1/2	Mid to dark reddish/orange brown. Frequent small voids and well sorted manganese(Fe?) inclusions. Swirls of buff clay.	Pallet moulded.	17th – 18th	17th	3.2
41	3	235x115x51	9 1/4x 4 1/2 x 2	Orange red fabric. Possibly organically tempered (voids in fabric), occasional inclusions of poorly sorted buff material and angular stones.	Slop moulded. Straw imprints – base and on side from stacking.	16th – 17th	17th	3.2
41	5	235x118x55	9 1/4x 4 9/ 16 x 2 3/16	Mid orange to red fabric. Organically tempered (voids in fabric). Occasional inclusions of poorly sorted buff material and angular stone.	Probably slop molded. Stacked on chaff/ straw.	16th – 17th	17th	3.2
43	1	210x100x57	8 3/8x 4 x 2 1/4	Fine mid reddish brown fabric. Moderate to frequent inclusions of small iron or manganese particles. Occasional large stone fragments. Dark purple (over fired) patches.	Pallet moulded.	16th – mid 17th	17th	3.2
43	1	220x110x55	8 5/8x 4 3/8 x 2 3/16	Fine mid reddish brown fabric with moderate to frequent inclusions of small iron or manganese particles. Occasional large stone fragments. Dark purple (over fired) patches.	Pallet moulded	17th	17th	3.2
43	1	225x115x68	8 7/8x 4 1/2 x 2 1/2	Mid reddish brown, very fine fabric with frequent inclusions of small quartz/ sand particles. Large voids in fabric and has glossy appearance.	Slop moulded.	17th	17th	3.2

Context	Count	Dimensions (mm)	Dimensions (inches)	Fabric description	Method of manufacture and specific features	Date of manufacture?	Period dating	Period
43	1	235x115x55	9 1/4x 4 1/2 x 2 3/16	Fine orange fabric with occasional inclusions of small iron-manganese particles.	Slop moulded.	16th – mid 17th	17th	3.2
43	1	235x115x60	9 1/4x 4 1/2 x 2 3/8	Dark reddish brown, sandy fabric with occasional small voids.	Possibly overfired. Extremely rough exterior.	17th	17th	3.2
43	1	240x115x55	9 7/16x 4 1/ x 2 3/16	Mid orange to red, fabric. Organically tempered (voids in fabric), even fabric with some voids and occasional poorly sorted angular stone inclusions.	Moulded brick with straw imprints to base.	16th – 17th	17th	3.2
44	1	230x105x60	9 1/16x 4 1/8 x 2 3/8	Purple colour and oxidized throughout. Rare small voids which may be the result of over firing as brick has distorted appearance.	Undetermined method of manufacture.	Mid 17th – early 18th	17th	3.2
44	1	234x120x69	9 1/4x 4 3/4 x 2 3/4	Mid reddish brown, Frequent inclusions of Iron particles, poorly sorted.	Early frog imprinted by finger on one surface.	Late 17th – early 18th	17th	3.2
44	1	235x112x70	9 1/4x 4 3/8 x 4 3/4	Mid reddish brown fabric. Frequent inclusions of poorly sorted Iron particles. Occasional flecks of buff clay.	Appears to be frame moulded. Early frog imprinted by finger on one surface. Needs further research to clarify date.	Mid 17th – early 18th	17th	3.2
44	1	235x115x65	91/4x 4 1/2 x 2 1/2	Deep reddish brown sandy fabric. Occasional clay pellets, occasional voids and occasional small iron-like inclusions and stones.	Moulded but slightly iregular at ends.	17th – 18th	17th	3.2
44	1	235x115x65	9 1/4x 4 1/2 x 2 1/2	Fine mid pinkish orange brown sandy fabric. Occasional small voids. Moderate inclusions of iron particles. Also bands of yellow/buff clay.	Pallet moulded. Base with twig like frog impression.	Late 17th – early 18th	17th	3.2
44	1	235x115x65	9 1/4x 4 1/2 x 2 1/2	Mid reddish brown fabric. Frequent inclusions of Iron particles, poorly sorted. Occasional flecks of buff clay.	Moulded.	Late 17th – 18th	17th	3.2
44	1	235x120x70	9 1/4x 4 3/4 x 2 3/4	Mid reddish brown fabric. Frequent inclusions of Iron particles and poorly sorted.	Moulded brick. Early frog imprinted by finger on base.	Late 17th – early 18th	17th	3.2
120	1	220x110x50-75	8 5/8x 4 3/8 x 2-3	Highly over fired so fabric unidentifiable.	Appears to be 2" moulded brick that has expanded along it's length	16th – mid 17th	17th	3.2
120	1	230x120x70	9 1/16x 4 3/4 x 2 3/4	Fine mid to dark Brown fabric. Frequent small voids and moderate inclusions of what appears to be iron particles.	Pallet moulded.	mid 17th – 18th	17th	3.2
120	1	235x115x65	9 1/4x 4 1/2 x 2 1/2	Pale to mid brown sandy fabric. Occasional voids, frquent poorly sorted angular stones and small to medium buff particles.	Pallet moulded.	Mid 17th – 18th	17th	3.2
120	1	240x105x55	9 7/16x 4 1/8 x 2 3/16	Dark reddish brown and very fine fabric. Frequent inclusions of small quartz/ sand particles. Large voids in fabric and has glossy appearance (overfired?).	Poorly shaped brick due to over firing. Rough finish to all surfaces.	16th – mid 17th	17th	3.2
127	1	240x120x60	9 7/16x 4 3/ 4 x 2 3/8	Fine mid to dark orange fabric. Frequent small voids and moderate inclusions of what appears to be iron particles. Occasional grains of sand.	Pallet moulded.	16th – mid 17th	17th	3.2
142	1	240x120x53	9 7/16x 4 3/ 4 x 2 1/8	Mid to dark reddish brown sandy fabric. Frequent inclusions of small iron like particles and small voids.	Probably slop moulded. Base has chaff imprints.	17th	17th	3.2

Appendix 1: Brick Catalogue 257

Context	Count	Dimensions (mm)	Dimensions (inches)	Fabric description	Method of manufacture and specific features	Date of manufacture?	Period dating	Period
157	1	235x115x60	9 1/4x 4 1/2 x 2 3/8	Fine mid-dark orange fabric. Frequent small voids and moderate inclusions of what appears to be iron particles.	Appears slop moulded. Frog is on sanded side so may be the result of placing something (twig ?) within the mould.	Late 17th – mid 18th	17th	3.2
158	1	237x117x55	9 5/16x 4 3/4 x 2 3/16	Retained as intact sample.	Has child finger prints on base from carrying after moulding.	(?) 16th – mid 17th	17th	3.2
159	1	235x120x50	9 1/4x 4 3/4x 2	Mid orange to reddish sandy fabric. Occasional small angular stone inclusions and occasional small voids.	Slop moulded. Side stacked with finger indents	16th – mid 17th	17th	3.2
159	1	245x120x65	9 5/8x 4 3/4 x 2 1/2	Mid to dark reddish brown sandy fabric. Frequent inclusions of small to medium iron like particles.	Pallet molded.	mid 17th – mid 18th	17th	3.2
167	1	230x111x50	9 1/16x 4 3/8 x 2	Pale to mid brown sandy fabric. Occasional voids, frquent poorly sorted angular stones and small to medium buff particles.	Slop moulded.	16th – mid 17th	17th	3.2
212	1	233x115x60	9 3/16x 4 1/2 x 2 3/8	Fine dark reddish orange fabric. Frequent small voids and moderate inclusions of what appears to be iron particles.	Roughly made with distorted proportions (curving of brick and irregular surface finish).	17th	17th	3.2
212	2	235x115x60	9 1/4x 4 1/2 x 2 3/8	Fine dark reddish orange fabric. Frequent small voids and moderate inclusions of what appears to be iron particles.	Roughly made with distorted proportions (curving of brick and irregular surface finish).	17th	17th	3.2
220	1	233x115x60	9 3/16x 4 1/2 x 2 3/8	Mid to dark reddish brown sandy fabric. Frequent inclusions of small iron like particles and small voids.	Solid brick with smooth but slighty irregular surfaces. Rudimentry frog.	mid 17th – 18th	17th	3.2
226	1	230x110x50	9 1/16x 4 3/8 x 2	Fine mid to dark orange fabric. Frequent small voids and moderate inclusions of what appears to be iron particles. Occasional grains of sand.	Pallet moulded.	17th – (?) 18th	17th	3.2
227	1	225x110x60	8 7/8x 4 3/8 x 2 3/8	Moulded brick, Dark reddish brown, sandy fabric occasional small voids.	Pallet moulded.	17th	17th	3.2
228	1	230x115x62	9 1/16x 4 1/2 x 2 3/16	Pale orange buff, sandy fabric, with frequent small voids.	Slop moulded. Possibly side stacked.	17th	17th	3.2
242	1	230x110x50	9 1/16x 4 3/8 x 2	Dark reddish brown flakey fabric with frequent small voids.	Slop moulded.	17th	17th	3.2
242	1	235x95x55	9 1/4x 3 3/4 x 2 3/16	Mid to dark reddish orange fabric. Frequent inclusions of small iron particles(?).	Pallet moulded.	17th – 18th	17th	3.2
242	1	235x115x55	9 1/4x 4 1/2 x 2 3/16	Dark reddish brown, sandy fabric with occasional small voids.	Possibly overfired. Extremely rough exterior.	17th	17th	3.2
242	1	235x120x50	9 1/4x 4 3/4 x 2	Fine mid to dark orange fabric. Frequent small voids and moderate inclusions of what appears to be iron particles. Occasional large inclusions of grog and lime.	Slop moulded.	(?) 16th – 17th	17th	3.2
242	1	245x115x55	9 5/8x 4 1/2 x 2 3/16	Fine mid to dark orange fabric. Frequent small voids and moderate inclusions of what appears to be iron particles. Occasional large inclusions of grog and lime?	Slop moulded.	17th	17th	3.2
243	2	240x120x51	9 7/16x 4 3/4 x 2	Fine mid to dark brown fabric. Frequent small voids and moderate inclusions of what appears to be iron particles.	Slop moulded. Base is rough with grass/chaff imprints.	17th – early 18th	17th	3.2

Context	Count	Dimensions (mm)	Dimensions (inches)	Fabric description	Method of manufacture and specific features	Date of manufacture?	Period dating	Period
243	1	245x115x45	9 5/8x 4 1/2 x 1 3/4	Mid to dark reddish brown sandy fabric. Frequent inclusions of small iron like particles.	Slop moulded. Base has rudimentry frog and is rough with grass/chaff imprints.	17th – early 18th	17th	3.2
243	1	245x120x50	9 5/8x 4 3/4 x 2	Fine mid-dark Brown fabric. Frequent small voids and moderate inclusions of what appears to be iron particles.	Covered in mortar.	17th – early 18th	17th	3.2
270	2	235x120x47	9 1/4x 4 3/4 x 1 7/8	Fine orange fabric with occasional inclusions of small iron-manganese particles.	Slop moulded.	16th – mid 17th	Late 17th – 18th	3.3
304	1	230x115x51	9 1/16x 4 1/2 x 2	Mid orange sandy fabric with occasional small angular stone inclusions and occasional small voids.	Pallet moulded .	16th – 17th	18th – early 19th	4
304	1	230x115x55	9 1/16x 4 1/2 x 2 3/16	Fine mid pinkish orange brown sandy fabric. Occasional small voids. Moderate inclusions iron particles. Also bands of yellow/buff clay.	Pallet moulded.	16th – mid 17th	18th – early 19th	4
304	1	230x115x60	9 1/16x 4 1/2 x 2 3/8	Pale to mid brown sandy fabric. Occasional voids, frquent poorly sorted angular stones and small to medium buff particles.	Pallet moulded	(?) 17th	18th – early 19th	4
304	2	235x119x55	9 1/4x 4 1/2 x 2 3/16	Reddish orange fabric with frequent small voids and occasional small pale clay/grog pellets, well fired.	Possible slop moulded. Also potential rudimentary frog.	Late 17th – early 18th	18th – early 19th	4
304	1	240x115x51	9 7/16x 4 1/2 x 2	Mid orange sandy fabric occasional small angular stone inclusions and occasional small voids	Pallet moulded.	16th – 17th	18th – early 19th	4
304	2	240x120x60	9 7/16x 4 3/4 x 2 3/8	Reddish orange fabric with frequent small voids and occasional small pale clay/grog pellets.	(?) Slop moulded.	Late 17th – early 18th	18th – early 19th	4
304	1	242x124x56	9 1/2x 4 3/4 x 2 1/2	Reddish orange fabric with frequent small voids and occasional small pale clay/grog pellets.	Mould made brick, Possible finger indented frog.	Late 17th – early 18th	18th – early 19th	4
319	1	230x115x53	9 1/16x 4 1/2 x 2 1/8	Light to mid orange sandy fabric. Frequent small voids and occasional small grog pellets and buff clay pellets.	Pallet moulded.	16th – mid 17th	17th	3.2
376	1	240x115x60	9 7/16x 4 1/2 x 2 3/8	Mid to dark reddish brown sandy fabric. Frequent inclusions of small iron like particles and small voids.	Pallet moulded.	16th – mid 17th	17th	3.2
382	2	213x105x60	8 3/8x 4 1/8 x 2 3/8	Deep reddish brown sandy fabric. Occasional clay pellets, occasional voids and occasional small iron particles and stones.	Slop moulded.	17th – (?) 18th	17th	3.2
382	3	235x113x65	9 1/4x 4 1/2 x 2 1/2	Fine mid to dark orange fabric. Frequent small voids and moderate inclusions of what appears to be iron particles and sand grains.	Slop moulded	17th – (?)18th	17th	3.2
390	1	233x115x58	9 3/16x 4 1/2 x 2 1/4	Dark reddish brown and very fine fabric. With frequent inclusions of small quartz/ sand particles. Large voids in fabric.	Pallet moulded.	16th – mid 17th	17th	3.2
390	1	240x118x57	9 3/8x 4 9/16 x 2 1/4	Mid to dark orange brown sandy fabric. Frequent inclusions of small iron like particles and small voids and occasional buff clay inclusions.	Slop moulded.	16th – mid 17th	17th	3.2
404	1	230x115x52	9 1/16x 4 1/2 x 2 1/16	Mid brown coarse fabric with patches of darker brown. Flakey appearance.	Slop moulded.	16th – mid 17th	17th	3.2
408	1	240x115x52	9 7/16x 4 1/2 x 2 1/16	Light-mid orange sandy fabric. Frequent small voids and occasional small grog and buff clay pellets.	Slop moulded.	16th – mid 17th	17th	3.2

Appendix 1: Brick Catalogue 259

Context	Count	Dimensions (mm)	Dimensions (inches)	Fabric description	Method of manufacture and specific features	Date of manufacture?	Period dating	Period
418	1	230x110x58	9x 4 3/8 x 2 1/4	Reddish orange fabric with frequent small voids and occasional small pale clay/grog pellets, well fired.	Rough sides, sanded base with finger indents (three fingers) at ends of base. Smooth upper surface.	16th – mid 17th	17th	3.2
421	1	230x115x60	9 1/16x 4 1/2 x 2 3/8	Dark reddish brown, sandy fabric occasional small voids.	Possibly overfired. Extremely rough exterior. One stretcher side slightly smoother- possibly from side stacking.	17th	17th	3.2
421	1	235x115x72	9 1/4x 4 1/2 x 2 3/4	Reddish pink fabric. Frequent poorly sorted bands of buff clay. Frequent small rounded to sub angular stones (includes quartz).	Pallet moulded.	17th	17th	3.2
428	1	238x120x55	9 3/8x4 3/4 x 2 3/16	Light to mid pinkish orange sandy fabric. Frequent small voids occasional small grog pellets and buff clay pellets.	Slop moulded.	16th – mid 17th	Late 17th – 18th	3.3
428	1	240x110x60	9 7/16x 4 3/8 x 2 3/8	Mid to dark Reddish brown sandy fabric. Frequent inclusions of small to medium iron like particles.	Moulded brick. Rough finish all surfaces, possibly over fired.	16th – mid 17th	Late 17th – 18th	3.3
428	1	240x120x55	9 7/16x 4 3/4 x 2 3/16	Light-mid pinkish orange sandy fabric. Frequent small voids occasional small grog and buff clay pellets.	Slop moulded	16th – mid 17th	Late 17th – 18th	3.3
428	1	242x115x55	9 1/2x 4 1/2 x 2 3/16	Light to mid pinkish orange sandy fabric. Frequent small voids occasional small grog and buff clay pellets.	Slop moulded.	16th – mid 17th	Late 17th – 18th	3.3
428	1	242x120x54	9 1/2x 4 3/4 x 2 1/8	Light to mid pinkish orange sandy fabric. Frequent small voids occasional small grog and buff clay pellets.	Slop moulded.	16th – mid 17th	Late 17th – 18th	3.3
452	1	230x111x50	9 1/16x 4 3/8 x 2	Dark reddish brown and very fine fabric. Frequent inclusions of small quartz/ sand particles and Iron. Large voids in fabric and has glossy appearance.	Pallet moulded.	Early – mid 17th	Late 17th – 18th	3.3
452	1	245x120x52	9 5/8x 4 3/4 x 2 1/16	Light to mid orange sandy fabric. Frequent small voids and occasional small grog and buff clay pellets.	Pallet molded.	16th – mid 17th	Late 17th – 18th	3.3
460	2	245x120x52	9 5/8x 4 3/4 x 2 1/16	Fine mid-dark orange fabric. Frequent small voids and moderate inclusions of what appears to be iron particles.	Pallet moulded.	17th – 18th	Late 17th – 18th	3.3
471	1	235x115x55	9 1/4x 4 1/2 x 2 3/16	Fine orange fabric with occasional inclusions of small iron-manganese particles.	Probably pallet moulded. Sanded base with grass or chaff imprints. All other surfaces sanded to a lesser degree.	16th – mid 17th	17th	3.2
471	1	240x117x52	9 7/16x 4 3/4 x 2 1/16	Fine mid reddish brown fabric. Moderate to frequent inclusions of small iron or manganese particles. Occasional large stone fragments.	Slop moulded. Base has diagonal twig imprints.	16th – 17th	17th	3.2
471	1	248x115x54	9 3/4 x 4 1/2 x 2 1/8	Fine mid orange brown fabric. Occasional inclusions of small buff clay and frequent small voids.	Pallet moulded.	16th – 17th	17th	3.2
471	2	248x120x57	9 3/4x 4 3/4 x21/4	Light to mid pinkish orange sandy fabric. Frequent small voids, small grog and buff clay pellets.	Slop moulded.	17th – early 18th	17th	3.2
473	1	240x120x55	9 7/16x 4 3/4 x 2 3/16	Reddish orange fabric with frequent small voids and occasional small pale clay/grog pellets.	Pallet moulded.	17th	17th	3.2
478	1	230x112x60	9 1/16x 4 3/8 x 2 3/8	Mid to dark reddish brown sandy fabric. Frequent inclusions of small iron like particles and small voids.	Pallet moulded.	16th – mid 17th	18th – early 19th	4

Context	Count	Dimensions (mm)	Dimensions (inches)	Fabric description	Method of manufacture and specific features	Date of manufacture?	Period dating	Period
483	1	237x120x54	9 5/16x 4 3/4 x 2 3/16	Mid orange brown sandy fabric. Frequent inclusions of silica and occasional angular stones.	Pallet moulded.	(?) 16th – mid 17th	Late 17th – 18th	3.3
484	1	237x116x54	9 5/16x 4 1/2 x 2 1/4	Mid orange brown sandy fabric. Frequent inclusions of silica and occasional angular stones and possible buff clay pellets. Frequent small voids. Flakey texture.	Pallet moulded.	(?) 16th – mid 17th	Late 17th – 18th	3.3
485	1	230x115x55	9 1/16x 4 1/2 x 2 3/16	Moulded brick, Fine orange fabric with occasional inclusions of small iron-manganese particles.	Possibly slop moulded	16th – mid 17th	Late 17th – 18th	3.3
485	1	270x110x60	10 1/2x 4 3/8 x 2 3/8	Mid to dark orange brown sandy fabric. Frequent inclusions of small iron like particles and small voids occasional buff clay inclusions.One large stone inclusion.	Deformed by over firing, irregular surfaces and 'blown-out' at both ends. Upper surface smooth, base rough with straw indents.	Mid 17th – late 18th	Late 17th – 18th	3.3
487	1	210x120x65	8 3/8x 4 3/4 x 2 1/2	Light-mid orange sandy fabric. Frequent small voids and occasional small grog pellets and buff clay pellets.	Pallet moulded.	17th	Late 17th – 18th	3.3
488	1	235x120x60	9 1/4x 4 3/4 x 2 3/8	Mid to dark reddish brown sandy fabric. Frequent inclusions of small to medium iron like particles.	Pallet moulded.	17th – mid 18th	Late 17th – 18th	3.3
492	1	240x110x60	9 7/16x 4 3/8 x 2 3/8	Fine dark reddish to orange fabric. Frequent small voids and moderate inclusions of what appears to be iron particles.	Moulded brick. Slightly crude form (irregularities to surface). All surfaces smooth but irregular.	17th	Late 17th – 18th	3.3
498	1	260x120x55	10 1/4x 4 3/4 x 2 3/16	Moulded brick, Unable to id fabric as overfired and vitrified.	Extremely hard. Distorted and splitting/exploded.	Early 17th – (?) mid 17th	Late 17th – 18th	3.3
499	1	240x105x64	9 7/16x 4 1/8 x 2 1/2	Mid brown to darker reddish brown, coarse fabric. Frequent small inclusions of buff clay and iron particles.	Slop moulded. Probable rudimentary frog. Appears over fired (purpling and small bubble holes). Base is sanded and deeply finger indented.	Late 17th – mid 18th	Late 17th – 18th	3.3
499	1	240x120x60	9 7/16x 4 3/4 x 2 3/8	Mid orange brown coarse fabric. Occasional stone inclusions, small buff clay particles and voids.	Very crude brick Sanded base with twig impression and deep finger imprints. Upper surface smoother but has large distorted thumb imprint.	17th – 18th	Late 17th – 18th	3.3
499	1	245x110x62	9 5/8x 4 3/8 x 2 1/2	Dark reddish brown fabric, bands of buff clay occasional large stone inclusions and frequent, poorly sorted iron(?) particles.	Pallet moulded.	Late 17th – 18th	Late 17th – 18th	3.3
499	2	245x110x62	9 5/8x 4 3/8 x 2 1/2	Dark reddish brown fabric, bands of buff clay, occasional large stone inclusions and frequent, poorly sorted iron(?) particles	Pallet moulded. Bases with frog indent most likely from twig/stick.	Late 17th – mid 18th	Late 17th – 18th	3.3
515	1	235x110x52	9 1/4x 4 3/8 x 2 1/16	Fine mid-dark orange fabric. Occasional small voids and moderate inclusions of what appears to be iron particles. large sub rounded quartz stones to 10mm evident in base.	Pallet moulded.	16th – mid 17th	Late 17th – 18th	3.3
516	1	123x60	4 7/8x 2 3/8	Coarse orange brown fabric, flakey appearance, frequent small voids, occasional small stones and small buff particles.	Fragmented lengths of brick window mullion. Two chamfered edges, over all well finished with some decay. Used as wall foundation.	16th – 17th	18th – early 19th	4
521	1	230x110x55	9x 4 3/8 x 23 /16	Mid orange brown sandy faric. Frequent inclusions of silica and occasional angular stones and possible buff clay pellets.	Moulded brick, covered in mortar.	(?)17th	Late 17th – 18th	3.3

Appendix 1: Brick Catalogue   261

Context	Count	Dimensions (mm)	Dimensions (inches)	Fabric description	Method of manufacture and specific features	Date of manufacture?	Period dating	Period
529	1	245x115x65	9 5/8x 4 1/2 x 2 1/2	Highly over fired and vitrified, unable to ID fabric type.	Grossly distorted.	17th	Late 17th – 18th	3.3
537	1	225x120x50	8 7/8x 4 3/4 x 2	Dark brown course fabric (grossly overfired). Frequent small angular stone inclusions.	Overfired, distorted and crumbling.	?		3.3
537	2	235x115x55	9 1/4x 4 1/2 x 2 3/16	Mid orange, sandy fabric with occasional voids. Occasional small stones and frequent small maganese/iron particles.	Pallet moulded.	Late 17th – early 18th	Late 17th – 18th	3.3
537	1	240x120x50	9 7/16x 4 3/4 x 2	Mid orange sandy fabric with occasional voids. Occasional small stones and frequent small maganese/iron particles.	Pallet molded.	(?) 16th – 17th	Late 17th – 18th	3.3
541	1	235x115x57	9 1/4x 4 1/2 x 2 1/4	Fine mid to dark orange fabric. Frequent small voids and moderate inclusions of what appears to be iron particles	Pallet molded.	17th – 18th	18th – early 19th	4
546	1	225x108x70	8 7/8x 4 1/4 x 2 3/4	Mid to light orange brown sandy fabric. Frequent inclusions of small iron like particles and small voids occasional buff clay inclusions.	Pallet moulded.	18th	17th	3.2
546	1	230x110x60	9 1/16x 4 3/8 x 2 3/8	Mid to dark reddish brown sandy fabric. Frequent inclusions of small to medium iron like particles.	Moulded and poorly finished with frequent straw impressions and all over rough textured appearance .	16th – mid 17th	17th	3.2
546	1	237x115x60	9 5/16x 4 1/2 x 2 3/8	Fine orange fabric with occasional inclusions of small iron-manganese partcles.	Pallet moulded.	Mid 17th – 18th	17th	3.2
546	1	240x110x55	9 7/16x 4 3/8 x 2 3/16	Mid toDark Reddish brown sandy fabric, frequent inclusions of small to medium iron like particles.	Moulded brick. Possible rudimentary frog, slightly distorted from over firing.	17th	17th	3.2
558	1	237x115x54	9 5/16x 4 1/2 x 2 1/4	Retained as intact sample.	Has animal paw and finger imprints.	(?) 16th – mid 17th		5
564	1	240x115x55	9 7/16x 4 1/2 x 2 3/16	Light-mid orange sandy fabric. Frequent small voids and occasional small grog and buff clay pellets.	Slop moulded. Drops of glaze on base edge. Fired with glazed floor tiles. Probable kiln brick.	16th – mid 17th	16th – 17th	3.1
565	1	235x115x55	9 1/4x 4 1/2 x 2 3/16	Fine mid to dark orange fabric. Frequent small voids and moderate inclusions of what appears to be iron particles.	Pallet moulded.	Early – mid 17th	18th – early 19th	4
565	1	235x115x60	9 1/4x 4 1/2 x 2 3/8	Mid to dark reddish brown sandy fabric, frequent inclusions of small to medium iron like particles and buff inclusions.	Slop molded with side stacking. Appears to have rudimentary frog.	Late 17th – 18th	18th – early 19th	4
565	1	235x115x65	9 1/4x 4 1/2 x 2 1/2	Mid to dark orange brown Sandy fabric, frequent inclusions of small iron like particles and small voids occasional buff clay inclusions.One large stone inclusion.	Severly over fired and distorted as frequent twig impressions to one surface. Surfaces rough and uneven.	mid 17th – mid 18th	18th – early 19th	4
565	1	240x115x58	9 7/16x 4 1/2 x 2 1/4	Coarse mid reddish brown fabric with flakey appearance. Inclusions of frequent sand, occasional voids, and frequent small buff clay inclusions (pellets).	Possible extruded brick.	16th – mid 17th	18th – early 19th	4
565	1	245x110x50-80	9 5/8x 4 3/8 x 2-3	Mid to dark orange brown sandy fabric. Frequent inclusions of small iron like particles and small voids and occasional buff clay inclusions.	Moulded brick, Severly over fired and distorted.	16th – mid 17th	18th – early 19th	4
567	2	235x113x55	9 1/4x 4 1/2 x 2 3/16	Mid orange to reddish sandy fabric. Occasional small angular stone inclusions and occasional small voids.	Moulded brick. Base sanded with twig/ straw impression.	16th – mid 17th	17th	3.2

Context	Count	Dimensions (mm)	Dimensions (inches)	Fabric description	Method of manufacture and specific features	Date of manufacture?	Period dating	Period
567	1	235x113x55	9 1/4x 4 1/2 x 2 3/16	Fine mid reddish brown fabric. Moderate to frequent inclusions of small iron or manganese particles. Occasional large stone fragments.	Distorted shape. All surfaces smooth except for base which is sanded and has diagonal twig imprints.	16th – mid 17th	17th	3.2
571	1	233x110x70	9 3/16x 4 3/8 x 2 3/4	Dark reddish brown and very fine fabric. With frequent inclusions of small quartz/ sand particles. Large voids in fabric.	Slop moulded.	M17-18C	17th	3.2
571	1	235x117x68	9 1/4x 4 1/4 x 2 3/4	Fine orange fabric with occasional inclusions of small iron-manganese particles.	Slop molded..	17th	17th	3.2
571	1	240x115x55	9 1/2x 4 1/2 x 2 3/16	Mid orange brown sandy fabric. Frequent inclusions of sand, occasional angular stones and possible buff clay pellets.	Pallet molded.	16th – mid 17th	17th	3.2
574	1	225x115x50	8 7/8x 4 1/2 x 2	Fine mid-dark orange fabric. Frequent small voids and moderate inclusions of what appears to be iron particles. Occasional grains of sand.	Slop moulded.	16th – mid 17th	17th	3.2
574	2	240x114x60	9 7/16x 4 1/2 x 2 3/8	Fine mid to dark orange fabric. Frequent small voids and moderate inclusions of what appears to be iron particles.	Moulding is of poor standared. Probably pallet moulded.	17th	17th	3.2
574	1	240x115x51	9 7/16x 4 1/2 x 2	Light-mid orange sandy fabric. Frequent small voids and occasional small grog and buff clay pellets.	Slop moulded.	16th – mid 17th	17th	3.2
577	1	230x105x70	9 1/16x 4 1/8 x 2 3/4	Mid orange sandy fabric with occasional voids. Occasional small stones and frquent small maganese/iron particles.	Possibly slop moulded.	18th	18th – early 19th	4
577	1	230x115x50	9 1/16x 4 1/2 x 2	Fine mid to dark brown fabric. Frequent small voids and moderate inclusions of what appears to be iron particles.	Pallet moulded.	17th – 18th	18th – early 19th	4
577	1	230x115x50	9 1/16x 4 1/2 x 2	Fine mid-dark reddish brown fabric, frequent small voids and moderate inclusions of what appears to be iron particles. Occasional large inclusions of grog and line.	Pallet moulded.	17th – 18th	18th – early 19th	4
577	1	232x120x60	9 1/8x 4 3/4 x 2 3/8	Fine mid pinkish orange brown sandy fabric. Occasional small voids. Moderate inclusions iron particles. Also bands of yellow/ buff clay.	Pallet moulded.	17th – 18th	18th – early 19th	4
577	1	246x112x60	9 5/8x 4 3/8 x 2 3/8	Fine mid-dark reddish brown, sandy fabric. Occasional small voids and iron particles. No visable inclusions.	Pallet moulded.	17th	18th – early 19th	4
580	1	230x105x55	9 1/16x 4 1/8 x 2 3/16	Mid to dark orange sandy fabric. Occasional large stone and small stone inclusions. Flakey appearance to fabric.	Slop moulded.	16th – mid 17th	17th	3.2
580	1	230x105x55	9 1/16x 4 1/8 x 2 3/16	Mid to dark orange fabric with frequent small voids and moderate inclusions of what appears to be iron particles.	Slop molded. Appears to have rudimentary frog or tally mark on upper surface.	Mid 17th – early 18th	17th	3.2
584	1	240x115x57	9 7/16x 4 1/2 x 2 1/4	Mid to light Reddish brown Sandy fabric, frequent inclusions of small iron like particles and small voids occasional buff clay inclusions.	Slop moulded.	16th – mid 17th	18th – early 19th	4
589	1	228x110x68	9x 4 3/8 x21/2	Mid to dark reddish brown sandy fabric, frequent inclusions of small to medium iron like particles.	Probably slop moulded. Large dog paw print on upper surface.	18th	18th – early 19th	4
589	3	230x110x58	9 1/16x 4 3/8 x 2 1/4	Dark reddish brown sandy fabric. Occasional small voids, occasional small rounded white sand grains.	Pallet moulded.	18th	18th – early 19th	4

Appendix 1: Brick Catalogue 263

Context	Count	Dimensions (mm)	Dimensions (inches)	Fabric description	Method of manufacture and specific features	Date of manufacture?	Period dating	Period
589	1	235x115x60	9 1/4x 4 1/2 x 2 3/8	Mid orange brown, fine sandy fabric. Frequent small voids and frequent small flecs of iron/manganese.	Pallet moulded.	17th – 18th	18th – early 19th	4
591	1	235x115x50	9 1/4x 4 1/2 x 2	Light-mid pinkish orange sandy fabric. Frequent small voids, small grog pellets and buff clay pellets.	Slop moulded.	16th – 17th	18th – early 19th	4
592	1	230x115x50	9 1/16x 4 1/2 x 2	Light to mid pinkish orange sandy fabric. Frequent small voids occasional small grog pellets and buff clay pellets.	Slop moulded with finger indents at ends of one sanded side (side stacked).	16th – 17th	18th – early 19th	4
606	1	235x115x50	9 1/4x 4 1/2 x 2	Mid reddish brown and very fine fabric. Frequent inclusions of small quartz/ sand particles. Large voids in fabric and has glossy appearance.	Slop moulded.	16th – mid 17th	18th – early 19th	4
606	1	245x105x60	9 5/8x 4 1/8 x 2 3/8	Light-mid orange sandy fabric. Frequent small voids and occasional small grog and buff clay pellets.	Slop moulded.	16th – mid 17th	18th – early 19th	4
606	1	245x120x65	9 5/8x 4 3/4 x 2 1/2	Dark purple, nearly vitrified, over fired so unable to ID fabric.	Rough distorted sides.	??	18th – early 19th	4
606	1	250x120x75	9 3/4x 4 3/4 x 3	Dark reddish/purple brown, course sandy fabric. Frequent voids, frequent poorly sorted inclusions of dark purplish material(?) and pale clay inclusions. Orange brown band running lengthway along sanded base edge.	Pallet moulded.	Late 18th – 19th	18th – early 19th	4
606	1	262x120x70	10 1/4x 4 3/4 x 2 3/4	Dark reddish/purple brown, course sandy fabric. Frequent voids, frequent poorly sorted inclusions of dark purplish material(?) and pale clay inclusions. Orange brown band running lengthway along sanded base edge.	Pallet moulded.	18th – 19th	18th – early 19th	4
618	1	235x115x57	9 1/4x 4 1/2 x 2 1/4	Fine mid-dark orange fabric, frequent small voids and moderate inclusions of what appears to be iron particles.	Pallet moulded.	17th – 18th	18th – early 19th	4
619	1	210x115x65	8 3/8x 4 1/2 x 2 1/2	Rudimentary frog. Dark reddish brown fabric, bands of buff clay occasional large stone inclusions and frequent, poorly sorted iron(?) particles.	Covered in mortar but appears to have rudimentary shallow frog.	18th	18th – early 19th	4
664	1	240x115x53	9 7/16x 4 1/2 x 2 1/8	Light-mid orange sandy fabric. Frequent small voids and occasional small grog and buff clay pellets.	Slop moulded.	16th – mid 17th	17th	3.2
724	1	230x114x55	9 1/16x 4 1/2 x 2 3/16	Mid to dark reddish brown sandy fabric. Frequent inclusions of small iron like particles and small voids.	Pallet moulded.	17th	Late 17th – 18th	3.3
724	1	250x115x65	9 3/4x 4 1/2 x 2 1/2	Fine mid to dark Brown fabric. Frequent small voids and moderate inclusions of what appears to be iron particles.	Pallet moulded. Distorted due to over-firing.	17th	Late 17th – 18th	3.3
833	2	220x115x60	8 5/8x 4 1/2 x 2 3/8	Mid orange sandy fabric occasional small angular stone inclusions and occasional small voids.	Pallet moulded.	Mid 17th – 18th	18th – early 19th	4
833	1	222x115x60	8 3/4x 4 1/2 x 2 3/8	Mid orange brown, fine but flakey fabric. Large stone inclusions and occasional small buff clay particles.	Hard and well made, all sides have rough texture.	17th – 18th	18th – early 19th	4
833	1	228x110x52	9x 4 3/8 x 21/16	Mid to dark reddish brown sandy fabric, frequent inclusions of small to medium iron like particles.	Slop moulded.	16th – mid 17th	18th – early 19th	4
833	1	230x110x60	9 1/16x 4 3/8 x 2 3/8	Mid to light reddish brown sandy fabric, frequent inclusions of small iron like particles and small voids.	Slop moulded and partially burnt (re used).	(?) 16th – mid 17th	18th – early 19th	4

Context	Count	Dimensions (mm)	Dimensions (inches)	Fabric description	Method of manufacture and specific features	Date of manufacture?	Period dating	Period
833	1	240x115x50	9 7/16x 4 1/2 x 2	Mid to dark orange sandy fabric. Occasional large stone and small pebble inclusions.	Slop molded.	16th – mid 17th	18th – early 19th	4
833	1	240x120x65	9 7/16x 4 3/ 4x 2 1/2	Pale to mid brown sandy fabric. Occasional voids, frequent poorly sorted angular stones, small to medium buff particles.	Slop moulded.	Mid 17th – 18th	18th – early 19th	4
833	1	242x120x52	9 1/2x 4 3/4 x 2 1/16	Mid to light reddish brown sandy fabric. Frequent inclusions of small iron like particles and small voids.	Slop moulded.	16th – mid 17th	18th – early 19th	4
842	1	215x105x52	8 1/2x 4 1/8 x 2 1/16	Mid to dark reddish brown sandy fabric. Frequent inclusions of small to medium iron like particles.	Hard brick, poorly finished with frequent straw impressions all over and rough texture.	Mid 15th – 16th	Late 17th – 18th	3.3
842	2	235x110x51	9 1/8x 4 3/8 x 2	Fine mid pinkish orange brown sandy fabric. Moderate inclusions of iron particles. Also bands of yellow/buff clay.	Pallet moulded.	Early – mid 17th	Late 17th – 18th	3.3
842	1	240x116x53	9 7/16x 4 1/2 x 2 1/8	Coarse fabric, light pinkish brown colour. Occasional very small voids, frequent small buff particles and reddish brown grog (lumps).	Pallet moulded.	17th – 18th	Late 17th – 18th	3.3
844	2	220x110x75	8 5/8x 4 3/8 x 2 7/8	Dark purple exterior. Dark reddish brown core, frequent inclusions of small subrounded and angular stones.	Machine made engineering brick. Extremely hard brick, well formed with slightly rough exterior	19th	18th – early 19th	4
844	1	225x110x75	8 7/8x 4 3/8 x 2 7/8	Dark purple exterior with dark reddish brown core. Frequent inclusions of small subrounded and angular stones.	Machine made engineering brick. Extremely hard brick, well formed with slightly rough exterior.	19th	18th – early 19th	4
844	2	230x110x75	9x 4 3/8x 3	Dark purple exterior with reddish brown core. Frequent inclusions of small subrounded and angular stones.	Machine made engineering brick. Extremely hard brick, well formed with slightly rough exterior.	19th	18th – early 19th	4
848	1	240x110x65	9 7/16x 4 3/8 x 2 1/2	Pale to mid brown sandy fabric. Occasional voids, frquent poorly sorted angular stones, small to medium buff particles.	(?) Pallet moulded.	Mid 17th – late 18th	18th – early 19th	4
849	1	230x115x50	9 1/16x 4 1/2 x 2	Coarse orange brown fabric, flakey appearance, frequent small voids, occasional small stones and small buff parcles.	Possible pallet moulded. Sanded base with grass or chaff imprints. All other surfaces sanded to a lesser degree.	17th	18th – early 19th	4
849	1	230x115x55	9 1/16x 4 1/2 x 2 3/16	Fine orange fabric with occasional inclusions of small iron-manganese partcles.	Pallet moulded. Sanded base with grass or chaff imprints. All other surfaces sanded to a lesser degree.	17-M18C	18th – early 19th	4
849	1	235x110x70	9 1/4x 4 3/8 x 2 3/4	Brick is grossly over fired.	Moulded brick. Lumpy and irregular finish.	18th	18th – early 19th	4
849	1	235x115x50	9 1/4x 4 1/2 x 2	Light-mid pinkish orange sandy fabric. Frequent small voids, small grog pellets and buff clay pellets.	Slop moulded.	16th – 17th	18th – early 19th	4
849	1	235x115x70	9 1/4x 4 1/2 x 2 3/4	Fine mid to dark brown fabric. Frequent small voids and moderate inclusions of what appears to be iron particles.	Pallet moulded.	18th	18th – early 19th	4
850	1	245x120x60	9 5/8x 4 3/4 x 2 3/8	Fine mid-dark orange fabric, frequent small voids and moderate inclusions of what appears to be iron particles.	Pallet molded.	16th – mid 17th	18th – early 19th	4

Appendix 1: Brick Catalogue 265

Context	Count	Dimensions (mm)	Dimensions (inches)	Fabric description	Method of manufacture and specific features	Date of manufacture?	Period dating	Period
851	1	230x115x47	9 1/16x 4 1/2 x 2	Fine mid to dark reddish brown fabric, frequent small voids and moderate inclusions of what appears to be iron particles. Occasional large inclusions of grog and lime.	Pallet moulded.	17th	18th – early 19th	4
851	1	230x115x49	9 1/16x 4 1/2 x 2	Lght to mid orange sandy fabric. Frequent small voids and occasional small grog pellets and buff clay pellets.	Pallet moulded.	16th – 17th	18th – early 19th	4
851	1	235x115x52	9 1/4x 4 1/2 x 2 1/16	Fine mid-dark reddish brown fabric. Frequent small voids and moderate inclusions of what appears to be iron particles. Occasional large inclusions of grog and lime.	Pallet moulded.	17th	18th – early 19th	4
851	1	235x115x58	9 1/4x 4 1/2 x 2 1/4	Fine mid-dark reddish brown fabric. Frequent small voids and moderate inclusions of what appears to be iron particles. Occasional large inclusions of grog and lime.	Pallet moulded.	17th	18th – early 19th	4
851	1	239x120x50	9 3/8x 4 3/4 x 2	Mid orange brown sandy fabric. Occasional small voids. Inclusions require further research.	Slop molded.	(?) 16 – 17th	18th – early 19th	4
853	1	237x110x72	9 5/16x 4 3/8 x 2 3/4	Fine mid-dark orange fabric, frequent small voids and moderate inclusions of what appears to be iron particles.	(?) Machine manufactured.	Late 18th – 19th	18th – early 19th	4
853	2	240x110x75	9 7/16x 4 3/8 x 3	Fine mid to dark orange fabric. Frequent small voids and moderate inclusions of what appears to be iron particles.	Machine manufactured brick.	Late 18th – 19th	18th – early 19th	4
854	1	220x110x50	8 5/8x 4 3/8 x 2	Coarse fabric, light pinkish brown in colour. Occasional small voids, frequent small buff particles and reddish brown grog.	Slop moulded.	16th – mid 17th	18th – early 19th	4
854	1	230x100x50	9 1/16x 4x 2	Coarse fabric with light pinkish brown colour. Occasional very small voids, frequent small buff particles and reddish brown grog (lumps).	Pallet Moulded.	(?) 16th – mid 17th	18th – early 19th	4
854	3	242x115x67	9 1/2x 4 1/2 x 2 3/4	Mould made brick, Dark orange brown. Fine sandy fabric. Frequent inclusions of small iron particles.	Possibly machine pressed or slop moulded.	19th	18th – early 19th	4
855	1	225x115x60	8 7/8x 4 1/2 x 2 3/8	Dark reddish brown very fine fabric with frequent inclusions of small quartz/ sand particles. Large voids in fabric.	Slop molded.	Mid 17th – 18th	18th – early 19th	4
855	1	235x110x65	9x 4 3/8x21/2	Dark reddish brown very fine fabric. Frequent inclusions of small quartz/ sand particles. Large voids in fabric.	Slop moulded. Base also has chaff or grass indents as does one side.	Mid 17th – 18th	18th – early 19th	4
855	1	235x114x60	9 1/4x 4 1/2 x 2 3/8	Dark reddish brown and very fine fabric. Frequent inclusions of small quartz/ sand particles. Large voids in fabric.	Slop moulded	Mid 17th – 18th	18th – early 19th	4
855	1	235x115x65	9 1/4x 4 1/2 x 2 1/2	Dark reddish brown and very fine fabric. Frequent inclusions of small quartz/ sand particles. Large voids in fabric.	Slop molded. Base has chaff or grass imprints.	Mid 17th – 18th	18th – early 19th	4
856	1	230x110x85	9 1/16x 4 3/ 8x 3 3/8	Homogeneous reddish brown fabric. Frequent small reddish rounded to angular stones. Moderate small voids.	Machine moulded brick well shaped and squared, all surfaces smooth.	Late 18th – 19th	18th – early 19th	4
856	1	235x110x70	9 1/4x 4 3/8 x 2 3/4	Light pinkish orange fabric. Coarse texture with frequent small voids and sub rounded stone inclusions. Occasional buff clay pellets.	Machine Moulded brick. Well shaped and squared, all surfaces smooth.	Late 18th – 19th	18th – early 19th	4
857	5	234x110x85	9 1/4x 4 3/8 x 3 3/8	Light pinkish orange fabric. Coarse texture with frequent small voids and sub rounded stone inclusions. Occasional buff clay pellets.	Appears to be extruded, mechanised brick. All sides have a slightly rough texture and appears to be wire cut.	19th – early 20th	18th – early 19th	4

Context	Count	Dimensions (mm)	Dimensions (inches)	Fabric description	Method of manufacture and specific features	Date of manufacture?	Period dating	Period
883	1	235x115x55	9 1/4x 4 1/2 x 2 3/16	Homogeneous reddish brown fabric. Frequent small reddish rounded/angular stones. Moderate small voids.	Slop moulded.	16th – mid 17th	17th – 18th	3.2/3
885	1	235x115x57	9 1/4x 4 1/2 x 2 1/4	Coarse fabric with light pinkish brown colour. Occasional very small voids, frequent small buff particles and reddish brown grog (lumps).	Pallet molded.	16th – mid 17th	17th – 18th	3.2/3
885	1	255x120x55	10x 4 3/4 x 2 3/16	Coarse fabric, light pinkish brown colour. Occasional very small voids, frequent small buff particles and reddish brown brick fragments.	Pallet moulded.	16th – mid 17th	17th – 18th	3.2/3
901	1	220x120x55	8 5/8x 43/4W x 2 3/16	Fine mid reddish brown fabric with moderate to frequent inclusions of small iron or manganese particles. Occasional large stone fragments.	Slop molded. Base has diagonal twig imprints.	16th – mid 17th	16th – 18th	3
901	2	225x115x65	8 7/8x 4 1/2 x 2 1/2	Mid tod ark reddish brown sandy fabric, frequent inclusions of small to medium iron like particles and buff inclusions.	Slop moulded.	17th	16th – 18th	3
901	1	230x120x58	9 1/16x 4 3/4 x 2 1/4	Fine orange fabric with occasional inclusions of small iron-manganese particles.	Poorly moulded. Upper surface smooth but all others irregular. Base is sanded and has diagonal twig imprints.	16th – mid 17th	16th – 18th	3
901	1	230x120x65	9 1/16x 4 3/4 x 2 1/2	Fine orange fabric with occasional inclusions of small iron-manganese particles.	Poorly moulded. Upper surface smooth but all others irregular. Base is sanded and has diagonal twig imprints.	17th	16th – 18th	3
901	1	245x125x55	9 5/8x 4 7/8 x 2 3/16	Light to mid orange sandy fabric. Frequent small voids and occasional small grog and buff clay pellets.	Pallet moulded. Large dogs paw print in centre.	16th – mid 17th	16th – 18th	3
908	3	230x115x55	9 1/16x 4 1/2 x 2 3/16	Mid to dark reddish brown sandy fabric. Frequent inclusions of small to medium iron like particles.	Roughly shaped 'patted brick'. Extremely rough base (sandy) covered in straw impressions. One side has occasional straw imprints. All surfaces roughly finished, though upper surface is slightly smooth.	(?) 14th – (?) 15th	16th – 18th	3
908	1	230x115x60	9 1/16x 4 1/2 x 2 3/8	Mid to dark reddish brown sandy fabric. Frequent inclusions of small to medium iron like particles.	Roughly shaped 'patted brick'. Extremely rough base (sandy) covered in straw impressions. One side has occasional straw imprints. All surfaces roughly finished though upper is slightly smooth.	(?) 14th – (?) 15th	16th – 18th	3
908	1	230x120x60	9 1/16x 4 3/4 x 2 3/8	Mid to dark reddish brown sandy fabric. Frequent inclusions of small to medium iron like particles.	Roughly shaped 'patted brick'. Extremely rough base (sandy) covered in straw impressions. One side has occasional straw imprints. All surfaces roughly finished though upper is slightly smooth.	(?) 14th – (?) 15th	16th – 18th	3
915	1	235x105x51	9 1/4x 4 1/8 x 2T	Moulded brick, Mid orange brown sandy faric. Frequent inclusions of silica and occasional angular stones and possible buff clay pellets.	Pallet moulded.	16th – mid 17th	Late 17th – 18th	3.3
915	1	235x110x60	9 1/4x 4 3/8 x 2 3/8	Coarse fabric with dark brown core and patchy black and blue grey 'crust'. Frequent inclusions of sub rounded and angular stones.	Slop moulded.	16th – mid 17th	18th – early 19th	4

Appendix 1: Brick Catalogue 267

Context	Count	Dimensions (mm)	Dimensions (inches)	Fabric description	Method of manufacture and specific features	Date of manufacture?	Period dating	Period
915	1	235x115x60	9 1/4x 4 1/2 x 2 3/8	Mid orange brown sandy fabric. Frequent inclusions of sand, occasional angular stones and possible buff clay pellets.	Pallet moulded.	16th – mid 17th	18th – early 19th	4
915	1	240x120x60	9 7/16x 4 3/8 x 2 3/8	Coarse orange brown fabric, flakey appearance. Frequent small voids, occasional small stones and small buff particles.	Slop moulded.	Mid 17th – 18th	18th – early 19th	4
915	1	240x120x68	9 7/16x 4 3/4 x 2 5/8	Mid orange brown sandy fabric. Frequent inclusions of silica, occasional angular stones and possible buff clay pellets.	Pallet moulded.	17th	18th – early 19th	4
928	1	240x120x55	9 7/16x 4 3/4 x 2 3/16	Light-mid orange sandy fabric. Frequent small voids and occasional small grog and buff clay pellets.	Slop moulded	16th – mid 17th	Late 17th – 18th	3.3
928	1	243x122x53	9 1/2x 4 3/4 x 2 1/4	Light to mid orange sandy fabric. Frequent small voids and occasional small grog and buff clay pellets.	Slop moulded.	16th – mid 17th	Late 17th – 18th	3.3
928	1	245x125x53	9 5/8x 4 7/8 x 2 1/4	Light to mid orange sandy fabric. Frequent small voids and occasional small grog and buff clay pellets.	Slop moulded.	16th – mid 17th	Late 17th – 18th	3.3
967	3	240x115x57	9 7/16x 4 1/2 x 2 1/4	Reddish orange fabric with frequent small voids and occasional small pale clay/grog pellets.	Slop moulded.	16th – mid 17th	16th – 17th	3.1
967	1	247x115x57	9 3/4x 4 1/2 x 2 1/4	Reddish orange fabric with frequent small voids and occasional small pale clay/grog pellets.	Slop moulded.	16th – mid 17th	16th – 17th	3.1
973	1	235x115x60	9 1/4x 4 1/2 x 2 3/8	Mid to dark orange/brown sandy fabric. Occasional large stone and small stone inclusions. Flakey appearance to fabric.	Pallet moulded.	16th – mid 17th		Late 4
984	1	250x130x50	9 3/4x 5 1/8 x 2	Coarse fabric, light pinkish brown colour, occasional very small voids, frequent small buff particles and reddish brown grog (lumps).	Slop moulded. Small irregular indents to upper surface caused by exposure to gentle rain.	16th – mid 17th	17th	3.2
988	1	235x115x53	9 1/4x 4 3/8 x 2 1/8	Light to mid orange sandy fabric. Frequent small voids and occasional small grog pellets and buff clay pellets. Occasional small angular stones.	Pallet moulded.	16th – mid 17th	Late 17th – 18th	3.3
988	1	240x110x55	9 7/16x 4 3/8 x 2 3/16	Light to mid orange sandy fabric. Frequent small voids and occasional small grog and buff clay pellets. Occasional small angular stones.	Pallet moulded.	16th – mid 17th	Late 17th – 18th	3.3
993	1	230x110x60	9 1/16x 4 3/8 x 2 3/8	Mid reddish brown and very fine fabric. Frequent inclusions of small quartz/ sand particles and Iron? Small buff clay pellets. Large voids in fabric and has glossy appearance (overfired?).	Pallet moulded.	(?)17th	16th – 17th	3.1
993	1	240x120x55	9 7/16x 4 3/4 x 2 3/16	Mid reddish brown very fine fabric with frequent inclusions of small quartz/ sand particles and Iron? Small buff clay pellets. Large voids in fabric and has glossy appearance (overfired?).	Pallet moulded.	16th – mid 17th	16th – 17th	3.1
993	2	240x120x60	9 7/16x 4 3/4 x 2 3/8	Mid reddish brown and very fine fabric. Frequent inclusions of small quartz/ sand particles and Iron? Small buff clay pellets. Large voids in fabric and has glossy appearance (overfired?)	Pallet moulded.	16th – mid 17th	16th – 17th	3.1
1035	1	220x115x55	8 5/8x 4 1/2 x 2 3/16	Partial brick, broken length, Pale to mid brown sandy fabric. Occasional voids, frequent poorly sorted angular stones, small to medium buff particles.	Slop molded. Has drips of dark green glaze along sides.	(?) Late 15th – 16th	Late 17th – 18th	3.3

Context	Count	Dimensions (mm)	Dimensions (inches)	Fabric description	Method of manufacture and specific features	Date of manufacture?	Period dating	Period
1035	1	245x115x55	9 5/8x 4 1/2 x 2 3/16	Light to mid orange sandy fabric. Frequent small voids and occasional small grog and buff clay pellets.	Pallet moulded.	16th – mid 17th	Late 17th – 18th	3.3
1035	1	247x115x55	9 3/4x 4 1/2 x 2 3/16	Pale to mid brown sandy fabric. Occasional voids, frequent poorly sorted angular stones and small to medium buff particles.	Slop moulded. Has drips of dark green glaze along sides.	mid 15th – 16th	Late 17th – 18th	3.3
1035	1	250x110x52	9 3/4x 4 3/8 x 2 1/16	Pale to mid brown sandy fabric. Occasional voids, frequent poorly sorted angular stones and small to medium buff particles.	Slop molded. Has drips of dark green glaze along sides.	mid 15th – 16th	Late 17th – 18th	3.3
1035	1	250x113x52	9 3/4x 4 1/2 x 2 1/16	Reddish orange brown fabric. Fine sandy with moderate inclusions of sub rounded pebbles and frequent small (unidentified) buff particles.	Pallet moulded.	16th – mid 17th	Late 17th – 18th	3.3
1041	1	235x115x55	9 1/4x 4 1/2 x2 3/16	Homogeneous reddish brown fabric. Frequent small reddish rounded-angular stones. Moderate small voids.	Slop moulded.	16th – mid 17th	17th	3.2
1041	1	235x120x56	9 1/4x 4 3/4 x 2 3/16	Mid orange to brown sandy faric. Frequent inclusions of sand and occasional angular stones and possible buff clay pellets. Frequent small voids. Flakey texture.	Pallet moulded.	16th – mid 17th	17th	3.2
1041	1	237x115x50	9 5/16x 4 1/2 x 2	Fine mid to dark orange fabric. Frequent small voids and moderate inclusions of what appears to be iron particles.	Pallet moulded.	17th	17th	3.2
1132	1	230x120x50	9 1/16x 4 3/4 x 2	Coarse orange brown fabric with flakey appearance. Frequent small voids, occasional small stones and small buff particles.	Pallet moulded.	16th – mid 17th	18th – early 19th	4
1137	1	235x115x50	9 1/4x 4 1/2 x 2	Homogeneous reddish brown fabric. Frequent small reddish rounded-angular stones. Moderate small voids.	Pallet moulded.	16th – mid 17th	17th	3.2
1137	1	240x118x53	9 7/16x 4 9/16 x 2 1/8	Light-mid orange sandy fabric. Frequent small voids and occasional small grog and buff clay pellets.	Pallet moulded.	16th – mid 17th	17th	3.2
1137	1	240x120x55	9 7/16x 4 3/4 x 2 3/16	Mid to dark orange brown sandy fabric, frequent inclusions of small iron like particles and small voids. Occasional buff clay inclusions.	Pallet moulded.	16th – mid 17th	17th	3.2
1137	1	245x125x50	9 5/8x 5x 2	Coarse fabric, light pinkish brown in colour. Occasional very small voids, frequent small buff particles and reddish brown grog (lumps).	Slop moulded. Chamfered end (retained).	16th – mid 17th	17th	3.2
1140	1	220x110x50	8 5/8x 4 3/8 x 2	Mid to dark orange brown sandy fabric. Frequent inclusions of small iron like particles and small voids. Occasional buff clay inclusions.	Slop molded.	16th – mid 17th	17th	3.2
1140	1	228x110x55	9x 4 3/8 x 2 3/16	Mid to dark orange fabric, occasional small stones, single reddish brown clay inclusion, and frequent small voids.	Pallet moulded.	16th – mid 17th	17th	3.2
1140	1	230x110x55	9 1/16x 4 3/8 x 2 3/16	Mid to dark orange brown sandy fabric. Frequent inclusions of small iron like particles and small voids. Occasional buff clay inclusions.	Slop moulded.	16th – mid 17th	17th	3.2
1140	1	232x110x58	9 1/8x 4 3/8 x 2 1/4	Mid to dark orange fabric. Occasional small stones, single reddish brown clay inclusion and frequent small voids.	Pallet moulded. Has small hoof imprints.	16th – mid 17th	17th	3.2
1147	1	210x110x55	8 3/8x 4 3/8 x 2 3/16	Coarse orange brown fabric with flakey appearance. Frequent small voids, occasional small stones and small buff particles.	Pallet moulded.	16th – mid 17th	17th	3.2

Appendix 1: Brick Catalogue 269

Context	Count	Dimensions (mm)	Dimensions (inches)	Fabric description	Method of manufacture and specific features	Date of manufacture?	Period dating	Period
1147	1	215x110x55	8 1/2x 4 3/8 x 2 3/16	Mid to very dark brown coarse fabric. Frequent inclusions requiring further identification.	Pallet moulded.	16th – mid 17th	17th	3.2
1151	1	240x125x65	9 7/16x 5 x 2 1/2	Mid orange brown sandy fabric. Occasional small voids, moderate sand and small angular stones.	Pallet moulded. Specialised brick bent to form curve. Well or arch brick. Bent in upwards direction shortly after moulding. Surface has secondary smoothing.	Late 17th – 18th	Late 17th – 18th	3.3
1151	1	247x112x62	9 3/4x 4 3/8 x 2 1/2	Pale to mid brownsandy fabric. Occasional voids, frequent poorly sorted angular stones, small to medium buff particles.	Pallet moulded.	Late 17th – 18th	Late 17th – 18th	3.3
1156	1	235x110x62	9 1/4x 4 3/8 x 2 3/8	Dark reddish/purple brown, coarse sandy fabric. Frequent voids, frequent poorly sorted inclusions of dark purplish material(?) and pale clay inclusions. Orange brown band running lengthway along sanded base edge.	Pallet moulded. Early frog impression.	Early 18th	17th – 18th	3.2/3
1156	1	240x110x60	9 7/16x 4 3/8 x 2 3/8	Mid toDark Reddish brown sandy fabric. Frequent inclusions of small to medium iron like particles.	Pallet moulded. Rudimentary frog impressed with stick to base.	Early 18th	17th – 18th	3.2/3
1156	1	240x110x62	9 7/16x 4 3/8 x 2 3/8	Dark reddish/purple brown, coarse sandy fabric. Frequent voids, frequent poorly sorted inclusions of dark purplish material(?), pale clay inclusions. Orange brown band running lengthway along base edge.	Pallet moulded. Rudimentary frog impressed with stick to base.	Early 18th	17th – 18th	3.2/3
1156	1	242x115x55	9 1/2x 4 1/2 x 2 3/16	Fine mid-dark orange fabric, frequent small voids and moderate inclusions of what appears to be iron particles.	Pallet moulded. Rudimentary frog impressed with stick into sanded base.	Early 18th	17th – 18th	3.2/3
1156	1	242x115x55	9 1/2x 4 1/2 x 2 3/16	Dark reddish/purple brown, course sandy fabric. Frequent voids, frequent poorly sorted inclusions of dark purplish material(?) pale clay inclusions. Orange brown band running lengthway along sanded base edge.	Pallet moulded.	Early 18th	17th – 18th	3.2/3
1158	1	235x115x65	9 1/4x 4 1/2 x 2 1/2	Coarse fabric with pinkish orange crust. Core is orange/brown in colour. Frequent small voids with occasional rounded buff grog and angular stone inclusions.	Moulded. Well formed but distorted (some lumping of sides due to over firing).	Mid 17th – 18th	17th – 18th	3.2/3
1158	1	245x115x52	9 5/8x 4 1/2 x 2 1/16	Fine dark reddish orange fabric. Frequent small voids and moderate inclusions of what appears to be iron particles.	Moulded brick with mortar on all surfaces.	16th – mid 17th	17th – 18th	3.2/3
1166	1	230x100x60	9 1/16x 4 x 2 3/8	Highly unusual fabric with multi coloured swirls to fabric. Requires further analysis.	Uneven surfaces with sanded finish. All edges are rounded.	(?) 17th	Late 17th – early 19th	3.3/4
1230	1	230x110x52	9 1/16x 4 3/8 x 2 1/16	Light brown sandy fabric, frequent small dark brown claypellet inclusions.	Slop moulded.	16th – mid 17th	16th – 17th	3.1
1231	1	230x110x50	9 1/16x 4 3/8 x 2	Mid brown fabric with reddish tinge around edges. Occasional buff pellets, white sand grains and iron/manganese.	Pallet moulded.	16th – mid 17th	16th – 17th	3.1
1242	1	250x118x50	9 3/4x 4 9/16 x 2	Reddish orange fabric with frequent small voids and occasional small pale clay/grog pellets.	Pallet moulded	16th – mid 17th	Late 17th – 18th centur	3.3
1250	2	230x105x65	9 1/16x 4 1/8 x 2 1/2	Fine dark reddish orange fabric with frequent small voids and moderate inclusions of what appears to be iron particles.	Moulded brick covered in mortar.	Mid 17th – late 18th	Late 17th – 18th	3.3

Context	Count	Dimensions (mm)	Dimensions (inches)	Fabric description	Method of manufacture and specific features	Date of manufacture?	Period dating	Period
1250	1	235x115x70	9 1/4x 4 1/2 x 2 3/4	Mid to dark orange brown sandy fabric. Frequent inclusions of small iron like particles, small voids and occasional buff clay inclusions.	Machine moulded brick. Well shaped with all surfaces lightly sanded.	18th	Late 17th – 18th	3.3
1250	1	245x110x52	9 5/8x 4 3/8 x 2 1/16	Pale to mid brown sandy fabric. Occasional voids, frequent poorly sorted angular stones and small to medium buff particles.	Pallet moulded.	17th	Late 17th – 18th	3.3
1260	1	245x125x60	9 5/8x 4 7/8 x 2 3/8	Coarse orange brown fabric. Flakey appearance with frequent small voids, occasional small stones and small buff particles.	Pallet molded.	17th	Late 17th – 18th	3.3
1265	1	235x115x57	9 1/4x 4 1/2 x 2 1/4	Mid orange brown sandy faric. Frequent inclusions of silica and occasional angular stones and possible buff clay pellets. Frequent small voids. Overall flakey texture.	Pallet moulded.	Early – mid 17th	Late 17th – 18th	3.3
1265	1	240x120x65	9 7/16x 4 3/4 x 2 1/2	Mid to dark brown, coarse sandy fabric. Frequent small buff inclusions (grog?).	Pallet moulded.	Mid 17th – 18th	Late 17th – 18th	3.3
1265	1	245x115x65	9 5/8x 4 1/2 x 2 1/2	Mid to dark reddish brown, sandy fabric. Stone inclusions, frequent sand and iron particles. Patches of grey reduction.	Moulded brick.	mid 17th – 18th	Late 17th – 18th	3.3
1265	1	250x115x53	9 3/4x 4 1/2 x 2 1/8	Coarse fabric, light pinkish brown colour. Occasional very small voids, frequent small buff particles and reddish brown grog (lumps).	Slop moulded.	16th – mid 17th	Late 17th – 18th	3.3
1269	1	205x105x55	8 1/8x 4 1/8 x 2 3/16	Mid to very dark brown course fabric. Frequent inclusions. Requires further fabric analysis	Pallet moulded.	16th – mid 17th	17th	3.2
1269	1	215x110x50	8 1/2x 4 3/8 x 2	Coarse orange brown fabric with flakey appearance. Frequent small voids, occasional small stones and small buff particles.	Pallet moulded. Two small kitten paw prints on upper surface.	16th – mid 17th	17th	3.2
1269	1	225x110x55	8 7/8x 4 3/8 x 2 3/16	Mid to dark orange brown sandy fabric, frequent inclusions of small iron like particles and small voids, occasional buff clay inclusions.	Pallet moulded.	16th – mid 17th	17th	3.2
1269	1	230x110x60	9 1/16x 4 3/8 x 2 3/8	Mid to dark orange fabric with occasional small stones, single reddish brown clay inclusion and frequent small voids.	Pallet moulded.	16th – mid 17th	17th	3.2
1280	1	240x120x55	9 7/16x 4 3/4 x 2 3/16	Mid to dark reddish brown and sandy fabric. Stone inclusions, frequent sand and iron particles. Patches of grey reduction.	Moulded brick.	16th – mid 17th	16th – 17th	3.1
1280	1	240x120x55	9 7/16x 4 3/4 x 2 3/16	Extremely dark brown fabric with frequent inclusions. Requires further research	Moulded brick	16th – mid 17th	16th – 17th	3.1
1289	1	234x120x57	9 1/4x 4 3/4 x 2 1/4	Not cut as has glaze dribbled across the surface.	Pallet moulded. Has glaze dribbles side flowing onto upper surface. Possible kiln brick.	16th – mid 17th	Late 17th – 18th	3.3
1289	1	235x115x57	9 1/4x 4 1/2 x 2 1/4	Fine mid-dark orange fabric. Frequent small voids and moderate inclusions of what appears to be iron particles. Occasional grains of sand.	Pallet moulded.	16th – mid 17th	Late 17th – 18th	3.3
1289	1	235x115x65	9 1/4x 4 1/2 x 2 1/2	Fine mid-dark orange fabric. Frequent small voids and moderate inclusions of what appears to be iron particles. Occasional grains of sand.	Pallet moulded.	Mid 17th – mid 18th	Late 17th – 18th	3.3

Appendix 1: Brick Catalogue 271

Context	Count	Dimensions (mm)	Dimensions (inches)	Fabric description	Method of manufacture and specific features	Date of manufacture?	Period dating	Period
1289	1	235x120x55	9 1/4x 4 3/4 x 2 3/16	Fine mid to dark orange fabric. Frequent small voids and moderate inclusions of what appears to be iron particles. Occasional grains of sand.	Pallet moulded.	Mid 17th – mid 18th	Late 17th – 18th	3.3
1321	1	216x104x70	8 1/2x 4 1/8 x 2 3/4	Fine mid-dark orange fabric. Frequent small voids and moderate inclusions of what appears to be iron particles.	Pallet moulded.	18th	Late 17th – early 19th	3.3/4
1321	1	225x100x70	8 7/8x 4x 2 3/4	Mid to dark reddish brown sandy fabric. Frequent inclusions of small iron like particles and small voids.	Highly fired.	18th	Late 17th – early 19th	3.3/4
1321	1	235x120x55	9 1/4x 4 3/4 x 2 3/16	Light to mid orange sandy fabric. Frequent small voids and occasional small grog pellets and buff clay pellets.	Pallet moulded.	17th	Late 17th – early 19th	3.3/4
1321	2	240x115x55	9 7/16x 4 1/2 x 2 3/16	Reddish orange brown fabric. Fine sandy with moderate inclusions of sub rounded pebbles and frequent small (unidentified) buff particles.	Pallet moulded.	16th – mid 17th	Late 17th – early 19th	3.3/4
1321	37	123x60	4 7/8x 2 3/8	Coarse orange brown fabric, flakey appearance, frequent small voids, occasional small stones and small buff parcles.	Fragmented lengths of brick window mullion. Two chamfered edges, well finished, some with substantial decay. Re-used as wall foundation.	16th – 17th	Late 17th – early 19th	3.3/4
1338	1	220x115x65	8 5/8x 4 1/2 x 2 1/2	Mid orange brown sandy faric. Frequent inclusions of sand, occasional angular stones and possible buff clay pellets. Frequent small voids. flakey texture.	Pallet moulded.	17th	Late 17th – early 19th	3.3/4
1338	1	240x115x52	9 7/16x 4 1/2 x 2 1/16	Mid orange brown sandy faric. Frequent inclusions of sand and occasional angular stones and possible buff clay pellets. Frequent small voids. Flakey texture.	Pallet moulded.	16th – mid 17th	Late 17th – early 19th	3.3/4
1338	1	240x115x55	9 7/16x 4 1/2 x 2 3/16	Fine mid-dark orange fabric. Frequent small voids and moderate inclusions of what appears to be iron particles and white sand grains.	Pallet molded.	16th – mid 17th	Late 17th – early 19th	3.3/4
1338	1	240x120x50	9 7/16x 4 3/4 x 2	Light to mid orange sandy fabric. Frequenr small voids and occasional small grog and buff clay pellets.	Slop moulded.	16th – mid 17th	Late 17th – early 19th	3.3/4
1338	1	250x110x50	9 3/4x 4 3/8 x 1 3/4	Dark orange brown sandy fabric. Frequent inclusions of small iron like particles and small voids. Occasional buff clay inclusions.One large stone inclusion.	Slop moulded.	16th – mid 17th	Late 17th – early 19th	3.3/4
1398	1	222x110x60	8 3/4x 4 3/8 x 2 3/8	Fine mid-dark orange fabric, frequent small voids and moderate inclusions of what appears to be iron particles.	Pallet Moulded	Mid 17th – 18th	Late 17th – early 19th	3.3/4
1398	1	223x110x65	8 3/4x 4 3/8 x 2 1/2	Fine mid-dark orange fabric, frequent small voids and moderate inclusions of what appears to be iron particles.	Pallet moulded.	Mid 17th – 18th	Late 17th – early 19th	3.3/4
1398	1	237x115x53	9 1/4x 4 1/2 x 2 1/8	Dark reddish brown and very fine fabric. Frequent inclusions of small quartz/ sand particles, Iron, and small buff clay pellets. Large voids in fabric and has glossy appearance (overfired?).	Pallet moulded.	16th – mid 17th	Late 17th – early 19th	3.3/4
1398	1	238x115x60	9 3/8x 4 1/2 x 2 3/8	Unrecorded.	Pallet moulded.	Mid 17th – 18th	Late 17th – early 19th	3.3/4

Context	Count	Dimensions (mm)	Dimensions (inches)	Fabric description	Method of manufacture and specific features	Date of manufacture?	Period dating	Period
1398	1	240x120x55	9 7/16x 4 3/4 x 2 3/16	Reddish orange fabric with frequent small voids and occasional small pale clay/grog pellets.	Slop moulded.	16th – mid 17th	Late 17th – early 19th	3.3/4
1398	1	123x60	4 7/8x 2 3/8	Coarse orange brown fabric, flakey appearance, frequent small voids, occasional small stones and small buff particles.	Fragmented lengths of brick window mullion. Two chamfered edges, over all well finished, some decay. Re-used as wall foundation.	16th – 17th	Late 17th – early 19th	3.3/4
1400	1	230x115x70	9 1/16x 4 1/2 x 2 3/4	Dark reddish brown sandy fabric. Occasional small voids, occasional small rounded white sand grains.	Well shaped with All surfaces lightly sanded.	Mid 17th – late 18th	Late 17th – early 19th	3.3/4
1400	2	235x120x70	9 1/4 4 3/4 x 2 3/4	Dark reddish brown sandy fabric. Occasional small voids, occasional small rounded white sand/quartz grains.	Moulded brick. Well shaped with all surfaces smooth.	Mid 17th – late 18th	Late 17th – early 19th	3.3/4
1400	1	240x110x63	9 7/16x 4 3/8 x 2 1/2	Dark reddish brown sandy fabric Occasional small voids with occasional small rounded white sand grains.	(?) Slop moulded..	Mid 17th – late 18th	Late 17th – early 19th	3.3
1444	1	230x120x65	9 1/16x 4 3/4 x 2 1/2	Mid orange to reddish sandy fabric. Occasional small angular stone inclusions and occasional small voids.	Pallet moulded.	mid 17th – 18th	Late 17th – early 19th	3.3/4
1444	1	235x118x55	9 1/4x 4 9/16 x 2 3/16	Mid orange to reddish sandy fabric. Occasional small angular stone inclusions and occasional small voids.	Pallet moulded. All base edges have been rounded off.	16th – mid 17th	Late 17th – early 19th	3.3/3.4
1444	1	240x125x60	9 7/16x 5 x 2 3/8	Coarse fabric, mid to dark brown with frequent inclusions of small angular stones, poorly sorted.	Pallet moulded.	Late 17th – 18th	Late 17th – early 19th	3.3/3.4
1444	1	245x110x70	9 5/8x 4 3/8 x 2 3/4	Mid orange brown sandy fabric. Frequent inclusions of sand, occasional angular stones and possible buff clay pellets.	Pallet moulded.	Late 17th – early 18th	Late 17th – early 19th	3.3/3.4
1509	2	240x120x57	9 7/16x 4 3/4 x 2 1/4	Reddish orange fabric with frequent small voids and occasional small pale clay/grog pellets.	Pallet moulded. Possible finger indented frog.	16th – mid 17th	Late 17th – early 19th	3.3/4
1512	1	235x120x52	9 1/4x 4 3/4 x 2 1/16	Homogeneous reddish brown fabric. Frequent small reddish rounded-angular stones. Moderate small voids.	Pallet moulded.	16th – mid 17th	Late 17th – early 19th	3.3
1512	1	245x125x50	9 5/8x 5x 2	Fine mid-dark orange fabric Frequent small voids and moderate inclusions of what appears to be iron particles. Occasional grains of sand.	Pallet molded.	16th – mid 17th	Late 17th – early 19th	3.3
1526	1	240x115x50	9 7/16x 4 1/2 x 2	Brown fabric with frequent inclusions. Fabric requires further research.	Pallet moulded.	16th – mid 17th	Late 17th – early 19th	3.3
1526	1	255x125x52	10x 4 7/8 x 2 1/16	Mid orange brown sandy fabric. Frequent inclusions of sand, occasional angular stones and possible buff clay pellets. Frequent small voids. Flakey texture.	Pallet moulded.	16th – mid 17th	Late 17th – early 19th	3.3
1545	1	215x100x70	8 1/2x 4 x 2 3/4	Mid to dark reddish orange. Frequent inclusions of small iron particles.	Pallet moulded.	Mid 17th – 18th	17th	3.2
1545	1	240x120x60	9 7/16x 4 3/4 x 2 3/8	Moulded brick, vitrified, bubbled and deep purple in colour.	N/A	Early – mid 17th	17th	3.2
1545	3	245x120x60	9 5/8x 4 3/4 x 2 3/8	Vitrified, bubbled and deep purple. Overfired with body distortion.	Appears to be pallet moulded.	Early 17th – mid 17th	17th	3.2

Appendix 1: Brick Catalogue 273

Context	Count	Dimensions (mm)	Dimensions (inches)	Fabric description	Method of manufacture and specific features	Date of manufacture?	Period dating	Period
1591	2	230x102x70	9 1/16x 4 x 2 3/4	Dark reddish brown sandy fabric. Occasional small voids, occasional small rounded white sand grains.	Possibly machine manufactured. Slighty rough texture to all surfaces.	18th – early 19th	18th – early 19th	4
1591	4	245x110x70	9 5/8x 4 3/8 x 2 3/4	Fine mid-dark brown fabric. Frequent small voids and moderate inclusions of what appears to be iron particles.	(?) Pallet moulded. Specialist curved brick for well.	18th	18th – early 19th	4
1599	1	240x110x70	9 7/16x 4 3/8 x 2 3/4	Mid to dark reddish orange. Frequent inclusions of small iron particles.	Slop moulded.	Mid 17th – late 18th	17th	3.2
1599	1	245x110x70	9 5/8x 4 3/8 x 2 3/4	Mid to dark reddish orange fabric. Frequent inclusions of small iron particles.	Slop moulded.	mid 17th – mid 18th	17th	3.2
1635	1	237x115x50	9 5/16x 4 1/2 x 2	Lght to mid orange sandy fabric. Frequent small voids, occasional small grog pellets and buff clay pellets.	Pallet moulded.	16th – mid 17th	17th	3.2
1636	1	240x115x50	9 7/16x 4 1/2 x 2	Light to mid orange sandy fabric. Frequent small voids and occasional small grog and buff clay pellets.	Pallet molded. Finger prints – base.	16th – mid 17th	17th	3.2
1779	1	240x115x50	9 7/16x 4 1/2 x 2	Mid to dark reddish brown sandy fabric. Frequent inclusions of small iron like particles and small voids	Pallet moulded.	Early – mid 17th	17th	3.2
1779	1	240x115x57	9 7/16x 4 1/2 x 2 1/4	Dark reddish brown very fine fabric with frequent inclusions of small quartz/ sand and Iron particles. Large voids in fabric and has glossy appearance (overfired?).	Pallet moulded.	16th – mid 17th	17th	3.2
1779	1	240x120x57	9 7/16x 4 3/4 x 2 1/4	Mid to dark brown smooth sandy fabric. Occasional small voids, frequent inclusions of limestone and or shell. One rounded stone.	Slop moulded.	16th – mid 17th	17th	3.2
1779	1	255x120x55	10x 4 3/4 x 2 3/16	Mid to dark reddish brown sandy fabric. Frequent inclusions of small iron like particles and small voids.	Pallet moulded.	17th	17th	3.2
1788	1	240x115x60	9 7/16x 4 1/2 x 2 3/8	Mid to dark orange/brown sandy fabric. Occasional large stone and small stone inclusions. Flakey appearance to fabric.	Pallet moulded.	17th	17th	3.2
1914	1	220x110x57	8 5/8x 4 3/8 x 2 1/4	Mid to dark reddish brown sandy fabric. Frequent inclusions of small iron like particles and small voids.	Pallet moulded. Has rudimentry frog on lower sanded surface.	Late 17th – early 18th	17th	3.2
1914	1	225x100x65	8 7/8x 4 x 2 1/2	Mid to dark reddish brown sandy fabric. Frequent inclusions of small iron like particles and small voids.	Over all surface appearance is smooth but has slightly sandy texture. Unable to determine method of manufacture	Late 17th – 18th	17th	3.2
1958	1	240x120x55	9 7/16x 4 3/4 x 2 3/16	Homogenous reddish brown fabric. Frequent small reddish rounded-angular stones. Moderate small voids.	Slop moulded	16th – mid 17th	17th	3.2
1958	1	242x115x50	9 1/2x 4 1/2 x 2	Not cut as 'special' brick, retained as sample.	Slop moulded. Special brick with rounded corner.	16th – mid 17th	17th	3.2
1958	1	245x115x50	9 5/8x 4 1/2 x 2	Coarse flakey fabric. Mid to reddish orange with occasional grog inclusions and small angular and rounded stones..	Slop moulded.	16th – mid 17th	17th	3.2
1995	2	235x110x53	9 1/4x 4 3/8 x 2 1/8	Mid to very dark brown course fabric. Frequent inclusions which need further research.	Pallet moulded.	16th – mid 17th	16th – 17th	3
2072	1	235x110x55	9 1/4x 4 3/8 x 2 3/16	Mid to dark Reddish brown sandy fabric, frequent inclusions of small iron like particles and small voids.	Pallet moulded.	17th – (?) 18th	17th	3.2

Context	Count	Dimensions (mm)	Dimensions (inches)	Fabric description	Method of manufacture and specific features	Date of manufacture?	Period dating	Period
2072	2	240x115x63	9 7/16x 4 1/2W x 2 1/2T	Fine mid-dark reddish brown and sandy fabric. Occasional small voids and iron particles. No visable inclusions.	Roughly cast brick with slight surface irregularities	Mid – late 17th	17th	3.2
2072	1	250x115x63	9 3/4x 4 1/2 x 2 1/2	Light to mid orange sandy fabric. Frequent small voids and occasional small grog and buff clay pellets.	Roughly cast brick with slight surface irregularities.	Early 17th – (?) mid 17th	17th	3.2
2075	1	245x120x50	9 5/8x 4 3/4 x 2	Light-mid orange sandy fabric. Frequent small voids and occasional small grog and buff clay pellets.	Pallet moulded. Chamfered corner (retained).	16th – mid 17th	16th – 17th	3.1
2075	1	245x125x50	9 5/8x 4 7/8 x 2	Light to mid orange sandy fabric. Frequent small voids and occasional small grog and buff clay pellets.	Pallet molded.	16th – mid 17th	16th – 17th	3.1
2075	1	255x122x50	10x 4 3/4x 2	Coarse fabric, light pinkish brown colour. Occasional very small voids, frequent small buff particles and reddish brown grog (lumps).	Slop moulded. Retained as has chamfered corner.	16th – mid 17th	16th – 17th	3.1
2075	2	255x122x50	10x 4 3/4x 2	Light to mid orange sandy fabric. Frequent small voids and occasional small buff clay pellets.	Slop molded.	16th – mid 17th	16th – 17th	3.1
2170	1	240x115x50	9 7/16x 4 1/2 x 2	Mid brown core with patchy black and blue grey 'crust'. Frequent inclusions of sub rounded and angular stones.	Slop moulded.	16th – mid 17th	16th – 17th	2.5/3.1
2170	1	240x120x50	9 7/16x 4 3/4 x 2	Mid to dark orange brown sandy fabric. Frequent inclusions of small iron like particles and small voids and occasional buff clay inclusions.	Slop moulded.	16th – mid 17th	Late 14th – 17th	2.5/3.1
2170	2	240x120x53	9 7/16x 4 3/4 x 2 1/8	Mid to dark orange brown sandy fabric. Frequent inclusions of small iron like particles and small voids and occasional buff clay inclusions.	Slop moulded.	16th – mid 17th	Late 14th – 17th	2.5/3.1
2170	1	245x120x55	9 5/8x 4 3/4 x 2 3/16	Mid to dark orange brown sandy fabric. Frequent inclusions of small iron like particles, small voids and occasional buff clay inclusions.	Slop moulded.	16th – mid 17th	Late 14th – 17th	2.5/3.1
2330	1	230x120x55	9 1/16x 4 3/4 x 2 3/16	Mid to dark orange fabric. Occasional small stones, single reddish brown clay inclusionand frequent small voids.	Pallet moulded.	16th – mid 17th	17th	3.2
2335	3	235x115x50	9 1/4x 4 1/2 x 2	Fine mid-dark orange fabric. Frequent small voids and moderate inclusions of what appears to be iron particles.	Slop moulded.	16th – mid 17th	17th	3.2
2335	1	235x115x55	9 1/4x 4 1/2 x 2 3/16	Fine mid-dark orange fabric. Frequent small voids and moderate inclusions of what appears to be iron particles.	Slop moulded. Base is sanded with four small finger indents, brick has been clasped in upright position by a left hand	16th – mid 17th	17th	3.2
2365	1	240x115x55	9 7/16x 4 1/2 x 2 3/16	Reddish orange fabric with frequent small voids and occasional small pale clay/grog pellets.	Pallet moulded.	16th – mid 17th	17th	3.2
2366	1	222x115x50-55	8 3/4x 4 1/2 x 2-2 3/16	Moulded brick. Not cut as unusual shape (retained).	Pallet molded. Wedge shaped-possible arch or ledge brick.	16th – mid 17th	17th	3.2
2366	2	238x113x50	9 3/8x 4 1/2 x 2	Mid to dark orange brown sandy fabric. Frequent inclusions of small iron like particles and small voids, occasional buff clay inclusions.	Pallet moulded.	16th – mid 17th	17th	3.2

Appendix 1: Brick Catalogue 275

Context	Count	Dimensions (mm)	Dimensions (inches)	Fabric description	Method of manufacture and specific features	Date of manufacture?	Period dating	Period
2366	1	240x120x53	9 7/16x 4 3/4 x 2 1/8	Mid to dark orange brown sandy fabric, frequent inclusions of small iron like particles and small voids and occasional buff clay inclusions.	Slop molded. Base is rough with grass/chaff imprints	16th – mid 17th	17th	3.2
2408	1	230x115x55	9 1/16x 4 1/2 x 2 3/16	Fine mid-dark orange fabric, frequent small voids and moderate inclusions of what appears to be iron particles. Occasional grains of sand.	Slop moulded.	16th – mid 17th	17th	3.2
2408	1	235x115x55	9 1/4x 4 1/2 x 2 3/16	Fine mid to dark orange fabric. Frequent small voids and moderate inclusions of what appears to be iron particles. Occasional grains of sand.	Slop moulded.	16th – mid 17th	17th	3.2
2408	1	235x120x55	9 1/4x 4 3/4 x 2 3/16	Fine mid to dark orange fabric. Frequent small voids and moderate inclusions of what appears to be iron particles. Occasional grains of sand.	Pallet moulded. Probable childs finger indents on one base to width end.	16th – mid 17th	17th	3.2
2408	1	240x115x50	9 7/16x 4 1/2 x 2	Fine mid to dark orange fabric. Frequent small voids and moderate inclusions of what appears to be iron particles.	Slop molded. One stretcher side is sanded which may be the result of stacking.	16th – mid 17th	17th	3.2
2408	1	240x115x55	9 7/16x 4 1/2 x 2 3/16	Fine mid to dark orange fabric. Frequent small voids and moderate inclusions of what appears to be iron particles.	Slop moulded.	16th – mid 17th	17th	3.2
2408	1	245x125x50	9 5/8x 5x 2	Fine mid-dark orange fabric. Frequent small voids and moderate inclusions of what appears to be iron particles.	Pallet molded.	16th – mid 17th	17th	3.2
2408	1	240x115x55	9 7/16x 4 1/2 x 2 3/16	Fine mid to dark orange fabric. Frequent small voids and moderate inclusions of what appears to be iron particles.	Slop moulded.	16th – mid 17th	17th	3.2
2456	1	230x110x53	9 1/16x 4 3/8 x 2 1/8	Homogeneous reddish brown fabric. Frequent small reddish rounded to angular stones. Moderate small voids.	Slop moulded.	16th – mid 17th	17th	3.2
2518	1	235x115x55	9 1/4x 4 1/2 x 2 3/16	Homogeneous reddish brown fabric. Frequent small reddish rounded-angular stones. Moderate small voids.	Slop moulded.	16th – mid 17th	17th	3.2
2518	1	240x115x57	9 7/16x 4 1/2x 2 1/4	Homogenous reddish brown fabric. Frequent small reddish rounded-angular stones. Moderate small voids.	Slop moulded.	16th – mid 17th	17th	3.2
2518	2	240x120x57	9 7/16x 4 3/4 x 2 1/4	Homogenous reddish brown fabric. Frequent small reddish rounded-angular stones. Moderate small voids.	Slop moulded.	16th – mid 17th	17th	3.2
2519	1	220x105x57	8 5/8x 4 1/8 x 2 1/4	Fine mid-dark reddish brown fabric. Frequent small voids and moderate inclusions of what appears to be iron particles. Occasional large inclusions of brick fragments.	Pallet molded.	16th – mid 17th	17th	3.2
2519	1	220x105x60	8 5/8x 4 1/8 x 2 3/8	Fine mid-dark reddish brown fabric. Frequent small voids and moderate inclusions of what appears to be iron particles. Occasional large inclusions of brick fragmentsand possibly limestone.	Pallet molded.	16th – mid 17th	17th	3.2
2519	2	225x105x57	8 7/8x 4 1/8 x 2 1/4	Fine mid-dark reddish brown fabric. Frequent small voids and moderate inclusions of what appears to be iron particles. Occasional large inclusions of brick fragments and possible limestone.	Pallet moulded.	16th – mid 17th	17th	3.2

Context	Count	Dimensions (mm)	Dimensions (inches)	Fabric description	Method of manufacture and specific features	Date of manufacture?	Period dating	Period
2519	1	240x120x57	9 7/16x 4 3/4 x 2 1/4	Coarse fabric with pinkish orange crust. Core is orange/brown. Frequent small voids with occasional rounded buff grog and angular stone inclusions.	Pallet moulded.	16th – mid 17th	17th	3.2
2521	2	220x110x60	8 5/8x 4 3/8 x 2 3/8	Coarse reddish brown fabric, possible small grog particles and frequent small angular, reddish stones.	Pallet moulded.	17th	17th	3.2
2521	2	230x110x60	9 1/16x 4 3/8 x 2 3/8	Fine mid-dark reddish brown fabric. Frequent small voids and moderate inclusions of what appears to be iron particles. Occasional large inclusions of grog and possibly lime.	Pallet moulded.	17th	17th	3.2
2628	1	220x110x60	8 5/8x 4 3/8 x 2 3/8	Mid orange sandy fabric with occasional voids. Occasional small stones and frequent small iron particles.	Pallet moulded.	16th – mid 17th	17th	3.2
2628	1	225x110x66	8 7/8x 4 3/8 x 2 1/2	Homogeneous reddish brown fabric. Frequent small reddish rounded-angular stones. Moderate small voids.	Pallet moulded.	(?) Mid 17th	17th	3.2
2689	1	235x120x60	9 1/4x 4 3/4 x 2 3/8	Homogeneous reddish brown fabric. Frequent small reddish rounded-angular stones. Moderate small voids.	Pallet moulded.	16th – mid 17th	16th – mid 17th	3.1
2762	1	235x115x55	9 1/4x 4 1/2 x 2 3/16	Homogeneous reddish brown fabric. Frequent small reddish rounded-angular stones. Moderate small voids.	Slop moulded.	16th – mid 17th		3

References

Primary references

CC Church Commissioners
    FF8 33722 All Saints'

Guildhall
    Newport St file 1/3
    Newport St file 1/9
    Newport St file 1/14

NA National Archives
    E179/200/131
    E179/200/147
    Will Thomas Lilly Prob 11/655

WCL Worcester Cathedral Library
    A7(ii) 13th July 2 & 4 Phil & Mary (1556)
    A7(iv) 19th Nov Elizabeth (1576)
    A7(xiii)
    A7(xvii) 25th November 1674
    B119a
    B1113
    B1114
    B1117
    B1124
    B3081
    1421a
    Dean and Chapters Houses All Saints', p.27 (transcript in WRO)

WHS Worcestershire Historical Society
    Bond, S. *The Chamber Order Book of Worcester 1602–1650*
    Hearth Tax 1678 (Meekings *et al.* 1984)

WRO Worcestershire Record Office
    496.5 BA 9360 Liber Recordum A2 Box 1
    496.5 BA 9360 Lib Rec A2/1 1670
    496.5 BA 9360 Shelf A2/4 Court Books
    496.5 BA 9360 A6/4 View of Frankpledge Poor Rate Assessment
    496.5 BA 9360 A10 1563
    496.5 BA 9360 A10 1624
    496.5 BA 9360 A14
    496.5 BA 9360 A14 Chamber Ord. Bk I f. 158, 177
    496.5 BA 9360 A14 Chamber Ord. Bk III 1656–1664
    496.5 BA 9360 A17
    496.5 BA 9360 A17 Rent Roll
    496.5 BA 9360 A17/2 Rent Roll for 1662
    496.5 BA 9360 B9
    496.5 BA 9360 B9 purpresture records
    496:5 BA 9360 B10 purpresture records
    496.5 BA 9360 B10 Victuallers' Recognisances
    496.5 BA 9360 B10 Court Leet Book
    496.5 BA 9360 B10 City Leet Bk 1773–1776
    496.5 BA 9360 Cab 16/11, Bridge Book of Orders 1770 10th Jan
    496.5 BA 9360 Cab 25/18
    496.5 BA 9360 Cab 25/23
    496.5 BA 9360 Cab 25/25
    496.5 BA 9360 Cab 25/26
    496.5 BA 9360 Cab 25/41
    496.5 BA 9360 Enrolments 4 1772
    496.5 BA 11241/b14
    705.27 BA 385/31
    705.27 BA 385/44 abuttals
    889.81 BA 1180
    899.81 BA 4893/7 Will John Wylmington
    899:81 BA 4893/7, Will Robert Leddington, 1654
    899.82 BA 4893/7 Will Thomas Hill, 1662
    899.749 BA 87822/14
    989.9:16 BA 8306
    BA 4600/1032
    BA 7996 Hearth Tax 1666 Microfilm
    Bentley's Directory for 1841
    Berrow's *Worcester Journal*
    City of Worcester compulsory purchase surveys 1936
    Grundy's Directory for 1792, 1794
    Kidderminster Parish Settlement papers 3.2.1731
    Will William Dodynge 1554
    Will William Parker 1624/201
    Will Ralph Yates 20th Oct. 1671
    Will Edward Hurdman 6th July 1682
    Will John Lilly 4th Feb. 1690

Will John Southall 27th Dec. 1709
Will and inventory, John Kinsey 1st Mar. 1722/3
Will John Sowden 9th Nov. 1727
Will Richard Lilly 24th Jan. 1739
Will William Herbert 11th Dec. 1744
Will Margaret Herbert 11th Nov. 1747
Will Ann Higgins 15th April 1771
Will Richard Hinksman 1775
Will Abraham Lingham 1784

Bibliography

AA (Archenfield Archaeology) 2003 *Newport Street, Worcester: A report on archaeological monitoring of a borehole survey* Unpublished report **AA/03/61**

AA (Archenfield Archaeology) 2004a *Newport Street, Worcester: An archaeological assessment* Unpublished report **AA/04/61**

AA (Archenfield Archaeology) 2004b *Newport Street, Worcester: A survey of the standing buildings* Unpublished report (un-numbered)

Albarella, U. 1995 'Depressions on sheep horncores', *J. Archaeol. Sci.* **22**, 699–704

Alcock, N.W. 2005 'Housing the Urban Poor in 1800: courts in Atherstone and Coventry, Warwickshire', *Vernacular Architecture* **36**, 49–60

Allan, J.P. and Morris, C.A. 1984 'Wooden objects', in Allan, J.P., *Medieval and post-medieval finds from Exeter, 1971–1980* Exeter Archaeology Report **3**, 305–15

Allies, J. 1852 *The Ancient British, Roman, and Saxon Antiquities and Folk-lore of Worcestershire* (2 edn) London and Worcester

Amphlett, J. and Rea, C. 1909 *The Botany of Worcestershire* Birmingham, Cornish Brothers

Anon 1981 *The Fibre Structure of Leather* Northampton, Leather Conservation Centre

Armstrong, P. 1977 *Excavations in Sewer Lane, Hull, 1974* E Riding Archaeol. **3**/ Hull Old Town Report Series **1**

Armstrong P. and Evans D.H. 1991 *Excavations at Lurk Lane, Beverley 1979–1982* Sheffield Excavation Report **1**

Arnold, J. 1988 *Queen Elizabeth's Wardrobe Unlock'd* Leeds, Maney

Atkinson, D.R. 1975 *Tobacco Pipes of Broseley Shropshire* Essex, Hart-Talbot

Baker, J. and Brothwell, D. 1980 *Animal diseases in archaeology* London, Academic Press

Baker, N.J. 1996 *Medieval archaeology and urban morphology* St Clement's Gate Urban Design Campaign Paper **2**, Worcester City Council

Baker, N. and Holt, R. 2004 *Urban Growth and the Medieval Town: Gloucester and Worcester* Aldershot, Ashgate Publishing

Baker, N., Morriss, R.K. and Stamper, P. 2006, 'Shrewsbury Market Place and Hall', *Archaeol. J.* **163**, 180–232

Barber, K.E. 1976 'History of Vegetation', in S.B. Chapman (ed.), *Methods in Plant Ecology* Oxford, Blackwell, 5-83

Barker, D. and Majewski, T. 2006 'Ceramic studies in historical archaeology', in Hicks, D. and Beaudry, M.C. (eds), *The Cambridge Companion to Historical Archaeology* Cambridge, Cambridge University Press, 205–31

Barker, P. 1969a 'The archaeological context of Worcester', in 'The origins of Worcester', *Trans. Worcestershire Archaeol. Soc. 3 ser.* **2**, 9–19

Barker, P. 1969b 'Excavations on the Lich Street development site, 1965–66', in 'The origins of Worcester', *Trans. Worcestershire Archaeol. Soc. 3 ser.* **2**, 44–60

Barron, C.M. 1989 'The fourteenth-century poll tax: returns for Worcester', *Midland Hist.* **14**, 1–29

Barton, K.J. 1968 'The pitcher imported from Saintonge found at Lich Street, Worcester', *Trans. Worcestershire Archaeol. Soc. 3 ser.* **1**, 45–7

Bassett, S. 1989 'Churches in Worcester before and after the conversion of the Anglo-Saxons', *Antiq. J.*, **69 (2)**, 225–56

Beardsmore, C. 1980 'Documentary evidence for the history of Worcester city defences', in Carver (ed.) 1980a, 53–64

Behrensmeyer, A.K. 1978 'Taphonomic and ecologic information from bone weathering', *Paleobiology* **4 (2)**, 150–62

Bennett, J. 1980 'Excavation and survey on the city wall, 1973', in Carver (ed.) 1980a, 65–85

Bennett, K.D. 1994 *Annotated Catalogue of Pollen and Pteridophyte Spore Types of the British Isles* Unpublished report, Department of Plant Sciences, University of Cambridge

BGS (British Geological Survey) 1993 *Geological survey of England and Wales sheet 199: Worcester* 1:50,000

Blair, J. and Ramsay, N. (eds), 1991 *English Medieval Industries* London, The Hambledon Press

Boessneck, J. 1969 'Osteological differences between sheep (Ovis aries Linné) and Goat (Capra hircus Linné)', in Brothwell and Higgs (eds) 1969, 331–58

Bridges, T. 2000 *Churches of Worcestershire* Logaston, Logaston Press

Bridges, T. and Mundy, C. 1996 *Worcester. A Pictorial History* Chichester, Phillimore and Co. Ltd

Brooks, A. and Pevsner, N. 2007 *The Buildings of England: Worcestershire* London, Yale University Press

Brothwell, D.R. 1976 'Further evidence of bone chewing by ungulates: the sheep of North Ronaldsay, Orkney', *J. Archaeol. Sci.* **3**, 179–82

Brothwell D.R. and Higgs E.S. (eds) 1969 *Science in archaeology* London, Thames and Hudson

Brown, A.G. 1997 *Alluvial Geoarchaeology: Floodplain Archaeology and Environmental Change* Cambridge, Cambridge University Press

Brown, D. and Lawson, G. 1990 'Toggles', in Biddle, M. (ed.), *Object and Economy in Medieval Winchester* Winchester Studies **7 (2)**, 589–91

Brown, D.H. 1999 *Pottery of the Beauvaisis* Unpublished typescript. Imported medieval pottery training course, University of Southampton

Brown, D.L. 1990 *Evaluation at County Furnishings, Silver Street, Worcester*, Hereford and Worcester County Council Archaeological Service, unpublished report **52**

Brunskill, R.W. 1997 *Brick Buildings in Britain* London, Gollancz

Bryant, V. 2004 'The medieval and early post-medieval pottery', in Dalwood and Edwards 2004, 281–339

Bryant, V. and Dalwood, H. 2004 'Consumption: goods', in Dalwood and Edwards 2004, 96–100

Burnham, B.C. and Wacher, J. 1990 *The 'small towns' of Roman Britain* London, Batsford

Buteux, V., Pearson, E. and Ratkai, S. 1994 *Watching brief at the Hop Pole, Leominster* Hereford and Worcester County Council, Archaeological Service unpublished report **290**

Butler, S. and Cuttler, R. (eds) 2011 *Life and Industry in the Suburbs of Roman Worcester* Brit. Archaeol. Rep. Brit. Ser. **533**/Birmingham Archaeology Monograph Ser. **8**, Oxford, Archaeopress

CA (Cotswold Archaeology) 1996 *Cotswold Archaeology Technical Manual 1: Excavation Recording Manual* Unpublished CA report

CA (Cotswold Archaeology) 2003 *Cotswold Archaeology Technical Manual 2: the Taking of Samples for Palaeoenvironmental and Palaeoeconomic Analysis from Archaeological Sites* Unpublished CA report

Cappers, T.R.J., Bekker, R.M. and Jans, J.E.A. 2006 *Digitale Zadenatlas van Nederland: Digital seed atlas of the Netherlands* Groningen, Groningen Archaeological Studies **4**, Barkhuis Publishing and Groningen University Library

Carver, M.O.H. (ed.) 1980a 'Medieval Worcester: an Archaeological Framework. Reports, Surveys, Texts and Essays.' *Trans. Worcestershire Archaeol. Soc. 3 ser.* **7**

Carver, M.O.H. 1980b 'An archaeology for the city of Worcester, 680–1680 AD', in Carver (ed.) 1980a, 1–12

Carver, M.O.H. 1980c 'The site and settlements at Worcester', in Carver (ed.) 1980a, 15–29

Carver, M.O.H. 1980d 'The excavation of three medieval craftsmen's tenements in Sidbury, Worcester', in Carver (ed.) 1980a, 155–219

CAS (County Archaeological Service) 1995 *Manual of Service Practice: Fieldwork Recording Manual* County Archaeological Service, Hereford and Worcester County Council, unpublished report **399**

Cave T., and Wilson R.A. (eds) 1924 *The Parliamentary Survey of the Lands and Possessions of the Dean and Chapter of Worcester* Worcester, Worcestershire Historical Society

Colledge, S. and Greig, J. 1992 'Environment', in Woodiwiss (ed.) 1992, 96–105

Cooke, W.D. and Lomas, B. 1990 'The evidence of wear and damage in ancient textiles', in J.P. Wild J.P. and Bender Jørgensen L. (eds), *NESAT III: Textiles in Northern Archaeology* NESAT III: Textile Symposium in York, 215–26

Corpus of Romanesque Sculpture in Britain and Ireland 2008 *The Chevron Guide* http://www.crsbi.ac.uk/the-chevron-guide/ (accessed 30 July 2010)

Crawford, A. 2007 'Pottery', in Miller, Crawford and Dalwood 2007, 22–30

Crowfoot, E., Pritchard, F. and Staniland, K. 1992 *Textiles and Clothing c.1150–c.1450: Medieval Finds from Excavations in London* **4** London, HMSO

Cunliffe, B. 1991 *Iron Age Communities in Britain* (3 edn) London, Routledge

Dalwood, C.H. 1992 'Salvage recording of a medieval stone undercroft and cellars at 48–85 High Street, Worcester', *Trans. Worcestershire Archaeol. Soc. 3 ser.* **13**, 167–72

Dalwood, C.H., Buteux, V.A. and Darlington, J. 1994 'Excavations at Farrier Street and other sites north of the City Wall, Worcester 1988–1992', *Trans. Worcestershire Archaeol. Soc. 3 ser.* **14**, 75–114

Dalwood, H. 2004a 'Settlement morphology: streets and plot layout', in Dalwood and Edwards 2004, 78–81

Dalwood, H. 2004b 'Buildings', in Dalwood and Edwards 2004, 81–5

Dalwood, H. 2004c 'Chronological synthesis', in Dalwood and Edwards 2004, 36–76

Dalwood, H. and Bryant, V. 2004 'Urban households and urban societies', in Dalwood and Edwards 2004, 88–91

Dalwood, H. and Edwards, R. 2004 *Excavations at Deansway, Worcester, 1988–89: Romano-British small town to late medieval city* Counc. Brit. Archaeol. Res. Rep. **139**, York, Council for British Archaeology

Daniell, P. 1988 'The Brick Children', in *British Brick Society Information, Compilation Volume 1 1973–1981*, 43, http://www.arct.cam.ac.uk/Downloads/bbs/bbs-1-25.pdf (accessed 14 July 2010)

Darlington, J. and Evans, J. 1992 'Roman Sidbury, Worcester: Excavations 1959–1989', *Trans. Worcestershire Archaeol. Soc. 3 ser.* **13**, 6–104

Davenport, P. forthcoming *Medieval and Later Redcliffe: Excavations at 3 Redcliff Street, Bristol*

Dobney, K. 2001 'A place at the table: the role of vertebrate zooarchaeology within a Roman research agenda for Britain', in James S. and Millett M. (eds), *Britons and Romans: advancing an archaeological agenda* Counc. Brit. Archaeol. Res. Rep. **125**, York, Council for British Archaeology, 36–45

Dobney, K. and Rielly, K. 1988 'A method for recording archaeological animal bones: the use of diagnostic zones', *Circaea* **5,** 79–96

Drinkwater, N. 1991 'Domestic stonework', in Saunders P. and Saunders E. (eds), *Salisbury Museum Medieval Catalogue Part 1*, Salisbury and South Wiltshire Museum, 169–83

Drury, P.J. 1975 'Post-medieval brick and tile kilns at Runsell Green, Danbury, Essex', *Post-Medieval Archaeol.* **9**, 203–11

Drury, P.J. 1981 'The production of brick and tile', in D.W. Crossley, *Medieval Industry* Counc. Brit. Archaeol. Res. Rep. **40**, York, Council for British Archaeology, 126–42

Dunning, G.C. 1967 'Pottery roof finials found at Worcester and Pershore', *Trans. Worcestershire Archaeol. Soc. 3 ser.* **1**, 48–54

Dunning, G.C. 1968 'Berichten van de Rijksdienst voor het Oudheidkundig Bodemonderzoek', *Proceedings State Service for Archaeol. Investigation Netherlands* **18**, 209–25

Dunning, G.C. 1975 'The roof fittings', in Platt C. and Coleman-Smith R. (eds), *Excavations in Medieval Southampton, 1953–69, 2: The Finds* Leicester, Leicester University Press, 186–8

Dyer, A.D. 1973 *The City of Worcester in the Sixteenth-Century* Leicester, Leicester University Press

Dyer, C. 1980 *Lords and Peasants in a Changing Society: the Estates of the Bishop of Worcester, 680–1540* Cambridge, Cambridge University Press

Dyer, C. 1991 *Hanbury: Settlement and Society in a Woodland Landscape* Leicester, Leicester University Press

Eames, E. 1980 *Catalogue of the Medieval Lead Glazed Earthenware Tiles in the Department of Medieval and Later Antiquities* London, British Museum

Edwards, R. and Bryant, V. 2004 'Note on the later post-medieval pottery', in Dalwood and Edwards 2004, 339

Edwards, R., Griffin, L. and Dalwood, H. 2002 'Excavations on the site of the new Police Station, Castle Street, Worcester', *Trans. Worcestershire Archaeol. Soc. 3 ser.* **18**, 103–32

Egan, G. 1998 *The Medieval Household: Daily Living c.1150–c.1450: Medieval Finds from Excavations in London* **6** London, HMSO

Egan, G. 2005 *Material Culture in London in an Age of Transition: Tudor and Stuart Period Finds c.1450–c.1700 from Excavations at Riverside Sites in Southwark* MoLAS Monograph **19**, London, Museum of London

Esdaile, K.A. 1946 *English Church Monuments 1510–1840* London, Batsford

Evans, D.H. 1979 'Gravel-tempered ware: a survey of published forms', *Medieval and Later Pottery in Wales* **2**, 18–29

Evans, D.H. and Tomlinson, D.G., 1992 *Excavations at 33–35 Eastgate, Beverley, 1983–86* Sheffield Excavation Reports **3** Sheffield, J.R. Collis

Evans, D., Jackson, R. and Dalwood H., 2007 *Land at Newport Street Worcester Worcestershire Post-Excavation Assessment and Updated Project Design* Unpublished CA Report **06137**

Fagan, L. 2004 'Medieval roof tiles', in Dalwood and Edwards 2004, 342–61

Fisher, S.W. 1970 *English Pottery and Porcelain Marks* Slough, W. Foulsham

Foreman, M. 1991 'The wood', in Armstrong and Evans 1991, 174–82

Forester, H. 1972 *Medieval Gothic Mouldings* Chichester, Phillimore

Fox, R. and Barton, K.J. 1986 Excavations at Oyster Street, Portsmouth, Hampshire, 1968–71, *Post-Medieval Archaeol.* **20**, 31–255

Galloway, P. 1990 'Combs of bone, antler and ivory', in M. Biddle (ed.), *Object and Economy in Medieval Winchester*, Winchester Studies **7 (2)**, 665–78

Geddes, J. 1991 'Iron', in Blair and Ramsay (eds) 1991, 167–88

Giorgi, J. 1997 'Diet in late medieval and early modern London: the archaeobotanical evidence', in Gaimster D. and Stamper P. (eds), *The Age of Transition: the Archaeology of English Culture 1400–1600,* Society for Medieval Archaeology Monograph **15**/Oxbow Monograph **98**, 197–213

Giorgi, J. 1999 'Archaeobotanical evidence from London on aspects of post-medieval urban economies', in Egan G. and Michael R.L. (eds), *Old and New Worlds: Historical/post-medieval Archaeology Papers from the Societies' Joint Conferences at Williamsburg and London 1997* Oxford, Oxbow, 342–8

Global Probing and Sampling Ltd 2004 *Technology* http://www.globalsampling.co.uk/page1.htm (accessed 7 February 2006)

Goad, J., Head, K. and Crawford, A. 2004 *Archaeological excavation at Bourn Brook, Selly Oak, Birmingham,* Historic Environment and Archaeology Service, Worcestershire County Council, unpublished report **1253**

Grant, A. 1982 'The use of tooth wear as a guide to the age of domestic ungulates', in Wilson, Grigson and Payne 1982, 91–108

Greaves, S.J. 1976 *Finds from Woodbank Street, Burslem* City Stoke-on-Trent Mus. Archaeol. Soc. Rep. **10**

Green, V. 1796 *The History and Antiquities of the City and Suburbs of Worcester* London, Bulmer and Co.

Greig, J. 1981 'The investigation of a medieval barrel-latrine from Worcester', *J. Archaeol. Sci.* **8**, 265–82

Greig, J.R.A. 1991 *The Plant Remains in the Roman Well Fill from Droitwich, Bay's Meadow (Worcestershire)* Ancient Monuments Laboratory Report New Series **65/91**

Greig, J. 1996 'Archaeobotanical and historical records compared – a new look at the taphonomy of edible and other useful plants from the 11th to the 18th centuries A.D.', *Circeae* **12 (2)**, 211–47

Greig, J.R. 2004 'Buried soil pollen', in Dalwood and Edwards 2004, 556–8

Grew, F. and de Neergaard, M. 1988 *Shoes and Pattens: Medieval Finds from Excavations in London* **2** London, HMSO

Grieve, M. 1931 *A Modern Herbal* Sydney, Savvas Publishing

Griffin, L. 2002a 'Pottery', in Jackson *et al.* 2002, 76–82

Griffin, L. 2002b 'The medieval floor tiles', in Jackson *et al.* 2002, 85–87

Griffin, L. 2004a 'The Pottery', in Griffin *et al.* 2004, 72–89

Griffin, L. 2004b 'Ceramic building material', in Miller *et al.* 2004a, 10–14

Griffin, L. 2004c 'Ceramic building material', in Miller *et al.* 2004b, 11–15

Griffin, L. 2007 'Medieval floor tiles', in Miller *et al.* 2007, 32–8

Griffin, S., Jackson, R., Atkin, S., Dinn, J., Griffin, L., Hughes, P., Hurst, D., Pearson, E., and Vince, A. 2004 'Excavation at City Arcade, High Street, Worcester', *Trans. Worcestershire Archaeol. Soc. 3 ser.* **19**, 45–109

Grimm, E.C. 1990 'TILIA and TILIA.GRAPH. PC spreadsheet and graphics software for pollen data', INQUA Working Group on Data-handling Methods, *Newsletter* **4**, 5–7

Grimm, E.C. 2004 *TGView 2.0.2 graphics software*

Guyatt, D. 1994 'Early pipe-making in Worcester', *Soc. Clay Pipe Research* **45**, 24

Hall, R.A. and Hunter-Mann, K. 2002 *Medieval Urbanism in Coppergate: Refining a Townscape* The Archaeology of York **10 (6)**, York, Council for British Archaeology

Hammond, M. 1998 *Bricks and Brickmaking* Buckinghamshire Shire Publications Ltd

Hart, J. forthcoming *Medieval and Later Redcliffe: Excavations at 1–2 Redcliff Street, Bristol*

Hartley, D. 1954 *Food in England* London, Little, Brown Book Group

Head, K. 2005a 'The pollen evidence', in Goad J., *Archaeological watching brief at Waitrose, Saltway, Droitwich, Worcestershire (SAM 30097),* Historic Environment and Archaeology Service, Worcestershire County Council, Unpublished report **1303**

Head, K. 2005b *Environmental Remains from Friar Street, Worcester,* Historic Environment and Archaeology Service, Worcestershire County Council, internal report **1371**

Head, K. 2006 'Environmental remains', in A. Mann, C. Patrick and D. Hurst, *Archaeological investigations at the former MG Rover North Works car park, Longbridge, Birmingham,* Historic Environment and Archaeology Service, Worcestershire County Council, Unpublished report **1445**

Head, K. and Wilkinson, K. 2005 *Environmental remains from Coventry Transport Museum, Hales Street, Coventry, Warwickshire,* Historic Environment and Archaeology Service, Worcestershire County Council, Unpublished report **1370**

Head, K. and Wilkinson, K. 2006 *A palaeoenvironmental assessment at Far Gosford Street, Coventry, Warwickshire,* Historic Environment and Archaeology Service, Worcestershire County Council, Unpublished report **1455**

Henshall, A.S. and Maxwell, S. 1952 'Clothing and other articles from a late 17th–century grave at Gunnister, Shetland', *Proc. Soc. Antiq. Scot.* **86**, 30–42

Higgins, D. 1987 *The Interpretation and Regional Study of Clay Tobacco Pipes: A Case Study of the Broseley District* Unpublished PhD thesis, University of Liverpool

Higham, M.C. 1989 'Some evidence for 12th and 13th century linen and woollen textile processing', *Medieval Archaeol.* **33**, 28–53

Hillman, G.C. 1981 'Reconstructing crop processing from charred remains of crops', in Mercer, R. (ed.), *Farming Practice in British Prehistory* Edinburgh, Edinburgh University Press

Hirst, S. 1980 'Excavations behind the City Wall at Talbot Street, 1975', in Carver (ed.) 1980a, 97–106

Hooke, D. 1980 'The hinterland and routeways of late Saxon Worcester: the charter evidence', in Carver (ed.) 1980a, 39–49

Howard-Davis, C. 2001 'Artefacts', in Newman *et al.* 2001, 211–24

Hughes, P. 1980 'Houses and property', in Carver (ed.) 1980a, 269–92

Hughes, P. 2007 *Newport Street, Worcester: A history of the Excavated Area in Newport Street* Unpublished report (un-numbered), held in archive at Worcestershire Historic Environment and Archaeology Service

Hurst, J.D. 1990 'Documentary evidence for medieval potters in Worcestershire Some further evidence', *Trans. Worcestershire Archaeol. Soc. 3 ser.* **12**, 247–50

Hurst, J.D. 1992a 'The pottery', in Woodiwiss (ed.) 1992, 132–54

Hurst, J.D. 1992b 'Ceramic building material', in Woodiwiss (ed.) 1992, 155–7

Hurst, J.D. 1994 'A medieval ceramic production site and other medieval sites in the parish of Hanley Castle; the results of fieldwork in 1987–1992', *Trans. Worcestershire Archaeol. Soc. 3 ser.* **14**, 115–28

Hurst, J.D. (ed.), 1997a *A Multi-Period Salt Production Site at Droitwich: Excavations at Upwich,* Counc. Brit. Archaeol. Res. Rep. **107**, York, Council for British Archaeology

Hurst, J.D. 1997b 'Wooden artefacts', in Hurst (ed.) 1997a, 106–11

Hurst, J.D. 2002 *Castle Moat, Leominster* Leominster, Orphans Press

Hurst, J.D. and Rees, H. 1992 'Pottery fabrics; a multi-period series for the county of Hereford and Worcester', in Woodiwiss (ed.) 1992, 200–9

Hurst, J.G., Neal, D.S. and Van Beuningen, H.J.E. 1986 *Pottery Produced and Traded in North-west Europe 1350–1650* Rotterdam Papers **6**

Hussey, D. 2000 *Coastal and River Trade in Pre-industrial England: Bristol and its Region 1680–1730* Exeter, University of Exeter Press

Jackson, R. 2004 'Production: Roman ironworking', in Dalwood and Edwards 2004, 100–5

Jackson, R., Dalwood, H., Bretherton, J., Hughes, P., Griffin, L., Hurst, D., Jordan, D., Pearson, E., Robson-Glyde, S. and Roe, F. 2002 'Excavation, survey and watching brief at Warner Village Cinemas, Friar Street, Worcester', *Trans. Worcestershire Archaeol. Soc. 3 ser.* **18**, 53–101

Jackson, R.G. 2006 'Archaeological Investigations at the former Courage Brewery, Bath Street, Bristol, 2000–2001', *Bristol and Avon Archaeol.* **21**, 1–58

Jackson, R.G. and Price, R.H. 1974 *Bristol Clay Pipes* Bristol City Museum Research Monograph **1**

Jacobs, A. 2005 *Pottery from 16–18 Sansome Street, Worcester, Worcestershire* Worcestershire Historic Environment and Archaeology Service, Worcestershire County Council, unpublished report **2476**

Jacobs, A. 2006 'Post-medieval pottery', in *Pottery from Worcester Porcelain Works development site*, WHEAS typescript for Archenfield Archaeology

Jacobs, A. (undated) *Worcester Porcelain Works, final report* Worcestershire Historic Environment and Archaeology Service, Worcestershire County Council, unpublished report **P2804**

John Parkhouse Partnership 2004 *Proposed redevelopment off Newport Street, Worcester: assessment of effects of construction on archaeology* Unpublished report

Jones, A.P., Tucker, M.E. and Hart, J.K. 1999 'Guidelines and recommendations', in Jones, A.P., Tucker, M.E. and Hart J.K. (eds), *The Description and Analysis of Quaternary Stratigraphic Field Sections,* Quaternary Research Association Technical Guide **7**, 27–76

Jones, E. and Vyce, D. 2000 *Worcester Magistrates Court, Castle Street, Worcester. An Interim Statement of an Archaeological Excavation* Archaeological Investigations Limited, Herefordshire Archaeology Series **475**

Jones, L. 2001 'The pottery', in Lockett N. and Jones, L., *Archaeological Evaluation at 19 Cowl Street, Evesham, Worcestershire*, Historic Environment and Archaeology Service, Worcestershire County Council, internal report **914**, 9–10

Keen, L. 1978 'The medieval decorated tile pavements at Worcester', *Medieval Art and Architecture at Worcester Cathedral. British Archaeological Association Conference Transactions 1975*, 144–60

Kiesewalter, L. 1888 *Skelettmessungen am Pferde als Beitrag zur theoretischen Grundlage der Beurteilungslehre des Pferdes* Unpublished thesis, Leipzig University

Lentowicz, I.J. 1997 'Pottery', in Hurst 1997a, 68–88

Lewis, J.M. 1999 *The Medieval Tiles of Wales* Cardiff, National Museum of Wales

Lilley, K. D. 2002 *Urban life in the Middle Ages, 1000–1450* Basingstoke, Palgrave

Lobel, M.D. and Carus-Wilson, E.M. 1975 'Bristol', in Lobel, M.D. (ed.), *The Atlas of Historic Towns Vol 2* London, Scolar Press/Historic Towns Trust

Lyman, R.L. 1994 *Vertebrate Taphonomy* Cambridge, Cambridge University Press

McCarthy M.R. and Brooks C.M. 1988 *Medieval Pottery in Britain AD 900–1600* Leicester, Leicester University Press

McDonnell, J.G. and Swiss, A. 2004 'Ironworking residues', in: Dalwood and Edwards 2004, 368–78

MacGregor, A. 1985 *Bone, Antler, Ivory and Horn: The Technology of Skeletal Materials since the Roman Period* London, Croom Helm

Macklin, M.G., Johnstone, E. and Lewin, J. 2005 'Pervasive and long-term forcing of Holocene river instability and flooding in Great Britain by centennial-scale climate change', *The Holocene* **15.7**, 937–43

Macphail, M. 2004 'Soils and land-use history: results and potential of soil micromorphology', in Dalwood and Edwards 2004, 77–9

Maddy, D. 1999 'English Midlands', in Bowen, D.Q. (ed.), 'A revised correlation of Quaternary deposits in the British Isles', *Geological Society Special Report* **23**, 28–44

Margeson, S. 1993 *Norwich Households: The Medieval and Post-Medieval Finds from Norwich Survey Excavations 1971–78,* E. Anglian Archaeol. Report **58**

Marsden, P. 1971 'A seventeenth-century boat found in London', *Post-Medieval Archaeology* **5**, 88–98

Matolcsi, J. 1970 'Historische Erforschung der Körpergrösse des Rindes auf Grund von ungarischen Knochenmaterial', *Zeitschrift für Tierzüchtung und Züchtungsbiologie* **87**, 89–137

Mawer, A. and Stenton, F.M. 1927 *The Place-names of Worcestershire* Cambridge, Cambridge University Press

Meekings, C.A.F., Porter S. and Roy I. (eds) 1984 *The Hearth Tax Collectors' Book for Worcester 1678–1680* Worcestershire Historical Society, n.s., volume 11, Worcester, Worcestershire Historical Society

Miller, D., Crawford, A. and Dalwood, H. 2007 *Excavations at the Commandery, Worcester, 2005–6*, Historic Environment and Archaeology Service, Worcestershire County Council, unpublished report **1549**

Miller, D., Crawford, A., Dalwood H., Griffin, L., McHugh, G. and Robson-Glyde, S. 2007 *Excavation and Building recording at The Commandery, Sidbury, Worcester, in 2004–6*, Historic Environment and Archaeology Service, Worcestershire County Council, unpublished report **1549**

Miller, D., Griffin, L. and Pearson, E. 2004a *Programme of Archaeological Work at 9–10 The Tything, Worcester,* Archaeological Service, Worcestershire County Council, unpublished report **1150**

Miller, D., Griffin, L. and Pearson, E. 2004b *Archaeological investigations at Church Lane, Hallow, Worcestershire*, Historic Environment and Archaeology Service, Worcestershire County Council, unpublished report **1174**

Mitchiner, M. 1988 *Jetons, Medalets and Tokens 1: The Medieval Period and Nuremberg* London, Seaby

Moffett, L. 1992 'Fruits, vegetables, herbs and other plants from the latrine at Dudley Castle in central England, used by the Royalist garrison during the Civil War', *Review Palaeobotany and Palynology* **73**, 271–86

Moffett, L. 1995 'An Archaeobotanical View of *Cucurbita* spp. in Britain and Europe', in Kroll, H. and Pasternak, R. (eds), *Res archaeobotanicae, the 9th symposium of the IWGP*, 219–27

Moffett, L. 2004a 'Consumption and site environment', in Dalwood and Edwards 2004, 91–4

Moffett, L. 2004b 'Botanical remains', in Dalwood and Edwards 2004, 537–56

Monckton, A. 2006 'An archaeological resource assessment and research agenda for environmental archaeology in the East Midlands', in Cooper N.J. (ed.), *The Archaeology of the East Midlands: An Archaeological Resource Assessment and Research Agenda*, Leicester Archaeology Monograph **13**, 259–86

Moore, P.D., Webb, J.A. and Collinson, M.E. 1991 *Pollen Analysis* (2 edn) Oxford, Blackwell Scientific Publications

Morris, E.L. 1980 'Medieval and post-medieval pottery in Worcester: a type series', in Carver (ed.) 1980a, 221–54

Morris, L. 1974 'The site of Worcester: its geology and geomorphology', in Adlam B.H. (ed.) *Worcester and its Region: Field Studies in the Former County of Worcestershire* Worcester, Geographical Association, 24–34

Mould, Q, Carlisle, I and Cameron, E. 2003 *Leather and Leatherworking in Anglo-Scandinavian and Medieval York* The Archaeology of York: The Small Finds, **17/16**, York Archaeological Trust

Mundy, C.F. 1985 *Trial Excavations in Worcester 1985* Hereford and Worcester County Council, Archaeological Service unpublished report (unnumbered)

Mundy, C.F. 1986 'Worcester, Blackfriars', *West Midlands Archaeol.* **29**, 10–11

Munsell Color 2000 *Munsell Soil Color Charts* Munsell Color, New Windsor, New York

Napthan, M. 2006 *Archaeological Evaluation, Excavation and Watching-brief at the former Pickfords Warehouse Site, 16–18 Sansome Street, Worcester* Mike Napthan Archaeology Report

Newman, R. with Cranstone D. and Howard-Davis, C. 2001 *The Historical Archaeology of Britain c.1540–1900* Stroud, Sutton Publishing

Nicholson, R. and Scott, S. 2004a 'Animal remains', in Dalwood and Edwards 2004, 506–37

Nicholson, R. and Scott, S. 2004b 'Animal husbandry and exploitation', in Dalwood and Edwards 2004, 94–6

Nockert, M. 1997 *Bockstenmannen, Och Hans Dräkt* Halmstad/Varberg, Sweden, Stiftelsen Hallands Länsmuseer

Noël Hume, I. 1969 *Pottery and Porcelain in Colonial Williamsburg's Archaeological Collections* Colonial Williamsburg Archaeological Series **2**

Noël Hume, I. 2001 *If These Pots Could Talk: Collecting 2,000 Years of British Household Pottery* Chipstone Press/University Press of New England

Nørlund, P, 1924 'Buried Norsemen at Herjolfsnes', *Meddelelser om Grønland* **67**, 87–190

North, J.J. 1991 *English Hammered Coinage, 2: Edward I to Charles II, 1272–1662* (3 edn) London, Spink

Nye, S. 1989 'Botanical remains', in Murphy, K., 'Analysis of a cess pit fill from the Tudor Merchant's House, Tenby, Dyfed', *Bull. Board Celtic Stud.* **36**, 249–52

O'Connor, T, 2000 *The archaeology of animal bones* Stroud, Sutton Publishing

O'Keeffe, T. and Yamin, R. 2006 'Urban Historical Archaeology', in D. Hicks and M. Beaudry (eds) 2006, *The Cambridge companion to historical archaeology*, 87–103

Orr, S. 1922 'Clothing found on a skeleton at Quintfall Hill, Barrock Estate, near Wick', *Proc. Soc. Antiq. Scot.* **55**, 213–21

Østergård, E. 2004 *Woven into the Earth: Textiles from Norse Greenland* Aarhus, Aarhus University Press

Panter, I. 2009 *Worcester Library and Heritage Centre, The Butts: requirements for deposit monitoring?* Unpublished document, York Archaeological Trust

Parker-Hore 2004 *An Archive of Paving tiles in the Parker-Hore Collection, Worcester and in the Ashmolean Museum, Oxford* http://tileweb.ashmolean.museum/

Payne, S. 1985 'Morphological distinctions between mandibular teeth of young sheep *Ovis* and goats *Capra*' *J. Archaeol. Sci.* **12**, 139–47

Peacey, A.A. 1979 *Clay Tobacco Pipes in Gloucestershire* Committee for Rescue Archaeology in Avon, Gloucestershire and Somerset, Occasional Paper **4**

Peacey, A.A. 1996 *The development of the clay tobacco pipe kiln in the British Isles*, The Archaeology of the Clay Tobacco Pipe **14** (series ed. Davey P.), Brit. Archaeol. Rep. Brit. Ser. **246**, Oxford

Peacey, A.A. forthcoming *Pipe Aston. A Seventeenth Century Community of Clay Tobacco Pipe Makers in North Herefordshire* Brit. Archaeol. Rep. Brit. Ser.

Pearson, E. 1995 *Assessment of Environmental Remains from Worcester Cathedral* Hereford and Worcester County Council, Archaeological Service Unpublished report **377**

Pearson, E. 1999 *Environmental Remains from a Watching Brief at 14–19 Bridge Street, Hereford*, Worcestershire County Council, Archaeology Service report **753**

Pearson, E. 2001 *Environmental archaeology in the West Midlands in the early post-medieval period*, West Midlands Regional Research Framework for Archaeology, Seminar 6, http://www.birmingham.ac.uk/schools/historycultures/departments/caha/research/arch-research/wmrrfa/seminar6.aspx

Pearson, E. 2003 *Assessment of Environmental Remains from wet-sieved samples from the former Mead and Tompkinson site, 19–22 Bridge Street, Hereford*, Worcestershire County Council, Historic Environment and Archaeology Service Unpublished report **1146**

Pearson, E. 2006 *Environmental Remains from an Evaluation at Mary-le-Port, Bristol*, Worcestershire County Council, Historic Environment and Archaeology Service Unpublished report **1467**

Pearson, E., Head, K. and Smith, D. 2005 *Environmental Remains from an Excavation at Mill Street, Leominster, Herefordshire*, Worcestershire County Council, Historic Environment and Archaeology Service Unpublished report **1341**

Perrin, J.R. 1999 'Roman Pottery from Excavations at and near to the Roman Small Town of Durobrivae, Water Newton, Cambridgeshire, 1956–58', *J. Roman Pottery Stud.* **8**

Platt, C. and Coleman-Smith, R. 1975 *Excavations in Medieval Southampton 1953–1969, 2: The Finds* Leicester, Leicester University Press

PortCities, Bristol (undated) 'Bristol and the East African slave trade' http://discoveringbristol.org.uk/slavery/routes/places-involved/east-indies/bristol-east-african-slave-trade (accessed 13/9/2013)

Price, R., Jackson, R. and Jackson, P. 1981 *Bristol Clay Pipe Makers* Privately published, Bristol

Quiney, A. 1974 'Hatchett's Farm, No. 735 Staines Road, Bedfont, London Borough of Hounslow (Middlesex)', *Post-Medieval Archaeol.* **8**, 108–12

Richardson, L. 1964 *The River Severn between Upper Arley and Gloucester* Privately printed

Roach, F.A. 1985 *Cultivated Fruits of Britain: their Origin and History* Oxford, Blackwell

Robinson, M.A. 1992 'Environment, archaeology and alluvium on the river gravels of the South Midlands', in Needham, S. and Macklin M.G. (eds), *Alluvial Archaeology in Britain,* Oxford, Oxbow Monograph **27**, 197–208

RockWare 2005 *RockWorks v2004* http://www.rockware.com (accessed 7 February 2006)

Roe, F. 2004 'Worked stone', in Dalwood and Edwards 2004, 462–86

Schweingruber, F.W. 1982 *Microscopic Wood Anatomy* Zurich, F. Fluck-Wurth

Silver, I.A. 1969 'The ageing of domestic animals', in Brothwell and Higgs (eds) 1969, 283–302

Sim, A. 1977 *Food and Feast in Tudor England* Stroud, Sutton Publishing

Snyder, J.B. 1992 *Flow Blue* Pennsylvania, Schiffer

Soiltechnics 2003 *Proposed Development off Newport Street Worcester: Ground Investigation Report* Soiltechnics unpublished report (un-numbered)

Stace, C. 1991 *New Flora of the British Isles* (1st edn) Cambridge, Cambridge University Press

Stace, C. 1997 *New Flora of the British Isles* (2nd edn) Cambridge, Cambridge University Press

Stamp, A.H. 1988 'The Brick Children', in *British Brick Society Information, Compilation Volume 1 1973–1981*, 40–2

Stenton, F.M. 1924 'City of Worcester', in Willis-Bund 1924, 376–420

Sworn, S. forthcoming *Archaeological excavations at University of Worcester, City Campus, Castle Street, Worcester*

Sworn, S. and Phear, S. 2007 *Archaeological Evaluation of the New Library and History Centre, The Butts, Worcester*, Worcestershire County Council, Historic Environment and Archaeology Service unpublished report **1408**

Teichert, M. 1975 'Osteometrische Untersuchungen zur Berechnung der Wideristhohe bei Schafen', in Clason, A.T. (ed.), *Archaeological Studies* Amsterdam, Elsevier, 51–69

Trinder, B. 2005 *Barges and Bargemen: a Social History of the Upper Severn Navigation 1660–1900* Chichester, Phillimore

Tucker, M.E. 1982 *Sedimentary Rocks in the Field* Chichester, Wiley

Vaughan, J.G. and Geissler, C. 1997 *The new Oxford book of food plants* Oxford, Oxford University Press

Vince, A. 1977 'The medieval and post-medieval ceramic industry of the Malvern region: the study of a ware and its distribution', in Peacock, D.P.S. (ed.), *Pottery and Early Commerce: Characterization and Trade in Roman and Later Ceramics* London, Academic Press, 257–305

Vince, A. 1984 *The Medieval Ceramic Industry of the Severn Valley* Unpublished PhD thesis, University of Southampton

Vince, A. 1985 'The ceramic finds', in R. Shoesmith (ed.), *Hereford City Excavations 3: The Finds* Counc. Brit. Archaeol. Res. Rep. **56**, London, Council for British Archaeology, 65–9

von den Driesch, A. 1976 *A Guide to the Measurement of Animals from Archaeological Sites* Peabody Museum of Archaeology and Ethnology Bulletin **1**

von den Driesch, A. and Boessneck, J. 1974 'Kritische Anmerkungen zur Widerristhohenberechnung aus Langenmassen vorn und frühgeschichtlicher Tierknochen', *Säugetierkundliche Mitteilungen* **22**, 325–48

Walton, P. 1981 'The textiles', in Harbottle, B. and Ellison, M., 'An excavation in the Castle ditch, Newcastle upon Tyne, 1974–76', *Archaeol. Aeliana* 5 ser. **9**, 190–228

Walton, P. 1991 'Textiles', in Blair and Ramsay (eds) 1991, 319–54

Walton, P. and Eastwood, G. 1989 *A Brief Guide to the Cataloguing of Archaeological Textiles* (1 edn) York 1983; (4 edn) London 1989

Walton Rogers, P. 1998. 'Textiles and costume', in Drinkall, G. and Foreman, M. (eds), 'The Anglo-Saxon Cemetery at Castledyke South, Barton-upon-Humber', *Sheffield Excavation Reports* **6**, 274–9

Warman, S. 2007a 'Animal Bone', in Evans *et al.* 2007, 40–2

Warman, S. 2007b 'Animal Bone', in Pickard, C., *Broadmead Expansion; Assessment Area 3. Post-Excavation Assessment* Cotswold Archaeology and Pre-Construct Archaeology joint report, 88–92

Warry, P. 2006 *Tegulae: Manufacture, Typology and Use in Roman Britain* Brit. Archaeol. Rep. Brit. Ser. **417**, Oxford

Watts, M. 2002 *The Archaeology of Mills and Milling* Stroud, Tempus

WCC (Worcester City Council) 2007 *An Outline Resource Assessment and Research Framework for the Archaeology of Worcester*, (consultation draft version 2.5), Worcester Urban Archaeological Strategy, Worcester City Council

Webster, P.V. 1976 Severn Valley Ware: A Preliminary Study, *Trans. Bristol Gloucestershire Archaeol. Soc.* **94**, 18–46

Webster, P.V. 1996 *Roman Samian Pottery in Britain* Counc. Brit. Archaeol. Practical Handbook in Archaeology **13**

Wenham, L.P. 1964 'Hornpot Lane and the horners of York', *Annual report of the Yorkshire Philosphical Society* 1964, 23–56

WHEAS (Worcestershire Historic Environment and Archaeology Service) 2004 *Archaeological evaluation at Newport Street, Worcester, Worcestershire* Typescript Report **1237**

WHEAS (Worcestershire Historic Environment and Archaeology Service) 2011 *Excavation and building recording at the Hive (Worcester Library and History Centre), The Butts, Worcester: Archaeological Assessment and Updated Project Design* Worcestershire County Council, Historic Environment and Archaeology Service unpublished report **P3031**

WHEAS/CA (Worcestershire Historic Environment and Archaeology Service and Cotswold Archaeology) 2005 *Written Scheme of Investigation: Land at Newport Street and All Saints Road, Worcester: Excavation and Evaluation* WHEAS/CA unpublished report (un-numbered)

White, R. and Barker, P. 1998 *Wroxeter. Life and Death of a Roman City* Stroud, Tempus

Whitehead, D. 1989 *Urban Renewal and Suburban Growth: the Shaping of Georgian Worcester* Worcestershire Historical Society Occasional Publication **5**

Whitehead, D.B. 1976 *The Book of Worcester* Chesham, Barracuda

Whitehouse, D.B. 1962 'Post-medieval pottery from Worcester', *Trans. Worcestershire Archaeol. Soc.* 2 ser. **39,** 33–47

Wilkinson, K. and Marter, P. 2006 *The Butts, Worcester: a Geoarchaeological Assessment*, ARCA Report **0506–5**, Department of Archaeology, University of Winchester

Wilkinson, K. 2007 *Newport Street, Worcester: Borehole Survey: Analytical Report*, ARCA Report **0708–4**, Department of Archaeology, University of Winchester

Williamson, G.C. 1891 *Trade Tokens issued in the Seventeenth Century: A New and Revised Edition of William Boyne's work* **2** London, Elliot Stock

Willis-Bund J.W. (ed.), 1924 *Victoria History of the Counties of England: Worcestershire* **4**

Wills, J. 1980 'Excavation and salvage recording at Friars Gate, Union Street, 1976', in Carver (ed.) 1980a, 107–11

Wills, L.J. 1938 'The Pleistocene development of the Severn from Bridgnorth to the sea', *Quart. J. Geological Soc.* **94**, 161–242

Wilson, B., Grigson, C. and Payne, S. 1982 *Ageing and Sexing Animal Bones from Archaeological Sites* Brit. Archaeol. Rep. Brit. Ser. **109**, Oxford

Withers, P. and Withers, B. 1999 *British Copper Tokens 1811–1820 including those of Ireland, the Isle of Man and the Channel Islands* Llanfyllin, Galata Print

Woodfield, P. 1964 'Yellow glazed wares of the 17th century', *Trans. Birmingham Warwickshire Archaeol. Soc.* **81**, 78–86

Woodiwiss, S. (ed.) 1992 *Iron Age and Roman Salt Production and the Medieval Town of Droitwich* Counc. Brit. Archaeol. Res. Rep. **81**, London, Council for British Archaeology/Hereford and Worcester County Council

Worcester City Museum Archaeology Section. 2005 *Brief for archaeological mitigation (excavation, watching brief and building recording), land at Newport Street and All Saints Road, Worcester* Worcester City Council, brief **05/7**

Worcestershire On-line Ceramic Database www.worcestershireceramics.org

Index

Page numbers in *italics* denote illustrations. Places and locations are in Worcester unless indicated otherwise.

Aberry, Elizabeth 103
Agberrow, Richard 101
agriculture 200, 225, 231
air raid shelter *71*, 78
alembic 117
All Hallows' Square 232
All Saints' Church 93, 100, 134, 157, 232
All Saints' parish 8, 9, 232, 233
All Saints' Road 18, 109, 236, 242, 247
Allen, Robert & Co. Ltd. 190, 191
alleys *see* passageways/alleys
Allies, Jabez 3
Allsopp's Ltd. 191
alluvium
  discussion 228, 229–31, 234, 252
  environmental evidence 225
  geoarchaeology 36–7, 38–40
  research objectives 19
Amicus of Eport 8
Amphlett, H. 95
The Anchor 15
Andrews, Joseph 94, 188
Angel Place 190
animal bone
  analysis
    age at death 219–20
    burning 223
    butchery 222
    gnawing 222–3
    pathology 222
    size 220–2
    weathering 222
  assemblage 216
  correlation with documentary evidence 224
  discussion 224–5
    Roman 223
    medieval 223, 225, 227, 243, 247, 249
    post-medieval 223–4, 226, 248
  methodology 27
  results
    Roman 216, 217
    medieval 216–17, 218, 219
    post-medieval 217–19, 220, 221
  see also fish bone

anvil stone 88
apple/crab apple (*Malus sylvestris/domestica*) 202, 209, 213
Applebury, William 96
Appleby, William 94
architectural stonework
  assemblage 146
  catalogue 146–51, *147*, *148*, *149*, *150*, *151*, *152–5*, *156*
  discussion 151–7
arrowhead, iron 82, 163, *164*
ash boxes *57*, *59*, *68*, *75*, 91
Axell, William 94

Bach, John 9
Badland, Elizabeth 96
Baggett, Richard 101
bakehouses
  discussion 238, 240, 241, 245, 250, 253
  documentary evidence 99, 103, 105
  excavation evidence 41, 70
Baker family
  Francis 94, 182–7, 188
  Francis junior 187
  Joseph 187
  Mary 187
  Richard 187
  Robert 94
  Samuel 187
bakers/baking
  discussion 229, 241, 245, 246, 251
  documentary evidence 10, 11, 12, 15, 10
    Hope and Anchor/Severn View 93, 96
    no. 8 109
    nos 10–12 108
    no. 24 103
    no. 32/34 94, 99
  see also bakehouses
Baldwin, Elizabeth 94
Baldwin, Thomas 93, 94
Band, William 94
Band's Marine Store 97
Barber, Francis 182–7
barge owners 106, 110
barley (*Hordeum vulgare*) 201, 209
Barnes, Nancy 99

Barnes, Samuel 94, 99, 101
Barnett, Cora 95
Barnett, John 94
Bate, Thomas 93, 94
Baxter Street, Shambles 11
beads, glass 189
Bean, Arnold 15
Beardmore, Thomas 187, 188
Beasons, Philip 108
bell, copper-alloy 165, *165*
Benbow, James 94
Bennett, George 94
Benthall (Shrops), clay pipe production 172
Bevere (Worcs), Severn 230
Beverley (E. Yorks), vat 243
Bezar, Philip 108
Billings, - 94
Birch, Ed 95
Birmingham (W. Mids)
    pollen analysis 200
    pottery production 115
Bissell, William 100
black mustard (*Brassica nigra*) 209, 213, 249, 250
black pepper (*Piper nigrum*) 209, 215, 216, 226, 248
blackberry/bramble (*Rubus*) 202, 209, 213, 214, 249
Blackfriars Priory
    architectural fragments 157
    excavations 3
    floor tiles 134
    gift to 8
    location *4*
    properties 8, 9, 10, 93, 97, 100
Blackmore/Blakemore, John 94
blacksmiths 105
Bland & Co. 191
Blew, Richard 95, 101, 108, 110
board offcut, wooden 197
Boar's Head 15, *16*, 61, 95, *98*, 104, 247
Boar's Head Yard 104
bone, conservation methodology 25; *see also* animal bone
Bordesley Abbey (Worcs), floor tiles 132
bosses/fittings
    copper-alloy 165, *165*
    iron 164, 165, *165*
boundaries *see* property boundaries
Bowen, Humphrey 95
Bowers, - 94
bowl, wooden
    description 195, 196, *196*, 197
    discussion 244, 247, 250
    excavation evidence 55–6
Bowles, Abraham 106
Bradley, Henry 172
Bradley, John 95
Bragg, Henry 95
bramble *see* blackberry/bramble
Brassica 209
Brassy, Richard 100
Braunesford, John de 97
brewers/brewing 11, 103, 108, 245–6, 251
brewhouses
    discussion 240, 241, 245–6, 250

documentary evidence
    nos 10–12 108, 109
    no. 14 107
    no. 18 106
    no. 20 105
    no. 22 104
    no. 24 103
    no. 30 102
    excavation evidence 70, 77
Breynton, John and Jane 17, 93, 94
Brian, Francis 182–7
brick
    assemblage 140–2
    catalogue 255–76
    description 142
        late medieval–early post-medieval 142–3, 145, *145*
        17th–18th centuries 143–4
        19th–20th centuries 144
    discussion 68, 144–5, 236, 239–40, 241, 253
bricklayers 95, 104, 106, 247
brickmaker 94
Bridge Street 11, *12*, 17, 105, 231–2
Bristol
    clay pipes 172, 182, 246
    development 234–5
    hearths 244
    trade 226, 249
Bristow, James 93, 94
The Britannia 15, 17
Brittain (Briton), - 187
Broad Street 3, *4*, 232
Broadfield, A. 95, 108
Bromyard (Worcs), clay pipes 182, 188
Broseley (Shrops), clay pipes 172–82, 188, 246, 248
Brown, Joseph 110
Browning, - 95
Browning, Edmund 95, 104
Browning, Thomas 95, 101, 104, 105
Browning's Passage 235, 237
Buck, Richard 95, 104
buckles
    copper-alloy 163, 164, *164*, 165, *165*, 166, *166*
    iron 164
Buckley (Flints), clay pipes 182
buckwheat (*Fagopyrum esculentum*) 209–13
buildings
    concordance of buildings with land-use 32–5
    discussion
        Roman 236–7
        medieval 237–8, 249, 253
        post-medieval 238–42, 250, 251, 253
buildings excavated
    Building 1
        discussion 235, 236, 239, 240, 242, 246
        excavation evidence
            Period 3.1 40–1, *41*, *54*
            Period 3.3 41–2, *42*, *58*
            Period 5 43–4, *43*
    Building 2
        discussion 229, 235, 239
        excavation evidence 45, *45*, *54*

Building 3
    discussion 241
    excavation evidence 46–7, *46*, *47*, *58*, *60*, *71*
Building 4
    discussion 235, 237–8, 239, 240, 244, 249
    excavation evidence *51*, 52–3, *52*, *53*
    spindle whorls 157
Building 5
    discussion 229, 238, 240, 242
        colonisation and property division 235, 236
        industry and craft 244
        status and wealth 249
    excavation evidence
        Period 2.4–2.5 *51*, 53–5
        Period 2.5–3.1 *51*, *54*, 55–6, *56*
        Period 3.1–3.2 *54*, *57*, 59
        Period 4–5 59–61, *60*
Building 6 *57*, *58*, 59
Building 7 *57*, 59
Building 8 59–61, *60*
Building 9 *54*, 65, 66, 245
Building 10 *60*, 67
Building 11 *57*, *60*, 66, 235, 239
Building 12 *60*, 66, 67, *71*, 235, 241
Building 13 *60*, 67, *71*, 246
Building 14
    discussion 236, 240
    excavation evidence *57*, *58*, 69, 70, 71–2
Building 15
    discussion 236, 240–1, 245
    excavation evidence
        Period 3.3–4 *58*, 70–2, *70*, *73*
        Period 4 *70*, 72–3
        Period 5 *71*, 73
Building 16
    discussion 240, 241, 242
    excavation evidence 70, 71, 72, *72*, 73
Building 17 *60*, 75–6, *76*, 246
Building 19 *58*, 75, 236, 239, 240
Building 20 *54*, 75, 240
Building 21 *71*, 76, 246
Building 22 76, 77, *86*, 239, 240
Building 23 76, 77, *90*, 241, 246
Building 24 *71*, 78
Building 26 76, *86*, 239
Building 27 77, *90*
Building 29 84–5
Building 30 85, *90*, 246
Building 31 *81*, *86*, 237, 238, 240, 243
Building 32 *81*, 87, 237, 238
Building 33
    discussion 237, 238, 240
    excavation evidence *83*, *86*, 89–91, *91*
Building 34 *89*, 91–2, 240, 245, 246
Building 35 *71*, 92, 238
Building 36 47, 48, *71*, 241
Building 37 48, *71*, 251
Building 39 *54*, 68
Building 40 77, *88*, *90*, 246
Building 41 *50*, *51*, 67–8, 236, 237, 238
Building 42 *50*, 61, 237, 238
building stone 235

Bull, William 94
Bullock, Frederick 95
burh 5, 232, 233
bus station 18, 236, 241, 242, 247
butchers 11, 95, 101, 106, 109
butchers' shops 11
butchery 216, 218, 219, 222, 223
button, bone 197, 198
button maker 109
The Butts 3, *4*, 37, 38, 39, 231
buzz bone 197, 198, *198*

cabinet maker 94, 102
Cahill, Elizabeth 95
Callowhill, Thomas and Francis 95, 104
candleholders, stone 158–9, 162, *162*
candlesticks, ceramic 122, 126, *127*
car park 236, 242, 247
Careless, Anthony 9–10, 93, 94
Careless, Mary 94
carpenters 70, 104, 106, 246, 247, 250
carriagemaker 95, 109
carrot (*Daucus carota*) 209, 213
cart house 239
Castle Street University Campus 3, *4*
cat 216, 217, 223
Cathedral
    floor tiles 131, 134
    Leddington memorial 100
    plant remains 215
    stonework 155, 156
cattle
    Roman 216, 219, 220–1, 223, 224
    medieval 216, 217, 219, 220–1, 223
    post-medieval 218, 219, 223, 224, 248
        age at death 219, 220
        pathology 222
        size 220–1, 226
cattle market 232
Cauldwell, Mary 110
causeway 232
cellars
    discussion
        Period 2 229, 237–8, 249, 253
        Period 3 239, 250
        Period 4 241, 250
    documentary evidence
        Hope and Anchor/Severn View 96
        no. 14 106, 107
        no. 16 106
        no. 18 106
        no. 20 105
        no. 22 104
        no. 30 102
        no. 32/34 99
    excavation evidence
        Plot 3 51–3, *51*, *52*, *53*, *57*, *58*, 59
        Plots 8–9 *71*, 76
        Plots 10–11 77
        Plots 12–13 85, *90*
        Plot 14 *71*, *83*, *86*, 89–91, *90*, 92

cess pits
    discussion 238, 245, 249
    environmental evidence 209, 213, 215, 216, 226
    excavation evidence
        Plot 1 41, 42
        Plot 2 47, *47*, 48, *58*
        Plot 3 55–6, *55*, *57*, 59
        Plots 4–5 *57*, *60*, 65, 66, 67
        Plots 6–7 *54*, *57*, 69
        Plots 10–11 77, 77–8
    see also privies
Chance, Richard 101
chandler 94, 100
chapman 102, 103
Chapman family 95
    William 95
Chelsea pensioner 95
Cheltenham (Glos), clay pipes 188
cherry (*Prunus cerasus*) 209, 213, 215, 225, 249
Chetle, William, token 167
chicken
    Period 1 216
    Period 2 216, 217, 249
    Period 3 218, 219, 223, 224, 226, 227, 248
china painter 106
City Arcade
    excavation 3, 5
    location *4*
    pottery 112, 113, 115, 116
City Depot 18
City Walls Road 3
Civil War 15–17, 99, 100
Clark, Jane 94
Clarke, Henry 109
Clarke, Lewis & Co. 190, 191
Clarke, Sarah 93
Clarke, Thomas 95
clay tobacco pipes
    assemblage 169–72
    discussion 188, 246, 248
        early forms (1630–50) 172, *173*
        late 17th–early 18th-century forms 172–82, *174–80*
        mid–late 18th-century forms *180–1*, 182
        makers' stamps 182, *183–4*, 185–7
Clements, Thomas 94, 102
Clempson family 101
Cleobury Mortimer (Shrops), clay pipe production 172
Clifton Quarry (Worcs) 231
cloister, stonework from 148, *151*, 156
cloth industry 8, 9–10, 100, 250, 251
clothiers
    discussion 241, 242, 244, 245
    documentary evidence 9, 10
        Hope and Anchor/Severn View 93, 94
        no. 24 102
        nos 26–30 100
        no. 32/34 99
clothing fragment 192–5, *194*, *195*
coach-house 102, 241
coal merchant 106
coal yard 48, 102, 106, 247, 251
coffee house 108, 246, 250

coins
    assemblage 166
    medieval 166, 167
    post-medieval 167, 168
    post-medieval–modern 168, 169
combs
    bone 197, 198
    ivory 197–8, *197*, 250
    wooden 55, 195–6, *196*, 250
The Commandery
    excavation 3, *4*
    floor tiles 132, 134
    pottery 122, 123, 124, 125
Constance, Ed 95
Cooksey family 15
coopers 94, 95, 102, 247
Copenhagen Street 232
coppicing 200
coriander (*Coriandrum sativum*) 209
Corker, Ann and Richard 93
corn chambers/lofts 12, 41, 99, 105, 236, 241
corndealer 105
counter, ceramic 146, *146*
Countess of Huntingdon's School 43, 99, 236, 242
courts 229
    Court 1 *97*
    Court 2 *97*, 106
    Court 3 *72*, *97*, 105, 242
    Court 4 61, *62*, *97*, *98*, 102, 241, 242
    Court 5 42–3, *60*, *97*
    Court 6 242
    Court 7 *97*
    Court 8 48, *71*, *97*, *98*, 102
    Court 9 106, 108–9
Coventry (W Mids)
    pollen analysis 200
    trade 247
Cozens, - 246, 250
Cozens, Stephen 95, 101, 109
crab apple see apple/crab apple
Cresswell (Creswell), Charles 95, 109
Crocketts Ltd. 191
The Cross 9, 232
cross base 9
Crowle woods 99
Crump family
    Joseph 95, 101, 108
    Joseph junior 108
    Mary 108
cucumber (*Cucumis sativa*) 209, 213, 215, 226, 248, 250
currant/gooseberry (*Ribes* sp) 209, 213, 214, 215, 225, 246

Dagget/Daggett family 17, 102
    Elizabeth 94, 100–2
    John 94, 100, 101
Dalby, John 94
Dallow, Thomas 100
Dance, William 95, 108
Dark, Edward 95
daub 240
Davis, Andrew 94
Davis, James (apprentice) 188

Davis family (of 22 Newport Street) 105
   Elizabeth Webb 95, 105
   J. 95
   John 95, 105
   Joseph 105
Dax, Henry 94
Dean and Chapter 93, 97, 99
Deansway, excavation 3, *4*, 8
   agriculture, Roman 5
   animal bone 220, 223, 224, 225, 226, 227, 247
   buildings 253
   defences 5
   flint 3
   ironworking 192, 244
   mortars 158
   plant remains 215, 227, 247
   pollen analysis 200
   pottery 112, 113, 114, 115, 116, 126, 247
   roof tiles 136, 137, 138, 139
   trade and consumption 247
Dedicott, Humphrey 9, 15
defences
   Roman 5, *6*
   medieval 5, *7*, 8, 232, 233–4
Denson, Roger 95, 104
diet 248, 249–50
Diglis (Worcs), Severn 230
distillers 12, 66, 103, 108, 215, 226, 246
distilling 66, 103, 215, 226, 251
documentary evidence
   general account 8–18, *9*, *10*, *11*, *12*, *13–14*, *15*, *16*, *17*
   individual properties 93, 94–5, *97*, *98*
      nos 2–8 109–10
      nos 10–12 108–9
      nos 14–18 105–8, *107*
      nos 20–22 104–5
      no. 24 102–4
      nos 26–30 99–102
      no. 32/34 97–9
      nos 40–44 96–7
      nos 54–36 93–7, *96*
   methodology 24
   property ownership *c*1550–1925 94–5
Dodynge family 100, 250
   Thomas 94, 99, 100, 239, 245
   William 10, 40, 94, 99, 100, 239, 245
Dolday
   buildings 229, 234, 235, 239, 250–1, 252, 253
   documentary evidence
      properties 100–2, 103, 104, 106
      summary 8, *10*, 11, 15, 17, *43*, *74*
   evaluation 229, 230
      excavation evidence *see* Newport Street, excavation evidence, Plot 2
   origins and function 8, 232, 233, 235, 250–1
   trade and industry 245, 247, 251
dolphin bone 217, 223, 226
Dovey, Catherine 188
drains
   Plot 1 43
   Plots 4–5 67
   Plots 6–7 72
   Plots 14 *81*, 87
Droitwich (Worcs)
   pollen analysis 200
   pottery 113, 115, 116
   salt trade 247
The Drum 15, 94
Dudley (W. Mids), plant remains 215
dye-vat hearths 243, 244
dyeing 11, 214, 225, 243, 244
Dyer, David 9
Dyer, Henry 95
Dyer, John 8
dyers 8–9, 11, 12, 15, 242, 243, 244
dyer's rocket (*Reseda luteola*) 209, 214, 243

East India Company 216
Ecclesiastical Commissioners 99
Edmund, J. 94
Edwards, Samuel 95, 101, 106
eggshell 209, 213, 249
elderberry (*Sambucus nigra*) 202, 209
environmental evidence, synthesis
   compared 226–7
   correlation with documented households 226
   description
      early deposits 225
      medieval 225
      post-medieval 225–6
   trade 226
Eport Street 8, 9, 231, 232
Erroll, Jas 94
Esther Brothers 94
Evans, Henry 95, 104
Eversleigh family 109
Evesham (Glos), pottery 115
Ewport Street 8

Farmer, J. 94
Farmer, W. 94
Farrier Street 3, *4*, 233
Featherstone, John 102
Featherstone, William 106
feltmaker 94
fence 236
fennel (*Foeniculum vulgare*) 209, 213, 250
Field, Joseph 94, 95, 108
fig (*Ficus carica*) 202, 209, 213, 248, 249
Fincher family 17, 100, 102
   Robert 94
finial, ceramic 139, 140, *141*
fireplaces 238, 240
   Plot 2 47
   Plots 4–5 66
   Plots 6–7 68
   Plots 8–9 75
   Plot 14 92
fish bone
   medieval 216, 217, 223, 226, 249
   post-medieval 218, 223, 224, 226
fisherman 103
fittings *see* bosses/fittings
Fitzer, Henry 101, 102

flax (*Linum usitatissimum*) 209, 214, 243
flax retting 214, 243
The Fleet 95
Fleet, Thomas 95, 101
Flinn, Judiah 109
Flokesmud, H. 8
flooding 17, 225, 228, 230–1, 233, 234
floor tiles, medieval
   assemblage 130–1
   description 131–2, *133*
   discussion 132–4
Foregate Street suburb 252
fort, Roman 5
Friar Street
   buildings 8
   floor tiles 132–4
   pottery 112, 113, 115, 116
fruiterer 95, 109
fullers 8, 40, 236, 239, 242, 244, 245
furnaces 70, 99, 103, 105, 108, 109, 246

garden soils 44, 51, 68, 85
gardens
   discussion 239, 240
   documentary evidence 99, 100, 102, 103, 104, 109, 110
Gardiner, F. 95, 109
Gardner Bros Fruiters, token 168
Garway (Herefs), church 155–6
Gear, Mrs 94
geoarchaeology
   discussion 40, 229–30
     chronology 39
     depositional environments 38–9
     river behaviour and impact on human activity 39–40
     topography of stratigraphy 38, *39*
   methodology 20, *22*, 23, 25–6
   stratigraphy 31–6, *37*
     alluvium (Power House and Elmore Members) 36–7, 225
     made ground 38
Gibbs (Gibbes) family 15
   William 17, 95, 101, 106, 250
   William junior 106
glass vessels
   assemblage 189
   medieval 189, 250
   16th–18th centuries 189, 190, *190*
   modern 190–1
   stamp 189
Gloucester (Glos)
   clay pipes 172, 182, 188, 246
   pottery 114
Glover family
   Mrs - 94
   James senior 102
   James 96, 102, 106
glovers 95, 105, 108
gloving industry 8
goose
   Period 2 216, 217, 223
   Period 3 218, 223, 224, 248
Gosling, Hugh 100

grains of paradise (*Aframomum granum-paradisi*) 55, 213, 215–16, 226, 248, 249
grape (*Vitis vinifera*) 209, 213, 214, 249
Great Malvern (Worcs), tiles 131, 138
Green, William 95
Green Dragon 10, 94, 96–7, 102, 106
Griffiths, William 95
grinding mill 72
grindstone 156
grocer 110
Grove, Elizabeth 101
Gummery, Joseph 110
Gwynn, Charles 95

Haden family 17, 95, 101, 103, 105, 108
   Beatrix 46, 103
   Moses 15, 95, 101, 103–4
   Thomas 95, 101, 103, 245–6, 250
   William 103–4
Hafod family 103
   John 94, 103
Haines, Harold William 102
hairdresser 97
Hall, Frederick 95
Hall, William 108
Hallow (Worcs), roof tiles 139
Hanbury (Worcs), settlement 231
Hand, James 94
handles
   bone 197, 198
   copper-alloy 165, *165*
   iron 163, *164*
Hanley Swan (Worcs), pottery production 113, 114
Hanwell, George 94
Hardwick, C. 188
Hardwick, G. 188
Harper family 95
   William 95, 101, 108
Harris *see* Hewins/Harris
Harston, William 94
Hart, Francis 103
Harvord, Mr 99
Hay, James 94
Haytor, Charles 94
hazelnut (*Corylus avellana*) 213
hearths
   discussion 229, 235, 236, 237, 238, 243–4
   documentary evidence 99, 100, 102, 104, 106, 108
   excavation evidence
     Plot 2 44–5, *44*
     Plot 3 51, 51–2, *52*, 53, 56, 59
     Plots 4–5 62–3, *64*, 65
     Plots 6–7 67, 68, 68–9, 70
     Plots 10–11 77
     Plot 14 *83*, 87, 87–8, *87*, 91
Heath family 95, 101
   Thomas 101, 102
Heepox, Thomas 188
Heming, - 94
Heming, Richard 106
Hemming, Thomas 94
Hemmings, John 101

hemp house 10, 40, 99, 236, 239, 245
Herbert family 101
   Margaret 107–8
   Mary 95, 101
   William 95, 101, 105, 106–8
Hereford (Herefs)
   clay pipes 182, 187, 188
   plant remains 214, 225
   pottery 116
Hereford, Robert de 97
Herefordshire House 95, 109–10
Hewins/Harris, Charlotte 188
Hewlett, Elizabeth and Robert 188
Hickman, Charles 95
Higgins family 95, 101, 106
   Ann (Nancy) 106
   Michael 106
   Sarah 106
High Street 5, 10, 53, 100
Hill family 244, 250
   Daniel 104
   Mary 102
   Patience 104
   Richard 101
   Thomas 10, 95, 102–3, 104, 241, 245
   Thomas the younger 245
   William 102
Hinksman family
   Henry 110
   Judith 109
   Mary 109, 110
   Richard 95, 101, 106, 109–10
   Robert 109
Hiron, Sarah 94
Holder, Mary 95, 101
Hole, William 95
Holt, William 108
Hooker, John 95
hop (*Humulus lupulus*) 209–13
Hope and Anchor 15, 17, 93, 94, 246
Hopkins, Thomas 187–8
horncores
   cattle 218, 222, 225, 243
   sheep 217, 223, 225, 226, 243
hornworkers 97, 242
Horridge, John 94
horse 216, 218, 221–2, 224, 226
hose fragment 192–5, *194, 195*
House of Industry, tokens 168
house of office 93
household consumption *see* trade
Hughes, George 94
Humphries, Chas 94
Huntbach family
   Joan 105
   William 104, 105
Huntsman, Richard 95
Hurdman family
   Edward 66, 95, 101, 102, 103, 215, 226, 246
   John 106
   Mary 101
Huxley, Thomas 94

Hyde family 94, 102
   John 102, 104
Hymulton woods 99

Ibies Coffee House 95, 108
Ibole/Ibull, John 100
industry and craft
   Roman 242
   medieval 225, 237, 242–5, 253
   post-medieval 245–6, 253
   18th century 246
   19th–20th centuries 246–7
inns/public houses 10, 12–15, 17–18; *see also* individual inns/public houses by name
ironmonger 94
ironworking
   Roman 5, 228, 242, 249
   medieval 87, 88, 229, 236, 237, 243
   see also slag
ivory, conservation methodology 25

James & Son 95
James, Francis 93
jettons 166–8
John le Deyzare 9
John le Pynnare 97, 242
Jones, Joshua 95

Kardonia factory 3, *4*
Kempson family
   George 95
   J.W. 95
   Mary 95
key, iron 164, 165, *165*
Kings, Humphrey 100
King's Head 12, *13*, 17, 96
Kinsey family
   Ann 104
   John 70, 72, 95, 101, 103, 104–5, 246, 250
kitchens
   discussion 236, 238, 239, 240, 241
   excavation evidence 55, 56, 59, 77
Knapp, John Junior, token 168
Knowles, C. 94
Kyte, - 105

Laiton, Thomas 187, 188
land reclamation 8, 230, 231, 232, 234, 252
Lane, Thomas 110
Langford, J. 188
Langland, William 215
Leak, Henry 95
leather, conservation methodology 25
leather fragments 55, 192–3
leatherworkers 11
leatherworking 192–3, 244
Ledbury (Herefs), floor tiles 132
Leddington/Luddington family 10, 17, 94, 96, 103, 216, 224, 226
   John 100
   Robert (17th century) 100
   Robert the elder 10, 100

Leddington/Luddington family (cont.)
 Robert the younger 10, 99, 100
 William 94
Lee, Richard 188
Lekhulle, Thomas 9
Lench, John 95, 101, 109
Leominster (Herefs)
 clay pipes 172, 188
 plant remains 214
 pollen analysis 200
 priory, floor tiles 132
Leppynton, John 100
Lewes, Robert 102
Lewis, Edward and Elizabeth 172
Lewis, William 108
Lewtry, - 95
Lewtry, Edmund and John 106
Lich Street 3, *4*
lid/cap, copper-alloy 163, *164*
Lilleshall Abbey (Shrops), floor tiles 132
Lilly family 17, 101, 250
 Aaron 95, 101, 108
 John 17, 95, 101, 103, 108, 245, 246
 Margaret 102, 103
 Moses 108
 Richard 103
 Thomas 94, 101, 102, 103
linen smoother 189–90, *190*
Lingham family 17, 101, 250
 Abraham 12, 73, 95, 105, 106, 241
 C. 95
 Elena 95, 105
 Ephraim 105
 Joseph 105
 Thomas 105
Link, Henry 95
Link, Thomas 95
Linton, - 95, 101
Lissaman family 95, 101
 Mrs - 106
 John 101
Lockley, John 95, 104
Lokier, Francis 94
London Brick Company 144
Longmore, Ed 101
Lowe family 17, 95, 101
 Abigail 109
 Mary 109
 Oliver 109
 Samuel 95, 101, 109
 Samuel junior 109
Lower Quay 11, 15, 232
Lucy family
 Mrs - 95
 Emily 104
 Jos 95
Luddington *see* Leddington
Lynall, John 95, 108

machinery fixings 43, 246
Maddox, William 9
Maddox slip 8

Magistrates' Court 3, *4*
Malpas, Henry 94
malthouses
 discussion 235, 236, 240–1, 245–6, 250, 253
 documentary evidence 12, *97*, 103, 105, 106, 108
 excavation evidence
  Period 3.3–4 *58*, 70–2, *70*, *73*
  Period 4 *70*, 72–3
  Period 5 *71*, 73
malting 241, 243, 245, 246, 247, 251
maltsters 12, 95, 99, 108, 250
Mann, Pretty 108
marbles, glass 189
Marduckes Slip 11
marine stores 94
Marker 8
market gardening 226
Marston, Thomas 106
Martin son of Marker 8
Martin, James 94
Mason, Thomas 95
Mathews, Richard 182
Mayes, John 188
medlar (*Mespilus germanica*) 209, 213, 215, 226
Meeke, - 95, 101
Meeke, Thomas 105
Mence, Richard 109
mercer 104
Merryday, G. 95
metal artefacts
 medieval 163–4, *164*
 post-medieval 164–6, *165*
 modern and unassigned 166
Middleton, Jos 187
Millard, John 15
mills 240, 245
millstones
 description and discussion 158, 161–2, *161*, 240–1, 245
 excavation evidence 72, *73*
Molyneux, Nicholas 106, 239
Moreton, Thomas 95, 106
Moreton, William 95, 108
Morley, John 187
mortar, medieval 158, 162, *162*
Moule family 96
mouse 216
Much Wenlock (Shrops), clay pipe production 172

nails, iron 163, 164
Needs, - 102
New Quay *see* Upper Quay
New Street 8
Newemon, William 9
'Newly' 100
Newport Street
 no. 2 109, 110, 236
 no. 4 109–10, 236
 no. 6 109, 110, 236
 no. 8 109, 236
 no. 10 108, 109, 236, 245, 246; excavation evidence *see* Plot 14

Newport Street (cont.)
  no. 12
    buildings 242
    colonisation and property division 235, 236
    documentary evidence 12, 108–9
    excavation evidence *see* Plot 14
    industry and craft 245, 246
    wealth and status 251
  no. 14
    buildings 241
    colonisation and property division 235, 236
    documentary evidence 12, 105–6, 106–8
    excavation evidence *see* Plots 12–13
    industry and craft 244, 246, 247
    wealth and status 250
  no. 16
    buildings 239, 241
    colonisation and property division 235, 236
    documentary evidence 12, 105–6, *107*
    excavation evidence *see* Plots 10–11
    industry and craft 247
  no. 18
    buildings 239, 240, 241
    colonisation and property division 235, 236
    documentary evidence 12, 15, 105–6, *107*
    excavation evidence *see* Plots 10–11
    industry and craft 247
  no. 20
    buildings 239, 240, 241, 242
    colonisation and property division 235, 236
    documentary evidence 12, *16*, 104–5
    excavation evidence *see* Plots 8–9
    industry and craft 244, 245, 246,
    wealth and status 250
  no. 22
    buildings 240, 241, 242
    colonisation and property division 235, 236
    documentary evidence 12, *16*, 104–5
    excavation evidence *see* Plots 6–7
    industry and craft 245, 246, 247
    wealth and status 250
  no. 24
    buildings 229, 237, 239–40, 241, 242
    colonisation and property division 235, 236
    documentary evidence 10, 12, 15, *16*, 102–4
    excavation evidence *see* Plots 4–5
    industry and craft 244, 245, 246
    wealth and status 250
  no. 26
    buildings 237, 239–40, 241, 242
    colonisation and property division 235, 236
    documentary evidence 10
    industry and craft 244, 247
  nos 26–30 10, 99–102, 224, 235, 236, 245
  no. 26/28 *16*, 226; excavation evidence *see* Plot 2; Plot 3
  no. 28 10, 236, 237, 239–40, 241, 242, 247, 249
  no. 30
    buildings 237, 239–40, 241, 242
    colonisation and property division 235, 236
    documentary evidence 10, *16*
    excavation evidence *see* Plot 3
    wealth and status 251
  no. 32 235, 236, 241, 242, 246
  no. 32/34
    buildings 240, 241, 242
    colonisation and property division 235, 236
    documentary evidence 10, 12, *16*, 97–9, *97*, *98*
    excavation evidence *see* Plot 1
    industry and craft 245
    wealth and status 249
  no. 36 12, 15, 245
  no. 42 96–7
  no. 42/44 10
  no. 44 96–7
  no. 48 93–6
  no. 50 93, 96
  no. 52 93, 96
  no. 54 9, 12, 93
  chronological overview 228–9
  discussion
    buildings 236–42
    consumption and urban households 247–9
    industry and craft 242–7
    wealth and social change 249–51
  documentary evidence *see* documentary evidence
  excavation evidence 30–1, *31*, 32–5, *36*
    Plot 1 32, 40
      Period 3.1 40–1, *41*, 54
      Period 3.3 41–2, *42*, *43*, 58
      Period 4 42–3, *60*
      Period 5 43, *43*, *71*
    Plot 2 32, 43–4
      Period 2 44, *50*
      Period 3.1 44–6, *44*, 54
      Period 3.2–4 46–7, *57*–*8*, *60*
      Period 5 47–8, *71*
    Plot 3 32, 48–9
      Period 1 *48*, 49, *49*
      Period 2.1 *48*, 49–50, *49*
      Period 2.3 50–1, *50*
      Period 2.4–2.5 51–5, *51*, *52*, *53*
      Period 2.5–3.1 *51*, 54, 55–6, *55*
      Period 3.1–3.2 54, 56–9, *57*
      Period 4–5 59–61, *60*
    Plots 4–5 33, 61
      Period 2.3 *50*, 61–3, *63*
      Period 2.4–2.5 *51*, 63–4, *64*, *65*
      Period 2.5–3.1 *51*, 54, 65
      Period 3.2–3.3 *57*–*8*, 65–6
      Period 4 *60*, 66
      Period 4–5 *60*, 66–7, *71*
    Plots 6–7 33, 67
      Period 2.3–2.5 *50*, *51*, 67–8
      Period 3.1 *54*, 68
      Period 3.1/3.2 *54*, *57*, 68–9
      Period 3.2 *57*, 69–70
      Period 3.3–4 *58*, *60*, 70–2, *70*, *73*
      Period 4 *60*, 70, 72–3
      Period 5 *71*, 73
    Plots 8–9 34, 73–4
      Period 2 *50*, *51*, 74–5
      Period 3 *54*, *57*–*8*, 75
      Period 4 *60*, 75–6
      Period 5 *71*, 76

Newport Street, excavation evidence (cont.)
    Plots 10–11 34–5, 76
        Period 3 76–7, *86, 88, 89*
        Period 3.2–3.3 77, *88, 89*
        Period 4 77, *90*
        Period 5 *71*, 77–8
    Plots 12–13 35, 78
        Period 1 78–80, *78, 79, 80*
        Period 2.1 *78, 79*, 80–1, *80*
        Period 2.2 *79*, 81
        Period 2.3 81–2, *81*
        Period 2.4 82–4, *83, 84*
        Period 2.5 *83, 84*, 85
        Period 3.1 84–5, *86*
        Period 4–5 85, *90*
    Plot 14 35, 85–6
        Period 2.3 *81*, 86–7
        Period 2.4–2.5 *83*, 87–91, *87*
        Period 3.1 *86*, 91
        Period 3.3–4 *89, 90*, 91–2, *91*
        Period 5 *71*, 92
  see also geoarchaeology
excavation project
  archive 29
  background 1–2, *2*
  conclusions 252–3
  methodologies 20–7, *21, 22*
  objectives/research priorities 19–20
  retrospective view 27–9
  location *xvi, 1, 2, 4*
  origins 231, *232, 233,* 234–5
Nixon, Thomas 95, 106
Norman, Mrs 94
Norris, S.A. 94
North Parade 17
North Quay *see* Upper Quay
Norwich (Norfolk), hearths 244

oat (*Avena* sp) 209
oatmeal maker 12, 73, 105
Okely, Edward 188
Old Red Lion 76, 77, 95, 106, 250
Oliver family 17
  Abigail 95, 101, 109
Ombersley (Worcs) 231
ovens/oven bases
  discussion 10, 12, 93, 229, 235, 236
    Period 2 237, 238, 243, 244
    Period 3 240, 241, 245
  excavation evidence
    Plot 2 44–5
    Plot 3 56, *56*, 59
    Plots 4–5 *51*, 62, 63–4, *63, 64, 64*, 65
    Plots 6–7 *57*, 67, 68, 69, *71*
    Plots 8–9 *58*, 75
    Plots 12–13 *81*, 82, *83*, 84, *84*, 85
    Plot 14 *64*, *83*, 86, 87, 88, 91, *91*

Packham and Co. Ltd. 130
Parker family 245
  Jone 236, 245

  Margery 100
  Thomas 99
  William 10, 94, 100, 109, 250
passageways/alleys
  discussion 235, 237, 240
  Plot 2 46, 47, 48
  Plot 3 55, 56, 59
  Plots 4–5 61–2, 65–6, 66
  Plots 6–7 68, 72
  Plots 8–9 75
  Plots 10–11 77
pastry cooks 95, 109, 110
pawnbroker 95, 109
pea (*Pisum sativum*) 209
Pearcy, Edward 95, 101, 109, 110
Pearcy, Jervice 95, 101
peg, wooden 197
Pelworth, William 10
Perkins family 95, 101
  Benjamin 95, 108, 246
Perless, John 94
perukemaker 106
Philips, John 94
Philips, William 95, 101, 188
Phillips, Vincent and Mary 93
Philpotts, George 94
pig
  Roman 216, 223, 224
  medieval 216, 217, 219, 222, 223
  post-medieval 218, 219–20, 223, 224
pig sties 236
piles 8, 240
  Plot 1 40, *41*, 239
  Plots 4–5 66
  Plots 6–7 70, 71, 72
pillar base 84
pinmakers 97, 242
pins
  bone 197, 198, *198*
  copper-alloy 164, 165, *165*
Pipe Aston (Herefs), clay pipes 172, 182, 187, 188, 246
Pirton (Worcs), church 143
Pitchcroft 11, 230
pits
  discussion 228
  Plot 1 41, 42
  Plot 2 44, 46
  Plot 3 56
  Plots 4–5 62, 63, 66
  Plots 6–7 72
  Plots 10–11 76, 77, *86, 88*
  Plots 12–13 78–9, 80–1, *80*, 82, *83, 83*, 84
  Plots 14 87, 91
Pitt, Francis 95
Pitt, William 95, 101, 105
plant remains
  compared 226–7
  discussion
    Roman 214, 225
    medieval 214, 225, 243, 247, 249–50
    post-medieval 214–16, 225–6, 246, 248

plant remains (cont.)
　methodology 26–7, 201–2
　results 203
　　Roman 201–2, 204
　　medieval 202–9
　　post-medieval 209–13
plasterers 95, 105, 247, 250
plum/damson/bullace (*Prunus domestica*) 202, 209, 213, 214, 215, 225, 249
plumb bob, lead 165, *165*, 166
plumber 95
Police Station 3, *4*
pollen analysis
　discussion 230, 231
　　late prehistoric–Romano-British 199–200, 225
　　medieval 200, 225
　methodology 26
　results 198, *199*
　　Zone 1 198
　　Zone 2 198–9
　　Zone 3 199
Poole, Benjamin and Hester 104
population 8
Porcelain Works 3, 122, 123, 124, 125
pottery, Romano-British
　assemblage 110–11
　discussion 111, 119
pottery, medieval–early post-medieval
　analysis
　　imported wares 116–17, 119, *119*
　　local and regional wares 111–14, 117, *118*
　　non-regional wares 115–16, 117–19, *118*, *119*
　　unidentified wares 117, 119, *119*
　assemblage 111
　catalogue 117–19, *118*, *119*
　discussion
　　medieval 119–20, 247–8
　　early post-medieval 120–1, 248
pottery, post-medieval
　analysis
　　agate ware 125
　　brown glazed speckled ware 122, 126, *127*
　　Creamware 125
　　Midlands purple ware 126, 129, *129*
　　Midlands yellow ware 122, 126, *127*
　　North Devon gravel-tempered and gravel-free wares 121–2
　　Nottingham stoneware 124
　　post-medieval buff ware 125–6, 129, *129*
　　post-medieval red ware 123, 126–9, *127–9*
　　Staffordshire stoneware 124, 129, *129*
　　stonewares 123
　　tin-glazed ware 124–5, 129, *129*
　　Westerwald stoneware 123–4
　　white salt-glazed stoneware 124, 129, *129*
　　miscellaneous 126, 129, *129*
　assemblage 121
　discussion 126, 248–9
pottery, modern 129–30
pottery manufacture 244–5, 248–9
Powell, Griffith 172
Powell, Joseph 95, 109

Powell, Mary 187
Powell, Richard 95
Pratt family
　John 101, 105
　Rob 95, 101, 109
　Widow 95, 101, 103
Price, Elizabeth 188
Prince of Wales 95, 105, 241
printer 95
Pritchett, John 94, 96
Pritchett, Joseph 101, 105
privies 96, 104, 105, 241, 242
promontory fort, Iron Age 3
property boundaries
　discussion 30, 228–9, 233, 234–6, 237, 252–3
　excavation evidence
　　Plot 1 40, 42
　　Plot 2 44, 45, 46, 47, 48
　　Plot 3 49, 55, 59
　　Plots 4–5 61, 66, 67
　　Plots 6–7 67
　　Plots 12–13 82, 83–4, 84
　　Plot 14 87, 88–9, 91
pumpkin/squash (*Cucurbita maxima*) 209, 213, 215, 226, 248
pumps
　discussion 242
　documentary evidence 102, 106
　excavation evidence 72, 73, 77, 158
purpresture payments 45, 101

Quakers 17, 105, 109
Quay Street 105, 108
Queen Street
　location *4*
　pottery 122, 123, 124, 125
querns 82, 157–8, 159–61, *160*, 243

ragmerchant 95
raisins 248
Randle family 96
　Henry 96
raspberry (*Rubus* sp) 209, 215
Rea, John 99, 245
Red Lion 106, 246
Reeve Bros 191
Richards, W.H. 94
road system 5, *6*, 8, 233
roads
　discussion 228, 230, 231, 232–3, 234
　environmental evidence 225, 228
　excavation evidence *48*, *49*, *78*, *79–80*, *80*
roof furniture 139
roof tiles, Roman 134–5, *134*
roof tiles, medieval–modern
　assemblage 135–6
　discussion by period
　　medieval 139–40
　　post-medieval 140
　　18th century 140
　　19th–20th centuries 140

roof tiles, medieval–modern (cont.)
  fabrics
    Fabric 1 136
    Fabric 2a 136, 140, *141*
    Fabric 2b 136–7, 140, *141*
    Fabric 2c 137–8, 140, *141*
    Fabric 2d 138
    Fabric 3 138–9, 140, *141*
    Fabric 5 139
  makers' stamps 136, 138, 140, *141*
rose (*Rosa* sp) 209, 213, 215, 246
Rose and Shamrock 106
Ross-on-Wye (Herefs), clay pipes 188
Rowlands, John 93
Rowlands, Richard 94
Rowley, Benjamin 94
Rowley, John 95, 108
Rudde, James 103
Runsell Green (Essex), brick 143
Russell, John 188
rye (*Secale cereale*) 199, 200, 225

St Albans Abbey (Herts), floor tiles 131
St Clement's Church *11*, *13*
  foundation date 232, 233
  location 9, 234
  stonework 157
St Clement's Gate 11
St Clement's parish 188
St Helen's Church 5
St Nicholas's parish 187, 188
St Oswald's Almshouse 143
St Swithin's parish 187
St Wulstan's Hospital 9
salt trade 247
Sambach, Mrs 109
Sansome Street
  excavation 3
  location *4*
  pottery 122, 123, 124, 125
Saracen's Head 15
Saunders, Francis 94
Saunders, Richard 15
schoolteacher 95, 105
Sefton
  Mrs - 106
  Thomas 95
  W. 95
Severn, river
  bridges
    medieval 5, *7*, 8, *13*, 15, 228, 232–3, 234
    post-medieval 11, *12*, 17, 250
  ford 5, *6*, 8, 232–3
  geology 38–40, 229–31, 234
  industry 8, 11, 242
  trade 215, 216, 226, 247, 248–9
  see also alluvium; flooding; Lower Quay; Upper Quay
Severn carrier 95, 108
Severn Galley 16, 61, 95, *98*, 104
Severn Street 8
Severn View *13*, 15, 17, 93, 97
Seys, Widow 101

Shambles 11, 109
Sheen, Richard 95
sheep/goat
  Roman 216, 223, 224
  medieval 216, 217, 223, 224
    age at death 219
    pathology 222, 226
    size 221
  post-medieval 218, 223, 224
    age at death 219, 220
    size 221, 226
sheet fragment, copper-alloy 165, *165*
Sheffield, Ann 94
Shepherd, William & Co. 188
Shipman, Henry 94, 101
Shipman, William 94, 99
shoe fragments 192–3, 244
shoemakers/shoemaking 8, 94, 95, 242, 244, 251
Showells Brewery Company Ltd. 191
Shrawley 100
Shrewsbury (Shrops), development 234–5
Shutter, Amelia and Amelia junior 188
Shutter, H. & Co. 188
Sidbury
  excavations 3, *4*
  plant remains 215, 227
  pottery 113, 122, 123, 124, 125
  Shambles 11
silk weavers 10, 103, 108, 109, 245, 246, 250
Silver Street, tile production 131
Singleton, John 15
Singleton, Thomas 94, 95
Slade family
  Edward 101, 109
  John 95, 101, 109
slag
  analysis 191–2
  assemblage 191
  borehole evidence *37*, 38
  discussion 192, 228, 234
  excavation evidence 79, 80, 87
slave trade 226
sloe (*Prunus spinosa*) 202, 209, 213, 214, 225, 249
Smith family 104
  George 143
  John 95, 101, 108
  Richard 187
  William 109
smithy/forge 88, 192, 237, 243–4
solicitor 95
Soule, John 94
Southall family 17, 41
  John 94, 99, 101, 102, 105
  Joseph 110
  Margery 102
  Philip 99, 101
  Sarah 99
Sowden, John 70, 72–3, 95, 101, 104, 105, 242
Spares, - 94
spindle/spindle fragment, bone 197, 198
spindle whorls 52, 157, 159, *159*, 244
spoons, pewter 56, 163–4, *164*, 250

Spreckley's Brewery 104, 191
spurs 51, 163, *164*
stables
 discussion 236, 239, 241, 242
 documentary evidence
  Hope and Anchor/Severn View 93
  no. 2 110
  no. 10 109
  no. 12 108
  no. 18 106
  no. 24 103
  nos 26–30 99, 100, 102
  nos 31–33 104
  no. 32/34 99
 excavation evidence 41, 42, 78
The Star 109
status and social change 249, 253
 Roman 249
 medieval 249–50
 post-medieval 250–1
Stead, - 246
Steede, Henry 99
Stinton, John 108
Stoke-on-Trent (Staffs), pottery 115, 122
Stokes, Berry 94
Stokes, John 95, 109, 110
strainer/skimmer, copper-alloy 166, *166*
strap fittings, copper-alloy 164, 165, *165*
strawberry (*Fragaria vesca*) 213, 214, 249
street pattern 5, 231–4
Strickland, Henry 95
Strickland, James 109
summer savory (*Satureja hortensis*) 209, 214

tailor 95
tanks, brick 69, 72, 75
tanners 8, 242, 253
tanning 192, 214, 225, 243
Taylor, George 94
Taylor, Richard 95
Taylor, Samuel 95, 101, 104, 105
Tewkesbury (Glos), clay pipes 188
textile fragments 56, 192–5, *194*, *195*
thimbles 164–5, *165*, 166, *166*
Thomas the dyer 9
Thomas, Lewis 188
Thorborrow, Elizabeth 95
tiles *see* floor tiles; roof tiles
tokens
 assemblage 166
 post-medieval 167, 168–9
 late post-medieval–modern 168, 169
tomb fragments
 catalogue 147, 148, 149, 150, *151*, *152*, *153*, *155*
 discussion 156, 157
town planning, medieval 231–2, 252
Townsend, William 94
trade
 Roman 5
 medieval 247, 247–8
 post-medieval 216, 226, 227, 248–9, 251

trades
 medieval 8, 242–3, 244, 253
 post-medieval 245–6, 247, 250, 253
 see also individual trades
Trevett, Ann 109
troughs, stone 159, 162, *162*
Trow, J. 94
Tybridge Street 232
The Tything
 brick 142, 143, 144
 excavation 3
 location *4*
 tiles 131, 132, 134, 137, 138

Upper Quay (North/New Quay) 11–12, 15, 17, 232

Vaulx, Thomas 11

Walker, Isabel 9
Walker, John 8
walkers 8, 9, 10, 40, 94, 239, 242
walnut (*Juglans regia*) 213, 226
Walsgrove, Thomas 100
Walshe, Seabright 99
Walter of Eport 8
Wanklyn family
 - 101, 103
 Richard 101
 Widow 105
warehouses
 discussion 239, 241, 247, 253
 documentary evidence 12, 99, 106, 108
 excavation evidence 40
Warner Village Cinemas 3
wash-houses 96, 106, 109, 241, 242
water supply 242
waterworks *10*, 11
Watkins, Charles 188
Watton, William 11
Watts, John 15
wealth *see* status and social change
weavers 9–10, 94, 99, 103, 244, 245
Webb, Elizabeth 242
wells
 capping 72, *73*, 158, 241
 discussion 228, 231, 233, 234, 242, 246
 excavation evidence
  Plot 2 48
  Plot 3 49–50, 59
  Plots 4–5 *60*, 66
  Plots 6–7 69, 70, 72, 73, *73*
  Plots 8–9 *60*, 75
  Plots 10–11 76, 77, *86*
  Plots 12–13 82
Wells family
 Walter 94, 100
 Widow 94, 99
West, Samuel 95, 101, 108
Westhead, S. 94
wheat (*Triticum* sp) 201, 209
wheel ruts *48*, 49
Wheeler, - 94

Whieldon, Thomas 125
White, George 95, 109
White, Isaac 99
White, Richard 94
Whitehead, Mrs 95, 110
Whitsones (Worcs) 231
Whittall, George 95, 106
Whittall, James 101
whittawing 225
Wigfall, Thomas 95, 101
Wilding, Thomas 101
William le Horner 242
William son of William le Horner 97
Williams, Cordelia 105
Williams, Robert 182
Williams, Thomas 95
Willis, John 94
Willoughby, Thomas 102
Wilson family 95
   William 109
window glass 189
wine trade 247
winemaking 215
Winsmore family 108
   William 105
wood turning 244
wooden artefacts 195–7, *196*
woodland clearance 225, 228
Woodsall, Richard 100
Worcester
   archaeological and historical frameworks 3–8, *6*
   archaeological investigations 3, *4*
   clay pipemakers 182–8, 246
   colonisation and property division 234–6
   see of 5
   street system and town planning 231–4

workshops/workhouse 8, 65, 236, 237, 240, 245
Wormington, John 104
Writer family 17
   Clement 17, 99
   Ellen 94, 99
   John 12, 41, 94, 99
   Thomas 94, 99, 241, 245
Wye, Henry 95, 101
Wylmington, John 100

yards
   discussion 229, 235, 236, 237, 238, 241
   documentary evidence
      Hope and Anchor/Severn View 96
      no. 4 110
      no. 10 109
      no. 18 106
      no. 24 103
      nos 26–30 99, 100, 102
      nos 31–33 104
      no. 32/34 99
   excavation evidence
      Plot 1 41, 42
      Plot 3 59
      Plots 4–5 62
      Plots 6–7 72
      Plots 8–9 75
      Plots 10–11 77, 78
      Plot 14 87, 91, 92
Yarnold family 101
   George 101, 103
Yarranton, - 15
Yeates (Yates), Ralph 94, 96